Hellenic Studies 29

THE ORAL PALIMPSEST

THE ORAL PALIMPSEST

Exploring Intertextuality in the Homeric Epics

Christos C. Tsagalis

Center for Hellenic Studies
Trustees for Harvard University
Washington, DC
Distributed by Harvard University Press
Cambridge, Massachusetts, and London, England
2008

The Oral Palimpsest: Exploring Intertextuality in the Homeric Epics
by Christos C. Tsagalis
Copyright © 2008 Center for Hellenic Studies, Trustees for Harvard University
All Rights Reserved.
Published by Center for Hellenic Studies, Trustees for Harvard University,
   Washington, DC
Distributed by Harvard University Press, Cambridge, Massachusetts, and
   London, England
Production Editor: Ivy Livingston
Editorial Assistant: Emily Collinson
Cover Design and Illustration: Joni Godlove

EDITORIAL TEAM:
Senior Advisors: W. Robert Connor, Gloria Ferrari Pinney, Albert Henrichs,
   James O'Donnell, Bernd Seidensticker
Editorial Board: Gregory Nagy (Editor-in-Chief), Christopher Blackwell,
   Casey Dué (Executive Editor), Mary Ebbott (Executive Editor), Olga
   Levaniouk, Anne Mahoney, Leonard Muellner, Ross Scaife
Production Editors: M. Zoie Lafis, Ivy Livingston, Jennifer Reilly
Web Producer: Mark Tomasko

LIBRARY OF CONGRESS CATALOGING-IN-PUBLICATION DATA

The oral palimpsest: exploring intertextuality in the Homeric epics /
by Christos C. Tsagalis
      p. cm. — (Hellenic studies series; 29)
   Includes bibliographical references and index.
   ISBN 978-0-674-02687-2
1. Homer—Criticism and interpretation. 2. Homer. Iliad. 3. Homer. Odyssey.
   4. Intertextuality. I. Title. II. Series.
   PA4037.T7895 2007
   833'.01—dc22
                              2007037296

For Pietro Pucci

Contents

Foreword ix
Preface xi
Acknowledgments xxv
Note on Transliteration and References xxvii

Part I: Intertextuality between Recognizable Traditions

1 Ἀνδρομάχη μαινομένη: The Dionysiac Element in the *Iliad* 1
2 Χαρίεσσα and στυγερὴ ἀοιδή: The Self-Referential Encomium
   of the *Odyssey* and the Tradition of the *Nostoi* 30
3 Nausicaa and the Daughters of Anius: Terms and Limits of
   Epic Rivalry 44
4 Intertextual Fissures: The Returns of Odysseus and the New Penelope 63

Part II: Intertextuality and Meta-Traditionality

5 Ἀχιλλεὺς Ἑλένην ἐπιθυμεῖ θεάσασθαι: From the *Cypria* to the *Iliad* 93
6 Viewing from the Walls, Viewing Helen: Language and
   Indeterminacy in the 'Teichoscopia' 112
7 Time Games: The 'Twenty-Year' Absent Hero 135

Part III: Intertextuality and Diachronically Diffused Relations

8 The Formula νυκτὸς ἀμολγῷ: Homeric Reflections of an
   Indo-European Metaphor 153
9 Genealogy and Imagery of a Homeric Formula: πεφυζότες
   ἠΰτε νεβροί 188

Contents

Part IV: Intertextuality and Intratextual Sequences

10 The Rhetorics of Supplication and the Epic Intertext (*Iliad* I 493–516).... 209
11 Intertextuality and Intratextual Distality: Thetis' Lament in
    Iliad XVIII 52–64 239
12 Mapping the Hypertext: Similes in *Iliad* XXII 272

Bibliography 287
Index Locorum 313
Index of Subjects 321

Foreword

THE TITLE OF THIS BOOK (*The Oral Palimpsest*) with its learned oxymoron and its allusion to analogously oxymoronic titles (for instance *Written Voices and Spoken Signs* edited in 1997 by E. Bakker and A. Kahane) might seem no more than a smart appeal to the sophisticated reader, but in fact it announces the various paradoxical, mysterious and enigmatic aspects of Homeric poetry. Christos Tsagalis is a virtuoso interpreter of this poetry, as he has shown in his book *Epic Grief* (Berlin-New York 2004), and in this new endeavour he straddles felicitously the contradictory, ungraspable aspects of the Homeric poems, as he moves on the razor's edge that holds united the fluctuating Homeric diction, always completely traditional and yet completely new. Specifically, the palimpsest image refers to Tsagalis' careful pursuit of the traces of rival poetic versions that the *Iliad* and the *Odyssey* let emerge and simultaneously exclude. Just as the erased text of a palimpsest still carries traces of a previous writing, so the Homeric texts reveal their knowledge of rival versions in the act of producing the signs of their erasure. Tsagalis' title is impressively precise.

By this strategy, the two poems yield extraordinary results. They manifest on the one hand their absolute control of the traditional epic songs, and on the other, by the exclusion of alternative variants, the selectivity and unitary force of their narratives. By eliminating the themes, the tones, the shades that would obscure or corrupt the fundamental coherence of their poetic effect and significance, the poems throw light on the image of their poetic self-awareness. Of course many other features, characters, and scenes (lamentation, representation of Achilles, Helen, Penelope, etc.) point to this same awareness.

The idiosyncratic, unique interpretation of the heroic *kleos*, the odd poetic liminality of Achilles within the Iliadic plot, the upsetting and paradoxical gesture whereby Thetis puts her son Achilles within the reach of death, and the desperate disparity between the goddess-mother and Achilles are some of the closely-knit poetic themes in the *Iliad*. These themes, however, are not simply described and elaborated as the thematic nucleus of the poem, but they are shown to mirror the direction and the goal of poetic activity. As Thetis sends Achilles to Troy and asks Zeus to restore his lost *time* (honor), she delivers her son to death, and "figuratively asks Zeus to make Achilles the hero of the *Iliad*, to allow the poem to make of him its subject matter." Every scene and every character, in Tsagalis' analysis, mirrors the poetic tenets and thrust making their *staging* possible and endowing them with the *Iliad's* particular tragic inflection. For the *Odyssey* Tsagalis illuminates "not the unfailing fame conveyed by *kleos aphthiton*, but the unfailing memory of enchanting and pleasing song."

The author moves with great caution upon the slippery and treacherous ground of formulaic diction and intertextuality. As he writes, the formulaic diction opens "labyrinthine paths" leading us either to the alluring and enriching meanings of intertextuality, or to nets of senseless and ultimately infinite connections. How to control this game of references and allusions? He succeeds with convincing resolution thanks to the precise principles he adopts and his extraordinary sensitivity in symbiosis with a thorough knowledge of the epic language. He finds the right expression to define this ground of research when he attributes to the language of the poems "a fluctuating regularity": the technical and critical language in this book is of admirable precision and originality. When confronting the thorny question of how to treat the poems, as texts or oral compositions, Tsagalis engages in a creative dialogue with Nagy's theory about textualized oral song-cultures, showing that in fact oral intertextuality is possible within the complex web of myth. Intertextual analyses are precise and rigorous: he begins by distinguishing four types of intertextuality and then illustrates how each of them works through richly commentated case-studies, replete with the author's special feeling for Homeric style.

Tsagalis is constantly in dialogue with the critics and writers of our time: he seems not to exclude any scholar from whom he may learn something useful and exciting. This on-going dialogue opens the vast panorama of our present studies on Homer that reflect the enormous complexity, the mysterious and fascinating power of his poetry.

Pietro Pucci
Professor of Classics
Cornell University

Preface

Homeric studies have shown a remarkable dynamism as they still stand (more than 200 years after Wolf's seminal *Prolegomena ad Homerum*) at the forefront of scholarly research in the field of Classics. During the second half of the last century, the evolution of Homeric studies has been primarily, though not solely, boosted by the exploration of the oral nature of archaic epic and the subsequent study of orality as a phenomenon opposed to literacy. The study of oral poetics has opened the door to the world of oral or oral-based cultures and has subsequently paved the way for understanding and appreciating a new form of Poetics, long needed in order to glance into a culture so different, and yet so similar to our own.

The title of this Book (*The Oral Palimpsest*) is based on a deliberately employed oxymoron. Notwithstanding the fact that the word palimpsest[1] (*codex rescriptus*) belongs to the realm of manuscript and not oral tradition, I regard it as an apt metaphor for describing the scope of this work. During a long process of shaping, the Homeric tradition has absorbed, altered, disguised, and reappropriated mythical, dictional, and thematic material of various sorts and from different sources. In that sense it is like an oral palimpsest, "to be 'erased' and re-'written' in accordance with traditional structure and within the limits of the multiform idiom."[2] Mythical fragmentation and dictional ellipsis[3] constitute two useful gateways leading to multiple other traditions that need to be retrieved in order to comprehend, evaluate, and appreciate the level of sophistication epic song-traditions display. Muellner's powerful insights about the interlocking of Homeric (Iliadic) and Hesiodic (Theogonic) narratives with respect to the patterning of 'wrath' (μῆνις) have

---

[1] See *OCD* s.v. palimpsest; Reynolds and Wilson 1991:85–86, 192–195.
[2] Foley 1990:31.
[3] For ellipsis as both a 'metaphor' and a 'metonym' not only of "specific stylistic conventions," but also of "the deep structure of meanings constantly at reactivation at all linguistic levels," see Nagy 2004:157–175.

Preface

opened the way for a redefinition of intertextuality in oral traditions.[4] More recently, Burgess has convincingly argued that the individual poems that later became parts of the Epic Cycle "would have been continually re-created and eventually crystallized in performance traditions of the Archaic Age."[5] Within this framework, cross-references and some form of quoting must have been possible, the more so since 'Theogonic', 'Theban', and 'Trojan' material formed integral phases of what we might call 'the past'. Oral epic traditions grew out of a continuous interaction and reshaping of traditional material, which had already been arranged by consistent bardic performance.

The retrieval of other rival traditions is possible through the epics of the Cycle, which are later than the Homeric poems but represent oral traditions antedating the shaping of both the *Iliad* and the *Odyssey*. Burgess, who discerns three levels of narrative (cyclic myth, cyclic epic, Homeric epic), has argued that "cyclic epic is an epic version of cyclic myth and Homeric epic exists as a self-conscious extension of cyclic myth and cyclic epic."[6] Although in this sense Homeric epic may be called 'meta-cyclic', I would prefer Finkelberg's term 'meta-epic',[7] since the oral traditions it employs and alludes to are recoverable not *only* by the cyclic poems but also by their oral predecessors.

Under this scope, I have decided to keep to the term 'intertextuality' which has been well established in Homeric studies[8] and refrain from introducing another scientific coin. Homeric song-making even has a word for intertextuality. *Poikilia* refers to a variegated, many-colored process by which an artifact becomes *poikilos* (varied, inwrought with something else). Furthermore, *poikilia* designates the interweaving of various fabrics which interact, answer, contradict, or rival other fabrics, resulting in a thick web of associations metaphorically epitomized in the word *intertext*, a system or set of interwoven fabrics whose constituent parts are interrelated.[9]

The web of myth, whose primary manifestation poetry is, may even be seen as a hypertextual upsetting and disrupting of textual linearity, the mental corollary of our *writing culture*. The interrelated fabrics of myth allow

---

[4] So Nagy in his foreword to Muellner 1996. For intertextuality in general, see Allen 2000 and Fowler, D. 2000.
[5] Burgess 2001:172.
[6] Burgess 2006:148–149.
[7] See Finkelberg 1998:154–155; 2002:160; 2003:79.
[8] See Pucci 1987.
[9] See Bakker 2001c:149–160. See also Burgess 2006:148–189, who rightly argues for an oral, intertextual neoanalysis. According to his view, which I fully endorse, "motif transference can be understood as a type of intertextuality ... not between texts but between the Homeric poems and pre-Homeric oral traditions" (177).

the audience of epic song access to multiple variants, alternative versions of a story, incidents, or given episodes. They function like nodes opening up the entire horizon of diverse mythical traditions in which the listeners have been immersed during their entire lives. To us this process seems, and truly is, *labyrinthine*, since we will always be in need of a thread that will allow us to find our way out. For an ancient audience, the web of myth constitutes their own *universe of signifieds*, an open-ended, decentered world, offering both the oral poet and themselves multiple points of entrance and exit.[10]

In fact, the very idea of the classical author is intricately connected to the idea of the poet as maker, a concept directly relevant to the emergence of the medium of writing that is responsible for the transmission of Homeric poetry in later times. Conversely, in an ancient song-culture the person who weaves the song, the bard or the singer, does not have complete control of the various pathways opened by unraveling the mythical fabric he uses. Like internet-oriented browsing on the web, ancient listeners are able to exercise their control over the multiple paths emerging as the song is expressed. This result stems from the very nature of the web of myth, whose decentralization and multifariousness invites the audience to create their own referential avenues, beyond the control of the singer. Such an evaluative process is an inherent part of the very performance of epic song, since there is no almighty author but an omnipotent song-tradition weaving its own nexus of associations, evoking other traditions or versions at will, immersing its listeners to an *intertext* of mythical cross-references.

The emergence of Homeric poetry brought about an evolutionary process of standardization and regulation of divergent traditions,[11] whose shortcomings had become irresolvable during a period of *proliferation of meaning*, to apply Foucault's apt term to the Archaic period.[12] By creating a firm trajectory, Homeric poetry aimed at regulating its reception, at controlling and directing the course of its own distribution and diffusion. 'Homer', then, reflects the concerted effort to create a Pan-Hellenic canon of epic song. His unprecedented success is due, I maintain, not to his making previous epichoric traditions *vanish* but to his *erasing* them from the surface of his narrative while *ipso tempore* employing them in the shaping of his epics. It is at this crucial point that the hypertextual web of multiple, conflicting local traditions is replaced by the *intertextual network* of Homeric song.

---

[10] See Bakker 2001c:149–160.
[11] See Nagy 1996a.
[12] Foucault 1979:141–160.

Preface

By exploring intertextuality, I attempt to map out and discuss (a) relations between recognizable song-traditions, (b) epic self-reflexive tendencies, i.e. meta-traditional intertextuality, (c) diachronically diffused associations between 'Homer' and non-identifiable traditions reconstructed by the exploration of older Indo-European strata, and (d) intertextual allusions which explain intratextual 'sequences', i.e. combinations of interacting parts acquiring their full meaning only when placed within a wider intertext.

In Part One of this book, I engage in an examination of intertextual relations between recognizable song-traditions. All four chapters of this first part focus on female figures in both the *Iliad* and *Odyssey*. The search for a general *female reading* of Homer is bound to bear all the interpretive extremities its analogous male-centered approach has reached in the past. Instead of suggesting an alternative female-based pattern for an overall analysis of the poems, I explore one of the ways the Homeric tradition uses principal female characters—to conjure up other rival traditions whose vagaries it overcomes by interweaving them into its own song. Bearing the mythological armature of the male protagonists but not necessarily their epic *Weltanschauung*, women allow the epic to complete, enrich, and even redetermine its cross-textual relations with other song-traditions. They open intertextual windows by which bard and audience can temporarily glance at other mythical versions, whose varied fabrics have been stitched up by the *poikilia* of Homeric song-making. In this light, the Iliadic and Odyssean song-traditions have surpassed an initial gender-based scissiparity between male and female heroes based on plot-requirements, only to turn it into a sophisticated mechanism of inter-textual 'play'.

Chapter One[13] sets out to explore the origin and function of the sparse Dionysiac references in the *Iliad* in relation to Andromache's maenadic associations. Extending Seaford's interpretation, which was based on the connotations of a Dionysiac metaphor, namely that of the dissolution of the household, the entire mythical spectrum of Andromache's non-Iliadic epic life is now meticulously examined. The regularly invoked memory of Hypoplakian Thebes in Asia Minor as Andromache's city of origin, mythical references to her father Eetion, her 'Amazonian' name, and her inseparable bond with Hector—to mention only some of the multiple elements examined—should, it is contended, be treated in unison to the frugal Dionysiac references restricted to her in the *Iliad*. In this light, we can discern a rival Theban tradition of epic

---

[13] Originally published as "'Ἀνδρομάχη μαινομένη: το διονυσιακό στοιχείο στην Ιλιάδα." *Hellenika* 52 (2002): 199–225. Permission to reprint from the Society of Macedonian Studies.

poetry in the mainland, in which Andromache and Dionysus would normally partake.

Chapter Two[14] is a study of Agamemnon's speech to Amphimedon in *Odyssey* xxiv 192–202. I argue that the disparity between the physical (Amphimedon) and notional (Odysseus) addressee of the speech is an elaborate epic technique aiming to create an intertextual framework. As Agamemnon speaks to Amphimedon, also addressing the physically absent but notionally present Odysseus, so the song-tradition of the *Odyssey* exploits the verbally overt but notionally covert function of its main protagonists, Odysseus and Penelope, 'reading' them not as simple plot-agents but as trademarks of its own poetic authority.

To ascertain its poetic supremacy over rival 'Return-songs', the *Odyssey* skillfully invents an intertextual metalanguage. To this end, Agamemnon, hero of the *Nostoi*, ironically becomes the very mouthpiece of the *Odyssey*'s declaration of its poetic status. Here, as in the aforementioned cases, the process of reconstructing the whole mythical nexus is effectuated by understanding that the *Iliad* is using *female figures* not only as plot agents but also as intertextual pathways leading to the retrieval of necessary information. Using a suitable analogy from the field of textual criticism and transposing it to the field of the study of myth in an oral tradition, we can see how epic poetry encapsulates material from other mythical traditions. Deprived of the means available to a modern editor (the printed page, the footnoted text, the character and font variations), oral epic traditions create their own referential avenues. Under this scope, Penelope's positive evaluation through her loyalty to Odysseus is emphatically opposed to Clytaemestra's negative coloring through her paragonal betrayal of Agamemnon. These two female figures emblematize the sophisticated vocabulary of the Odyssean intertextual metalanguage, which is further strengthened by heavy-loaded metapoetic terminology such as 'pleasing song' (χαρίεσσα ἀοιδή) and 'hateful song' (στυγερὴ ἀοιδή). In this way, intertextual cross-referencing becomes the metonymical vehicle through which the *Odyssey* bolsters its self-referential encomium.

In Chapter Three, I apply this approach to the Nausicaa-Odysseus episode in *Odyssey* vi and show how the Odyssean visualization of their meeting in Scheria reflects the poem's 'treatment' of a rival poetic tradition, reflected later on in the epic poem *Cypria*. When Odysseus compares Nausicaa to a shoot (ἔρνος) he had seen in Delos (*Odyssey* vi 163), the *Odyssey* is alluding to

---

[14] Originally published as "Odyssey 24.191–202: A Reconsideration." *WS* 116 (2003): 43–56. Permission to reprint from the Österreichische Akademie der Wissenschaften.

Preface

the episode of his visit to Apollo's sacred island, in order to bring to Troy the daughters of Anius. These are called Oinotropoi, since they have received from their ancestor Dionysus the gift of producing olive-oil (Elais), wine (Oino), and seed (Spermo). By scrutinizing the entire mythical intertext upon which this cross-reference is based, I suggest that we should rethink the function of mythical allusion and broaden the range of its application. Under the light of these observations, I attempt (a) to explore how the *Odyssey* might not have erased all traces of the version offered by the *Cypria*-tradition and (b) to show how the Nausicaa-Odysseus episode represents a fusion of the *Cypria*-oriented episode of the Oinotropoi with features pertaining to an Odyssean visualization of Odysseus.

Chapter Four is a study of a different kind of cross-reference. After the meeting between Odysseus and Penelope at the end of the *Odyssey*, Odysseus informs his wife about his desire to leave her once more, in order to fulfill a prophecy given to him by Teiresias. Given that ancient audiences would have been familiar with Odysseus' 'post-Odyssean' adventures, I suggest that the song-tradition of the *Odyssey*, at a point when its song has almost been completed, avails its main hero, the very trademark of Odyssean poetics, of a rather 'provocative' statement threatening the very tradition he typically emblematizes. By alluding to another song-tradition where Odysseus travels to foreign lands and is married again, the *Odyssey* engages its audience in a profound intertextual game, allowing Odysseus to 'menace' the very tradition that has made him the great hero of Return. At this crucial juncture, a female figure, Penelope, takes the floor and becomes the mouthpiece of Odyssean poetics. Odysseus may well 'entertain' the thought of extending his poetic life to another tradition, but he is fooling himself if he thinks that he will remain in that tradition, *Odyssey*-like, the great hero of Return. Penelope's ironical coda is both a covert cross-reference to a rival song-tradition, later reflected in the *Telegony*, and an expression of the *Odyssey's* ultimate ruse: this time, its 'victim' will be Odysseus himself, and Penelope the very means for her husband's 'duping'.

In Part Two, intertextuality is examined under the scope of self-reflexive strategies employed by Homeric epic. Until now, self-reflexivity has been rightly considered a preeminent characteristic of the Odyssean song-tradition. In the three chapters included in this part, I present three cases where Iliadic Helen is used as a vehicle for intertextual rivalry and subsequently as a metaphor for the supremacy of the Iliadic tradition. Helen's suitability to this role stems from the fact that she does not really 'belong' to the Iliadic plot. By narratively 'squeezing' her into the *Iliad*, the Homeric tradition turned her into an effective intertextual tool, the more so since her very presence would have easily triggered in the audience's mind alternative versions or possibilities within the larger framework of the Trojan war and its aftermath. Helen was, after all, the basic mythical figure, a 'thread' woven into the fabric of all the phases of the Trojan myth, since she featured in the pre-war saga, the war itself, and the post-war traditions. To usurp a term coined by Georg Danek that felicitously epitomizes her role, Helen is the ultimate 'Zitat'[15] or referential quotation of the Iliadic tradition.

In Chapter Five,[16] I offer a thorough examination of a rather brief reference made by Proclus to a meeting between Achilles and Helen in the *Cypria*. By reconstructing the particulars of this episode, one can also discover and subsequently evaluate the reasons for which such an episode could have never featured in the plot of the *Iliad*. Achilles and Helen seem to be 'incompatible' given the Iliadic perception of the critical turning point at which the world of heroes is placed. This 'mutual exclusion' endorsed by the *Iliad* may be seen as a stylized technique of mythical selection. The romantic episode of a rival song-tradition between Achilles and Helen, later reflected in the post-Homeric *Cypria*, may well explain why the *Iliad* refuses to reconcile itself with the idea of a meeting between the 'best of the Achaeans' and the 'best of women'. Instead, it avails itself of a dramatic encounter between Andromache and Hector in *Iliad* VI. Romance is thus replaced by tragedy, female beauty and male might by deep love and care. The *Iliad* invites its audience to experience a profound transformation of Achilles' desire to stop the Achaeans from returning to Greece (featured in a rival *Cypria*-tradition) into Hector's willingness to 'return' to the battlefield from which he will never 'return' to Troy. By allowing Achilles to refer to Helen only once (XIX 325), the *Iliad* deftly accepts his and, by inference, its own 'personal', dramatic glance at the heroic world. In this light, Helen's emblematic status as the καλλίστη γυναικῶν becomes the stepping-stone for a bold manifestation of the Iliadic credo: Achilles, the tradition's greatest hero, fights a doomed war against the Trojans for the sake of 'accursed Helen'. The stark rejection of a rival tradition's viewpoint acquires its full interpretive potential through a female-oriented cross-reference.

Chapter Six[17] explores how the Iliadic song-tradition manages to accommodate a female figure in its war-oriented structure. In the case of Helen,

---

[15] Danek 1998.
[16] Originally published as "'Ἀχιλλεὺς Ἑλένην ἐπιθυμεῖ θεάσασθαι: από τα *Κύπρια* στην *Ιλιάδα*." *Hellenika* 54 (2004): 7–26. Permission to reprint from the Society of Macedonian Studies.
[17] Originally published as "Viewing from the Walls, Viewing Helen: Language and Indeterminacy

problems stemming from generic restrictions were reinforced by those originating from plot confinements. As the *Iliad* focuses on the theme of Achilles' wrath, i.e. on a specific episode situated at the tenth year of the war, it should not have a place for Helen, since she was only linked to the beginning and end of the Trojan myth. On the other hand, Helen was such an indispensable part of the entire mythical nexus concerning the Trojan War, that it was unthinkable to offer an ancient audience a version without her. Excluding Helen would significantly and, perhaps, decisively undermine any Iliadic claim to poetic supremacy.

Helen's apostrophes of self-blame emotionally punctuate her Iliadic presence. Her language bears the mark of a personal vocal timbre that lays special emphasis on her inner upheaval. At the same time, her fragmented speech allows the poem to explore part of her mythical landscape and, without attempting the complete effacement of a rival tradition of her defamation, to avail itself of certain chronological detours[18] pointing to her past life. In view of the fact that discontinuities or irregularities that accommodate mythical material stemming from other epic traditions may result in narrative hiatuses, the *Iliad* manages to skip the annoying spot of another abduction of Helen and linger over the fertile soil of Menelaus' and Odysseus' past visit to Troy. To this end, this visit is narratively unfolded not by Helen but by Antenor, one of the Trojan elders. Through Helen's rebus-like speech, coupled with her genre-mixing syntax and formulaic misuse, the poem indulges in a profound game with the traditional dilemma of her innocence or guilt. Helen refuses to abide by the epic rules and pigeonhole herself in Iliadic or Odyssean nomenclature. The deliberate dysfluencies of her language, being by-products of her intertextual filtering, have a significant effect on shaping her exceptional Iliadic cast. Socially displaced, marginalized and confused, oscillating between past and present, Sparta and Troy, Menelaus and Paris, Helen is at the same time a dictional outsider and a poetic immigrant of the main action. By guilefully exploiting her idiosyncratic use of layered language and intertextual allusions, the *Iliad* achieves the unthinkable: it elevates her from the status of a character of the plot to that of an internal commentator on the tradition.

Chapter Seven[19] centers its focus on a notorious Iliadic non-sequitur concerning Helen's autobiographical information during her mournful coda in

---

in the 'Teichoscopia'." *EEAth* 34 (2002–2003): 167–193. Permission granted from the Scientific Annual of the School of Philosophy of the University of Athens.

[18] On ancient sources discussing chronological inconsistency in Greek epic, see Else 1957:586; Rengakos 2004:277–304.

[19] Originally published as "Time Games: Helen, Odysseus, and Intertextuality." *EEAth* 35 (2003–

Iliad XXIV 765. Chronological deviations of this sort have troubled Homerists for ages, from the times of the Mouseion to the present. Intertextual affinities are built upon associative links, which are in their turn triggered by repetition, the *Lydian stone* of poetic semiosis in a formulaically loaded environment. Thus, the reiteration of the expression "this is the twentieth year, since ..." in both the *Iliad* and the *Odyssey* reveals a common intertext, shared by its respective speakers, Iliadic Helen and Odyssean Odysseus. These are emblematic figures that stand for the tradition they represent: Odysseus is the 'twenty-year' hero of the 'twenty-year' epic, the *Odyssey*. The control that the two rival traditions exercise over their material is truly remarkable: by employing an Odyssean expression, in *Iliad* XXIV 765, Iliadic Helen becomes the epic's mouthpiece, uttering its polemical cry against the *Odyssey*. To the *Odyssey*'s appropriation of Iliadic time (Odysseus spends ten years in Troy and ten more years returning to Ithaca), the *Iliad* suggests its own usurpation of the *Odyssey*'s Pan-Hellenic *diffusion and authority*, of the *Odyssey*'s undisputed (for any ancient audience) time-span of 'twenty-years'.

The intertextual hermeneutics of this approach are—of course—based on one of the most fundamental—but often misunderstood, not to say distorted—tenets of oral theory. As epic rivalry[20] operates constantly on the level of song-traditions and not crystallized texts fixed by writing, one can appreciate the subtle technique of this extensive and internally cohesive reference-system in disclosing the refined sophistication with which the Iliadic tradition does, in fact, allude to its Odyssean counterpart. Female figures constantly participate in elaborate cross-textual games in ways complementary to those used by male protagonists. The case of Helen, though, may be paragonal, for she regularly calls upon the intertextual reservoir of the audience. Infusing her speech with chronological detours and engaging in dictional transvestism, she renegotiates our familiarity with the entire epic tradition. Thus, Helen's temporal anisochrony[21] is not a textual protrusion needing philological remedy, but a sophisticated poetic ruse of the *Iliad* aiming at fending off Odysseus' preeminence and, through him, the supremacy of his own epic, the *Odyssey*.

Part Three focuses attention on the intertextual pathways created by the formula, an exclusive trademark of Homeric diction standing at the very

---

2004): 109–125. Permission granted from the Scientific Annual of the School of Philosophy of the University of Athens.

[20] On diachronic changes of different performance traditions engaged in agonistic rivalry, see Aloni 1986; Burgess 2002:234–245; Marks 2002:1–24; 2003:209–226.

[21] See Tsagarakis 1982:61–72.

heart of epic song-making. The formula is not an external characteristic of epic language but a *symbiotic* feature operating on multiple levels and guiding us into a labyrinthine path of associations and interconnections. Formulaic diction is a mechanism whose surviving traces in Homeric epic cannot be attributed to recognizable traditions but to a *diachronically diffused set of relations* going back to Indo-European strata. The reconstruction of this framework helps us explore the deep structure of the epics by looking beyond the elliptical shape into which originally complex imagery has been crystallized during the process of shaping epic song.

In Chapter Eight[22] I examine the meaning and function of the Homeric formula νυκτὸς ἀμολγῷ. Through detailed examination of mythical 'parallels' stemming from a wide variety of cultures (Old Indic, Iranian, Irish and Roman), I attempt to reconstruct a 'hybrid imagery', mainly of Indo-European origin. The formula νυκτὸς ἀμολγῷ is linked to the myth of the Cattle of the Sun. It has 'survived' as a condensed, highly elliptical formulaic expression, placed at the most traditional part of the dactylic hexameter, the terminal adonic. Given these parameters, one is able to comprehend why this dictional and semantic fossil is always attested, within the Homeric epics, in contexts alluding to a solar imagery and implying imminent danger.

Chapter Nine[23] examines the formula πεφυζότες ἠΰτε νεβροί comprising part of a larger simile, which has acquired a context-free semantic aura disclosing Homeric eschatological beliefs. The preverbal *Gestalt*, to employ Nagler's apt term, nascent in the formula πεφυζότες ἠΰτε νεβροί, was that of the terrified, panic-stricken young deer being attacked by some carnivorous predator as they drank water. The participles πεφυζότες and τεθηπότες determine the imagery's framework including two temporally distinct phases of the realization of the *Gestalt*: confusion and daze before the imminent menace (τεθηπότες) and panic-stricken flight (πεφυζότες). Building on the interpretive foundations of Nagy, who has shown that the πόντος-notion connotes the concept of *dangerous transition* and the water imagery that of *destruction and imminent death*, I maintain that the elliptical nature of the simile is only a 'surface-level' by-product of a long process of reshaping and adaptation in Homeric diction and that the full semantic and functional range of this formula may be attained only when its *deep* structure is retrieved.

---

[22] Originally published as "The Homeric Formula νυκτὸς ἀμολγῷ." *Classica et mediaevalia* 54 (2003): 5–40. Permission to reprint from Museum Tusculanum Press.

[23] Originally published as "Πεφυζότες ἠΰτε νεβροί: Genealogy and Poetic Imagery of a Homeric Formula." *Symbolae Osloenses* 76 (2001): 113–129. Permission to reprint from Taylor & Francis.

In Part Four, I argue that intertextuality is stimulated not only by associations with extra-Homeric complementary material but also by the activation of intratextual sequences. In this form of intertextuality, the referential character of Homeric epic entails a renegotiation of alternative versions or possibilities generated or at least enhanced by 'Homeric' (Iliadic or Odyssean) thematic arrangement. Fragmented parts or *disiecta membra* are subsequently organized by the Homeric tradition into chains representing or reflecting aberrant intertextual variants. Under this scope, one can see that Homeric epic gives interpretive clues or hints to its audience, for whom foreknowledge of alternative and complementary versions must be taken for granted, by turning allusions into intratextual series, whether proximal (Thetis' two consecutive appeals to Zeus in *Iliad* I) or distal (personal laments scattered throughout the entire poem). In this type of intertextuality, the important notion is that of thematically associated parts forming a chain and emphasizing performance sequences. This form of intertextuality is effectuated between orderly combinations of interacting parts creating a meaningful whole. These *syntagmatic* relations stress the *sequential* associations between traditions. They may at times have to do with a recognizable tradition, but the emphasis is on the revelation of rules or conventions underlying the production of an epic scene.

In Chapter Ten,[24] I explore how the deliberate paradox of Thetis' request to Zeus in *Iliad* I 493–516 is interwoven with another song-tradition in which Thetis had saved Zeus from the usurpation of his preeminence by his divine rivals. Intertextuality takes here the form of dictional allusion, i.e. it is reflected on the very formulation and *staging* of the supplication scene between Thetis and Zeus. Conversely, given that Greek myth was familiar with an archetypal rivalry between Zeus and Achilles, who might have overthrown the father of gods if Thetis had been married to an immortal instead of Peleus, it becomes clear that the *Iliad* invites the audience to reconstruct a tradition against which its own version must be measured. In particular, the disparity between the immortality of the mother (Thetis) and the short life-span of her son (Achilles) becomes a central theme around which the *Iliad* evolves and by which the epic differentiates itself from other rival songs. By studying the structure, diction, and deployment of this scene, one is able to comprehend its 'structuration', i.e. its coming into being. The first paradox of Thetis' supplication lies in the fact that her request seems quite annoying to Zeus, who occu-

---

[24] Originally published as "Construction, Sound and Rhythm: Thetis' Supplication to Zeus (*Iliad* 1.493–516)." *Arethusa* 34.1 (2001): 1–29. Permission to reprint from Johns Hopkins University Press.

pies, within the Olympian pantheon, a position equivalent to the one taken by Agamemnon among the other Achaean kings.

Thetis' appeal to Zeus has another, figurative dimension. Achilles' proximity to the divine culminates in a second, this time dramatic, paradox: his immortal mother (Thetis) asks Zeus to grant her mortal son *time* (honor), the one thing that will lead to his death. By requesting Zeus to 'kill' Achilles in terms of mortality, she figuratively asks him to make Achilles the hero of the *Iliad*, to allow the poem to create its own subject-matter. It is clear that the *Iliad* is using Thetis as a poetic vehicle in order not to sidestep the vexed paradox of her request but to tailor it to its needs. By creating a profound narrative tease, the epic renegotiates its audience's familiarity with rival epic traditions through abbreviated mythical tatters creeping up in the plot. Thetis is thus rebaptized in the Iliadic narrative pool, concocting, in fact, an Achillean plan. The divine ruse of Zeus will be devised upon *female* connivance, harking back to an earlier mythical phase which the *Iliad* will narratively exploit through a masterful analeptical ploy.

In Chapter Eleven,[25] Thetis' personal lament is placed under scrupulous examination. Formulaic deviation constitutes a sophisticated epic strategy of creating meaning, used either as a cross-referencing device, a footnoting mechanism, or a means of authority-conferring. The style of Thetis' language, the reuse of traditional formulas, the creation of new dictional coins such as the famous *hapax legomenon* δυσαριστοτόκεια make her γόος deviate from the typical lament pattern employed by the *Iliad*. The peculiarities of this lament bespeak the epic's sophisticated absorption of the theme of Achilles' death, which was once a significant episode of a rival tradition, but has now become the renovated emblem of the *Iliad*. The dictional, stylistic, and formulaic idiosyncrasies of her personal lament for Achilles not only reflect the marginalization and liminality of the poem's greatest hero, but also form part of an intertextual 'answer' of the Iliadic γόος for Achilles to its 'Aethiopic' rival.

In Chapter Twelve, I explore the extended Homeric simile as a form of imagery performed on a special rhythmic register. The interpretation of similes stands at the crossroads between two conflicting approaches. On the one hand, the singer or storyteller aims at guiding his listeners to a specific interpretation of the similes according to his narrative blueprint. He, therefore, creates a 'narrative indexing' of the similes by such means as *intratextual sequencing*. On the other hand, since similes refer to the physical world

---

[25] Originally published as "The Poetics of Sorrow: Thetis' Lament in *Iliad* 18.52-64." QUCC 76 (2004): 9–32. Permission to reprint from *Istituti Editoriali e Poligrafici Internazionali*.

and not to the epic past, they conjure up, in the listeners' minds, multiple mental image-mappings. The condensed or abbreviated form of Homeric similes engages the audience in an active interplay, since the mental template of each listener will allow him to visualize the simile's short story according to his own experiential storage. Similes reactivate mental images in such a vivid manner that they enable listeners to explore a deeper meaning, especially a meaning in the making, located not just within the simile's framework but also in connection to their own mental world. Under this scope, similes function on a *hypertextual* level, directing the audience to multiple conceptual strata from which they can easily 'return' to the main narrative. It is exactly at the juncture between the mental multiformity of the audience's image-mappings on the one hand, and the storyteller's attempt to help his listeners visualize similes in a way consonant to his narrative blueprint on the other that the special nature of the Homeric simile lies. To this extent, similes are imbued with an endless intertextuality, which is neither tradition-dependent nor diachronically activated. In fact, this form of *hypertextuality* leads Homeric listeners through conceptual pathways to the mentally reconstructed hyper-world of image-mappings and, once the simile is completed, back again to the main narrative.

Acknowledgments

THIS BOOK IS DEDICATED TO PIETRO PUCCI, whose scientific acumen, unstinting encouragement, and unfailing guidance have been a constant support for me during these last fifteen years. He stands at the head of a small but precious group of scholars, who have guided me in search of my scholarly pathway.

Through the years, I have incurred some special debts of professional and personal gratitude, which I am truly happy to acknowledge. My deepest thanks go to Gregory Nagy, whose profound understanding of epic song-traditions have shaped the way many people, including myself, approach Homeric poetry. Egbert Bakker's groundbreaking contributions to Homeric studies over the years have also left a lasting imprint on my work. On the European side of the Atlantic, Georg Danek's and Antonios Rengakos' work on intertextuality and Homeric Poetics have also enlightened the way I study Homer. I am also grateful to the latter, who suggested to me the Hellenic Series published by the Center for Hellenic Studies as the ideal 'Homeric' place to submit my work for publication.

I am also glad to thank the anonymous reader for helpful comments and the entire editorial team at CHS for making the process of turning my manuscript into a book a pleasing experience. Needless to say, I am entirely responsible for the errors and shortcomings that remain.

Christos C. Tsagalis
Athens, January 2007

Note on Transliteration and References

WHILE FOR GREEK PERSONAL NAMES I have used their anglicized forms (Achilles, not Akhilleus), for Greek place names I have opted for their hellenicized –*os* endings (Delos, Scyros). When using someone else's translation, I have remained faithful to the author's transliteration system, hence the lack of absolute consistency and the discrepancy between e.g. Kallidice and Callidice, Trophonios and Trophonius. Internal cross-references indicate chapter numbers.

Part One

INTERTEXTUALITY BETWEEN RECOGNIZABLE TRADITIONS

1
Ἀνδρομάχη μαινομένη:
The Dionysiac Element in the *Iliad*

THE ALMOST COMPLETE ABSENCE OF DIONYSUS from the *Iliad* is well known, as it is commonly recognized that the heroic epic singing the κλέα ἀνδρῶν does not have a place for the god of wine, ecstasy, and bacchic frenzy. Dionysus appears in the *Iliad* only twice: the first time in the myth of Lycurgus (*Iliad* VI 132, 135) and the second in the episode of Zeus' deception (*Iliad* XIV 325), within a small catalogue of Zeus' extramarital relationships. However, the Dionysiac element is latently present in the *Iliad* through Andromache, who is characterized twice (*Iliad* VI 389: μαινομένη εἰκυῖα, *Iliad* XXII 460: μαινάδι ἴση) by terminology with covertly Dionysiac overtones.

The use of Dionysiac, or rather maenadic, associations has been studied primarily by Privitera and Seaford. The former argues that the Dionysiac myths formed part not only of heroic epic but also of the complex mythical nexus developed around the Trojan War. The adventures of Dionysus had thus been the subject of epic poetry, as can also be argued from the study of Eumelus' *Europia*.[1] Moreover, the name of Dionysus is already attested in Linear B, which proves that the god was known and, probably, worshiped by the Mycenean aristocracy.[2] Seaford[3] has rightly argued that the marginalized and almost liminal presence of Dionysus as well as of the maenadic references to Andromache in the *Iliad* are the result of the enactment and subsequent annulment of the nuptial ritual in general and of marriage in particular, which this epic tradition fosters and systematically pursues. Each time Andromache, the Iliadic paragon of the noble wife on the human level, is mentioned (*Iliad*

---

[1] *PEG* 1, fr. 11 = *EGF* fr. 1. On the possible connection of Eumelus' *Europia* to Boeotia, see West 2002:126–128. There was also another *Europia* by Stesichorus (fr. 195, *PMGF*) concerning the foundation of the city of Thebes by Cadmus.
[2] Privitera 1970:14–15, 20–21.
[3] Seaford 1993:115–146.

VI, XXII, XXIV), the image of either a past or an impending catastrophe (referring to Hector's death and the dissolution of his marriage) lurks in the background. According to Seaford,[4] Andromache is the only Iliadic figure to whom a Dionysiac metaphor is attributed, because both in *Iliad* VI and XXII she leaves, maenad-like, her οἶκος. In this light, she virtually annuls (especially in *Iliad* XXII) both the wedding ritual and marriage itself, which Dionysus also overturns in myth, forcing women to resist any form of institutionally legitimized obedience, as symbolized by marriage, one of the most representative forms of female submission to male-controlled civic authority.

This chapter aims to widen the horizon of Seaford's aforementioned theory by presenting an evolutionary model of interpretation according to which the questions "Why is Dionysus excluded from the *Iliad*?" and "Why is Andromache presented as a maenad connected with a Dionysiac metaphor?" are complementary. The central problem to these questions concerns the relationship of the Iliadic tradition to another rival tradition, that of Thebes, which the *Iliad* artfully conceals, though unable to avoid making implicit allusions to it.

This chapter is divided into two parts. In the first I deal with those elements 'shared' by the two "Dionysiac" scenes in *Iliad* VI (the episode of Lycurgus and the meeting between Hector and Andromache), as well as the end of *Iliad* XXII, where Andromache, running to the walls in order to face the sight of her dead husband, is compared to a maenad. In the second part, I examine the Theban allusions and hints, overt and covert alike, that recur in *Iliad* VI and relate to the two aforementioned 'Dionysiac' scenes, that of Lycurgus and of the meeting between Hector and Andromache. I make the case that two allegedly distinct features of the *Iliad* (the absence of the god Dionysus and the systematic and almost exclusive correlation between Andromache and Dionysus) constitute a by-product of the epic rivalry between song-traditions aiming at prevailing upon one another by adopting a policy of selective compilation.

The Myth of Lycurgus

The most important allusion to Dionysus in the *Iliad* is attested in the myth of Lycurgus. I quote the relevant passage (*Iliad* VI 130-140):

οὐδὲ γὰρ οὐδὲ Δρύαντος υἱός, κρατερὸς Λυκόοργος,
δὴν ἦν, ὅς ῥα θεοῖσιν ἐπουρανίοισιν ἔριζεν·

---

[4] Seaford 1993:116–117.

Ἀνδρομάχη μαινομένη

ὅς ποτε μαινομένοιο Διωνύσοιο τιθήνας
σεῦε κατ' ἠγάθεον Νυσήϊον, αἳ δ' ἅμα πᾶσαι
θύσθλα χαμαὶ κατέχευαν, ὑπ' ἀνδροφόνοιο Λυκούργου
θεινόμεναι βουπλῆγι. Διώνυσος δὲ φοβηθείς
δύσεθ' ἁλὸς κατὰ κῦμα, Θέτις δ' ὑπεδέξατο κόλπῳ
δειδιότα· κρατερὸς γὰρ ἔχε τρόμος ἀνδρὸς ὁμοκλῇ.
τῷ μὲν ἔπειτ' ὀδύσαντο θεοὶ ῥεῖα ζώοντες,
καί μιν τυφλὸν ἔθηκε Κρόνου πάϊς· οὐδ' ἄρ' ἔτι δήν
ἦν, ἐπεὶ ἀθανάτοισιν ἀπήχθετο πᾶσι θεοῖσιν.

Since even the son of Dryas, Lykourgos the powerful, did not
live long; he who tried to fight with the gods of the bright sky,
who once drove the fosterers of rapturous Dionysos
headlong down the sacred Nyseian hill, and all of them
shed and scattered their wands on the ground, stricken with an
    ox-goad
by murderous Lykourgos, while Dionysos in terror
dived into the salt surf, and Thetis took him to her bosom,
frightened, with the strong shivers upon him at the man's
    blustering.
But the gods who live at their ease were angered with
    Lykourgos,
and the son of Kronos struck him to blindness, nor did he live
    long
afterwards, since he was hated by all the immortals.

The above passage constitutes a mythological *exemplum* or *paradeigma*.[5] The speaker Diomedes tells Glaucus the story of Lycurgus, who attacked Dionysus and his nurses so fiercely that the god was only able to escape by plunging into the sea, where he was welcomed and comforted by Thetis.[6] By exploiting the rich content of this mythological example, Diomedes covertly denotes his intention to avoid the confrontation with the gods on the battlefield, so as not to share Lycurgus' fate, who lost first his sight and then his life. The tone of the mythological example is rather dissuading, as it is placed within the context of Diomedes' attempt to find out whether his battlefield

---

[5] For the general use and function of the mythological model in the Homeric epics, see Willcock 1964:141–154.
[6] Dionysus and Thetis are mythologically connected through a golden amphora Dionysus gave her as a wedding gift. It was this same amphora the goddess later used to keep the bones of Achilles (*Odyssey* xxiv 73–76).

opponent, Glaucus, is a god or a man, so as to decide to either avoid battle or launch an attack against him.

Diomedes' reference to Dionysus follows his *aristeia* in *Iliad* V, where the son of Tydeus has wounded and put into flight even the pro-Trojan gods. Diomedes' excellence in battle is context-dependent as it is he, together with the greater Ajax, who acts as surrogate of Achilles, filling the void Thetis' son has left for the Greek side. The mythological example of Lycurgus is, of course, adapted to suit the narrative needs of the scene in which it belongs, but it simultaneously initiates the beginning of an internal cycle brought to an end only with the meeting of Hector and Andromache in *Iliad* VI. Interestingly enough, this internal cycle is brought to the fore once more, at the end of *Iliad* XXII, just after Hector's death.

The episode of Diomedes and Glaucus stands as a prelude to any overt or covert allusions to the maenadic elements in *Iliad* VI. In fact, the scene between Diomedes and Glaucus and the meeting between Hector and Andromache, placed respectively at the beginning and end of *Iliad* VI, are symmetrically balanced with respect to their Dionysiac connotations. This structural analogy does not necessitate thematic cohesion, but it nevertheless indicates the significance of the Dionysiac overtones in *Iliad* VI, in the single—I dare say—Dionysiac Book of the *Iliad*.

Detecting and analyzing Dionysiac features, explicit and implicit alike, does not only contribute to appreciating the structural model upon which *Iliad* VI has been built but also allows for a deeper understanding of Andromache's overall Iliadic presentation. Turning my attention to the mythological model of Lycurgus, I will attempt to pinpoint a series of Dionysiac elements that have particular meaning for the function of Andromache in the *Iliad*.

(a) The participle μαινομένοιο (*Iliad* VI 132) referring to Dionysus does not, contrary to Iliadic practice, have any warlike overtones. The verb μαίνεσθαι and the noun μένος are used almost exclusively in terms of war, as they signify the fighting frenzy warriors display during the havoc of battle.[7] Seaford[8] has correctly observed that there are only six cases in the *Iliad* and

---

[7] The verb μαίνεσθαι is attested 20 times in the *Iliad* (V 185; V 717; V 831, VI 101; VI 132; VI 389; VIII 111; VIII 355; VIII 360; VIII 413; IX 238; XV 128; XV 605; XV 606; XVI 75; XVI 245; XXI 5; XXII 460 (μαινάς); XXIV 114; XXIV 135) and 4 times in the *Odyssey*: ix 350, xi 537, xviii 406, xxi 298. The noun μαινάς is attested only once in the *Hom. Hymn to Demeter* (2) 386: ἤϊξ' ἠΰτε μαινὰς ὄρος κάτα δάσκιον ὕλῃ. μένος pertains to male behavior and is regarded as a primary component of the warrior's military talent. However, it is not used exclusively for men, (*Iliad* XXI 411; *Iliad* XXI 482; *Iliad* XXI 488). See also Hershkovitz 1998:57 (with relevant bibliography), 143.

[8] Seaford 1993:143–144.

the *Odyssey*, where frenzy does not have warlike connotations. I will focus only on three instances of this phenomenon.⁹

In the first case (*Iliad* XXII 70-71), Priam uses the verb ἀλύσσω (οἵ κ' ἐμὸν αἷμα πιόντες ἀλύσσοντες περὶ θυμῷ // κείσοντ' ἐν προθύροισι) when referring to the dogs that will drink the blood and then, in their anger, lie down in Priam's courts. Seaford¹⁰ rightly points to verses 337-339 of Euripides' *Bacchae*, designating Actaeon's miserable death, who is torn to pieces by the very same dogs he has reared (... τὸν Ἀκταίωνος ἄθλιον μόρον, // ὃν ὠμόσιτοι σκύλακες ἃς ἐθρέψατο // διεσπάσαντο ...), and verse 977 of the same play, indicating that Pentheus will be dismembered by the fast dogs of Madness (θοαὶ Λύσσας κύνες).

The second case is that of *Iliad* XXIV 114 (φρεσὶ μαινομένῃσιν), in which Zeus expresses displeasure because Achilles refuses to return Hector's body, instead keeping it next to the ships, thus inviting the rage of the gods, and most of all that of Zeus (*Iliad* XXIV 113-114: ... ἐμὲ δ' ἔξοχα πάντων // ἀθανάτων κεχολῶσθαι, ...). Zeus' fury recalls the rage of the gods in the myth of Lycurgus (*Iliad* VI 140: ... ἐπεὶ ἀθανάτοισιν ἀπήχθετο πᾶσι θεοῖσιν) and belongs to the same thematic framework as *Iliad* XXII 70-71. Likewise, it "threatens the performance of the death ritual," only because this time, as Seaford¹¹ accurately notes, the threat relates to the disfigurement of the body not by the dogs, as in the case of Priam, but by a human being, Achilles, who is figuratively transformed into a 'dog eating raw-flesh' (ὠμηστὴς κύων). The horrific echoes of the Iliadic proem could hardly have resounded with greater emphasis (*Iliad* I 4-5: ... αὐτοὺς δὲ ἑλώρια τεῦχε κύνεσσιν // οἰωνοῖσί τε πᾶσι, ...¹².

A third case, where μαίνεσθαι has no warlike overtones whatsoever is found in *Odyssey* xviii 406, where Telemachus accuses the suitors (δαιμόνιοι, μαίνεσθε ...). Even in this context, μαίνεσθε alludes to imminent threat and the overturning of both the wedding ritual and marriage at large. In fact, the suitors' determination to marry Penelope as well as their obstinate insistence on making her choose one of them as her new husband indicates that the menace imposed on Odysseus' household is keyed on a Dionysiac tone.¹³ Combining all of the non-warlike uses of μαίνεσθαι in the *Iliad* and the *Odyssey*,

---

⁹ The three other Iliadic deviations from the typical warlike-colored terms relating to μαίνεσθαι and μένος refer to Dionysus (*Iliad* VI 132: μαινομένοιο Διωνύσοιο) and Andromache (*Iliad* VI 389: μαινομένῃ εἰκυῖα, *Iliad* XXII 460: μαινάδι ἴση). For these cases, see the introductory comments in this chapter. For Andromache as a maenad, see Gagliardi 2006:16-19.
¹⁰ Seaford 1993:143.
¹¹ Seaford 1993:144.
¹² For the theme of the mutilation of the body in the *Iliad*, see Segal 1971b.
¹³ Seaford 1993:144.

Seaford argues that each one is connected "with one or more of the elements of our tragic complex of ideas: violence within household, the negation of ritual and the Dionysiac."[14]

After this detailed analysis of the non-warlike uses of μαίνεσθαι, one can plausibly claim that the participle μαινομένοιο (*Iliad* VI 132), which is used to characterize Dionysus, inaugurates a Dionysiac use of the term, which in the *Iliad* appears to be particular to Andromache and her presence and function in epic.

(b) In the mythological example employed by Diomedes, Lycurgus assaults the nurses of frenzied Dionysus at Nyseion, a mountain in Thrace (*Iliad* VI 132-133).[15] The *Iliad* refrains from mentioning what exactly the women were doing at Nyseion. Instead, it focuses on the throwing of their branches to the ground in a state of panic. However, according to Eumelus, who gives a detailed account of this myth in his *Europia*,[16] the nurses (who, as in *Iliad* VI 132, are called τιθῆναι) were celebrating orgies, together with Dionysus (ἐτύγχανον αὐτῷ [sc. Διονύσῳ] συνοργιάζουσαι). This comparison makes it clear that these nurses (τιθῆναι) are maenads, in spite of the fact that the Iliadic tradition does not use this term for them. Moreover, the same word employed for the women who accompany Dionysus (τιθῆναι) is also used in the meeting between Hector and Andromache (*Iliad* VI 389: μαινομένῃ εἰκυῖα· φέρει δ' ἅμα παῖδα τιθήνη; *Iliad* VI 467-468: ἂψ δ' ὁ πάϊς πρὸς κόλπον ἐϋζώνοιο τιθήνης // ἐκλίνθη ἰάχων, ...), even though earlier, in *Iliad* VI 399, the same maid, who accompanies Andromache on the walls and is present at the meeting scene between husband and wife, is characterized by the more common, in terms of Iliadic diction, and more general term 'maid' (ἀμφίπολος). The word 'nurse' (τιθήνη) is also used in *Iliad* XXII 503 (ἐν ἀγκαλίδεσσι τιθήνης). Privitera has rightly observed that the term τιθήνη[17] deviates from the typical way the *Iliad* refers to a nurse (τροφός). This stylistic differentiation becomes all the more important, since all four attestations of the word τιθήνη are placed in

---

[14] Seaford 1993:145.

[15] The mountain is named Nysa in Euripides *Bacchae* 556. According to Kirk 1990:174: "There were many mountains of that name – from India to Babylon, Arabia and Libya according to Hesychius – associated with or named after the god, but [the scholia] bT were right in taking this one to be in Thrace because Thetis is nearby (136), since she lived in an underwater cave between Samos, i.e. Samothrace, and Imbros according to 24.77-84." Thrace is the correct choice because it is compatible with the widespread mythological concept that Dionysus originated from Thrace.

[16] *PEG* 1, fr. 11 = *EGF* fr. 1.

[17] The word τιθήνη is attested only 4 times in the *Iliad* (VI 132; VI 389; VI 467; XXII 503). See Privitera 1970:61n18.

contexts with Dionysiac connotations. Aside from the mythological example of Lycurgus, all three other instances of Iliadic maenadism involve Hector, Andromache, or Astyanax. The use of τιθήνη in these three passages adds a covert Dionysiac element to the overt Dionysiac terms μαινομένοιο (*Iliad* VI 132), μαινομένη (*Iliad* VI 389) and μαινάδι (*Iliad* XXII 460) and reveals the existence of a *selective affinity* of this terminology to Andromache, the only character in Iliadic epic constantly connected with Dionysiac allusions.

(c) In the myth of Lycurgus, greater emphasis should be placed on the latent connections between Hector and Andromache. Lycurgus is characterized by the epithet 'man-slaying' (*Iliad* VI 134: ἀνδροφόνοιο), which, together with the noun it modifies, forms a typical noun-epithet formula placed either in verse-initial or terminal position. The epithet ἀνδροφόνος is attested 16 times in the *Iliad*,[18] of which 13 are in the genitive case[19] and only three in the accusative[20] (designating the murderous hands of Achilles). From the 13 times this epithet is found in the genitive case, 11 refer to Hector (ὑφ' Ἕκτορος ἀνδροφόνοιο or Ἕκτορος ἀνδροφόνοιο), one to Ares (*Iliad* IV 441: Ἄρεος ἀνδροφόνοιο) and one to Lycurgus (*Iliad* VI 134: ὑπ' ἀνδροφόνοιο Λυκούργου). As a result, by forming an integral part of a Hector-related formula, the epithet ἀνδροφόνοιο conjures up these latent connotations not only to the singer's mind but also to that of the audience. Formulaic expressions of this sort have acquired a secondary, 'elliptical' meaning, one that has been registered in the collective awareness of the tradition. The context-free formulaic input of ἀνδροφόνοιο allows Hector to be present even when not referred to by name. Thus, the formula ὑπ' ἀνδροφόνοιο Λυκούργου recalls Hector, as the *Iliad* attributes to a figure mentioned only once an epithet traditionally employed for an epic protagonist.[21] In the meeting between Andromache and Hector in *Iliad* VI, Hector is also designated by the same epithet (*Iliad* VI 498: Ἕκτορος ἀνδροφόνοιο). In this way, the *Iliad* invites its audience to associate the myth of Lycurgus with the meeting between Hector and Andromache, which will follow later in *Iliad* VI. The epithet ἀνδροφόνοιο, however, is joined to the fate

---

[18] It is attested only once in the *Odyssey* (i 261).
[19] *Iliad* I 242; *Iliad* IV 441; *Iliad* VI 134; *Iliad* VI 498; *Iliad* IX 351; *Iliad* XVI 77; *Iliad* XVI 840; *Iliad* XVII 428; *Iliad* XVII 616; *Iliad* XVII 638; *Iliad* XVIII 149; *Iliad* XXIV 509; *Iliad* XXIV 724. See n22.
[20] *Iliad* XVIII 317; *Iliad* XXIII 18; *Iliad* XXIV 479.
[21] This is confirmed by the use of the fundamental, nuclear idea of the formula, the preverbal *Gestalt* according to Nagler 1967:269–311; 1974:8. In similar cases, the use and combination of metrical, morphological and semantic elements (or their formulaic allomorphs) creates an interpretive pattern that is recalled under the same or similar contextual parameters. See Kahane 1994:43–79.

of Andromache in a unique way, as becomes evident from the wordplay in *Iliad* XXIV 723-724: τῇσιν δ' Ἀνδρομάχη λευκώλενος ἦρχε γόοιο, // Ἕκτορος ἀνδροφόνοιο κάρη μετὰ χερσὶν ἔχουσα.[22] In these two verses introducing the lamentation of the spouse for her dead husband, the bond between the dead Hector and Andromache is deepened, highlighting the common fate shared by the deceased and the mourner. It is this motif that the widow of the most famous Trojan warrior had already mentioned in *Iliad* XXII 477-479: Ἕκτορ, ἐγὼ δύστηνος· ἰῇ ἄρα γεινόμεθ' αἴσῃ // ἀμφότεροι, σὺ μὲν ἐν Τροίῃ Πριάμου κατὰ δῶμα, // αὐτὰρ ἐγὼ Θήβῃσιν ὑπὸ Πλάκῳ ὑληέσσῃ. Simultaneously, the expression μετὰ χερσὶν ἔχουσα alludes to the murderous hands (ἀνδροφόνους χεῖρας) of Achilles, which had caused the death of Hector. In this light, the epithet ἀνδροφόνος has evolved into an Iliadic metonymy for both Hector and for his relationship with Andromache, in the name of whom (Ἀνδρο-μάχη) it is partly reflected.

(d) Another element in the Lycurgus myth bearing similarities to the scene of the meeting between Hector and Andromache is that of fear. In *Iliad* VI 135 and 137, we learn that Dionysus, in a state of fear (φοβηθείς), plunged into the sea where, still afraid (δειδιότα), he was welcomed into Thetis' arms. In *Iliad* VI 467-469 the infant Astyanax, frightened by the bronze armor and the crest of Hector's helmet, 'was welcomed' in the embrace of his nurse who held him in her arms (ἂψ δ' ὁ πάϊς πρὸς κόλπον ἐϋζώνοιο τιθήνης // ἐκλίνθη ἰάχων, πατρὸς φίλου ὄψιν ἀτυχθείς, // ταρβήσας χαλκόν τε ἰδὲ λόφον ἱππιοχαίτην).

(e) The analogy between the fear experienced by Dionysus and by Astyanax is strengthened by the fact that, just as the frightened god is welcomed into Thetis' lap (*Iliad* VI 136: δύσεθ' ἁλὸς κατὰ κῦμα, Θέτις δ' ὑπεδέξατο κόλπῳ), so Astyanax is either hidden in the arms of his nurse (*Iliad* VI 467-468: ἂψ δ' ὁ πάϊς πρὸς κόλπον ἐϋζώνοιο τιθήνης // ἐκλίνθη ἰάχων, ...) or 'is received' in the arms of his mother, Andromache (*Iliad* VI 483: ... ἣ δ' ἄρα μιν κηώδεϊ δέξατο κόλπῳ)[23] or finds comfort in the embrace of his nurse (*Iliad* XXII 503: ἐν ἀγκαλίδεσσι τιθήνης).[24]

(f) The expression δύσεθ' ἁλὸς κατὰ κῦμα (*Iliad* VI 136) and, more significantly, the use of the verb δύομαι presents a latent analogy to the phrase

---

[22] I have adopted, contra West, the reading ἀνδροφόνοιο offered by the manuscript family Ω*.

[23] In the episode of Hector and Andromache in *Iliad* VI, the word κόλπος is used in order to highlight the image of the young and frightened Astyanax (*Iliad* VI 400: παῖδ' ἐπὶ κόλπῳ ἔχουσ' ἀταλάφρονα, νήπιον αὔτως). Andromache proleptically refers to a similar image in *Iliad* XXII 503, though the word κόλπος is not stated: εὕδεσκ' ἐν λέκτροισιν, ἐν ἀγκαλίδεσσι τιθήνης.

[24] Privitera 1970: 61-62, and, most importantly, 61n18.

χθόνα δύμεναι used by Andromache when she wishes to sink into the earth rather than live without Hector (*Iliad* VI 411). The form δύμεναι is used four times in the *Iliad*, three of which have warlike implications (*Iliad* VI 185: μάχην [...] δύμεναι ἀνδρῶν; *Iliad* XIV 62-63: πόλεμον ... // δύμεναι; *Iliad* XIX 313: ... πολέμου στόμα δύμεναι αἱματόεντος). Conversely, this (*Iliad* VI 411) is the only case where it is used with the noun χθόνα. A comparable example is γαῖαν ἐδύτην (*Iliad* VI 19). The formula (κατα)δῦναι ὅμιλον, which is mainly used in battle scenes, provides the spark for the creation of a verbal parallelism between the two passages. Furthermore, since the context of this scene presupposed a peaceful meeting between the two spouses on the walls of Troy before their definitive separation, the formula (κατα)δῦναι ὅμιλον needed to be adapted to its new 'environment'. The result was the creation of the formulaic allomorph χθόνα δύμεναι (*Iliad* VI 411), which also echoes the expression δύσεθ' ἁλὸς κατὰ κῦμα (*Iliad* VI 136).[25]

(g) The dramatic space where the episodes of Lycurgus and Hector-Andromache unfold is described in detail. Lycurgus chases Dionysus and his maenads on the Nyseion mountain, a space situated outside the boundaries of the city, symbolizing the figurative distance from human civilization since it is imbued with an unusual and charming wildness. Consequently, the framework of the Lycurgus episode immediately transports us to a "different" place, into the realm of Dionysiac 'otherness', where the god and his maenads are found as they travel from the city into the wild. The mountain is not simply a geographic point but rather the symbol of a 'transition' from the rational to the irrational, from the 'civilized' space of the *polis* to a realm where the power of Dionysus prevails.

Similar observations can be made concerning the meeting scene between Hector and Andromache in *Iliad* VI.[26] The fact that the two spouses meet on the walls of Troy is narratively highlighted, the more so since they were both compelled to leave the space of their own proper domain, Andromache her 'house' (οἶκος) and Hector the battlefield. In this light, the walls of Troy constitute a 'transitional' space, one that belongs neither to the city nor to the

---

[25] The phrase (κατα)δῦναι ὅμιλον // δόμον is attested 8 times in the *Iliad* (*Iliad* III 322; *Iliad* VII 131; *Iliad* X 231; *Iliad* X 433; *Iliad* XI 537; *Iliad* XIII 307; *Iliad* XV 299; *Iliad* XX 76). For the allomorph ἀναδῦναι ὅμιλον, see *Iliad* VII 217-218. See also *Iliad* X 338 (κάλλιφ' ὅμιλον) and *Iliad* XVI 729 (δύσεθ' ὅμιλον ἰών) referring to Apollo and recalling *Iliad* VI 136 (δύσεθ' ἁλὸς κατὰ κῦμα). Segal 1971a: 33-57 has argued that the second portion of *Iliad* XXII 462 (καὶ ἀνδρῶν ἷξεν ὅμιλον) "is clearly modeled after δῦναι (καταδῦναι) ὅμιλον, common in the battle scenes" (48). It is indeed noteworthy that the protagonist in this episode is, once more, Andromache.
[26] See Maronitis 1990:105-123.

battlefield and, by extension, neither to Andromache nor to Hector. This place is especially important for the *Iliad*, since it forms a metaphorical threshold where space and time are suspended in order to narratively immobilize these two important plot-characters, on which half of the Iliadic tragedy is based. When the tragic cycle is drawn to a close, the *Iliad* will once more bring the walls of the city to the narrative surface. It is there that the drama of Hector will be finally played out, as Andromache, maenad-like, panic-stricken and with disheveled hair, will watch her husband's body being dragged by Achilles' chariot in the battlefield.[27] In this tragic scene, we encounter many of the motifs also found in *Iliad* VI. Andromache rapidly moves through the palace (*Iliad* XXII 460: μεγάροιο διέσσυτο) with her heart pounding (*Iliad* XXII 461: παλλομένη κραδίην). She then runs to the walls, where she will see the dead body of Hector dragged by Achilles' chariot. In her panic she metaphorically loses her sight, collapses, and her heart becomes weak (*Iliad* XXII 466–467: τὴν δὲ κατ' ὀφθαλμῶν ἐρεβεννὴ νὺξ ἐκάλυψεν, // ἤριπε δ' ἐξοπίσω, ἀπὸ δὲ ψυχὴν ἐκάπυσσεν). Then she throws off the headbands and veils symbolizing her marriage to Hector (*Iliad* XXII 468–470). In her ensuing dirge[28] she does not fail to recall the same persons and themes she has already mentioned in her proleptic γόος in *Iliad* VI 407–439: her wedding, her father Eetion, Hector, with whom she shared the same doomed fate, and, last but not least, Astyanax.[29]

The walls of Troy constitute the emotional topography for the presentation of the last meeting between the two spouses. Under this scope, it is their early narrative connection to the episode of Andromache and Hector in *Iliad* VI that confers their special, *Iliad*-specific definition as a dramatic space of timely meaning.[30] But what exactly is the relationship between this dramatic space and the Dionysiac metaphor?

Following Segal, who, in his discussion on Greek tragedy, uses the terms 'horizontal' and 'vertical' axes in order to define all that is familiar in the life of the city and all that is foreign,[31] we can examine the space where the

---

[27] See *Iliad* XXII 460–465.

[28] See Tsagalis 2004:129–133.

[29] Seaford 1993:118–119 has rightly emphasized that in this scene certain typical elements of the wedding ritual, such as the μακαρισμός and the new home where the newlyweds will live, have been inverted or completely destroyed. See also Tsagalis 2004:118–129.

[30] The importance of the walls for the plot of the *Iliad* is overtly but systematically underscored. All of the scenes related to the future of Troy take place either at the walls or at the Skaian gates, not inside the city (the 'Teichoscopia' in *Iliad* III, the meeting of Hector and Andromache in *Iliad* VI, Priam and Hecuba's warnings to Hector in *Iliad* XXII, the laments for Hector in *Iliad* XXII). See Scully 1990:42–43.

[31] Segal 1997:78.

Ἀνδρομάχη μαινομένη

episode of Hector and Andromache unfolds. By fostering such an interpretive approach, we may be able to determine the interplay between the Dionysiac metaphor in the myth of Lycurgus (*Iliad* VI 130-140) and the meeting between Andromache and Hector (*Iliad* VI 390-493).

The 'horizontal' axis includes both the meeting at the walls and the movement of the two spouses. Schadewaldt[32] believes that the emphasis here is on the mutual movement, as Hector is looking for Andromache in her own space, the 'house' (οἶκος), while she is looking for Hector in his own space, the walls.[33] Even though the walls define an intermediate space, as the Trojans in the *Iliad* almost always go out to the plain to fight against the Achaeans (there is never actually a siege), Schadewaldt's observation is valid, since it underscores the importance of the 'mutual approach' of husband and wife. This approach consists of three phases: the *search*, the *meeting*, and the final *separation*.[34] In this light, the audience is encouraged to follow the shift from the speed of an initial anguished dash to an ensuing immobility. Andromache 'has gone in speed to the wall, like a woman gone mad' (*Iliad* VI 388-389: ... ἐπειγομένη ἀφικάνει // μαινομένη εἰκυῖα ...)[35] on the one hand, and Hector 'hastened from his home / backward by the way he had come through the well-laid streets' (*Iliad* VI 390-391: ... ὃ δ' ἀπέσσυτο δώματος Ἕκτωρ // τὴν αὐτὴν ὁδὸν αὖτις ἐϋκτιμένας κατ' ἀγυιάς) on the other. The remaining passage is replete with similar accounts: 'as he had come to the gates on his way through the great city, the Skaian gates, whereby he would issue into the plain, there at last his own generous wife came running to meet him' (*Iliad* VI 392-394: εὖτε πύλας ἵκανε διερχόμενος μέγα ἄστυ // Σκαιάς, τῇ ἄρ' ἔμελλε διεξίμεναι πεδίονδε, // ἔνθ' ἄλοχος πολύδωρος ἐναντίη ἦλθε θέουσα). When the two spouses meet and find themselves face to face, the action stops and the focus is digressively turned to Andromache's origins (*Iliad* VI 395-398). The term ἀπέσσυτο, which was used for Hector (*Iliad* VI 390), will be slightly repeated in *Iliad* XXII 460 (διέσσυτο), occupying the same place in the hexameter, albeit this time designating Andromache.[36] The deliberate emphasis on the theme of movement on the *horizontal axis* of the dramatic space is related to the motif of *arrival* in terms of Dionysiac epiphany. In Euripides' *Bacchae*, the play begins

---

[32] Schadewaldt 1965⁴:214-215.
[33] Schadewald 1965⁴:215-217.
[34] Schadewaldt 1965⁴:215. The verb σεῦε is also used in *Iliad* VI 133 for the attack Lycurgus launched against Dionysus and his maenads.
[35] In this case, I have not adopted West's edition, in which *Iliad* VI 388 is considered to be an interpolation.
[36] Segal 1997:48.

with the unexpected advent of the god: ἥκω Διὸς παῖς τήνδε Θηβαίαν χθόνα // Διόνυσος ... (1–2).[37] This arrival is usually underscored by the κατ' ἐνώπιον (face to face) presence of Dionysus before humans.[38] Likewise, by presenting Andromache as coming in haste to meet Hector (*Iliad* VI 394: ἐναντίη ἦλθε θέουσα) and highlighting the family-reunion scene at the walls (*Iliad* VI 399: ἥ οἱ ἔπειτ' ἤντησ'; *Iliad* VI 404: ἰδὼν ἐς παῖδα; *Iliad* VI 405: οἱ ἄγχι παρίστατο), the *Iliad* emphasizes the face-to-face meeting between husband and wife.

The Dionysiac metaphor is also manifested in the *vertical* axis. In the episode of Lycurgus, Dionysus is given a warm welcome in the arms of Thetis, after he plunges into the sea to save himself (*Iliad* VI 136: δύσεθ' ἁλὸς κατὰ κῦμα). In the meeting between Hector and Andromache, the wife of the Trojan hero prefers to sink to the ground than to live without her beloved husband (*Iliad* VI 411: χθόνα δύμεναι). The use of the same verbal type in both passages points to a well-known Dionysiac metaphor, according to which the god is linked with both the watery and chthonic realms. In fact, the submersion into the sea represents, within a Dionysiac context, a transition to another state of being. The mythological tradition supporting one such interpretation is remarkably rich. The lake of Lerne, where Perseus throws the dead body of Dionysus, is commonly considered the entrance into Hades.[39] According to Diodorus,[40] who offers a mythological variation of the story of Lycurgus, the nurses of Dionysus were thrown into the sea in order to save themselves, while Boutas dies by falling into a well. Another well-known story is that of the Ἁλίαι, women murdered by Perseus. In the context of the ritual reenactment of their deaths in the water, Dionysus ἁλιεύς is immersed in water.[41] Moreover, as Daraki correctly observes, "the only swimming contests we are aware of in Greece were held in honor of Dionysus, in the area around lake Lerne, not far away from Hermione in the Argolid.[42] The word κόλυμβος, designates both a

---

[37] Ἥκω is often used in the first verse of Euripidean prologues but this does not undermine the fact that Dionysus' arrival has specific religious connotations.

[38] For the 'arrival' of Dionysus, the 'face-to-face' encounter with the god and the function of vision (ὁρᾶν) and appearance (φαίνεσθαι) in a Dionysiac context, see the seminal discussion of Vernant in Vernant and Vidal-Naquet 1986:237–270 (vol. 2).

[39] Pausanias II 37.5. See also Socrates of Argos (*FGrHist* 310, F 2), Pollux IV 861, scholia on Lycophron's *Alexandra* 212 (Scheer), scholia vetera on *Iliad* XIV 319 (Erbse).

[40] See Diodorus Siculus V 50.

[41] Pausanias II 20.4 and 22.1, scholia vetera on *Iliad* VI 130 (Erbse).

[42] See Daraki 1985:35. See also Sourvinou-Inwood 2005:204–205, who argues that the recurrence of bou- elements in the mythological nexuses of Boutas, Lycurgus (bouplex), and Lerna (Dionysus bougenes) "provides some confirmation for the notion that the Homeric Lykourgos and the Lerna nexus were indeed transformations (as was the Boutas myth) of earlier mythicoritual material that had involved a mortal's attack on Dionysos and Dionysos plunging in water." (205)

swimming contest and diving, and the nautical contest in Hermione had been placed under the protection of μελάναιγις Dionysus, a god of the darkness with chthonic characteristics."[43] The expression χθόνα δύμεναι (*Iliad* VI 411) used by Andromache constitutes a death wish. Simultaneously, however, it is inscribed in the context of the Dionysiac metaphor pertaining to this particular scene, since the metaphorical submersion into the earth is known not only from the worship of Dionysus but also from the myth of the abduction of Kore by Hades/Plouton. In the Lenaia, Dionysus is recognized as a god of the Underworld and is virtually compared to Plouton,[44] while the Cretan tradition presents him as the son of Zeus and Persephone having the Underworld as his realm.[45]

(h) Another covert connection, which should not necessarily be pressed a great deal, concerns the way the two passages emphasize the massiveness of the destruction. In *Iliad* VI 133–134, Dionysus' nurses all throw their branches to the ground (... αἳ δ᾽ ἅμα πᾶσαι // θύσθλα χαμαὶ κατέχευαν ...). In the episode of Hector and Andromache, the image of an impending or past disaster is expressed in a similar way: *Iliad* VI 409–410: ... τάχα γάρ σε κατακτενέουσιν Ἀχαιοί // πάντες ἐφορμηθέντες ...; *Iliad* VI 416: ... κατὰ δ᾽ ἔκτανεν Ἠετίωνα; *Iliad* VI 418–419: ἀλλ᾽ ἄρα μιν κατέκηε σὺν ἔντεσι δαιδαλέοισιν // ἠδ᾽ ἐπὶ σῆμ᾽ ἔχεεν· ...; *Iliad* VI 422–423: οἳ μὲν πάντες ἰῷ κίον ἤματι Ἄϊδος εἴσω· // πάντας γὰρ κατέπεφνε ποδάρκης δῖος Ἀχιλλεύς.

The Theban Connection

After having examined the Dionysiac element in the meeting between Hector and Andromache and its relation to the episode of Diomedes and Glaucus, I will place all the above-mentioned Dionysiac connections into a larger perspective. In particular, I will attempt to clarify the relation of Hector and Andromache to Thebes and, through this, to Dionysus.

The episode of Hector and Andromache contains Theban-colored features either concerning the protagonists of the episode directly (Hector, Andromache, Astyanax) or consisting of 'secondary' references, which seem inexplicable or are, at least, difficult to explain, since they appear outside of their original framework.

---

[43] The translation is my own.
[44] See Heraclitus B15 (D-K): —Ὠυτὸς δὲ Ἀίδης καὶ Διόνυσος, ὅτεῳ μαίνονται καὶ ληναΐζουσιν.
[45] See Daraki 1985:51n58-60. See also Hesiod *Works and Days* 126, where the dead of the golden age are called πλουτοδόται (wealth-giving), just like Dionysus.

Chapter One

The Protagonists

Andromache's name recalls an Amazon.[46] She is the one 'fighting against men' while representing matriarchal conceptions,[47] evidenced by the fact that her mother (*Iliad* VI 425) reigned (βασίλευεν) in Plakos. In sixth-century iconography, she is sometimes depicted either along with other Amazons fighting against Heracles or holding a spear in order to protect Astyanax after the fall of Troy.[48] Her abilities in war and her military knowledge are not unknown in Homeric epic. In *Iliad* VI 431–439 she demonstrates her knowledge of war when advising Hector on how to place the army at that portion of the wall where there was a wild fig tree (ἐρινεός), right at the spot the best of the Achaeans had attacked in the past. Andromache is also associated with other military activities: she takes care of Hector's horses (*Iliad* VIII 187–189) and, according to Zeus' foreshadowing (*Iliad* XVII 207–208), she will never take the famous weapons of Achilles from Hector's hands after his return from the battlefield. She is the only daughter of Eetion among seven brothers, which strengthens the 'male' aspect of her character, in contrast, for example, to the 'effeminized' Dolon, who is the only son among five sisters.[49] The reference to her mother in the list of her personal losses (*Iliad* VI 425–428) does not only belong to the typical motif of 'the scale of affection for one's beloved persons'[50] but also makes it possible for Andromache to be found completely alone, so that Hector can act as father, mother, and brothers, that is, embody her entire lost family as well as her new marital home.[51] Furthermore, her mother's death recalls both Artemis' murder of Laodameia in the story of Bellerophon (*Iliad* VI 205) and the murder of Ariadne, executed according to Dionysus' orders (*Odyssey* xi 321–325).[52] In Homer, the death of Andromache's

---

[46] The use of a name expressing hostility towards men does not necessarily prove that it belongs to an Amazon (cf. the name Alexandros). The name Andromache is not necessarily of Amazonian origin and so I prefer the term 'recalls' rather than 'denotes' an Amazon. However, given the relevant Iliadic passages, iconographical representations and mythological evidence, the hypothesis of Andromache's Amazonian origin becomes all the more likely.
[47] Pomeroy 1975:16–19.
[48] See von Bothmer 1957 plates 1, 3, 8, 11, 25, 106, 129–146, 179 (black-figure vases) and plates 3, 4, 8–9, 12 (red-figure vases); Touchefeu-Meynier 1981:772; Devambez and Kauffmann-Samaras 1981:586–653. See also the scholia vetera on *Iliad* III 189 (Erbse), where the name Ἀνδρομάχη features in an Amazon-list. I owe this point to Wathelet 1988:1214. Moreover, Andromache's name reflects the basic Homeric epithet attributed to the Amazons (*Iliad* III 189: ἀντιάνειραι).
[49] See Wathelet 1988:282.
[50] For the effect of 'ascending climax' within such a list, see Kakridis 1949:49–64.
[51] See Tsagalis 2004:118–129; Gagliardi 2006:11–46.
[52] See Wathelet 1988:282.

Ἀνδρομάχη μαινομένη

mother by Artemis is not explained, because the epic remains silent about a possible infringement infuriating the goddess. Jeanmaire has rightly observed that, in myth, Dionysus functions as a god of the underworld, since by making Artemis murder his beloved Ariadne, he brings the latter under his control.[53] Notwithstanding this murder, Dionysus subsequently deifies his beloved one, lifting her to the sky. Mother and beloved exchange roles and function as 'dual' companions, like the two goddesses in Eleusis, for whom Dionysus is 'lover' and 'son'. In this light, one may inquire whether it is mere chance that the festival of Ἡρωΐς, celebrating the ascent of Dionysus' mother, Semele, who is identified with Kore, is held in Boeotia.[54]

Andromache's covert, Amazon-oriented Iliadic associations point to Ares, as the Amazons are the cherished beings of the god of war.[55] To state another typical example from Greek epic, let us recall that the Amazon Penthesileia, who in the *Aethiopis* comes from Thrace to assist the Trojans, is Ares' daughter. Ares' Theban connections stem from Harmonia, the daughter he had with Aphrodite. Harmonia becomes, in myth, the wife of Cadmus, the mythical founder of Boeotian Thebes.[56] In view of the aforementioned associations, Ares is the mythical 'filter' through which Andromache's link to Boeotian Thebes is effectuated.

---

[53] See Jeanmaire 1951:225. Block 1995:310–311 argues that Artemis kills Laodameia in order to avenge the annihilation of the Amazons by Bellerophon. If this was the case, then why does Artemis kill (inexplicably) the mother of an Amazon like Andromache? The explanation given by Block leaves this question unanswered. One of the two sons of Bellerophon, Isandros, is murdered by the Solymoi and Ares. Artemis who kills Laodameia is characterized by the epithet χρυσήνιος (*Iliad* VI 205), which Homeric epic only ascribes to Ares (Block [1995] 311n58). Given that Ares and Artemis have complementary roles and that *Iliad* VI 190 (πάντας γὰρ κατέπεφνεν ἀμύμων Βελλεροφόντης) and *Iliad* VI 423 (πάντας γὰρ κατέπεφνε ποδάρκης δῖος Ἀχιλλεύς) are formulaically equivalent, it could be plausibly argued that the story of Bellerophon, which is embedded in the episode of Diomedes and Glaucus, is analogous to the embedded story of Eetion in the episode of Hector and Andromache in *Iliad* VI. Just as Bellerophon murders all of his foes (and the Amazons), so Achilles murders almost the entire family of the 'Amazon' Andromache. In a similar way, just as Artemis led the daughter of Bellerophon to disaster, so she kills Andromache's mother. However, the list of those murdered by Bellerophon is profoundly reminiscent of the list of those Achilles had killed in the embedded story of *Iliad* VI 414–428. Alden 2000:135n37 has argued that the word Ἀλήϊον (*Iliad* VI 201) perhaps echoes the verb ἀλᾶτο (*Iliad* VI 201) in the story of Bellerophon. Under this light, one may maintain that this is also the case with Διωνύσοιο (*Iliad* VI 132) and Νυσήϊον (*Iliad* VI 133) in the embedded story of Lycurgus. Needless to say, aural similarities of this kind are enhanced by the textual proximity of the aforementioned words, which are placed either in the same (*Iliad* VI 201) or in ensuing (*Iliad* VI 132–133) verses.

[54] See Daraki 1985:222.
[55] Daraki 1985:222.
[56] For Dionysus Cadmeius of Thebes, see Mikalson 2005:91–99.

Chapter One

Hector's Theban connections are based on both the transfer of his bones to Thebes and his Iliadic associations to Ares. Dümmler was the first to have argued for the Theban origin of Hector.[57] This theory has been strongly supported by some, and furiously opposed by others.[58] However, as is often the case in Homeric studies, the scholarly debate focused more on the criticism of the method of each hermeneutical approach rather than on the core issue supported by the various schools. This is not the forum to present in detail the variety of different views argued thus far, but a brief account of the basic components of the theory supporting Hector's Theban connections can be easily given: numerous ancient and Byzantine sources (Aristodemus of Thebes,[59] Lycophron,[60] a sepulchral epigram attested in pseudo-Aristotle's *Peplos*,[61] Pausanias,[62] and Tzetzes)[63] speak of the transfer of Hector's bones from Troy to Boeotian Thebes, to protect against plague (Tzetzes), war (Lycophron), or another disaster (Aristodemus of Thebes). The main argument supporting Hector's Boeotian connection is that if Hector was not from Thebes and if he were not some local hero, then the Thebans would not have cared to transfer his bones from Troy to their own city in Boeotia.[64] Additional information refers to the existence of a historically identified person named Hector on the

---

[57] The Amazons are characterized as ἀντιάνειραι (*Iliad* III 189). According to Block 1995:221, the form of the epithet may have been determined by the word ἀντιθέοιο (*Iliad* III 186), which is attested in the same passage and occupies the same metrical position (the terminal adonic). Is it really a coincidence that the name of Andromache is suspiciously similar to a characteristic epithet (ἀνδροφόνοιο) used for Hector in the *Iliad*? In *Iliad* XXIV 723-724, the two words are found in subsequent verses (... Ἀνδρομάχη / / Ἕκτορος ἀνδροφόνοιο ...). Note also that the name of the Amazon Πενθεσίλεια reflects (etymologically but also acoustically as far as its second part is concerned) the name of Achilles (Ἀχιλλεύς).

[58] Dümmler 1890:194-205. See all previous bibliography in Sakellariou 1958:193n6.

[59] *FGrHist* 383 F 7 (Jacoby). See Sakellariou 1958:194n1. For this topic, see also Wathelet 1988:1326-1328 with additional bibliography.

[60] *Alexandra* 1189-1213.

[61] Fr. 640.46 (Rose).

[62] IX 18.5.

[63] Scholia on Lycophron's *Alexandra* 1194 (Scheer).

[64] This seems to be a *petitio principii* (since the bones of Hector were transferred to Boeotian Thebes, therefore Hector was of Theban origin). The transfer of the bones of other heroes, such as Theseus to Athens and Orestes to Sparta, does not support the analogy. Sakellariou (1958:195) correctly notes: "*Thésée était une figure attique; Oreste appartenait au Peloponnèse, et les Lacédémoniens s' efforçaient de se presenter eux-mêmes commes les continuateurs du régime achéen. L' Héctor homérique était un prince étranger à Thèbes. Par quelle sorte de raisonnement les Thébains auraient-ils été amenés à demander, au moment d'un danger, la protection d'un héros lointain, auquel rien ne les aurait liés dans le passé?*" Therefore, the only valid explanation may be that Hector was a local Theban hero, whose name epic poetry had used for the famous Trojan prince. The dissemination and cultural domination of epic poetry concerning the Trojan War almost obliterated the 'Theban' Hector and resulted in the aforementioned 'paradox'.

island of Chios at the time the island became part of the Ionian League.⁶⁵ The activity of this Hector, fourth descendant of Amphiclus, is connected to the war "against the Abantes and those Carians who had settled in Chios."⁶⁶ Hector, after having killed many of his enemies, forced the rest of them to desert the island. Then, he made Chios part of the Ionian League. The supporters of this view believe that Hector was initially a Greek hero of Theban origin⁶⁷ and that the historical person, Hector, in Chios in the sixth century BC, was an emigrant of Boeotian origin, a case that is further supported by the fact that the Boeotian element was rather strong on the island, as proven by the multitude of place names of Boeotian provenance and by the mythological connections between the two places, such as that of Orion.⁶⁸

In the *Iliad*, Hector seems to be covertly associated to Ares, since the epithets κορυθαιόλος, ἀνδροφόνοιο, and ὄβριμος attributed to the former are also employed for the latter. In *Iliad* V 590–595, Ares and Enyo, together with Hector, lead the Trojans into battle, and Ares' huge spear recalls Hector's spear (*Iliad* VII 244, *Iliad* VIII 494, *Iliad* XXII 289).⁶⁹ However, of more interest to us, Ares is linked to Thebes in Boeotia since, as I have already mentioned, his daughter Harmonia, the child of his marriage with Aphrodite, married Cadmus, the mythical founder of Thebes. In this foundation myth, Ares' son was a dragon that Cadmus slayed, and whose teeth Cadmus subsequently planted in the ground, from which the Spartoi grew, i.e. the earth-born warriors.⁷⁰ The cult of Ares, whose name is attested already in Linear B, was not at all widespread in Greece during the Archaic period. However, he was venerated in Boeotian Thebes. Finally, the names of Hector and Ares display an interesting relation. The name e-ko-to (Hector) and its derivative e-ko-to-ri-jo (Hectorean), which are attested in Linear B (PY Eb 913.1, En 74.7, Eo 276.6, En 74.17, Eo 247.2, Ep 212.3, 705.8), designate a person who wins, conquers, or protects.⁷¹ The military connotations of Hector's name bear a striking similarity to the name Ares, which may well be an antiquated form of a noun

---

⁶⁵ See Sakellariou 1958:195, and for the relevant bibliography, 195n2. See also Ion of Chios *FGrHist* 392 F1 = Pausanias VII 4.9.
⁶⁶ See Sakellariou 1958:192.
⁶⁷ See Bethe 1922:79–83, who has observed that Hector's opponents in the Iliadic plot come from central Greece (where Thebes is situated).
⁶⁸ See Sakellariou 1958:188.
⁶⁹ See also *Iliad* V 703–710, where Hector and Ares go to war together. Among others, they kill Oresbius ὅς ῥ' ἐν Ὕλῃ ναίεσκε μέγα πλούτοιο μεμηλώς, // λίμνῃ κεκλιμένος Κηφισίδι· πὰρ δέ οἱ ἄλλοι // ναῖον Βοιωτοί, μάλα πίονα δῆμον ἔχοντες (*Iliad* V 708–710).
⁷⁰ Burkert 1985:169–170.
⁷¹ Chantraine 1968–1980 s.v. Ἕκτωρ.

Chapter One

meaning 'war', without excluding the possibility that the word ἕκτωρ was initially an invocation of war,[72] as Wathelet has suggested.[73]

The Theban associations are evident not only in the two protagonists of this scene (Andromache, Hector) but also in the whole of *Iliad* VI, both in the myth of Lycurgus (*Iliad* VI 130–140) and in the story of Bellerophon.[74] Murray[75] has suggested that the myth of Lycurgus, which is also found in Eumelus' *Europia* (*PEG* 1, fr. 11 = *EGF* fr. 1), is to be related to another epic by the same poet, the *Korinthiaka*, where we learn about Sisyphus and Glaucus, Bellerophon's ancestors. Consequently, it is possible that Eumelus depends on the same oral tradition that was also the source for the Iliadic episode of Glaucus and Diomedes.

Secondary References

Mountain-nymphs (νύμφαι ὀρεστιάδες)

When Andromache refers to the murder of her father by Achilles, she adds that the Achaean warrior respected his dead body and buried it accordingly. Subsequently, "... the nymphs of the mountains, / daughters of Zeus who brings the thunderstorm,[76] planted elm trees about it." Nymphs are found in the *Odyssey* (xiii 356: νύμφαι νηϊάδες; xvii 240: νύμφαι κρηναῖαι), where they are called 'daughters of Zeus' (κοῦραι Διός). The formula κοῦραι Διός is also found in *Odyssey* vi 105 and *Odyssey* ix 154, but the phrase νύμφαι ὀρεστιάδες is only used in *Iliad* VI 420 and in the *Homeric Hymn to Pan* (19) 19.[77] Given that

---

[72] Burkert 1985:169n1–2 with bibliography.
[73] Wathelet 1988:504.
[74] For the Theban references to the embedded story of Bellerophon, see Alden 2000:131–142.
[75] Murray 1934⁴:176.
[76] For the interpretation of the epithet αἰγιόχοιο, see West 1978:366–368. The translation is that of Lattimore with the exception of the epithet αἰγίοχος.
[77] See also *Homeric Hymn to Aphrodite* (5) 257: νύμφαι μιν θρέψουσιν ὀρεσκῷοι βαθύκολποι. Kirk 1990:215 remarks that the elm trees placed in the *Iliad* at the banks of Scamander may well have had funerary associations. Interestingly, in *Iliad* VI 402 Astyanax is called Scamander by his father Hector. The nymphs, as Kirk correctly argues, add to the status of Eetion (as it is the case with the Nereids for Achilles in *Odyssey* xxiv 47). For mountain-nymphs in tragedy in a Dionysiac context, see Sophocles *Antigone* 1128–1129 (... ἔνθα Κωρύκιαι // στείχουσι Νύμφαι Βακχίδες); Euripides *Cyclops* 4 (Νύμφας ὀρείας ἐκλιπὼν ᾧχου τροφούς) and 68–69 (οὐδ᾽ ἐν Νύσᾳ μετὰ Νυμφᾶν // ἴακχον ἴακχον ...); Euripides *Suppliants* 993 (ὠκυθόαι νύμφαι†). The interpretation of Kirk is followed, although not overtly stated, by Larson 2001:23, who asks herself whether Eetion is an Asian aristocrat connected to a nymph or if we are simply faced with the participation of nature in his mourning. Additionally, she argues (2001:4–5) that the nymphs are related to the element of water, which is also the case for Dionysus and Artemis. In *Iliad* VI

Ἀνδρομάχη μαινομένη

Eetion ruled the city of Hypoplakian Thebes, situated at the feet of mount Plakos in the Troad, and that he was killed by Achilles in this same city, it is likely that the mountain-nymphs who planted elm trees around his grave must also be placed at mount Plakos above the city Eetion ruled. This reference provokes justified questions: "Who are these mountain-nymphs?" and more importantly, "What is Eetion doing in this mythical context?"

In order to answer these questions, we have to interpret the function of three different mythological threads skillfully interwoven in the Iliadic tradition:[78]

(a) Eetion's identity: Eetion is the son of Zeus and Electra, the daughter of Atlas who lived in Samothrace.[79] The other two children from Zeus' marriage to Electra were Dardanus, mythical founder of Troy, and Harmonia, who married Cadmus, the mythical founder of Thebes. Because Eetion slept with Demeter, Zeus killed him with his thunderbolt,[80] exactly as in the story of Iasion and Demeter in *Odyssey* v 125-128. Hesiod (*Theogony* 969-974) places this myth in Crete and presents Ploutos as the offspring of the union of the two lovers. Of particular importance, in the *Theogony* (975-978) the union of Iasion and Demeter is immediately followed by the marriage of Cadmus and Harmonia. This catalogue-organized sequence may well be an argument *ex silentio* about the interconnection between the two traditions. Needless to say, Harmonia is also known to have been the daughter of Ares and Aphrodite. The common element between the mythical versions pertaining to the aforementioned three couples is *hierogamia* (marriage between a mortal and an immortal) as well as the motif of divine intervention.[81] Eetion's connection to Thebes can be also seen through his mother Electra, after whom the gates of Thebes were named (Ἠλεκτρίδες πύλαι).

428, Artemis kills the mother of Andromache, while Thetis, who receives Dionysus into her arms as he is being chased by Lycurgus, (*Iliad* VI 130-140) is a Nereid, the sea-equivalent of a mountain-nymph. See Carpenter 1986:76-77, who observes that in an Attic black-figure vase painted by Cleitias depicting the marriage of Peleus and Thetis, Dionysus is accompanied by Silenoi and Nymphs.

[78] For the mythological and religious elements used in the following three remarks I rely upon Wathelet 1988:566-569, and Burkert 1985:281-285.

[79] See Zarker 1965-1966:110-114, who does not attempt to trace the mythical ramifications of Eetion's identity. Even if a pre-Iliadic song-tradition referred to Achilles' 'Great Assault' against Thebe and Lyrnessos, as Zarker and others seem to believe, the use of Eetion's name still remains unexplained. On Eetion and Samothrace in the Hesiodic *Catalogue of Women*, see West 1985:160-161.

[80] See *Catalogue of Women*, fr. 177 (M.-W.). See also Hellanicus (*FGrHist* 4 F 23 = *EGM* fr. 23) and Idomeneus (*FGrHist* 547 F 1). I owe these references to Wathelet 1988:566.

[81] Wathelet 1988:568.

(b) The Cabiri: the origin of the myth of Eetion seems to be related to the Cabiri, who were worshipped in Lemnos, Samothrace, and Boeotia. Hephaestus, by whose name there was a city in Lemnos, is related to Dionysus who had helped him return to Olympos after his fall.[82] The link between Electra, Eetion's mother, and Samothrace points to the Cabiri, who were local underworld deities related to fertility, *prosperity*, and the working of metals. Their relationship with Demeter, Dionysus, and Hephaestus is obvious.[83] In the *Iliad*, Eetion is a very *wealthy* man (after all, his daughter, Andromache, is referred to as πολύδωρος) and reigns in Hypoplakian Thebes, in the area of Troy.[84] In view of all the information presented above, it can hardly be a simple coincidence that the city of Thebes in Boeotia has a rich tradition in the cult of the Cabiri. In Boeotian Thebes a Cabirion has been excavated and there is strong evidence for the cult of Cabirian Demeter. In addition, votive objects from the temple were intended for a Cabirus, who is represented as a beardless Dionysus reclining in order to drink.[85]

(c) Achilles: In the *Iliad*, Eetion is killed by Achilles, who is related to Zeus through his mother Thetis and who sometimes acts in the place of the father of gods and men (like Asteropaius).[86] It has been suggested[87] that the *Iliad* has replaced Zeus with Achilles in this episode, adapting the old myth to its own plot requirements. Whereas Zeus had killed Eetion because of his affair with Demeter in the Hesiodic tradition[88] and perhaps in another oral tradition, in the *Iliad* Achilles causes his death. The substitution of Zeus by Achilles ties in well with the more general strategy of the Iliadic tradition to replace Zeus' 'wrath' (μῆνις) by Achilles' 'wrath' (μῆνις).[89] Furthermore (and in accordance to this epic's narrative blueprint), as in the past Achilles had killed Andromache's entire family (father and brothers), so in the future he will kill her beloved husband, Hector.

Eetion's various associations point to the city of Thebes in mainland Greece, not only through Andromache but also through his affair, as Iasion, with Demeter, who is considered, along with Dionysus, one of the main deities

---

[82] See Burkert 1985:281, to whom I owe the references to Alcaeus 349 (Voigt) and Aeschylus' *Cabiri* fr. 97 (*TrGF* 3, Radt). See also Harrison 1991³:652, who draws attention to the shards of a black-figure vase depicting Dionysus (holding a kantharos) as a bearded Cabiros (inscription).
[83] Wathelet 1988:566.
[84] Wathelet 1988:568–569.
[85] Wathelet 1988:568.
[86] See Burkert 1985:281, who refers to Nilsson (1967³) plate 48.1.
[87] See Wathelet 1988:568.
[88] See *Catalogue of Women*, fr. 177 (M.-W.).
[89] See chapter 10.

of Boeotian Thebes.⁹⁰ In this light, I would argue that we must interpret the reference to the mountain-nymphs within the complex nexus created by the three aforementioned mythical threads. The mountain-nymphs seem peculiar within their Iliadic context,⁹¹ but their eccentricity can be screened out, if they are intertextually linked to another oral tradition where Eetion was not the king of Hypoplakian Thebes but was connected to Boeotian Thebes. His death as the result of Zeus' divine anger would easily explain the presence of mountain-nymphs at his funeral, especially if one assumes that the father of gods and men has been replaced by Achilles in *Iliad* VI.⁹²

High-Gated Thebes (Θήβη ὑψίπυλος)

The argument presented above must be placed within the general framework of the connection between Boeotian Thebes and Hypoplakian Thebes in the area of Troy.⁹³ In *Iliad* VI 415–416, Hypoplakian Thebes is designated as one of the cities conquered by Achilles in the region of the Troad. The *Iliad* employs the same formula (τείχεα Θήβης) both for Thebes in Boeotia (*Iliad* IV 378) and for Hypoplakian Thebes (*Iliad* II 691). Moreover, the adjective ἱερός is used both for Hypoplakian Thebes (*Iliad* I 366) and for the walls of Boeotian Thebes (*Iliad* IV 378). Additionally, in *Iliad* VI 416 Hypoplakian Thebes is described as 'high-gated' (ὑψίπυλος),⁹⁴ which is also employed for Troy (*Iliad* XVI 698 = *Iliad* XXI 544). The epithet 'high-gated' (ὑψίπυλος) seems to have been 'influenced' by the tradition of the Seven-Gated Boeotian Thebes, which the *Iliad* explicitly mentions in IV 406 within the context of Diomedes' analeptic cross-reference to the expedition of the Epigoni against Thebes. It is highly unlikely that all these similarities are purely accidental, the more so since Hypoplakian Thebes

---

⁹⁰ See Wathelet 1988:569.
⁹¹ What happens to Dionysus, who is saved by a sea-nymph (Thetis) in extra-Iliadic myth, is applied to Eetion who dies but is honored by the mountain Nymphs. Since 'Nymphs' were "associated with an ambiguous kind of immortality" and are a rather "elastic concept" (Sourvinou-Inwood 2005:100), the Lycurgus-Dionysus-Thetis versus Achilles-Eetion-'mountain Nymphs' nexuses may well represent two different versions of 'nymphic' immortality. In fact, the former constitutes an example of *greater* immortality [as it is the case with water Nymphs, especially those with "a distinct persona, such as Thetis" (Sourvinou-Inwood 2005:105)], while the latter stands for a case of *lesser* immortality, "primarily drifted to Nymphs associated with trees" (Sourvinou-Inwood 2005:105).
⁹² Larson 2001:23 explains the presence of nymphs in Eetion's funeral as an example of a pathetic fallacy, "whereby the natural world, personified in the nymphs, expresses its sorrow at [Eetion's] death"..."Andromache's father was such a great man that even his enemy honored him, while the nymphs came out of the mountains to do the same."
⁹³ See Pindar *Isthmian* 7.3. See also Torres-Guerra 1995:55–57.
⁹⁴ See also *Iliad* I 366-367 with Kirks comment's (1990:215) ad *Iliad* VI 415–416.

was an unimportant and small city, which could not have been famous for being 'high-gated' (ὑψίπυλος).⁹⁵

The wild fig tree (ἐρινεός)

The wild fig tree is attested four times in the *Iliad* (*Iliad* VI 433, *Iliad* XI 167, *Iliad* XXI 37, *Iliad* XXII 145), always in relation to a threat the Trojan army faces on the battlefield. Topographical details of this sort have acquired a secondary, metonymical function given the dramatic framework of the plot. Under this scope, a single spot on the Trojan plain has 'evolved' into a sophisticated topographical metonymy for Trojan-oriented impending danger. In *Iliad* XI 166-168, Agamemnon chases his enemies and, after passing by the tomb of Ilus and the wild fig tree, he heads towards Troy. Prior to Agamemnon's ἀριστεία,⁹⁶ the poet has artfully withdrawn Hector from the battle (*Iliad* XI 163), since the wild fig tree is also specially linked to him. In *Iliad* XXI 37, Lycaon, taken captive by Achilles while cutting branches next to the wild fig tree and subsequently sold into slavery in Imbros, meets his doom. Likewise, in *Iliad* XXII 145, Achilles, chasing Hector around the walls of Troy, passes by the wild fig tree. At this point, the epic carefully mentions two springs, one of cold water, the other warm. This *prima facie* trivial detail should not be taken at face value, since Iliadic topography does not conform to geographical but to poetic rules. On the other hand, one is tempted to draw an analogy between the two springs of Forgetfulness (Λήθη) and Remembrance (Μνημοσύνη) in the oracle of Zeus Trophonius in Boeotia (Pausanius IX 39.9).

In *Iliad* VI 433, Andromache refers to the ἐρινεός by stressing that the Achaeans know it to be found at the weakest part of the walls of Troy. She adds that either a seer gave them this information or that they followed their intuition when they attacked this part of the walls (*Iliad* VI 438–439). But why would a seer have given the Achaeans the information? Why would someone with access to the will of the gods have revealed that the wild fig tree indicated a weakness at a single spot on the walls? Is there some latent religious significance linked to this tree, or is the *Iliad* making a covert intertextual reference to another assault on a wall-protected city? Andromache's words are quite inappropriate not only in respect to the awkwardness of a woman giving military advice⁹⁷ but also because the *Iliad* never refers to an assault on the walls of Troy by the Achaean army. On the contrary, war always takes place on either

---

⁹⁵ On 'Theban' motifs in the *Iliad*, see Torres-Guerra 1995:51–64.
⁹⁶ Thornton 1984:152–153.
⁹⁷ See scholia vetera on *Iliad* VI 433–439 (Erbse) with Aristarchus' comments.

Ἀνδρομάχη μαινομένη

the battlefield outside the walls of Troy or, when things go bad for the Greeks, in front of the Achaean Wall and then inside the Achaean camp.

The 'weak spot on the walls' might have been a direct borrowing from an unknown eastern source, given that eastern influence on mythical material concerning city-siege might be due to the fact that wall-protected cities had been built in Mesopotamia long before Greece. Herodotus offers a typical example (I 84) in the description of the siege and ensuing sack of Sardis by a Persian army led by Cyrus. In this case, the spot on the walls that seems least vulnerable to attack, the steepest part of the fortification, becomes the 'weak spot' Hyroeades uses to enter the citadel. Herodotus makes explicit reference to a prophecy given to Meles, the ancient king of Sardis, by the Telmessians, telling him to carry around the walls the lion cub his concubine had born to him, in order to make the city impregnable. Assuming that this particular spot on the walls was so steep that no enemy could climb it and enter the city, Meles failed to carry the lion cub over it. The situation in *Iliad* VI 433-439[98] explicitly refers to a weak spot on the walls of Troy, *which the best of the Achaeans have already attacked three times either because some seer had revealed it to them or because their heart urges them to do so*. The reference to a seer, when taken together with the 'magical' number three (designating the attacks on the wall), shows that the Iliadic tradition has used material of intertextual provenance, which it has subsequently tailored to its needs. If we endorse Aristarchus' athetesis of these verses,[99] then the 'weak spot' feature becomes all the more intriguing. Pindar (*Olympian* 8.31-46) relates that the weak spot was placed at that part of the wall built by the mortal Aiacus, whereas the rest of the walls were made impenetrable by Apollo and Poseidon. If this information reflects an oral tradition predating the Epic Cycle,[100] and given the 'Theban' context of all this episode, it would be advisable to look more closely into the construction of the walls of Troy by Apollo and Poseidon.

Amphion and Zethus, the Boeotian Dioskouroi[101] (*Odyssey* xi 260-265), represent a more recent, rival Boeotian tradition according to which the walls of Thebes had been built by 'non-Thebans' instead of the 'thebanized' Cadmus, who belonged to the Theban version. The similarities between the building of the walls in Thebes of Boeotia by Amphion and Zethus[102] and the building

---

[98] See Tsagalis 2004:125-127.
[99] See scholia vetera on *Iliad* VI 433-439 (Erbse).
[100] Kirk 1990:218.
[101] This is how they have been called by Vian 1963:69.
[102] Amphion and Zethus are builders of ramparts par excellence. See Eumelus' *Europia* fr. 13 (*PEG* 1) = fr. 3 (*EGF*); *Catalogue of Women* fr. 182 (M.-W.). I owe this information to Vian 1963a:72n2.

of the walls in Troy by Apollo and Poseidon are striking. First, the building of the walls in Troy takes place when Laomedon, the son of the city founder, Ilus, is king, just as Amphion and Zethus build the Theban walls after Cadmus had founded the city. Second, Amphion and Apollo share a number of similarities: they are both twins, they love pastoral life and music, they possess a magic lyre, a gift of Hermes or of the Muses. Amphion's house is destroyed by Apollo's arrows when Niobe compares herself to Leto, and he finds his death attempting to burn the Ismenos temple. Apollo is founder of cities par excellence, and in Thebes he has passed his powers on to Amphion. The seven sons and daughters of Niobe and Amphion were later linked to the tradition of the seven warriors and the seven gates of Thebes. Interestingly enough, both Zethus and Poseidon are linked to the earth.[103]

Similarities of this sort cannot be coincidental. The 'Theban' connection between the mythical tradition of the building of Thebes' walls by Amphion and Zethus on the one hand, and of Troy's walls by Apollo and Poseidon on the other, becomes even stronger when one considers how large the Achaean Wall looms in the *Iliad*. The 'turning' of the Achaeans from besiegers of Troy into the besieged gives the Iliadic tradition the opportunity to describe, at length, an assault on a besieged 'city', in this case the very camp of the Achaeans. Singor has convincingly shown that the Seven-Gated city of Thebes lurks in the background of the Iliadic depiction of the Achaean Wall and that the latter's seven gates with their seven guardians have been created under the influence of their Theban antecedent.

> The epic parallel of a battle on and around the walls of a besieged city, described from the perspective of and with a certain sympathy for the besieged, is clearly the war against Boiotian Thebes. Parts of 'Theban epic', probably not from the *Thebais* but from the oral epic that must have preceded it in the manner that oral epic on the Trojan War preceded our *Iliad*, could quite easily have been borrowed or 'transposed' to yield some material for the siege of the Greeks in their camp before Troy.[104]

I would go even further than Singor by arguing that the strong 'Theban' overtones of the Achaean Wall constitute a narrative of the abbreviated reference to the six-warrior attack on the weak spot of the Trojan wall in *Iliad* VI 433–439. The 'Theban' oral epic tradition on which the *Iliad* is drawing knew of

---

[103] Vian 1963a:69–75.
[104] Singor 1992:404.

Ἀνδρομάχη μαινομένη

the famous siege of Boeotian Thebes by seven warriors who were killed in front of its seven gates. The Iliadic tradition could not exploit the rich intertextual background offered by the Theban oral tradition *with respect to an assault on Troy* because war in the *Iliad* virtually takes place on the battlefield and not on or around the walls of Troy. In other words, one of the most essential features of Theban war, i.e. the siege of a walled city, was *inappropriate* given the plot-line of Iliadic epic. Since the *Iliad* was obviously aware of material linked to its past (like the building of its ramparts by Apollo and Poseidon in the manner Amphion and Zethus had built the walls of Thebes), it exploited the 'Theban' background of the siege *by reverting its actants*. In this way, Hector (a hero of 'Theban' connections) became the primary attacker of the Achaean Wall and the Achaeans who were initially besieging Troy were turned into the besieged. In this light, Andromache's reference to an otherwise unknown attack of six Achaean warriors at the weak spot of the walls of Troy must be placed within the much larger framework of the aforementioned cross-reference to a Theban oral epic tradition. In fact, the very number six used for these warriors (the two Atreides, Idomeneus, the two Aiantes, and Diomedes) can be explained, if we take into account the Iliadic deviation from the Theban pattern of this episode. In the Theban oral tradition, Amphion has seven sons with Niobe, i.e. as many as the number of warriors attacking Thebes, and, of course, as many as killed by Apollo after Niobe's insult to Leto. In the Iliadic tradition (XXIV 603-604), Niobe has six sons (from Amphion) who are subsequently killed by Apollo, i.e. as many as the warriors who attack the weak spot on the walls.[105] The internal discrepancy between the seven gates and seven guardians of the Achaean Wall on the one hand, and the six sons of Niobe and Amphion on the other, may be due to the existence of variant versions of this story, some of which made the number of attacking warriors and guardians of the city match the sons of one of the city's builders, while others did not.

In this light, Willcock's theory of *ad hoc invention*, or *Augenblickserfindung*, in reference to this episode is, I maintain, off the mark.[106] The *autoschediasmata* of the Iliadic tradition do indeed arise from the composition of Homeric epic, but the exploitation of traditional mythical material is not invented to suit only immediate needs. In fact, the very term *autoschediasmata* is only valid *intratextually*, when examined from the point of view of the deployment of the plot. *Intertextually*, *autoschediasmata* are a 'surface-phenomenon', which ceases

---

[105] See the *Catalogue of Women*, fr. 183 [M.-W.] (= Apollodorus *Library* III [45] 5.6 (120.3 Wagner), Aelian *Varia Historia* XII 36.
[106] Willcock 1977:41-53.

to exist when seen as the compositional *exploration*, not *invention*, of mythical diversity widely diffused by living oral epic traditions. Intratextually perceived invention is nothing more than intertextually oriented exploration.

The Origins of Dionysus

The *Iliad* (XIV 325: ἢ δὲ Διώνυσον Σεμέλη τέκε, χάρμα βροτοῖσιν) is familiar with the myth of the birth of Dionysus from Semele, who is related to Thebes (as she is, along with Ino, Agaue, Autonoe and Polydorus, a child of Cadmus and Harmonia, the mythical founder of Thebes and the daughter of Ares and Aphrodite, respectively). I shall not deal more with this brief reference, and perhaps I should not have even mentioned it were it not for the fact that it is indirectly relevant to Dionysus' Theban connection. When Zeus, in a long priamel in *Iliad* XIV, offers a list of his previous lovers, he considers it necessary to refer also to the offspring he had with them. In his extended catalogue, Semele is naturally presented as the mother of Dionysus. However, this reference to Dionysus is related to Zeus' previous mention of Heracles, his son from Alcmene[107] (*Iliad* XIV 323: οὐδ' ὅτε περ Σεμέλης, οὐδ' Ἀλκμήνης ἐνὶ Θήβῃ). The common point between these two love affairs of the father of gods with mortal women is anything but the city of Thebes. The juxtaposition of the two 'mythical items' in this catalogue may well have been triggered by some sort of mental link they created in the bard's mind, as they both had Theban associations.

The Festival of the Agrionia

The mythical version of Lycurgus's attack against Dionysus used in *Iliad* VI 130–140 is related to the feast of Agrionia in Orchomenos of Boeotia. According to some ancient sources,[108] the daughters of Minyas (Leukippe, Arsipe, and Alkithoe) offended Dionysus by refusing to take part in the dancing performed in his honor. As a result, the angry god 'visited' the Minyads when they were weaving at the loom. Suddenly, leaves of ivy and vine appeared on their tools, snakes came out of their baskets, and drops of wine started dripping from the

---

[107] See also the Hesiodic *Catalogue of Women*, in which the last part devoted to Helen's suitors (a shorter catalogue within a larger catalogue) is preceded by a 'Theban part' ending with Alcmene's twin sons, Heracles and Iphicles. See Cingano 2005:118-152, and in particular 123-124.

[108] See Aelian *Varia Historia* III 42, and Antoninus Liberalis *Metamorphoses* X 3.

ceiling of the room. Then the girls, who realized what was going on, cast lots to select the one who would try to appease the wrath of the god. When the lot fell to Leukippe, she sacrificed her son, Hippasus, to Dionysus, dismembered him with the assistance of her sisters, and made her way to the mountains together with the other Minyads. At the feast of the Agrionia in Boeotia, the priest of Dionysus chases the women of the city, who represent the Minyads, and kills the one who falls in his hands. Burkert[109] associates the myth of Lycurgus with the ritual of the Agrionia, suggesting that Lycurgus is *a ritual surrogate of Dionysus' priest*. Indeed, during a sacrifice to Dionysus, an armed man appears and chases the god and his maenads to the sea. He then turns a weapon recalling Lycurgus' ox-goad (*Iliad* VI 135: θεινόμεναι βουπλῆγι ...) around in his hand, and in later versions even kills his own children in a state of uncontrollable frenzy.

The Temple of Athena

Hector, upon his return to Troy, does not find Andromache in the temple of Athena with the other women. Praying to the pro-Greek Athena in order to stop Diomedes' fierce attack against their city and even having a temple dedicated to Athena in Troy is noteworthy. Is this reference to be related to the cult of Oncaian and Ismenian Athena in Thebes? In Thebes, Athena is neither the goddess of the acropolis nor its patron goddess. The temple of Pallas Onca, found near the walls and, more specifically, near the Oncaian Gate, is devoted to Athena 'of the gates' (πυλαΐτις).[110] The cult of Pallas Onca is based on her ancient relationship to Demeter ἐν Ὀγκείῳ in Arcadia and Boeotian Demeter, who also share a special relationship to Thebes.[111] In this light, the description of a supplication scene in Athena's temple in *Iliad* VI may owe much to its intertextual background in a Theban oral tradition, where such a scene would have made greater sense. The Cyclic *Epigoni* might have also featured a homologous scene, which should have been based on a pre-Iliadic Theban epic. The Iliadic tradition is exploiting a scene pertaining to a lost Theban tradition, where a supplication to Athena, protectress of the Oncaian gate, carried out by the women of the city in order to avert the assault of Diomedes, son of Tydeus and one of the Epigoni, would have been at home.[112]

---

[109] Burkert 1985:164-165. See also Burkert 1983:168-179.
[110] Vian 1963a:139-141.
[111] See Vian 1963a:139-140.
[112] See Torres-Guerra 1995:59-61.

Chapter One

An Evolutionary Hermeneutical Model

The above remarks show that the references to Diomedes (whom the *Iliad* knows as one of the Epigoni, conquerors of Thebes), the episode of Dionysus, and the origin of Andromache and Hector unravel a narrative web that allows for the presentation of an evolutionary model of Iliadic maenadism. The main aim of this chapter has been to answer the question of why the maenadic and, consequently, the Dionysiac references in the *Iliad* are related to Andromache and are extremely scarce, or perhaps marginalized.

The maenadic references to Andromache in Books VI and XXII result from the Iliad's sophisticated use of older mythical material, where the Dionysiac allusions would be at home and where Andromache, Hector, and the mythological context they are placed in would be related to Dionysus and Thebes. Therefore, the *Iliad* refers to Dionysus only occasionally because the mythological material related to him belongs not simply to another poem (perhaps Eumelus' *Europia*)[113] but also to another tradition, that of Boeotian Thebes. This rival epic tradition seems to have been well known to the Ionian poets, who had every reason to refrain from highlighting it.

Under this scope, Andromache's maenadic associations and, by extension, Dionysiac allusions should be placed within the intertextual framework of an older Theban epic tradition, of which Eumelus' *Europia* is only a later, post-Homeric reflection. The entire 'Theban part' of the *Iliad* indicates the existence of intertextual relationships in one of the most fertile and strong epic traditions developed in the Greek world during the Archaic period. Throughout its evolution and shaping, the Iliadic tradition 'transferred' Theban epic heroes and events to its own story. Within this process, the so-called 'Theban features' evolved into Iliadic ones, the more so since the *Iliad* was able to tailor them to its needs and accommodate them to its plot requirements. Still, 'Theban features' have left the traces of their 'earlier', non-Iliadic past in the form of intratextual ruptures, which can be filled by intertextually retrieved material.

One of the reasons, perhaps the most important, why the *Iliad* has been recognized since antiquity as a monumental epic composition is the fact that it embedded, incorporated, and adapted various rival song-traditions to its basic myth. By filtering these traditions, the *Iliad* managed to surpass them, changing (as far as Andromache is concerned) an Amazon with maenadic and warlike origins into a suffering wife and mother, and the great, mythologi-

---

[113] On Eumelus' *Europia*, see Lecomte 1998:71–79; West 2002:109–133.

cally renowned Thebes of Boeotia into a small, unimportant city of the Troad, Hypoplakian Thebes. The new poetry of Ionia was thus able to speak about its own places with its own traditional but also innovative voice.

2

Χαρίεσσα and στυγερὴ ἀοιδή: The Self-Referential Encomium of the *Odyssey* and the Tradition of the *Nostoi*

ONE OF THE MAIN ARGUMENTS in favor of those who think that the *Odyssey* ends in xxiii 296[1] (since both Odysseus' brief recounting to Penelope of his adventures and the whole of book xxiv are considered later additions) relies on Agamemnon's speech to Amphimedon in xxiv 192-202. The aim of this chapter is to scrutinize this particular passage and examine thoroughly all the problems related to it in an attempt to reconsider its function within the second Nekyia and the *Odyssey* as a whole.

Before embarking I would like to forestall any objections raised, with respect to the fact that the aforementioned passage forms part of a larger thematic unit, the second Nekyia, and therefore cannot be examined in isolation. This is certainly so, but my focus on this passage in particular has emanated from both the need to explore it in depth and the lack, at least to my knowledge, of any convincing suggestion facing what has been considered an unsurpassable difficulty to its authenticity and, consequently, that of the second Nekyia as a whole.[2]

The examination of *Odyssey* xxiv 191-202 will deal with the following problems associated with the doubts about the authenticity of this passage, raised by both soft and hard core analysts: i) the connection between the formulaic introduction to Agamemnon's speech and the first two verses, in

---

[1] See Heubeck 1992:353-354 for a comprehensive summary; Oswald 1993; Kullmann 1992, 1995:41-53.

[2] See Sourvinou-Inwood 1996:100-101, who argues that "[t]here is no plausible reading that can in any way explain away the more serious difficulty involved in vv. 191-202. Agamemnon is supposed to be addressing Amphimedon; in fact, he addresses Odysseus in the second person singular and praises Penelope's virtue and again compares his own case, having a treacherous wife, to that of Odysseus who was happy to have married such an excellent woman and faithful spouse."

which he addresses Odysseus in the second person; ii) the praise of Penelope and its relevance to the Odyssean plot; iii) the function of this passage for the poetics of the *Odyssey*.

Physical and Notional Presence: Addressing an Absent Addressee

In *Odyssey* xxiv 191, Agamemnon's speech to Amphimedon is introduced by the standard formulaic expression: τὸν δ' αὖτε ψυχὴ προσεφώνεεν Ἀτρεΐδαο, which is attested five times[3] in Book xxiv of the *Odyssey*. The oddity of this formulaic introduction lies in its lack of conformity with the first two verses of the ensuing speech, which is addressed to Odysseus despite the fact that Agamemnon is speaking to Amphimedon, and Odysseus is not in the underworld but in Ithaca.

The most thorough account of this textual oddity has been given by Sourvinou-Inwood who adopts an analytical stance against the authenticity of this speech.[4] Sourvinou-Inwood[5] refers to the comments of Heubeck concerning this particular problem: "Even Heubeck who believes in the authenticity of *Odyssey* 24 acknowledges the difficulty (Heubeck 1992:380 *ad* 24.191), though he very much underplays it: 'the formulaic line is unusual here because it names Amphimedon (τόν) as the listener to whom the speech is addressed, whereas in fact it introduces a speech directed to the absent son of Laertes'; nonsensical rather than unusual would have been a more apposite description. In addition, the address to the absent Odysseus is in itself not unproblematic, especially in this particular context."

Heubeck's term "unusual" refers to the lack of regularity with respect to the pair 'introductory formula v. initial speech-address', whereas Sourvinou-Inwood's "nonsensical" pertains to the absurdity of the situation. In other words, Heubeck thinks that such a phenomenon is unusual, not regularly

---

[3] See *Odyssey* xxiv 23; xxiv 35; xxiv 105; xxiv 120; xxiv 191. Verses 35 and 191 contain the formula τὸν δ' αὖτε ψυχὴ προσεφώνεεν Ἀτρεΐδαο; verse 105 τὸν προτέρη ψυχὴ προσεφώνεεν Ἀτρεΐδαο; verse 23 τὸν προτέρη ψυχὴ προσεφώνεε Πηλεΐωνος; and verse 120 τὸν δ' αὖτε ψυχὴ προσεφώνεεν Ἀμφιμέδοντος. I consider all of these to be allomorphs of the same formula, since they constitute manifestations of the same metrical and syntactical pattern and realizations on the synchronic level of the same preverbal *Gestalt*. For the notion of preverbal *Gestalt* in Homeric poetry, see Nagler 1967:269–311, 1974:8.

[4] See Sourvinou-Inwood 1996:100–101; see also her previous discussion in the same chapter. For relevant scholia from ancient authorities on the two Nekyiai, see Petzl 1969 and, in particular for the passage under discussion, 65–66.

[5] See Sourvinou-Inwood 1996:100n254.

Chapter Two

observed, while Sourvinou-Inwood argues that it does not make sense. Before committing ourselves to one of these two sides, it is worthwhile to examine whether such or an equivalent phenomenon is attested anywhere else in the *Odyssey*.

Verses x 456 and x 504 (Διογενὲς Λαερτιάδη, πολυμήχαν' Ὀδυσσεῦ) are omitted by the majority of manuscripts (x 456 is also missing in Eustathius). x 456 seems to be an interpolation based on x 400–401 (ἡ δέ μευ ἄγχι στᾶσα προσηύδα δῖα θεάων· // Διογενὲς Λαερτιάδη, πολυμήχαν' Ὀδυσσεῦ); but, whereas in x 400–401 Circe is speaking in the presence of Odysseus alone, in x 456 she is speaking to a group of people (x 464: ὑμῖν; x 466: ἡμῖν)[6] so her address to Odysseus seems odd, to say the least. The reverse of this phenomenon can be observed in x 504, where Circe is indeed addressing only Odysseus (cf. μελέσθω [505], στήσας [506], πετάσσας [506] etc.),[7] but the introductory formula διογενὲς Λαερτιάδη, πολυμήχαν' Ὀδυσσεῦ is also omitted by a large number of manuscripts. Early critics, such as Ameis-Hentze[8] and Ludwich,[9] favored the omission of the introductory formula, but Heubeck[10] rightly pointed to the existence of a whole pattern of thought, which is at work in the three speeches of Circe to Odysseus. In Heubeck's own words, "... 456 is prepared by μευ ἄγχι στᾶσα, and the poet wanted to underline the parallelism between Circe's three speeches (456–65, 488–95, 504–40) by beginning them all in the same way (456 + μηκέτι νῦν ... 457; 488 + μηκέτι νῦν ... 489; 504 + μή τί τοι ... 505)." Through this parallelism one can see that the correspondence between an introductory formula and the first verse of an address is not always observed. On the contrary, some flexibility is allowed when a speech is pigeonholed within a larger framework (like that of Circe's encounter with Odysseus).[11]

In the same manner, we can draw the line between the physical addressee of a speech designated by the introductory formula and the notional addressee, the character whom the speaker has in his mind when uttering the speech. It is now time to turn to xxiv 191, where we encounter an equivalent (albeit odder) situation, since in x 456 Odysseus is present (although as member of the group of his comrades), whereas in the second Nekyia he is physically absent from the underworld. But, at least now we have paved the way towards the notion

---

[6] Cf. the second person plural forms ὄρνυτε (x 457), πάθετ' (x 458), ἄγετ' ἐσθίετε ... πίνετε (x 460), λάβητε (x 461), ἐλείπετε (x 462), πέπασθε (x 465), and the nominative plural participle μεμνημένοι (x 464).

[7] Cf. also the second person pronoun τοι (x 505).

[8] See Ameis and Hentze 1889.

[9] See Ludwich 1889.

[10] See Heubeck 1992:67 ad *Odyssey* x 456.

[11] On speech introductions, see Edwards 1970:1–36; Beck 2005:13–15, 32–43, 130–131, 263–266.

of irregularity as opposed to that of absurdity and senselessness. The text to be discussed runs as follows (xxiv 191–202):

> Τὸν δ' αὖτε ψυχὴ προσεφώνεεν Ἀτρεΐδαο·
> "ὄλβιε Λαέρταο πάϊ, πολυμήχαν' Ὀδυσσεῦ,
> ἦ ἄρα σὺν μεγάλῃ ἀρετῇ ἐκτήσω ἄκοιτιν·
> ὡς ἀγαθαὶ φρένες ἦσαν ἀμύμονι Πηνελοπείῃ,
> κούρῃ Ἰκαρίου, ὡς εὖ μέμνητ' Ὀδυσῆος,
> ἀνδρὸς κουριδίου. τῷ οἱ κλέος οὔ ποτ' ὀλεῖται
> ἧς ἀρετῆς, τεύξουσι δ' ἐπιχθονίοισιν ἀοιδὴν
> ἀθάνατοι χαρίεσσαν ἐχέφρονι Πηνελοπείῃ,
> οὐχ ὡς Τυνδαρέου κούρη κακὰ μήσατο ἔργα,
> κουρίδιον κτείνασα πόσιν, στυγερὴ δέ τ' ἀοιδὴ
> ἔσσετ' ἐπ' ἀνθρώπους, χαλεπὴν δέ τε φῆμιν ὀπάσσει
> θηλυτέρῃσι γυναιξί, καὶ ἥ κ' εὐεργὸς ἔῃσιν."

"Son of Laertes, shrewd Odysseus!" the soul of Agamemnon, son of Atreus,
cried. "You are a fortunate man to have won a wife of such pre-eminent virtue!
How faithful was your flawless Penelope, Icarius' daughter! How loyally she kept
the memory of the husband of her youth! The glory of her virtue will not fade
with the years, but the deathless gods themselves will make a beautiful song for
mortal ears in honour of the constant Penelope. What a contrast with
Clytaemnestra, the daughter of Tyndareus, and the infamy she sank to when she
killed me, the husband of her youth. The song men will sing of her will be one of
detestation. She has destroyed the reputation of her whole sex, virtuous women
and all."

The formula πολυμήχαν' Ὀδυσσεῦ is attested seven times in the *Iliad* and 16 times in the *Odyssey*, localized always in the second hemistich after the penthemimeral caesura. It is preceded by the phrase διογενὲς Λαερτιάδη, thus forming a single-verse formulaic address to Odysseus. *Odyssey* xxiv 192 is the

Chapter Two

only case where the formula πολυμήχαν' Ὀδυσσεῦ is preceded by the phrase ὄλβιε Λαέρταο πάϊ instead of διογενὲς Λαερτιάδη.[12] This is a clear case of deviation from a formulaic pattern, which is widely attested in both the *Iliad* and the *Odyssey*. This irregularity is connected to the other irregularity, that of the *non sequitur* between xxiv 191 and xxiv 192, which Heubeck[13] has characterized as "unusual" and Sourvinou-Inwood[14] as "nonsensical."

Odyssey xxiv 192 (ὄλβιε Λαέρταο πάϊ, πολυμήχαν' Ὀδυσσεῦ) recalls[15] *Odyssey* xxiv 36 (ὄλβιε Πηλέος υἱέ, θεοῖς ἐπιείκελ' Ἀχιλλεῦ) that seems to be the pattern upon which the former verse has been composed. There are striking correspondences between these two verses, the more so since they constitute praise to the ὄλβοι of Achilles and Odysseus respectively. It is clear that the tradition of the *Odyssey* wants to compare the fate of Achilles to that of Odysseus as it had done throughout the epic, and especially in the two Nekyiai, where the negative fate of Agamemnon had been compared to the positive and fortunate fate of Odysseus.[16]

In fact, in the last part of the first speech of Agamemnon to Amphimedon in the second Nekyia (*Odyssey* xxiv 106–119, esp. 114–119), the name of Odysseus creeps twice on the surface. Amphimedon mentions Odysseus no less than eight times in his answer to Agamemnon's questions about how he got to Hades. This high frequency of uttering Odysseus' name results in Odysseus' notional presence in the scene, through his reactivation in the minds of the audience. This point needs further elaboration:

It has been argued that, in the *Iliad*, Patroclus "is the character whose actions are preordained and determined by forces stronger than himself."[17] This acute observation is of extreme importance for understanding a superficially unexplained phenomenon in the older epic, namely the interchangeability[18] of Patroclus as audience of Achilles (e.g. *Iliad* IX 186–191) with the

---

[12] Rutherford 1992:52 argues that only in xxiv 191 "is Odysseus in a situation where that epithet [sc. ὄλβιος] could be used without absurdity."

[13] See Heubeck 1992:67 ad *Odyssey* x 456.

[14] See Sourvinou-Inwood 1996:100n254.

[15] See Heubeck 1992:381 ad *Odyssey* xxiv 191.

[16] The adjective ὄλβιος when used for Achilles and Odysseus in the vocative means "blessed" (2 times in the *Odyssey*). In the nominative case, ὄλβιος can mean both "blessed" and "wealthy" (6 times in the *Odyssey*), whereas in the accusative it always means "blessed" (5 times in the *Odyssey*).

[17] Bakker 1997:172.

[18] See Frontisi-Ducroux 1986:23–25; Nagy 1990a:202, 1996a:72; Russo and Simon 1968:483–498. For a discussion of the function of the narrator's tendency to address Patroclus in the second person, see Martin 1989:235–237. On apostrophe in general and its effects, see Kahane 1994:153–155.

audience of the *Iliad*. This process is, I argue, at work in the second Nekyia as well. Instead of trying to adduce some metrical explanation for the xxiv 191-192 *non sequitur* or explain it as a gap in the formulaic system (i.e. as the dictional by-product of some ambiguous reworking of an older version in which Odysseus would have been physically present in Hades), it is preferable to look for poetic motivation, which often makes irregularity narratively functional. Odysseus is the hero *par excellence* of the *Odyssey*. As such, his epiphany does not require a staging formula, since he is already present in the performance, constituting the notional internal audience of this particular scene. As a result, the voice of Agamemnon, who is the physical speaker in xxiv 192-202, reflects the singer's perspective while addressing his audience. By drawing on the performative reality of Homeric song, the bard is able to turn Odysseus into a listener in the performance, just as we are.

Odysseus cannot make a normal appearance at this point, for he is, after all, physically absent. His summoning is unusual, the more so since he is addressed in a *victorious, triumphant* manner. But as the pronoun τόν in xxiv 191 becomes an allusive starting point (designating Amphimedon although referring to Odysseus), so the staging formula acquires a new, meta-traditional function. It is not so much the soul of Agamemnon who speaks, but *the tradition of the Odyssey* addressing its main hero, Odysseus, who is notionally present in the underworld. By addressing Odysseus, the Odyssean tradition 'erases' the personae of Agamemnon and Amphimedon, who are physically present, and summons on stage not the narrative Odysseus, but the Odysseus of all time, the one who has surpassed the limits of the action and has become the trademark of the collective consciousness of the tradition.

Agamemnon's voice does not become the singer's, but gets to be understood as such by the audience. Agamemnon serves here as the mouthpiece of the tradition which, through this device, is able to make a comment about itself. Besides, the interchangeability phenomenon discussed above occurs in the very last of the speeches belonging to the scene in the underworld. After its completion, the second Nekyia is over and the listeners are transferred back to Ithaca. By placing Agamemnon's speech at a crucial juncture between the underworld episode and the continuation of the plot in Ithaca, the tradition of the *Odyssey* intrudes into the narrative and makes explicit what was implicit in the whole of the second Nekyia, namely the presence of Odysseus. Alluded to by the Achilles-Agamemnon speeches, foreshadowed by the Agamemnon-Amphimedon dialogue, the fate of Odysseus is slowly but carefully revealed by the poet, who has been artfully moving towards his goal, i.e. the presentation of his hero's happy fate in comparison to that of his epic comrades. Now, at the end of the whole scene, it is time for the singer to remove the curtain and cease the shadows from speaking. It is the moment for the tradition to make its own voice heard at last.

The Song of Praise: Penelope and the Encomium of the *Odyssey*

The basic problem of this passage (*Odyssey* xxiv 191-202) refers to the multiple addressees of the speech, which is uttered by the shadow of Agamemnon in the presence of Amphimedon, but is surprisingly addressed to the absent Odysseus, though most of its content (aside from the first two verses) is "a (long overdue) encomium of Penelope (192-202)."[19] The existence of three different addressees has prompted the theory of a Continuator, who, influenced by "the taste of the archaic age for more katabasis literature" was "led to the desire to add a second Nekyia at the end."[20]

The undoubtable kernel of this speech is the eulogy for Penelope, who is praised for her 'virtue' (ἀρετή). The high sophistication of this encomium is due to the epic's most emphatic and explicit statement dealing with her κλέος as the subject of a 'pleasing song' (χαρίεσσα ἀοιδή) in opposition to the 'evil fame' (χαλεπὴ φῆμις) of Clytaemestra, which will form the subject of a 'hateful song' (στυγερὴ ἀοιδή). Before embarking on a discussion pertaining to the function of the speech in relation to the figures of Odysseus and Penelope, I shall begin with a detailed structural analysis of this passage.

Structure of the speech

I. Introduction (192-193)

192: (address to Odysseus) ὄλβιε Λαέρταο πάϊ, πολυμήχαν' Ὀδυσσεῦ,
193: (link between Odysseus and Penelope) ἦ ἄρα σὺν μεγάλῃ ἀρετῇ ἐκτήσω ἄκοιτιν·[21]

---

[19] See West 1989:113-143 and, for the citation, 123.

[20] See Sourvinou-Inwood 1996:102. West 1989:132 places the addition of the Epilogue (xxiii 297-xxiv 548) by the Continuator (who is not to be confused with the B-poet or final redactor) at the Panathenaic festival in Athens. She thus tries to cater to newer tastes and beliefs such as those concerning the impunity of a king (Odysseus) who has slaughtered those trying to usurp his power in his absence, as well as the question of final harmony.

[21] According to West 1989:124, who follows Shipp 1972²:360, we must take σὺν μεγάλῃ ἀρετῇ with ἄκοιτιν and not with ἐκτήσω. In that case we have an unparalleled Homeric feature. Other abnormalities found in the passage under discussion are the Attic brachylogical comparison in xxiv 199 (οὐχ ὡς Τυνδαρέου κούρη) and the genitive Τυνδαρέου which is considered by both

II. Praise of Penelope (194-198)

194: ὡς ἀγαθαὶ φρένες ἦσαν ἀμύμονι Πηνελοπείῃ,
195: κούρῃ Ἰκαρίου· ὡς εὖ μέμνητ' Ὀδυσῆος,
196: ἀνδρὸς κουριδίου. τῷ οἱ κλέος οὔ ποτ' ὀλεῖται
197: ἧς ἀρετῆς, τεύξουσι δ' ἐπιχθονίοισιν ἀοιδὴν
198: ἀθάνατοι χαρίεσσαν ἐχέφρονι Πηνελοπείῃ,

III. Blame of Clytaemestra (199-202)

199: οὐχ ὡς Τυνδαρέου κούρη κακὰ μήσατο ἔργα,
200: κουρίδιον κτείνασα πόσιν, στυγερὴ δέ τ' ἀοιδὴ
201: ἔσσετ' ἐπ' ἀνθρώπους, χαλεπὴν δέ τε φῆμιν ὀπάσσει
202: θηλυτέρῃσι γυναιξί, καὶ ἥ κ' εὐεργὸς ἔῃσιν.

The parallelism between the fate of Penelope and that of Clytaemestra is highlighted throughout the speech in the following ways:

a. The encomium of Penelope is juxtaposed to the blame of Clytaemestra
b. Parts II and III of the speech have almost the same length (5:4 verses)
c. Parts II and III are symmetrically developed:

1.	κούρῃ Ἰκαρίου	Τυνδαρέου κούρη
2.	εὖ μέμνητ'	κακὰ μήσατο ἔργα
3.	ἀνδρὸς κουριδίου	κουρίδιον ... πόσιν
4.	οἱ κλέος οὔ ποτ' ὀλεῖται	χαλεπὴν δέ τε φῆμιν
5.	ἐπιχθονίοισιν	ἐπ' ἀνθρώπους
6.	χαρίεσσαν ἀοιδήν	στυγερὴ δέ τ' ἀοιδή

The thematic units corresponding to the above structural analysis are the following:

1. Characterization of both women by their patronymics to emphasize the family element
2. Good 'memory' (μνήμη) of Penelope vs. evil intelligence (μῆτις) of Clytaemestra
3. Connection to their husbands
4. Imperishable 'fame' (κλέος) vs. evil reputation

Shipp 1972[2]:55 and Chantraine 1986-1988[6] (1948-1953):197 (GH 1) to be a late feature. It is out of the scope of this chapter to examine peculiar linguistic features in Odyssey xxiv 191-202, since this would entail a general study of the linguistic abnormalities of the second Nekyia. Here, it suffices to say that "late" features do not necessitate "late" composition.

5. Impact on mortal men
6. Pleasing song versus hateful song

By presenting Penelope's ἀρετή as paragonal and by linking it specifically with the memory of her husband Odysseus, the epic tradition of the *Odyssey* bestows on the daughter of Icarius κλέος that will never perish (*Odyssey* xxiv 196). The expression οὔ ποτ' ὀλεῖται has a temporal dimension,[22] since it refers to the everlasting duration of Penelope's κλέος. At the same time, the epic defines itself retrospectively as a divine deed and as a song of Penelope, whose persona has literally become the unfailing memory of Odysseus.[23]

Memory is of prime importance for Odyssean poetics. It is through memory that Odysseus becomes an ἀοιδός, it is through the memory of Penelope that he seeks his νόστος, and through memory that he manages to escape from Calypso's world, the world of forgetfulness. Throughout his adventures Odysseus is faced with various perils whose common denominator is the danger of oblivion, of forgetting Ithaca and Penelope. His quest is both external and internal: he has to fight against strange beings, to employ his polytropic νόησις, his μῆτις, in order to survive. What his adventures represent is not limited to external physical danger, but includes the danger of forgetting who he really is, of loosing his identity. It is the memory of Penelope that helps him recover and return home.

At the same time, Penelope is faced with equivalent dangers. If she were to marry one of the suitors, she would forget Odysseus and abandon her past. By remaining loyal she makes the *Odyssey* possible, giving meaning to her husband's return.[24] On a poetic level, Penelope resembles the Odyssean Muse "*non seulement parce qu' elle inspire en Ulysse le désir du nostos mais aussi*

---

[22] The expression οὔ ποτ' ὀλεῖται refers to time, whereas οὐρανὸν ἵκει (the other modifier of κλέος) denotes extent. See Edwards 1985:76 citing Schmitt 1967:8, who has argued that duration and extent conventionally modified 'fame' (κλέος) in Indo-European heroic poetry.

[23] See Papadopoulou-Belmehdi 1994:40.

[24] Katz 1992:194 maintains that "Agamemnon endeavors to stabilize the indeterminacy of the narrative around a polarity of good and bad woman ... But Penelope resists conformity to the conventions of both sexual fidelity and character representation" and "[her] *kleos* ... is never fully stabilized." Katz deliberately underplays the fixity of Penelope's figure by suggesting that only on the denotative level of meaning is Penelope's 'fame' (κλέος) based on her loyalty to Odysseus; on the connotative level, her 'fame' (κλέος) is a problematic concept. This seems unreasonably vague to me, as Katz fails to explain satisfactorily the *Problematik* of Penelope's 'fame' (κλέος). Pucci 1987:217 puts the problem on the right track: "Such a limited concession to Penelope's husband is set against the preceding celebration of Achilles' *kleos* in its Iliadic splendor... The contrast is striking: Odysseus' *kleos* is debased to a generic reputation for his share and merits in Penelope's domestic virtues."

parce que la Muse est une expression métaphysique de la mémoire du poète épique."[25] Since memory in archaic poetry generates the creation of poetry itself,[26] it is Penelope's memory of Odysseus that generates "a most pleasing song (χαρίεσσα ἀοιδή)" offered by the gods to mortal men.[27] Likewise, Penelope's memory of Odysseus is the source of immortal fame, of a new type of κλέος, which is no longer based on glorious deeds as in the *Iliad*, but produces "enchantment (θέλξις) or a song-tale (μυθολογεύειν xii 450, 453)."[28]

The κλέος of both Odysseus and Penelope is based not only on memory, but also on δόλοι (*Odyssey* ix 19–20; xix 137), which both husband and wife employ to overcome the dangers with which they are faced. Clytaemestra uses δόλοι as well (*Odyssey* xi 422, xi 439), only, to "pour down shame on herself and on all women after her" (*Odyssey* xi 433–434).[29] Thus, the second Nekyia stands for the metapoetic *locus*, where the correlation of the δόλοι and κλέος of Odysseus with the cunningness and good fame of Penelope becomes clear. Odysseus and Penelope have cooperated in making possible Odysseus' final revenge against the suitors not through a common plan, but through poetic direction. The faithful wife uses her 'intelligence' (μῆτις) to put off the suitors and give Odysseus the opportunity to once again become her husband and the king of Ithaca.[30] Using the expression κακὰ μήσατο ἔργα (xxiv 199) for Clytaemestra,[31] the Odyssean song-tradition points to her δόλος, by which she

---

[25] Papadopoulou-Belmehdi 1994:170.

[26] See Vernant 1965:80–107.

[27] See Kullmann 1995:51, who argues that "the entire second Nekyia amounts to the prophecy of a famous song about Penelope. This is the only reason for its composition that can be found, unless we mean to understand it as a weak duplicate of the first Nekyia, for which we have no cause." This careful statement epitomizes the importance of Penelope's encomium and, consequently, of the passage we are discussing as a whole.

[28] Pucci 1997:168.

[29] The Odyssean tradition employs twice the same (xi 434 = xxiv 202) formula for Clytaemestra's shame. Interestingly enough, the same formula (*Odyssey* xv 422) is used by Odysseus in one of his false stories, in which he refers to a woman abducted by Phoenician sailors. For linguistic evidence about the antiquity of this formulaic expression, see Hoekstra 1989:259 ad *Odyssey* xv 422.

[30] See Edwards 1985:81: "[t]he κλέος of each is dependent upon the action of the other." He also argues that "[t]he *Odyssey* incorporates Iliadic κλέος within its narrative as the κλέος from a hero's death. The λόχος for the killing of the suitors has demonstrated that the *Odyssey* appropriates the *Iliad's* view of that strategy" (90).

[31] Nagy 1979:37, §13n3 is right in observing that "[t]hese themes correspond to the actual name *Klutaiméstra*, a form indicating that the wife of Agamemnon is 'famed' (*Klutai-*, from the same root **kleu-* as in *kléos*) on account of what she 'devised' (*-méstra*, from verb *médomai*). The element *méstre*, from *médomai* 'devise', corresponds to the theme of κακὰ μήσατο ἔργα 'she devised [*médomai*] evil deeds' at verse 199. As for the element *Klutai-* 'famed', it corresponds to the theme of στυγερή ... ἀοιδή 'hateful song' at verse 200. This hateful song will be not

Chapter Two

murders Agamemnon upon his return from Troy. Conversely, the *Odyssey* uses the doom of Agamemnon not simply as the negative reflection of Odysseus' fate, but also as the basis upon which it will define both heroism and happiness. By linking the narratively separate δόλοι of Odysseus and Penelope, aiming to restore both their οἶκος and κλέος,[32] the *Odyssey* redefines its own poetic κλέος by diverging from its renowned Iliadic predecessor as well as from the tradition of the *Nostoi*. It is exactly the generation of a 'pleasing song' (χαρίεσσα ἀοιδή) by this new Odyssean κλέος that announces the perennial nature of the *Odyssey*.

The new Odyssean epic song (νεωτάτη ἀοιδή) is opposed to that of Clytaemestra, whose evil intelligence (μῆτις) prompted the murder of her husband Agamemnon upon his return from Troy. Both her lack of 'fame' (κλέος) and the 'hateful fame' (χαλεπὴν φῆμιν) she has bestowed on women will be also transferred to her song (στυγερὴ ἀοιδή). This direct and emphatic opposition between the fate of Penelope and Clytaemestra is consonant with the general picture the *Odyssey* consistently draws about the comparison of the fates of Agamemnon and Odysseus.[33]

Penelope is not simply the model of the loyal wife and good queen, waiting for the return of her husband. She is the vehicle that redefines 'fame' (κλέος) in such a way that it becomes a condition for the creation of the poem's own subject matter. In this highly sophisticated passage, Penelope emerges in a metapoetic cloth, becoming the emblem[34] for the poetics of Odyssean κλέος. By absorbing Agamemnon's voice, the tradition of the *Odyssey* is able

---

simply about the wife of Agamemnon. Rather, the song is being presented as the very essence of *Klytaiméstre*."

[32] See Segal 1994:94–95.

[33] Felson-Rubin 1994:106 is right in arguing that Agamemnon makes Clytaemestra "a fitting scapegoat for his own (supposedly) undeserved destiny," but she makes too much, I think, out of "the folly and narrowness of his [Agamemnon's] male gaze" (107). After all, the song of blame for Clytaemestra exists just because there should be a song of praise for Penelope. It is because the *Odyssey* desires to praise itself that the *Nostoi* must be undermined.

[34] Finley 1978:3 has argued that "Agamemnon's statement in the second Nekyia "comes near making our *Odysseia* a *Penelopeia*," and Murnaghan 1987:124, repeating the same view, maintains that "[n]ot only does Penelope provide the most powerful potential threat to Odysseus' enterprise, but she threatens to usurp his poem as well." I would not go that far as Finley and Murnaghan. Penelope's role is no doubt crucial in redefining κλέος but from xxiv 192–202 it is clear that her encomium is subjugated to her husband's praise. Odysseus is ὄλβιος, among other things because he had a wife of great virtue (σὺν μεγάλῃ ἀρετῇ). Likewise, Agamemnon's doom is determined by his wife Clytaemestra. The presence of the wives in this passage is a means for one more comparison not only between Odysseus and Agamemnon, but also between two oral epics in which these figures would have formed part of the plot (see Kullmann, 1992:298).

to offer its own point of view, its own focalization. In this focalization, as the husband is saved by his wife, so the *Odyssey*, the χαρίεσσα ἀοιδή, is saved from oblivion through redefining its own subject matter, which is no longer the unfailing fame conveyed by Iliadic 'imperishable fame' (κλέος ἄφθιτον), but the Odyssean unfailing memory of enchanting and pleasing song.[35]

The Supremacy of the *Odyssey*

This exceptionally refined passage (xxiv 192-202) has a special importance for the poetics of the *Odyssey*, since it deals with κλέος, which "entails not only a relationship between heroes, but one between poems as well."[36]

From this comparison, which transcends the limits of the plot and reaches the level of song and poetry, Odysseus cannot be absent. The tradition of the *Odyssey* wants him there, which is the reason that the idea of the souls of the suitors flocking Hades has been presented in such detail. The suitors symbolize the Odyssean tradition encountering the non-Odyssean[37] (Iliadic, Aethiopic, and that of the *Nostoi*). The portrayal of Achilles and Agamemnon,[38] who talk about their own deaths, is natural for a scene in the underworld, but at the same time it points to the narrative of Amphimedon, who is only a "vehicle" for presenting Odysseus' fate to his Trojan comrades.

---

[35] See de Jong 2006:188-207, and in particular 197, 203-206. She rightly argues that "by connecting the *Odyssey* with the gods, the Homeric narrator enhances his status and authority, and by having Agamemnon [...] predict the *Odyssey*, he heightens the effectiveness of this 'metaleptic' move." See also Murnaghan 1987:125; Goldhill 1991:101; Danek 1998:487.

[36] Edwards 1985:90. Nagy 1979:37, §13n4 has even traced within this passage an allusion to an audience listening to poetry: "... instances of *epì* + accusative in the sense of 'among' are restricted in Homeric diction to *anthrópous* 'humans' as the object of the preposition. This syntactical idiosyncrasy can be correlated with an interesting thematic association: the expression *ep' anthrópous* 'among humans' is conventionally linked with *kléos* (X 213, i 299, xix 334, xxiv 94) and its derivatives (XXIV 202, xiv 403). It is also linked with *aoidé* 'song' at xxiv 201. Because of this parallelism between *kléos* and *aoidé*, and because *kléos* designates the glory conferred by poetry ... I infer that *ep' anthrópous* 'among humans' in these contexts indicates an audience in general listening to poetry in general."

[37] The Iliadic and Aethiopic traditions are represented by Achilles, Patroclus and Antilochus in the underworld, whereas that of the *Nostoi* by Agamemnon. See Kullmann 1992:298.

[38] See Bassett 1923:49-51. Moulton 1974:167 maintains that "[t]he second *nekuia*, in particular, seems to round out the Homeric picture of Achilles, and explicitly emphasize his *kleos*. In this episode, we see Agamemnon and Achilles, the two great adversaries of the *Iliad*, for the last time. Achilles rues his premature death, while Agamemnon contrasts his own fatal homecoming with the funeral honors paid Achilles at Troy." On the contrast between the homecoming of Odysseus and Agamemnon, which seems to preoccupy the poet of the *Odyssey* from beginning to end, see *Odyssey* i 32-43, 298-300; iii 194-198, 303-310; iv 519-537; xi 385-461; xiii 383-385. On the importance of this topic for the whole poem, see Klinger 1964:75-79; Hölscher 1967:1-16.

Chapter Two

The placement of this whole scene in the underworld becomes the ultimate metaphor for the crystallization of the older part of the tradition, which seems to be firmly established at the moment of the completion of our epic. The tradition of the *Odyssey* is trying to achieve a twofold goal: first, to put its hero in the highest position among the other epic heroes, with respect to his ὄλβος, by means of creating a tri-level climax with Agamemnon at the bottom, Achilles in the middle, and Odysseus in the top position. Second, since epic heroes stand for entire song-traditions, the *Odyssey* is able to emphatically express its qualitative superiority over its epic counterparts. In this context, intertextuality has become the foil for self-reflexivity and epic rivalry. Odysseus' supremacy is based on a new, comprehensive measuring of epic fame (κλέος). Agamemnon has neither won 'imperishable fame' (κλέος ἄφθιτον), since he did not die in Troy, nor has he fulfilled his νόστος, since when he arrived at Mycenae he was murdered by his wife, Clytaemestra. Achilles won 'imperishable fame' (κλέος ἄφθιτον) by dying at Troy, but failed to fulfill his νόστος. Odysseus, the poem's hero, both won 'imperishable fame' (κλέος ἄφθιτον), since he was responsible for the sack of Troy, and fulfilled his νόστος, since he returned home to his faithful wife Penelope and was reestablished as a king in Ithaca.

In particular, the presentation of Penelope and Clytaemestra does not postulate a distinction between *praise* versus *blame poetry*, as Nagy has argued.[39] The difference consists, rather, in the content of the poems and its evaluation by the audience.[40] The comparison that takes place in the underworld deals more, as Danek has neatly put it,[41] with "*poetische Stoff*" than "*poetische Form.*" It thus becomes a pretext for the Odyssean tradition to praise its own version against other competitive versions as well as other competitive traditions. The *Odyssey* inscribes the contrast between Penelope and Clytaemestra and, therefore, between Odysseus and Agamemnon within the larger framework of contrasting its song with other epic songs.[42] In Agamemnon's reply to Amphimedon, self-reference and intertextuality[43] are effectively combined, making this passage emblematic not only for the Odyssean plot, but also for the place the *Odyssey* wants to occupy within the epic tradition. This line of

---

[39] See Nagy 1979:36–38, 222–242, 254–256.
[40] Danek 1998:486.
[41] Danek 1998:487.
[42] Cf. Rutherford 2000:95, who asks the question whether the 'pleasing song' that the gods will weave for Penelope is the *Odyssey* itself or *ehoie*-poetry, "the genre in which female virtue is the established theme." See also de Jong 2001:573–574.
[43] See Kullmann 1992:297: "*Eine Selbstreferenz ist also mit einem intertextuellen Bezug gekoppelt.*"

interpretation is in agreement with the high probability that epic singing was competitive, which would have inevitably resulted in making heroes of epic poetry compete and rival one another.

Thus, the *Odyssey* not only joins the rest of the epic tradition, but surpasses it by becoming *the poem of poems*. It has incorporated and absorbed the entire Trojan—and Post-Trojan—War tradition to such an extent that it can place itself at a level superior to other already shaped and established epic songs. Like its hero, the *Odyssey* proves itself to be truly multileveled (πολύτροπος), of many devices (πολυμήχανος), and, most of all, a pleasing song (χαρίεσσα ἀοιδή) whose κλέος οὔ ποτ' ὀλεῖται (fame will never perish).[44]

---

[44] See also Marg 1956:16–29; Hölscher 1967:9–10; Rüter 1967:253; Nagy 1979:39. All these scholars have argued that the *Odyssey* places itself at the same level as the *Iliad*. Edwards 1985:91n39, following Pucci 1979:121–132 (= 1997:1–9), maintains that the *Odyssey* expresses its disavowal towards the authority and prestige of the *Iliad*, since it describes it as a song of death.

3

Nausicaa and the Daughters of Anius: Terms and Limits of Epic Rivalry

INTERTEXTUAL ASSOCIATIONS are based on the repetition of material treated in text A and whose reuse in text B will immediately allow the reader to make the connection to text A. In this way, a new 'reading' will emerge, one which does not depend solely on text A or text B, but on their *symbiosis* in a new intertext, AB, that will emerge in the reader's mind. In oral poetry, such a *symbiosis* is not created by helping the listener evoke a 'specific' text representing the crystallization of a given episode or version. Epic songs may be alluding to themes or topics falling outside their plot-framework but belonging to the plot-framework of other epic traditions. Since these traditions may be reconstructed due to later, post-Homeric treatments of the same mythical material, then we may be able to reconsider latent allusions to other versions of an episode or incident that the Homeric song-tradition deliberately leaves lurking in the background. Intertextuality is here not the result of an authorial, poet-centered policy, but an almost in-built characteristic of oral poetry. Selecting their material from multiple traditions concerning Odysseus, the bards who decide to sing his ante- and post-Iliadic mythical lore are well equipped to incorporate characteristics alluding to non-Odyssean episodes of Odysseus' heroic saga. Post-Homeric epics, whose content scholars have meticulously tried to reconstruct using material from various sources, are a valuable aid, since they are undoubtedly based on epic versions that were uninterruptedly sung during the formative period of the Homeric poems.[1]

In this light, cross-referencing may well be at work in traditional oral poetry, provided that we understand cross-references not as indicating text-oriented allusions but tradition-dependent associations. Nagy has eloquently summarized this viewpoint in the following way:

---

[1] This is the second phase in the evolutionary model of Homeric poetry suggested by Nagy 1996a:110, 1996b:42, and 2004:27.

Even if we were to accept for the moment the dubious notion that parts of the Homeric Cycle are drawn from some other text that predates our *Iliad* and *Odyssey*, the fundamental objection remains the same: when we are dealing with the traditional poetry of the Homeric (and Hesiodic) compositions, it is not justifiable to claim that a passage in any text can refer to another passage in another text. Such a restriction of approaches in Homeric (and Hesiodic) criticism is one of the most important lessons to be learned from the findings of Milman Parry and Albert Lord on the nature of traditional "oral" poetry. I will confine myself, then, to examining whether a poem that is composed in a given *tradition* may refer to other *traditions* of composition. Thus, for example, our *Odyssey* may theoretically refer to the traditional themes that are central to the stories of the *Cypria*—or even to stories of the *Iliad*, for that matter. But even in that case, such traditional themes would have varied from composition to composition. There may theoretically be as many variations on a theme as there are compositions. Any theme is but a multiform [that is, a variant], and not one of the multiforms may be considered a functional "*Urform*". Only by hindsight can we consider the themes of our *Iliad* to be the best of possible themes.[2]

One important issue in respect to cross-references of the type described above is their sequence-ignoring character. The very notion of intertextuality is,[3] in fact, consonant to this very idea. It has been argued that by evoking a single aspect or incident of a story not exploited by the Homeric epics at the moment of performance, the bard does not demand from his audience to have mastered enormous quantities of mythological material, but to focus their attention on a single point.[4] Compressed narrative, on the other hand, disrupts the chronological sequence in which a given episode is placed and conjures in the audience's mind not just the particular detail at hand, but also the framework and, perhaps, even the tradition with which this incident is associated. Since familiarity with characters and the entire mythical nexus concerning a given hero is required, I strongly reject the idea of a poet imposing a heavy interpretive burden on his audience's shoulders. When talking about traditional mythical material, we do not need to think

---

[2] Nagy 1979:42–43. Taken from Nagy 1996b:133. See also Pucci 1987:240–242.
[3] Having clarified the meaning of intertextuality in an oral traditional medium such as archaic epic, I prefer to keep the term (intertextuality) unchanged.
[4] Scodel 2002:153–154.

Chapter Three

of an audience comprised of well-informed students of Greek myth. Such a distorted picture is typical of the modern sense of 'mythology', according to which acquaintance with mythical material is attained only after meticulous study of the relevant myths. An ancient audience was able to fill the gaps every time they were presented with a compressed narrative, because that was the process mythical material developed. There was no compendium of myths from which a given poet would select a story and tailor it to his needs. Links and aberrations, associations and deviations among various mythical traditions, grew out of their performative use in oral contexts, one of which was epic singing. We do not need to postulate a supremely competent audience to argue that the average listener must have heard many epic performances. In fact, what we define as 'competence' within a performance-context is simple acquaintance.

It is as if, to employ a metaphor from the field of textual criticism, we are dealing with a *palimpsest* (a *codex rescriptus*), which has been re-written in the same place as an earlier text that has been now erased. Thus, the codex we possess can help us read two texts, both the earlier and the present one. To that extent, the two texts, which may well be completely unrelated, share a peculiar form of *symbiosis* through the medium on which they have been written. Traces of the older text may be still discernible, provided that we look 'below' the present text to recover the erased one. Extending this analogy to the field of oral poetics, I employ the oxymoronic term 'oral palimpsest' in order to allude to the co-existence, in our *Iliad* and *Odyssey*, of episodes or incidents belonging to other song-traditions current during the formative period of the Homeric epics. Like the erased text on a *palimpsest*, traces of other song-traditions may be still recovered in the *Iliad* and the *Odyssey*. This time, though, such recovery can be achieved not through modern laser techniques, as it is the case in palaeography, but through a sophisticated system of cross-referencing, which involves what Martin has happily called a 'selection-of-detail' principle.[5] Selecting details from a mythical episode known to the audience presupposes a process of suppression of certain aspects that the current version wants to eliminate. The reasons explaining this suppression-policy often have to do with the particular mythical version a given epic intends to foster and promote, as well as with its effort to differentiate itself from other traditions to which it may be related through its interest in the same characters. The tradition of the *Odyssey*, to state a relevant example, may have aimed at 'usurping' Odysseus from all other rival traditions dealing with the

---

[5] Martin 1989:130n78; Nagy 1996b:136.

same hero. In all other traditions where Odysseus is present, the king of Ithaca hardly features as the main character. He is one of many heroes, whose fate is connected either to the preparation and departure for Troy or the Trojan War itself, or his adventures after his reunion with Penelope. Making Odysseus the main hero of a whole song-tradition such as the *Odyssey*, though, was not the only means by which this tradition attempted to highlight its importance. Odysseus had to become the hero of the *Odyssey* by acquiring characteristics that would distinguish him not only from other heroes of the tradition of the Trojan War, but also from his rival epic personas featured in other epic songs. Under this scope, a positively evaluated Odysseus may have been the 'narrative product' of the Odyssean song-tradition that aimed at promoting its 'one man's show', i.e. a version with only Odysseus as the protagonist. Selecting the appropriate details and suppressing others became, therefore, an effective policy on the part of the Odyssean tradition, so as to highlight the importance of its own Odyssean Odysseus.

The compressed narrative the hero offers to Nausicaa in *Odyssey* vi 160–167 is one case in which the mechanics of cross-referencing are amply employed in order to conjure a rival version of Odysseus' mythical lore and subsequently appropriate it to an Odyssean perspective.

The Palm Tree

One of the most impressive features of the meeting between Nausicaa and Odysseus in *Odyssey* vi is the hero's reference to his journey to Delos and the young palm-tree he saw next to Apollo's altar there. This piece of information has instigated a serious debate concerning both its origin and its function in the Nausicaa-Odysseus episode. The relevant verses run as follows (*Odyssey* vi 160–167):

> "οὐ γάρ πω τοιοῦτον ἐγὼ ἴδον ὀφθαλμοῖσιν,
> οὔτ' ἄνδρ' οὔτε γυναῖκα· σέβας μ' ἔχει εἰσορόωντα.
> Δήλῳ δή ποτε τοῖον Ἀπόλλωνος παρὰ βωμῷ
> φοίνικος νέον ἔρνος ἀνερχόμενον ἐνόησα·
> ἦλθον γὰρ καὶ κεῖσε, πολὺς δέ μοι ἕσπετο λαός
> τὴν ὁδὸν ᾗ δὴ μέλλεν ἐμοὶ κακὰ κήδε' ἔσεσθαι.
> ὣς δ' αὔτως καὶ κεῖνο ἰδὼν ἐτεθήπεα θυμῷ
> δήν, ἐπεὶ οὔ πω τοῖον ἀνήλυθεν ἐκ δόρυ γαίης."

> "Never have I set eyes on any man or woman like you. I am overcome with awe

> as I look at you. Only in Delos have I seen the like, a fresh young
> palm tree
> shooting up by the altar of Apollo, when my travels took me
> there—with a fine
> army at my back, that time, though the expedition was doomed
> to end so fatally
> for me. For a long time I stood spellbound at the sight, for no
> such sapling ever
> sprang from the ground."

According to Hainsworth, "Odysseus appears to allude to his voyage to Troy (or Aulis), but a visit to Delos is otherwise quite unknown."[6] There is, however, a scholium by Aristarchus (EPQ ad *Odyssey* vi 164) referring to a visit of Odysseus and Menelaus (followed by the entire Greek fleet) to Delos to seek the daughters of Anius, who were able to relieve the famine of the Greek army by producing food:

> λέγοι δ' ἂν πολὺν λαὸν οὐ τὸν ἴδιον στόλον, ἀλλὰ τὸν Ἑλληνικόν, ὅτ' ἀφηγούμενος εἰς Δῆλον ἦλθε Μενέλαος σὺν Ὀδυσσεῖ ἐπὶ τὰς Ἀνίου θυγατέρας, αἳ καὶ Οἰνότροποι ἐκαλοῦντο).

> By *a great army* he refers not to his own fleet, but to the Greek one, when Menelaus, after taking up the command, went to Delos together with Odysseus in search for the daughters of Anius, who were called Oinotropoi.

The study of the myth of the Oinotropoi is of central importance for exploring the mythical apparatus upon which Odysseus' compressed narrative at *Odyssey* vi 160–167 is founded. The following is a list of all the ancient sources referring to this episode:

(a) In the scholia on Lycophron's *Alexandra* 570 (197 Scheer) we read about an incident that, according to Pherecydes (*FGrHist* 3 F 140 = *EGM* fr. 140), belonged to the plot of the lost epic *Cypria* (*PEG* 1, fr. 29 = *EGF* fr. 19). Lycophron's *Alexandra* 570 (197 Scheer):

> Σταφύλου τοῦ υἱοῦ Διονύσου θυγάτηρ γίνεται Ῥοιώ. ταύτῃ ἐμίγη Ἀπόλλων, αἰσθόμενος δὲ ὁ Στάφυλος ἔβαλεν αὐτὴν εἰς λάρνακα καὶ ἀφῆκε κατὰ τὴν θάλασσαν. ἡ δὲ προσεπελάσθη τῇ Εὐβοίᾳ καὶ ἐγέννησεν αὐτόθι περί τι ἄντρον παῖδα, ὃν Ἄνιον ἐκάλεσε διὰ τὸ

---

[6] Hainsworth 1988:304. See Danek's criticism 1998:132–133.

ἀνιαθῆναι αὐτὴν δι' αὐτόν. τοῦτον δὲ Ἀπόλλων ἤνεγκεν εἰς Δῆλον, ὃς γήμας Δωρίππην ἐγέννησε τὰς Οἰνοτρόπους Οἰνώ, Σπερμώ, Ἐλαΐδα, αἷς ὁ Διόνυσος ἐχαρίσατο, ὁπότε βούλονται, σπέρμα λαμβάνειν. Φερεκύδης (FGrHist 3F 140) δέ φησιν ὅτι Ἄνιος ἔπεισε τοὺς Ἕλληνας παραγενομένους πρὸς αὐτὸν αὐτοῦ μένειν τὰ θ' ἔτη· δεδόσθαι δὲ αὐτοῖς παρὰ τῶν θεῶν τῷ δεκάτῳ ἔτει πορθῆσαι τὴν Ἴλιον. ὑπέσχετο δὲ αὐτοῖς ὑπὸ τῶν θυγατέρων αὐτοῦ τραφήσεσθαι. ἔστι δὲ τοῦτο καὶ παρὰ τῷ τὰ Κύπρια πεποιηκότι.

Staphylus, son of Dionysus, had a daughter, Rhoio, with whom Apollo had intercourse. As soon as Staphylus realized this, he put her into a chest and sent her down to the sea. She approached Euboea and in this place, around some cave, gave birth to a son, whom she named Anius because of the pain she experienced for his sake. Apollo brought him to Delos. He [Anius] married Dorippe and had born to him the Oinotropoi, Oino, Spermo, [and] Elais. Dionysus gave freely to them the ability to receive seed, whenever they wanted. Pherecydes (*FGrHist* 3 F 140 = *EGM* fr. 140) relates that Anius persuaded the Greeks, who came to him, to stay in this place [Delos] for nine years; [he foretold] that it would be granted to them by the gods to sack Ilium in the tenth year. He also promised them that they would be nourished by his daughters. This story is narrated by the poet of the *Cypria*.

Two other scholia on Lycophron's *Alexandra* 580 (200 Scheer) and 581 (200 Scheer) are also relevant:

αἱ Οἰνότροποι ἐκαλοῦντο Οἰνώ, Σπερμώ, Ἐλαΐς. αὗται ἔλαβον παρὰ Διονύσου δῶρον, ἵνα, ὅτε θελήσουσι, καρπὸν τρυγῶσι· καὶ ἡ μὲν Οἰνώ τὸν οἶνον ἐποίει, ἡ δὲ Σπερμώ τὰ σπέρματα, τὸ ἔλαιον δὲ ἡ Ἐλαΐς. αὗται καὶ τοὺς Ἕλληνας λιμώττοντας ἐλθοῦσαι εἰς Τροίαν διέσωσαν.

The Oinotropoi were named Oino (wine-girl), Spermo (seed-girl), Elais (oil-girl). They received from Dionysus the gift of being able to reap fruit, whenever they want. Oino created the wine, Spermo the seeds, Elais the oil. It is they who went to Troy and saved the Greeks who were starving.

Lycophron's *Alexandra* 580 (200 Scheer)

Chapter Three

Ἀγαμέμνων γὰρ τῶν Ἑλλήνων λιμῷ συνεχομένων μετεπέμψατο αὐτὰς διὰ τοῦ Παλαμήδους, καὶ ἐλθοῦσαι εἰς τὸ Ῥοίτειον ἔτρεφον αὐτούς.

For, Agamemnon, since the Greeks were affected by famine, summoned them [the Oinotropoi] by Palamedes, and when they [the Oinotropoi] arrived at Rhoiteion, they fed them [the Greeks].

Lycophron's *Alexandra* 581 (200 Scheer)

(b) There was also a lost epyllion by the neoteric Hellenistic poet Euphorion, whose title was *Anius*.[7] This poem's content had to do with Dionysus' priest, Anius, who was able to feed the entire Greek army through the help of his daughters, the Oinotropoi. Since Euphorion is known for his taste in episodes and characters featured in the Epic Cycle, it can be plausibly argued that he would have drawn some of the material concerning Anius from the *Cypria*.[8]

(c) According to Tzetzes' scholia (on Lycophron's *Alexandra* 570 [198 Scheer]: μέμνηται δὲ καὶ Καλλίμαχος τῶν Ἀνίου θυγατέρων ἐν τοῖς Αἰτίοις and 580 [200 Scheer]: μαρτυρεῖ δὲ ταῦτα καὶ Καλλίμαχος) Callimachus too dealt with the story of the Oinotropoi in the *Aetia* (fr. 188 Pf.).

(d) Apollodorus (*Epitome* 3.10) refers to the daughters of Anius, who had received from Dionysus the gift of producing olive, seeds, and wine: θυγατέρες Ἀνίου τοῦ Ἀπόλλωνος Ἐλαΐς Σπερμὼ Οἰνώ, αἱ Οἰνότροποι λεγόμεναι· αἷς ἐχαρίσατο Διόνυσος ποιεῖν ἐκ γῆς ἔλαιον σῖτον οἶνον.[9]

(e) Ovid (*Metamorphoses* XIII 632–674) refers to the four daughters of Anius who were commanded by Agamemnon to feed the Greek army. In order to escape, two of them fled to Euboea and two to Andros. In a state of complete desperation, they prayed to Dionysus (669: '*Bacche pater, fer opem!*'), who transformed them into white doves.[10]

---

[7] *CA* fr. 2 = fr. 4 (van Groningen).

[8] Sistakou 2004:178–181 rightly observes that in Euphorion's idyll Anius played the key role, as can be inferred from the idyll's title (179). Euphorion may have focused his attention on the first visit of the Greek fleet to Delos, and it may also be the case that the indirect discourse in Lycophron's version of the Anius episode may also be reflecting the priest's original direct speech in Euphorion's idyll. On this point see Holzinger 1895:257 ad 575. I owe this reference to Sistakou 2004:180.

[9] 'The daughters of Anius, who was priest of Apollo, were Elais (Olive-girl), Spermo (Seed-girl), Oino (Wine-girl). It is to them that Dionysus gave the ability to produce olive, seed and wine from the earth.

[10] See Forbes Irving 1990:233–234.

The above information concerning the episode of the Oinotropoi clearly shows that there were at least two different versions of this story. Divergence is based on two aspects: (a) the place where the Oinotropoi saved the Greeks from starvation, and (b) the person or persons who played a key-role in summoning them.[11] According to the first version, which is mainly based on the scholia by Tzetzes on Lycophron's *Alexandra*, the Oinotropoi saved the Greeks after coming to cape Rhoiteion, in the Troad. In this first version, it is either Palamedes (scholia on Lycophron's *Alexandra* 581 [200 Scheer]), who follows the orders of Agamemnon and summons them to Troy, or Menelaus and Odysseus (EPQ ad *Odyssey* vi 164). According to the second version, which is also based on Tzetzes' scholia on Lycophron's *Alexandra*, Pherecydes (*FGrHist* 3 F 140 = *EGM* fr. 140) narrated the story of Anius, who, having prophesied to the Greeks that Troy would fall only in the tenth year after the departure of the Greek fleet from Aulis, suggested that they should stay with him at Delos. Anius reassured them that the Oinotropoi, his daughters, would nourish the Achaeans for nine years, after which they would sail to Troy and sack the city. This story, according to Tzetzes' scholium, was told by the poet of the *Cypria*.

Some scholars[12] endorse the accuracy of Tzetzes' scholium about Pherecydes' narrating that the episode of the Oinotropoi was part of the *Cypria*, but others seem quite skeptical about it. Welcker[13] has argued that the Pherecydes-fragment did *not* belong to the *Cypria*, since Tzetzes' scholium leaves no other alternative[14] but to believe that Anius indeed convinced the Greeks to stay at Delos for nine years. Immisch argues fiercely against Welcker by stating that one should not trust Tzetzes (as Welcker did) and should therefore read the conative imperfect ἔπειθε instead of the aorist ἔπεισε in Pherecydes (*FGrHist* 3 F 140 = *EGM* fr. 140).[15] This conjecture makes much more sense, since it is assumed that the Greeks did not stay at Delos but continued their voyage towards Troy. The scholium, in fact, does not say that the Greeks stayed at Delos for nine years and were subsequently fed by Anius' daughters, but simply that Anius promised (ὑπέσχετο) the Greeks that *if* they stayed in

---

[11] Ovid's version does not fall into the aforementioned categories. It is the only attestation of the story of Anius, in which the Oinotropoi do not save the Greek fleet. Such a divergence is, of course, due to the 'transformation pattern' employed in the *Metamorphoses*.

[12] Severyns 1928:309–313; Kullmann 1955:269; Jouan 1966:354–357; *PEG* 1, fr. 29 = *EGF* fr. 19; Danek 1998:132–134.

[13] Davies 1989:45.

[14] 1882:108.

[15] It is unlikely that ἔπεισε may mean '*chercha à persuader*', as Severyns 1928:310 translates this passage.

Chapter Three

Delos, his daughters would be able to feed the army.[16] Moreover, since the episode of the Oinotropoi is summarized in the aforementioned fragment in relation to the *Cypria*, it may have formed part, as Welcker had thought, of an isolated Delian myth. Immisch tries to corroborate his own view by arguing that, in the phrase μέμνηται δὲ τούτων καὶ ὁ τὰ Κύπρια συγγραψάμενος added by Tzetzes at the end of the scholium, the genitive τούτων refers to the daughters of Anius and not to the entire preceding passage.[17] Therefore, he concludes that the Pherecydes-fragment belonged to the *Cypria*.

The majority of modern scholars believe that the Pherecydes-fragment indeed refers to an episode that formed part of the *Cypria*. Still, there are a number of thorny issues that need to be convincingly solved. In fact, the question 'Did the Oinotropoi episode form part of the plot of the *Cypria*?' is linked to the question 'In which part of Proclus' summary should it be located?' Before I embark on a detailed examination of all the relevant material, let me point to the fact that only the scholium on Lycophron's *Alexandra* 570 (197 Scheer) is followed by an explicit reference to the *Cypria*. In the scholia on verses 580 (200 Scheer) and 581 (200 Scheer) the *Cypria* are not mentioned. Moreover, only Pausanias (X 31.2) explicitly refers to the drowning of Palamedes by Diomedes and Odysseus as belonging to the *Cypria*.[18] I will deal in due course with all of the suggestions made thus far and state all the problems linked with each proposal:

(a) If the Pherecydes-fragment formed part of the *Cypria*, then it would have to be placed, in all probability, *after* the first gathering of the army at Aulis and *before* the arrival of the Greek fleet at Teuthrania.[19] If one accepts the explanation offered by Immisch, who changed the aorist ἔπεισε into the imperfect ἔπειθε in the Pherecydes-fragment, then Anius' prophecy would have to be placed exactly *after* Calchas' prophecy, which also referred to *the very same matter, namely the duration of the war*. Calchas, in the episode coming just before the Teuthranian expedition, had prophesied to the Greeks (by interpreting the omen of the snake and the sparrows) what would happen to them. Prophecy[20]

---

[16] Immisch 1889:302: "*quam historiam voluit* [Welckerus] *intellegi Deliacam quandam semotam a reliqua memoria fabellam.*"
[17] Immisch 1889:302: "τούτων *enim in verbis Tzetzae feminini generis esse et spectare ad filias Anii, non ad universa, quae praecedant.*"
[18] Pausanias X 31.2: Παλαμήδην δὲ ἀποπνιγῆναι προελθόντα ἐπὶ ἰχθύων θήραν, Διομήδην δὲ τὸν ἀποκτείναντα εἶναι καὶ Ὀδυσσέα ἐπιλεξάμενος ἐν ἔπεσιν οἶδα τοῖς Κυπρίοις.
[19] Immisch 1889:303; Severyns 1928:312; Kullmann 1992:47.
[20] Kullmann 1960:221–223 lists all the prophecies contained in the Epic Cycle, which amount to seventeen. The number of prophecies that might have formed part of the *Cypria* varies from

constitutes a principal feature of the *Cypria*, which clearly have a 'hieratic' tone. The potential narrative juxtaposition of two prophecies on *exactly the same matter* should not, though, raise suspicions about the authenticity or placement of the Anius episode, since in the *Cypria* there is another example of two prophecies placed one next to the other while *foreshadowing the same events*. According to Proclus' summary, both Helenus (91–92 Severyns = 5 Kullmann: καὶ Ἕλενος περὶ τῶν μελλόντων αὐτοῖς προθεσπίζει) and Cassandra (93–94 Severyns = 7 Kullmann: καὶ Κασσάνδρα περὶ τῶν μελλόντων προδηλοῖ) clarify in advance what is going to happen.

(b) A more serious problem is connected to the episode of Palamedes' death. If Pausanias is right in stating that he read in the *Cypria* that Palamedes was drowned by Diomedes and Odysseus while fishing (Pausanias X 31.2), then how are we to explain his (Palamedes') summoning of the Oinotropoi from Delos (Lycophron *Alexandra* 581 [200 Scheer]) to relieve the Greeks from a famine at Troy? Almost every modern authority on the matter has interpreted Palamedes' fishing as a sign of famine in the Greek camp.[21] If Palamedes was then killed by Diomedes and Odysseus *during a famine*, he must have already summoned the Oinotropoi from Delos according to Agamemnon's order. In that case, what were the Oinotropoi doing in Troy if there was still a famine? If, on the other hand, we suppose that Palamedes' summoning of the Oinotropoi to Troy was *not* narrated in the *Cypria*,[22] then the narrative function of the Greek army's visit at Delos would be reduced only to a reiteration of the prophecy concerning the duration of the war. The only reasonable alternative is based on Kullmann's suggestion, that interprets Palamedes' fishing as indicating his effort to relieve the Greek army from a *second* famine,[23] which

---

six to eight. On the function of prophecy in the Epic Cycle, see Stockinger 1959:90–94; Griffin 1977:48; Davies 1989:38–39, 42, 45; Rengakos 2004:283–284.

[21] Robert 1920⁴:1130n4; Finsler 1924³:11; Severyns 1928:312n4; Jouan 1966:357; Davies 1989:48.

[22] This is the opinion of Jouan 1966:357–358, who thinks that the summoning of the Oinotropoi to Troy by Palamedes did *not* occur in the *Cypria* but was added later on from a source containing Palamedes-oriented mythical material. Conversely, Severyns 1928:312 had argued that the Palamedes episode did belong to the plot of the *Cypria*, but the visit of the Greek army to Delos was only mentioned as an analepsis *at the occasion of Palamedes' death* (312: "à l' occasion de la mort de Palamède"). Severyns's opinion is much more effective than that of Jouan, who fails to explain the function of the Anius episode. The visit of the Greek army at Delos acquires its full narrative potential only if the Oinotropoi are to be summoned, later on, to Troy. I tend to side with Kullmann's aforementioned explanation for the following reasons: (a) Kullmann has revealed a narrative pattern (the 'double-motifs') within which these two episodes fall; (b) Severyns' suggestion does not explain why the Oinotropoi had not saved the Greeks from the famine, since Palamedes resorted to fishing in order to fight starvation.

[23] Kullmann 1960:224.

Chapter Three

occurred towards the end of the *Cypria, after* the Oinotropoi had saved the Greek army from the first famine and only *after* the daughters of Anius had returned to Delos. The two famines should not make us suspicious about their authenticity, since Kullmann has rightly highlighted "an idiosyncrasy of the Cyclic Epics", their fondness for *Motivdubletten*,[24] for example the double explanation of Achilles' death and the double causation of Troy's destruction by the summoning of both Philoctetes from Lemnos and Neoptolemus from Scyros etc.[25]

So, we may now return to the episode between Odysseus and Nausicaa in *Odyssey* vi, particularly to the reference of a palm tree Odysseus had seen in Delos next to Apollo's altar. The ancient scholiast explains this by referring to a visit made to Delos by Menelaus and Odysseus to summon the daughters of Anius (ἐπὶ τὰς Ἀνίου θυγατέρας). This scholium (EPQ on *Odyssey* vi 164) points to a version of the myth of the Oinotropoi in which Menelaus and Odysseus have taken the place of Palamedes, who features in the *Cypria*. The phrase ἐπὶ τὰς Ἀνίου θυγατέρας, αἳ καὶ Οἰνότροποι ἐκαλοῦντο suggests that this can *not* be the Greek fleet's visit to Delos narrated in the *Cypria*, as the Greeks did not go to Delos *for* the daughters of Anius (ἐπὶ τὰς Ἀνίου θυγατέρας), but found out about their extraordinary abilities only *after* Anius' prophecy. Why, then, does the scholiast refer to Menelaus and Odysseus, but not to Palamedes? Obviously, because he employs a version that makes sense only as an exegetical scholium to the text of the *Odyssey*, where Odysseus refers, in an abbreviated narrative, only to himself as leader of the Greek fleet going to Delos. The *Odyssey* has every reason to 'erase' Palamedes, who is the great rival of Odysseus in the field of cunningness, but the question still remains as to what incident the scholiast is referring. In other words, why did the scholiast 'avoid' referring to Odysseus' first visit to Delos with the Greek army, which was narrated in the *Cypria*? The answer is perfectly compatible, I think, with the aforementioned analysis. The scholiast could not have explained Odysseus' abbreviated narrative by referring to the visit of the Greek army at Delos because at that point *the Greek army was not suffering from starvation*. The cross-textual reference the *Odyssey* unravels is based on the analogy the audience is expected to draw once

---

[24] Kullmann 1960:224: "*Eine weitere Eigentümlichkeit der kyklischen Epen besteht darin, dass sie zahlreiche Motivdubletten enthalten.*"

[25] As far as the function and placement of a dispute between Achilles and Odysseus (*Odyssey* viii 73–82) is concerned, I do not believe that it formed part of the *Cypria*. On this issue, I side with Danek 1998:142–150, who has argued, partly following Nagy 1979:15–65, that the conflict between βίη and μῆτις epitomized in the figures of Achilles and Odysseus may well be referring to the end of the war, at least to that part of the war following the death of Hector.

Nausicaa and the Daughters of Anius

Odysseus mentions the palm tree at Delos. Therefore, we are clearly dealing with two rival traditions[26] concerning the episode of the Oinotropoi, one belonging to the *Cypria* in which Palamedes summoned Anius' daughters from Delos to Troy, and the other stemming from another oral tradition, unknown to us, where it was Menelaus and Odysseus who played the role Palamedes had undertaken in the *Cypria*.[27] The abbreviated form of Odysseus' narrative to Nausicaa in *Odyssey* vi 160–167 implicitly indicates that the Delos incident was familiar to the audience. As a matter of fact, Odysseus' condensed reference acquires its full semantic potential only when its intertextual perspective is taken into account.

Comparative Analysis

In order to recover the intricate nexus of associations Odysseus' abbreviated narrative conjures up, we need to place this reference within the entire encounter with Nausicaa. The following table shows the narrative similarities between the myth of the Oinotropoi and the Nausicaa-Odysseus episode:

Story of the Oinotropoi	Nausicaa-Odysseus episode
Hunger of the Greek army	Hunger of Odysseus
The Oinotropoi feed the Greeks	Nausicaa gives food to Odysseus
The Oinotropoi descend from Dionysus	The Nausicaa episode is replete with Dionysiac elements

In both stories, starvation plays a key role. The Greeks (led by Menelaus and Odysseus) search for the Oinotropoi, who will be able, according to Anius' promise, to feed the army. Odysseus arrives at Scheria in a state of complete devastation and in urgent need of food. The hero's feeling of hunger pangs constitutes a well-known feature of this episode, reflected even in later iconographical representations of Odysseus and Nausicaa, in which the Ithacan king is depicted as having a humped back.[28] Odysseus' hunger can be clearly seen in: (a) *Odyssey* vi 133 (κέλεται δέ ἑ γαστήρ), when he is compared to a hungry

---

[26] See Danek 1998:133.
[27] I am very skeptical about the possibility that the *Cypria* might have featured another embassy to Delos by Menelaus and Odysseus, after the death of Palamedes, once a second famine had occurred in the Greek camp at Troy.
[28] See Shapiro 1995, plates 24–26.

Chapter Three

lion ready to attack cattle or sheep and (b) *Odyssey* vi 249-250 (ἦ τοι ὁ πῖνε καὶ ἦσθε πολύτλας δῖος Ὀδυσσεύς // ἁρπαλέως· δηρὸν γὰρ ἐδητύος ἦεν ἄπαστος).

The Oinotropoi produced food and saved the Greek army.[29] In *Odyssey* vi 248 (πὰρ δ᾽ ἄρ᾽ Ὀδυσσῆϊ ἔθεσαν βρῶσίν τε πόσιν τε), Nausicaa and her attendants offer food to Odysseus.

The Oinotropoi are the great-great-grand-daughters of Dionysus (Dionysus > Staphylus > Rhoio [+ Apollo] > Anius [+ Dorippe] > Oinotropoi). In Lycophron's *Alexandra* 577, it is explicitly stated that they were 'taught' by their great-great-grand father, Dionysus (called Πρόβλαστος in Lycophron's text), 'how to produce food crushed in a mill, how to make wine and ointment from oil' (578-580). In the Odysseus-Nausicaa episode, Alden has traced a number of Dionysiac elements, which give a Dionysiac overtone to the story.[30] In fact, the overt references to Artemis are coupled with multiple covert associations to Dionysiac cult.[31] I offer the following list, which is based on Alden's analysis:[32]

(a) The box (κίστη) containing the food Arete gives to Nausicaa (*Odyssey* vi 76)[33] is commonly used in Dionysiac ritual for the customary meal.[34]

(b) The removal of the headdresses by Nausicaa and her attendants also points to Dionysiac associations. In *Iliad* XXII 468-470, Andromache's removal of her headband and veil implies that she is in a state of ecstatic frenzy, 'like a maenad' (μαινάδι ἴση).[35]

(c) The Nymphs are associated both with Artemis and Dionysus.[36] Before the 6th century BC the Nymphs occupy a prominent place, but they are subsequently substituted by the Maenads.[37] When amidst dancing female company,

---

[29] See Lycophron *Alexandra* 581-583: αἳ καὶ στρατοῦ βούπειναν ὀθνείων κυνῶν // τρύχουσαν ἀλθανοῦσιν, ἐλθοῦσαί ποτε // Σιθῶνος εἰς θυγατρὸς εὐναστήριον. According to the scholia on Lycophron's Alexandra 580 (200 Scheer) αὗται (sc. αἱ Οἰνότροποι) καὶ τοὺς Ἕλληνας λιμώττοντας ἐλθοῦσαι εἰς Τροίαν διέσωσαν. See scholia on Lycophron's *Alexandra* 581 (200 Scheer): καὶ ἐλθοῦσαι (sc. αἱ Οἰνότροποι) εἰς τὸ Ῥοίτειον ἔτρεφον αὐτούς.

[30] Alden 1995:335-351.

[31] Artemis and Dionysus are not easily discerned in cult practice. See Alden 1995:343n56.

[32] Alden 1995:342-348.

[33] See Theocritus 26.1-9; Aristophanes *Lysistrata* 1182-1185.

[34] See Burkert 1983:271-272.

[35] On Andromache's Dionysiac associations in the *Iliad*, see chapter 1. Alden points to the par excellence Dionysiac removal of headdress in Euripides' *Bacchae* 1115-1116.

[36] Henrichs 1987:99-106; Jameson 1993:45-46; Cole 1993:281-282. Seaford 1993:122 rightly observes that the earliest example of Artemis' association with Dionysus is *Odyssey* xi 325, where it is stated that Artemis, who was informed by Dionysus, killed Ariadne. Artemis and Dionysus are usually connected by way of their rites being celebrated in the wild, far away from the civilized world.

[37] Jameson 1993:45.

Dionysus' sexuality is latent. Likewise, Odysseus' sexuality in this episode is rather covert. Interestingly enough, the entire episode places special emphasis on Odysseus' bath, which is made possible by 'the soft olive-oil in a golden flask' (vi 215: ... χρυσέῃ ἐν ληκύθῳ ὑγρὸν ἔλαιον) Arete has given to Nausicaa and her attendants.

(d) The disruption of the game with the ball, the shrieking of the girls (vi 117), Odysseus' awakening from sleep (vi 117), the hero's sudden appearance (vi 127), the panic-stricken attendants running here and there (vi 138), the face-to-face meeting between Odysseus and Nausicaa, all these features taken together have Dionysiac overtones. They correspond fairly well to the anguished cries of the maenads, the awakening of the infant Dionysus by the Thyiads in Delphi, the frenzied attendants occupied by the spirit of the god, the face-to-face encounter with the *'kommende Gott'*.[38]

(e) The branch or leafy bough[39] that Odysseus breaks from the thicket to conceal his nudity is, of course, very apt for the occasion, due to its practical use. At the same time, such a leafy bough recalls the well-known θύρσος, which is typical in Dionysiac cult. The θύρσοι, which are often used by those participating in cultic practice, have a special significance for Dionysus. Alden rightly observes that Nausicaa's attendants strikingly resemble Dionysus' maenads, who run in panic chased by Lycurgus or pursued by Dionysus' priest in the festival of the Agrionia in Orchomenos.[40] In two vases from Madrid, Dionysus is depicted carrying a tree[41] and in the famous Attic red-figure neck-amphora attributed to the Nausicaa Painter, Odysseus wears garlands of leaves on his head and holds two branches.[42]

(f) The palm[43] tree Odysseus refers to in *Odyssey* vi 163 is placed next to Apollo's altar at Delos. Apollo is also linked to the story of the Oinotropoi, since he slept with Dionysus' granddaughter, Rhoio, and was the father of Anius. The palm tree[44] is one of the most interesting features of this episode. It was

---

[38] Alden 1995:345. Cf. the maxim *'der liebe Gott steckt im détail'* (god lies in the particulars) by the art historian Warburg. See Henrichs 1993:40n71.

[39] Alden 1995:345n74 argues for an analogy between Odysseus' uncovered face beyond the branch and the Dionysiac mask or masks upon a column with branches sprouting out from his body. See Burkert 1983:235–237 and plate 7.

[40] Alden 1995:345–346.

[41] *CVA* Madrid 2, III 1 C plate 15 1a (Madrid 32656). Schauenburg 1957:222 and plate VIII, n13. See also Alden 1995:345n80.

[42] See Alden 1995:346; Shapiro 1995, plate 24.

[43] See Sourvinou-Inwood 1991:99–143.

[44] It was believed that Leto was supported by a palm tree while trying to give birth to Apollo and Artemis at Delos. See Hainsworth 1988:304.

Chapter Three

very often used in art "as an iconographic representation of the eternal recycling of life."[45] In Minoan-Mycenaean art, the sacred tree was often depicted as a fig or olive tree associated with a female deity, but "the palm tree seems to have been confined to other representations in which the female deity is not depicted."[46] In Early Greek art, tree cult was not overtly expressed but was implicit, especially when the sacred tree became a recognizable feature of a sanctuary, like the osier tree at Hera's sanctuary at Samos, the olive tree on the Acropolis at Athens, and Leto's palm tree at Delos. In certain cases the sacred tree became synonymous to an oracle, as was the case with the oak in the oracle of Zeus at Dodona or the bay tree at Delphi.[47] In Archaic and later Greek art, the iconographic representation of a palm tree by an altar proliferated and was used, under the pressure of the aristocracy's desire to activate its past, within the framework of myths, epics, and popular religious beliefs.[48] As the old tree on an altar is progressively replaced by the new motif, Dionysus and the vine make their appearance. The famous cup by Exekias depicting Dionysus aboard a ship is the best example of this change. Dionysus is surrounded (above) by seven bunches of grapes springing from the ship's mast, which becomes a huge vine tree, and (below) by seven dolphins. The symbolism is more than explicit: Dionysus and the vine have replaced the Great Goddess of Minoan-Mycenaean art and the sacred tree. What lies beyond this representation is the cult of Dionysus *Dendritis*.[49] Dionysus has a special link to tree cult. The unmarried girls at Karyai in Laconia dance around a walnut tree, led by Artemis *Karyatis*. According to legend, Karya was a princess from Lacedaemon who was loved by Dionysus and was subsequently metamorphosed into a tree. The young girls who are called *Karyatides*[50] (daughters of the walnut tree, i.e. daughters of Dionysus) dance around the nut-bearing tree (καρύα) and hang themselves from its branches as an act of mimetic identification with this 'Dionysiac' tree.[51] The palm tree Odysseus mentions is called a φοίνικος νέον ἔρνος ἀνερχόμενον (fresh young palm tree shooting up). This rising palm tree may well be indicative of the theme of vegetation connected

---

[45] Kourou 2001:31. See also Evans 1901:99–204; Unger 1926:261–262; Danthine 1937; James 1966; Yarden 1972; Cook 1978; Kepinski 1982; Brosse 1993.
[46] Kourou 2001:34.
[47] Brosse 1993:71; Kourou 2001:38.
[48] Kourou 2001:48.
[49] Brosse 1993:113; Veneri 1986:415. See also Sourvinou-Inwood 2005:104, who observes that in Boeotia Dionysus was called Ἔνδενδρος (Hesychius s.v.).
[50] In Athens the *Karyatides* in the Erechtheion were called Καρυάτιδες δυσμαῖναι (Caryatids in madness). See Calame 1977:273n199.
[51] Burkert 1995:151; Daraki 1985:90.

to the myth of the Oinotropoi. A growing fresh shoot of a palm tree next to Apollo's altar bridges the beginning of the story of the Oinotropoi (Apollo impregnating Rhoio who is subsequently exiled by her father, Staphylus, the son of Dionysus) with the arrival of Anius at Delos. Dionysus has recompensed his granddaughter's (Rhoio's) exile by endowing her own granddaughters, the Oinotropoi, with the ability of producing food. The symbolism of vegetation inherent in the sacred tree next to an altar blends in effectively with the covert Dionysiac associations lying in the background of the myth of the daughters of Anius.

(g) Once Odysseus washed and dressed himself, Athena "made him taller and sturdier and caused the bushy locks to hang from his head thick as the petals of a hyacinth in bloom."[52] Odysseus' long hair bears a striking similarity with the long hair Pentheus acquires after being turned into a maenad by Dionysus.[53] Odysseus has, like Dionysus, acquired a greater stature; he has been changed into an almost new condition. All of this occurs only *after* Odysseus has washed off "the salt that encrusted his back and his broad shoulders, and [scrubbed] his head free of the scurf left by the barren sea."[54] Likewise, the daughters of Proetus were saved from madness by Melampus, priest of Dionysus, "in the temple of Artemis at Lousoi, the place of washing."[55]

(h) Nausicaa foresees that if she carries Odysseus upon her wagon, the people of Phaeacia might take him for a god who, having heard her prayers (πολυάρητος θεὸς ἦλθεν), has come from heaven to take hold of her.[56] The coming god ('*der kommende Gott*'),[57] carried upon a ship-wagon from the sea[58] to the city before his intended sacred marriage (ἱερὸς γάμος) to the daughter of the ἄρχων βασιλεύς,[59] bears a striking similarity to Odysseus. He also comes from the sea, and, if carried upon Nausicaa's wagon, he may be taken as the god who had listened to her prayers or as her would-be husband (*Odyssey* vi 282-284). Dionysus is considered hostile to endogamy. The myths of Erigone, Icarius' daughter, and of Althaea, Oineas' wife, as well as the ritual practice of the *Anthesteria* in Athens attest to this.[60] Odysseus, although posing a threat to

---

[52] *Odyssey* vi 230-231.
[53] See Euripides *Bacchae* 821, 928-929, 935-939.
[54] *Odyssey* vi 225-226.
[55] Burkert 1985:223.
[56] *Odyssey* vi 280-281.
[57] Otto 1933:74.
[58] On Dionysus coming from the sea, see Kerényi 1976:139-144. For a list of ancient sources, see Alden 1995:342n48.
[59] Simon 1983:96-98.
[60] Daraki 1985:101-103; Seaford 1993:138; Alden 1995:342.

Nausicaa's future wedding with one of the Phaeacians (since he is after all a ξένος), will depart with a ship, Dionysus-like, from his Phaeacian hosts.

(i) The word συνέριθος (*Odyssey* vi 32–33: καί τοι ἐγὼ συνέριθος ἅμ' ἕψομαι, ὄφρα τάχιστα // ἐντύνεαι ...), employed for Athena as a disguised companion of Nausicaa, is also used for the same goddess as a 'helpful servant' of Dionysus by Telestes[61] in his *Argo* (quoted by Athenaeus, see *PMG* [805 (c)]: ἂν συνεριθοτάταν Βρομίῳ παρέδωκε σεμνᾶς // δαίμονος ἀερόεν πνεῦμ' αἰολοπτέρυγον // σὺν ἀγλαᾶν ὠκύτατι χειρῶν (It was handed over as a most helpful servant / to Bromios by the uplifted wing-flashing breath / of the august goddess with the swiftness of her glorious hands).[62]

The Recovered Intertext

The wealth of Dionysiac associations found in the Nausicaa-Odysseus episode cannot be explained as an instant reflex of the narrative coordinates of the encounter between the Phaeacian princess and the king of Ithaca. The comparative examination of the myth of the Oinotropoi, who have clear Dionysiac overtones, and of the covert Dionysiac elements in the Nausicaa-Odysseus episode points to a lost oral tradition featuring the story of Odysseus' visiting Delos in order to summon the daughters of Anius. In this tradition, which is partly reflected in the story of the Oinotropoi presented in the *Cypria*, the first visit of the Greek army at Delos as well as Odysseus' and Menelaus' second visit would have, in all probability, included numerous Dionysiac elements connected to the Oinotropoi and their relation to Dionysus. In this version, just as in the *Odyssey*, Odysseus arrived by sea, faced a terrible famine, and was in need of urgent help.

The *Odyssey*'s preoccupation with Dionysiac elements in the Nausicaa-Odysseus episode is in marked contrast to the complete absence of Dionysiac overtones in the rest of the epic.[63] The Odyssean tradition has employed material pertaining to an episode not featured in its plot (that of the Oinotropoi) and has narratively 'accommodated' it within the framework of the Nausicaa-Odysseus encounter.

In the first part of this chapter, I emphasized the difference between the roles of Palamedes in the *Cypria* and of Odysseus in another oral tradition,

---

[61] See Wilson 1999:66–68.
[62] The translation is based on Campbell 1993.
[63] The only exception is a brief reference to Dionysus and Ariadne in Naxos at the first *Nekyia* (*Odyssey* xi 325).

alluded to in the *Odyssey* through Odysseus' abbreviated narrative about the palm tree he had seen at Delos. The *Cypria* may well reflect a rival oral tradition in which Palamedes, as Agamemnon's envoy to Delos to summon the daughters of Anius, played Odysseus' role. Are we able to trace even a single element showing or at least entertaining the possibility that the oral tradition of the *Odyssey* was aware of a rival oral tradition featuring Palamedes in the place of Odysseus, as is the case in the *Cypria*? In other words, are we able to find in the *Odyssey* a hint of a tradition endorsing the *Cypria*'s version of the story of the Oinotropoi?

This is an impossible jigsaw puzzle to solve. Still, there is a single feature that is, I hope, worth stating. Palamedes and his entire mythical entourage are associated with names pertaining to the world of the sea. His father was Nauplius and their family ruled over the area of Nauplion. His two brothers were Oeax and Nausimedon. Palamedes was famous for promoting human civilization (invention of numbers, alphabet, measures, and distribution of goods). Likewise, the Phaeacians in the *Odyssey* are also connected to the sea, as indicated by their names and their unsurpassed nautical proficiency. Moreover, the Phaeacians experience not only a high state of civilization, but also an unprecedented abundance of goods lavished incessantly upon them by the gods.[64] Is it then plausible that the *Odyssey* places the cross-textual reference of Odysseus' visit to Delos within a Phaeacian framework because it aims, even more, at downplaying the preeminent role of Palamedes in the story of the Oinotropoi *as presented by* a rival oral tradition? I do not mean at all that the Phaeacian idyllic world has been invented for that reason, but that the Odyssean tradition has made Odysseus embed his Oinotropoi-oriented narrative in the Nausicaa episode (and not, say, in his false stories) in an attempt to more effectively 'erase' Palamedes' presence in this myth. The abbreviated form of Odysseus' reference to Delos is in stark contrast to the epic's detailed presentation and description of the Phaeacian world to its audience. This may be an implicit indication that the former myth (Oinotropoi) was well known, whereas the latter (Phaeacians) was completely unknown.[65] Granted that the Phaeacian world was 'invented' by the Odyssean tradition, it becomes more plausible that an introduction to the idyllic world of Scheria would have been more appropriate if this world did not, Palamedes-like, pose a threat to the poem's main hero. In this sea-oriented Phaeacian world, abundance is acquired not through Palamedian inventions and labor, but through a god-

---

[64] *Odyssey* vii 114–132.
[65] Lowenstam 1993:207–228; Danek 1998:131.

Chapter Three

sent cornucopia. In fact, the Phaeacians are the only people Odysseus does not have to compete with. Their unparalleled proficiency at sea is almost ironically presented by the *Odyssey*, since their ships quickly fly to the ends of the world, thereby making Odysseus' last journey on a Phaeacian ship from Scheria to Ithaca contrast his long, unsuccessful efforts to get home by his own means.

Thus, I maintain that both rival versions of the summoning of the Oinotropoi might have been known to the tradition of the *Odyssey*. Over centuries of compositional and thematic shaping, this epic tradition had incurred many poetic debts, which it adjusted to its own aim and scope. The epic's ability to select, rework, and tailor various rival traditions to its own subject matter has once again been effectuated through a female figure, Nausicaa, who has been shaped not only intratextually but also intertextually. In this light, one can apprehend why the epic refuses to apologize for offering only vestigial remains of fragmented myths, turning the technique of appropriating just the required mythical material into a demonstration of its own preeminence.

4

Intertextual Fissures:
The Returns of Odysseus and the New Penelope

THE AIM OF THIS CHAPTER is (a) to consider the function of intertextual fissures with respect to Odysseus' return and reunification with his wife, and (b) to explore how a crucial element of this scene, the story of the Sailor and the Oar, can assist us in examining the relationship between the *Odyssey* and other rival traditions. Gender-studies[1] and intertextuality[2] feature two of the most prominent modern approaches to such multifaceted texts as the *Odyssey*. Polar oppositions like presence—absence, old οἶκος—new οἶκος, γάμος—ἀγαμία, as well as key terms like μετοικεσία and ἀποδημία, may in fact suggest a bold re-reading of Penelope's condition when Odysseus finally returns to Ithaca. These binary pairs stand for semantic frames, representing antithetical states of affairs, between which Odysseus oscillates throughout the entire poem. This ever-changing condition of the poem's main hero is one of the hallmarks of the Odyssean interpretation of the heroic world approaching its end, but at the same time it is exploited by the *Odyssey* at full length as a matrix for the equally ever-shifting condition of Penelope. Instead of offering a new, holistic explanation model, I would like to discuss the possibility that Odysseus' future wanderings are treated by the *Odyssey* as a mirror

---

[1] Murnaghan 1987; Winkler 1990:129–161; Katz 1991; Wohl 1993; Felson-Rubin 1994; Doherty 1995; Holmberg 1995; Clayton 2004.

[2] Most notably Pucci 1987; Nagy 1990a:70–79; Muellner 1996; Danek 1998; Bakker 2001c:149–160; Burgess 2006:148–189. Intertextuality and oral tradition may seem incompatible to many. The scholars mentioned above, with whom I side, have in fact redefined intertextuality by making it encompass song traditions that show traces of *textualization* long before they become actual, written texts. Despite the fact that the term intertextuality contains the word 'text', I can see no more apt a term for describing the process of cross-reference between rival song traditions. See Nagy 1996b:40, whose definition of *textualization* I fully endorse: "I continue to describe as *text-fixation* or *textualization* the process whereby each composition-in-performance becomes progressively less changeable in the course of diffusion–with the proviso that we understand *text* here in a metaphorical sense."

Chapter Four

where Penelope's relationship to and definition of herself is reflected. The epic indulges in such a profound game with the couple's self-oriented disfluencies that it guilefully exploits the limits of its main protagonists, thus questioning even the most elementary tenets it seems to take for granted, such as the very idea of sameness once Odysseus and Penelope are reunited. As Odysseus and Penelope exist as character trademarks of the *Odyssey*, the window of allusion opened through their reunion scene allows the audience to gaze at another tradition in which both Odysseus and Penelope are molded in a very different cast.[3]

Male and Female δόλοι

Gender-based studies have highlighted the importance of Odysseus' and Telemachus' absences for Penelope's undertaking of a more active role in the palace.[4] Both Odysseus and Telemachus function as protective shields for the powerless female queen, wife of the former and mother of the latter. A closer look, though, at the way the epic treats the theme of presence—absence reveals that the absence of the male household guardians shifts Penelope's role and function. In this particular case, the important absence is that of Telemachus,[5] since Odysseus is away from Ithaca for half of the poem and, when there, does not reveal his identity for most of its second part. When Telemachus is in the palace, he assumes the role of Penelope's guardian and at times gets involved in bitter verbal exchanges with the suitors, whereas the mother-queen seems to be marginalized. Conversely, during Telemachus' absence Penelope becomes emancipated and manages to impose her presence on the suitors, not to the extent of restraining their gluttonous and insulting proclivities, but at least to that of reminding them that their are guests in another man's house.

The litmus test for Penelope's undertaking of a more active role is, of course, her δόλος, the devising of a cunning plan according to which Laertes' shroud[6] is woven and unwoven endlessly in order to postpone the date of

---

[3] The cast of Odysseus' and Helen's characters has been recently studied by Worman 2003, who explores how verbal mannerism and appearance have shaped the aforementioned literary figures.

[4] Gender studies have been understandably prolific in respect to the figure of Penelope in the *Odyssey*. Felson-Rubin 1994 has interpreted Penelope's connection to multiple plots as a sign of both her being an active agent and of reflecting the bardic activity of the poet.

[5] See Manakidou 2002:69–86.

[6] According to Papadopoulou-Belmehdi 1994:20, the shroud Penelope weaves is a coded language representing the poem's major themes: "la mémoire et l' oubli, le mariage et la mort, la ruse."

Intertextual Fissures

her selection of one of the suitors as her husband. This ruse is, of course, the paragonal example of the cunningness not just of Penelope, but also, and probably preeminently, of the poetic tradition of the *Odyssey*. Through this plan Penelope resembles not only Odysseus, her cunning husband, whose μῆτις has been the interpretive trademark of this whole epic, but even the Odyssean song-tradition. By weaving, unweaving, and reweaving the shroud, Penelope (whose name may even suggest through its etymology this very idea)[7] mirrors the poem's most inherent characteristic, a sign true to its poetic nature, namely its open-endedness and indeterminacy.[8] The continuous opening and re-opening of various possibilities and courses of action, to which the *Odyssey* guilefully alludes, as well as its deeper *mouvance*[9] and diachronic openness[10] aimed at leaving its ancient audiences as well as its modern readers always with unanswered questions rather than with definite, clear-cut answers.[11]

In order to decode the function of Penelope's δόλοι we first need to deal with questions pertaining to what certain critics have called Penelope's 'failed feminism'. The rise of feminist studies concerning the figure of Penelope in the *Odyssey* has acquired a rather negative coloring over time, in the sense that feminist critics themselves have argued that Penelope's feminism fails in the end, or is overshadowed, at least, by Odysseus' final triumph. Seen through male eyes as playing an active role only to be later 'subjugated' to Odysseus, Penelope gradually undergoes a process of 'emasculation' by adopting a male point of view.[12] For these critics the *Odyssey* is a kind of *Siren Song*, "a perilous temptation to betray one's feminist ideals."[13] My point of departure is a deviation from this 'failed-feminist' approach.[14] According to my interpretive stance, the *Odyssey* uses the figure of Penelope as a means for intertextual

---

[7] The name Penelope may have originated either from the word πήνη ('woof' or 'shuttle') or from a water-bird, the πηνέλοψ. See Levaniouk 1999:95–100.

[8] See Katz 1991.

[9] The term *mouvance* was coined by Zumthor 1972:73. For its application to Homeric poetry, see Nagy 1996a:1–38.

[10] See Kahane 2005:55, who speaks about "a tension between claims to textual closure and authorial fixity versus the diachronic openness and *mouvance*."

[11] See Rengakos 2006:74–84 (= 2002:87–98), who shows how the first four Books of the *Odyssey*, the so-called 'Telemachy', function as a foil for intratextual and intertextual misdirections. Whereas in the *Iliad* advance mentions and proleptic statements turn the '*Spannung auf das Was*' into a '*Spannung auf das Wie*', in the *Odyssey* the extended retardation caused by Telemachus' initial inertia and long absence results in the 'duplication' of the epic's beginning with the two divine assemblies in Books 1 and 5. See also Hölscher 1990:78–85.

[12] Doherty 1995:177.

[13] Clayton 2004:17 commenting on Doherty's *Siren Songs* 1995.

[14] Holmberg 1995.

play. The epic's almost obsessive preoccupation with stories, storytelling, and intertextuality represents a sophisticated way in which the poem thematizes the 'female'. There is no question of failure or of Penelope's subjugation as an emblem of feminism under the yoke of Odysseus, who again becomes master of the household. In fact, the scene I am about to discuss shows that the *Odyssey*, by allowing the audience to gaze at a post-Odyssean rival epic tradition, identifies with Penelope rather than with Odysseus. In other words, Penelope is factored into the *Odyssey* not so much as a figure challenging male values and androcentric ideology, but as a metaphor for the tradition's self-referentiality.[15] The ideological debate between male and female power is not absent from the *Odyssey* but it should be seen, I maintain, in light of the poem's constant search for its own identity, for delineating its limits and placing itself in a preeminent position among other epic songs. The *Odyssey's* refusal of closure[16] transcends the innate dichotomy between male and female, redirecting traditional gender-based opposition towards a search for self-consciousness and identity. Gender-polarity is thus turned into intertextual rivalry.

The Intertextual Horizon

The refusal of closure that characterizes the queen of Ithaca is effectuated, in the episode of the reunion between Odysseus and Penelope, through crosstextual associations between the Odyssean and the Thesprotian-Telegonian epic traditions. The persistence of uncertainty and indeterminacy that critics have often discussed has been interpreted in structuralist[17] or gender-based[18] terms. Intertextuality, a complex system of references, associations, and allusions determining the relations between different texts, acquires a profound meaning in the case of Penelope because of her special metapoetic role in the *Odyssey*. Since Penelope is undoubtedly not only a key figure in the plot, but also a preeminent trademark of the epic's obsession with the question of poetics, it can be plausibly argued that her participation (together with the other key figure of the plot, Odysseus) in an intertextual dialogue with another rival tradition *at such a critical point* in the plot is of unprecedented importance in respect to the *Odyssey's* preoccupation with bardic activity. Penelope creates fissures in the epic by opening "intertextual windows" that lead the

---

[15] See Austin 1975:7–8.
[16] Katz 1991:194.
[17] Pucci 1987; Peradotto 1990.
[18] Winkler 1990; Katz 1991; Felson-Rubin 1994; Clayton 2004.

audience to other epic traditions. Being the primary "source of suspense in the *Odyssey*,"[19] the cause of endless uncertainty through her connection with multiple plots,[20] Penelope's intertextual games set a real challenge for the audience, as they question the poem's self-consciousness as well as its place in the entire epic tradition.

The intertextual hermeneutics of this approach are based on one of the most fundamental—but often misunderstood, not to say distorted—tenets of oral theory. As epic rivalry operates constantly on the level of song-traditions and not texts crystallized by writing, one can appreciate the subtlety and refined sophistication with which the *Odyssey*, as an extensive and internally cohesive reference-system, alludes to its counterparts. But is it possible for the *Odyssey* to allude to 'later' texts such as those belonging to the Epic Cycle? This is, of course, an unanswerable question, should one adopt the approach of hardcore literary critics, who see the entire corpus of archaic poetry as a collection of epic texts fixed (or even composed) by writing. On the other hand, one must keep in mind that this linear approach has made an important group of scholars (the Neoanalysts) hypothesize the existence of precursors to some of the epics belonging to the Epic Cycle, the *Aethiopis* being the most famous example. These scholars realized that a number of thematic disfluencies could be explained if the poems were influenced by other preexisting epics, and in order to screen out all problems of relative chronology, they argued that the *Aethiopis* (for example) was based on another, hypothetical, pre-Iliadic epic, the *Memnonis or the *Achilleis. Neoanalysis,[21] for all its undoubted contribution to the study of the origins and sources of the Homeric epics, has thus silently, but clearly, attempted to bypass the chronological barrier.

Oral poetry has followed a different course. Here the emphasis lies on song-traditions continuously reshaped during the Archaic and (according to some) Classical periods. These traditions must be treated as open systems that incorporate material from other rival song-traditions within a framework of continuous reforming. Oralists, both hard- and soft-core, do not deny the historicity of the Epic Cycle. They simply argue that what later became the Cycle, attributed to specific poets (although, as usual, the tradition is far from unanimous about the individual poets), reflects a more fluid state of epic traditions in the Archaic period.[22] In other words, it is much more plausible

---

[19] Felson-Rubin 1994:67.
[20] Clayton 2004:14.
[21] See Pestalozzi 1945; Kakridis 1949; Schadewaldt 1966⁴; Kullmann 1960.
[22] On the importance of making the distinction between the Cyclic Epics and the traditions they represent and stem from, see Burgess 2001:1–46.

Chapter Four

that the *Aethiopis*, the *Little Iliad*, or the *Telegony* mirror equivalent song-traditions than that they reflect other unattested, hypothetical poems preceding the Homeric epics, also composed by writing, *about whose existence we hardly possess anything.*

Oral poetry does not engage in mythical parsing. An *ecology of variation*—to use Foley's apt expression—is on constant display for the audience, enabling the recovery of the entire mythical intertext. In the case of Penelope, the process of reconstructing the whole mythical nexus is effectuated by understanding that the *Odyssey* is using a *female figure* not only as a plot agent, but also as an intertextual pathway leading to the retrieval of relevant mythical material. Using a suitable analogy from the field of textual criticism and transposing it to the field of the study of myth in an orally derived text, we can see how epic poetry encapsulates material from other mythical traditions. Deprived of the means available to a modern editor (the printed page, the footnoted text, the character and font variations), oral epic traditions create their own referential avenues. Surpassing the built-in limitations of a conventional *reading*, Penelope's allusions to alternative plots are treated as *variae lectiones on the level of myth*, enabling us to reconstruct an *apparatus fabulosus*.[23] In this way, we can discern a rival song-tradition of epic poetry, in which Odysseus and Penelope, the two protagonists of the reunion scene, would normally partake.

In the Cyclic *Telegony*,[24] one of Penelope's Odyssean 'guardians' (Odysseus) dies, whereas the other (Telemachus) becomes, together with Penelope, immortal. In fact, the *Telegony* eliminates the two Odyssean 'pillars' of Penelope, her husband Odysseus and her son Telemachus. This is made possible by death and two new marriages. The death of Odysseus signifies only the partial end of the old household. If the Cyclic *Telegony* had ended there, then the audience would have been confronted with a situation similar to that of the *Odyssey*, in which Odysseus is considered dead but Telemachus, who is supporting his mother, is alive. Conversely, the Cyclic *Telegony* needs to 'eliminate' Telemachus as 'son and protector' of Penelope. In order to achieve this goal, it devises the stratagem of the double marriages to completely dissolve Odysseus' household. By having Penelope marry Telegonus and Telemachus marry Circe (who

---

[23] The intertextual game between the *Odyssey* and the Thesprotian-Telegonian tradition is possible for those who adopt the stance and beliefs of oral poetics because the aforementioned epics are considered to represent song traditions rather than texts fixed by writing. In fact, I am siding with Danek 1998:456, who believes in a wider 'Telegonian' tradition, whose reflection is the Cyclic *Telegony*. On orality and intertextuality, see Burgess 2006:148–189.

[24] Burgess 2001:11 argues that the Cyclic *Telegony* may be dated with some certainty after the foundation of Cyrene in the seventh century B.C, especially if Penelope's son Arcesilaus was the mythical forbearer of the Battiads. See *Telegonia PEG* 1, fr. 3 = *EGF* fr. 2.

never meet in the *Odyssey*), the Cyclic *Telegony* aims at 'destroying' the very foundations upon which the edifice of the *Odyssey* has been built: a faithful wife, a husband striving to return home, a loyal son, the re-foundation of the Ithacan household. The polemical cry that the Cyclic *Telegony* utters against the *Odyssey* is so intense that it resounds even in the *Odyssey*, which is aware of a Thesprotian-Telegonian rival tradition, as I will show. The relevant scene is *Odyssey* xxiii 263–287:

> Τὴν δ' ἀπαμειβόμενος προσέφη πολύμητις Ὀδυσσεύς·
> "δαιμονίη, τί τ' ἄρ' αὖ με μάλ' ὀτρύνουσα κελεύεις
> εἰπέμεν; αὐτὰρ ἐγὼ μυθήσομαι οὐδ' ἐπικεύσω.
> οὐ μέν τοι θυμὸς κεχαρήσεται· <u>οὐδὲ γὰρ αὐτός</u>
> <u>χαίρω, ἐπεὶ μάλα πολλὰ βροτῶν ἐπὶ ἄστε' ἄνωγεν</u>
> <u>ἐλθεῖν, ἐν χείρεσσιν ἔχοντ' εὐῆρες ἐρετμόν,</u>
> <u>εἰς ὅ κε τοὺς ἀφίκωμαι οἳ οὐ ἴσασι θάλασσαν</u>
> <u>ἀνέρες, οὐδέ θ' ἅλεσσι μεμιγμένον εἶδαρ ἔδουσιν·</u>
> <u>οὐδ' ἄρα τοὶ ἴσασι νέας φοινικοπαρῄους,</u>
> <u>οὐδ' εὐήρε' ἐρετμά, τά τε πτερὰ νηυσὶ πέλονται.</u>
> <u>σῆμα δέ μοι τόδ' ἔειπεν ἀριφραδές,</u> οὐδέ σε κεύσω.
> ὁππότε κεν δή μοι ξυμβλήμενος ἄλλος ὁδίτης
> φήῃ <u>ἀθηρηλοιγὸν</u> ἔχειν ἀνὰ φαιδίμῳ ὤμῳ,
> καὶ τότε μ' ἐν γαίῃ πήξαντ' ἐκέλευσεν ἐρετμόν,
> ἔρξανθ' ἱερὰ καλὰ Ποσειδάωνι ἄνακτι,
> ἀρνειὸν ταῦρόν τε συῶν τ' ἐπιβήτορα κάπρον,
> οἴκαδ' ἀποστείχειν, ἔρδειν θ' ἱερὰς ἑκατόμβας
> ἀθανάτοισι θεοῖσι, τοὶ οὐρανὸν εὐρὺν ἔχουσι,
> πᾶσι μάλ' ἑξείης· <u>θάνατος δέ μοι ἐξ ἁλὸς αὐτῷ</u>
> <u>ἀβληχρὸς μάλα τοῖος ἐλεύσεται, ὅς κέ με πέφνῃ</u>
> <u>γήρᾳ ὕπο λιπαρῷ ἀρημένον· ἀμφὶ δὲ λαοί</u>
> <u>ὄλβιοι ἔσσονται·</u> τὰ δέ μοι φάτο πάντα τελεῖσθαι."
> Τὸν δ' αὖτε προσέειπε περίφρων Πηνελόπεια·
> "εἰ μὲν δὴ <u>γῆράς</u> γε θεοὶ τελέουσιν ἄρειον,
> ἐλπωρή τοι ἔπειτα <u>κακῶν ὑπάλυξιν</u> ἔσεσθαι."

"What a strange woman you are!" said the quick-witted
    Odysseus. "Why press
me so insistently? However, I will tell you all, holding nothing
    back. Not that
you will find it to your liking, any more than I do! *Teiresias told
    me to carry a*

> *well-balanced oar and wander on from city to city, till I came to a people who*
> *know nothing of the sea, and never use salt with their food, so that crimson*
> *painted ships and the long oars that serve those ships as wings are quite beyond*
> *their experience. He gave me this infallible sign* (which I now reveal to you)—
> *when I met some other traveler who referred to the oar I was carrying on my*
> *shoulder as a "winnowing-fan",* then, he said, the time would have come for me
> *to plant my oar in the earth and offer the Lord Poseidon the rich sacrifice of a*
> *ram, a bull, and a breeding boar. After that I was to go back home and make*
> *ceremonial sacrifices to the everlasting gods who live in the far-flung heavens,*
> *to all of them this time, in due precedence. As for my end, he said that Death*
> *would come to me away from the sea, and that I would die peacefully in old age,*
> *surrounded by a prosperous people.* He assured me that all this would come
> true." "If the gods make your *old age* a happier time," the sagacious Penelope
> replied, "there is a hope of an *end to your troubles*."

Odysseus' speech harks back to Teiresias' prophecy in *Odyssey* xi 100–137 about Odysseus' future. Teiresias' speech refers to the Cattle of the Sun, to Odysseus' return to Ithaca and subsequent punishment of the suitors, and to his post-Odyssean future up to the hero's death.[25] A close comparison of the two speeches is therefore needed in order to pinpoint any deviation, expansion or reduction.

---

[25] See Peradotto 1990:65-70, who argues that "the prophecy can be conceived as a narrator's grid of possibilities." Peradotto (1990:67) highlights the fact that Teiresias' prophecy does not so much "see future events" but "states conditional probabilities" and "clarifies the framework within which it operates."

Intertextual Fissures

In the part of Teiresias' speech devoted to Odysseus' post-Odyssean future (xi 121-137), the hero's wanderings are expressed by the phrase '[t]ake a well-cut oar and go on till you reach a people who know nothing of the sea' (xi 121-122: ἔρχεσθαι δὴ ἔπειτα, λαβὼν εὐῆρες ἐρετμόν, // εἰς ὅ κε τοὺς ἀφίκηαι οἳ οὐ ἴσασι θάλασσαν), whereas in Odysseus' speech in xxiii 264-284, Odysseus presents a 'fuller' version of Teiresias' prophecy that also contains a vague reference to other 'post-Ithacan' adventures preceding the story of the oar: '[Teiresias] told me ... to wander on from city to city ...' (xxiii 267-268:... ἐπεὶ μάλα πολλὰ βροτῶν ἐπὶ ἄστε' ἄνωγεν // ἐλθεῖν, ...). The difference is anything but trivial, because the diction employed by Odysseus recalls the epic's proem and the language of the external narrator (*Odyssey* i 3: πολλῶν δ' ἀνθρώπων ἴδεν ἄστεα καὶ νόον ἔγνω).[26] Given the *Odyssey's* intense emphasis on Odysseus' bardic activity on the one hand, especially in the 'Apologoi' (Books ix-xii) where the poem's main protagonist displays his singing abilities at length, and the metapoetic coloring of the proem on the other, the verbal echo between the hero's and the narrator's language becomes all the more significant. By invoking the proem, Odysseus puts Teiresias' advice into a larger perspective. He will, superficially imitating his Odyssean self, wander again in the many cities of men, thus challenging the authority of an Odyssean tradition that has made him the paragonal wanderer. This new Odysseus is, of course, the creation of the Odyssean tradition, which, in a remarkable display of self-consciousness, lets Odysseus, its main hero and symbol of its subject matter, entertain the thought of escaping from his own song-tradition, of testing the *Odyssey's* very limits. The usurpation of the external narrator's language, which has left its lasting imprint on the epic's identity, is deliberately 'entrusted' to Odysseus and not to Teiresias. Odysseus is made to speak as the external narrator so that his litmus test on the epic becomes all the more ironical, since it is the *Odyssey* that intentionally questions its own identity, limits, and value.

The *Odyssey's* sophisticated mechanism of turning literary semiosis into an active engagement with the question of its own limits is exemplified in the scene of the reunion between Odysseus and Penelope. Placed at a crucial juncture, which Aristophanes of Byzantium and Aristarchus regarded as the πέρας τῆς Ὀδυσσείας, this reunion scene is full of surprises. Odysseus informs his wife that he will place an oar on his shoulder and leave again. He will wander until he finds someone ignorant of the sea, someone who will take his oar for a winnowing fan (ἀθηρηλοιγός).[27] At that place he will plant his oar in the earth,

---

[26] "He saw the cities of many people and he learnt their ways."
[27] The word ἀθηρηλοιγός ('chaff-ravager' or 'chaff-wrecker' for winnowing fan) is a kenning and

Chapter Four

offer sacrifices to Poseidon, and return to Ithaca, where he will live in happiness. Death will come for him at a late age ἐξ ἁλός, either 'from the sea' or 'away from the sea,' and it will be a light and easy one. The people of Ithaca will gather around him, in a state of ὄλβος. Once Odysseus has explained why he will leave again, Penelope takes the floor and replies in bitter irony (*Odyssey* xxiii 286–287): εἰ μὲν δὴ γῆράς γε θεοὶ τελέουσιν ἄρειον, // ἐλπωρή τοι ἔπειτα κακῶν ὑπάλυξιν ἔσεσθαι.[28]

The *Odyssey* is the epic of the sea par excellence, and its main hero, Odysseus, the Man who 'suffered great anguish on the high seas in his struggles to preserve his life and bring his comrades home' (*Odyssey* i 4–5: πολλὰ δ' ὅ γ' ἐν πόντῳ πάθεν ἄλγεα ὃν κατὰ θυμόν, // ἀρνύμενος ἥν τε ψυχὴν καὶ νόστον ἑταίρων). By referring to another journey not across the sea, but across various lands, not in search of his way home, not trying to return to Ithaca and Penelope, Odysseus virtually informs his wife, as well as the external audience, that he will transform himself into the hero of another poem, that he is going to abandon the ship of the *Odyssey* and evolve into the hero of a post- and non-Odyssean tradition. His oar is about to become a winnowing fan.

Odysseus refers to his old age and depicts an almost idyllic picture of his last days. Surrounded by his people, in full happiness, he will enjoy an easy (ἀβληχρός) death.[29] Conversely, the plot of the Cyclic *Telegony* refers to another Man of the Sea, a Man 'born' afar (Telegonus), the son whom the *Odyssey*'s Man of the Sea begot from Circe who, like Odyssean Telemachus, comes looking for his father. Odysseus will die by Telegonus' spearhead, which is made by a turtledove (τρυγών). The divergence between the last part of Odysseus' extra-textual proleptic statement in the *Odyssey* and the second part of the Cyclic *Telegony* is telling. A closer analysis of Odysseus' speech shows that the *Odyssey* deliberately has him employ the ambivalent expression ἐξ ἁλός

---

is used in the place of πτύον ('winnowing shovel'). Peradotto 1990:66 regards this kenning as "a spell-breaking formula that anticipates its own enactment, but never merely silently presumes it." Kennings, as Hansen 1990:254–255 observes, are typical not of oracular language (i.e. of Teiresias' speech) but of rustic, provincial wit. Like Hesiod's φερέοικος and ἀνόστεος, they should be regarded as substitute expressions of a descriptive character. See Waern 1951; West 1966:89.

[28] 'If the gods make your old age a happier time, there is a hope of an end to your troubles.'

[29] Burgess 2001:153–154 rightly observes that the τρυγών (stingray) might have been a very effective weapon due to its poisonous tail, which inflicts incurable wounds (Aelian *De Natura Animalium* I 56). He even argues that Odysseus' 'gentle' death might have been caused by the venomous tail of the stingray. Burgess, with whom I side on this issue, claims that "[t]he Cyclic poem has not misused a Homeric passage; The Homeric poem is alluding to a traditional story of misinterpreted oracle that the *Telegony* happened to narrate" (153–154).

Intertextual Fissures

in order to 'play' with the sea-element, i.e. to make Odysseus oscillate for a moment between the *Odyssey* and the Thesprotian-Telegonian tradition. At the same time, the epic indulges in a profound game with its hero's polytropic nature, cunningness, and δόλοι. Even at this last moment in which the *Odyssey* has reached its πέρας,[30] Odysseus attempts to trick. This time his δόλος is not against a character of the plot, but against the tradition, whose very Hero he is. Countering Odysseus' attempt to deceive the epic by fostering the viewpoint of its rival Thesprotian-Telegonian tradition, the *Odyssey* replies with an even more cunning ruse.[31] By allowing Odysseus to entertain the idea that after abandoning Ithaca, the sea, Penelope, and their poetic embodiment, the *Odyssey* itself, he may return once again and live in happiness, it suppresses the hero's dreadful end in the Thesprotian-Telegonian tradition; namely, it silences the fact that this rival epic tradition will not treat Odysseus the way the *Odysssey* did. In a remarkable display of careful planning, the *Odyssey* will reward Penelope by allowing *her* to allude to the real death of Odysseus, through a cunning irony that is expressed in timely fashion.[32] Penelope thus becomes the mouthpiece of the *Odyssey* and informs the arrogant Odysseus that the 'end of troubles' (ὑπάλυξις κακῶν) will be actually granted to *her*, not to *him*, through *immortality* when she makes the intertextual leap to the

---

[30] Purves 2006:5 rightly argues that the *Odyssey* uses the semantically related words πέρας, πεῖραρ, and περάτη in order to make "the outer limits (πείρατα) or horizon (περάτη) of Odysseus' world reflect on the status of the ending (πέρας) of the *Odyssey* itself, but also on their connection to the limits (πέρας) of Odysseus' suffering." Furthermore, the author shows how the expressions 'we have not yet come to the end of our trials' (*Odyssey* xxiii 248-249: ... οὐ γάρ πω πάντων ἐπὶ πείρατ' ἀέθλων // ἤλθομεν, ...) and '[t]here lies before me still a great and hazardous adventure' (*Odyssey* xxiii 249: ... ἀλλ' ἔτ' ὄπισθεν ἀμέτρητος πόνος ἔσται) both have a rich metapoetic resonance. Drawing on the Hesiodic connection between the act of sailing and the art of poetry, Purves (15) argues that once the epic hero is cut loose from the *Odyssey* he will be disorientated. Unlike Elpenor in Odyssey xi 76 (cf. what is said for Hector's opponent in *Iliad* VII 86), his σῆμα, as indicated by the oar planted in the ground, will mark an anonymous identity. On the poetics of the Nautilia section in Hesiod's *Works and Days* with a special emphasis on the metapoetic meaning of μέτρα, see Nagy 1982:65–66; Rosen 1990:99–113; Tsagalis 2006:103–113, 121–124.

[31] The σῆμα ἀριφραδές, which Odysseus gives to Penelope while repeating Teiresias' words, is a coded sign or clue. Just as Penelope tested Odysseus before (xxiii 105-110), now Odysseus will try to test Penelope. Conversely, the *Odyssey* implies to its audience that these signs have a figurative meaning. The oar test is a *sema* only for those participating in the *Odyssey* and sharing the basic tenets of this epic tradition. Once out of this tradition, the oar, the *sema* of Odyssean poetics and the trademark of the *Odyssey* loses its sense. The audience needs therefore to interpret the *sema* on a figurative level, as the sign indicating Odyssean identity. On this interpretation of *sema*, see Pucci 1987:90.

[32] See Peradotto 1990:73, who regards Penelope's response as the best, albeit ambivalent, guide to the interpretation of Teiresias' prophecy.

Chapter Four

Thesprotian-Telegonian tradition.³³ It is in that tradition that wives do not wait or endlessly mourn their husbands, but get married to younger ones, where virginity and old age are not the matrix upon which faith and loyalty are judged, where Penelope carries out her ultimate δόλος against Odysseus' arrogance by becoming the heroine of the Thesprotian-Telegonian tradition. Through this scene, the *Odyssey* implicitly states that only within its own poetic borders can Odysseus be the great hero of return, that only within its own framework will Telemachus be the good son and Penelope the faithful and patient wife, and that in the end only the Odyssean song-tradition will be able to grant Odysseus what he was seeking: neither an easy life nor physical immortality,³⁴ but poetic immortality through keeping him next to the person that allows him to be his real self, Penelope. By reminding the audience that the lack of personal knowledge about the future enables the transmission of transcendental knowledge, Penelope is made to resemble the epic bard. The abdication of the personal authority of her husband allows her to channel to the listeners the higher knowledge of the tradition as a whole, knowledge that no mortal can ever possess.³⁵

Odysseus' wanderings with the oar make a profound metapoetic statement, which the *Odyssey* contrives in order to compete against the Thesprotian-Telegonian epic tradition.³⁶ In most of the folktale versions of this story, as Hansen has shown, the sea is contrasted to the land not only as a geographical boundary, but also as a semantic entity, the former signifying danger, weariness, or even immorality, the latter standing for safety, ease, and morality. Greek epic has transformed the nexus of such bipolar antitheses into a thick web of poetic associations. In fact, the *Odyssey* has epitomized sea adventures as its metaphorical trademark so as to oppose the Thesprotian-Telegonian tradi-

---

[33] On the concept of immortality, see Burgess 2001:167, who has argued that the Cyclic poems (and in our case the post-Homeric *Telegony* by Eugammon of Cyrene) do not mirror a post-Homeric world.

[34] Burgess 2001:167, 255n148 rightly argues that immortalization is not a post-Homeric concept and that (167) the *Odyssey's* treatment of immortality is unusual, not primary. In fact, Odysseus' rejection of the immortality offered him by Calypso reflects the *Odyssey's* interest in promoting Odysseus as a man who prefers Penelope and Ithaca to Calypso and immortality. Having promoted its hero, the *Odyssey* entertains, as it comes to its end, the thought of an Odysseus attempting, now that the Odyssean tradition had offered him all it has, to exit the poem.

[35] See Kahane 2005:35.

[36] The story of Odysseus and the oar is not mentioned by the scholia on Lycophron's *Alexandra* (ad 815 Scheer) or Apollodorus' *Epitome* or Proclus' summary. Most commentators believe that it is implicit in these sources, since they all refer to the performance of the sacrifices commanded by Teiresias. This is a quite complex issue, which has not been fully studied. On this topic, see the following pages.

tion, which the *Odyssey* 'treats' as a land-adventure. The very scene of Odysseus carrying the oar on his shoulder is presented in a metapoetic cloth, since the oar is the poetic trademark of his Odyssean adventures, the metonymical sign of the tradition of the *Odyssey*. Therefore, the entire scene of his wandering in a foreign land is a poetic iter to another, non-Odyssean tradition. Odysseus is carrying, oar-like, the *Odyssey* itself on his shoulder, asking the people he meets the following questions: "Do you recognize this epic?" and "Does this poetic tradition make any sense to you?" By allowing Odysseus to even entertain his escape from the poem, the *Odyssey* actually undermines the plot's happy ending, leaving open fissures for cross-textual associations. The open-endedness of the Odyssean tradition exploits the final reunion of the separated couple by fusing Odysseus' and Penelope's ever-changing identities in a husband-wife scene, a metaphorical epic amalgam of the rival traditions the *Odyssey* boldly mixes.

The Sailor and the Oar

The Sailor and the Oar is a well-known traditional story, which can be subdivided into two groups.[37] The first group contains texts, which relate the story as a past event: a sailor who has experienced significant hardships at sea decides to travel inland carrying an oar. When he meets a man or men who are unable to state the name of the tool the mariner is carrying, he decides to end his journey and settles down in the same place this man or community live. In the second group, the story of the Sailor and the Oar is presented as a future event: the mariner declares that one day in the future he will abandon the hardships of a seaman's life, take an oar, and travel inland until he comes across a man who does not know what the oar is. Once he meets such a person he will settle down.

The differences between the two groups do not only refer to narrative time (past versus future), but also to narrative form. In the first group, the story is related in the third-person, in the second group in the first-person since the narrator is the mariner himself. The emphasis is rather different in the two groups despite the fact that scholars have basically subdivided these tales into the same typical features (the cause of the mariner's departure, the oar, the mariner's goal, the oar test, the ignorant inlander, the inlander's error, the mariner's response, the aetiological coda).[38]

---

[37] Hansen 1990:239–272. My analysis is heavily based on Hansen's findings.
[38] Hansen 1990:249–260. The aetiological coda is only attested in the first group of stories concerning the Sailor and the Oar.

Chapter Four

Hansen[39] makes the interesting observation that a number of informants report the story of the Sailor and the Oar only when they want to comment upon seafaring as a trade, evaluating it as a way of life. Even a Greek sailor, in the case of commenting on the hardships of his trade, attempts to make St. Elias a reflection of his own self, i.e. a troubled fisherman. Is it possible then that we can reconstruct the context of the narration backwards by stating that Odysseus conjures up the story of the oar *when he wants to evaluate seafaring as a way of life, namely when he implicitly evaluates the Odyssey*? The narrative situation is similar, since even the present-day tellers imply that they report the story of the oar when they desire to make a more general statement referring to their relationship with the sea. This kind of reasoning leads to another equally important question. The story of the Sailor and the Oar would no doubt have formed part of the Thesprotian-Telegonian tradition of which the *Odyssey* was aware, but would it have had any meaning in the Cyclic *Telegony*, where a local Thesprotian genealogical myth (that of Callidice) had taken the place of the story of the oar, which ends, in all the folktale material Hansen has studied, with the sailor settling down away from home? The Cyclic *Telegony*, contrary to the Thesprotian-Telegonian tradition, has used Odysseus' exile from Ithaca as the reason for his travels to Elis and Thesprotia.[40] Once we have drawn the line between the Thesprotian-Telegonian tradition and the Cyclic *Telegony*, we may begin to explore the thick web of associations between these two traditions and the *Odyssey*.

The Open-Ended Perspective

The study of the reunion scene between Odysseus and Penelope is an excellent opportunity for opening up the discussion and considering, albeit briefly, how the closure of the *Odyssey* may be replete with loose ends pointing to Odysseus' post-Odyssean adventures, of which "*die kyklische Telegonie stell hier nur den punktuellen Reflex einer breiten älteren Tradition dar.*"[41] The scope of such a tradition, which we may call Thesprotian-Telegonian, was much wider than the Cyclic *Telegony*,[42] whose thematic skeleton we possess due to Proclus'

---

[39] Hansen 1990:266.
[40] See Merkelbach 1969:146.
[41] Danek 1998:456.
[42] On the Cyclic *Telegony*, see Welcker 1882²:303–304; Svoronos 1888:257–280; Vürtheim 1907:183–216; Hartmann 1915, 1917; Phillips 1953:53–67; Huxley 1960:23–28; Severyns 1962:15–24; Stanford 1963²:81–89; Merkelbach 1969:142–155; Danek 1998:454–457; Burgess 2001:153–154, 167, 170.

summary (306–330 Severyns = 114–130 Kullmann) and Apollodorus' mythical compendium.

Τηλεγονίας β΄ Εὐγάμμωνος

Μετὰ ταῦτά ἐστιν Ὁμήρου Ὀδύσσεια· ἔπειτα Τηλεγονίας βιβλία δύο Εὐγάμμωνος Κυρηναίου περιέχοντα τάδε.

(§ 114) οἱ μνήστορες ὑπὸ τῶν προσηκόντων θάπτονται·
(§ 115) καὶ Ὀδυσσεὺς θύσας Νύμφαις εἰς Ἦλιν ἀποπλεῖ ἐπισκεψόμενος τὰ βουκόλια,
(§ 116) καὶ ξενίζεται παρὰ Πολυξένῳ δῶρόν τε λαμβάνει κρατῆρα,
(§ 117) καὶ ἐπὶ τούτῳ τὰ περὶ Τροφώνιον καὶ Ἀγαμήδην καὶ Αὐγέαν.
(§ 118) ἔπειτα εἰς Ἰθάκην καταπλεύσας τὰς ὑπὸ Τειρεσίου ῥηθείσας τελεῖ θυσίας.
(§ 119) καὶ μετὰ ταῦτα εἰς Θεσπρωτοὺς ἀφικνεῖται,
(§ 120) καὶ γαμεῖ Καλλιδίκην βασιλίδα τῶν Θεσπρωτῶν.
(§ 121) ἔπειτα πόλεμος συνίσταται τοῖς Θεσπρωτοῖς πρὸς Βρύγους, Ὀδυσσέως ἡγουμένου·
(§ 122) ἐνταῦθα Ἄρης τοὺς περὶ τὸν Ὀδυσσέα τρέπεται, καὶ αὐτῷ εἰς μάχην Ἀθηνᾶ καθίσταται·
(§ 123) τούτους μὲν Ἀπόλλων διαλύει.
(§ 124) μετὰ δὲ τὴν Καλλιδίκης τελευτὴν τὴν μὲν βασιλείαν διαδέχεται Πολυποίτης Ὀδυσσέως υἱός,
(§ 125) αὐτὸς δ' εἰς Ἰθάκην ἀφικνεῖται·
(§ 126) κἂν τούτῳ Τηλέγονος ἐπὶ ζήτησιν τοῦ πατρὸς πλέων ἀποβὰς εἰς τὴν Ἰθάκην τέμνει τὴν νῆσον·
(§ 127) ἐκβοηθήσας δ' Ὀδυσσεὺς ὑπὸ τοῦ παιδὸς ἀναιρεῖται κατ' ἄγνοιαν.
(§ 128) Τηλέγονος δ' ἐπιγνοὺς τὴν ἁμαρτίαν τό τε τοῦ πατρὸς σῶμα καὶ τὸν Τηλέμαχον καὶ τὴν Πηνελόπην πρὸς τὴν μητέρα μεθίστησιν·
(§ 129) ἡ δὲ αὐτοὺς ἀθανάτους ποιεῖ,
(§ 130) καὶ συνοικεῖ τῇ μὲν Πηνελόπῃ Τηλέγονος, Κίρκῃ δὲ Τηλέμαχος.

The contents of the Cyclic *Telegony* based on Proclus' summary and the relevant fragments[43] show that this two-book epic could be organized into three parts:

---

[43] See *Telegonia*, PEG 1, frs. 1–5 = EGF frs. 1–2.

Chapter Four

a. (§ 114–118): The suitors are buried by their relatives. And Odysseus, having sacrificed to the Nymphs, sails off to Elis to look at his herds and is entertained by Polyxenos, receiving as a gift a krater; and on this was the story of Trophonios, Agamedes, and Augeas. Then sailing back to Ithaca, he accomplishes the sacrifices spoken of by Teiresias.

b. (§ 119–125): And after these events he arrives at the Thesprotians and marries Kallidike, the queen of the Thesprotians. Then war occurs between the Thesprotians and the Brygians, with Odysseus leading. Then Ares routs the followers of Odysseus, and Athena battles him. Apollo separates these. After the death of Kallidike, Polypoites the son of Odysseus receives the kingship, and Odysseus returns to Ithaca.

c. (§ 126–130): Meanwhile Telegonus, sailing in search of his father, lands at Ithaca and ravages the island. Odysseus in defense is killed by his unwitting son. Telegonus upon realizing his error takes the body of his father and Telemachus and Penelope to his mother. She makes them immortal, and Telegonus lives with Penelope; Telemachus with Circe.[44]

Apollodorus' mythological compendium does not refer to Eugammon's Cyclic *Telegony*, but offers a prose summary of Odysseus' adventures after the killing of the suitors. Apollodorus is important to the extent that he elucidates certain elements that remain unclear from Proclus' summary. Apollodorus' aim is rather different from that of Proclus, since the former is interested in offering as much information as possible about his topic, whereas the latter simply wants to summarize the content of the Cyclic *Telegony*. Therefore, the focus of the following presentation will be only on those points of Proclus's summary that can be better understood by comparison to Apollodorus' text.[45]

Ἐπιτομή 7.34–37:[46]

(§ 34) θύσας δὲ Ἄδῃ καὶ Περσεφόνῃ καὶ Τειρεσίᾳ, πεζῇ διὰ τῆς Ἠπείρου βαδίζων εἰς Θεσπρωτοὺς παραγίνεται καὶ κατὰ τὰς τοῦ Τειρεσίου μαντείας θυσιάσας ἐξιλάσκεται Ποσειδῶνα. ἡ δὲ βασιλεύουσα τότε Θεσπρωτῶν Καλλιδίκη καταμένειν αὐτὸν ἠξίου

---

[44] The paragraph divisions in Burgess' translation (which came to my knowledge only after I had argued for a *Telegony* in three moves) is an *argumentum ex silentio* about the three parts of this epic.

[45] See Hartmann 1917:61–62.

[46] The rest of Apollodorus' text (§ 38–40) is excluded from analysis because I believe that it reflects a different, non-Telegonian tradition. Penelope's rape by Antinoos, her pregnancy by Hermes, and her death at the hands of Odysseus because of her seduction by Aphinomus are all elements referring to later traditions concerning a non-Telegonian future for Penelope. Likewise for the stories concerning Odysseus' exile (§ 40).

τὴν βασιλείαν αὐτῷ δοῦσα. καὶ συνελθοῦσα αὐτῷ γεννᾷ Πολυποίτην. (§ 35) γήμας δὲ Καλλιδίκην Θεσπρωτῶν ἐβασίλευσε καὶ μάχῃ τῶν περιοίκων νικᾷ τοὺς ἐπιστρατεύσαντας. Καλλιδίκης δὲ ἀποθανούσης, τῷ παιδὶ τὴν βασιλείαν ἀποδιδοὺς εἰς Ἰθάκην παραγίνεται, καὶ εὑρίσκει ἐκ Πηνελόπης Πολιπόρθην αὐτῷ γεγεννημένον. (§ 36) Τηλέγονος δὲ παρὰ Κίρκης μαθὼν ὅτι παῖς Ὀδυσσέως ἐστίν, ἐπὶ τὴν τούτου ζήτησιν ἐκπλεῖ. παραγενόμενος δὲ εἰς Ἰθάκην τὴν νῆσον ἀπελαύνει τινὰ τῶν βοσκημάτων, καὶ Ὀδυσσέα βοηθοῦντα τῷ μετὰ χεῖρας δόρατι Τηλέγονος <τρυγόνος> κέντρον τὴν αἰχμὴν ἔχοντι τιτρώσκει, καὶ Ὀδυσσεὺς θνήσκει. (§ 37) ἀναγνωρισάμενος δὲ αὐτὸν καὶ πολλὰ κατοδυράμενος, τὸν νεκρὸν <καὶ> τὴν Πηνελόπην πρὸς Κίρκην ἄγει, κἀκεῖ τὴν Πηνελόπην γαμεῖ. Κίρκη δὲ ἑκατέρους αὐτοὺς εἰς Μακάρων νήσους ἀποστέλλει.

(§ 34) After sacrificing to Hades and Persephone and Teiresias, [Odysseus] marching on foot through Epiros arrives at the Thesprotians and in accordance to the oracles of Teiresias appeases Poseidon after performing sacrifices. Callidice, who was at the time queen of the Thesprotians deemed him worthy of residing there by offering him the kingdom. After coming together with him in love, she gives birth to Polypoites. (§ 35) After marrying Callidice [Odysseus] ruled as king of the Thesprotians and defeats in battle those of the neighboring inhabitants who marched against him. After the death of Callidice, Odysseus gives back the kingdom to his son and goes to Ithaca. And he finds Poliporthes being born to him from Penelope. (§ 36) And Telegonus after learning from Circe that he is the son of Odysseus, sails out in search of his father. When he arrives in Ithaca he drives away some of the cattle and with a spear having a head made of a <turtle-dove's> sting wounds Odysseus, who came against him. Odysseus dies. (§ 37) After recognizing his father and bewailing a great deal, he takes his dead father and Penelope to Circe, and there he gets married to Penelope. Circe sends both of them to the Isles of the Blessed.

The tripartite structure of the Cyclic *Telegony* is based on the two inland journeys and Odysseus' deadly dramatic encounter with Telegonus in Ithaca. In order to explore the scope and aim of the Cyclic *Telegony*, we need to focus our attention on matters concerning its content. Why does this epic insist on two separate journeys by Odysseus? What do these journeys contribute to this new Odysseus whom the Cyclic *Telegony* strives to promote? A close analysis

Chapter Four

of the content of the Cyclic *Telegony* shows that there are important analogies between the first and third parts and that each part aims at highlighting a specific aspect of Odysseus' personality, which is presented in stark contrast to his Odyssean character.

In the first inland journey Odysseus goes to Elis to visit his herds and stays at the home of Polyxenus, who offers him a mixing-bowl as a gift. At this point, complications arise, as Proclus' summary makes special reference to what must have been in the Cyclic *Telegony* a long *ekphrasis*, the detailed description of a work of art (the mixing-bowl), and, in particular, of the representations on it.[47] A reasonable speculation concerning the content of this episode would have included an embedded narrative by Polyxenus, Augeias' grandson, who would have replied to Odysseus' inquiries with respect to the scenes depicted on the mixing-bowl. The key to the function of this first part might have been the myth of Trophonius, Agamedes, and Augeias.[48] Trophonius and Agamedes were famous architects, and Augeias had asked them to build his treasury. They placed a fake stone on the building in such a skillful manner that nobody would notice. They then removed the stone, stole part of Augeias' treasures, and placed the stone back in its position. But Augeias realized what had happened and decided to punish the thieves. Agamedes was caught in a trap, and Trophonius, in an attempt to save himself, decapitated his accomplice so that he could not reveal that Trophonius had helped him steal the king's treasures. Then, a chasm suddenly opened in the earth and Trophonius fell in. After the punishment of the two thieves, Augeias lived happily for many years and was especially honored by his people.[49] The similarities to the Odyssean Odysseus are obvious, since Odysseus too punished the suitors who were destroying his household and expressed his hope to live happily with his people in his old age. By offering the mixing-bowl to Odysseus, Polyxenus[50] is implicitly expressing his wish that his guest will also live in happiness, just like Augeias.

In the second inland journey, Odysseus travels to the land of the Thesprotians and gets married to their queen, Callidice. There is no mention of the story with the oar (explicitly foreshadowed in *Odyssey* xxiii), but one is

---

[47] On the misunderstanding of the expression ἐπὶ τούτῳ, see Severyns 1962:15–24.
[48] See Hartmann 1917:65–70, who studies in detail the relation between the Trophonius-Agamedes myth and its Egyptian parallel by drawing attention to the story of Rhampsinitus in Herodotus II 121.
[49] See Grimal 1986 s.v. Agamedes and Augeias.
[50] Polyxenus is also known from Homeric epic. In *Iliad* II 623–624, Polyxenus (Πολύξεινος) is mentioned as the fourth leader of the forces coming from Bouprasion and Elis. He is the son of Agasthenes and grandson of Augeias.

entitled to believe that this element formed an integral part of the much wider scope of the Thesprotian-Telegonian tradition from which the post-Homeric Cyclic *Telegony* undoubtedly stems. In fact, the absence of a male king in the kingdom of the Thesprotians is a clear sign that the Thesprotian-Telegonian tradition deliberately aimed at creating the conditions for Odysseus to become a permanent resident in the land of the Thesprotians, which is a basic tenet in the story of the Sailor and the Oar.[51] The argument about Odysseus' permanent or, at least, extended residence among the Thesprotians is further corroborated by the fact that, after the war against the Brygians and Callidice's death, Polypoites (Odysseus' son with Callidice) becomes king. Since Polypoites had to be old enough to take the rule, this is an *argumentum ex silentio* concerning Odysseus' long stay in the land of the Thesprotians. The cause of Callidice's death remains unknown, but one may connect it to Odysseus' departure. Callidice's death, following Odysseus' inability to triumph in war (he is almost defeated, and it is on the one hand Athena helping the Thesprotians and on the other the intervention of Apollo,[52] who brings the fighting to an end, that win the day), signifies in the most emphatic way his failure as a Hero of the Land (he is not successful in ground fighting and is unable to live a happy life beside Callidice). The key elements in this second inland journey are Odysseus' marriage to Callidice and his having a new son with her. Both the Thesprotian-Telegonian tradition and the Cyclic *Telegony* emphasize Odysseus' lack of interest in Penelope. Conversely, in the *Odyssey* Odysseus' extra-marital affairs are downplayed, as not only are Penelope and Ithaca constantly in his mind, but there are also no offspring from his erotic adventures who would overshadow Telemachus' preeminence as Odysseus' son.

In the third part, Telegonus arrives in Ithaca in search of his father. He has, in all probability, followed the advice his mother Circe gave him in order to find this island, but he has never seen his father. Telegonus is presented as laying the land waste or driving away the cattle,[53] which stands in marked

---

[51] Once the sailor comes across a man who would mistake an oar for a winnowing fan, then he has to put it in the ground and make there his new home.

[52] The intervention of Apollo in the battle is reminiscent of Athena's intervention in *Odyssey* xxiv 531–532, when the fighting between Odysseus and his family against the relatives of the suitors was abruptly stopped.

[53] The driving away of the cattle by Circe's son, Telegonus (according to Apollodorus' version), and Odysseus' visit to the βουκόλια of Augeias (according to Proclus' summary) bear a striking similarity to a part of Teiresias' prophecy (*Odyssey* xi 106–109) concerning Odysseus' journey to Thrinacia, where his comrades will eat the Cattle of the Sun. Interestingly enough, both Circe and Augeias are the daughter and the son of Helios, respectively. In all these stories, a crucial event in Odysseus' life is connected with Helios.

Chapter Four

contrast to Odysseus' friendly visit in Elis in the first part of this epic. This time, a second son is introduced into the plot, a son this poem conjures up from one of Odysseus' Odyssean adventures, of which the Odyssey is completely unaware. In opposition to the story of Trophonius and Agamedes, the plunderer is not punished, but he even kills his own father. We are not able to say whether the detail about Telegonus' spearhead being made by the sting of a turtledove belonged to the Thesprotian-Telegonian tradition[54] or was invented by Sophocles in his Ὀδυσσεὺς ἀκανθοπλήξ,[55] but the story about the double marriages between Telegonus and Penelope on the one hand and Telemachus and Circe on the other, as well as their immortalization, need not be a feature pertaining to the literary taste of a late age.[56] By the double marriages, the Thesprotian-Telegonian tradition is able to completely dissolve the idyllic picture of Odysseus' family that the Odyssey has so consistently strove to support. After Odysseus' failure as a Man of the Land in the Thesprotian-Telegonian tradition, the time has come to rip his poem, the Odyssey, even of the great hero's last resources, a faithful wife and a single son, heir to his Ithacan kingdom.

Teiresias and the Cyclic Telegony

The narrative blueprint of the reconstructed Thesprotian-Telegonian tradition would then be in direct contrast to the Odyssean tradition, especially with respect to the treatment of the hero's fate, which moves in a completely opposite direction. The same is the case *mutatis mutandis* with the Cyclic Telegony, which is simply a reflex of the Thesprotian-Telegonian tradition; see the table on the facing page.

These similarities should in no way lead us into a tautology between the Thesprotian-Telegonian tradition and the Cyclic Telegony, since there are certain elements that are treated differently. These elements are centered on the figure of Teiresias and his prophecy to Odysseus, part of which consists of the Sailor and the Oar story.

Teiresias' prophecy to Odysseus (*Odyssey* xi 100–137) contains two proleptic foreshadowings: the Thrinacia episode and the Sailor and the Oar story. Later (*Odyssey* xii 37–141), Odysseus will receive information and advice

---

[54] The ἐξ ἁλός conundrum, which is attested in *Odyssey* xi 134 and xxiii 281, may indicate that this is a very old feature. See Burgess 2001:153–154.
[55] See *TrGF* 4 (Radt), frs. 453–461a.
[56] See Burgess 2001:167, 255n148.

Intertextual Fissures

Odyssey	Thesprotian-Telegonian tradition / Cyclic *Telegony*
a. The Hero faces many dangers at sea	a. He seems to have no trouble in his first inland journey (Cyclic *Telegony*).
b. He overcomes the difficulties and prevails as Man of the Sea	b. He fails as Man of the Land, since he is unable to defeat the Brygians
c. He has no extra-marital sons despite his love-affairs	c. He has sons by other women, such as Polypoites (by Callidice) and Telegonus (by Circe)
d. He lives happily with his wife, Penelope	d. He dies and his wife is married again to his killer (Telegonus), who is the son Odysseus had with Circe.

from Circe about his future adventures. It is obvious from the content of the two 'prophecies' that Teiresias' speech is oracular and concerned with the topic of 'life and death', whereas Circe's advice is not prophetic but future-oriented, specific, more accurate, full of names and details, replete with practical advice, and much longer. There are two interesting questions linked to these two predictions, both of which are significant for the Cyclic *Telegony*. The first question concerns Teiresias' selectivity: Why does he only refer to the Cattle of the Sun episode? The second is relevant to the Sailor and the Oar story: Why is this story deprived of any names and details? I believe the two questions are interconnected and that once we answer them, we will be able to clarify certain aspects of the Cyclic *Telegony*.

The Thrinacia episode is the hallmark of Odysseus' adventures in the *Odyssey*. It has been singled out already in the epic's proem (*Odyssey* i 8–9) as the last and most crucial adventure, the one that will lead all of the hero's comrades into destruction.[57] Likewise, the story of the Sailor and the Oar,

---

[57] See Olson 1997:7–9, who has argued that there is an etymological connection between the word Θρινακία (*Odyssey* xi 107) and θρῖναξ, the latter being a gloss (like πτύον 'shovel') for the kenning ἀθηρηλοιγός employed by Teiresias in his prophecy to Odysseus (*Odyssey* xi 128). Under this scope, the oar will be mistaken for 'a destroyer of chaff' (ἀθηρηλοιγός), which alludes to the 'Winnowing-Shovel Island' (Θρινακία), where Odysseus will be separated from his comrades. In this way, according to Olson's interpretation, the Thrinacia episode becomes intricately linked to Odysseus' last post-Odyssean adventure.

Chapter Four

which would feature in the Thesprotian-Telegonian tradition, is the last of Odysseus' adventures. After that, he would return to Ithaca, only to meet his doom at the hands of Telegonus. Apart from the symmetrical placement of the two episodes in the *Odyssey* and the Thesprotian-Telegonian tradition, the true linchpin between them is their connection to Helios, the Sun-god. In Thrinacia, it is Helios' punishment that brings death to Odysseus' companions. In the Thesprotian-Telegonian tradition it was Telegonus, Circe's son and the grandson of Helios, who kills Odysseus. Therefore, Teiresias' selection only of the Thrinacia episode depends on the *Odyssey's* intention to create a link with the Thesprotian-Telegonian tradition. Exploiting the ambivalent and non-specific nature of oracular speech, on the one hand, and its desire to allude to a rival tradition by simultaneously underplaying it, on the other, the *Odyssey* made Teiresias prophesize Odysseus' non-Odyssean final adventure and death as an analogy to his last journey in the *Odyssey*.

Circe's and, through her, Telegonus', connection to Helios is revealing, considering that both the first and last episode of the Cyclic *Telegony* involve Helios in one way or another. Odysseus' first journey to Elis to visit the Cattle of Augeias seems to be a positive version of the Thrinacia episode. Augeias, whose name is related to αὐγή (bright light of the sun) might have once been the Sun-god himself.[58] In *Iliad* XI 739, Nestor, while relating his story of helping the Pylians[59] defeat the Epeians (who come from Elis), explicitly states that he killed Moulios, the son-in-law of Augeias. Moulios was married to Agamede, who was familiar with all manner of drugs (*Iliad* XI 741: ἣ τόσα φάρμακα εἴδη ὅσα τρέφει εὐρεῖα χθών). Agam*ede*, whose name is indicative of knowledge and sound thinking, seems to be a kind of *Medea*, granddaughter of Helios, who is also knowledgeable in drugs. Augeias is also connected to the story of the Cattle of the Sun (Helios), both through Nestor's killing of Itymoneus, the guardian of the Cattle (*Iliad* XI 672-673), and driving them to Pylos, and through Heracles, as Theocritus' *Idyll* 25 amply states (7, 29, 36, 43, 54, 108, 129-144, 160, 193).[60] What has escaped attention is that Agam*ede's* name, echoed in Agam*edes* (i.e. the Trophonius-Agamedes episode), features in the Cyclic *Telegony* with respect to the mixing-bowl that Polyxenus donates to Odysseus.[61] Likewise, Circe is closely related to Helios;[62] she is his daughter.

---

[58] Frame 1978:88.
[59] Both Elis and Pylos feature in *Odyssey* xxiv 430-431 as places where Odysseus might flee. See Merkelbach 1969:150.
[60] See Frame 1978:88-90. See chapter 8.
[61] This time it is employed as a man's name designating Trophonius' companion Agamedes.
[62] Eliade 1963:143; Frame 1978:38-53.

Intertextual Fissures

Her own name, which comes from κρίκος or the metathesized κίρκος (ring), may perhaps refer to the circular path the sun follows in the sky.⁶³ Circe has both a negative and a positive side, as can be seen from the threat she poses to Odysseus and his comrades on the one hand, and from the help she offers them at the end of the 'Apologoi' on the other. The fact that the first and last part of the Cyclic *Telegony* were implicitly connected with Helios may have been a reflex of the Odyssey's emphasizing of the Thrinacia episode, which is linked, in Teiresias' prophecy, to the story of the Sailor and the Oar.⁶⁴

Now that we have established a link between Teiresias' first part of the prophecy and the contents of the Cyclic *Telegony*, it is time to investigate the second part of the prophecy concerning the story of the Sailor and the Oar.⁶⁵

A close analysis of the contents of the Cyclic *Telegony* shows that there is an important problem with the unfolding of the plot. Odysseus is presented as performing the sacrifices Teiresias had indicated to him in Ithaca, after his first journey to Elis. Only then does he depart for the land of the Thesprotians, without any mention of the story of the Sailor and the Oar. Interestingly enough, whereas in the first journey Proclus explicitly states the reason for Odysseus' journey to Elis (ἐπισκεψόμενος τὰ βουκόλια), the reason for the second voyage is not given. Since the sacrifices Teiresias had asked Odysseus to perform can be none other than those stated in *Odyssey* xi 130–134, then why does the hero go to the land of the Thesprotians? Scholars have suggested two solutions to this problem, both of which, I maintain, are false. Huxley has argued that Odysseus had traveled inland to Elis, not to Thesprotia, despite the fact that Proclus says nothing about this.⁶⁶ He explains his argument in the following manner:⁶⁷

---

⁶³ Frame 1978:50.
⁶⁴ In this respect, Odysseus' meeting with Elpenor in the Underworld becomes all the more relevant. This scene has been rightly regarded (Ahl and Roisman 1996:123–125) as an ironical comment on the part of Odysseus' narrative, since poor Elpenor unwillingly arrives earlier than Odysseus at Hades. Moreover, when Teiresias prophesies Odysseus' future journey with an oar on his shoulder, the audience is expected to make the connection with the scene immediately preceding, in which it is stated that Elpenor's grave will be marked by an oar. The oar, being a symbol of seamanship and a trademark of Odyssean poetics, is used as the ironical link between the two episodes. The *Odyssey* is wittily employing the story of the Sailor and the Oar at a point where heroic fame has just been questioned through Elpenor's unheroic death and hasty arrival at the Underworld. A more profound criticism will be presented later in the same Book (*Odyssey* xi 488–491) through Achilles' denunciation of heroic ideals.
⁶⁵ In the analysis above, I have attempted to explain the presence of the Helios element (through Thrinacia and Circe) in both 'prophecies'.
⁶⁶ 1960:23–28.
⁶⁷ Huxley 1960:26.

Chapter Four

It follows that in the *Telegony* the sacrifices to Poseidon were made before Odysseus returned from Polyxenus in Elis to Ithaca. Proclus does not mention them, but it can be shown that in the *Telegony* Odysseus did indeed sacrifice far from the sea before he left Elis for Ithaca. The Arcadians were well known for their ignorance of maritime matters: accordingly Eugamon was able to send Odysseus to sacrifice to Poseidon in Arcadia. To confirm that he did so, the coins of Mantineia include types depicting Odysseus bearing an oar on his shoulder; there, then, in central Peloponnese, according to one interpretation of the prophecy of Teiresias, Odysseus sacrificed to Poseidon far from the sea. To conclude the reasoning thus far: Odysseus sacrificed to Poseidon far inland before he returned to make the sacrifices in Ithaca. Before he came back to Ithaca in the *Telegony*, he was in the Peloponnese, and the representation of Odysseus with an oar on the coins of Mantineia shows that in the *Telegony* the hero went to Arcadia to sacrifice to Poseidon far inland. Then he went back to Ithaca, after seeing Polyxenus in Elis, and sacrificed to all the immortals. Proclus mentioned only the sacrifices in Ithaca.

Huxley's arguments have two basic flaws:[68] First, he treats the archaeological evidence as proof for an unattested literary episode of the Cyclic *Telegony*, namely the sacrifices of Odysseus in Elis. He thus fails to explain why Proclus did not mention that these sacrifices took place in Elis,[69] although Proclus is anything but tacit concerning the performance of sacrifices in the Cyclic *Telegony*[70] since he explicitly refers to the sacrifices Odysseus performed to the Nymphs[71] before departing for Elis and those performed once he returned

---

[68] Huxley could have also mentioned the fact that, according to one tradition, Trophonius and Agamedes, whose story features in the Cyclic *Telegony* when Odysseus travels to Elis, had built a temple for Poseidon in Mantineia, where archaeologists had found coins depicting Odysseus with the oar.

[69] Malkin 1998:131 rightly argues that "Thesprotia in the *Odyssey* and Elis in both the *Telegony* and the *Odyssey* seem to indicate both an allusion of the *Odyssey* to its sequels and alternatives and a reflection of Ithaca's multiple real-world connections with its various mainland (Epirus and the Peloponnese)."

[70] I disagree with Malkin 1998:123, who thinks that since Odysseus sacrifices to all the Olympian gods after his return from Elis to Ithaca, then we should believe that the "condition of the oar had been fulfilled." In other words, Malkin seems to accept that the story of the Sailor and the Oar formed part of the Cyclic *Telegony* and that it occurred in Elis.

[71] In the *Odyssey*, as soon as Odysseus arrives in Ithaca, Athena reminds him of the cave of the Nymphs where he used to offer sacrifices (*Odyssey* xiii 347–351). Odysseus immediately raises

from Elis to Ithaca. It is much more plausible to argue that the Mantineian[72] coins and the myth about the temple of Poseidon built by Trophonius and Agamedes in Mantineia reflect local claims against the older Thesprotian-Telegonian tradition, which depicted Odysseus wandering in Thesprotia with the oar on his shoulder and subsequently performing sacrifices to Poseidon. The second flaw in Huxley's theory is a *petitio principii*. He wants to screen out the problem of the sacrifices ordered by Teiresias because these sacrifices have to follow the story of the Sailor and the Oar. In other words, the need to locate the sacrifices appears only when one believes that the story of the Sailor and the Oar formed part of the Cyclic *Telegony*. The question, though, still remains: Why did Proclus pass over such an important episode, and, moreover, why does he have Odysseus travel to the land of the Thesprotians after he had accomplished Teiresias' prophecy? To this second issue I will soon return, after examining the second solution by Merkelbach.[73]

Merkelbach argued that the reason for Odysseus' first journey to Elis was not his desire to fulfill Teiresias' prophecy but his exile[74] because of the killing of the Suitors.[75] He rightly pointed out that the Cyclic *Telegony* implicitly indicates this outcome, since it begins with the burial of the Suitors by their relatives. This reminds one of the last part of the *Odyssey*, where the anger of the Suitors' relatives against Odysseus prominently features. In order to deal with the problem of the sacrifices held in Ithaca, Merkelbach has argued that Proclus made a mistake and instead of writing ἔπειτα εἰς τὴν Ἤπειρον καταπλεύσας τὰς ὑπὸ Τειρεσίου ῥηθείσας τελεῖ θυσίας, he wrote ἔπειτα εἰς

---

his hands towards the sky and prays to the Nymphs (*Odyssey* xiii 355–360). In both Proclus's summary and in Apollodorus' *Epitome*, Odysseus' first journey begins with sacrifices either to the Nymphs (Proclus) or to Hades, Persephone, and Teiresias (Apollodorus). Malkin 1998:104 argues that Odysseus' sacrifice to the Nymphs in the beginning of the Cyclic *Telegony* has been 'inherited' from a seventh century poem, the *Thesprotis*. By adducing significant archaeological information concerning the cave of the Nymphs at Polis Bay, he maintains that this cave was considered to be the point of both Odysseus' return and second departure from Ithaca.

[72] The same applies to Pausanias' (VIII 44.4) information concerning the remains of a temple dedicated to Athena and Poseidon, which had been supposedly built by Odysseus on his way home from Troy. See Hansen 1977:33.

[73] 1969:145–147.

[74] Malkin 1998:129

[75] See Merkelbach 1969:146. Odysseus' exile is explicitly mentioned by two ancient sources, Plutarch's *Moralia* 294 CD (*Aetia Romana et Graeca* 14 = Aristotle fr. 507 R.) and Apollodorus' *Epitome* VII 40. According to these versions, the suitors' relatives stood up against Odysseus, and Neoptolemus was summoned as a mediator (διαιτητής). Odysseus, who was subsequently exiled, traveled to Aetolia, where he married the daughter of king Thoas and had a son with her, Leontophonus. Odysseus died in Aetolia in his old age.

Chapter Four

Ἰθάκην καταπλεύσας τὰς ὑπὸ Τειρεσίου ῥηθείσας τελεῖ θυσίας. In this way, Merkelbach was able to place the sacrifices in Thesprotia, in Epirus,[76] and explain Odysseus' second journey as a result of the exile that is over only when Odysseus returns to Ithaca for the final time, after giving the kingdom of the Thesprotians to Polypoites, the son he had from Callidice.

Merkelbach's first observation seems perfectly plausible. The exile of Odysseus[77] explains his first journey to Elis well and matches appropriately the end of the *Odyssey*, where features belonging to the older Thesprotian-Telegonian tradition and reflected in the Cyclic *Telegony* are abundantly attested. The fact that Proclus describes as the reason for Odysseus' trip the hero's intention to visit the cattle of Polyxenus (ἐπισκεψόμενος τὰ βουκόλια) does not undermine the value of Merkelbach's argument. Once Odysseus was banned from Ithaca, he started wandering and went first to Elis (as predicted by Eupeithes in *Odyssey* xxiv 430-432) and then to Epirus. Merkelbach's theory is thus far correct, but from this point he makes the same mistake as Huxley. In his attempt to have Odysseus perform in Epirus the sacrifices Teiresias had foretold, he changes the text of Proclus' summary. This approach seems to me very forced and is bound to be incorrect for the following reasons: first, it can hardly be explained how εἰς τὴν Ἤπειρον had been changed into εἰς Ἰθάκην; second, the participle καταπλεύσας used in Proclus' summary cannot mean 'sail out to' (namely from Elis to Epirus as Merkelbach wants the text to state). Καταπλεύσας means 'sail from the high sea to the shore', 'sail back', and so it designates a journey of return, i.e. Odysseus' return to Ithaca.[78] Moreover, Merkelbach's textual change has originated from the same wrong assumption as Huxley's. In order to place the story of the Sailor and the Oar inland (in Thesprotia and not in Elis as Huxley has suggested), he needed to have Odysseus perform Teiresias' sacrifices in Epirus, whence he resorted to the aforementioned solution. Despite that, there are crucial questions Merkelbach's theory is unable to answer: Is it not awkward to have Odysseus first travel inland to accomplish Teiresias' prophecy and only then arrive to

---

[76] According to my view, Lycophron's *Alexandra* 795-804 does not point to the Cyclic *Telegony* but to the older Thesprotian-Telegonian tradition, in which Odysseus performed the sacrifices in Epirus. See scholia on Lycophron's *Alexandra* 815 [Scheer]: Ὀδυσσεὺς δὲ εἰς Εὐρυτᾶνας ἔθνος Ἠπείρου κατὰ χρησμὸν ἐλθὼν θύει τὰ νενομισμένα καὶ γηραιὸς ἄγαν κτείνεται παρὰ Τηλεγόνου, τοῦ ἐκ Κίρκης αὐτῷ γεννηθέντος υἱοῦ. καὶ τὰ μὲν κατὰ τὸν Ὀδυσσέα οὕτως ἔχει. One of Lycophron's sources may have been Aristotle's Ἰθακησίων πολιτεία, where it is stated (according to Tzetzes) that the Eurytanes honored Odysseus by having founded an oracle dedicated to him. See Stephanus Byzantius *Ethnica* s.v. Βούνειμα.

[77] See Malkin 1998:123-124. Cf. *Odyssey* xxiv 482-486.

[78] Notice that Proclus used the form ἀποπλεῖ to refer to Odysseus' journey's to Elis.

the land of the Thesprotians?⁷⁹ In addition, why did Proclus fail to mention the story of the Sailor and the Oar, which is the prerequisite for the sacrifices Teiresias mentions to Odysseus, but then explicitly refer to the sacrifices?

In order to answer these questions we need to free ourselves from the basic assumption common to the mistakes of both Huxley and Merkelbach. This mistaken assumption is that the Cyclic *Telegony* contained the story of the Sailor and the Oar. The study of living, oral folk-traditions⁸⁰ has shown that the crucial function in the performance of the story of the Sailor and the Oar is its aetiological coda. In other words, the person narrating the story manipulates its details in such a way that the story explains either why St. Elias chapels are found on mountain tops in Modern Greece or how much a sailor desires to leave behind him the hardships of the sea. Therefore, what is inherent in the deep structure of this folk-tale, as mentioned by Teiresias in *Odyssey* xi and repeated by Odysseus in *Odyssey* xxiii, is its explanation of Odysseus' new wanderings as an effort to escape from his sufferings and appease Poseidon's anger. If, then, the Cyclic *Telegony* explained Odysseus' journey to Elis and Thesprotia as the result of his exile from Ithaca, the story of Odysseus and the Oar would have been redundant and pointless. Proclus does not mention the story of Odysseus and the Oar because it simply did not feature in the Cyclic *Telegony*.⁸¹ In fact, there is no need to resort to witty but false suggestions in order to explain the problem of Odysseus' performance of Teiresias' sacrifices, for the sacrifices mentioned by Proclus are independent from the story of Odysseus and the Oar.

When Teiresias in *Odyssey* xi 130–134 refers to the story of the Sailor and the Oar, he speaks of two sets of sacrifices: one set performed for Poseidon in the land where people are ignorant of the sea (ῥέξας ἱερὰ καλὰ Ποσειδάωνι ἄνακτι, // ἀρνειὸν ταῦρόν τε συῶν τ' ἐπιβήτορα κάπρον), and a second set of sacrifices to all the gods after Odysseus' return to Ithaca (οἴκαδ' ἀποστείχειν ἔρδειν θ' ἱερὰς ἑκατόμβας // ἀθανάτοισι θεοῖσι, τοὶ οὐρανὸν εὐρὺν ἔχουσι, // πᾶσι μάλ' ἑξείης· ...). Therefore, even in the Odyssean allusion to the Thesprotian-Telegonian tradition, there were two sets of sacrifices, one in Thesprotia, the other in Ithaca. It is plausible that the Cyclic *Telegony* is simply reflecting the second set of sacrifices in Ithaca, which Odysseus would perform once he had accomplished his wanderings. He began his journey to Elis by

---

⁷⁹ Καὶ μετὰ ταῦτα εἰς Θεσπρωτοὺς ἀφικνεῖται.
⁸⁰ Hansen 1977.
⁸¹ See Hansen 1977:37, who argues that "Homer's account has not passed into or reentered oral tradition."

Chapter Four

sacrificing to the Nymphs and he concludes his return home with a sacrifice to the other gods. When Proclus states that in the Cyclic *Telegony* Odysseus τὰς ὑπὸ Τειρεσίου ῥηθείσας τελεῖ θυσίας, we may be dealing with a deflected feature of both the *Odyssey* and the Thesprotian-Telegonian tradition. The sacrifices had, through the process of time, become intricately connected to Teiresias, even when their prerequisite, the story of the Sailor and the Oar, was not employed. One substitution does not necessarily or automatically lead to another, as is often the case with mythical material. This principle might well be the explanation for Odysseus' second journey. Our hero's travel to the land of the Thesprotians reflects the Thesprotian-Telegonian tradition of Odysseus' journey to Epirus.[82] Once more, despite the disappearance of the Sailor and the Oar story, Thesprotia features in the plot. We are in no position to say whether the story of Callidice formed part of the old Thesprotian-Telegonian tradition, but we can plausibly maintain that this story serves well as an aition for Odysseus' long stay among the Thesprotians as a result of his exile.

Eugammon combined various traditions in the Cyclic *Telegony* concerning the post-Odyssean adventures of Odysseus. He seems to have aimed at creating a poem in which the older Thesprotian-Telegonian substratum[83] and Odysseus' death by Telegonus would be fused together with the other, later versions of Odysseus' wanderings. From these versions, an Aetolian and a Peloponnesian one, both of which reflect Ithaca's historical connections with the mainland, Eugammon has selected the second one. The double sacrifices, to the Nymphs before Odysseus' departure from Ithaca to Elis and to the Olympians after his return from Elis to Ithaca, implicitly indicate that it is the journey to Elis that has been added to the older substratum. This argument is further corroborated by the fact that Proclus does not feel the need to explain to his readers the reason for Odysseus' first and second departures from Ithaca (probably due to a στάσις), but he does choose Elis as an itinerary destination in his first journey (εἰς Ἦλιν ἀποπλεῖ ἐπισκεψόμενος τὰ βουκόλια). After all, Odysseus' first voyage is a trip, whereas the second to Thesprotia is a real adventure.

---

[82] On Thesprotia, see Malkin 1998:126–134. Merkelbach 1969 rightly claims that the *Odyssey's* false stories of the Cretan Odysseus are a kind of intertextual pathway to other versions of Odysseus' return.

[83] See Kullmann 1992:341.

Part Two

INTERTEXTUALITY AND META-TRADITIONALITY

5

Ἀχιλλεὺς Ἑλένην ἐπιθυμεῖ θεάσασθαι: From the *Cypria* to the *Iliad*

THE AIM OF THIS CHAPTER is to examine Proclus'[1] brief mention in his *Chrestomathy* of a meeting between Achilles and Helen, which featured as an episode in the *Cypria*. The relevant passage (157–158 Severyns = 41 Kullmann) runs as follows:

> καὶ μετὰ ταῦτα Ἀχιλλεὺς Ἑλένην ἐπιθυμεῖ θεάσασθαι, καὶ συνήγαγεν αὐτοὺς εἰς τὸ αὐτὸ Ἀφροδίτη καὶ Θέτις.

> And after these events Achilles desires to look upon Helen, and Aphrodite and Thetis brought them together.

Unus testis, bonus testis: The Reliability of a Single Source[2]

The first problem that we must examine, concerning the authenticity of the abovementioned episode, is fundamental for the ensuing analysis. If Proclus did not consult the *Cypria* but had at his disposal a synopsis of the epic, then we can assume that the meeting between Achilles and Helen possibly echoes the aesthetic perceptions of a new era and is therefore a rather later addition.[3]

The love element in the Cyclic epics must have been substantial, but must not have been used frequently. Aside from the meeting between Achilles

---

[1] The question of Proclus' identity has yet to be completely resolved, that is to say, whether the second century AD grammarian or the well-known fifth century AD Neo-Platonic philosopher are concerned. For the problematic identification of Neo-Platonic Proclus with the author of the *Chrestomathy* see the crucial comments of Sicherl 1956:210n1, who argues that this identification is supported exclusively by an observation of Tzetzes (codex Ottob. Gr. 58). For Proclus, see Severyns 1938, 1953, 1963.
[2] The allusion to the well-known expression *unus testis, nullus testis* is apparent and deliberate.
[3] These sorts of 'objections' have been raised by Rzach 1922:2391 (*RE* s.v. Kyklos). See Forsdyke 1956:131; Griffin 1977:43–45; Jouan 1980:102.

Chapter Five

and Helen, we know that Thersites ridiculed Achilles for his attraction to Penthesileia, the queen of the Amazons.[4] According to Quintus Smyrnaeus *Posthomerica* I 671–674 (καὶ δ' Ἀχιλεὺς ἀλίαστον ἑῷ ἐνετείρετο θυμῷ, // οὕνεκά μιν κατέπεφνε καὶ οὐκ ἄγε δῖαν ἄκοιτιν // Φθίην εἰς εὔπωλον, ἐπεὶ μέγεθός τε καὶ εἶδος // ἔπλετ' ἀμώμητός τε καὶ ἀθανάτῃσιν ὁμοίη), Achilles was incessantly distressed inside his own heart because he killed Penthesileia instead of taking her as his divine wife to Phthia, since with respect to her size and beauty she was both impeccable and similar to the immortal goddesses.[5]

The meeting between Achilles and Helen in the *Cypria* should be compared to similar love scenes attested in Proclus' summary of the Cyclic epics. I have just mentioned the episode in the *Aethiopis* (178–181 Severyns = 54–55 Kullmann), in which Thersites mocks Achilles for his rumored love for Penthesileia and then pays for his mockery with his life. The most interesting element in this case is the στάσις (revolt, rebellion) of the Achaeans against Achilles immediately after the murder of Thersites. The picture is rather different at the end of the *Telegony* (327–330 Severyns = 128–130 Kullmann), since, after the double marriages of Telegonus to Penelope and of Telemachus

---

[4] See Proclus's *Chrestomathy* 178–181 Severyns = 54–55 Kullmann: καὶ Ἀχιλλεὺς Θερσίτην ἀναιρεῖ, λοιδορηθεὶς πρὸς αὐτοῦ καὶ ὀνειδισθεὶς τὸν ἐπὶ τῇ Πενθεσιλείᾳ λεγόμενον ἔρωτα. See also: (1) the ancient scholia on Sophocles' *Philoctetes* 445 (364, 12–15 Papageorgius): φονευθείσης γὰρ τῆς Πενθεσιλείας ὑπὸ Ἀχιλλέως ὁ Θερσίτης δόρατι ἔπληξε τὸν ὀφθαλμὸν αὐτῆς· διὸ ὀργισθεὶς ὁ Ἀχιλλεὺς κονδύλοις αὐτὸν ἀνεῖλεν. (2) Apollodorus *Epitome* V 1: Πενθεσίλεια, Ὀτρήρης καὶ Ἄρεως, ἀκουσίως Ἱππολύτην κτείνασα καὶ ὑπὸ Πριάμου καθαρθεῖσα, μάχης γενομένης πολλοὺς κτείνει, ἐν οἷς καὶ Μαχάονα· εἶθ' ὕστερον θνήσκει ὑπὸ Ἀχιλλέως, ὅστις μετὰ θάνατον ἐρασθεὶς τῆς Ἀμαζόνος κτείνει Θερσίτην λοιδοροῦντα αὐτόν. (3) Eustathius, in B 220 (208. 1–3 van der Valk): Ἡ δὲ νεωτέρα ἱστορία καὶ ἀναιρεθῆναι τὸν Θερσίτην ὑπ' Ἀχιλλέως λέγει κονδυλισθέντα, ὁπηνίκα τὴν Ἀμαζόνα Πενθεσίλειαν ἐκεῖνος ἀνελὼν οἶκτον ἔσχεν ἐπὶ τῇ κειμένῃ. (4) Tzetzes on Lycophron *Alexandra* 999 (Scheer): (a) μετὰ θάνατον Πενθεσιλείας ἠράσθη αὐτῆς ὁ Ἀχιλλεύς, ὁ δὲ Θερσίτης λαθὼν ἐξώρυξε τοὺς ὀφθαλμοὺς αὐτῆς, ὁ δὲ νεανίας ὀργισθεὶς ἀνεῖλεν αὐτῷ πλήξας κονδύλῳ, οἱ δὲ τῷ δόρατι (312, 4–11); (b) οἱ μὴ εἰδότες φασὶν Ἀχιλέα ἀνελόντα Πενθεσίλειαν μετὰ θάνατον αὐτῆς ἐρασθῆναι, ἧς τοὺς ὀφθαλμοὺς ὁ Θερσίτης λαθὼν ἐξώρυξεν. ὁ δὲ Ἀχιλλεὺς ὀργισθεὶς ἀνεῖλεν αὐτὸν μὲν πλήξας δόρατι, κατ' ἐμὲ δὲ καὶ τοὺς λοιποὺς κονδύλῳ ἤτοι γρόνθῳ μηδὲ διὰ τὸ ἐξορύξαι τοὺς ὀφθαλμοὺς ἀλλ' ὅτι αἰσχροὺς λόγους κατ' Ἀχιλλέως ἀπέρριπτεν ὡς δῆθεν ἐρῶντος συγγενέσθαι νεκρᾷ τῇ Πενθεσιλείᾳ (312, 4–17); (a) + (b): ἀντιμαχησάμενος γὰρ Ἀχιλλεὺς ἐκείνῃ καὶ πολλάκις ὑπ' αὐτῆς ἡττηθείς, μόλις δέ ποτε περιγενόμενος καὶ ἀνελὼν αὐτὴν θαυμάζων τὴν ῥώμην ἐκείνης ὁμοῦ καὶ τὸ κάλλος καὶ τὸ νεαρὸν τῆς ἡλικίας ἐδάκρυε καὶ τοὺς Ἕλληνας παρεκάλει ταφῆς ἀξιοῦν τὴν νεάνιδα. ἐφ' οἷς Θερσίτης συμπλάττων καὶ λέγων μίξεις ἀθέσμους καὶ ἔρωτας γρόνθῳ ὑπ' αὐτοῦ πληγεὶς ἀναιρεῖται (312, 18–24)]. (5) scholia vetera on *Iliad* II 220 (Erbse): ὅτι Ζηνόδοτος τοῦτον καὶ τοὺς μετ' αὐτὸν τρεῖς (B 221-3) ἠθέτηκεν. πρὸς ὑπόθεσιν δέ τινα λέγονται. For the death of Thersites, see also Sodano 1951:68; Vian 1959:20; Griffin 1977:44.

[5] The translation is my own.

Ἀχιλλεὺς Ἑλένην ἐπιθυμεῖ θεάσασθαι

to Circe, they are all transported to Aiaia,[6] the island of Circe, who grants them immortality.[7]

Certain features of the first and second aforementioned erotic episodes are comparable[8] to those in the scene of the meeting between Achilles and Helen in the *Cypria*. The result of Achilles' murder of Thersites (which presupposes his infatuation with Penthesileia) in the *Aethiopis* is the στάσις (revolt, rebellion) of the army, while in the *Cypria*, the result of the meeting between Achilles and Helen is Achilles' attempt to stop another mutiny (στάσις) of the army, which seems willing (just as in *Iliad* II) to return to Greece. These two scenes seem to be in inverse proportion to their results, even though they are both based on the same factors, namely the erotic element and the involvement of Achilles. Moreover, as is the case with the *Cypria*, the *Telegony* (329 Severyns = 129 Kullmann) specifically refers to the divine intervention of Circe, who grants immortality to Penelope and Telemachus, while the mythographer Hyginus (*Fabulae* 127) states that Circe sends Telegonus to search for his father (*Telegonus Ulixes et Circes filius, missus a matre ut genitorem quaereret* ...).[9]

---

[6] See Hyginus *Fabulae* 127.5-6: "*quem postquam cognovit qui esset, iussu Minervae cum Telemacho et Penelope in patriam reduxerunt, in insulam Aeaeam.*" In Hyginus, the intervention of Athena-Minerva is as vital for the transportation of Telemachus and Penelope to Aiaia, the island of Circe, as it is for the subsequent double marriages (127.8-9: *eiusdem Minervae monitu Telegonus Penelopen, Telemachus Circen duxerunt uxores*).

[7] See Proclus' *Chrestomathy* 327-330 Severyns = 128-130 Kullmann: Τηλέγονος δ' ἐπιγνοὺς τὴν ἁμαρτίαν τό τε τοῦ πατρὸς σῶμα καὶ τὸν Τηλέμαχον καὶ τὴν Πηνελόπην πρὸς τὴν μητέρα μεθίστησιν· ἡ δὲ αὐτοὺς ἀθανάτους ποιεῖ, καὶ συνοικεῖ τῇ μὲν Πηνελόπῃ Τηλέγονος, Κίρκῃ δὲ Τηλέμαχος.

[8] By the term "comparable", I designate those features that are linked by either similar or different connections, that is to say, analogies, and are neither converging nor diverging. This observation is crucial for my reasoning. It is clear that there is a difference between the *Aethiopis* and the *Cypria*, since in the former the στάσις ('revolt') was due to the murder of Thersites and not to Achilles' love for Penthesileia, while in the latter Achilles' determination to prevent the Achaeans from returning to their homeland is a result of his meeting with Helen. Revolt (στάσις) is, indeed, recurrent in epic poetry, forming a sort of motif commonly used in order to carry out the narration (see the episode with Thersites in *Iliad* II and Nestor's narrative in *Odyssey* iii 135-150 and 160-166 about the two strifes in the Achaean camp). However, what interests us here is that the analogies (the convergent and divergent connections) between the meeting of Achilles and Helen and the abovementioned episodes undoubtedly authenticate the meeting.

[9] According to Hyginus (*Fabulae* 127), the arrival of Telemachus and Penelope in Aiaia and the double marriages between Telegonus and Penelope, on the one hand, and Telemachus and Circe, on the other, are equally dependent on the orders and advice (respectively) of Athena (*iussu Minervae - Minervae monitu*). Proclus' summary does not mention anything about the intervention of Athena. We are not in a position to know the source of Hyginus. The similarities detected in the wording of Hyginus and Proclus (ἐπὶ ζήτησιν τοῦ πατρός - *ut genitorem quaereret*, Ὀδυσσεὺς ὑπὸ τοῦ παιδὸς ἀναιρεῖται κατ' ἄγνοιαν - *Ulixes et Telemachus ignari*

Chapter Five

Conversely, it could be argued that the thematic similarities shared by the *Aethiopis* and the *Telegony*, concerning the treatment of a love story and divine intervention respectively, do not necessarily mean that the *Cypria* must have also dealt with such an episode in the same way. In other words, the argument of analogy that I presented earlier has only relative worth. However, this way of thinking is rather circular, since it cannot be proven that every erotic episode attested in Proclus' summary of the Epic Cycle, *must be a later addition because Proclus or his source may have been influenced by new aesthetic conceptions.*[10] In this light, we can safely assume that Proclus' account of a meeting between Achilles and Helen in the *Cypria* is credible.

Reconstruction and Interpretation

The second issue to be considered regards the reconstruction of and justification for the meeting between Achilles and Helen as well as its incorporation into the plot of the *Cypria*. We know that Achilles had never seen Helen before and that he was not one of her suitors.[11] In fact the scene of their meeting in the *Cypria* seems to cater to this problem, and, therefore, Achilles' desire to see the abducted queen of Sparta is a narrative reflex of the poet's plan to justify to his audience that Achilles will also fight the Trojans for her sake,[12] as can be inferred from his restraining the Achaeans, who attempt to return to their homeland (Proclus' *Chrestomathy* 159–160 Severyns = 42 Kullmann).[13]

---

arma contulerunt. Ulixes a Telegono filio est interfectus, Τηλέγονος δ' ἐπιγνοὺς τὴν ἁμαρτίαν τό τε τοῦ πατρὸς σῶμα καὶ τὸν Τηλέμαχον καὶ τὴν Πηνελόπην πρὸς τὴν μητέρα μεθίστησιν - *quem postquam cognovit qui esset, iussu Minervae cum Telemacho et Penelope in patriam reduxerunt*, καὶ συνοικεῖ τῇ μὲν Πηνελόπῃ Τηλέγονος, Κίρκῃ δὲ Τηλέμαχος - *eiusdem Minervae monitu Telegonus Penelopen, Telemachus Circen duxerunt uxores*) indicate that they have both drawn material from a mythological compendium or synopsis in Greek. The intervention of Athena is reminiscent of the function of a *dea ex machina*, which leaves us unable to exclude the possibility that Hyginus (or his Greek mythological source) drew his material from some now unknown tragedy. However, godlike intervention is also at work in Proclus' summary (329 Severyns = 129 Kullmann: ἡ δὲ [Κίρκη] αὐτοὺς ἀθανάτους ποιεῖ).

[10] On immortalization, see Burgess 2001:167, 255n148.

[11] See Hesiod *Catalogue of Women* fr. 204.89–92 (M.-W.). On the so-called 'Tyndaric Oath', see *Iliad* II 339 (though this oath may be referring to all the soldiers, cf. Latacz 2003:103); Hesiod *Catalogue of Women* fr. 204.78–85 (M.-W.); Stesichorus fr. 190 (*PMGF*). For a balanced discussion of the 'Tyndaric Oath' in the Hesiodic *Catalogue of Women*, see Cingano 2005:128-130.

[12] See Kullmann 1960:153n1.

[13] Griffin 1977:44 believes that "[h]ere we have re-using and transformation of an Iliadic motif." This Neoanalytical approach presupposes a linear theory of epic tradition, with the *Iliad* being a text that preceded and influenced the later *Cypria*.

Ἀχιλλεὺς Ἑλένην ἐπιθυμεῖ θεάσασθαι

Is it possible to fully exploit the brief extract of the *Chrestomathy* and reconstruct the entire Achilles-Helen scene? The involvement of the two goddesses, Aphrodite and Thetis, probably depending on their close connection to Helen and Achilles respectively,[14] constitutes a traditional narrative means of making the meeting possible. One may even infer that there was a transitional scene Proclus does not mention, in which Achilles would have revealed to his Nereid-mother, Thetis (who perhaps would emerge from her abode in the bottom of the sea), his strong desire to see Helen, the beautiful wife of Menelaus for whom the entire expedition was taking place. Later on, Thetis may either have come directly in contact with Aphrodite or have asked for the intervention of Zeus, who owed her (Thetis) a favor because she saved him from a plot that had been engineered against him by Hera, Poseidon, and Athena.[15]

Before selecting between the two aforementioned possibilities, we must examine the likely mythological connection between Thetis and Aphrodite. Would it have ever been possible for Thetis to ask Aphrodite for a favor? In the *Aethiopis* (Proclus' *Chrestomathy*, 184-190 Severyns = 57-61 Kullmann), Eos and Thetis, the mothers of Memnon and Achilles respectively, are not only associated with the actual fighting between their two sons, but also with their plea to Zeus in the *psychostasia* scene, the 'weighing of lives', which is not attested in Proclus' summary, but which almost certainly constituted an integral part of the *Aethiopis*. Such a claim is supported by the following evidence:

(a) In the *Iliad* there are two *psychostasiai* or *kerostasiai* scenes: the first, in *Iliad* VIII 69-74, in which Zeus weighs the fates of the Achaeans and the Trojans, and the second, in *Iliad* XXII 209-213, in which Zeus weighs the fates of Achilles and Hector. It has been strongly argued that the *kerostasia* scene in *Iliad* XXII has been influenced by an equivalent *psychostasia* scene featuring in a pre-Homeric *Memnonis, which can be reconstructed on the basis of the plot of the post-Homeric *Aethiopis*, where Memnon, the son of Eos (Dawn) was one of the principal figures.[16]

---

[14] Aphrodite would easily have transported Helen close to the ships where she would meet Achilles. Although Aphrodite rescues Paris twice by transporting him far from the battlefield (*Iliad* III and XX, respectively), Helen refers ironically (*Iliad* III 400-401) to Aphrodite in terms of her ability to transport Helen to one of the goddess' best loved cities. See Clader 1976:73-74.

[15] See *Iliad* I 396-406, where Achilles reminds Thetis that he often heard her speaking of how she had saved Zeus, whom Hera, Poseidon, and Athena had planned to put in chains. Thetis asked for the help of Briareos, the hundred-hander Agaion, who came to Olympos and rescued Zeus. On this episode, see chapter 10.

[16] See Schadewaldt 1965[4]:155-202, especially 155-158.

Chapter Five

(b) The *psychostasia* scene formed part of the tragedy *Psychostasia* by Aeschylus.[17]

(c) There is significant iconographical material depicting the *psychostasia* scene, where Eos and Thetis implore Zeus to save the lives of their children, Memnon, and Achilles. These representations are hereby presented:[18]

A. Black-figure pottery

(1) Attic *dinos*, Vienna, Kunsthist. Mus. IV 3619, found in Caere of Etruria, ci. 540 BC (*LIMC* I.2, 799:135). Zeus is seated, with Hermes to his right holding scales that weigh the souls of Achilles and Memnon. Eos is to the right of Hermes and Memnon is behind her. Memnon's charioteer is standing behind him with his chariot. Thetis is depicted to the right of Hermes, and Achilles is behind her with his charioteer, Automedon, and his chariot behind him.

(2) Ionic *hydria*, Rome, Villa Giulia, found in Caere of Etruria, ci. 520 BC (*LIMC* I.2, 804:136).[19] Zeus is seated, holding scales with the souls of the two heroes, Achilles and Memnon. Their mothers plead before him, one (probably Eos, given the tunic that covers her head) kneeling and touching Zeus.

B. Red-figure pottery

(1) *Kylix*, Rome, Villa Giulia 57912, found in Caere of Etruria, with the signature of the painter Epictetus, ci. 520–510 BC. Hermes, who holds scales with the souls of dead men, is depicted between Achilles and Memnon. Eos and Thetis, who stand before Zeus and Hera, are portrayed behind Memnon. The seated divine couple is about to listen to the supplication of the two mothers.

(2) Bell-shaped *krater*, Palermo, Mus. Reg. V 779, found in Akragas, the work of the painter of Oreithyia, ci. 480–470 BC (*LIMC* III.2, 296:580). Zeus is seated with Eos to his left and Thetis to his right. The two goddessess supplicate Zeus with outstretched arms. The scales, though a typical feature of any *psychostasia* scene, are not depicted.

---

[17] See Radt, *TrGF* 3, frs. 279–280a. It is not clear whether the scene of the *psychostasia* would have featured in Aeschylus' *Memnon* (Radt, *TrGF* 3, frs. 127–130). If it belonged to the same tetralogy as the play *Psychostasia* (Radt, *TrGF* 3, TRI B VI, 1–5), this possibility is decisively discounted. Sophocles also wrote a tragedy, the *Aethiopis*, in which Achilles and Memnon were the main characters (Radt, *TrGF* 4, frs. 28–33), but it is extremely risky to postulate on these grounds a scene of *psychostasia* in this play.

[18] For iconography referring to the scene of the *psychostasia*, see *LIMC* III, 1:781-783, s.v. Eos. See also Burkert 1985:121n24.

[19] See Laimou 1999–2000:11–50 (34).

Ἀχιλλεὺς Ἑλένην ἐπιθυμεῖ θεάσασθαι

(3) *Stamnos*, Boston, Museum of Fine Arts 10.177, from Cyme, the work of the painter of Syracuse, ci. 470–460 BC (*LIMC* I.2, 800:135). Eos and Thetis stand to the right and left, respectively, of Hermes.

(4) *Amphora*, Campania, Leiden, Rijkmus AMM I, the work of the painter Ixion, ci. late 4th century BC (*LIMC* I.2, 805:136). Hermes stands above the two fighters (Achilles has hurled his javelin and wounded Memnon, who is depicted across from him). Next to Hermes is a tree from which scales holding the souls of the two heroes are suspended. Thetis is portrayed above Achilles, and Eos, pulling her hair in an act of grief, above Memnon.

C. Bronze sculpture

Votive offering of the people of Apollonia, Olympia, early classical period (non-extant), described by Pausanias (V 22.2-3). Zeus with the two goddesses and their two heroes-sons (Achilles and Memnon). Eos is named Ἡμέρα (Day) in Pausanias.

Under the scope of the above examples, it becomes clear that the goddesses Eos and Thetis supplicating Zeus in the *psychostasia* scene form a typical iconographic pair.[20] This observation, strengthened by the fact that in myth these two divinities are constantly presented as opponents, makes it highly unlikely that there would be another song-tradition in which Thetis would have asked Eos for a favor. *Mutatis mutandis*, one may maintain that the same argument would be valid for Aphrodite, who plays an active role in effectuating the meeting between Achilles and Helen in the *Cypria*. In order to corroborate this analogical reasoning even more, we need to clarify the relationship between Eos and Aphrodite.

Eos belongs to the oldest mythical substratum and stands for the most representative Greek equivalent of *Ausos, the archetypal Indo-European goddess of Dawn.[21] In archaic epic, especially in the *Iliad*, Aphrodite has inherited a fair number of features originally associated with the Indo-European divinity of Dawn, as reconstructed on the basis of a comparative study of the function of Indic Uṣas and Greek Eos.[22] Eos and Aphrodite are goddesses of

---

[20] It is worth emphasizing that the two black-figure vases (A1-2) and the red-figure *kylix* (B1), which are dated to the sixth century, belong to the pre-Aeschylean period. Consequently, the *psychostasia* of Memnon and Achilles and the supplication of their mothers to Zeus formed an integral part of the mythical tradition of the Archaic period, which makes it highly likely that this episode was already treated in epic poetry.

[21] This deity is represented in the Old Indic mythological tradition by the goddess Uṣas. See Slatkin 1991:28.

[22] See the extensive studies of Boedeker 1974; Friedrich 1978.

Chapter Five

concealment.²³ They are able to transport those whom they wish to save from one place to another. Thus, Tithonus is swept away by Eos (*Homeric Hymn To Aphrodite* [5] 218-238), while Alexandros (*Iliad* III 380-382) and Aeneas (*Iliad* V 311-318) are swept away by Aphrodite.²⁴

Given that Homeric Aphrodite represents the epic surrogate of Eos, we can search for latent connections with Thetis, the more so since Thetis is also able to save those she cares for. According to Proclus' summary of the *Aethiopis* (199-200 Severyns = 66 Kullmann), Thetis takes the dead body of Achilles from the pyre and transports it to the island of Leuke '' (καὶ μετὰ ταῦτα ἐκ τῆς πυρᾶς ἡ Θέτις ἀναρπάσασα τὸν παῖδα εἰς τὴν Λευκὴν νῆσον διακομίζει).²⁵ The similarities between these goddesses are not restricted to their ability to save their loved ones; they extend to their love affairs with mortals (Eos with Tithonus and Orion, Aphrodite with Anchises and Phaethon, Thetis with Peleus), with whom they beget famous sons (Eos-Memnon, Aphrodite-Aeneas, Thetis-Achilles)²⁶ In this light, it could be argued that both Aphrodite and Thetis might well have transferred their loved ones from one place to another, making the meeting between Achilles and Helen possible. Conversely, Thetis' supplication to Zeus in *Iliad* I 493-516 constitutes such a strong parallel that we may plausibly opt for an intermediate scene in which Thetis would have asked Zeus to fulfill Achilles' desire to see Helen (Ἀχιλλεὺς Ἑλένην ἐπιθυμεῖ θεάσασθαι). Even the use of the verb ἐπιθυμεῖ postulates the intermediate scene. This argument is further corroborated by the fact that, given Aphrodite's overt support of the Trojan side and her opposition to Thetis,²⁷ as we may infer from Eos' function in the *Aethiopis* and in the scene between

---

²³ The rescue of mortals is carried out by the typical method, especially in the Greek epic tradition, of divine intervention into human affairs (see e.g. Poseidon's interventions in *Iliad* XI 751-752 and XX 325 and Apollo's in *Iliad* XX 443-444). The difference here is that in the case of Eos and Aphrodite it is the erotic element, either directly or indirectly, that determines their intervention.

²⁴ See also Kakridis 1986:232.

²⁵ See Nagy 1990b: 242-257. Slatkin 1991:26 explains: "The tradition represented by the *Aethiopis* and by our iconographic examples thus posits an identity not only between Achilles and Memnon but between Thetis and Eos, based on their roles as immortal guardians and protectors of their mortal children. From a narrative standpoint this parallelism is more than an instance of the Cycle's fondness for repetition or doublets." See Howald 1937; 1946:125.

²⁶ For a detailed presentation of the mythical lore shared by these goddesses, see Boedeker 1974:68-70.

²⁷ The mythological variant of Charis as Hephaestus' wife (instead of Aphrodite in *Odyssey* viii) is perhaps due to the difficulties created by Thetis' desire to give her son a new suit of armor. Ancient audiences might have felt quite uncomfortable if Achilles' new armor was made by the god Hephaestus, whose wife was unsympathetic towards the Achaeans. The substitution of Aphrodite by Charis removes the problem altogether.

Ἀχιλλεὺς Ἑλένην ἐπιθυμεῖ θεάσασθαι

Aeneas and Achilles in *Iliad* XX 205-212,[28] it would have been quite unlikely that the two goddesses would have cooperated to make the meeting possible, had Zeus not intervened.

On the other hand, one might argue that in an analogous case, specifically in the *Aethiopis* (189-190 Severyns = 61 Kullmann), Proclus refers to Eos meeting with Zeus in order to ensure the immortality of her son Memnon. Why then would another such scene relating to Aphrodite in the *Cypria* not be mentioned? The arguments that one could give in response to this valid question are the following:

(a) The scene of the *Aethiopis* is different from that of the *Cypria*. It does not include an intermediate phase, only the final stage of the conflict between Achilles and Memnon. One might even argue that its function is to counterbalance the victory of Achilles (and indirectly Thetis) while offering some benefit for Eos and Memnon.

(b) Eos asks for Zeus's help because she is not able to ensure the gift of immortality on her own. In this case, the intervention of Zeus is necessary.

We can now reconstruct an intermediate supplication scene between Thetis and Zeus, on the basis of *Iliad* I. Following that scene, Zeus would ask Aphrodite to transport Helen to the camp of the Achaeans, to a place where she would have been visible only by Achilles.[29]

Proclus (*Cypria*, 158 Severyns = 41 Kullmann) refers to the actual meeting between Achilles and Helen with the expression 'and Aphrodite and Thetis brought them together' (καὶ συνήγαγεν αὐτοὺς εἰς τὸ αὐτὸ Ἀφροδίτη καὶ Θέτις). Yet, what is the exact meaning of this phrase? The verb συνάγειν is used in this way only one other time in the entire corpus of Proclus. Interestingly enough, this case too comes from the *Cypria* (100-102 Severyns = 11 Kullmann):

---

[28] ὄψι δ' οὔτ' ἄρ πω σὺ ἐμοὺς ἴδες οὔτ' ἄρ' ἐγὼ σούς. // φᾶσι σὲ μὲν Πηλῆος ἀμύνονος ἔκγονον εἶναι // μητρός τ' ἐκ Θέτιδος καλλιπλοκάμου ἁλοσύδνης· // αὐτὰρ ἐγὼν υἱὸς μεγαλήτορος Ἀγχίσαο // εὔχομαι ἐκγεγάμεν, μήτηρ δέ μοί ἐστ' Ἀφροδίτη. // τῶν δὴ νῦν ἕτεροί γε φίλον παῖδα κλαύσονται // σήμερον· οὐ γάρ φημ' ἐπέεσσί γε νηπυτίοισιν // ὧδε διακρινθέντε μάχης ἐξ ἀπονέεσθαι. (I have never with my eyes seen yours parents, nor have you seen mine. / For you, they say you are the issue of blameless Peleus / and that your mother was Thetis of the lovely hair, the sea's lady; / I in turn claim I am the son of great-hearted Anchises / but that my mother was Aphrodite; and that of these parents / one group or the other will have a dear son to mourn for / this day. Since I believe we will not in mere words, like children, / meet, and separate and go home again out of the fighting.)

[29] As she did with Paris in *Iliad* III 380-382. For Thetis, see Slatkin 1991:44: "Thetis, like Kalypso and Aphrodite, is associated by the *Iliad* with impenetrable clouds and with veils and with concealment."

Chapter Five

ἐν τούτῳ δὲ Ἀφροδίτη συνάγει τὴν Ἑλένην τῷ Ἀλεξάνδρῳ. καὶ μετὰ τὴν μίξιν τὰ πλεῖστα κτήματα ἐνθέμενοι νυκτὸς ἀποπλέουσι.

Meanwhile Aphrodite brings Helen and Alexander together, and after their union they sail off in the night with a great load of treasure.

The verb συνάγειν together with the noun μίξις and the intervention of Aphrodite overtly designate an erotic context. Is it possible to argue that the erotic element is latent in the meeting between Achilles and Helen, given that two of the three aforementioned features (συνάγειν and Aphrodite) are also present? Let us first look at certain other sources indicating that there was an erotic relationship between Achilles and Helen:

(1) According to the 'Hesiodic' *Catalogue of Women* (frs. 204.87-92 [M.-W.]), Menelaus would have never been able to marry Helen, if, during the period she was meant to acquire a husband, Achilles had been among her suitors:

> ... Χείρων δ' ἐν Πηλίῳ ὑλήεντι
> Πηλείδην ἐκόμιζε πόδας ταχύν, ἔξοχον ἀνδρῶν,
> παῖδ' ἔτ' ἐόν[τ'·] οὐ γάρ μιν ἀρηΐφιλος Μενέλαος
> νίκησ' οὐδέ τις ἄλλος ἐπιχθονίων ἀνθρώπων
> μνηστεύων Ἑλένην, εἴ μιν κίχε παρθένον οὖσαν
> οἴκαδε νοστήσας ἐκ Πηλίου ὠκὺς Ἀχιλλεύς.

> Cheiron in woody Peleion was rearing the son of Peleus, swift-footed, best of
> men, [but] still a child; for neither Menelaus who is dear to Ares nor some other
> among mortal men would have won in marrying Helen, if swift Achilles found
> her still unmarried, after returning home from Peleion.[30]

This testimony may be an *argumentum ex silentio* demonstrating that archaic epic was 'familiar' with a possible erotic connection between Achilles and Helen.

(2) According to Euripides (*Helen* 98-99), Achilles was considered one of Helen's suitors: τὸν Πηλέως τιν' οἶσθ' Ἀχιλλέα γόνον; // ναί· // μνηστήρ ποθ' Ἑλένης ἦλθεν, ὡς ἀκούομεν. This is the only ancient source that makes such a reference. The crucial point here lies in the interpretation of the phrase ὡς

---

[30] The translation is my own.

Ἀχιλλεὺς Ἑλένην ἐπιθυμεῖ θεάσασθαι

ἀκούομεν (99). From where does Euripides draw this information? Even in later sources such as Apollodorus (*Bibliotheca* III 10.8) and Hyginus (*Fabulae* 81) Achilles is not included among Helen's suitors.³¹ Wilamowitz and Schubart attempted to interpret the aforementioned Euripidean passage 'internally,' that is to say, they tried to explain Helen's words based on her role in this particular tragedy. Thus, they argued that Euripides' aim was to emphasize Helen's vanity in her desire to present Achilles as one of her suitors.³² Other scholars attempted to solve this riddle 'externally,' that is, they looked for the origins of the aforementioned information in earlier texts or authors. Mayer believed that Euripides' source was Stesichorus.³³ Jouan³⁴ adopted the view of Wilamowitz, while Kannicht³⁵ argued that Euripides' source was the *Cypria*, specifically the passage examined in this study: καὶ μετὰ ταῦτα Ἀχιλλεὺς Ἑλένην ἐπιθυμεῖ θεάσασθαι, καὶ συνήγαγεν αὐτοὺς εἰς τὸ αὐτὸ Ἀφροδίτη καὶ Θέτις (157–158 Severyns = 41 Kullmann). Kannicht's explanation does not refute Wilamowitz's and Schubart's 'internal' explanation. On the contrary, it adds an interpretive color, since he shows that Euripides exploited the mythical narrative of the *Cypria* only to adapt it to his own tragedy. Helen, in a highly provocative display of female arrogance and vanity, aims at including among her suitors even Achilles, whom the epic tradition had notoriously excluded from the long list of male competitors flocking Tyndareus' palace only to become the victims of her beauty and subsequently heroes of the Trojan War.³⁶

(3) According to Pausanias (III 19.11–13),³⁷ Ptolemaeus Chennus (*Kaine Historia* 4.3 [in Photius, *Bibliotheca* 149a19]),³⁸ and Philostratus (*Heroicus* 54.8–

---

³¹ Pausanias (III 24.10–11) attempts (by using complex reasoning not withstanding scientific inquiry) to demonstrate that Achilles could never have been included in the list of Helen's suitors. Pausanias' account is only worth mentioning in that it attests to the growing interest (mainly, but not exclusively in the imperial years) in response to the silence of the mythical tradition regarding the relationship between Achilles and Helen. The best of the Achaeans had somehow been connected to the most beautiful woman.

³² See Wilamowitz-Moellendorff and Schubart 1907:39.

³³ Mayer 1883:20.

³⁴ See Jouan 1966:161.

³⁵ See Kannicht 1969:45–46 (ad 99). Kannicht refers to Lycophron's *Alexandra* 143 and 146, which alludes to Helen's five husbands, Theseus, Paris, Menelaus, Deiphobus, and Achilles. On the contrary, Pattichis 1978:15–16 and 198 (ad verse 99) states that we are in the dark concerning the source Euripides might have used in his *Helen*, in order to present Achilles as Helen's suitor.

³⁶ See also Kullmann 1960:153: "Das Schauen der Helena in den Kyprien ist für Achill also die nachgeholte 'Freite um Helena'." See also Lange 2002:122–125; Pallantza 2005:265–275; Tsagalis 2008.

³⁷ Pausanias, III 19.11–13.

³⁸ καὶ ὡς Ἑλένης καὶ Ἀχιλλέως ἐν μακάρων νήσοις παῖς γεγόνοι, ὃν διὰ τὸ τῆς χώρας εὔφορον Εὐφορίωνα ὠνόμασαν. Despite the spread of 'deceptive literature' during this era, Ptolemaeus

13), Achilles[39] and Helen lived on the island of Leuke in the Black Sea, near the mouth of the Ister.[40] Philostratus' text, the most valuable piece of information among the aforementioned authors, runs as follows:

> ἐνταῦθα εἶδόν τε πρῶτον καὶ περιέβαλον ἀλλήλους Ἀχιλλεύς τε καὶ Ἑλένη, καὶ γάμον ἐδαίσαντό σφων Ποσειδῶν τε αὐτὸς καὶ Ἀμφιτρίτη, Νηρηίδες τε ξύμπασαι καὶ ὁπόσοι ποταμοὶ καὶ δαίμονες <ἐσ>έρχονται τὴν Μαιῶτίν τε καὶ τὸν Πόντον. οἰκεῖν μὲν δὴ λευκοὺς ὄρνιθας ἐν αὐτῇ φασιν, εἶναι δὲ τούτους ὑγρούς τε καὶ τῆς θαλάττης ἀπόζοντας, οὓς τὸν Ἀχιλλέα θεράποντας αὑτοῦ πεποιῆσαι κοσμοῦντας αὐτῷ τὸ ἄλσος τῷ τε ἀνέμῳ τῶν πτερῶν καὶ ταῖς ἀπ' αὐτῶν ρανίσι· πράττειν δὲ τοῦτο χαμαὶ πετομένους καὶ μικρὸν τῆς γῆς ὑπεραίροντας. ἀνθρώποις δὲ πλέουσι μὲν τὸ τοῦ πελάγους χάσμα ὁσία ἡ νῆσος ἐσβαίνειν, κεῖται γὰρ ὥσπερ εὔξεινος νεῶν ἑστία· οἶκον δὲ μὴ ποιεῖσθαι αὐτὴν πᾶσί τε ἀπείρηται τοῖς πλέουσι καὶ τοῖς περὶ τὸν Πόντον Ἕλλησί τε καὶ βαρβάροις. δεῖ γὰρ προσορμισαμένους τε καὶ θύσαντας ἡλίου δυομένου ἐσβαίνειν μὴ ἐννυχεύοντας τῇ γῇ, κἂν μὲν τὸ πνεῦμα ἕπηται, πλεῖν, εἰ δὲ μή, ἀναψαμένους τὸ πλοῖον ἐν κοίλῳ ἀναπαύεσθαι. ξυμπίνειν γὰρ δὴ λέγονται τότε ὁ Ἀχιλλεύς τε καὶ ἡ Ἑλένη, καὶ ἐν ᾠδαῖς εἶναι, τόν ἔρωτά τε τὸν ἀλλήλων ᾄδειν καὶ Ὁμήρου τὰ ἔπη τὰ ἐπὶ τῇ Τροίᾳ καὶ τὸν Ὅμηρον αὐτόν. τὸ γὰρ τῆς ποιητικῆς δῶρον, ὃ παρὰ τῆς Καλλιόπης τῷ Ἀχιλλεῖ ἐφοίτησεν, ἐπαινεῖ Ἀχιλλεὺς ἔτι καὶ σπουδάζει μᾶλλον, ἐπειδὴ πέπαυται τῶν πολεμικῶν.

There Achilles and Helen first saw and embraced one another, and Poseidon himself and Amphitritê hosted their wedding feast, along

---

Chennus may be an exception. See Kullmann 1960:141n1, who uses Ptolemaeus Chennus as a possible source. For a systematic study of the sources of Ptolemaeus Chennus and of the literary value of his work, see Tomberg 1968, and in particular for Achilles and Helen on the Isles of the Blessed according to the variant found in Ptolemaeus Chennus, 108–109, 124–125, 166.

[39] Apart from the *Aethiopis*, the account of Achilles' relocation to and stay on the Isles of the Blessed (with no mention of Helen) is provided by Pindar (*Olympian* 2.79–80, *Nemean* 4.49–50), Ibycus (fr. 291 *PMGF*), Simonides (fr. 558 *PMG*), Euripides (*Andromache* 1260–1262, *Iphigenia in Tauris* 435–437), Plato (*Symposium* 179e). Achilles' transfer to the island of Leuke must be seen in light of Thetis' consistent attempts to prevent his death, either by not sending him to Troy (Achilles is hidden in the island of Scyros disguised as a woman) or by making him immortal (she plunges him in the waters of Styx). For this topic, see Waldner 2000:96–101 with bibliography.

[40] This tradition must be connected to Achilles' post mortem transfer to the island of Leuke by Thetis, which featured in the Cyclic *Aethiopis* (199–200 Severyns = 66 Kullmann).

Ἀχιλλεὺς Ἑλένην ἐπιθυμεῖ θεάσασθαι

with all the Nereids and as many rivers and water-spirits as flow into the Sea of Maiôtis and the Pontus. They say that white birds live on the island and that these marine birds smell of the sea. Achilles made them his servants, since they furnish the grove for him with the breeze and raindrops from the wings. They do this by fluttering on the ground and lifting themselves off a little bit above the earth. For mortals who sail the broad expanse of the sea, it is permitted by divine law to enter the island, for it is situated like a welcoming hearth for ships. But it is forbidden to all those who sail the sea and for the Hellenes and barbarians from around the Pontus to make it a place of habitation. Those who anchor near the island and sacrifice must go onboard when the sun sets, so that they do not sleep on its land. If the wind should follow them, they must sail, and if it does not, they must wait in the bay after mooring their ship. Then Achilles and Helen are said to drink together and to be engaged in singing. They celebrate in song their desire for one another, Homer's epics on the Trojan war, and Homer himself. Achilles still praises the gift of poetry which came to him from Calliope, and he pursues it more seriously, since he has ceased from military activities.

(4) According to the most likely interpretation of the following iconographic representations on two vases, Achilles and Helen 'lived' together in the Isles of the Blessed.

(a) One amphora (the well-known Portland Vase)[41] from the 1st century BC (ci. 30 BC), now in the British Museum, depicts Peleus, Thetis, and Poseidon on one side, and on the other Achilles, Helen and Aphrodite (with a tree in the background) in the Isles of the Blessed. Helen is holding a torch, which indicates that she is in the underworld, as can also be concluded from the fact that the vase was intended for funeral use.[42] Ashmole has proposed an interesting reading of the iconographic representation that links the tree with the ancient worship of Helen as a goddess of vegetation. In addition, he rightly points to a similar reference to a plane tree that is mentioned in connection to Helen in Theocritus' *Idyll* 18.43-48. According to Theocritus, who may well be

---

[41] See table 1 with caption: *The Portland Vase*, British Museum, London (from: *JHS* 87 [1967], table II).

[42] The bibliography in relation to the interpretation of the figures on the famous Portland vase is immense. See Haynes 1975²:27-32, whose figure identification I have followed. In spite of the many alternative interpretations, I think that the arguments of Haynes 1995:146-152 and Hind 1995:153-155 are more than convincing.

relying on an epithalamion by Stesichorus for Helen, her female companions sing that they will hang the lotus wreath from a plane tree and carve above it in the Doric dialect the phrase 'σέβευ μ'· Ἑλένας φυτόν εἰμι' (Adore me; I am Helen's tree).[43]

(b) In a marble relief (end of the 1st century BC), which was found in "the house of Telephus" in Herculaneum (now in the National Archaeological Museum in Naples [76/128]), a young man is depicted (Achilles?) with a sword beside him, leaning on his spear. Next to him is a woman (Helen?) wearing sandals, a tunic, and a cloak. The rocks in the background indicate that the man and the woman are on an island (just as in the previous representation), which may well be one of the Isles of the Blessed.[44]

In any case, the meeting between Achilles and Helen in the *Cypria* must have had a significant influence on Achilles, since according to Proclus' summary, "[t]hen Achilles restrains the Achaeans in their desire to return home" (159–160 Severyns = 42 Kullmann: εἶτα ἀπονοστεῖν ὡρμημένους τοὺς Ἀχαιοὺς Ἀχιλλεὺς κατέχει). Achilles' zeal in restraining the Greeks who want to return home can be explained only in light of a latent erotic atmosphere in the scene of his meeting with Helen. The best of women with respect to beauty has 'captured' the best of the Achaeans regarding valor and military might. *Arma cedunt Helenae.*

Rival Traditions: The *Iliad* and the *Cypria*

The meeting scene between Achilles and Helen in the *Cypria* directly contrasts with the fact that Achilles and Helen almost never refer to each other in the *Iliad*.[45] The reasons lying behind this are worth considering, all the more so since they may tell something about the relationship between the poetic traditions that the *Iliad* and the *Cypria* represent.

Before embarking on answering these questions, it will be useful first to study the context of the meeting between Achilles and Helen in the *Cypria* and then to search for similarities with the scene of Helen's first Iliadic appearance, in the 'Teichoscopia' (*Iliad* III 161–244).

---

[43] See Ashmole 1967:1–17, especially 11–14. Theocritus' text (18.43–48) runs as follows: πρᾶταί τοι στέφανον λωτῶ χαμαὶ αὐξομένοιο // πλέξαισαι σκιαρὰν καταθήσομεν ἐς πλατάνιστον· // πρᾶται δ' ἀργυρέας ἐξ ὄλπιδος ὑγρὸν ἄλειφαρ // λαζύμεναι σταξεῦμες ὑπὸ σκιαρὰν πλατάνιστον· // γράμματα δ' ἐν φλοιῷ γεγράψεται, ὡς παριών τις // ἀννείμῃ Δωριστί· 'σέβευ μ'· Ἑλένας φυτόν εἰμι.'

[44] See *LIMC* IV.1:554 s.v. Hélène [L. Ghali-Kahil].

[45] The only exception is *Iliad* XIX 325: εἵνεκα ῥιγεδανῆς Ἑλένης Τρωσὶν πολεμίζω.

Ἀχιλλεὺς Ἑλένην ἐπιθυμεῖ θεάσασθαι

The meeting between Achilles and Helen in the *Cypria* is framed by an embassy to the Trojans asking them to return Helen along with the possessions Paris had stolen,[46] and by Achilles' restraining the Achaeans who are eager to return to Greece, respectively.[47]

Are there any scenes or episodes in the *Iliad* that correspond to those framing the meeting between Achilles and Helen in the *Cypria*? In *Iliad* III, the Achaeans ask the Trojans to return Helen and the κτήματα (possessions) Alexandros took with him when leaving Sparta. The Trojans refuse to give Helen back but agree that the whole matter should be decided by a single conflict between the two rivals, Menelaus and Alexandros. The episode of the 'Teichoscopia' constitutes an effective interlude, allowing for the introduction of Helen (the prize of the duel) into the plot. The phrase τὴν Ἑλένην καὶ τὰ κτήματα ἀπαιτοῦντες 'demanding Helen and her possessions', which is employed by Proclus (152-153 Severyns = 38 Kullmann), is also used, albeit slightly altered, by Alexandros in *Iliad* III 70: συμβάλετ' ἀμφ' Ἑλένῃ καὶ κτήμασι πᾶσι μάχεσθαι 'to fight together for the sake of Helen and all of her possessions'. Interestingly enough, the ensuing conflict, which results from the breach of the oaths by the Trojans when Pandarus wounds Menelaus, recalls the resumption of battle in the *Cypria* after the Trojan refusal to return Helen and her possessions to the Achaeans: 'when they refuse, they then attack the walls' (153-154 Severyns = 39 Kullmann: ὡς δὲ οὐχ ὑπήκουσαν ἐκεῖνοι, ἐνταῦθα δὴ τειχομαχοῦσιν). As far as the events following the meeting between Achilles and Helen in the *Cypria* are concerned, i.e. (a) the restraining of the Achaeans who wish to return to Greece, (b) the oxen of Aeneas and the capture of Lyrnessos and Pedasos, the following comments can be made:

(a) In *Iliad* II, just as in the *Cypria*, the Achaean army is eager to depart for Greece. Kullmann[48] has convincingly argued that the source for this Iliadic episode was the story of a famine, a reflex of which we can see in the *Cypria*. In *Iliad* II Achilles is absent, and it is Odysseus and Nestor who restrain the Achaeans.

(b) The oxen of Aeneas are briefly mentioned in *Iliad* XX 89-92, where Aeneas speaks to Apollo, who has taken the form of Lycaon and urged the son

---

[46] See 152-156 Severyns = 38-40 Kullmann: [the Achaeans] καὶ διαπρεσβεύονται πρὸς τοὺς Τρῶας, τὴν Ἑλένην καὶ τὰ κτήματα ἀπαιτοῦντες. ὡς δὲ οὐχ ὑπήκουσαν ἐκεῖνοι, ἐνταῦθα δὴ τειχομαχοῦσιν. ἔπειτα τὴν χώραν ἐπεξελθόντες πορθοῦσι καὶ τὰς περιοίκους πόλεις ("[they] send an embassy to the Trojans, demanding Helen and the goods back. When those refuse, they then attack the walls. Then setting out, they plunder the land and surrounding cities").
[47] See 159-160 Severyns = 42 Kullmann: εἶτα ἀπονοστεῖν ὡρμημένους τοὺς Ἀχαιοὺς Ἀχιλλεὺς κατέχει ("Then Achilles restrains the Achaeans in their desire to return home").
[48] Kullmann 1955:253-273.

of Anchises to face Achilles: οὐ μὲν γὰρ νῦν πρῶτα ποδώκεος ἄντ' Ἀχιλῆος // στήσομαι, ἀλλ' ἤδη με καὶ ἄλλοτε δουρὶ φόβησεν // ἐξ Ἴδης, ὅτε βουσὶν ἐπήλυθεν ἡμετέρῃσιν, // πέρσε δὲ Λυρνησσὸν καὶ Πήδασον· ... (Since this will not be the first time I stand up against swift-footed / Achilleus, but another time before now he drove me / with the spear from Ida, when he came after our cattle / the time he sacked Lyrnessos and Pedasos).[49] Apollo's response to Aeneas is revealing. The god reminds Aeneas of his divine origin (he is the son of Aphrodite and Anchises) and emphasizes, precisely on the basis of this origin, his superiority over Achilles (Iliad XX 106–107): ... κεῖνος δὲ χερείονος ἐκ θεοῦ ἐστιν· // ἣ μὲν γὰρ Διός ἐσθ', ἣ δ' ἐξ ἁλίοιο γέροντος (... but Achilleus was born of a lesser goddess, / Aphrodite being daughter of Zeus, Thetis of the sea's ancient).

Concluding Remarks

The comparative analysis between the *Iliad* and the *Cypria* shows that the *Iliad* contains episodes or scenes similar to the context that frames the meeting between Achilles and Helen in the *Cypria*. The Iliadic tradition makes occasional use of material that hardly fits its plot requirements, when not at odds with its basic interpretive viewpoint. Although the reference to a pre-Iliadic incident, the stealing of Aeneas' oxen, for example, was not at all necessary and could have been easily omitted, the *Iliad* still incorporates it, since it does not downplay any of the *Iliad*'s fundamental narrative tenets.

Achilles would not, of course, have been on the battlefield in the episode of the 'Teichoscopia', when Helen stood on the walls of Troy and described the major Achaean leaders to Priam. The plot of the poem rules out this possibility. As we know, Achilles had withdrawn from the battlefield after his quarrel with Agamemnon in *Iliad* I. However, the epic is able to bypass such difficulties when necessary. A characteristic example is Helen's reference to her brothers, Castor and Polydeuces (*Iliad* III 236–238), who would not have been able to participate in the Iliadic war because they had already died before the expedition to Troy. In fact, the very episode of Castor's death, Polydeuces' subsequent killing of Idas and Lynceus and Zeus' bestowing alternative immortality upon the Dioscuri (by allowing each one return to the world of the living every other day) formed part of the *Cypria* (106–109 Severyns = 14–16 Kullmann). In

---

[49] Kullmann 1960:285 has rightly argued that the details concerning the destruction of Lyrnessos can hardly fit the Iliadic plot, and so it is possible that the poet of the *Iliad* might have taken this information from a source consonant with the content of the *Cypria*.

the 'Teichoscopia' the *Iliad* alludes to a well-known episode stemming from a tradition reflected in the post-Homeric *Cypria*, an episode that had nothing to do with the plot of the *Iliad* whatsoever. Likewise, the *Iliad* would have been able to avoid the technical difficulty of Achilles' absence from the battlefield and the fact that Helen does not know what the Achaean hero looks like, since she has never seen him. It would have been possible in the 'Teichoscopia' (e.g.) for Priam to ask Helen to show him Achilles, the renowned Achaean hero, the more so since Priam is unaware of the conflict between Achilles and Agamemnon as well as Achilles' subsequent decision to withdraw from the battlefield. Alternatively, Helen herself may have inquired about Achilles, just as she inquired about Castor and Polydeuces.

    I would like to argue that there are several other reasons explaining the *Iliad*'s silence when it comes either to a meeting between Achilles and Helen or even to any reference made by the one to the other. The one exception is *Iliad* XIX 325: εἵνεκα ῥιγεδανῆς Ἑλένης Τρωσὶν πολεμίζω (make war upon the Trojans for the sake of accursed Helen), which stands as a bold manifestation of the Iliadic *Weltanschauung*. The *thelxis* by which Achilles is attracted to Helen after their meeting in the *Cypria* has been replaced by his tragic outlook on the heroic code as embodied in the world of the *Iliad*. The love episode of the meeting between the ἄριστος Ἀχαιῶν and the καλλίστη γυναικῶν does not have a place in the *Iliad*, given the critical turning point that Iliadic heroes face.[50] Mythical nomenclature does not necessitate identical epic behavior; the names of the heroes and heroines may be the same, but the characters they represent and the way they behave may well be different. Thus, Achilles and Helen cannot 'coexist' in the *Iliad*, since the presence of one of them rules out the presence of the other.[51] The *Iliad* is the poem of the wrath (μῆνις)

---

[50] Achilles and Helen form a unique but illicit pair. Schmidt 1996:23–38 maintains that the genealogical, catalogue-based tradition has substituted Achilles for Patroclus as the suitor of Helen. The tradition repeatedly attempts to connect the best of the Achaeans with the most beautiful woman, even indirectly. Schmidt 1996:38 argues that their coexistence on the Isles of the Blessed, the wedding of Neoptolemus with Hermione, daughter of Helen and Menelaus (*Odyssey* iv 3–9; Euripides *Andromache* 29), and also the incorporation of Patroclus into the catalogue of Helen's suitors must be interpreted in this light. In this way, Patroclus becomes Achilles' surrogate. Even if unable to win the heart of Helen, he wins, in the Iliadic tradition, a place in Achilles' heart, as his best friend.

[51] On the contrary, in the *Cypria* the meeting between Achilles and Helen is perfectly justifiable. See also Ghali-Kahil (1965) 34: "*Car Achilles, trop jeune pour avoir été l'un des Prétendants n'avait point connu Hélène, et l'auteur pouvait logiquement supposer qu'il désirait la voir, pour donner un sens à sa participation à la guerre; après l'entrevue, Achille empêchera les Achéens de lever le siège de Troie. De toute façon ne fallait-il pas mettre en présence le héros principal de la guerre et l'héroïne qui en était la cause? Le plus fort ne devait-il pas au moins apercevoir la plus belle?*"

Chapter Five

of Achilles that systematically refuses to abide by 'Cyclic' standards and accommodate romantic scenes. The two most important meetings between husbands and wives in the *Iliad*, namely those between Helen and Alexandros in *Iliad* III and between Hector and Andromache in *Iliad* VI, are anything but romantic. In the first, Alexandros is bitterly scorned by Helen, whereas in the second Andromache's and Hector's life stories converge at the fulcrum of an impending danger leading to an inevitable end. Achilles and Helen cannot coexist in the *Iliad* because their meeting appears to be linked inseparably with the content and viewpoint of another epic tradition reflected in the post-Homeric *Cypria*, one that the monumental composition of the *Iliad* is trying to surpass. The *Iliad* would have betrayed its own idiosyncratic, though unique, interpretation of heroic κλέος if Helen and Achilles were brought together.

I attempted to demonstrate that we must treat archaic epic more from the perspective of song-traditions than as a set of texts fixed by writing and bound by absolute chronological termini. The selection of the episode between Achilles and Helen was mainly intended to show how the rival poetic traditions of the *Cypria* and the *Iliad* can be studied from either side, as they coexisted and were simultaneously shaped during the Archaic period. By way of the particular episode that I examined, I tried to explore how the *Iliad* differentiated itself from mythical material that did not suit its plot or its perspective on the heroic world. Being, at present, encumbered with a lack of information, we are unable to trace all the details of the meeting between Achilles and Helen in the *Cypria*, to know exactly what the Achaean hero saw, how he was filled with such strong admiration that he did not hesitate to restrain the Achaeans who were willing to return home. Conversely, by reconstructing this lost episode and exploring the implications it puts forth, we are able to comprehend how the *Iliad* zoomed its interpretive lens on the relevant scene between Achilles and Helen that featured in a rival tradition.

A 'specular reading' between the *Cypria* and the *Iliad* reveals their mutual referentiality, which can be explained if it is assumed that they developed simultaneously within the larger context of oral traditional poetry.[52] Marks[53] has argued that inconsistencies arising at the junction between the *Cypria* and the *Iliad* reflect "a clash between their narrative strategies." This claim, which I fully endorse, holds true for the entire epic traditions represented by

---

[52] For a 'specular reading' between epic traditions, see Pucci 1987:41–43. For the *Cypria* versus the *Iliad*, see Marks 2002:4.
[53] Marks 2002:1–24.

Ἀχιλλεὺς Ἑλένην ἐπιθυμεῖ θεάσασθαι

the *Cypria* and the *Iliad*. In fact, a meeting between Achilles and Helen[54] may also (like Zeus' plan to alleviate the Trojans from Achilles' presence[55] or the earth from too many humans[56] in the *Cypria*) reflect both contact with Near-Eastern traditions and epichoric contexts, where Aphrodite would have been better evaluated by a local, Cypriot audience, as a principal actor in this scene. A 'specular reading', finally amounting to an intertextual reading, of these two traditions shows that we may be dealing with tensions between an epichoric tradition (*Cypria*) and a Pan-Hellenic one (*Iliad*).

In this light, intertextuality as a system of simple (quotations) or complex (allusions) cross-references allows the audience to evaluate each song-tradition by its relation to other song-traditions. Helen thus acquires a meta-traditional function, as she emblematizes an oral tradition that is incompatible with the tragic notion of the heroic world thematized by Iliadic Achilles. In the *Iliad*, Achilles 'erases' his admiration for Helen as reflected in the *Cypria*. When the listeners hear the son of Thetis say εἵνεκα ῥιγεδανῆς Ἑλένης Τρωσὶν πολεμίζω (*Iliad* XIX 325), they are invited to recall the meeting scene between the most beautiful woman in the world and the best of the Achaeans and to realize that the erotic framework of the *Cypria* tradition has been turned into a lament scene in the Iliadic tradition. Beautiful Helen is now coined 'accursed' (ῥιγεδανή), whereas infatuated Achilles has become a mourner. He no longer desires to see Helen, but wishes simply to lament.

---

[54] See Mayer 1996:1–15, who speaks for "Zeus' double device of Achilles and Helen" (14), "a πῆμα for mankind" (12).
[55] 167–168 Severyns = 49 Kullmann.
[56] *PEG* 1, fr. 1 = *EGF* fr. 1.

6

Viewing from the Walls, Viewing Helen: Language and Indeterminacy in the 'Teichoscopia'

Introduction

WHEN WE DISCUSS THE ROLE OF HELEN in the *Iliad*, we should always keep in mind that she is situated in the midst of the Iliadic war and myth, which differs in its plot from Trojan lore, albeit their obvious connection.[1] The Iliadic myth is not simply a miniature of its Trojan predecessor, but a sophisticated selection and reworking of certain episodes with a change of emphasis and scope. To this extent, the case of Helen is paradigmatic. For in the Trojan myth Helen was the protagonist (since both the beginning and end of the war were connected to her), whereas in its Iliadic version her importance became secondary.[2]

The literature on Helen in the *Iliad* is extensive, but it has been mainly concerned with questions of a genetic nature. Scholars have been interested in the dilemma concerning her innocence or guilt, trying to examine and trace its mythological origin. Even very recent efforts have adopted the basis for this dilemma, although they interpret it in terms of its poetic function.

The aim of this chapter is to examine Helen's language in the 'Teichoscopia' in an effort to determine its poetic mechanics and to disclose Helen's status and function in this episode. In other words, how does Helen's diction reflect her thematic marginalization within the Iliadic plot?

Arguing that speech is not uniform in the *Iliad* is no novelty. Although the oral nature of the Homeric poems presently seems fairly well established, the language of the poems shows what I would like to call a *fluctuating regularity*, since every song is *ipso tempore* completely traditional and completely new. This paradoxical term is imbued with an oxymoronic tone. It refers not only

---

[1] See Maronitis 1995:55–73.
[2] Cf. Zagagi 1985:63.

to the formularity and regularity of Homeric speech, but also to the personal linguistic styles of different characters, not to speak of the differences between narrator and characters.[3] All use language in different ways according to the content of their speech and the audiences they address. Moreover, different subgenres incorporated within the greater super-genre of epic have their own formulaic characteristics, the more so since they mirror corresponding social occasions of performance within a given community.[4]

From this theoretical perspective, I will try to show that the lack of consistency characterizing Helen's language in the *Iliad* is not only a reflection on the level of diction of her thematic marginalization but also the result of Iliadic preoccupation within the tradition of epic poetry. Helen's language in the 'Teichoscopia' reveals that the whole episode is not just a view from the walls, but a view of Helen herself, and through her a glance at the genre of epic poetry. I will argue that Helen's language is imbued with genre-mixing, formulaic misuse, and intertextual references, which have a profound effect on the way the whole poem 'views' the rest of the tradition as represented by key epic heroes described by Helen in the episode. This interpretation elevates Helen from the status of a character of the plot to that of an internal commentator of the tradition, making her layered language mirror the Iliad's meta-traditional criticism of its own art.[5]

Genre-Mixing and Formulaic Misuse

Helen's figurative death

When Priam tells Helen to identify a huge Achaean warrior in the battlefield looking like a king, she replies with a lengthy speech that has, in its larger part, nothing to do with the question the Trojan king had asked her (*Iliad* III 172–180):[6]

"αἰδοῖός τέ μοί ἐσσι, φίλε ἑκυρέ, δεινός τε.
ὡς ὄφελεν // θάνατός μοι ἀδεῖν κακός, // ὁππότε δεῦρο
υἱέϊ σῷ ἑπόμην, θάλαμον γνωτούς τε λιποῦσα

---

[3] See Griffin 1986:36–57.
[4] See Martin 1989:43–47.
[5] See Martin 1989:43–47; Pucci 2003:90. See also scholia vetera on *Iliad* III 126-127 (Erbse): ἀξιόχρεων ἀρχέτυπον ἀνέπλασεν ὁ ποιητὴς τῆς ἰδίας ποιήσεως.
[6] See the classification of formulas into "paradigmatic" and "syntagmatic" by Martin 1989:164–166. Double-underscored characters indicate "paradigmatic" formulas, underlinings indicate "syntagmatic", and italics Iliadic *hapax legomena*.

Chapter Six

παῖδά τε τηλυγέτην καὶ ὁμηλικίην // ἐρατεινήν.
ἀλλὰ τά γ' οὐκ ἐγένοντο· τὸ καὶ κλαίουσα τέτηκα.
τοῦτο δέ τοι ἐρέω, ὅ μ' ἀνείρεαι ἠδὲ μεταλλᾷς·
οὗτός γ' Ἀτρεΐδης εὐρὺ κρείων Ἀγαμέμνων,
ἀμφότερον βασιλεύς τ' ἀγαθὸς κρατερός τ' αἰχμητής.
δαὴρ αὖτ' ἐμὸς ἔσκε // κυνώπιδος, εἴ ποτ' ἔην γε."

"Always to me, beloved father, you are feared and respected;
and I wish bitter death had been what I wanted, when I came
    hither
following your son, forsaking my chamber, my kinsmen,
my growing child, and the loveliness of girls my own age.
It did not happen that way: and now I am worn with weeping.
This now I will tell you in answer to the question you asked me.
That man is Atreus' son Agamemnon, widely powerful,
at the same time a good king and a strong spearfighter,
once my kinsman, slut that I am. Did this ever happen?"

Helen begins her speech by addressing her father-in-law (ἑκυρέ)[7] with the epithets αἰδοῖος (III 172) and δεινός (III 172), which are only attested together here and in *Iliad* XVIII 394.[8] In *Iliad* III 172, the constituent items of the formula αἰδοῖός τε ... δεινός τε have been separated by the family term (ἑκυρέ); they notionally refer to (albeit in a different case) and present a new combination of the formula αἰδοίη τε φίλη τε. This lexical amalgam is an innovative use of traditional material because the dictional allomorph φίλη τε καὶ αἰδοίη / αἰδοίη τε φίλη τε is never previously employed with family terms. Αἰδοῖος acquires here a specific emotive force, since it does not simply mean 'revered'[9] but expresses a new connotation for a state of intimacy, not just veneration and respect, which emphasizes the integral part that Helen plays in Priam's

---

[7] The word ἑκυρέ (metrically *Fεκυρέ) is a family term. Cf. Chantraine 1986-1988⁶ (1948-1953):146 (*GH* 1). Helen constantly uses such terminology in her speeches (see especially her improvised lament for Hector in *Iliad* XXIV). She calls Hector (*Iliad* VI 344; *Iliad* XXIV 762) and Agamemnon (*Iliad* III 180) by the family term δαήρ.

[8] Αἰδοῖος is attested 14 times in the *Iliad*: II 514; III 172; IV 402; VI 250; X 114; XI 649; XIV 210; XVIII 386 = XVIII 425; XVIII 394; XXI 75; XXI 460; XXI 479; XXII 451. In respect to the 14 attestations of the epithet αἰδοῖος, three observations can be made: (1) Only once (X 114) does it modify a proper name. In all the other cases it is used as the complement of either a family term (6 times), or a simple noun (3 times), or together with φίλη without a noun (3 times), or finally on its own (1 time); (2) The epithet αἰδοῖος is used in the formula φίλη τε καὶ αἰδοίη or inverted as αἰδοίη τε φίλη τε; (3) The epithet αἰδοῖος is also employed in the expression δεινή τε καὶ αἰδοίη or inverted in separation as αἰδοῖός τε... δεινός τε.

[9] See Kirk 1985:289.

family.[10] Moreover, this expression of emotion unfolds a poetic strategy characterizing Helen's language throughout the poem: she constantly indicates her preference for Priam and Hector, who are the only people in Troy that show her respect despite the pain and grief she causes the Trojan people. Formulaic reshaping gives a personal touch to the beginning of her speech, underscoring her apologetic tone, which will acquire a climactic self-abusive pitch by the end of her speech.[11]

The next verse begins[12] abruptly with a heavily charged phrase, ὡς ὄφελεν θάνατός μοι ἁδεῖν κακός, constituting a death wish,[13] which is the trademark of a special kind of speech in the *Iliad*, namely the γόοι or personal laments.[14] Helen employs the death wish in all of her three speeches in the *Iliad* (III 173; VI 345–347; XXIV 764), so it seems that this extreme form of self-blame is particular to her language and style. In order to explore the full depth of meanings inherent in a death wish, one has to consider first its function and significance as a type of self-reproach and opprobrium.

By uttering a death wish, a speaker postulates his or her own death expressing a level of anxiety and desperation that virtually annuls the very notion of existence, the primary precondition for the utterance of speech. The speaking "I" adopts a self-destructive stance, wishing for its own effacement from life and, by extension, for its own poetic death. Nagy,[15] drawing on the iconoclastic work of Dumézil[16] in the field of Indo-European studies and

---

[10] See Autenrieth 1984 s.v. It should be noted that Priam has just addressed her as φίλον τέκος (*Iliad* III 162). The whole verse δεῦρο πάροιθ' ἐλθοῦσα, φίλον τέκος, ἵζε' ἐμεῖο (*Iliad* III 162) expresses Priam's intimacy with Helen, who is treated like a guest. Sitting next to the host is also an act pertaining to a hospitality scene. This is one more paradox concerning this presumed xenia and the fact that Helen is a member of Priam's family. Priam and the elders of Troy see her as a guest, albeit a special and beloved one, but Helen constantly employs family terms as a new member of the old king's family. Mackie (1996:38n80) rightly claims that "[t]he Teikhoskopia itself has the atmosphere of an Odyssean visit" and that Helen "abducted by Paris, whether willingly or unwillingly, and the cause of all the trouble at Troy, preserves her dignity by assuming the manners of a guest when she sits among the elderly Trojan men." Mackie rightly argues that the formula ἀνείρεαι ἠδὲ μεταλλᾷς, which is an Iliadic hapax (attested 5 times in the *Odyssey*: i 231; vii 243; xv 390; xv 402; xix 171), is typical of guest scenes, when the host asks the guest about his identity, his origin, etc.

[11] See Worman 2001:21–22.

[12] Furthermore, by wishing that she had died not only does she establish a pattern of diction pointing to self-blame and self-reproach, but she also introduces a stereotypical way of speaking that refrains from answering other people's questions directly.

[13] For the death wish in Homeric speeches, see Lohmann 1970:96–97.

[14] See Tsagalis 2004:42–44. Worman 2001:24n32 points to the use of the ὤφελλον expression in taunts and verbal counts. The death wish constitutes a typical feature of the Iliadic γόοι.

[15] Nagy 1979:222–242.

[16] Dumézil 1943.

Chapter Six

of Detienne[17] in the area of Greek culture, has convincingly shown that the old Indo-European bipolarity between praise and blame is also at work in Homeric poetry, which confers praise and blame to various heroes. Keeping this observation in mind, one can see how Helen takes a paradoxical stance by constructing her fictive death by means of language. As a creature of speech, she blames herself while being, *ipso tempore*, immortalized through the medium of poetry.[18] In the phrase ὡς ὄφελεν θάνατος the word θάνατος is modified by κακός. This is not the only use of the adjective κακός with θάνατος,[19] but it is the only expression of a death wish accompanied by the nominative of a noun qualified by an adjective.[20] The use of the aorist infinitive ἀδεῖν in juxtaposition to the phrase θάνατος κακός creates an oxymoronic effect, since ἀδεῖν means to "please", to "delight", to "gratify."[21] In the *Iliad* ἀνδάνω is used with a negative particle (I 24 = I 378: ἀλλ' οὐκ Ἀτρείδῃ Ἀγαμέμνονι ἥνδανε θυμῷ and XV 674: οὐδ' ἄρ' ἔτ' Αἴαντι μεγαλήτορι ἥνδανε θυμῷ),[22] indicating that something is not pleasing to one's heart. By speaking of Helen's imagined death, the *Iliad* looks back at her picture and reads it anew.[23] For Helen is supposed to be the mythical paragon of beauty bringing pleasure when people look at her. Some verses earlier in the same Book of the *Iliad*, e. g. when the old Trojan men look at Helen, stress her beauty: αἰνῶς ἀθανάτῃσι θεῇς εἰς ὦπα ἔοικεν (*Iliad* III 158),[24] since she recalls in their minds the picture of Aphrodite, the

---

[17] Detienne 1973²:18–27.

[18] Helen seems to be well aware of her poetic immortality. See *Iliad* VI 357–358.

[19] The word θάνατος is attested 75 times in the *Iliad* (22 times in the nominative, 29 times in the genitive, 24 times in the accusative). It is accompanied only 19 times by an adjective (9 times in the nominative, 8 times in the genitive and 2 times in the accusative). Θάνατος is modified by δυσηχής (3 times in the genitive), θυμοραϊστής (3 times in the nominative), κακός (2 times in the nominative and 2 times in the accusative), καταθύμιος (2 times in the nominative), μέλας (3 times in the genitive), πορφύρεος (2 times in the nominative), τανηλεγής (2 times in the genitive).

[20] An unfulfilled wish is often expressed in Homer by the formula ὤφελ(λ)ον // ὄφελες(ν) + infinitive. There are 6 death wishes expressed by this pattern in the *Iliad*. Only in III 40 and in III 173 does a nominative accompany the infinitive and only in III 173 is the nominative of a noun employed (θάνατος). On the use of the ὤφελ(λ)ον // ὄφελες(ν) + infinitive, see Chantraine 1986–1988⁶ (1948–1953):228 (*GH* 2).

[21] *LSJ*⁹ s.v.

[22] The imperfect ἥνδανε is also used in *Iliad* XVIII 510 without a negative particle, but there it means "acceptable". Ἑαδότα (*Iliad* IX 173) and ἅδε (*Iliad* XII 80, XIII 748) are also accompanied by datives without a negation.

[23] This deviation from formulaic standards observed in Helen's language can be also traced in the use of δεῦρο in *Iliad* III 173 which, as Kirk 1985:290 notes, "occurs only here at the verse-end out of 22 Iliadic uses (and only 1/21x *Od*.)."

[24] There is a brilliant wordplay between (III 158: ἀθανάτῃσι) and (III 173: θάνατος) contrasting divine immortality to the mortality of Helen. This contrast is multileveled, for it points to an

Viewing from the Walls, Viewing Helen

divine paragon of beauty. And yet she who is the most beautiful woman in the world, who is famous for a concept regarded as ἀρετή and praised accordingly, she is destined to bring grief to both Greeks and Trojans. The phrase θάλαμον γνωτούς τε λιποῦσα brings forth further associations triggered by the abundant use of lament terminology and inspires a tone reminiscent of funerary epigrams.²⁵ The phraseology employed by Helen alludes to the description of someone who has passed away.²⁶ It recalls an epitaph dedicated to a woman who has left behind husband, family, daughter and friends.²⁷ CEG 486 strikes a similar note:

[ἥ]δ' ἔθανεν προλιπõσα πόσιν καὶ μητ[έρα κεδνήν] |
[κ]αὶ κλέος ἀθάνατον σωφροσύνης [μεγάλης].²⁸ |
᾿Αριστοκράτεια Κορινθία. υυυ(υ) Θεόφ[ιλος].

This woman here has died after leaving behind her husband,
    her holy mother,
and the immortal glory of great sophrosyne. Aristocrateia
    from Corinth.
Theophilus.

The participle προλιπõσα, like the Homeric λιποῦσα, is a marked term employed for leaving behind dear ones or something belonging to the cycle of life. λιποῦσα is attested only three more times in the entire poem (*Iliad* XVI 857, XXII 363, XXIV 144):

---

oblique, even sinister aspect of things, since Helen has been actually regarded as similar in shape and beauty to the immortal goddesses (III 158). The whole death wish acquires here an oxymoronic, not to say, ironic tone. See Constantinidou 1990:49, who correctly notes that ἄλγεα πάσχειν in *Iliad* III 157 and πῆμα in *Iliad* III 160 "suggest the destructive nature of the extraordinary beauty which is meaningfully developed in verses 159-160."

²⁵ See Elmer 2005:1-39, who has extensively argued that the two tristichs spoken by Helen (*Iliad* III 178-180 and *Iliad* III 200-202) correspond to a particular subclass of epigram. Under the scope of Helen's meta-traditional role in Homeric epic, these 'epigrams' become the Iliadic tradition's 'vehicle' for expressing "its relation to other poetic genres and to poetry in general" (2).

²⁶ Elmer 2005:1-39 building on the work of Vox 1975:67-70 argues for Helen's *epigrammatic teichoscopic* style. He rightly discerns the different function of Helen's tristich and Hector's distich epigrams (*Iliad* VI 460-461 and *Iliad* VII 89-90). The use of οὗτος in the former and ὅδε//ἥδε in the latter indicates, according to Elmer, that Helen's tristichs are a *caption*, a *Beischrift*, whose 'autonomy' consists in that "they do not require the prior formulation of a demand or request." For Homeric οὗτος, see especially Bakker 1999:1-19.

²⁷ For more examples supporting the claim that these two verses of her speech (*Iliad* III 174-175) recall funerary epigrams, see Peek 1955.

²⁸ Pircher 1979:22 rightly says that "*Der Hexameter diese künstlerisch kaum beachtlichen Gedichtes erwähnt, dass die Frau gestorben ist und ihren Gatten sowie ihre Mutter (?) zurückgelassen hat.*"

> ὣς ἄρα μιν εἰπόντα τέλος θανάτοιο κάλυψεν·
> ψυχὴ δ' ἐκ ῥεθέων πταμένη Ἄϊδόσδε βεβήκει,
> ὃν πότμον γοόωσα, λιποῦσ' ἀνδροτῆτα καὶ ἥβην.
>
> He spoke, and as he spoke the end of death closed in upon him,
> and the soul fluttering free of the limbs went down into Death's house
> mourning her destiny, leaving youth and manhood behind her.
>
> *Iliad* XVI 855-857 = *Iliad* XXII 361-363

> "βάσκ' ἴθι, Ἶρι ταχεῖα, λιποῦσ' ἕδος Οὐλύμποιο"
>
> "Go forth, Iris the swift, leaving your place on Olympos"
>
> *Iliad* XXIV 144

In the first two cases the participle λιποῦσα is used in reference to the departure of Patroclus' and Hector's souls to Hades, whereas in the third (*Iliad* XXIV 144), it takes a literal object (ἕδος). In Helen's speech (*Iliad* III 174) the participle λιποῦσα, used in reference to her own advent to Troy and placed at the hexameter's end, is deviating from its typical localization right after the trochaic caesura. Helen once more misuses an expression by shifting its position within the verse and changing its function. This localization shift is accompanied by a semantic one. By saying that she has left behind family and friends, Helen virtually implies that she has gone to Hades, that Troy is *mutatis mutandis* a metonymy for her figurative death.[29]

It seems that Helen, like Penelope in the *Odyssey*, ravels and unravels her own figurative web of past memories and present sufferings, employing lamentation terminology and family vocabulary in an intricate verbal game that makes her speech remain endlessly suspended and unfinished. By oscillating between two equally plausible representations,[30] which can be resumed in the latent polarization between θάνατος and θάλαμος, she introduces a key opposition in her speech. The semantic fields expressed by both θάνατος and θάλαμος are extensive, since both terms contain a large number of allusive

---

[29] See also Alcaeus fr. 283.7-8 (Voigt) and Sappho fr. 16.7-11 (Voigt), where it is clear that there is no metaphoric use of the expression λίποισα + accusative object. I do not think that this observation undermines the argument stated above because both Sappho and Alcaeus intend to present and explain Helen's abandonment of her family as a result of the power of love. On the other hand, in *Iliad* III 174 Helen does not refer or allude to her falling in love with Paris. This is done only later on, in the scene with Aphrodite, but even then a polemical tone emerges in her language as she blames the goddess of love for her present sufferings.

[30] On Penelope's metaphorical web in the *Odyssey*, see Papadopoulou-Belmehdi 1994:113-116.

references that shed their light upon the particular lexical use of the term. θάνατος is always masculine[31] and, like its divine representation (Θάνατος), does not incarnate a horrible power of destruction[32] so much as express a state, a condition beyond the grave, a point of no return. The *Iliad* is also familiar with the other side of death, the horrible Κήρ, expressing the inexorable, pitiless divinity that incarnates a radical alterity and brings destruction to mortals. In the 'Shield of Achilles' Κήρ is represented as "… holding either a warrior still alive, despite his recent wound, or another still not wounded, or another already dead whom she drags by her feet into the fighting while she is wearing a cloth on her shoulders, made red by human blood."[33] The death Helen wishes for is rather a point of no return and not a horrible end at the hands of furious, bloodthirsty deities.[34] This distinction is important for understanding the intricate nexus between θάνατος and θάλαμος. The opposition on which their polarization is based is an antithesis of different conditions of being and not being, not of contradicting powers. θάλαμος encompasses a semantic field that includes a nuptial dimension on two distinct but complementary levels (that of her marriage and of her bridal competition) and an erotic dimension. It alludes not only to Helen's nuptial chamber and conjugal status as Menelaus' wife, but also to her bridal competition, which will soon be repeated in front of her eyes in Troy.[35] The juxtaposition of these two terms bespeaks their interconnection. Once the θάλαμος of Helen and Menelaus is abandoned, Helen must die, albeit a pleasing death.

Her bridal competition[36] is a *heterodiegetic* event lying outside the Iliadic plot, since it has taken place long before even the beginning of the Trojan War. The *Iliad* would, by definition, exclude the commemoration of such an event. Instead, what happens before the audience's eyes is a second contest for Helen, this time between her two husbands, Menelaus (the legitimate) and Alexandros (the illegitimate). This second contest may have acquired an ironic tone since Helen is the wife of both men, but the *Iliad* does not seem to bother with the oxymoronic nature of the situation. Helen considers her marriage with Paris illegitimate and seems to inhabit two different worlds: that of her

---

[31] I am hereafter basing my approach to θάνατος on Vernant 1996:131–152.
[32] See Vernant 1996:132.
[33] See *Iliad* XVIII 536–538.
[34] See Hesiod *Shield* 248–257.
[35] It is tempting to see in θάλαμος an allusion to death, since this word also means death chamber. On the other hand, this meaning is nowhere attested in Homer. Its first attestation is in Aeschylus' *Persians* 624 in the phrase θαλάμους ὑπὸ γῆς (the realms below).
[36] For her bridal competition, see the *Catalogue of Women* frs. 196–204 (M.-W.).

Chapter Six

desire and that of reality. On the level of desire she would prefer not to have left her husband and family, in other words to have remained Menelaus' lawful wife, but on the level of reality she blames herself for having followed Paris to Troy. Her desire remains suspended and does not find its resolution within the *Iliad*.[37]

Helen's speech alludes, through the use of the word θάλαμος, to a second contest for Argive Helen, and the 'Teichoscopia' may in fact be seen as the preparation for a reenactment of the bridal competition for the most beautiful woman in the world.[38] This time, though, there is a funerary finality emerging from Helen's speech, a finality reinforced by the specific Iliadic context, since the competition may end with the death of one of the two contestants. What in the pre-Iliadic tradition was an event of happiness has acquired a death-inspiring tone in the *Iliad*. The marriage (θάλαμος) has been *intertextually* transformed into impending death (θάνατος).

Formulaic deviation from the standard norm is also at work in the case of ὁμηλικίην ἐρατεινήν. ὁμηλικίην is attested five times in the *Iliad* (III 175; V 326; XIII 431; XIII 485; XX 465), but is only accompanied here by an epithet.[39] ἐρατεινήν is employed thirteen times in the entire epic. It usually (nine times)[40] modifies a place-name in verse-terminal position, whereas it accompanies a simple noun like ὁμηλικίη, ἠνορέη, ἀμβροσίη only four times. In this light ὁμηλικίην ἐρατεινήν (III 175) is a new coin based on the combination of two paradigmatic formulas giving a unique color to Helen's language.[41] The interpretation of the specific semantics of this formulaic deviation coincides with my previous claim about the figurative death of Helen. Through pattern deixis, which springs from formulaic localization at a specific slot within the hexameter and from the context-specific use of the cluster ὁμηλικίην ἐρατεινήν,[42] it may be plausibly argued that this expression offers a glance

---

[37] See Maronitis 1995:60. Worman 2001:22 is right to argue that her self-abuse is due to her tactics of cementing a good relationship with her interlocutor (esp. Priam and Hector), even if she has to employ covert seduction.

[38] Clader 1976:9 points to the oddity of Helen in presenting the Achaean heroes to Priam. The author believes that Helen's "catalogue of the troops" represents her own bridal competition back in Sparta. On the reshaping of the 'Teichoscopia' as a traditional catalogue of warriors, see Edwards 1980:81–105.

[39] The case of *Iliad* V 326 is somewhat different.

[40] Modifying a place-name: *Iliad* II 571; II 591; II 607; III 239; III 401; III 443; V 210; XIV 226; XVIII 291. Without a place-name: *Iliad* III 175; VI 156; XIX 347; XIX 353.

[41] In (*Iliad* III 239) Helen uses the epithet ἐρατεινῆς according to its standard function, namely modifying the place-name Λακεδαίμονος.

[42] The expression refers, in all probability, to her pre-marriage life. See Theocritus' term θῆλυς νεολαία (18.24).

at Helen's allusive language. Helen's affinity with her age-group[43] recalls the endearment typical of one's fatherland[44] but also points to her paradoxical situation, which is covertly expressed by the fact that she has also left behind her daughter,[45] who is fully grown or was, rather, born long ago. The epithets τηλυγέτη and ἐρατεινή refer to the chronemics[46] of Helen's language, i.e. not simply to time, but to its manipulation and perception by the speaker, who makes both temporal distality (τηλυγέτην)[47] and proximity (ὁμηλικίη) operate in order to create a sorrowful tone reminiscent of funerary epigrams.[48] Helen's chronemics, based on the innovative combination of the paradigmatic formulas τηλυγέτη and ὁμηλικίην ἐρατεινήν, specify that her perception of time is not linear but rather circular and mixed, underscored by emotional factors.

Helen's painful memory of the past impels her to utter another illogical, but poetically efficient expression denoting the eradication of her past life: "it did not happen that way."[49] Helen's memory annuls the epic code and refuses the conferring of κλέος on her. Conversely, it becomes a constant source of grief, finally turning out to be self-destructive. Τά γ' οὐκ ἐγένοντο is a second, albeit disguised, death wish that Helen employs in an attempt to 'ease' the dark side of her past.

The introduction of an Iliadic *hapax legomenon* (κλαίουσα τέτηκα)[50] marks her language with a sorrowful tone expressed at the moment when the self-addressed part of her speech comes to its destined end. Whereas κλαίουσα is a typical lament term recurrent in funerary epigrams and abundantly employed

---

[43] See Edwards 1991:341: "This natural affinity within an age-group, perhaps arising from shared puberty-rites, is often stressed in Homer, e.g. at [*Iliad*] 3.175, 5.325-6, *Od.* 3.363-4, 6.23, 15.197, 22.209."

[44] The epithet ἐρατεινός, which is employed 4 times in *Iliad* III (175, 239, 401, 443) suggests "a memory of a lost peace and fatherland" as Scully 1990:134 correctly suggests. Scully quotes Bowra 1960:17 and Vivante 1982:121, who both underscore the emotional weight of the above epithet as well as its special application to cities. Thus, according to Scully 1990:133, it is "particularly suited to the Catalogue of Book 2 and its invocation of the Greek homeland (cf. 2.532, 571, 583, 591, 607)." Scully also offers some euphonic reasons explaining the use of this epithet (see 1990:203n6 and compare his point with mine concerning the use of the epithet in Helen's speech in the 'Teichoscopia' proper).

[45] See Kirk 1985:290 ad *Iliad* III 174-175.

[46] For the term 'chronemics' and its function in Homeric poetry, see Lateiner 1995:291-296.

[47] For τηλυγέτη in the *Odyssey*, see Kakridis 1971:49-53.

[48] Grave epigrams regularly employ time as a grief-producing device concerning the premature death of the deceased (ἄωρος θάνατος–*mors immatura*). See Griessmair 1966; Vérilhac 1978. The term τηλύγετος introduces the 'single-child' motif. See Sistakou 2001:247-248.

[49] Lattimore 1951:105.

[50] See Pucci 2003:107n24.

Chapter Six

in the formulas capping the Iliadic γόοι, τήκω is an Iliadic *hapax*.[51] Thus, the use of a marginal and rare lament expression brings the first part of her speech to its end.[52]

Helen and Achilles

A significant part of Helen's linguistic marginalization in the 'Teichoscopia' proper is founded upon the use and function of the metanastic term τηλύγετος.[53] Achilles is the κάλλιστος and ἄριστος among the Achaeans in the masculine form; Helen is the most beautiful and the best in the woman's form.[54] Both are marginal figures in the sense that they are secluded and excluded from the main action for the largest portion of the poem, Achilles in his hut and Helen within the walls of Troy. They both have partly divine parentage (Helen is the daughter of Zeus, Achilles the son of Thetis) and as Helen is the cause of the Trojan War, so Achilles is the cause of its destructive change against the Achaeans. Achilles' γόος for his dead friend Patroclus (*Iliad* XIX 315–337) and Helen's speech to Priam (*Iliad* III 172–180) share the same preoccupation with the past, since Achilles remembers his father and his son, and Helen recalls her γνωτούς and her daughter. Achilles' speech is more elaborate, imbued with what has been called the 'expansion aesthetic',[55] a tendency for the Iliadic tradition to expand and refine ideas and feelings when they are attributed to the best of the Achaeans. In this way the best warrior becomes the best speaker, as if the tradition of the *Iliad* has reserved for the poem's main hero the privilege to distinguish himself not only through his might and subsequent marginalization within the action, but also through the medium of speech, thus making his liminality warlike as well as poetic. Helen shares a similar poetic and dictional liminality, which does not find the overflowing outburst of sensitivity characterizing Achilles' diction, but distin-

---

[51] Conversely, in the *Odyssey* it is widely employed in lament contexts. See *Odyssey* v 396; viii 522; xi 200–201; xix 136; xix 204–209; xix 264.

[52] Notice the absence of the most current diction of lament in this speech: ὀδύρομαι, στεναχίζω, ἄλγος, κῆδος, ὀλοφύρομαι, etc. For lament terms, see Anastassiou 1971; Mawet 1979; Derderian 2001; Alexiou 2002²; Tsagalis 2004.

[53] See Martin 1992:11–33; Tsagalis 2006:112–113.

[54] Austin 1994:27n5 argues that κάλλιστος and ἄριστος are synonymous in Homer and brings as evidence *Iliad* III 124, where Iris in the form of Laodike is described as εἶδος ἀρίστη ('best in physical form'). For some early non-Homeric references to Helen's beauty, see the Hesiodic *Catalogue of Women* frs. 196–204 (M.-W.); *Ilias Parva* (PEG 1, fr. 19 = EGF fr. 19); Herodotus VI 61; Ibycus S 151.5-7 (*PMGF*); Stesichorus 201 (*PMGF*).

[55] Martin 1989:206–230.

guishes itself by its abruptness of tone, its wavering hesitancy between past and present, its family-oriented wording, and, finally, its blameful self-referentiality. From this perspective, I am inclined to adopt a figurative reading of *Iliad* XIX 324-325, where Achilles uses such an emotionally weighty phrase: ... ὃ δ' ἀλλοδαπῷ ἐνὶ δήμῳ // εἵνεκα ῥιγεδανῆς Ἑλένης Τρωσὶν πολεμίζω. Helen is ῥιγεδανή (shrilling/bringing ῥῖγος) both dictionally and poetically.[56] Achilles presents himself as being in a foreign land (ἀλλοδαπῷ ἐνὶ δήμῳ), where the horror of a woman has made him fight an endless war. Likewise, he and Helen painfully realize that they are exiled in a foreign country literally and figuratively alike, both in plot and in diction.

The metanastic poetics[57] of the *Iliad* are centered on Achilles and his pedigree: both Phoenix (IX 478-482) and Patroclus (XXIII 89-90) were μετανάσται, gracefully welcome by Achilles' father, Peleus, in his palace in Phthia. Odysseus (IX 285) employs the term τηλύγετος 'growing son', when referring to Orestes, "who is brought up there in abundant luxury"[58] (ὅς οἱ τηλύγετος τρέφεται θαλίῃ ἔνι πολλῇ).[59] The same term (καί μ' ἐφίλησ', ὡς εἴ τε πατὴρ ὃν παῖδα φιλήσῃ // μοῦνον τηλύγετον πολλοῖσιν ἐπὶ κτεάτεσσι)[60] is used by Phoenix later on (*Iliad* IX 481-482), when he speaks of being raised by Peleus. The use of these metanastic politics is a rhetorical means for convincing Achilles to become Agamemnon's adopted son, cherished equally beside his true son, Orestes, and married to one of his beloved daughters (IX 283-289). Mackie,[61] drawing on the status and function of μετανάστης in Hesiodic poetry, examines the threats imposed on Achilles by μετανάσται such as Phoenix and Patroclus. She concludes that Achilles uses Hesiodic language to aim at various targets, the most important of which is "to question the very ideology of heroic epic."[62]

The metanastic politics of Helen, like those of Achilles, are based on the perception and symbolic function of the key epithet τηλύγετος. In the case of Orestes,[63] τηλύγετος was used by Odysseus with an aristocratic coloring[64] and a caring tone. Conversely, Achilles, determined not to accept Agamemnon's proposal, will not become an adopted son, like Phoenix or Patroclus, because

---

[56] See Helen's own words in *Iliad* XXIV 775: ... πάντες δέ με πεφρίκασιν.
[57] For the term metanastic poetics I am indebted to Martin 1992:11-33.
[58] Lattimore 1951:205.
[59] Mackie 1996:147.
[60] *Iliad* IX 481-482.
[61] Mackie 1996:148-152.
[62] Mackie 1996:151.
[63] For a detailed discussion of the figure of Phoenix in the *Iliad*, see Voskos 1974:47-69.
[64] Mackie 1996:147n77.

his metanastic hermeneutics are of a different kind, figurative rather than literal. In the same way, Helen's world is that of a μετανάστης.[65] She employs the marked term τηλύγετος, which has almost acquired a metonymic force, in order to point to her adopting the stance of a foreigner and a stranger in her new home in Troy.

This approach revolutionizes the very foundations of the traditional dilemma of Helen's innocence or guilt. She refuses to abide by the epic rules and thus agree to pigeonhole herself in Iliadic or Odyssean nomenclature, despite the general assumption that the *Iliad* depicts her as guilty, since she is presented as having deliberately followed Paris to Troy, whereas the *Odyssey* promotes her innocence. This taxonomical dichotomy reflects a canonistic model made up by scholars who are willing to see a correspondence between a tradition and the representation of a character. The innate linearity of this approach aims at accounting for the evolution of a poetic persona, but considerably fails to dovetail with the sort of synchronic multifariousness of which epic poetry is so fond. By employing the term τηλυγέτην Helen objects to her classification and expresses her negation of the role of Menelaus' good wife back in Sparta. The memory of the past discloses the deliberate paradox Helen herself ingenuously concocts, a paradox revealing her foreignness, both literally and metaphorically, to the world of the *Iliad*.

In this foreign, hostile world, both Achilles and Helen are isolated and liminal, since they oscillate between life and death, past and present. And if in the case of Achilles this marginalization has been turned by the Iliadic tradition into a dictional over-expressiveness,[66] then in the case of Helen it has been shifted into what I would like to call *the oscillation principle*, a tendency of her language to become aberrant and idiosyncratic, thus mirroring her 'resistance' to any effort to categorize. The *oscillation principle* is best observable in the way Helen uses diction belonging to different genres of speaking in order to remain marginal and elusive as a poetic persona.

Genre-Mixing

The second part of her speech begins with an Odyssean formula used as a reply pattern[67] (*Iliad* III 177: τοῦτο δέ τοι ἐρέω, ὅ μ' ἀνείρεαι ἠδὲ μεταλλᾷς),

---

[65] See Mackie 1996:38n80. The picture now becomes clearer. Helen is not simply a guest but a stranger (*xenos*), who has come to stay permanently in Troy. See also Martin 1992:11–33.

[66] I am referring to the well-known 'expansion aesthetic' that characterizes the language of Achilles. See Martin 1989:166–205.

[67] Higbie 1995:73 has shown that the naming pattern embedded in typical scenes like the *xenia* in

which should cue the following verses for the Homeric audience on a tone recurring in Odyssean *xenia*-scenes.[68] Surprisingly enough, the description of Agamemnon that follows in the next two verses is carried out in Iliadic terms, with a typical naming formula occupying the first verse and a new coin referring to his majestic grandeur in the second.

The whole part of this second verse describing Agamemnon stands in apposition to his name and modifies it through its chiastic order (*Iliad* III 179):

βασιλεύς τ' ἀγαθός
κρατερός τ' αἰχμητής

The noun-adjective/adjective-noun construction implies a strong parallelism but also alludes to a contrast, which has—after Book I—become a *locus communis* in the *Iliad*: Agamemnon is a great king but not such a great warrior, despite his future Iliadic *aristeia*. In this way, Helen looks back to the quarrel between Achilles and Agamemnon in *Iliad* I, engaging the audience to recall what had happened. Given that Helen describes Agamemnon in this way because she is ignorant of his quarrel with Achilles and has in mind the picture of Agamemnon that she knew before the war, it becomes clear how attached to the past she is, even when speaking about the present. These observations become all the more important, as they have been introduced by a truth-telling formula: τοῦτο δέ τοι ἐρέω, ὅ μ' ἀνείρεαι ἠδὲ μεταλλᾷς. Not only does Helen present Agamemnon in a manner that recasts the events of *Iliad* I, but she also corroborates her presentation as if she were a guest replying truthfully to the questions of her host.

The 'Teichoscopia' proper does indeed contain elements that pertain to the *xenia*-scenes of the *Odyssey* and, perhaps, to the *xenia* of Helen's suitors in the Hesiodic *Catalogue of Women*. On the other hand, the use of a *xenia*-formula (τοῦτο δέ τοι ἐρέω, ὅ μ' ἀνείρεαι ἠδὲ μεταλλᾷς) creates a subtle interplay between the disguised language of Helen and the potential tuning of her speech on an Odyssean note. This intertextual misdirection remains only an unexploited possibility.[69] On the contrary, the description of Agamemnon in Iliadic terms brings to the surface the intertextual play between the *Iliad* and the *Odyssey*. Iliadic Helen winks at her Odyssean self, who in *Odyssey* iv is also

---

the *Odyssey* contains–among other formulas–both τοῦτο δέ τοι ἐρέω, ὅ μ' ἀνείρεαι ἠδὲ μεταλλᾷς and the more flexible formula νημερτ- + ἐννέπω // εἶπον employed by Helen and Antenor, respectively. For Odyssean overtones in Helen's language in *Iliad* VI, see Kirk 1990:206.

[68] Higbie 1995:85–86.
[69] On intertextual and intratextual misdirection, see Rengakos 2006:77–82 and 82–83, respectively.

Chapter Six

ready to talk about the Greek heroes in Troy. Was Helen particularly linked to catalogues in epic poetry, as the Hesiodic 'Helen-Section' may imply? And if so, is Helen's 'poetic authority' for recounting the past indicating that she assumes the role of a bard or singer (ἀοιδός)?[70]

The term κυνώπιδος (*Iliad* III 180) points to the language of self-abuse,[71] making Iliadic Helen special among the rest of the poem's characters in that she is "the only character in the Homeric poems to engage in self-abuse; no one else turns such barbs against themselves."[72] Dog epithets, often used as flyting tools, are employed in the verbal dueling that recurs in epic poetry. Verbal dueling in the *Iliad* has become a highly conventionalized process, mainly between males,[73] suiting a need for triumph and self-confirmation felt particularly within a male-dominated warrior society. Helen's language thus imitates "the aggressive challenge of the hero in the battlefield"[74] and transfers her to an intermediate state of being, since she oscillates between male and female. As a female, Helen obviously cannot take part in the fighting. Heroic flyting is for her, by definition, only verbal, not martial. Yet her venomous auto-referential insults reveal the shared speech patterns she is capable of using in accordance with the larger frame of the *Iliad* (dogs, linked to Hades, are a metaphor for death).

Furthermore, Helen's dog language may have generic affiliations alluding to other competitive versions of the Trojan War that present her negatively. Graver[75] supposes the negative portrayals of Helen to have figured in the ancient kitharodic narrative and that her (Helen's) representation in Homeric epic reflects a defaming tradition, of which the *Iliad* is aware but tries to erase. It is likely that in *Iliad* VI 357–358 Helen is referring to this tradition precisely. Thus, dog language functions also on a meta-traditional level, since it marks the *Iliad's* preference for a different treatment of Helen on purely generic terms.

---

[70] See *Odyssey* iv 278–279. In addition, in *Iliad* VI 358 Helen says that she and Paris will be the subject of future songs for mankind. See Kirk 1990:207 ad loc.

[71] Nagy 1979:226 convincingly argues that "the language of praise poetry presents the language of unjustified blame as parallel to the eating of heroes' corpses by dogs. Significantly, the language of epic itself quotes the language of blame within the framework of narrative quarrels (cf. I 159 = κυνῶπα) and a prominent word of insult within such direct quotations is κύων 'dog' and its derivatives." See also Faust 1970:8–31, who examines the function of κύων in Homer according to the kind of text it belongs to. In narrative, dogs are presented as hunters, watchdogs or pets, in the similes as hunters and in the speeches (as well as the proem) as carrion-eaters. See also Vodoklys 1992:20–21.

[72] Worman 2001:21.

[73] Parks 1990:12–13.

[74] Worman 2001:26.

[75] Graver 1995:41–61.

Viewing from the Walls, Viewing Helen

The sophisticated interplay between male and female language adopted by Helen acquires new dimensions, referring not only to gender but also to nationality. The idea of Trojan effeminacy is not new. Mackie has argued that the Iliadic tradition feminizes Troy and the Trojans.[76] Nagler[77] has claimed that the rape of Troy is personified by the gestures of Hecuba (*Iliad* XXII 405–407) and Andromache (*Iliad* XXII 468–470). Rabel[78] has also maintained that the female's rape by the male is transferred to both an image of youths and maidens depicted on Achilles' shield and to the pursuit of Hector by Achillles in *Iliad* XXII.

Helen's language is double-bound, mirroring her effort to assimilate herself with the community, but to retain her independence at the same time. The radical instability of her diction, fluctuating between praise for Hector and Priam and self-blame, mimics the languages of both Greeks and Trojans in the *Iliad*. She adopts a defensive, Trojan-like stance for those she holds dear, but an aggressive, Greek-like stance towards herself, refusing to abide by the epic rules and hinting at her idiosyncratic disavowal of any effort of classification.

In this way, she avoids the dilemma of choosing sides and oscillates between not only the Achaean and Trojan communities, but also between male and female characteristics. By employing the language of blame with an auto-referential tone, Helen shifts nationality and gender at the same time: nationality because the language of νεῖκος is akin to the aggressive Achaean style, and gender because it is particular to the male warrior society.

Equally enigmatic is the expression εἴ ποτ' ἔην γε filling the terminal adonic after Helen's self abuse. This expression is used in both the *Iliad* and *Odyssey* and "regularly refers to irretrievable and irreparable loss, and most often that associated with death."[79] Referring to lost happiness, the above formula constitutes a liminal phrase resounding the blurred voice of Helen, whose life fluctuates between reality and imagination, thus making the 'Teichoscopia' an indeterminate, ambiguous account whose truthfulness and validity are put into doubt by its own internal narrator.[80] One can hardly find a more appropriate way for an ambiguous figure like Helen to bring her speech to a halt. Elusiveness of language becomes a key term for her postponed and incomplete utterance, which introduces her personal outlook at the world

---

[76] Mackie 1996:80.
[77] Nagler 1974:53–54. I owe this reference to Mackie 1996:80.
[78] Rabel 1989:90. I owe this reference to Mackie 1996:80.
[79] Katz 1991:142. The same formula is used by Nestor (*Iliad* XI 762), Priam (*Iliad* XXIV 426), Telemachus (*Odyssey* xv 268), Penelope (*Odyssey* xix 315), and Laertes (*Odyssey* xxiv 289).
[80] Helen's account in the 'Teichoscopia' is by no means complete. See Lynn-George 1988:33.

Chapter Six

of heroes (i.e. the world of the *Iliad*), while underscoring "that incomprehensible contradiction between memory and non-existence"[81] that speaks for her displacement within the *Iliad* itself.

The Silent Voice

After Agamemnon, it is Odysseus' turn to be described by Helen (*Iliad* III 199–202):

> τὸν δ' ἠμείβετ' ἔπειθ' Ἑλένη Διὸς ἐκγεγαυῖα·
> "<u>οὗτος δ'</u> // <u>αὖ</u> // <u>Λαερτιάδης</u> // <u>πολύμητις Ὀδυσσεύς</u>,
> <u>ὃς τράφεν</u> // <u>ἐν δήμῳ Ἰθάκης</u> // <u>κραναῆς</u> // περ ἐούσης,
> <u>εἰδὼς</u> // παντοίους τε // <u>δόλους</u> // <u>καὶ μήδεα πυκνά</u>."

Helen, the daughter descended of Zeus, spoke then in answer:
"This one is Laertes' son, resourceful Odysseus,
who grew up in the country, rough though it be, of Ithaka,
to know every manner of shiftiness and crafty counsels."

Helen's answer strikes with its laconic style. Her dictional thrift is at once opposed to Antenor's eloquence, who both describes in detail Menelaus[82] and Odysseus (III 204–224) and elaborates on the presentation of the king of Ithaca. The basic question concerns Helen's inability to talk minutely about Odysseus, a problem that the tradition solves by giving Antenor, one of the Trojan elders, the opportunity to fill the gap. A close look at Helen's answer speaks for the formularity[83] of her response, since these verses of "compressed biography and characterization"[84] are opposed to the rarity of giving Odysseus' patronymic in a case other than the vocative in the *Iliad*.[85]

---

[81] Lynn-George 1988:37.

[82] By giving Antenor the opportunity to talk in detail about Odysseus, the *Iliad* avoids an important 'technical' obstacle, namely making Helen talk about Menelaus (who is of course her first husband and ready to fight Paris in a duel in *Iliad* III). Thus, both Odysseus and Menelaus are well presented in the 'Teichoscopia' despite Helen's inability to talk about them in detail (Odysseus) or at all (Menelaus).

[83] Kirk 1990:293 ad loc. convincingly argues for the formularity of verses 201–202, the former being paralleled in the *Odyssey* and the latter "being an ad hoc amalgam of formular elements elaborating his [Odysseus'] description as πολύμητις" (294).

[84] Kirk 1990:293.

[85] Higbie 1995:106n36. The uneconomical speech introductions of *Iliad* III 171, 199 and 228 (all in the 'Teichoscopia') have been observed by Edwards 1969:81–87. Edwards thinks this is due to variation but Kirk 1990:293 explains the matter as a "rather tiresome departure, not perhaps to be imitated or repeated, from an established formular rhythm."

Viewing from the Walls, Viewing Helen

Helen and Odysseus constantly engage themselves in disguise, verbal and literal alike. These two paragonal beguilers met within Troy when Odysseus attempted to steel the Palladium (*Odyssey* iv 240-264). Helen recognized Odysseus, though did not betray him to the Trojans. Something similar happens when she mimics the voices of the wives of those Achaeans hidden within the Trojan Horse (*Odyssey* iv 278-279).[86] Odysseus is the one who recognizes her and advises his companions not to fall in her trap. Both Helen and Odysseus are paired as clever, eloquent, and verbally exceptional figures, each a match for the other.[87] They could very well have been rivals, but both the *Iliad* and the *Odyssey* make potential rivalry a congenial analogy, as both Helen and Odysseus are able to recognize and destroy each other (in the Palladium story and the Wooden Horse) but turn this dormant enmity into a silent, mutual understanding, as if sharing some special code akin only to themselves.[88]

Helen and Odysseus, just like Helen and Achilles, are mutually exclusive. There is no single scene in which they can be together. When it comes to Helen to describe Odysseus, she does so in a brief, laconic manner that is highly formulaic and colored with Odyssean formulas. This description, in opposition to Helen's first speech, employs paradigmatic and syntagmatic formulas in equal numbers, showing that she is not so innovative as before and relies more on the repeated phrase. Helen is incapable of developing her own language for Odysseus and follows the more secure, yet less creative solution of using the ready-made formulas. She is unable to describe Odysseus in detail because

---

[86] Kakridis 1971:47 plausibly argues that the poet of the *Odyssey* imagines Helen calling each Achaean warrior hiding in the Trojan Horse in his local dialect. He also calls attention to the fact that the virgins in Delos (*Homeric Hymn to Apollo* [3] 156-164) were known to have mimicked the voices of pilgrims. For Helen's 'polyphonic ability', see Martin's article "Synchronic Aspects of Homeric Performance: The Evidence of the *Hymn to Apollo*," *Proceedings of the First International Conference on Hellenism at the End of the Millennium*, LaPlata, Argentina. I owe this reference to Martin 2001:56n5.

[87] Worman 2001:34.

[88] The *locus classicus* for Helen's mimic ability is of course *Odyssey* iv 278-279, as Worman 2001:21 rightly suggests. I would like to argue that her extraordinary powers of mimicry are not only literal but also figurative. In the 'Teichoscopia', Helen describes certain Achaean heroes by using language that corresponds to her own perception of each of them. It is no coincidence that the two heroes (Menelaus and Odysseus) whom Antenor describes in detail are the ones (together with Diomedes) who are inside the Trojan Horse, when Helen mimics the voices of the wives of the Achaeans (*Odyssey* iv 278-279). Menelaus in *Odyssey* iv 266-289. frames his own tale in a way similar to the one Helen has just used. Ford 1992:72-74 and Worman 2001:33 emphasize the importance of the analogy between *Iliad* II 488 and *Odyssey* iv 240 attributing to Helen the authority of both Menelaus and the poet. Menelaus adopts a similar strategy attempting to invigorate his own story. All three characters (Helen, Menelaus and the absent Odysseus) share a preoccupation with speech either in epic tradition in general (Helen and Odysseus) or in the specific scene (Menelaus).

Chapter Six

he is the hero of speech par excellence, and so she has no language to rival him. She withdraws when the gifted speaker comes to mind, borrowing the tradition's voice to simply mention his name, his place of origin, and his well-known epic qualities. Antenor is then summoned by the *Iliad* to do what Helen herself cannot, namely to state, albeit indirectly, that Odysseus excels above other heroes with respect to his outstanding verbal ability (III 221-224):

> ἀλλ' ὅτε δὴ ὄπα τε μεγάλην ἐκ στήθεος εἵη
> καὶ ἔπεα νιφάδεσσιν ἐοικότα χειμερίῃσιν,
> οὐκ ἂν ἔπειτ' Ὀδυσῆΐ γ' ἐρίσσειε βροτὸς ἄλλος.
> οὐ τότε γ' ὧδ' Ὀδυσῆος ἀγασσάμεθ' εἶδος ἰδόντες.

> But when he let the great voice go from his chest, and the words came
> drifting down like the winter snows, then no other mortal
> man beside could stand up against Odysseus. Then we
> wondered less beholding Odysseus' outward appearance.

Intratextual and Intertextual Helen

Helen's third reply to Priam's question is, like the first, a long one (III 228-242):

> τὸν δ' Ἑλένη τανύπεπλος ἀμείβετο δῖα γυναικῶν·
> "<u>οὗτος δ'</u> // <u>Αἴας</u> // ἐστὶ // <u>πελώριος, ἕρκος Ἀχαιῶν.</u>
> <u>Ἰδομενεὺς</u> // <u>δ' ἑτέρωθεν</u> // <u>ἐνὶ Κρήτεσσι θεὸς ὣς</u>
> <u>ἕστηκ'</u>, // <u>ἀμφὶ δέ μιν</u> // <u>Κρητῶν ἀγοὶ</u> // <u>ἠγερέθονται.</u>
> <u>πολλάκι</u> // μιν // <u>ξείνισσεν</u> // <u>ἀρηΐφιλος Μενέλαος</u>
> <u>οἴκῳ ἐν ἡμετέρῳ,</u> // <u>ὁπότε</u> // <u>Κρήτηθεν</u> // <u>ἵκοιτο.</u>
> <u>νῦν δ'</u> // <u>ἄλλους μὲν πάντας</u> // <u>ὁρῶ</u> // <u>ἑλίκωπας Ἀχαιούς,</u>
> <u>οὕς</u> // <u>κεν ἐῢ</u> // <u>γνοίην</u> // <u>καί τ'</u> // <u>οὔνομα</u> // <u>μυθησαίμην,</u>
> <u>δοιὼ δ'</u> // <u>οὐ δύναμαι ἰδέειν</u> // <u>κοσμήτορε λαῶν,</u>
> Κάστορά θ' ἱππόδαμον καὶ πὺξ ἀγαθὸν Πολυδεύκεα,
> αὐτοκασιγνήτω, // <u>τώ μοι μία γείνατο μήτηρ.</u>
> ἢ' οὐκ ἐσπέσθην // <u>Λακεδαίμονος ἐξ ἐρατεινῆς,</u>
> ἢ // <u>δεῦρω</u> // μὲν // <u>ἕποντο</u> // <u>νέεσσ' ἔνι ποντοπόροισιν,</u>
> <u>νῦν αὖτ'</u> // <u>οὐκ ἐθέλουσι</u> // <u>μάχην</u> // <u>καταδύμεναι</u> // <u>ἀνδρῶν,</u>
> <u>αἴσχεα</u> // <u>δειδιότες</u> // καὶ // <u>ὀνείδεα</u> // <u>πόλλ'</u> // ἅ μοί ἐστιν."

> Helen with the light robes and shining among women answered him:
> "That one is gigantic Aias, wall of the Achaians,

and beyond him there is Idomeneus like a god standing
among the Kretans, and the lords of Krete are gathered about
him.
Many a time warlike Menelaos would entertain him
in our house when he came over from Krete. And I see them
all now, all the rest of the glancing-eyed Achaians,
all whom I would know well by sight, whose names I could tell
you,
yet nowhere can I see those two, the marshals of the people,
Kastor, breaker of horses, and the strong boxer, Polydeukes,
my own brothers, born with me of a single mother.
Perhaps these came not with the rest from Lakedaimon the
lovely,
or else they did come here in their sea-wandering ships, yet
now they are reluctant to go with the men into battle
dreading the words of shame and all the reproach that is on
me."

Helen's reply is virtually completed in the very first verse of her speech with the description of Ajax (*Iliad* III 229). The mention of Idomeneus, who stands nearby, is merely a pretext for what might seem to the eyes of a conservative critic an unnecessary autobiographical addition with no bearing on the situation. A closer look, though, shows that the reference to Idomeneus transfers Helen's thoughts back to Sparta, when she recalls that Menelaus had often offered hospitality to Idomeneus in their palace at home.

The *xenia*-scene relic plays a prominent role, since it gives Helen the opportunity to refer to Menelaus, who is presented in his typical Iliadic verbal vestiture, that of a great warrior. Helen ingeniously picks up ἀρηΐφιλος, just used by Antenor, (III 206: ... σὺν ἀρηϊφίλῳ Μενελάῳ) only to mimic his language:

... σὺν ἀρηϊφίλῳ Μενελάῳ· // τοὺς δ' ἐγὼ ἐξείνισσα καὶ ἐν μεγάροισι φίλησα,
Antenor: III 206–207

πολλάκι μιν ξείνισσεν ἀρηΐφιλος Μενέλαος // οἴκῳ ἐν ἡμετέρῳ ...
Helen: III 232–233

There are further examples corroborating the idea of a response or rather an echo coming from Antenor's previous speech:

> ἤδη γὰρ καὶ δεῦρό ποτ' ἤλυθε δῖος Ὀδυσσεύς (205)
> ἀλλ' ὅτε δὴ Τρώεσσιν ἐν ἀγρομένοισιν ἔμιχθεν (209)
> στάντων (210)
> στάσκεν (217)
>
> Antenor: III 205, 209
>
> ἔστηκ', ἀμφὶ δέ μιν Κρητῶν ἀγοὶ ἠγερέθονται (231)
> ... ὁπότε Κρήτηθεν ἵκοιτο (233)
>
> Helen: III 231, 233

These textual analogies are a clear sign of intratextual mirroring between Antenor's and Helen's speeches.[89] But since Helen speaks after Antenor and not vice versa, only her speech can implicitly allude to the preceding one. This may even hint at an indirect reply, because Helen skillfully uses the language of *xenia* to reshape and reformulate her past life. She consistently attempts to redefine her image by insisting on presenting her past in her own terms. In this way, she fosters the stance of the external narrator, as if she were rivaling a competitive song tradition that was fond of disparaging her through a negative portrayal.[90]

The blissful past, exactly as in her initial reply to Priam, is counterbalanced by a painful present to which she decides to return abruptly (νῦν δ'). The sudden change from paradigmatic formulas (which she employed when referring to Ajax and Idomeneus: III 230–231) to syntagmatic (when recalling her two brothers: III 236–239) mirrors her emotional shift. She uses the ready-made phrase to bring to the narrative surface those heroes she herself, not Priam, chooses to mention. But as the names of Castor and Polydeuces become a pretext for her divulging "the nemesis that others do not and cannot speak",[91] she resorts to paradigmatic formulas (III 240–242), showing her laborious effort to find the right words that can express her shame.

Helen has been watching a spectacle organized and performed for her sake,[92] but at the same time questions its validity, its very *raison d' être*. The typical blame vocabulary (αἴσχεα - ὀνείδεα: III 242) that she employs should not be simply taken at face value. By accusing and condemning herself, the cause and end of the war, as well as spectacle and viewer during the 'Teichoscopia', Helen generates a meta-traditional effect.

---

[89] 'Mirroring', 'framing', 'juxtaposition', and '*mise en abyme*' form the main intratextual associations. For intratextuality, see Sharrock and Morales 2000, and in particular Martin's contribution 2000:43–65.
[90] Graver 1995:59.
[91] Ebbott 1999:15.
[92] Austin 1994:48.

Viewing from the Walls, Viewing Helen

This last observation is of profound importance for understanding the level of self-knowledge that epic poetry exemplifies. The dazzling question after the 'Teichoscopia' concerns the value inherent in listening to a song tradition that deals with the struggle of two armies for the possession of a woman (Helen) who is the symbol of blame. The Iliadic tradition thus questions the very ontogeny of its subject matter and, by extension, of the genre it belongs to. Skillfully enough, there is a way out of the impasse. As only Helen can blame Helen,[93] so only is the *Iliad* allowed to question its own validity.[94]

By referring to her brothers (III 236–242), Helen connects the end of the 'Teichoscopia' to its beginning (III 144) and opens a window to intertextual[95] associations, which conjure up other competitive song-traditions.[96] The *Iliad* offers a hint of the variation of the 'Theseus as an abductor of Helen' story,[97] but keeps this version marginalized. Helen is looking for her own brothers to "save herself from the ignominy of epic,"[98] from the position she has placed herself in the *Iliad*.[99] These variants remain a possibility of which the Iliadic tradition is well aware, but which it carefully downplays. At the end of the scene, the external narrator caps Helen's words by putting an end to her vain effort to escape via another tradition: her brothers are dead in their fatherland (III 244).

The effect of such interplay is remarkable. Helen's language picks up the poet's vague reference to Aithra (III 144) and links it to her brothers. Through this allusive hint to a possible para-narrative[100] inextricably linked with the role Helen plays in the 'Teichoscopia' as an evaluating factor of epic poetry, a meta-traditional comment is being shored up. In the Catalogue of Ships in *Iliad* II, peoples and cities are localized and placed within the specific taxonomy of

---

[93] Achilles is a marginal exception (see *Iliad* XIX 325) even if we regard this term as derogatory.

[94] Collins 1988:57 has neatly put it: "... only Helen can blame Helen without exposing the paradox that the poem wishes to remain hidden, that the very act which necessitates a war over her also condemns her from the poem's point of view, and renders her an unworthy object of struggle."

[95] For intertextuality, see Pucci 1987.

[96] See Jenkins 1999:220n33, who writes that "Helen can be seen as a poetess in her own right, singing her own catalogue of warriors ... For the space of the *teikhoskopia*, Helen *is* a singer, responding to the audience of Priam."

[97] Herodotus IX 73; Apollodorus *Library* III 107, *Epitome* I 23. According to the scholia vetera on *Iliad* III 242 (Erbse) there was a version by the poet Alcman in which Theseus had abducted Helen. Euphorion of Chalkis and Alexander of Pleuron recited also this tale. See Jenkins 1999:209n5.

[98] Jenkins 1999:220. See also Austin 1994:48.

[99] See Stesichorus fr. 192 (*PMGF*); Pausanias III 19.11.

[100] For para-narratives in the *Iliad*, see Alden 2000.

Chapter Six

epic memory.[101] In the Hesiodic *Catalogue of Women*, the 'Helen-Section' (frs. 196-204 [M.-W.]) represents an expanded form of an initial episode of the Trojan myth, featuring Helen as the protagonist. In contrast to these aforementioned cases, Helen's 'Catalogue of Heroes' in *Iliad* III, which constitutes a brief reenactment of the beginning of the whole Trojan myth, is abruptly cut short by Helen's "ignorance of the mortal fate of those most clearly related to her, now most remote to her."[102]

This disturbing coda decreases the *authority* of Helen's speech, since the external narrator decides to take the floor again and put an end to the 'Teichoscopia'. It is time for Helen, the dictional outsider, the multi-faceted *female* poet-figure,[103] the 'poetic immigrant' of the *Iliad*, to recede into the background now that her role has been completed. After all, the epic's goal has been fulfilled: the 'Viewing from the Walls' has become a 'Viewing of Helen' and, through this beguiling and vague figure, a self-conscious view to the genre of epic poetry.

---

[101] For the resources of memory used by the Homeric poet to weave his tales, see Minchin 2001b; for the performance of lists and catalogues, see Minchin 2001b:73-99.
[102] Lynn-George 1988:33.
[103] See Elmer 2005:1-39, who rightly accentuates Helen's gender-based self-referentiality. On the other hand, I would prefer to interpret the fact that Helen produces a 'Catalogue of Warriors' instead of a straightforward epic *diegesis* as the result of the epic's refusal to put internally presented female singers on a par with their male counterparts. *Mutatis mutandis*, the same is the case with professional singers of lament as opposed to the next of kin, whose dirges are verbalized by the Iliadic tradition. See Tsagalis 2004:2-8.

7

Time Games: The 'Twenty-Year' Absent Hero

Introduction

GENETIC APPROACHES TO HOMERIC POETRY, whether they are Analytical, Unitarian, Neoanalytical, or adopting the viewpoint of historical positivism, have used repetition in different but often misleading ways. Analysts viewed repetition as a symptom of inferior poetic quality, a clear sign indicating multiple authorship. Unitarians tried to explain such repetitions by drawing analogous examples from other writers in whose case single authorship was uncontested, thus showing that repetition must not be necessarily linked to poetic inferiority nor should it be considered as a hint for suspecting the authenticity of a given passage. Neoanalysis attempted to trace the origins of such repetitions in earlier, pre-Homeric epics whose reflections can be still seen in the Homeric poems.[1] As such epics do not survive nor is there any information proving that they antedated the *Iliad* and the *Odyssey*, Neoanalysis had to reconstruct them on the basis of information found in the Homeric epics—in artistic representations of epic themes, in other poems of the Epic Cycle, and, at times, in later sources. Historical positivism adopted a different stance, which can be partly explained by the storming predominance of oral-traditional studies. As oral theory was gaining support, some scholars fostered its principal tenets, but not the necessary consequences stemming from such beliefs. Notwithstanding the serious implications of the Parry-Lord theory for studying epic songs in an oral culture, historical positivists explained certain oral features either as the result of a primitive form of style or as the proof for the existence of a master composer. Historical determinism had thus equated the old, analyst notion of *poetic quality* with the dogma of

---

[1] On Neoanalysis, see Kakridis 1949, 1971; Kullmann 1960, 1992; Pestalozzi 1945; Schadewaldt 1965[4], 1966[4]. Willcock 1996:174–189 is the most recent account of the impact of the Neoanalytical school on Homeric studies.

single authorship. The vicious circle of philological obsession with a historical Homer is now complete, as the phantom of an alleged monumental composer has returned by the back door. All of these approaches have virtually adopted a linear, genetic approach to Homer. In doing so, they have, despite their undeniable contribution to Homeric studies, failed to treat the *Iliad* and the *Odyssey* as *songs recomposed in performance* and, consequently, Homer not as a historical author but as an invented symbol of the tradition, "culture hero of all Hellenism, a most cherished teacher of all Hellenes, who will come back to life with every new performance of his *Iliad* and *Odyssey*."[2]

Oral theorists also had to face the protests of literary critics who complained that once the Parry-Lord theory was accepted, large chunks of Homeric text would have to be deprived of meaning, since formulas and type-scenes are bare means employed by the bard in order to sing or recite epic poetry. A careful study of the Homeric poems shows that oral poetry can be as technically complex and sophisticated as written poetry. In order to explain this *prima facie* paradox some scholars employed the special term *oralcy*, which refers to the coexistence of oral and written cultures.[3] To that extent, it is fair to say that the *Iliad* and the *Odyssey* are oral-traditional compositions displaying features which are also known from written poetry, but do not pertain solely to it.[4]

In the light of these observations, we need to rethink the meaning and function of repetition, the *Lydian stone* of all intratextual[5] and intertextual references. Iliadic and Odyssean quoting can take different forms (formulaic repetition ranging from noun-epithet formulas to single- and multiple-verse repetitions, homologous similes, type-scenes, etc.) that represent sophisticated mechanisms of incorporation, appropriation, absorption, and transformation. A modern reader may be on the horns of the dilemma between Barthian intertextuality[6] and a more critical approach[7] that strives to map out the limits of intertextual references. With this in mind, Pucci's use of the term

---

[2] Nagy 1996b:112.

[3] See Robb 1994:191, 218, 232.

[4] The bibliography on oral poetry is immense. The best account of previous research is Foley 1985. Edwards 1986:171–230, 1988:11–60 is excellent on metrical issues such as the origins of the dactylic hexameter, the formula and its localization within the verse as well as certain peculiarities of Homeric diction.

[5] On intratextuality, see Sharrock 2000:1–39. For an exemplary application in Homer, see Martin, 2000:43–65.

[6] See Barthes 1975, who attempted to break Balzac's text into elementary units that show no traces of a structural organization. I owe this reference to Sharrock 2000:15.

[7] On intertextuality in Homer, see Pucci 1987:18–19, 28–30, 51–52, 236–238.

allusion reflects exactly the effort to determine limits on the relational activity between texts, avoiding the interpretive impasse that originates from a utopian search of authorial intentionality and endless referentiality. *Ad infinitum* redistribution of textual material in a new text would necessarily lead to an endless spectrum of references. Likewise, a hopeless search for sibling texts would make equally plausible all interpretive readings of specific expressions, which would then lead to evoked contexts coloring the use of a formula. A subtle but critically restrained use of repetition would then help us see how a text grows through its *reading* of other texts. In the case of the *Iliad* and the *Odyssey*, which belong to equivalent song-traditions, formulaic repetition acquires an even more profound significance. Apart from the inevitability of stemming from the very nature of Homeric diction, formulaic repetition enhances a labyrinthine *reading* of the two poems,[8] a *reading* challenging progressive linearity as well as Iliadic or Odyssean autonomy. Conversely, it allows for an interactive link between the two epics that unconditionally engulfs the audience in a complex game of references. When comparing passages belonging to different texts, the problem of fragmentation comes to the foreground. Why is it that these two passages allude to one another? Reading thematic relevance into a passage's details may seem a matter of choice, but it is in fact not. Heath has convincingly shown how ancient readers tended to perceive texts centrifugally, i.e. they judged details of every sort not in relation to the work's center (which is a contestable idea anyway), but on their own basis.[9] Extending his idea further, I will try to show how the *Iliad* uses, in a specific case, formulaic repetition not simply to allude to an Odyssean passage where the same expression is more at home, but also to define itself through a relational process: by challenging the Odyssean perspective of a rival tradition, the *Iliad* incorporates a seemingly trivial detail and accommodates it to its polemical gesture against that other tradition.

To conclude I must submit a rather necessary caveat: Both the Aristotelian[10] "[j]ust as, therefore, in the other mimetic arts a unitary mimesis has a unitary object, so too the plot, since it is the mimesis of an action, should

---

[8] *Reading* is here used in its metaphorical sense.
[9] Heath 1989:59–70 has argued that ancient readers and audiences judged centrifugally (without paying special attention to details diverging from the alleged unity and cohesion of a thematic nucleus), whereas modern readers (and scholars) tend to 'read' centripetally (focusing on the connections between the parts and the whole, as if everything should be in orbit around a thematic center). Heath's observation is right, but one should not confuse the way ancient audiences 'read' and the way(s) a poetic composition flows.
[10] *Poetics* 1451a8. I have used the OUP edition of Kassel 1965.

Chapter Seven

be of a unitary and indeed whole action" (χρὴ οὖν, καθάπερ καὶ ἐν ταῖς ἄλλαις μιμητικαῖς ἡ μία μίμησις ἑνός ἐστιν, οὕτω καὶ τὸν μῦθον, ἐπεὶ πράξεως μίμησίς ἐστι, μιᾶς τε εἶναι καὶ ταύτης ὅλης) and the Horatian[11] *simplex dumtaxat et unum* refer to a final totality, which does not deny aesthetic value to the parts of any artifact, but describes "how the poet produces a work (and the reader reads a work) in which intratextual activity of the parts makes it a text—makes it readable."[12] Completeness is culturally determined. In fact, we—as modern readers—often interpret totality as a form of compacted wholeness, where the parts are subordinated to the *totum*. It is our Aristotelian and post-Aristotelian concept of totality that makes us complain when details do not fit into the whole the way we want them to. Homeric epic aims otherwise. Being both centripetal and centrifugal at the same time, the *Iliad* exploits the embarrassingly annoying non sequitur of Helen's idiosyncratic autobiographical trivia not by simply determining poetic debt, but by reshuffling the cards and indulging in a meta-traditional comment. It thus aims for a different kind of totality, one that encompasses other rival traditions and defines its own voice meta-traditionally, i.e. by retrieving fragmented connotations from the Odyssean intertext only to distort and, subsequently, to reconstruct it.

State of the Problem

Helen's time reference in *Iliad* XXIV 765 does not correspond to the traditional mythological pattern of the duration of the Trojan War. The death of Hector took place in the tenth and last year of the war, so the mention of a lapse of twenty years since Helen's arrival to Troy seems awkward. It also seemed strange to the ancients themselves, and they tried to explain this temporal inconsistency. Ancient and modern explanations[13] can be classified into categories, which are worth considering since they are, I will argue, part of the interpretive problem:

The addition theory: I have grouped under the heading *addition theory* all efforts to interpret literally Helen's reference to the twenty years she has been away from home. In the light of such an *a priori* belief, scholars, ancient and modern alike, have departed on the discovery of the *ten missing years*. The scholia vetera (on *Iliad* XXIV 765 Erbse[14] and Eustathius ad Ω 765)[15] argued that

---

[11] *Ars Poetica* 23.
[12] Sharrock 2000:18.
[13] A good survey of the problem is offered by Richardson 1993:358 ad loc.
[14] See scholia vetera on *Iliad* XXIV 765a (Erbse).
[15] See van der Valk 1987, IV, 984, 6–15.

the preparation for the war had lasted ten years,[16] whereas certain present-day Homerists of the Neoanalytical school think that in this Iliadic time-reckoning, the ten years of the so-called Teuthranian expedition against the Mysian king, Telephus (which took place before the Achaeans reached Troy), are implicitly taken for granted.[17] Whether waiting in Aulis or fighting against the Mysians, the Achaeans took ten years to reach Troy.

An extreme 'solution' was put forward by Welcker who proposed the omission of verses XXIV 765-766, since they could not fit any rationalized time-reckoning.[18] The false 'solution' of a would-be interpolation was, needless to say, typical of Welcker's time, but is rather incompatible with our present stance towards the Homeric text. Even West, who regards "references to Cyclic material that is otherwise unknown or ignored in the *Iliad*"[19] as a special category of minor interpolations, does not adopt Welcker's omission in his recent Teubner edition of the *Iliad*.

A crucial argument concerning the problematic number 'twenty' in *Iliad* XXIV 765 has been thoroughly presented by Reinhardt,[20] although the scholarly *invenit* belongs to Weber.[21] Reinhardt argued that the similarities between *Odyssey* xix 222-223 cannot be the key to our problem, since in the *Odyssey* these words are said "*von einem Zeitpunkt*" and not, as in the *Iliad*, "*von einer Zeitdauer*." There is a clear difference between the two situations, especially since Helen's νῦν μοι τόδ' in *Iliad* XXIV 765 underscores her personal account of time. Reinhardt drew attention to the change between first and third person in the Iliadic and Odyssean passages respectively, but he used it, I think, in the wrong direction. The "*Zeitpunkt*"—"*Zeitdauer*" distinction is not deprived of problems. The syntax of the Greek is identical and there is no reason to believe that both expressions do not verbalize the same basic idea, namely that "this is the twentieth year since I/he came from that place and I/he left behind my/his homeland."

Reinhardt's argumentation was rejected by Hooker,[22] who argued that the number 'twenty' "is used according to the familiar Greek idiom, whereby the speaker would rather say 'in the Xth year' than 'for a period of X years'."[23]

---

[16] This was also the opinion of Severyns 1948:433 (I owe this reference to Kullmann 1960:192n1. The original article was inaccessible to me).
[17] See Kullmann 1960:189-200; 1992:191-192.
[18] Welcker 1882²:265.
[19] West 2001:12.
[20] Reinhardt 1961:485-490.
[21] Weber 1925:341-343.
[22] Hooker 1986:111-113.
[23] Hooker 1986:111.

Chapter Seven

According to Hooker, "the epic employed 'twenty', as it employed 'twelve', to express the concept 'more than a few'."[24] By adopting this approach, Hooker expresses his disagreement towards Macleod, who supports the old *addition theory* by pointing to two Iliadic passages IV 28 and XI 770) that allude to the ten-year lapse for gathering the Achaean army before the beginning of the war.[25] Hooker argued that "by solving one problem Macleod has created another: namely, why *in this one passage* is Helen made to speak of a duration of twenty years?" What Hooker failed to see was that Macleod explicitly emphasized the importance of number twenty for the *Iliad*. 'Twenty' is for the poem 'greater than ten'.[26]

Although Macleod adopts an interpretation based on the *additive theory*, he is able to bypass the problems created by using strict chronological criteria in order to explain the number 'twenty' in *Iliad* XXIV 765. 'Twenty' is for him a typical time-reckoning device, which the *Iliad* prefers in order to express the idea of any large number.[27]

According to another line of interpretation, *Iliad* XXIV 765 echoes *Odyssey* xix 222–223, in which the same expression is used for Odysseus. The reference to the twenty years of absence seems to be at home in the Odyssean passage, as Odysseus has been wandering for ten years after the sack of Troy. Kakridis thought that this might be an ad hoc invention restricted to Helen's speech, but facilitated through the use of a 'typical' number like 'twenty' (10+10).[28] Willcock has argued along the same lines, maintaining that this explanation is in agreement "with the modern view that the pressure of formulaic composition leads to carelessness about details, although if this is an example, it is an extremely violent one."[29]

Textual Games

In *Iliad* XXIV 765–766, while uttering her γόος for Hector, Helen turns the focus on herself, who has been absent from her fatherland for a long time:

ἤδη γὰρ νῦν μοι τόδ' ἐεικοστὸν ἔτος ἐστίν
ἐξ οὗ κεῖθεν ἔβην καὶ ἐμῆς ἀπελήλυθα πάτρης

---

[24] Hooker 1986:112.
[25] Macleod 1982:154–155.
[26] Macleod 1982:154.
[27] Macleod 1982:154 offers a list of epic uses of the number 'twenty' as "an intensification of ten" (154). See *Iliad* IX 379.
[28] Kakridis 1960:407.
[29] Willcock 1984:321.

Time Games

And here now is the twentieth year upon me since I came
from the place where I was, forsaking the land of my fathers.

In *Odyssey* xix 222–223, Odysseus disguised as a beggar tells Penelope a false story about his meeting with "the real Odysseus," who is, of course, the fictive creation of Odysseus the storyteller:

εἰπέμεν· ἤδη γάρ οἱ ἐεικοστὸν ἔτος ἐστίν
ἐξ οὗ κεῖθεν ἔβη καὶ ἐμῆς ἀπελήλυθε πάτρης·
222 τόδ' P 99/ P.S.I. 979: οἱ *sive* μοι *sive* τοι *sive* μιν Ω

"[It is difficult for me] to speak [after parting so long ago];
and it is twenty years since he left my country."

The textual tradition shows some interesting variants. A single papyrus offers the reading τόδ' that has been adopted by von der Mühll's text.[30] Van Thiel prints οἱ,[31] which seems to be supported by *Iliad* XXIV 765 (see above) and *Odyssey* xxiv 309–310:

αὐτὰρ Ὀδυσσῆϊ τόδε δὴ πέμπτον ἔτος ἐστίν,
ἐξ οὗ κεῖθεν ἔβη καὶ ἐμῆς ἀπελήλυθε πάτρης

As for Odysseus, it is five years since he bade me farewell and
left my country.

The manuscript family Ω (*omnes codices*) offers three dative readings (οἱ, μοι, τοι) and one accusative (μιν). It seems that we are dealing here with two separate strands in the textual tradition: (a) that offering the dative singular and accusative readings and (b) the P 99/ P.S.I. 979 reading τόδ' which is consonant with the textually "safer" passages in *Iliad* XXIV 765 and *Odyssey* xxiv 309.

The variant reading τόδ' that is offered by the 'eccentric' papyrus P 99[32] does not contain "the ethic dative [which] is desirable and idiomatic here."[33] Both *Iliad* XXIV 765 and *Odyssey* xxiv 309 offer interesting parallels. However, they cannot be used as supporting evidence for the reading τόδ', for in both cases there is already the indispensable 'ethical dative' (μοι, Ὀδυσσῆϊ). Del Corno thought that the reading τόδ' had originated from a scribe's effort to

---

[30] Von der Mühll 1946 ad *Odyssey* xix 222.
[31] See van Thiel 1991 ad loc.
[32] See West 1967:272. This is a third century BC papyrus of unknown provenance, now in the Biblioteca Laurenziana in Florence. It was first edited by Vitelli and Norsa 1927:189, no. 979. See also Del Corno 1961:43. I owe these references to West 1967:270.
[33] West 1967:272. See also Chantraine 1986–1988⁶ (1948–1953):74 (*GH* 2) and Schwyzer 1950:152.

eliminate the hiatus before ἐεικοστόν.³⁴ There is no evidence which can either guarantee Del Corno's explanation or support von der Mühll's adoption of τόδ' in his *Odyssey* edition.³⁵

These textual issues notwithstanding, there is another explanation for this variant reading, an explanation that is of interest to our inquiry. The expression dative + τόδ(ε) + numeral + ἔτος ἐστίν is typical and recurrent in epic poetry. It is therefore plausible that the scribe was influenced first by *Iliad* XXIV 765 (which seems—textually—the default mode)³⁶ and secondly by *Odyssey* xxiv 309, where τόδε was also used with the same expression.

This line of interpretation shows how easily the two distantly located passages in *Iliad* XXIV 765-766 and *Odyssey* xix 222-223 could be linked through diction and theme.

The 'Twenty-Year' Absent Hero

In *Odyssey* xxiv 309-310, when Laertes eagerly asks a stranger standing in front of him about his son, Odysseus-the-stranger pretends to be Eperitus, son of Apheidantus, who has met Laertes' son (the real Odysseus) in the past:

αὐτὰρ Ὀδυσσῆϊ τόδε δὴ πέμπτον ἔτος ἐστίν,
ἐξ οὗ κεῖθεν ἔβη καὶ ἐμῆς ἀπελήλυθε πάτρης

As for Odysseus, it is five years since he bade me farewell and
    left my country.

Why is this the fifth year? The situation resembles that of Odysseus' false tale to Penelope in *Odyssey* xix 107-307, where Odysseus disguised as a beggar set his meeting with the supposedly 'real' Odysseus 'twenty' years ago. Are there any specific reasons for this different time reckoning? Metrical criteria have to be excluded, for the text could very well stand even if the number 'twenty' was used, e.g. αὐτὰρ Ὀδυσσῆϊ τόδ' ἐεικοστὸν ἔτος ἐστίν. The context is again that of lament, since Laertes performs acts pertaining to the ritual mourning for the dead (he pours dust over his head, he wails deeply and bitterly).³⁷ The answer lies in Odysseus' quick response to his father's tears (*Odyssey* xxiv 321-323):

---

[34] See West 1967:272 ad loc. to whom I owe the reference to Del Corno.
[35] Von der Mühll 1946 ad *Odyssey* xix 222.
[36] I consider *Iliad* XXIV 765 to be the default mode as it is a whole-verse expression containing the numeral ἐεικοστόν that is also used in *Odyssey* xix 222.
[37] See *Odyssey* xxiv 316-317: ἀμφοτέρῃσι δὲ χερσὶν ἑλὼν κόνιν αἰθαλόεσσαν // χεύατο κὰκ

> κεῖνος μέν τοι ὅδ' αὐτὸς ἐγώ, πάτερ, ὃν σὺ μεταλλᾷς,
> ἤλυθον εἰκοστῷ ἔτεϊ ἐς πατρίδα γαῖαν.
> ἀλλ' ἴσχεο κλαυθμοῖο γόοιό τε δακρυόεντος.

Father, here I am, the very man you asked about, home in my own land after twenty years. But no more tears and lamentation.

The new, true time reckoning is consonant with the disclosure of Odysseus' real identity. The initial false reckoning is employed in order to be nullified by the unveiling of Laertes' son. In *Odyssey* xix 222–223, Odysseus refrained from disclosing his identity to Penelope, whereas here his self-revelation happens right away. The *Odyssey* lets itself play with the idea of a five-year absence, only to allow its hero, Odysseus, to make a majestic disclosure of his identity, one that does not include his name (as it is the case with other recognition scenes throughout the poem), but that lets the hero define himself in terms of his 'twenty' years of absence, which have become an Odyssean alias to his persona, the symbolical trademark of his figure. A hero who is defined in terms of his absence is a hero using time in a centripetal manner, with a clear-cut, self-referential focus. By guilefully entertaining the five-year absence scenario only to refute and correct it, the *Odyssey* rightly earns a standing ovation for its technical sophistication in manipulating time.

The Common Intertext

Let us now look at the context within which the two passages are placed (*Iliad* XXIV 761–776):

> τῇσι δ' ἔπειθ' Ἑλένη τριτάτη ἐξῆρχε γόοιο·
> "Ἕκτορ, ἐμῷ θυμῷ δαέρων πολὺ φίλτατε πάντων·
> {ἦ μέν μοι πόσις ἐστὶν Ἀλέξανδρος θεοειδής,
> ὅς μ' ἄγαγε Τροίηνδ'· ὡς πρὶν ὤφελλον ὀλέσθαι·}
> ἤδη γὰρ νῦν μοι τόδ' ἐεικοστὸν ἔτος ἐστίν
> ἐξ οὗ κεῖθεν ἔβην καὶ ἐμῆς ἀπελήλυθα πάτρης,
> ἀλλ' οὔ πω σέ' ἄκουσα κακὸν ἔπος οὐδ' ἀσύφηλον,
> ἀλλ' εἴ τίς με καὶ ἄλλος ἐνὶ μεγάροισιν ἐνίπτοι
> δαέρων ἢ γαλόων ἤ' εἰνατέρων εὐπέπλων

κεφαλῆς πολιῆς, ἀδινὰ στεναχίζων. Even the whole-verse formula used by the external narrator (*Odyssey* xxiv 315: ὣς φάτο, τὸν δ' ἄχεος νεφέλη ἐκάλυψε μέλαινα) describes a situation of deep pain.

Chapter Seven

ἢ ἑκυρή - ἑκυρὸς δὲ πατὴρ ὣς ἤπιος αἰεί -
ἀλλὰ σὺ τόν γ' ἐπέεσσι παραιφάμενος κατέρυκες
σῇ τ' ἀγανοφροσύνῃ καὶ σοῖς ἀγανοῖς ἐπέεσσιν.
τὼ σέ θ' ἅμα κλαίω καὶ ἔμ' ἄμμορον ἀχνυμένη κῆρ·
οὐ γάρ τίς μοι ἔτ' ἄλλος ἐνὶ Τροίῃ εὐρείῃ
ἤπιος οὐδὲ φίλος, πάντες δέ με πεφρίκασιν."
ὣς ἔφατο κλαίουσ', ἐπὶ δ' ἔστενε δῆμος ἀπείρων.

Third and last, Helen led the song of sorrow among them:
"Hektor, of all my lord's brothers dearest by far to my spirit:
my husband is Alexandros, like an immortal, who brought me
here to Troy; and I should have died before I came with him;
and here now is the twentieth year upon me since I came
from the place where I was, forsaking the land of my fathers. In this time
I have never heard a harsh saying from you, nor an insult.
No, but when another, one of my lord's brothers or sisters, a fair-robed
wife of some brother, would say a harsh word to me in the palace,
or my lord's mother—but his father was gentle always, a father
indeed—then you would speak and put them off and restrain them
by your own gentleness of heart and your gentle words. Therefore
I mourn for you in sorrow of heart and mourn myself also
and my ill luck. There was no other in all the wide Troad
who was kind to me, and my friend; all others shrank when they saw me."
So she spoke in tears, and the vast populace grieved with her.

Odyssey xix 204–223:

τῆς δ' ἄρ' ἀκουούσης ῥέε δάκρυα, τήκετο δὲ χρώς.
ὡς δὲ χιὼν κατατήκετ' ἐν ἀκροπόλοισιν ὄρεσσιν,
ἥν τ' Εὖρος κατέτηξεν, ἐπὴν Ζέφυρος καταχεύῃ·
τηκομένης δ' ἄρα τῆς ποταμοὶ πλήθουσι ῥέοντες·
ὣς τῆς τήκετο καλὰ παρήϊα δάκρυ χεούσης,
κλαιούσης ἑὸν ἄνδρα παρήμενον. αὐτὰρ Ὀδυσσεὺς
θυμῷ μὲν γοόωσαν ἑὴν ἐλέαιρε γυναῖκα,

Time Games

ὀφθαλμοὶ δ' ὡς εἰ κέρα ἕστασαν ἠὲ σίδηρος
ἀτρέμας ἐν βλεφάροισι· δόλῳ δ' ὅ γε δάκρυα κεῦθεν.
ἡ δ' ἐπεὶ οὖν τάρφθη πολυδακρύτοιο γόοιο,
ἐξαῦτίς μιν ἔπεσσιν ἀμειβομένη προσέειπε·
"νῦν μὲν δή σευ, ξεῖνε, ὀΐω πειρήσεσθαι,
εἰ ἐτεὸν δὴ κεῖθι σὺν ἀντιθέοις ἑτάροισι
ξείνισας ἐν μεγάροισιν ἐμὸν πόσιν, ὡς ἀγορεύεις,
εἰπέ μοι ὁπποῖ' ἄσσα περὶ χροῒ εἵματα ἕστο,
αὐτός θ' οἷος ἔην, καὶ ἑταίρους, οἵ οἱ ἕποντο."
τὴν δ' ἀπαμειβόμενος προσέφη πολύμητις Ὀδυσσεύς·
"ὦ γύναι, ἀργαλέον τόσσον χρόνον ἀμφὶς ἐόντα
εἰπέμεν· ἤδη γάρ οἱ ἐεικοστὸν ἔτος ἐστίν
ἐξ οὗ κεῖθεν ἔβη καὶ ἐμῆς ἀπελήλυθε πάτρης·

... the tears poured from Penelope's eyes and drenched her
      cheeks. As the snow
that the West Wind has brought melts on the mountain tops
      when the East
Wind thaws it, and, melting, makes the rivers run in spate, so
      did the tears she
shed drench her fair cheeks as she wept for the husband who
      was sitting at her
side. But though Odysseus' heart was wrung by his wife's
      distress, his eyes, as if
made of horn or iron, remained steady between their lids, so
      guilefully did he
repress his tears. When Penelope had wept to her heart's
      content she said in
answer, "Now, stranger, I mean to test you and find out whether
      you really
entertained my husband and his godlike company in your
      palace as you say.
Tell me what sort of clothes he was wearing and what he looked
      like; and
describe the men who were with him." "My lady," replied the
      resourceful
Odysseus, "it is difficult for me to speak after parting so long
      ago; and it is
twenty years since he left my country."

Chapter Seven

The two passages share a common intertext, which is of prime importance for understanding the deeper intertextual play that they orchestrate. Unlocking the function of these two couplets, the Iliadic and the Odyssean, we should avoid the obstacle of determining the priority and antiquity of one of them at the expense of the other. Ramersdorfer[38] has studied the *singuläre iterata* of the first ten Books of the *Iliad* in comparison to the equivalent expressions found in the *Odyssey*, Hesiod, and the Homeric Hymns. His approach has been a linear one, trying to locate the 'first' passage upon which the 'second' one has been modeled. The approach undertaken here is rather different as the *Iliad* and the *Odyssey* are seen as open traditions, not as written texts crystallized and standardized during such an early period. The matter of priority is, therefore, nullified by the very nature of oral composition and recomposition in performance. In light of these observations, I propose a different reading of the two passages in question, with a keen eye for locating the common intertext they share and, then, determining the impact of this intertext in the process of creating a different kind of meaning, one based not just on contextual parameters but also on larger intertextual references. For the full meaning of this reformulated repetition can be grasped and appreciated once it is set anew within the true whole to which it belongs: that of epic poetry at large.

Before discussing the serious implications these references have, let us glance at the extended simile the *Odyssey* employs to describe Penelope's lamentation. In the first part of Odysseus' false tale to Penelope, Odysseus-the-beggar presents a fictive visit by the 'real' Odysseus to Crete, which takes place only ten or eleven days following their departure for Troy (xix 192–193). After receiving the king's hospitality and gifts, Odysseus and his comrades are ready to sail to Ilium. Unfortunately, they are prevented by the north wind, which makes them wait in Crete for twelve days, only to depart on the thirteenth day. At this point, the external narrator takes the floor and turns the narrative lens on Penelope. Odysseus' words make her tears fall, drench her cheeks, and make her body melt. The simile of the snow melting on the high mountain tops because of the west wind and becoming water that fills the rivers is indeed a powerful one. The downward motion of the falling tears and the melted snow is captivating, but one should not fail to connect the simile with the reference to the wind preventing the fictive Odysseus from sailing away from Crete as well as the text's preoccupation, one could even speak of obsession, with time. The external narrator thus makes a welcoming gesture to Odysseus' fictive narrative by using the winds as a device linking Odysseus'

---

[38] See Ramersdorfer 1981.

false tale with the description of his wife's feelings. Time is also emphasized in Odysseus' narrative, especially since Odysseus-the-narrator presents his fictive Odysseus as arriving at Crete soon after his departure towards Troy. Therefore, the meeting between the Cretan king and the fictive Odysseus takes place when our hero is within the realm of a war-epic.

I would like, therefore, to suggest that the aforementioned Odyssean lament context can help us locate similar resonances in the equivalent Iliadic lament context, namely that of Helen's lament for Hector in *Iliad* XXIV. Penelope's tears constitute her response to Odysseus' fictive narrative (xix 204: τῆς δ' ἄρ' ἀκουούσης ῥέε δάκρυα, τήκετο δὲ χρώς). Likewise, Iliadic Helen laments Hector, whose kind words always protected her amidst the unfriendly Trojans (*Iliad* XXIV 767–772: ἀλλ' οὔ πω σέ' ἄκουσα κακὸν ἔπος οὐδ' ἀσύφηλον, // ἀλλ' εἴ τίς με καὶ ἄλλος ἐνὶ μεγάροισιν ἐνίπτοι // δαέρων ἢ γαλόων ἢ εἰνατέρων εὐπέπλων // ἢ ἑκυρή - ἑκυρὸς δὲ πατὴρ ὣς ἤπιος αἰεί - // ἀλλὰ σὺ τόν γ' ἐπέεσσι παραιφάμενος κατέρυκες // σῇ τ' ἀγανοφροσύνῃ καὶ σοῖς ἀγανοῖς ἐπέεσσιν). One can see that from our initial point of departure, namely the reformulated two-verse repetition that originated from the 'problematic' use of number 'twenty' in *Iliad* XXIV 765, we have been able to locate an entire nexus of resonances between the corresponding Iliadic and Odyssean contexts. These textual echoes constitute the framework where this special time reckoning belongs.

In the *Iliad*, Helen 'invents' the detail of the twenty years in order to alleviate her position and ameliorate her place within a hostile Trojan community. Now that Hector is dead she has to evoke even more the sympathy of the audience, both external and internal. Helen, as an internal narrator, manipulates biographical details and invents her own autobiography, one not consonant with mathematically proven chronology, but one based on her own and the poem's perception of time. The *Iliad* here allows for a different kind of deception by allowing Helen to construct her own fictive and idiosyncratic chronology. In the Odyssean passage, Odysseus-the-beggar dupes Penelope with his false story, not with chronological trivia. In the Iliadic passage, Helen attempts to deceive the Trojan internal audience at a moment of deep pathos, during the lamentation for Hector. She therefore constructs a fictive internal narrative in a manner resembling the way Odysseus-the-beggar invents his own fictive self. There is no *Trugrede* here but a sophisticated use of chronemics that Helen employs, thus inviting the audience to flirt with the idea that she may also evoke sympathy, just like Penelope in the corresponding Odyssean passage.[39]

---

[39] See Clarke 1987, who in chapter 4 of his thesis explores the relation of the complementary

Chapter Seven

As Hector's death symbolizes the fall of Troy, Helen adopts a post-war focalization, which is that of the post-war epic par excellence, the *Odyssey*. The *Iliad* refrains from using its own, Iliadic time reckoning and adopts an Odyssean stance, facilitated by the context of the lament. Temporal reshuffling through a mixture of past, present, and future events mediated by anachronies, proleptic and analeptic alike, are common to lament narrative. By citing Odyssean time, the *Iliad* makes a gesture to the Odyssean tradition, since it insinuates that such a temporal input usurps the extended time-span of its rival epic. The essential question, however, lies ahead: How is this usurpation effectuated?

By using the number 'twenty' when referring to Odysseus' absence, the *Odyssey* implies that its own perspective includes that of the *Iliad*. The ten years of the Iliadic war (in Odyssean terms phase A of Odysseus' absence) are taken for granted and are regarded as an indisputable time-span guaranteed by the authority of the *Iliad*. They are consequently added to the other ten years of Odysseus' Odyssean adventures, his Odyssean absence with which the *Odyssey* systematically deals. Thus, the epic of return successfully incorporates Iliadic time into its own time, *in terms of Odysseus' absence from his fatherland*. This is a polemical gesture against the *Iliad*, intending to subordinate it to the extended time-frame of the *Odyssey*.

Helen's *reactivation* in the audience's mind of the time frame of the *Odyssey* entails important implications concerning questions of poetic authority. In a traditional medium like Homeric song-traditions, *authority* is not based on "a personalized subject (the 'author')" but "is invested in a set of impersonal rules (the narrative code) embodied in words."[40] By resisting *authorship*, oral song-cultures claim *authority* through sanctioning the medium of performing the given epic 'code'. Under this perspective, the Iliadic tradition claims its *authority* by pushing the narrative 'code' to its limits, i.e. by having a plot-character (Helen) attempt to 'master' one of the most central features of another song-tradition's narrative 'code', the 'twenty-year' time-span. Helen thus becomes, once more, a meta-traditional device, an internal reflection of an epic performer or skilled practitioner. Through the use of the meta-traditional number 'twenty', she depersonalizes the reiteration, making "irrelevant the obvious *change* ... in the reference of the speaking 'I' or other

---

figures of Penelope and Helen, different yet linked, with respect to language and poetry: i.e. Penelope and the bard Phemius, Helen recounting the fall of Troy, Penelope's loving lies before Odysseus.

[40] Kahane 2005:12.

shifters deliberately included in the text."[41] 'Twenty' thus becomes an almost 'magical word', whose repetition confers undisputed *authority*.

In light of these observations, we can now see how in XXIV 765–766 the *Iliad* employs an Odyssean expression to make an even more provocative statement, to utter, so to speak, its own polemical cry against the *Odyssey*; to the Odyssean usurpation of Iliadic time, the *Iliad* suggests its own usurpation of the *Odyssey's Pan-Hellenic diffusion and authority*, of the *Odyssey's* undisputed (for any ancient audience) time-span of 'twenty' years. Helen, as the speaker of the lament, acquires a meta-traditional role and situates herself in the overarching post-war epic intertext, which is at hand after Hector's death. Such an intertext encompasses both the war-epics (such as the *Cypria*, the *Iliad*, the *Aethiopis*, the *Little Iliad*, and the *Iliou Persis*) and the post-war epics (the *Nostoi*, the *Odyssey*, and the *Telegony*). Both Odysseus in the *Odyssey* and Helen in the *Iliad* are the *transitional links* between the war epics and the post-war epics, as her departure from Sparta initiated the former, whereas his return to Ithaca concluded the latter.[42]

If there is something that the scholia vetera can teach us on this issue, it is that there was an effort to explain the peculiarity of the number 'twenty'. The awkwardness of this number in respect to the *Iliad's* time-frame presupposes the *Odyssey's Pan-Hellenic impact and diffusion*, which had established the duration of the Trojan War as a ten-year period and Odysseus' adventures before his return to Ithaca as another ten-year period. Screening out the relative chronology of the two Homeric epics, we can see that one song-tradition with a Pan-Hellenic viewpoint attempts to match another one with a Pan-Hellenic prominence. The *Iliad* thus adopts the Odyssean viewpoint, namely that Helen has been away for as many years as the hero of the other Pan-Hellenic epos, the *Odyssey*.[43]

---

[41] Kahane 2005:13.

[42] Iliadic Helen and Odyssean Odysseus share at least two common features: an exceptional ability for disguise, verbal and literal alike, and a special beauty that is recognised as such by others. See Maronitis 1999:216–217; Worman 2001:34. See also chapter 6.

[43] The scholia and Eustathius missed this point, while Kullmann (1960:189–203) aimed at explaining the number 'twenty' by using the argument about the Teuthranian expedition. Neither considered the possibility that the mention of this expedition probably reflected and promoted local interests, probably of that part of the Troad where the Mysian king Telephus comes from. For a similar argument concerning the cities of Lyrnessos and Pedasos, see Dué 2002:21–36 (in particular 22–23).

Part Three

INTERTEXTUALITY AND
DIACHRONICALLY DIFFUSED RELATIONS

8

The Formula νυκτὸς ἀμολγῷ: Homeric Reflections of an Indo-European Metaphor

Introduction

THE AIM OF THIS CHAPTER is to explore a covert form of intertextuality through the study of the function, origin, and meaning of the formulaic expression νυκτὸς ἀμολγῷ. By intertextuality, I am hereby referring to the use of the same expression in *multiple* Greek and other Indo-European (and even Mesopotamian) traditions, which allow us to trace "parallel" texts in order to shed light on unintelligible Homeric attestations of a given expression. Intertextuality thus involves transcending the *single-tradition* barrier and opening up wider perspectives. The search is no longer about the *quotation* of or *allusion* to a given expression attested in two different traditions or texts. Rather, it concerns *diachronically diffused* relationships between 'Homer' and *various* other Indo-European strata, which help us retrieve the shared intertext of ancient imagery whose distant 'memory' has survived in Homeric poetry.

With respect to the formula νυκτὸς ἀμολγῷ, the situation we encounter in Homer is a relic of a much older use of imagery connected to the mythical pattern of the Cattle of the Sun. In Greek mythology this imagery symbolizes, at a surface level, the end of the day and the beginning of night. Notwithstanding their function in Greek tradition, cattle are allegorically linked to a prototypical opposition between light and darkness, between the Here and the Beyond, and, finally, between life and death, as we will see in surveying equivalent cattle myths in other Indo-European traditions. With a Dumézilian intention in mind,[1] we should not look for the preexistence of an Ur-Myth of the Cattle

---

[1] Dumézil 1958, 1968 was the first comparative mythologist to focus his attention on key structures of the Indo-European peoples and to emphasize the importance of isolating shared elements generating new myths. The Dumézilian approach highlights the dynamic appropriation

Chapter Eight

of the Sun, but rather for key elements of a solar imagery common to various poetic and mythical traditions of the Indo-European daughter languages and cultures.

On the other hand, the source and significance of νυκτὸς ἀμολγῷ does not account for its function within the Homeric epics. Genetic attempts to 'unlock' the meaning of this obscure phrase have two important but often neglected disadvantages, as they tend to ignore (1) the fact that this expression was, already in the Archaic period, unintelligible (as can be seen from the pleonastic use of μελαίνης νυκτὸς in what seems to be *a modernized version* of the old formula νυκτὸς ἀμολγῷ as well as from the confusion between twilight and dawn), and (2) that *iconyms* (words/expressions deprived of standard meanings) "are resistant to normal lexicographical procedures",[2] and interpretive methods, I would like to add.

I will, therefore, first study the thematic context[3] of this formula, in order to show that its function should be traced in its *symbiosis* with the rest of the narrative that contains thematic relics emanating from the old use of this imagery. These relics are not recognizable at a surface level, but do exist within the boundaries of the common poetic consciousness of the tradition.

Under such a methodological framework, the examination of the function of the fossilized νυκτὸς ἀμολγῷ may be of particular importance not only for determining its function within the narrative but also for the Homeric similes at large. It is a tempting hypothesis that formulaic expressions may be working quite differently under a *separate performance register* and, moreover, that this performance register creates meaning that, despite its condensed form, is replete with implicit associations shared by the singer and his audience because they belong to the realm of social memory.[4] The obscure formula νυκτὸς ἀμολγῷ would have hardly recalled the myth of the Cattle of the Sun in

---

of mythical material instead of aiming at a reconstructive process of an initial, closed tradition that has been altered by later additions and removals.

[2] Silk 1983:330. Doubts may be raised as to the use of such an impressionistic term as *iconym*, which has originated from a lexicographical study (see above). But *iconyms* do sometimes exist in specific contexts and can be restricted to them. This is the case of the formula under examination. Such formulaic expressions, especially in 'oral' texts like that of the *Iliad* and the *Odyssey*, have their own semantic aura acquired both by *traditional* and by *direct referentiality*. The former refers to a specific kind of metonymical relation that pulls on the narrative's surface the whole emotive range hidden in a formula, whereas the latter "is determined by both its position in the verse and its immediate thematic environment." For the term *traditional referentiality*, see Foley 1991:24; Danek 2002:3–19.

[3] Muellner 1990:59–101.

[4] Bakker 2001a:23.

the bard's and audience's mind, but it would still have kept a great part of its original metaphoric force, which epic tradition has, once more, successfully appropriated to its needs and means in order to effect surprising tropes in the narrative.

Narrative Function (*Iliad*)

In the *Iliad*, the expression νυκτὸς ἀμολγῷ is attested four times, always in similes. Two of these similes (in *Iliad* XI and XV) belong to the category of animal similes, whereas the other two (in *Iliad* XXII) are typical star/fiery similes.[5] The following table displays the typical features found in the Iliadic similes and the single Odyssean attestation of the aforementioned formula:

Features	*Iliad* XI 172–178	*Iliad* XV 323–326	*Iliad* XXII 26-32	*Iliad* XXII 317–319	*Odyssey* iv 841
Motion	+	+	+	+	+
Gleam	+	–	+	+	+
Fear	+	+	–	+	–
Simile	+	+	+	+	+
Terminal Adonic	+	+	+	+	+

A closer inquiry reveals the existence of an entire semantic texture partly shared and partly amplified by other Iliadic similes containing certain associative details.[6]

Lion similes

Two of the Iliadic attestations of the νυκτὸς ἀμολγῷ formula are found in lion similes. The first refers to Agamemnon (*Iliad* XI 172-178):

---

[5] Scott 1974.
[6] For a thorough examination of the function of similes in both the *Iliad* and the *Odyssey*, see Moulton 1977. Moulton treats exhaustively the topic of the narrative function of similes by examining them in sequences, pairs or dispersed throughout the entire epics.

> οἳ δ' ἔτι κὰμ μέσσον πεδίον φοβέοντο βόες ὥς,
> ἅς τε λέων ἐφόβησε μολὼν <u>ἐν νυκτὸς ἀμολγῷ</u>
> πάσας, τῇ δέ τ' ἰῇ ἀναφαίνεται αἰπὺς ὄλεθρος,
> τῆς δ' ἐξ αὐχέν' ἔαξε λαβὼν κρατεροῖσιν ὀδοῦσιν
> πρῶτον, ἔπειτα δέ θ' αἷμα καὶ ἔγκατα πάντα λαφύσσει·
> ὣς τοὺς Ἀτρεΐδης ἔφεπε κρείων Ἀγαμέμνων,
> αἰὲν ἀποκτείνων τὸν ὀπίστατον· οἳ δ' ἐφέβοντο.

> while others still in the middle plain stampeded like cattle
> when a lion, coming upon them *in the dim night*, has terrified
> the whole herd, while for a single one sheer death is emerging.
> First the lion breaks her neck caught fast in the strong teeth,
> then gulps down the blood and all the guts that are inward;
> so Atreus' son, powerful Agamemnon, went after them
> killing ever the last of the men; and they fled in terror.

A conventional method of interpreting this simile (and any simile) is to examine the relation between tenor and vehicle.[7] This approach fails, though, to cater to the function of elements which seem inappropriate or, rather, irrelevant to the narrative context. Are these elements mere additions of no importance, or do they contribute to our understanding of the function of the similes? In other words, is it possible to locate in other lion similes certain features also shared by the νυκτὸς ἀμολγῷ lion similes, which, in turn, can illuminate the *deep* structure of the expression within the Iliadic narrative? And what, to begin, is the relation of the lion simile containing the formula νυκτὸς ἀμολγῷ in *Iliad* XI 172–178 to other lion similes[8] in the same Book or even in the *Iliad* at large?

Some verses later in the same Book (*Iliad* XI 548–557), Ajax is compared to a lion attacking cattle that are protected by both dogs and men:

> <u>ὡς δ' αἴθωνα λέοντα βοῶν ἀπὸ μεσσαύλοιο
> ἐσσεύοντο</u> κύνες τε καὶ ἀνέρες ἀγροιῶται,
> οἵ τέ μιν οὐκ εἰῶσι βοῶν ἐκ πῖαρ ἑλέσθαι
> <u>πάννυχοι</u> ἐγρήσσοντες· <u>ὃ δὲ κρειῶν ἐρατίζων
> ἰθύει,</u> ἀλλ' οὔ τι πρήσσει· θαμέες γὰρ ἄκοντες
> ἀντίον ἀΐσσουσι θρασειάων ἀπὸ χειρῶν

---

[7] See Richards 1936 = 1971:90.
[8] For the difference between conventional/standard and metaphoric thematic context, see the illuminating discussion of Muellner 1990:61–62.

καιόμεναί τε δεταί, τάς τε τρέει ἐσσύμενός περ,
ἠῶθεν δ' ἀπὸ νόσφιν ἔβη τετιηότι θυμῷ·
ὣς Αἴας τότ' ἀπὸ Τρώων τετιημένος ἦτορ
ἤϊε, πόλλ' ἀέκων· περὶ γὰρ δίε νηυσὶν Ἀχαιῶν.

as when the men who live in the wild and their dogs *have driven
a tawny lion away from the mid-fenced ground of their oxen,
and will not let him tear out the fat of the oxen, watching
nightlong against him, and he in his hunger for meat closes in
but can get nothing of what he wants, for the raining javelins
thrown from the daring hands of the men beat ever against him,
and the flaming torches, and these he balks at for all of his fury
and with the daylight goes away, disappointed of desire;
so Aias, disappointed at heart, drew back from the Trojans
much unwilling, but feared for the ships of the Achaians.*

In this simile we encounter most of the typical characteristics displayed in the table above: the lion is modified by the term αἴθων, which can also mean 'glittering', 'gleaming'. The contrast between *light* and *darkness* is enhanced by the opposition between the rising of both dogs and men at night (πάννυχοι ἐγρήσσοντες) and the burning of the torches to keep the lion away (καιόμεναί τε δεταί). The rush of both groups (the dogs and men and the lion) is emphasized by the use of the words ἐσσεύοντο and ἐσσύμενος respectively, and the lion's fear is also stated (τρέει). In addition, 'at dawn' (ἠῶθεν) designates the temporal point of the lion's unwilling but final withdrawal. This is a significant detail that I would like to coin "additive". It adds, so to speak, some additional, at first glance rather trivial, information to the lion simile. Interestingly enough, this superficially unimportant detail will be a key point in the interpretation of the (for *Iliad* XI) initial lion simile containing the νυκτὸς ἀμολγῷ expression.

Another lion simile is that of *Iliad* XII 299–308, in which Sarpedon is compared to a mountain-raised lion attacking a flock of sheep:

βῆ ῥ' ἴμεν ὥς τε λέων ὀρεσίτροφος, ὅς τ' ἐπιδευὴς
δηρὸν ἔῃ κρειῶν, κέλεται δέ ἑ θυμὸς ἀγήνωρ
μήλων πειρήσοντα καὶ ἐς πυκινὸν δόμον ἐλθεῖν·
εἴ περ γάρ χ' εὕρῃσι παρ' αὐτόθι βώτορας ἄνδρας
σὺν κυσὶ καὶ δούρεσσι φυλάσσοντας περὶ μῆλα,
οὔ ῥά τ' ἀπείρητος μέμονε σταθμοῖο δίεσθαι,
ἀλλ' ὅ γ' ἄρ' ἢ ἥρπαξε μετάλμενος, ἠὲ καὶ αὐτὸς

Chapter Eight

> ἔβλητ' ἐν πρώτοισι θοῆς ἀπὸ χειρὸς ἄκοντι·
> ὥς ῥα τότ' ἀντίθεον Σαρπηδόνα θυμὸς ἀνῆκεν
> τεῖχος ἐπαΐξαι διά τε ῥήξασθαι ἐπάλξις.
>
> *he went onward like some hill-kept lion*, who for a long time
> has gone *lacking meat*, and the proud heart is urgent upon him
> *to get inside of a close steading and go for the sheepflocks*.
> And even though he finds *herdsmen in that place, who are watching
> about their sheep flocks, armed with spears, and with dogs*, even so
> he has no thought of *being driven from the steading* without some
>   attack made,
> and either makes his spring and seizes a sheep, *or else
> himself is hit in the first attack by a spear from a swift hand
> thrown*. So now his spirit drove on godlike Sarpedon
> to make a rush at the wall and break apart from the battlements.

This time, the harvest of thematic features common to the νυκτὸς ἀμολγῷ similes is not so rich. Nevertheless, both the movement of the lion (βῆ ῥ' ἴμεν // ἐλθεῖν // δίεσθαι) and the cattle's abode are repeatedly mentioned (ἐς πυκινὸν δόμον // σταθμοῖο). On the other hand, there is no reference to the interplay between light and darkness, while the role of the phrase ἠὲ καὶ αὐτός / ἔβλητ' ἐν πρώτοισι θοῆς ἀπὸ χειρὸς ἄκοντι remains rather obscure. In order to explore the function of this simile, we need to turn to lion imagery as depicted on Achilles' shield (*Iliad* XVIII 573–589):

> ἐν δ' ἀγέλην ποίησε βοῶν ὀρθοκραιράων·
> αἱ δὲ βόες χρυσοῖο τετεύχατο κασσιτέρου τε,
> μυκηθμῷ δ' ἀπὸ κόπρου ἐπεσσεύοντο νομόνδε
> πὰρ ποταμὸν κελάδοντα, παρὰ ῥαδαλὸν δονακῆα.
> χρύσειοι δὲ νομῆες ἅμ' ἐστιχόωντο βόεσσιν
> τέσσερες, ἐννέα δέ σφι κύνες πόδας ἀργοὶ ἕποντο·
> σμερδαλέω δὲ λέοντε δύ' ἐν πρώτῃσι βόεσσιν
> ταῦρον ἐρύγμηλον ἐχέτην· ὃ δὲ μακρὰ μεμυκὼς
> εἵλκετο, τὸν δὲ κύνες μετεκίαθον ἠδ' αἰζηοί.
> τὼ μὲν ἀναρρήξαντε βοὸς μεγάλοιο βοείην
> ἔγκατα καὶ μέλαν αἷμα λαφύσσετον· οἱ δὲ νομῆες
> αὔτως ἐνδίεσαν, ταχέας κύνας ὀτρύνοντες,
> οἳ δ' ἤτοι δακέειν μὲν ἀπετρωπῶντο λεόντων,
> ἱστάμενοι δὲ μάλ' ἐγγὺς ὑλάκτεον ἔκ τ' ἀλέοντο.
> ἐν δὲ νομὸν ποίησε περικλυτὸς Ἀμφιγυήεις

ἐν καλῇ βήσσῃ μέγαν οἰῶν ἀργεννάων,
σταθμούς τε κλισίας τε κατηρεφέας ἰδὲ σηκούς.

He made upon it *a herd of horn-straight oxen. The cattle
were wrought of gold and of tin, and thronged in speed* and with
    lowing
out of the dung of the farmyard to a pasturing place by a sounding
river, and beside the moving field of a reed bed.
The herdsmen were of gold *who went along* with the cattle,
four of them, and nine dogs *shifting their feet followed them.*
But among the foremost of the cattle two formidable lions
had caught hold of the bellowing bull, and he with loud lowings
was dragged away, as the dogs and the young men *went in
    pursuit* of him.
But the two lions, *breaking open the hide of the great ox,
gulped the black blood and the inward guts, as meanwhile the
    herdsmen
were in the act of setting and urging the quick dogs on them.*
But they, before they could get their teeth in, turned back from
    the lions,
but would come and take their stand very close, and bayed, and
    kept clear.
And the renowned smith of the strong arms made on it a meadow
large and in a lovely valley *for the glimmering sheepflocks,*
with *dwelling places upon it, and covered shelters, and sheepfolds.*

Now, the picture is much clearer. Fearful lions (σμερδαλέω λέοντε), cattle (βοῶν ὀρθοκραιράων), dogs and shepherds trying to protect them (κύνες // νομῆες), speedy movement (ἐπεσσεύοντο // ἐστιχόωντο // πόδας ἀργοὶ ἕποντο // μετεκίαθον // ἐνδίεσαν, ταχέας κύνας ὀτρύνοντες), returning home after grazing (ἀπὸ κόπρου ἐστιχόωντο νομόνδε), the opposition between light and darkness (μέλαν αἷμα // οἰῶν ἀργεννάων), and even the cave (σταθμούς τε κλισίας τε κατηρεφέας ἰδὲ σηκούς), all the pieces have been 'reassembled' in the aforementioned simile.[9]

---

[9] See Alden 2000:67–70, who rightly argues that this simile is *traditional* since it belongs to a *family* of relevant lion-similes. Within a total of 27 Iliadic similes describing lions attacking cattle, 19 portray herdsmen and dogs trying to protect the cattle by pushing back the carnivorous predator.

Chapter Eight

If we now combine the material shared by the lion similes presented above, we can see that what remained implicit in the first two of them (*Iliad* XI 172–178 and XI 548–557, respectively) becomes explicit, provided that they are thematically contextualized. Despite the apparent contextual divergence of the two similes in *Iliad* XI (the lion in *Iliad* XI 172–178 will first succeed in his attack, whereas the one in *Iliad* XI 548–557 will fail), both Agamemnon and Ajax (who are compared to these lions) will suffer the same fate. As *Iliad* XVIII 583 (ἔγκατα καὶ μέλαν αἷμα λαφύσσετον) makes clear, Agamemnon and Ajax will both face a great danger in battle.[10]

Likewise, what was obscure in the Sarpedon lion simile in XII 299–308 becomes clear when compared to the lion imagery described in *Iliad* XVIII 573–589. One can now grasp the full semantic range of the expression τεῖχος ἐπαΐξαι διά τε ῥήξασθαι ἐπάλξις used for Sarpedon in the simile quoted above (*Iliad* XII 308). A few verses earlier, almost the same expression had been used for both Hector and the Trojans (XII 291: τείχεος ἐρρήξαντο πύλας καὶ μακρὸν ὀχῆα). Under this scope, an equivalent expression in the description of the cattle on Achilles' Shield (XVIII 582: τὼ μὲν ἀναρρήξαντε βοὸς μεγάλοιο βοείην) enables us to reconstruct the thematic nexus of correlations motivating further associations for the bard and his audience. Sarpedon breaks the wall of the Achaeans Hector-like, but only superficially. The Iliadic tradition deliberately lets us play with the idea that Sarpedon may *only temporarily* become Hector's surrogate, a great hero who will destroy the Achaean wall. Like the lion in the 'Shield of Achilles', Sarpedon's achievement will be short-lived; he will be driven away and later killed.[11]

The other lion simile containing the formula νυκτὸς ἀμολγῷ refers to Hector and Apollo (*Iliad* XV 323–327):

> οἳ δ' ὥς τ' ἠὲ βοῶν ἀγέλην ἢ πῶϋ μέγ' οἰῶν
> θῆρε δύω κλονέωσι <u>μελαίνης νυκτὸς ἀμολγῷ</u>
> ἐλθόντ' ἐξαπίνης σημάντορος οὐ παρεόντος,
> ὣς ἐφόβηθεν Ἀχαιοὶ ἀνάλκιδες· ἐν γὰρ Ἀπόλλων
> ἧκε φόβον, Τρωσὶν δὲ καὶ Ἕκτορι κῦδος ὄπαζεν.

> And they, as when *in the dim of the black night* two wild beasts stampede a herd of cattle or a big flock of sheep, falling suddenly upon them, when no herdsman is by, the Achaians

---

[10] See *Iliad* XI 186–194, in which Zeus tells Iris to inform Hector that Agamemnon will be wounded and that only later on will he take control of things on the battlefield.

[11] For this simile, see also Minchin 2001b:155–156 and, for the useful term 'advance organizer', 155n63.

fled so in their weakness and terror, since Apollo drove
terror upon them, and gave the glory to the Trojans and Hektor.

This lion simile involves a 'superfluous' expression that seems a trivial addition to the nucleus of the simile, i.e. the dreadful attack of two beasts on a herd of oxen or a great flock of sheep (*Iliad* XV 323). This 'superfluous' expression highlights the powerlessness of the herbivorous animals attacked by a carnivorous predator, presenting them as defenseless due to their lacking a protector/shepherd (XV 325: σημάντορος οὐ παρεόντος).

Is this the only function of the 'superfluous' expression, or is it linked to other uses of the term σημάντωρ in the *Iliad*? Before embarking on an examination of the other attestations of this term throughout the poem, we should keep in mind that one less developed, albeit recurrent, feature of the myth of the Cattle of the Sun is the inability of their protector to safeguard them. In the story of Euenius in Herodotus IX 93–94, the wolves kill about sixty of the sheep of Helios while Euenius sleeps (κατακοιμήσαντος). Likewise in the *Odyssey*, Odysseus' comrades kill the Cattle of the Sun when the Sun-God is absent and Odysseus is sleeping. The same feature occurs in the Hercules-Cacus episode, in which the treacherous thief steals the cattle during Hercules' sleep.[12] Therefore, the defenselessness of the cattle seems to be a characteristic of the *deep structure* of this imagery. Let us now turn to the other two Iliadic attestations of the term σημάντωρ (*Iliad* IV 422–440):

ὡς δ᾽ ὅτ᾽ ἐν αἰγιαλῷ πολυηχέϊ κῦμα θαλάσσης
ὄρνυτ᾽ ἐπασσύτερον Ζεφύρου ὕπο κινήσαντος·
πόντῳ μέν τε πρῶτα κορύσσεται, αὐτὰρ ἔπειτα
χέρσῳ ῥηγνύμενον μεγάλα βρέμει, ἀμφὶ δέ τ᾽ ἄκρας
κυρτὸν ἰὸν κορυφοῦται, ἀποπτύει δ᾽ ἁλὸς ἄχνην·
ὣς τότ᾽ ἐπασσύτεραι Δαναῶν κίνυντο φάλαγγες
νωλεμέως πόλεμόνδε. κέλευε δὲ οἷσιν ἕκαστος
ἡγεμόνων· οἱ δ᾽ ἄλλοι ἀκὴν ἴσαν, οὐδέ κε φαίης
τόσσον λαὸν ἕπεσθαι ἔχοντ᾽ ἐν στήθεσιν αὐδήν,
σιγῇ, δειδιότες σημάντορας· ἀμφὶ δὲ πᾶσιν
τεύχεα ποικίλ᾽ ἔλαμπε, τὰ εἱμένοι ἐστιχόωντο.
Τρῶες δ᾽, ὥς τ᾽ ὄϊες πολυπάμονος ἀνδρὸς ἐν αὐλῇ
μυρίαι ἑστήκωσιν ἀμελγόμεναι γάλα λευκόν,
ἀζηχὲς μεμακυῖαι, ἀκούουσαι ὄπα ἀρνῶν,
ὣς Τρώων ἀλαλητὸς ἀνὰ στρατὸν εὐρὺν ὀρώρει·

---

[12] See the second part of this study.

οὐ γὰρ πάντων ἦεν ὁμὸς θρόος οὐδ' ἴα γῆρυς,
ἀλλὰ γλῶσσ' ἐμέμικτο· πολύκλητοι δ' ἔσαν ἄνδρες.
<u>ὦρσε δὲ τοὺς μὲν Ἄρης, τοὺς δὲ γλαυκῶπις Ἀθήνη</u>
<u>Δεῖμός τ' ἠδὲ Φόβος</u> καὶ Ἔρις ἄμοτον μεμαυῖα

As when along the thundering beach the surf of the sea strikes
beat upon beat as the west wind drives it onward; far out
cresting first on the open water, it drives thereafter
to smash roaring along the dry land, and against the rock jut
bending breaks itself into crests spewing back the salt wash;
so thronged *beat upon beat* the Danaans' close battalions
steadily into battle, with each of the lords commanding
his own men; and these went silently, you would not think
all these people with voices kept in their chests were marching;
silently, in fear of their commanders; and upon all
glittered as they marched the shining armour they carried.
But the Trojans, as sheep in a man of possessions' *steading*
stand in their myriads waiting *to be drained of their white milk*
and bleat interminably as they hear the voice of their lambs, so
the crying of the Trojans went up through the wide army.
Since there was no speech nor language common to all of them
but their talk was mixed, who were called there from many far
    places.
Ares drove these on, and the Achaians grey-eyed Athene,
and Terror drove them, and Fear, and Hate whose wrath is relent-
    less

    This simile chain in *Iliad* IV 422–440 offers a good departure point. The term σημάντορας is used for the leaders of the army, whose commands the ordinary soldiers fear. The reference to σημάντορας conjures up, in the singer's and audience's mind, a nexus of associations innate in their shared awareness and readily evoked by traditional language. Thus the ensuing simile comes as no surprise. The Trojans are compared to sheep standing in the yard of a rich man. They give white milk and bleat when they hear the voice of the lambs. The alternative meaning of σημάντωρ has been brilliantly explored here by the Iliadic tradition, which unravels certain elements belonging to the conventional frame of poetic experience. The fact that the first simile refers to the Danaans, who move in silence on the battlefield, whereas the second designates the Trojans, who march making much noise, is of no importance to the poetic technique of the *Iliad*. The tradition is able to combine features, forming part of the same imagery even when plot referents are contradictory. In a nutshell, Danaans and Trojans and their marching in battle may be antithetical, but the poetic means employed for their iconizing are the same.

The term σημάντωρ is also attested in *Iliad* VIII 127, when Diomedes kills Hector's charioteer, Eniopeus, son of Thebaius. As a result, the swift-footed horses shrink back, but Hector, for all his sorrow for the loss of his charioteer, has to let him lie dead and look for another driver (*Iliad* VIII 122–132):

> ἤριπε δ' ἐξ ὀχέων, ὑπερώησαν δέ οἱ ἵπποι
> {ὠκύποδες· τοῦ δ' αὖθι λύθη ψυχή τε μένος τε}.
> Ἕκτορα δ' αἰνὸν ἄχος πύκασε φρένας ἡνιόχοιο·
> τὸν μὲν ἔπειτ' εἴασε, καὶ ἀχνύμενός περ ἑταίρου,
> κεῖσθαι, ὃ δ' ἡνίοχον μέθεπε θρασύν· οὐδ' ἄρ' ἔτι δὴν
> <u>ἵππω δευέσθην σημάντορος</u>· αἶψα γὰρ ηὗρεν
> Ἰφιτίδην Ἀρχεπτόλεμον θρασύν, ὅν ῥα τόθ' ἵππων
> ὠκυπόδων ἐπέβησε, δίδου δέ οἱ ἡνία χερσίν.
> ἔνθά κε λοιγὸς ἔην καὶ ἀμήχανα ἔργα γένοντο,
> καί νύ κε <u>σήκασθεν</u> κατὰ Ἴλιον <u>ἠΰτε ἄρνες</u>,
> εἰ μὴ ἄρ' ὀξὺ νόησε πατὴρ ἀνδρῶν τε θεῶν τε·

> He fell out of the chariot, and the fast-footed horses
> shied away. And there his life and his strength were scattered.
> And bitter sorrow closed over Hektor's heart for his driver,
> yet grieving as he did for his friend he left him to lie there,
> and went on after another bold charioteer; and it was not
> long that *the horses went lacking a driver*, since soon he found one,
> Archeptolemos, bold son of Iphitos, and gave into his hands
> the reins, and mounted him behind the fast-running horses.
> And now there would have been fighting beyond control, and
>   destruction,
> now *they would have been driven and penned like sheep* against
>   Ilion,
> had not the father of gods and of men sharply perceived them.

In this case, the term σημάντωρ means horse driver (the one who leads the horses), charioteer. The detail about the horses shrinking back after the death of Eniopeus may seem trivial, but a scrupulous examination of the immediate context may help us get a clearer view of this apparently 'superfluous' reference. Before embarking on this examination, I propose to dwell momentarily on the figure of Nestor, who, together with Diomedes, attacks

Chapter Eight

Hector's chariot. Nagy,[13] drawing partly on the work of Frame,[14] has convincingly argued that *Odyssey* xxiv 11–12 (πὰρ δ' ἴσαν Ὠκεανοῦ τε ῥοὰς καὶ Λευκάδα πέτρην, // ἠδὲ παρ' Ἠελίοιο πύλας καὶ δῆμον ὀνείρων), referring to the souls of the suitors being brought to Hades by Hermes, is based on solar imagery. In fact, the Streams of the Ocean, the Gates of the Sun, and the District of Dreams are all situated in the far-west end of the known world. The gates '*pylai*' are paralleled with Homeric *Pylos*. Nagy carefully notes that "Frame's arguments are not used to negate a historical Nestor and the historical Pylos, but rather to show that the kernel of the epic tradition about Nestor and Pylos was based on local myths linked with local cults."[15] Nestor's name may be associated with the root **nes-* (of the verb νέεσθαι 'return to life and light'). Frame[16] uses *Iliad* XI 671–761, in which Nestor himself narrates how he retrieved the cattle of Pylos from the Epeians, to argue that this embedded Iliadic story is a *thematic analogue to the Cattle of the Sun*. The same might be the case with the seer Melampous,[17] who also has a solar significance. Frame goes so far as to suggest that the entire Odyssean series of Odysseus' famous efforts to return home is based on a solar metaphor.[18] Keeping these observations in mind, we can turn to *Iliad* VIII 122–129, in which Diomedes kills Hector's charioteer, Eniopeus, son of Thebaius.

Iliad VIII begins with a scene on Olympos, where Zeus asserts his command over the rest of the immortals and confirms his will to prevent them from participating in the war of mortal men at Troy. The entire scene, however, is replete with references to the structure of the cosmos. Within this 'topography' Olympos occupies the highest peak of the world, followed by the earth, and finally Hades and Tartaros situated far below. This cosmic geography sets the framework for the ensuing battle, which contains a specific cosmic, i.e. solar, allegory.

Zeus descends from Olympos by crossing the sky in a manner similar to Helios. His two horses are 'bronze-footed' (*Iliad* VIII 41), 'flying-footed' (*Iliad* VIII 42), 'with long manes streaming of gold' (*Iliad* VIII 42). He is also dressed in gold (*Iliad* VIII 43) and holds a golden lash (*Iliad* VIII 43–44). The horses

---

[13] See Nagy 1990b:225, and in particular 223–262.
[14] Frame 1978:81–115.
[15] Nagy 1990b:225.
[16] See Frame 1978:87–90.
[17] Frame 1978:91–92.
[18] Nagy 1990b:223–262 provides a brilliant illustration of how evidence from various Indo-European sources can be employed to discover the meaning and function of an obscure expression within the realm of Greek poetical and mythological tradition.

willingly obey their divine charioteer and fly between earth and the starry heavens (*Iliad* VIII 45-46).

As the battle begins at daybreak with great casualties on both sides, there is no sign as to the final outcome. But *when the sun arrives at mid-sky* (*Iliad* VIII 68), then Zeus weighs in his *golden scales* the fates of Achaeans and Trojans (*Iliad* VIII 69-71). The fates of the Achaeans "settled down towards the bountiful / earth, while those of the Trojans were lifted into the wide sky" (*Iliad* VIII 73-74). Moreover, Zeus thunders from Ida and a kindling light comes to the Achaeans, who are terrified upon seeing it. It is significant that the weighing of the fates temporally coincides with noon, namely the point of time when the Sun reaches the highest point in its course. According to Greek religious beliefs,[19] after midday, when Eos is not any longer present, the day starts to wane. By inference, the κηροστασία and what follows, i.e. the chariot fighting, are patterned upon solar imagery.

Then the real description of the battle starts, with Paris wounding one of Nestor's horses. The Pylian hero is virtually at the mercy of Hector, who drives by on his chariot. Diomedes comes to Nestor's rescue, helps him mount the chariot driven by the great horses of Aeneas (a gift from Aphrodite), attacks Hector, and kills Hector's charioteer. Diomedes would have killed Hector himself were it not for Zeus, who, in his turn, stops Diomedes' chariot with his thunderbolt.

All of these scenes, from the beginning of *Iliad* VIII up to this point, are connected to a solar imagery. In particular, the κηροστασία designates life and death in terms of the rising and setting of the sun. The fates of the Achaeans set towards the earth, whereas those of the Trojans rise to the heavens. Zeus, who has certain heliacal features in this episode, confirms with his σέλας (*Iliad* VIII 75-76) the outcome of the weighing of fates. It is within this framework that we come to the notable verse VIII 131: ... σήκασθεν ... ἠΰτε ἄρνες 'driven and penned like sheep' (in reference to the Trojans).

In a remarkable manner, life and death are expressed through solar imagery, which functions as a mythologically cohesive mechanism for the entire episode. Zeus, Helios-like, is the only figure endowed with the ability to drive his divine chariot successfully through the sky. In the world of mortals, all other charioteers are unable to drive their chariots: one of Nestor's horses is killed by Paris' arrow, one of Hector's charioteers is killed by Diomedes, and Diomedes' chariot is stopped by Zeus' thunderbolt while in pursuit of Hector. This polarity between divine ability and human helplessness is highlighted

---

[19] Nagy 1990b:252.

through a solar metaphor based on common beliefs about the movement of the Sun.[20]

In this light, the reference to the term σημάντωρ in this scene can be more fully appreciated if it is placed within the network of its other Iliadic attestations. For the singer and his audience, the word σημάντωρ seems to have been associated with powerlessness and fear, and both its meanings (leader and shepherd) were combined in the poetic memory that formed the basis of the Iliadic tradition. Now we can see the full range of associations latent in what seemed a 'superfluous' verse in the νυκτὸς ἀμολγῷ simile in *Iliad* XV 325: *the cattle and sheep are completely defenseless and, moreover, the result of the attack of the deadly predators is going to be destructive.*[21]

Examination of the lion similes containing the νυκτὸς ἀμολγῷ formula has shown that imminent danger is a recurrent feature of this imagery. In order to determine the contextual frame of the entire νυκτὸς ἀμολγῷ expression, we need to turn to its other two Iliadic attestations, both in fire similes.

Fire similes

In *Iliad* XXII 27-28 (ὅς ῥά τ' ὀπώρης εἶσιν, ἀρίζηλοι δέ οἱ αὐγαί // φαίνονται πολλοῖσι μετ' ἀστράσι νυκτὸς ἀμολγῷ) and *Iliad* XXII 317 (οἷος δ' ἀστὴρ εἶσι μετ' ἀστράσι νυκτὸς ἀμολγῷ), Achilles shines like a star gleaming in the night sky. However, the reference to νυκτὸς ἀμολγῷ does not simply create a contrast between *light* and *darkness*, but also symbolizes the coming of a disastrous event, since the appearance of the constellation of the Dog of Orion is a κακὸν δέ τε σῆμα ... δειλοῖσι βροτοῖσιν (XXII 30-31). Orion, associated with astral imagery, was a famous hunter killed by Artemis at the island of Ortygia (*Odyssey* v 121-124) because the goddess was jealous of Eos' love for him.[22] Later in *Iliad* XXII 188-193, Achilles is compared to a dog hunting a fawn. The allegory innate in the early reference to Orion in *Iliad* XXII 29-31 becomes

---

[20] Is it a coincidence that the formula νυκτὸς ἀμολγῷ is also attested in tragic plays (the first example is found in Aeschylus' *Heliades*, *TrGF* 3, fr. 69.7 (Radt) and the second in Euripides' *Alcmene*, *TrGF* 5.1, fr. 104 (Kannicht): ἀμολγὸν νύκτα), whose plot is connected to solar myths?

[21] The same observation can be made for another lion simile in *Iliad* XV 630-637. Hector is again compared to a lion attacking *defenseless* cattle. The defenselessness of the cattle is also stressed through the shepherd's inability to protect them:... ἐν δέ τε τῇσι νομεὺς οὔ πω σάφα εἰδώς // θηρὶ μαχέσσασθαι ἕλικος βοὸς ἀμφὶ φονῇσιν (*Iliad* XV 632-633). See Janko 1992:262-263.

[22] Eos was traditionally associated with mortal consorts (Cephalus, Cleitus, Tithonus, Ganymedes). See Heubeck, West, and Hainsworth 1988 ad loc.; Boedeker 1974. Nagy 1990b:253 argues about the existence of a sequence of events epitomized in what he calls *abduction/preservation followed by death*. He claims that "Orion's relation to Dawn is the inverse of the Sun's" (253) because "unlike the Sun, it [Orion] rises and sets at nighttime, not day-time" (253).

obvious as the dramatic hunting of Hector unfolds. Implied from a mythological point of view, Achilles, Orion-like, will meet his end (though not in the *Iliad*) through the action of the enraged god Apollo (Artemis' brother), who has been contested by Achilles' arrogance in these final scenes of the poem.[23]

In the other star simile in *Iliad* XXII 317-319, Achilles is compared to Hesperos, the evening star that stands out among all other stars in the night sky. No direct threat is expressed in this case, but Hesperos "evokes the idea of closing day and night drawing on, which fits the theme of Hector's coming death."[24] Achilles' marching onto the battlefield makes him look like a gleaming star, a clear sign of the coming of night. In *Iliad* XXII 466, a similar metaphor is used:[25] when Andromache rushes to the walls of the city and sees Hector's dead body being dragged by the victorious Achilles, *black night covers her eyes* (τὴν δὲ κατ' ὀφθαλμῶν ἐρεβεννὴ νὺξ ἐκάλυψεν).[26] As a result, in the case of the Hesperos simile, the formula νυκτὸς ἀμολγῷ could not have simply meant 'at the dead of night'. For, 'the dead of night' is just before dawn, not at twilight when Hesperos is visible in the sky.

Narrative Function (*Odyssey*)

The single Odyssean attestation of the formula νυκτὸς ἀμολγῷ poses a rather different problem. There is hardly any solar imagery here, not even in the 'usual' context of a simile (*Odyssey* iv 839-841):

> ... ἡ δ' ἐξ ὕπνου ἀνόρουσε
> κούρη Ἰκαρίοιο· φίλον δέ οἱ ἦτορ ἰάνθη,
> ὥς οἱ ἐναργὲς ὄνειρον ἐπέσσυτο <u>νυκτὸς ἀμολγῷ</u>.
>
> ... But Icarius' daughter, waking with a start, drew a warm sense
>   of comfort from
> the vividness of this dream that had flown to her in *the dark of
>   the night.*

---

[23] Hector will make this more than explicit in *Iliad* XXII 359-360:... ὅτε κέν σε Πάρις καὶ Φοῖβος Ἀπόλλων // ἐσθλὸν ἐόντ' ὀλέσωσιν ἐνὶ Σκαιῇσι πύλῃσιν. In cases like this the following proposal by Minchin (2001b:154), initially used for another occasion, becomes extremely valid: "I propose, therefore, that the poet has allowed the scene in his mind's eye (the scene of the simile) to run ahead of the narrative proper. And, forgetting that he must co-ordinate the two, he has continued to sing his simile-song."

[24] See Richardson 1993:138.

[25] For the functional equation between simile and metaphor, see Goodman 1968:77-78. See also Petergorsky 1982. I owe these references to Muellner 1990:60n2.

[26] This is my own translation.

Chapter Eight

Penelope wakes up from sleep with her heart softened after a vivid dream has rushed upon her νυκτὸς ἀμολγῷ. But what did the dream tell her? Only that Pallas Athena will be on her side, without revealing whether Odysseus is alive or dead. Earlier in the same Book, Penelope had also been compared to a lion trapped by men (*Odyssey* iv 791-792). Tormented by her fears, νήδυμος ὕπνος comes upon her (793: ἐπήλυθε) bringing a dream that emphasizes her fear of Telemachus' *nostos* (*Odyssey* iv 806-807).

Penelope's rising from sleep, from a condition of being and not being, is accompanied by her doubts concerning both Odysseus' and Telemachus' condition. Falling to sleep and waking up set a framework narratively paralleled to life and death, as can be inferred from the use of diction pertaining to a lament context (*Odyssey* iv 800-801, 805-806, 812-813). Expressions like ἐν ὀνειρείῃσι πύλῃσιν (*Odyssey* iv 809) and εἴδωλον ἀμαυρόν (*Odyssey* iv 824 and iv 835) allude to the interplay between light and darkness and indicate the passage to the world of the dead and the return from it.[27] In extension, I propose that the formula νυκτὸς ἀμολγῷ determines the end of Penelope's psychological oscillation between life and death. The interplay between light and darkness, which had been sustained throughout the entire episode, thus finds its temporary rest.

Narrative Function (*Homeric Hymn to Hermes* [4])

In the *Homeric Hymn to Hermes* (4), Maia of the beautiful locks of hair, who lived in a shadowy cave (6: ἄντρον ἔσω ναίουσα παλίσκιον), mingled with Zeus νυκτὸς ἀμολγῷ (7) while Hera was sleeping (8). The cave where the tryst takes place is the abode of the beautiful-haired nymph. It symbolizes the passage from one state of being to another, functioning as a protected space for Zeus and Maia. The background of this event is colored by the *imminent danger* posed by Hera, which is overcome (see above the *Odyssey* example with Penelope's dream) by sleep. In this particular case, the mating in the cave brings the new god Hermes to light and life (12: εἴς τε φόως ἄγαγεν, ἀρίσημά τε ἔργα τέτυκτο). His stealing of Apollo's cattle, "stepping over the threshold of the high-roofed cave" (23: οὐδὸν ὑπερβαίνων ὑψηρεφέος ἄντροιο) where the god's cattle are kept,[28] is presented as his final action *within the course of*

---

[27] The Gates of Dreams (*Odyssey* iv 809: ἐν ὀνειρείῃσι πύλῃσιν) recall the Gates of the Sun and the District of Dreams (*Odyssey* xxiv 12: Ἠελίοιο πύλας καὶ δῆμον ὀνείρων) which is the location where the passage to the underworld is situated. On the association between νόστος (root *nes-) and the return to life and light, see Frame 1978:81-115; Nagy 1990b:224-225.

[28] In the *Homeric Hymn to Hermes* (4) 14-15 Hermes is described as ἐλατῆρα βοῶν,

a single day: ἠῷος γεγονὼς μέσῳ ἤματι ἐγκιθάριζεν, // ἑσπέριος βοῦς κλέψεν ἑκηβόλου Ἀπόλλωνος (17-18). The reference to ἄντρον becomes all the more significant,[29] since the cave will be the focal point around which the last and most important part in the process of Hermes' stealing Apollo's cattle will take place. The cave, where Helios' cattle are also kept, is mentioned in Herodotus' *Histories*, the most notable source for both the Cave and the Cattle of the Sun. The story runs as follows (IX 93.1-2):

ἔστι ἐν τῇ Ἀπολλωνίῃ ταύτῃ <u>ἱερὰ Ἠλίου πρόβατα</u>, τὰ τὰς μὲν ἡμέρας βόσκεται παρὰ ποταμόν, ὃς ἐκ Λάκμονος ὄρεος ῥέει διὰ τῆς Ἀπολλωνίης χώρης ἐς θάλασσαν παρ' Ὤρικον λιμένα, τὰς δὲ νύκτας ἀραιρημένοι ἄνδρες οἱ πλούτῳ τε καὶ γένεϊ δοκιμώτατοι τῶν ἀστῶν οὗτοι φυλάσσουσι ἐνιαυτὸν ἕκαστος· περὶ πολλοῦ γὰρ δὴ ποιεῦνται Ἀπολλωνιῆται τὰ πρόβατα ταῦτα ἐκ θεοπροπίου τινός. (Ἐν δὲ

ἡγήτορα ὀνείρων, // νυκτὸς ὀπωπητῆρα ('thief of cattle, bringer of dreams, spy of the night'). Hermes is described as a "bringer of dreams," who employs his cunningness to deceive Apollo. In this aspect he recalls the cattle thief Cacus (see Roman evidence below) who also tries to take in Hercules after having stolen his cattle. See Dionysius of Halicarnassos *Roman Antiquities* I 39.3, and Small 1982:10-11n25-27.

[29] The cave has been constantly exploited by Greek and Roman poets as a symbol of inspiration, sanctity, or as a place of nurturing. On the other hand, it may have negative connotations: it can be a trap, a passage to the underworld, or a place of suffering. There are also multiple uses of the cave according to the ingenuity and innovation of each poet (see Paschalis 1981:30). The cave seems to be a typical element in the myth of the Cattle of the Sun and its variations. According to Heyden 1995:127, caves represent sacred space and stand for symbols of life and death. This is a liminal and allegorical space, a meeting point between earth and sky or earth and underworld, thus making possible the passage from one cosmic region to another. In Hesiod's *Theogony* 294 (but see the OCT edition of Hesiod by Solmsen 1970 ad loc.), Heracles drives off Geryon's cattle from a "gloomy stable (σταθμῷ ἐν ἠερόεντι)". In Apollodorus' *Library* I 6.1 it is the Giant Alcyoneus who drives off the Cattle of the Sun from the island of Erytheia (see Apollodorus' *Library* II 5.10, where it is stated that Heracles uses the cup of Helios in order to go to the island of Erytheia; see Frame 1978:46n23). According to Apollodorus, the gods were not allowed to kill a Giant on their own and so needed the help of a human. Thus, it was Heracles who became Athena's ally and helped kill Alcyoneus. What is also important is Zeus' trick against Gē, who suspected the plan of the Olympians against Alcyoneus and who was looking for a remedy/drug (ἐζήτει φάρμακον) to make the Giant's death by a mortal impossible. *Zeus after forbidding the Dawn and the Moon and the Sun to shine*, uproots beforehand the plant producing the drug (... Ζεὺς δ' ἀπειπὼν φαίνειν Ἠοῖ τε καὶ Σελήνῃ καὶ Ἡλίῳ τὸ μὲν φάρμακον αὐτὸς ἔτεμε φθάσας ...). In Apollodorus' account there is no mention of a cave but there is a prohibition (not a threat, and this time by Zeus to the Sun, not by the Sun to Zeus, as in *Odyssey* xii) concerning solar forces (the Dawn, the Moon, and the Sun). The cave may be relevant to the *adyton* (νυκτὸς ἀμολγῷ or Νυκτὸς ἀμολγῷ) mentioned in the Derveni Papyrus (col. XI 1-2) in reference to the place Νύξ prophesizes from (see Kouremenos-Parassoglou-Tsantsanoglou 2006:83, 116-117). Interestingly enough, the Derveni author explains ἄδυτον as 'that which cannot set', not 'that which cannot be entered'.

Chapter Eight

ἄντρῳ αὐλίζονται ἀπὸ τῆς πόλιος ἑκάς, ἔνθα δὴ τότε ὁ Εὐήνιος οὗτος ἀραιρημένος ἐφύλασσε, καί κοτε αὐτοῦ κατακοιμήσαντος τὴν φυλακὴν παρελθόντες λύκοι ἐς τὸ ἄντρον διέφθειραν τῶν προβάτων ὡς ἑξήκοντα).

In this town of Apollonia there is a *flock of sheep which is sacred to the Sun. By day* they graze along the banks of a river which rises on Mount Lacmon and flows through the countryside around Apollonia to the sea by the port of Oricus. *At night* it is up to the leading citizens, from the wealthiest and noblest families, to look after them; one of them is chosen for the job and does it for a year. The importance of this flock to the people of Apollonia is due to a prophecy they once received. (*The sheep spend the night in a cave which is some distance from the town.* This was the cave where Euenius was on the occasion in question, when it was his turn to guard the flock. One night *he fell asleep during his watch*, and wolves slipped past him into the cave and killed about sixty of the sheep).

In tragedy, the word ἀμολγός (ἱερᾶς νυκτὸς ἀμολγόν) is attested as a noun in Aeschylus' *Heliades*, TrGF 3, fr. 69.7 (Radt), where it must be assigned to the chorus,[30] and as an adjective in Euripides'[31] *Alcmene*, TrGF 5.1, fr. 104 (Kannicht): ἀμολγὸν νύκτα.[32] It is also found, as a noun, in the Orphic Hymns (34.12: γαῖαν δ' ὀλβιόμοιρον ὕπερθέ τε καὶ δι' ἀμολγοῦ 'and upon the rich earth you look upon through the twilight').[33]

The Origins of the Expression[34]

Lazzeroni has convincingly shown that the unintelligible and obscure Homeric expression νυκτὸς ἀμολγῷ can be explained by a parallel Indic tradition representing dawn and night as milk-producing cows in Vedic mytho-

---

[30] Due to metrical reasons. The meter is not iambic trimeter, and so the verse does not belong to the narrative parts of the play. It is not certain whether the meter is Ionic (see Radt TrGF 3, app. crit. ad fr. 69) but it would be interesting if we could trace a lyric tone here pertaining to the function of this formula. For this interpretive strategy, see the second part of this study on the function of the formula νυκτὸς ἀμολγῷ. See also Sideras 1971:19.

[31] Not in *Phaethon*, pace Sideras 1971:19. See Diggle 1970:144, who rightly rejects Hermann's conjecture ἀμολγόν, accepting Dobree's σταλαγμόν.

[32] See Hesychius s.v. ἀμολγόν: ζοφερὰν καὶ σκοτεινήν. οἱ δὲ μέρος καθ' ὃ ἀμέλγουσιν.

[33] Translation by Athanassakis 1977:49.

[34] The Cattle or Sheep of the Sun as a mythological motif are known in many cultures. See Thompson 1955, A 732.1.

logy.[35] Night is thus illuminated by the stars or by dawn, and milk represents either twilight or crepuscular light. I would like to add to his convincing interpretation substantial evidence from other Indo-European daughter-languages pointing to the common origins of this prototypical cosmic metaphor.

Vedic Evidence

The *Rig-Veda* offers a revealing analogy for the milking imagery inherent in the νυκτὸς ἀμολγῷ formula. Both the dawn and the night are symbolically represented as milk-producing cows:[36]

> *Rig-Veda* 1.186.4: ... uṣā́sānáktā ... sudúgheva dhenúḥ (the dawn and the night [are] like a cow [bearing] good milk).

> *Rig-Veda* 2.3 (321), 6: ... uṣā́sānáktā ... sudúghe páyasvatī (the dawn and the night, of good milk, milk-producing).

> *Rig-Veda* 3.40 (264), 14: máhi jyótir níhitaṁ vakṣáṇāsv āmā́ pakvám carati bíbhratī gaúḥ (a great light is stopped in front of the belly (of dawn); the cold cow will produce cooked/burnt milk).

> *Rig-Veda* 7.41 (557), 7: áśvāvatīr gómatīr na uṣā́so vīrávatīḥ sádaṁ ucchantu bhadrā́ḥ / ghr̥tám dúhānā viśvátaḥ prápītā (rich in horses, rich in oxen, rich in men, the dawns always bright gleam to us, sending forth everywhere the milk-butter shaft, those (dawns) that are full (of milk).

These dawns are in fact cows used by the god Indra as a depository of light in the form of warm, shining milk (*Rig-Veda* 1.62.9). Therefore, in Vedic mythology, milk and light are associated through the cattle/cow imagery we have referred to.[37] Vedic mythology offers an excellent parallel to the Greek myth of Helios' cattle, the more so since there is a strong connection between freeing the sacred cattle and sunrise. The god Indra releases the cattle of the Paṇis (demons living at the ends of the earth and keeping large numbers of cattle in a cave),[38] but it is through the intervention of certain priests that the

---

[35] See Lazzeroni 1971:45–47. See also Kretschmer 1921:108, 1924:166-167.
[36] See the discussion of Lazzeroni 1971:45–47 from whom I have drawn all the examples from the *Rig-Veda*. See also Jacoubet 1924:399-402; Wahrmann 1924:98-101.
[37] See Lazzeroni 1971:45–46.
[38] Cf. the Herodotean ἐν δὲ ἄντρῳ αὐλίζονται ἀπὸ τῆς πόλιος ἑκάς (IX 93). See also Frame 1978:46.

Chapter Eight

cows are really freed, Vala is cut asunder, and the sun shines again (*Rig-Veda* 2.24.3).

One other noteworthy element concerning the role of cattle in Vedic mythology is the special connection of cows and sheep to the god *Varuna*, their protector. He knows the thrice-seven secret names of the cows and claims that the one who knows their names will pass them to the next generation, functioning like an inspired poet (*Rig-Veda* 7.87.4: "The cow bears thrice seven names. / He who knows the track should tell them like secrets, / if he would serve as inspired poet to the later generation").[39] Moreover, 'cow imagery' represents human thoughts, kept in the mind just as cows are guarded in a cave or stall. Evocations of cow-like dawns accompany daily praises to *Varuna* in order to free humans from evil "as a calf from halter."[40] The solar element is not absent from the lore surrounding *Varuna*; he is the all-seeing god, whose watchful and undeceived vigilance nothing can escape. He is also, like the Greek Helios, able to extend his powers over both the living and the dead (see Helios threatening of Zeus in *Odyssey* xii 382–383 that if Odysseus' comrades are not punished he will shine upon the dead).

Roman Evidence

In Roman literature the closest equivalent to the myth of Helios's Cattle is that of Hercules driving away the cattle of Geryones and facing Cacus, a monstrous fire-breathing giant whose abode was the Aventine[41] or Palatine[42] hill in Rome. Cacus is thought to have been a local fire deity (the same applies to his sister Caca who is a religious predecessor of the goddess Vesta)[43] or a local seer,[44] who offered hospitality to a hero named not Hercules but Garanus or (T)recaranus.[45] The initial fight between a local fire-god and a local hero

---

[39] Jakobson 1985:41; Watkins 1995:72–73.
[40] Jakobson 1985:41.
[41] See Fontenrose 1959:339.
[42] See Ogilvie 1965:55.
[43] Fontenrose 1959:339.
[44] Small 1982:35 argues that the Palatine, the Aventine and the Forum Boarium, where the incident between Hercules and Cacus takes place, "provided the setting for two kinds of encounter: guest-friendship (the *ius hospitii*) and the cattle raids." Small 1982:35–36 also concludes that the foundation of the city of Rome offered the political background for the Romanization of everyone received in that place, whether it be the Etruscan Vibennae, the Greek Heracles, the Arcadian Evander, or the Trojan Aeneas. Cacus may well be of Italian origin, a figure of good for the Etruscans but of evil for the Romans.
[45] See *Origo gentis Romanae* VI 1 and Servius, ad *Aeneid* VIII 203.

became (after the fusion of Greek and Roman mythological material) part of Hercules' *nostos* and was eventually transformed into a fight between Hercules and Cacus. The story of Hercules and Cacus is only related by Roman authors (Livy, Virgil, Propertius, Ovid are the most important versions), with the exception of Dionysius of Halicarnassos, who deals with the Cacus myth in *Roman Antiquities* (I 38–42).[46] On the other hand, the tradition of Geryones is also known from Greek mythology,[47] but seems to have been of special interest to Roman poets of the Golden Age, the more so because Geryones was thought to live in Spain (an area of special weight in Roman history) and was brilliantly exploited by Augustan poets, who strove to use myth as a vehicle for political propaganda.[48] I will now offer, in a brief digression, an overview of the Geryones myth together with an analysis of its basic interpretive parameters. I have decided to also include in the Roman evidence some notes on the Stesichorean *Geryoneïs*, as they form an integral part of the Geryones myth used by Roman authors (mainly Augustan poets).

The Geryones myth

Geryones was a mythical creature, a three-headed, three-bodied giant living in the island of Erytheia,[49] which was situated at the western end of the world.

---

[46] The story of the Heracles and the cattle of Geryones (but not the episode with Cacus) is first attested in the following Greek sources: 1) Hesiod's *Theogony* 287–294, 982–983; 2) Stesichorus' *Geryoneis* (*PMGF* frs. 181–186 S7–S87); 3) early mythographers such as Agias and Dercylus of Argos (*FGrHist* 305 F 1 = *EGM* fr. 1), Hecataeus of Miletos (*FGrHist* 1 F26 = *EGM* fr. 26), Hellanicus of Lesbos (*FGrHist* 4 F 111 = *EGM* fr. 111), and Pherecydes of Athens (*FGrHist* 3 F 18b = *EGM* fr. 18b).

[47] In Hesiod's *Theogony* (287–294 and 979–983) Heracles kills Geryones and drives his cattle away from Eirytheia to Tiryns after crossing the straits of Oceanus and slaughtering Orthus and Eurytion in their *dark stable* (σταθμῷ ἐν ἠερόεντι). See also Apollodorus' *Library* II 106–112. For an exhaustive treatment of Heracles' journey to the western end of the world, see Jourdain-Annequin 1989:475–515.

[48] See *Enciclopedia Virgiliana* II, s.v. Gerione 698–699 and *Enciclopedia Oraziana*, s.v. Gerione 383–384. For Geryones, see also *Der Neue Pauly*, s.v. Geryoneus; *RE* 7.1286–1296, s.v. Geryoneus; *LIMC*, IV.1:186–190 s.v. Geryones. The myth of Cacus, on the other hand, does not become a favored subject of iconography during the Augustan period (namely when this theme is used as political propaganda in support of Roman origins and ancient victories against locals in the Italian peninsula), but begins to be iconographically represented from the Antonine era onwards. See *LIMC* III.1, 177–178, s.v. Cacus [Arce]. For the myth of Geryones, see also Adam 1985:577–609 with interesting observations on local Italic traditions of three-headed monsters. Blazquez Martínez 1983:21–38 is basically informative, whereas Brize 1980 examines iconographic representations of Stesichorus' *Geryoneïs* in early Greek art (mainly iconography).

[49] The localization of Erytheia was a matter of speculation and controversy in antiquity. Hecataeus (*FGrHist* 1 F 26) thought Erytheia was in Ambracia in Epirus, whereas Herodotus (IV

Chapter Eight

He was the son of Chrysaor (who is mythologically connected to the Sun) and Callirhoë, daughter of Oceanus. Geryones' sacred cattle were protected by the herdsman, Eurytion, with the help of the two-headed watchdog, Orthus. Hercules, after killing both Eurytion and Orthus, drove Geryones' cattle away with the aim of bringing them to Eurystheus at Argos or Tiryns. Of special importance for our investigation is the meeting between Helios and Heracles. Heracles, after being insulted by Helios, obtains an outstanding means of transport, Helios' own golden cup, with which he travels through the sky. Heracles uses this cup twice: first, on his own when he crosses the Ocean and arrives at Erytheia and, second, with the stolen cattle after Geryones' death, on his way back to Tartessos, where he meets Helios and returns it.[50] Burkert[51] has drawn our attention (by adopting a Proppian[52] model of analysis) both to the *motifematic patterns* and to the wealth of *local traditions* with which this myth has been associated.[53] The Geryones myth is mainly related to the western end of the world (probably due to the location of the place where the Sun sets). Cacus[54] was associated with the underworld, so stealing the sacred cows could be a metaphor for a threat against the regular order of the universe, alluding to a potential release of the dead. This brings us, surprisingly close to Helios'

---

8 *et aliter*) believed it was Gadeira itself (modern Cadiz in Spain). On the other hand, Ptolemy identified it with Mauritania.

[50] This account of the Heracles-Geryon myth is taken from Apollodorus' *Library* II 5.10. It is believed that this account reflects Stesichorus' *Geryoneïs*. See Page 1973:144, who owes this observation, as he says, to an unpublished lecture entitled *Stesichorus and the story of Geryon*, given by W. S. Barrett at a meeting of the Hellenic and Roman Societies at Oxford in September 1968 (138n1).

[51] Burkert 1979:84.

[52] See Propp 1975².

[53] Burkert 1979:84 refers to Heracles' participating in a war with Pylos (Isocrates *Archidamus* (6) 19; Agias *FGrHist* 305 F 1 = *EGM* fr. 1). Heracles, while driving the cattle of Geryones to Argos, meets in Epiros the shepherd Λαρίνος who, Cacus-like, steals the sacred cattle. Heracles sets them free and then offers some of them to Dodonean Zeus (Lycus Rheginus *FGrHist* 570 F 1b; Proxenus Epirota *FGrHist* 703 F 8 in Photius' *Lexicon*, vol. II litteras E-M continens, s.v. Λαρινοὶ βόες // λ 311 (Theodoridis 1998) and Suda, *Lexicon* s.v. Λαρινοὶ βόες // λ 311 (Adler 1933)). The ancient scholiast on Pindar (*Nemean* 4.84) links the otherwise isolated βουβόται in Pindar *Nemean* 4.52 with the story of Heracles and the Λαρίνου βόες. The same story is also alluded to in the scholia on Aristophanes' *Aves* 465c and probably 465d (Holwerda 1991), the scholia on Theocritus' *Idyll* 4.20 (Wendel 1914), and on Nicander's *Heteroeumena*, fr. 38 (22) (Gow and Scholfield 1953) attested in Antoninus Liberalis' *Metamorphoses* IV 13–14 (Cazzaniga 1962). It is also assumed by Hecataeus of Miletos *FGrHist* 1 F 26 (attested in Arrian's *Alexandri Anabasis* II 16.5–6 (Roos 1967)), by Scylax Caryandensis *GGM* 26, and by Ephorus Cumaeus, *FGrHist* 70 F 129b (quoted by Ps.-Scymnus' *Orbis Descriptio* (*ad Nicomedem Regem*) 152 (Müller 1855–1861).

[54] For Cacus, see *Der Neue Pauly*, Ark-Ci, 2.879, s.v. Cacus.

The Formula νυκτὸς ἀμολγῷ

threat against Zeus in *Odyssey* xii 377–383, as well as to the menacing words of the goddess Ishtar to Anu in *Gilgamesh*, VI iii-VII i (see Babylonian evidence below). As Davies[55] has neatly put it: "... the story of Heracles' mission to fetch the cattle of Geryon, like the tale of his descent to Hades to fetch Cerberus, is (though in more oblique form) a *Jenseitsfahrt*,[56] a heroic journey to the land of the dead." Heracles was traditionally associated with fighting monsters, death figures like Thanatos in Euripides' *Alcestis*, or Old Age in iconographical representations.[57] Geryones himself may have been, in an older version of the story, the shepherd of his own cattle (not Eurytion as in Apollodorus' version). Croon[58] goes as far as identifying him with the mythical Herdsman of the dead.[59] The myth of Geryones and his fatal encounter with Heracles seems to belong to an older mythical stratum, being added to the list of Heracles' labors at a later date, after it had lost its original color as standing for a visit to the underworld.[60] At that point, the analogy between the two dogs involved in two of Heracles' exploits, Cerberus (who formed part of an overt journey to the underworld) and Orthus (being part of the Geryones myth) had been obliterated.[61] Davies suggests a parallelism between Geryones and Nereus as well as between Geryones and Cacus.[62] Both Geryones and Cacus are associated with darkness, since they live in caves (see Hesiod, *Theogony* 294: σταθμῷ ἐν ἠερόεντι for Geryones, and Virgil's *Aeneid* VIII 254 *sub antro* for Cacus) where it is difficult to enter. Moreover, when Hercules[63] enters Cacus' dwelling, the

---

[55] Davies 1988b:278.

[56] The term was coined by Meuli 1921:15 (see *Gesammelte Schriften*, 2.604). Recently Davies 2002:5–43 examined important folk-tale elements of the *Iliad* and the *Odyssey* arguing (38–39) that "most of our earliest attested cycles of Greek myths, not only those of the *Iliad* and the *Odyssey* (the Trojan expedition and the hero's return), but also the Argonautic Expedition, many of the labours of Heracles, and Perseus' quest for the head of Medusa, reflect the primeval pattern of a heroic journey to the Underworld and a conquest over death." Davies rightly observes that the myth of the Cattle of the Sun also shares common elements with Circe's episode, thus corroborating their link with the underworld (27).

[57] Davies 1988b:279–280.

[58] See Croon 1952:27, 67, who distinguishes between a Chalcideian and a Corinthian version convincingly maintaining (65) that the tradition of the Herdsman of the Dead was strong among the Western Greeks. On the other hand, his attempt to localize the origins of the Geryones myth on the lower Spercheios valley near Hypata and Thermopylae is rather eccentric. Mythogenesis is a far more complicated phenomenon than Croon thinks, and, needless to say, it is almost absurd to try to reconstruct a canonical version of any given myth.

[59] See also Davies 1988b:281n23.

[60] This attractive suggestion was first made by Schweitzer 1922:132–135.

[61] See Davies 1988b:282; Schweitzer 1922:132; Kroll 1932:373.

[62] Davies 1988b:287.

[63] Hercules is used for the Roman figure and Heracles for the Greek hero.

terrible thief reacts like a beast: he bellows loudly (*Aeneid* VIII 248: *insueta rudentem*), acquiring a feature that recalls Geryones' name itself, Γηρυών, from the present participle γηρύων < γηρύω 'to roar'.[64] These fascinating features inherent in the tale of Geryones point to further similarities between Geryones, Alcyoneus, and Cacus, already noted by Wilamowitz,[65] who argues that the giant Alcyoneus was also a cattle-thief.[66] In fact, his stealing of Helios' (!) cattle, which Heracles brought back from Erytheia (!), caused an entire war between gods and men.[67]

The first extant reference to Hercules and the cattle of Geryones, though, is attested in Livy (I 7.4–8.1):

> Herculem in ea loca Geryone interempto boves *mira specie* abegisse memorant, ac prope Tiberim fluvium, qua prae se armentum agens nando traiecerat, loco herbido ut quiete et pabulo laeto reficeret boves et ipsum fessum via procubuisse. Ibi cum eum cibo vinoque gravatum sopor oppressisset, pastor accola eius loci, nomine Cacus, ferox viribus, captus pulchritudine boum cum avertere eam praedam vellet, quia si agendo armentum *in speluncam* compulisset ipsa vestigia quaerentem dominum eo deductura erant, aversos boves eximium quemque pulchritudine caudis *in speluncam traxit*. Hercules *ad primam auroram somno excitus cum gregem perlustrasset oculis* et partem abesse numero sensisset, *pergit ad proximam speluncam*, si forte eo vestigia ferrent. Quae ubi omnia foras versa vidit nec in partem aliam ferre, confusus atque incertus animi ex loco infesto agere porro armentum occepit. Inde cum actae boves quaedam ad desiderium, ut fit, relictorum mugissent, *reddita inclusorum ex spelunca boum vox Herculem convertit*. Quem cum vadentem ad speluncam Cacus vi prohibere conatus esset, ictus clava fidem pastorum nequiquam invocans mortem occubuit.

> Hercules, after slaying Geryones, was driving off his *wondrously beautiful cattle*, when, close to the river Tiber, where he had swum

---

[64] Davies 1988b:287.
[65] Wilamowitz 1895²:45n74.
[66] See Pindar *Isthmian* 6.32–33. and the relevant ancient *scholium ad versum* 6.32 (Drachmann).
[67] Davies 1988a:287–288n59. Geryones bears similarities also with Electryon ("the gleaming one") who is accidentally killed by Amphitryon, Heracles' father, after he (Electryon) had lost his cattle by the Taphians (Apollodorus *Library* II 4.6). Burkert 1979:84–87 offers an impressive bulk of information concerning Heracles' association with cattle, mainly representing local traditions.

The Formula νυκτὸς ἀμολγῷ

across it with the herd before him, he found a green spot, where he could let the cattle rest and refresh themselves with the abundant grass; and being tired from his journey he lay down himself. When he had there fallen into a deep sleep, for he was heavy with food and wine, a shepherd by the name of Cacus, who dwelt hard by and was insolent by reason of his strength, was struck with the beauty of the animals, and wished to drive them off as plunder. But if he had driven the heard *into his cave*, their tracks would have been enough to guide their owner to the place in his search; he therefore chose out those of the cattle that were most remarkable for their beauty, and turning them the other way, *dragged them into the cave* by their tails. *At daybreak Hercules awoke. Glancing over the herd*, and perceiving that a part of their number was lacking, *he proceeded to the nearest cave*, in case there might be foot-prints leading into it. When he saw that they were all turned outward and yet did not lead to any other place, he was confused and bewildered, and made ready to drive his herd away from that uncanny spot. As the cattle were being driven off, some of them lowed, as usually happens, missing those which had been left behind. *They were answered with a low by the cattle shut up in the cave, and this made Hercules turn back.* When he came towards the cave, Cacus would have prevented his approach with force, but received a blow from the hero's club, and calling in vain upon the shepherds to protect him, gave up the ghost.

Livy's account of the episode highlights certain themes, such as Hercules' sleep, the motif of deceit, and the *light-darkness* interplay. Hercules' initial theft of Geryones' cattle and their recovery from brigands have been compared to the Indic myth of the rescue of the *soma* cows by the god Indra.[68] Along these lines, Cacus is thought to be an analogue of Geryones, who, like Vritra, steals the cows,[69] which symbolize the power of life and light.

---

[68] This has been already observed by both Bréal 1863²:1-161 and Schroeder 1914.
[69] The text of the *OCT* for Livy refers to bulls and cows or only to bulls (since the masculine is used). Ogilvie 1965:58 notes that Stroth, followed by Kleine and Madvig, changed the text to *aversas boves eximiam quamque* keeping the reading of N (*consensus codicum Symmachianorum*) that offered feminine participles, that is to say *relictarum ... inclusarum*. This change is well founded on the striking similarities between the text of Livy and that of Dionysius of Halicarnassos (*Roman Antiquities* I 38). Ogilvie 1965:58 argues otherwise, disfavoring the view that Livy's source was either Ennius or the source used by Dionysius of Halicarnassos.

Chapter Eight

Virgil[70] in *Aeneid* VIII 200-275 has Evander narrate the episode of Cacus, who, after Hercules has driven away the Cattle of Geryones, steals four cows and four bulls.[71] Hercules kills this three-headed half-man and sets the cattle free. This is an embedded narrative with an aetiological aim of explaining the cult of Hercules and the foundation of the Ara Maxima. Moreover, it brings Aeneas (and Augustus) within the company of all mortals who will be deified.

In Virgil's narrative we encounter some of the typical elements of the myth of the Cattle of the Sun, such as the cave (*spelunca* or *antrum*) where the cattle are kept, the pursuit of Hercules, and the flight of Cacus, as well as the most noteworthy feature of this literary account, the opposition between *light and darkness* (the cave is called a *domus atra*).[72] The end of the Virgilian narrative speaks for itself (*Aeneid* VIII 262–267):

> panditur extemplo foribus *domus atra* revulsis
> abstractaeque boves abiurataeque rapinae
> *caelo ostenduntur*, pedibusque informe cadaver
> protrahitur. nequeunt expleri corda tuendo
> terribilis *oculos*, vultum villosaque saetis
> pectora semiferi atque *exstinctos* faucibus *ignis*.

> Straightaway the doors are torn off and the *dark den* laid bare;
>   *the stolen oxen*
> *and forsworn plunder are shown to heaven*, and the shapeless
>   carcass is dragged
> forth by the feet. Men cannot sate their hearts with gazing on
>   the terrible *eyes*,
> the face, the shaggy bristling chest of the brutish creature, and

---

[70] One should note that in Virgil's *Georgics* 1.477 we encounter the expression *sub obscurum noctis* which recalls the formula νυκτὸς ἀμολγῷ. This attestation becomes all the more intriguing for it is immediately followed by *pecudesque locutae*. I have decided not to include this reference to my main discussion because it is rather isolated even by Virgilian standards and can hardly be connected to any mythical pattern.

[71] See Paschalis 1997:291: "Evander tells the story of Hercules and Cacus *after* the company have sated their hunger on the roasted flesh of bulls from the sacrifice."

[72] Paschalis 1997:290 has rightly drawn our attention to the semantic link between *Cacus* and *caecus*. In his own words, "[t]he inrush of light leads to the defeat of 'Cacus'; vice versa, the darkness of sleep is a major threat to the vigilant gaze of 'Palinurus'." The interplay between Cacus and light/darkness probably originates from his being *Vulcanis filius* (see Servius ad *Aeneid* VIII 190 and, for the reference, O' Hara 1996:204). The evil side of this notorious thief was, according to Servius, reflected in his name (from Greek κακός with an accent shift [... *translato accentu Cacus dictus erat*]).

> *the quenched*
> *fires* of his throat.

The black cave opens as the doors are destroyed and the liberated cattle "are shown to the sky" (*caelo ostenduntur*), i.e. they are exposed to the open air.

Propertius IV 9 also refers to the sacred cattle driven from Erytheia to the Palatine hill in Rome,[73] where the thief Cacus steals the cattle and is then killed by Hercules. Some of the typical aspects of this myth are present in Propertius' account, which differs from Virgil's. The cave is only mentioned in brief (IV 9.12):[74]

> aversos cauda traxit *in antra* boves
>
> he dragged the cattle backwards by their tails *to the cave*

The opposition between light and darkness does not belong to the Cacus episode, but to another myth (that of Hercules' successful descent to the underworld) embedded in the following scene between Hercules and the maidens in the sacred grove (IV 9.41):

> atque uni *Stygias* homini *luxisse tenebras?*
>
> and how only to the mortal has the *Stygian darkness become light?*

The Hercules-Cacus story is also mentioned by Ovid in *Fasti* I 543–586,[75] where it is also used as an aetiological myth for the foundation of the Ara Maxima. The whole episode takes place at early dawn (I 547: *mane erat*). Hercules wakes up only to find that two of his bulls are missing. He looks in vain for any traces, while the external narrator seizes the opportunity to update the reader with all of the necessary information: the cattle had been stolen by Cacus, son of Mulciber, a monstrous creature leaving in a cave situated far away (I 553–556):

> dira viro facies, vires pro corpore, corpus
> grande (pater monstri Mulciber huius erat),

---

[73] Virgil places Cacus' cave on the Aventine hill. For a semantic allusion to *adventus* and *avis*, see Paschalis 1997:289.

[74] There are many Virgilian echoes in this part of the poem (like that of the cave and the grove, which recall, in all probability, *Aeneid* VI 9-13). See Spencer 2001:259-284 with further bibliography. For the function of Hercules in this episode, see both Cairns 1992:65-95 and Anderson's response (1992:96-103) in the same volume. For the blending of epic and elegy as well as the existence of elements belonging to the παρακλαυσίθυρον or κῶμος, see the seminal article of Anderson 1964:1-12.

[75] For comments, see Bömmer 1958.

> *proque domo longis spelunca recessibus ingens,*
> abdita, vix ipsis inveniendis feris;

Grim was his aspect, huge his frame, his strength to match; the monster's sire was Mulciber. *For house he had a cavern vast with long recesses*, hidden so that hardly could the wild beasts themselves discover it.

The cave is, of course, a typical element in this myth, but here we encounter a detail that had been emphasized in the Herodotean (IX 93.1-2) version of the story, i.e. that the cave is located at a distant place, even if the reader understands that it will be close to the Aventine hill where Cacus' abode is situated:

> (... ἔνθα δὴ τότε ὁ Εὐήνιος οὗτος ἀραιρημένος ἐφύλασσε, καί κοτε αὐτοῦ <u>κατακοιμήσαντος τὴν φυλακὴν</u> παρελθόντες λύκοι ἐς τὸ ἄντρον διέφθειραν τῶν προβάτων ὡς ἑξήκοντα).

This was the cave where Euenius was on the occasion in question, when it was his turn to guard the flock. One night *he fell asleep during his watch*, and wolves slipped past him into the cave and killed about sixty of the sheep.

The sound of the cattle reveals the cave's location to Hercules, where he fights against Cacus, who vomits flames from his mouth (*Fasti* I 572: *... et flammas ore sonante vomit*) like Typhoeus or Aetna. Despite the speed of fire (*Fasti* I 574: *et rapidum Aetnaeo fulgur ab igne iaci*), Hercules moves quickly and defeats the dreadful Cacus. He, then, sacrifices one bull to Jupiter and sets up the Ara Maxima in the place taking its name from an ox, later called Forum Boarium (*Fasti* I 582: *hic ubi pars Urbis de bove nomen habet*).[76]

Dionysius of Halicarnassos (*Roman Antiquities* I 39)[77] narrates the Hercules-Cacus episode, offering more or less the same details we have found in the aforementioned Roman authors. In the course of his return to Argos after having completed one of the labors set for him by Eurystheus, Hercules stopped at a προσεχὲς τῷ Παλλαντίῳ χωρίον in Rome to feed Geryones' cattle. While he was sleeping, the thief, Cacus, stole some of his cattle and hid them

---

[76] Bömer 1958:65 *ad versum* 582, notes that "*lag die Kultstätte nicht am Forum Boarium, sondern beim Circus Maximus.*"

[77] I have included the discussion of the Dionysius passage in the Roman evidence for methodological reasons (Dionysius deals with the myth of Geryones and in particular with the Hercules-Cacus confrontation in Rome).

in a cave (this time closely situated),[78] dragging them by their tails in order to deceive Hercules. When Hercules woke up and realized that some of the cattle were missing, he started looking for them, eventually arriving at the cave by following the traces of the cattle. Cacus pretended he knew nothing, but when Hercules thought of bringing the rest of the cattle inside the cave, the stolen ones ἀντεμυκῶντο ταῖς ἔκτοσθεν καὶ ἐγεγόνει ἡ φωνὴ αὐτῶν κατήγορος τῆς κλοπῆς (I 39.3 4). Subsequently, Hercules fights against Cacus and kills him with his club. He then founds an altar to Zeus Heuresios, sacrificing one of the cattle.

Dionysius' account does not refer to the monstrosity of Cacus, describing him only as a local thief (I 39.2: λῃστής τις ἐπιχώριος ὄνομα Κάκος), nor does it deal with the fiery element, which in the other versions is linked to Cacus' monstrosity. On the other hand, Dionysius' version does share features with Livy's account.

Iranian Evidence

The Avestan deity Ahura-Mazdāh is the equivalent of the Vedic Varuna Asura; both gods are endowed with special far-seeing capacities and have beasts under their control.[79] According to Nyberg,[80] Ahura-Mazdāh is an early form of a *Himmelsgott*. Herodotus (I 131) is the first Greek authority to observe that the Persians regard the sky-vault as Zeus: οἱ δὲ νομίζουσι Διὶ μὲν ἐπὶ τὰ ὑψηλότατα τῶν ὀρέων ἀναβαίνοντες θυσίας ἔρδειν, τὸν κύκλον πάντα τοῦ οὐρανοῦ Δία καλέοντες. The sky-vault has two aspects, the *day* and *night* sky, respectively.[81] The daily element is represented by Ahura-Mazdāh and the night element by Mithra, the night-god. The polarity between these two deities, both of cosmogonic significance, is typical in Iranian religious belief. This divine pair is of Indic origin, belonging to the Indo-Iranian stratum of Iranian religion. Both Varuna and Ahura-Mazdāh are called far-seeing (it comes as no surprise that the same ability applies to Varuna's son, Surya, the Sun-god). Varuna is closely linked to the Sun, his great miracle being that "*im Luftkreis stehend die Erde mit der Sonne wie mit einem Maße gemessen hat.*"[82] Since Ahura-Mazdāh shares common characteristics with the Indic Varuna, one expects to find mytho-

---

[78] See I 38.2: ὀλίγας δέ τινας ἐξ αὐτῶν εἰς τὸ ἄντρον, ἐν ᾧ πλησίον ὄντι ἐτύγχανε τὴν δίαιταν ποιούμενος.
[79] Jakobson 1985:42.
[80] See Nyberg 1966:98–100.
[81] Nyberg 1966:99.
[82] Nyberg 1966:100.

logical patterns common to both of them. One such mythological pattern is that of the sacred cattle. According to *Yasna* 29, the soul of the cattle has a sky connotation.[83] Earthly cattle are personified as heavenly, primeval entities, which, through the intervention of Ahura-Mazdāh and Asa, produce *āzûti* ("fluid", "pouring"), a sacral concept that together with milk constitutes a "*sakrales Begriffspaar*" [84] and forms the subject of exhortation. The soul of the cattle bears two elements, milk and urine, symbolizing the generation of life. This is an old Aryan tradition, reflected in both the Indic *soma* and in its Iranian analogue *haoma*.[85] These precious, heavenly gifts for mankind are linked to the cosmic significance of the sacred cattle as symbols of solar power procreating life.[86]

Irish Evidence

The metaphor of the 'water' (milk) of the dawn-cows may be, according to Watkins,[87] older than the *Rig-Veda* examples quoted above. The Vedic *vár* (water, milk) corresponds to Old Irish *fír* (milk). The old and obscure formula, *teora ferbba fíra* (three milk cows), referring to the dawn-cows, is offered by two separate traditions with both a mythological and a legal component: the first is from the *Cetharslicht Athgabala* (AL 1.64; CIH 325.25, 881.4, 1897.16), the second is a judgment of *Fachta mac Sencha* in Cormac's Glossary § 585. There might be, as Watkins argues, a connection with Modern Irish *bo bhainne* (milk-cows). Watkins is absolutely right in asserting that the apparent archaism of Old Irish *fír* "owes its preservation to being frozen in a formulaic epithet in a mythological nexus which is itself of Indo-European antiquity."[88] This may also be the case for the Homeric νυκτὸς ἀμολγῷ.

---

[83] Nyberg 1966:196.

[84] Nyberg 1966:198.

[85] Jamison 1991:22 notes that there were various forms of Indic rituals that took their names from the chief offering occuring at the right moment of the entire process. The *Haviryajñas* included oblations of animal and dairy products, whereas the *Somayajñas* dealt with the offering of a drink called *soma*. An important event in this sacrifice was the pressing of the *soma*, "straining it through a sheep's fleece, and mixing it with milk" (Jamison 1991:23). For the *soma*-drinking, see Jamison 1991:61–62, 65–66, 83–88, 101, 107. For the *soma*-pressing, see Jamison 1991:22–24, 149, 161–164, 166–167, 248.

[86] For Iranian religious beliefs and ritual practice, see Boyer et al. 1989:111–152.

[87] Watkins 1987:399–404. For a possible connection with Vedic *vár* in *usríyānām vár* (Rig-Veda 4.5.8) 'milk of the dawn cows', see also Watkins 1995:72.

[88] Watkins 1987:399–404.

The Formula νυκτὸς ἀμολγῷ

Babylonian Evidence

The myth of the Cattle of the Sun is also known from ancient Mesopotamia and the Babylonian epic, *Gilgamesh*.[89] After having killed the god-demon Humbaba (Tablet 5), Gilgamesh wins widespread fame and receives a sexual proposal from the goddess Isthar. Gilgamesh is unwilling to accept her offer, and Isthar, in her anger, asks the sky-god Anu to give her the Bull of Heaven to wreak vengeance upon Gilgamesh and the city of Uruk, where Gilgamesh and his beloved friend Enkidu reside (*Gilgamesh*, VI iii-VII i):[90]

> 'Father, please give me the Bull of Heaven, and
> let me strike Gilgamesh down!
> Let me ... Gilgamesh in his dwelling!
> If you don't give me the Bull of Heaven,
> I shall strike (?) [ ]
> I shall set my face towards the infernal regions,
> I shall raise up the dead, and they will eat the living
> I shall make the dead outnumber the living!'

Isthar's words recall Helios' threat against Zeus in *Odyssey* xii 377-383:

> "Ζεῦ πάτερ ἠδ' ἄλλοι μάκαρες θεοὶ αἰὲν ἐόντες,
> τῖσαι δὴ ἑτάρους Λαερτιάδεω Ὀδυσῆος,
> οἵ μευ βοῦς ἔκτειναν ὑπέρβιον, ᾗσιν ἐγώ γε
> χαίρεσκον μὲν ἰὼν εἰς οὐρανὸν ἀστερόεντα,
> ἠδ' ὁπότ' ἂψ ἐπὶ γαῖαν ἀπ' οὐρανόθεν προτραποίμην.
> εἰ δέ μοι οὐ τίσουσι βοῶν ἐπιεικέ' ἀμοιβήν,
> <u>δύσομαι εἰς Ἀΐδαο καὶ ἐν νεκύεσσι φαείνω</u>."

> "Father Zeus and you other blessed gods who live for ever, take vengeance on
> the followers of Odysseus, son of Laertes. They have criminally killed my cattle,

---

[89] I am very skeptical about the possible influence of the Gilgamesh epic to the *Odyssey*. Similarities may be explained by similar social conditions and analogous generic constraints rather than direct influence, which is a problematic notion for other reasons as well. This is not the place to discuss the matter in detail. See Tsagarakis 2000:19-26. For an alternative view, see Bakker 2001b:331-353.

[90] The translation is that of Dalley 1991:80. The same threat is uttered by Ishtar to the Janitor of the underworld in another Mesopotamian poem, *The Descent of Ishtar*, and by Ereshkigal in *Nergal and Ereshkigal*. The threat is the same but there is no mentioning of the Bull of Heaven. See Dalley 1991:129n62.

Chapter Eight

> the cattle that gave me such joy every day as I climbed the
>   starry sky and as I
> dropped down from heaven and sank once more to earth. If
>   they do not repay
> me in full for my slaughtered cows, *I will go down to the realm of
>   Hades and*
> *shine among the dead."*

There are no milking cows here, but both epics share the theme of punishment that will fall upon humans (the city of Uruk and Odysseus' companions) as well as the threat of "a reversal of the upper and lower worlds."[91] Therefore, the theme of fear, which recurs in all Iliadic attestations of the νυκτὸς ἀμολγῷ formula, prevails in the episode of the Bull of Heaven and the Cattle of the Sun, as narrated in the *Gilgamesh* and in the *Odyssey*, respectively.

Conclusion

The examination of Indo-European mythological cognates[92] concerning the isolated and obscure Homeric formula νυκτὸς ἀμολγῷ has revealed the existence of a "prototypical" imagery having as its kernel a set of complex conventional meanings connected to a solar metaphor.

1. Solar Imagery: the imagery is based on the intricate association of cattle with sunrise (which is of key importance in Vedic mythology).[93] In Greek mythology where this myth is found in fragmentary form, there is clearly a focus on versions where the cattle's abode is emphasized (*Odyssey* xii, *Homeric Hymn to Apollo* [3] and *to Hermes* [4], Herodotus), while the solar element is clearly downplayed. A noteworthy exception is the whole-verse expression 'when Helios returned towards the setting/time of unyoking his oxen' (*Odyssey* ix 58: ἦμος δ' ἠέλιος μετενίσσετο βουλυτόνδε). This phrase is indeed a *rara avis* among the attestations of solar imagery associated with cattle in Greek

---

[91] West 1997:417n43.

[92] The only example of Near Eastern provenance is from the Babylonian epic *Gilgamesh*. The threat of punishment and reversal are indeed closely comparable between the Cattle of the Sun and the Bull of Heaven, but I am not willing to equate them. There is clear reshaping here, since Isthar's threat aims at obtaining the bull, which will be the instrument of vengeance (I owe this observation to Prof. Christiane Sourvinou-Inwood through private communication). I have decided to include this example in the same section with those of Indo-European origin simply because of the remarkably similar form the solar penalty takes in both the Thrinacia episode in the *Odyssey* and the *Gilgamesh* epic.

[93] See Frame 1978:44–45.

mythology. It refers to the specific time the oxen are unyoked (i.e. at the end of the day).[94] The downplaying of the solar element is, in all probability, due to the fact that the Sun/Helios belongs to an older religious stratum which has been replaced by a newer one, that of the Olympian deities. This is obvious in both the Homeric and Herodotean versions. In both the *Iliad* and the *Odyssey*, Dawn (Ἠώς) is commonly mentioned in reference to the beginning and end of the day.[95] The formulaic system makes this quite plain, as it offers specific formulaic expressions used in both epics for the setting out and setting down of Dawn. In Herodotus, the mention of Helios' holy sheep (ἱρὰ Ἡλίου πρόβατα) is completely marginal, while Euenius plays the prominent role.

2. Imminent Danger: Imminent danger is a typical feature of all Iliadic attestations of the expression. As far as the two animal similes are concerned (*Iliad* XI and XV), the threat of the attacking predators is clearly stated. In the two solar/fiery similes in *Iliad* XXII, the deadly tone is expressed in a different way. In *Iliad* XXII 30-31, Sirius (gleaming in the night sky) is described as λαμπρότατος μὲν ὅ γ' ἐστί, κακὸν δέ τε σῆμα τέτυκται, // καί τε φέρει πολλὸν πυρετὸν δειλοῖσι βροτοῖσιν. Later, in *Iliad* XXII 317-319, the gleaming armor of Achilles is compared to Hesperos shining during the twilight. Once again, the simile is used as a foreshadowing of the threat imposed by Achilles upon Hector, who soon afterwards will meet his doom. In *Odyssey* iv 795-841, Penelope is visited by a vivid dream in which a black phantom (iv 824 and iv

---

[94] Helios' cattle and sheep are designated by the phrase ... ἠὲ βοῶν ἀγέλην ἢ πῶϋ μέγ' οἰῶν in *Odyssey* xii 299; (cf. *Iliad* XV 323). This may be another indication of the common elements shared by various manifestations of the cattle imagery. I disagree with Frame 1978:162-164, who argues that βουλυτόνδε should be etymologized from βοῦς + λούω and not from βοῦς + λύω, which is the standard interpretation. From a linguistic standpoint, all three arguments presented by Frame do not seem very strong to me. It is true, as Frame 1978:164 suggests, that the verbal adjective λυτός has a long υ in the penultimate syllable, but there are plenty of other forms of λύω in Homer with a variable length of υ. Secondly, time and place share common and alternating means of expression, even in Homer. Temporal and local *deixis* often converge, as can be seen in forms like ἠῶθεν ('from daybreak, at dawn') which is clearly temporal while using the deictic particle -θεν (expressing movement from a place). See Lyons 1977:718. Finally, a reconstructed *boulewotonde* or *boulowetonde* (Frame 1978:164-165) would have indeed produced a long close o, which is rather unlikely to have turned into a back closed rounded vowel [u]. There is, as far as I know, no inscriptional evidence for such a change. Moreover, we know (see Allen 1987[3]:66-67) that a change in the value of υ must have occured in Attic-Ionic at a very early date. So, "when the Boeotians adopted the Attic (Ionic) alphabet and its values around 350 B.C., they found the υ unsuitable for representing the genetically corresponding [u] vowels of their dialect, which they rendered instead by ου: e.g. π]ουθιω = Attic Πυθίου" (Allen 1987[3]:67).

[95] The formula ἦμος δ' ἠριγένεια φάνη ῥοδοδάκτυλος Ἠώς is constantly used in Homeric epic to indicate the beginning of day.

Chapter Eight

835: εἴδωλον ἀμαυρόν) tells her not to be afraid (iv 825: θάρσει, μηδέ τι πάγχυ μετὰ φρεσὶ δείδιθι λίην) and does not reveal, despite her asking (iv 833–834: ἤ που ἔτι ζώει καὶ ὁρᾷ φάος ἠελίοιο, // ἦ ἤδη τέθνηκε καὶ εἰν Ἀΐδαο δόμοισι), whether Odysseus is alive or dead. The element of fear for the menaces imposed on Odysseus' life is equally at work here, making Penelope wake up from her sleep (*Odyssey* iv 839). Imminent danger is also typical in the Vedic story of the Vala and the stealing of the sacred cows, referred to in the *Rig-Veda*, as well as in the epic of Gilgamesh, with Isthar threatening to do almost what Helios threatens in the *Odyssey*.

The examination of similes thematically relevant to those containing the νυκτὸς ἀμολγῷ formula has shown that the function of this fossilized phrase within the traditional medium of epic poetry is based on the opposition between *light and darkness as symbols of some imminent danger having a negative result*: Agamemnon in *Iliad* XI, Apollo in *Iliad* XV, and Achilles in *Iliad* XXII, all will bring destruction to their opponents. What initially formed part of a coherent imagery has 'survived' within the frame of the Homeric simile, leaving only certain traces on the poetic surface, but being shared by the members of the poetic community. The myth of the Cattle of the Sun has cosmogonic significance. In various Indo-European cultures cattle have been associated with the light of the sun and a process of regeneration and fertility. This symbolic interpretation belongs to a mythological substratum that epic poetry has somehow obliterated, as there is no real place for the Sun-god among the powerful Olympians. The Sun-god (Helios) is still referred to as an important deity of course, but one outside of the usually invoked Olympian pantheon. As Apollo has been virtually equated with him,[96] Helios' role has been marginalized. The same applies to the goddess of dawn (Eos), who is used to denote the coming of the day. With the exception of the episode of the Cattle of Helios in *Odyssey* xii, the Sun-god is virtually absent from epic poetry. Only some old formulaic expressions, such as *Odyssey* ix 58 and νυκτὸς ἀμολγῷ (four times in the *Iliad*, one time in the *Odyssey*), have been preserved in epic memory. The latter is a more complicated expression than the former, due to its isolation and obscurity. As I have tried to show, its full interpretation has to cater to both its origins and its placement within the framework of the Homeric simile. I would therefore like to argue, in extension, *that certain features of Homeric diction are poetically colored according to the register in which they are placed, and that the they are perceived as such by the audience because of their special coding*. If a formula is attested in only one rhythmic and thematic

---

[96] See Burkert 1985:120.

register (such as that of the Homeric similes), it obviously has a special relationship with this particular register. The essential observation here is that the contradictory semantic uses of the formula νυκτὸς ἀμολγῷ reveal, from a diachronic point of view, only its unintelligibility. Under this scope, the exploration of the formula νυκτὸς ἀμολγῷ has shown that its *traditional referentiality* can be fully retrieved through an *intertextual* search in other Indo-European and even Mesopotamian traditions, allowing us to map out the entire intertext of this obscure archaism. On the other hand, Homeric epic invites us to appreciate the subtle technique by which it has appropriated this dictional fossil to its scope and needs. Synchronically perceived, this ossified expression had a special color, *familiar to both poet and audience*. No scrupulous etymologizing was needed by ancient listeners to 'interpret' this formula as a sign of *imminent danger*. Its apt contextualization made its elliptical nature recognizable to the members of the poetic community.

9
Genealogy and Poetic Imagery of a Homeric Formula

THE PROCESS OF CRYSTALLIZATION of the dictional material in oral epic poetry is realized in three different levels: *reenactment*,[1] *theme*,[2] and *traditional referentiality*.[3] In this chapter, I will focus my attention on the term *traditional referentiality*, which refers to specific kinds of metonymical relations that pull up to the narrative's surface the whole emotive, often unexpressed, range of a formula. *Traditional referentiality* runs parallel to the *direct referentiality* of the formula, which is determined by both its position in the verse and by its immediate thematic environment. To put it figuratively, this whole process resembles a tide of memory recalling the latent semantic substratum of the formulaic expression that has sunk into oblivion (due to its antiquity) but is still alive, since it has become an integral part of the collective awareness of the tradition.

In this light, *traditional referentiality* may be seen as a diachronically diffused form of intertextuality, more so since the full semantic and emotive range of a formulaic expression can be reconstructed by the study of multiple intertextual references or various partial intratextual manifestations of a pre-verbal *Gestalt*. Cross-textual associations may go back to older, recognizable Indo-European traditions or may be based on unidentifiable strata. Diachronic diffusion has made it possible for elliptical or fragmented parts of mental icons to survive independently, preserving contextualized features that pertain to the *deep structure* of their initial thematic environment. In this sense, *traditional referentiality* reflects neither the *quoting* nor the *allusive* aspect of intertextuality. It makes notionally *present* what is dictionally *absent*, i.e. it makes the *text* yield to the *tradition*, the individual formula 'return' to the *family* of formulas from which it originated. Behind its condensed and abbrevi-

---

[1] See Martin 1989:12–37 and 231–239.
[2] For the term *theme* in Homer, see Lord 1960:68–98 and 1991:26–27.
[3] See Foley 1991:24; Danek 2002:3–19.

ated shape, the formula reveals a remarkable *structural unboundedness*, being tied to a series of relevant formulas that cannot be identified as belonging to any specific tradition.

In this chapter, I will explore the meaning and function of the simile ἠΰτε νεβροί by examining the full nexus of its Iliadic attestations. By zooming in on the *structure* of an *oral fossil* such as the formula, I will attempt to disclose its *structuration*, its coming into being. The dictional and metrical features pertaining to this fossilized expression are consonant with its 'pre-Homeric' past, i.e. with its forming part of a larger imagery, a mental *Gestalt* from which it has been detached.

Outer Metric

The participle πεφυζότες is attested four times in the *Iliad*, but never in the *Odyssey*:[4]

1. τῇ ῥ' οἵ γε προχέοντο πεφυζότες, ἠέρα δ' Ἥρη (XXI 6)
2. Τρῶες ἄφαρ κλονέοντο πεφυζότες, οὐδέ τις ἀλκή (XXI 528)
3. ἔλθωσι προτὶ ἄστυ πεφυζότες· ἦ γὰρ Ἀχιλλεύς (XXI 532)
4. ὣς οἳ μὲν κατὰ ἄστυ, πεφυζότες ἠΰτε νεβροί (XXII 1)

The metrical structure of these verses is the following:[5]

1. $---\,|\,\cup\cup-\cup\,^{tr}|\,\cup-\cup\cup\,|\,-\cup\cup--$ (XXI 6)
2. $-\cup\cup-\,|\,\cup\cup-\cup\,^{tr}|\,\cup-\cup\cup\,|\,-\cup\cup--$ (XXI 528)
3. $---\,|\,\cup\cup-\cup\,^{tr}|\,\cup-\cup\cup\,|\,-\cup\cup--$ (XXI 532)
4. $---\,|\,\cup\cup-\cup\,^{tr}|\,\cup-\cup\cup\,|\,-\cup\cup--$ (XXII 1)

I will start with a detailed metrical discussion of these verses, which is essential for an in-depth exploration of the *genealogy* of the participle πεφυζότες and, consequently, of the whole πεφυζότες ἠΰτε νεβροί simile.

1. All four verses follow the typical dactylic pattern with 24 *morae*. Verse XXI 528 has 17 syllables, whereas XXI 6, XXI 532 and XXII 1 have 16. It is clear that their syllabicity follows the basic pattern of the dactylic hexameter.[6]

---

[4] The form πεφυζότες is not attested in the *Odyssey* where one finds πεφευγότες instead. E.g. οἴκοι ἔσαν, πόλεμόν τε πεφευγότες ἠδὲ θάλασσαν (i 12).
[5] The single vertical bar (|) indicates the beginning and end of a colon, and the supra-linear index (tr) marks the trochaic caesura.
[6] For the concept of *syllabicity* and its role as determining factor, not only in the dactylic hexameter, but also in the reconstructed proto-Indo-European Ur-meter, see Foley 1993:54–63.

Chapter Nine

2. All four verses are characterized by the principle of *right justification*,[7] since their only metrical differentiation is localized in the first colon, where the initial dactyl has been substituted by a spondee.

Inner Metric

1. All four verses have a B2 caesura (i.e. after the third trochee). The participle πεφυζότες (⌣ – ⌣ ⌣) is invariably localized between caesuras B2 and C2,[8] namely between the feminine caesura and the bucolic diaeresis, before the terminal adonic (– ⌣ ⌣ – –).

2. All four verses have been developed upon four-colon patterns.[9] Moreover, XXI 532 and XXII 1 seem to be based on the same dictional template, as, in both of them, the participle πεφυζότες is preceded by a prepositional phrase including the noun ἄστυ. To some extent then, and as far as the second and third cola are concerned, one can also speak of the same syntactical, not only metrical, pattern.[10] Therefore, in view of their metrical structure, verses XXI 532 and XXII 1 are identical. The implications of this observation are essential for our examination of the genealogy of the formula containing the participle πεφυζότες. As a result, since the form πεφυζότες (⌣ – ⌣ ⌣) followed by

---

[7] The term *right justification* was coined by Foley 1993:56–59. Foley takes over from the work of Meillet 1923 and Jakobson 1952:21–66, who had detected this regulating metrical factor not only in the dactylic hexameter but also in the *deseterac*, the Serbo-Croatian heroic decasyllable employed in the traditional epic poetry of the peoples of former Yugoslavia. On this occasion, it can be briefly stated that the dactylic hexameter is comprised by an initial and terminal metrical sequence, which are marked out, the former by metrical flexibility and the latter by metrical rigidity. However, the gradual metrical rigidity of the hexameter verse, as we move from the beginning towards the end of the verse (from left to right, whence the term *right justification*), is only the visual imprint of this metrical divergence expressed in linear terms. It, therefore, does not mirror the diachronic evolution of the hexameter from an Ur-form of the archetypal Indo-European proto-language. This linear interpretation is, diachronically examined, inversely proportional to the evolution of the dactylic hexameter, which, as the terminal adonic (– ⌣ ⌣ – –) testifies, must have had in its archetypal Indo-European form a more rigid and standardized structure towards its end but a rather looser and flexible shape in its beginning. *Right justification* is also relevant to another tendency of the hexameter, namely that of the size of the cola. Cola 1 and 3 are considerably smaller than cola 2 and 4, since dactyls, according to Foley 1993:84, "migrate toward the ends of both verses and half-verses, making these terminal sections more expansive by both syllable- and morae-count and more densely populated by short syllables." See also O' Nolan 1969:17. For a detailed presentation of the dactylic hexameter in its entirety (from Homer to Nonnus), see v. Raalte 1986:28–103; Sicking 1993:69–82.

[8] See Fränkel 1926:197–229.

[9] For the concept of *pattern* in Homeric poetry, see Lord 1960:37.

[10] The poet of the *Iliad* and the *Odyssey* builds his verses not with words but with metrical cola and formulas, which often coincide with sense-breaks within the hexameter verse.

the terminal adonic (– ᴗ ᴗ – –) is placed in the second hemistich (after the B2 caesura), it will be less flexible and more rigid in its metrical form. Therefore, the metrical incongruity of the three syllables in the first colon is rather the outcome of *right justification* than the effect of the semantic disparity of the four aforementioned verses. This argument is further corroborated by the observation that the first colon of each of the four verses [τῇ ῥ' οἵ γε (– – –) // Τρῶες ἄφαρ (– ᴗ ᴗ –) // ἔλθωσι (– – –) // ὡς οἳ μὲν (– – –)] refers, despite its dictional and syntactic divergence, to the same subject, *the Trojans* (who are either named or understood by the syntax).

3. The colon is a metrical, not a phrase unit. The smallest phrase unit is the hemistich. As a result,[11] the expression πεφυζότες ἠΰτε νεβροί constitutes a phrase unit. Although the only fixed element in the four verses, with respect to morphology, is the participle πεφυζότες, we are in no position to classify it as a formula since it does not fulfill the Parryan "essential idea." According to Foley, we should coin it "a functional phrase element."[12] Pin-pointing an elementary structural unit in verses with similar phrase structure is a very difficult task. Foley maintains that "... no line or unit is ontologically primary. The phraseology does not merely present the possibility of multiformity; it actively is a multiform."[13]

Foley's theory is certainly functional on the synchronic level, but on the vertical axis of diachrony things can be different. When epic diction employs archaisms, it is possible to discern the survival of fossilized items[14] incorpo-

---

[11] See Foley 1993:132. This observation becomes obvious in cases where a specific combination of phrases prevents a caesura. All four verses have a B2 caesura (after the third trochee).

[12] See Foley 1993:132.

[13] Foley 1993:137.

[14] For the antiquity and other related problems of the participle πεφυζότες (*πεφυγϝότες > πεφυγϝόσες > πεφυγϝότες > πεφυζότες) that was formed in analogy to the noun φύζα after the loss of the digamma, see Chantraine (1968–1980), s.v. φεύγω 1. On the contrary, Trümpy 1950:276n614 and Schwyzer 1934–1939 argue that the participle πεφυζότες comes from the perfect of the verb *φύζω (lat. *fugio*) or from the noun φύζα, as the form μεμυζότε (Antimachus fr. 90 Wyss = fr. 63 Matthews) comes from the verb μύζω. But see Richardson 1993 and Rix 1976: § 238, § 258, who are in favor of a historical evolution of the form in the pattern of ἀρηρότα < ἀραρϝόσα < ἀραρϝοh-α < a-ra-ru-wo-a. See also Cuny 1936:395398, who thinks that it is wrong "*d' admettre le transfert, dans une forme nettement rattachée au verbe, d' un ζ qui, dans le nom, résulte d' une combinaison phonétique de g et de y*" (φύζα < *bhug-ya). According to Cuny (396), the result of the loss of the digamma 'produced' the form *πεφυγότες (which would have been scanned as a tribrach [ᴗ ᴗ ᴗ] but had to be placed in the fourth foot of the hexameter). In order to avoid the tribrach, the form was changed to πεφυζότες, which was, as a matter of fact, a barbarism on the level of writing, but because of its morphological idiosyncrasy it preserved the traces of an archaism that survived within the formulaic framework. The antiquity of the form πεφυζότες is also reinforced by the fact that it always has, contrary to the form πεφευγότες that is the form attested in the *Odyssey*, a passive sense in spite of its active form. An equi-

Chapter Nine

rated into formulaic constructions, which, due to their rigid morphology, invade the hexameter by occupying specific slots and 'produce' metrical clusters that are gradually crystallized in consonance with the metrical shape of the verse.[15]

This is the case with the formula πεφυζότες ἠΰτε νεβροί, which on a phrase level is expressed by the pattern *perfect participle* + ἠΰτε νεβροί (⏑ − ⏑ ⏑ − ⏑ ⏑ − −) and which constitutes on the vertical axis of diachrony[16] the archetypal formula from which the allomorphs of XXI 6, XXI 528 and XXI 532 have emanated.

This conclusion is further supported by the fact that, apart from the simile ἠΰτε νεβροί, all the other expressions occupying the metrical slot of the terminal adonic (− ⏑ ⏑ − −) are not coterminous and produce an enjambment effect.[17]

Coterminacy, i.e. the convergence of prosodic/metrical completion of the verse and semantic consummation (one verse, one idea),[18] constitutes, by and large, a typical characteristic of oral poetry. Enjambment (whose absence underscores the balanced symmetry between form and content) has its own peculiarities according to the form it takes. Consequently, *necessary-periodic* enjambment is a sign of the non-traditional style, whereas *adding-unperiodic* enjambment is typical of oral composition and seems to be traditional. The same phenomenon has been observed in other oral verse forms, such as the decasyllable/*deseterac* in the Serbo-Croatian return song[19] and the

---

valent development can be already observed in Linear B. See the participle te-tu-ko-wo-a₂ (θεθυχϝόα/PY Sa 682 al.), which has a transitive meaning. For more details on this point, see Chantraine 1927:52 and Shipp 1972²:114, who disagrees with Chantraine 1986-1988⁶ (1948-1953):429 (*GH* 1).

[15] See Nagy 1974; 1976:239-260.

[16] Diachronic and synchronic developments could be schematically represented by a cross, whose vertical axis stands for diachrony and its horizontal for synchrony.

[17] For a different view, see Bakker 1997:151-152 who argues: "... I suggest that we refrain from using the term 'enjambment' whenever the progression of speech units is in accordance with the metrical period."

[18] "Enjambment, the continuation of the sentence from one verse to the next, is characteristic of Homer, but the nature of the running-over of the sense is more restricted than in literate writers, and attempts have been made to use this feature to differentiate oral from literate poetry." This is the way Edwards 1986:171-230 sets the framework for his survey of the literature concerning enjambment in Homer. The bibliography is immense but the most important modern discussions can be limited to the following: Bassett 1926:116-148; Parry 1929:200-220 (= 1971:251-265); Lord 1948:113-24; Kirk 1966:105-52; Edwards 1966:115-179; Clayman and van Nortwick 1977:85-92; Barnes 1979:1-10; Bakker 1990:1-21; Higbie 1990; Clark 1994:85-114; Clark 1997; Friedrich 2000: 1-19.

[19] See Foley 1993:164.

fifteen-syllable verse of Modern Greek folk song.[20] The fact that verses XXI 6, XXI 528, and XXI 532 have a *necessary-periodic* enjambment preceded by internal punctuation at the end of the fourth foot and the introduction of a new subject at verse-end implicitly indicates that they cannot represent the *template* or *pattern* of the πεφυζότες ἠΰτε νεβροί formula. Conversely, XXII 1 has a *secondary* enjambment, which shows the presence of a slight pause at the point of sense completion. The lack of punctuation is, of course, only a printing convention of our written text, but it *graphically* represents the difference between the *adding-unperiodic* and the *secondary* enjambment, the former indicating a shorter pause expressed by *optional* punctuation at verse-end, whereas the latter points to a longer pause expressed by *compulsory* punctuation. Given that the enjambment in XXII 1 is secondary, the formula πεφυζότες ἠΰτε νεβροί may well be the *formulaic template* from which the allomorphs of XXI 6, XXI 528 and XXI 532 have originated. This argument is further reinforced by the fact that the formula τεθηπότες//-ας ἠΰτε νεβροί//-ούς (IV 243, XXI 29), which is also placed at verse-terminal position, is followed by no enjambment. In this light, it can be plausibly argued that the expression πεφυζότες ἠΰτε νεβροί constitutes the formulaic precursor to other Iliadic verses containing the form πεφυζότες. Besides, the attachment of the second part of the simile (ἠΰτε νεβροί) to the participle πεφυζότες must have preceded its joining the rest of the hemistiches (οὐδέ τις ἀλκή // ἦ γὰρ Ἀχιλλεύς // ἠέρα δ' Ἥρη). A diachronic viewpoint is absolutely vital for understanding the mechanics of the above-mentioned process. Enjambment is, by definition, a form of dissonance, which the set of rules we describe as Homeric diction has reorganized by "thoroughly integrating it into the system."[21] In other words, enjambed verses like XXI 6, XXI 528, and XXI 532 employing a word attested *as part of a word-group* that occupies the most traditional part of the dactylic hexameter (the terminal adonic) are likely to stand for historical *accretions* to or *aberrations* from a formulaic prototype. At the same time, since they have been effectively incorporated into the system, they are the best proof that the built-in *entropy* of Homeric diction coexists with a kind of *paradoxical taxonomy*. Diachronically seen, *incompatibility* has become masterfully *canonized*.[22]

In order to avoid any misunderstandings, I should make it clear that I am not arguing for the equation of any preverbal templates with actual phrases

---

[20] For enjambment, coterminacy, (and the concepts of *isometric parallelism* and *isometric oscillation*) in Modern Greek folk song, see Kyriakidis 1978:209–280; Baud-Bovy 1973:301–313; Sifakis 1988:136–164.
[21] Kahane 2005:70.
[22] See Kahane 2005:70–72.

Chapter Nine

endowed with specific metrical properties.²³ On the contrary, I draw attention to the fact that the part of XXII 1 following the trochaic caesura contains a *cataphoric* word-group that leads the flow of speech forward, whereas in XXI 6, XXI 528, and XXI 532, πεφυζότες is a 'sense-terminal' word, i.e. one marking the completion of a sense-group. The aforementioned *cataphoric* word-group metrically occupies the last two feet of the hexameter (– ⏑ ⏑ – –), which correspond to an identifiable and autonomous metrical unit, the adonic. Before going on, let us briefly consider the following 'evolutionary' model suggested by Nagy with respect to the relation between meter and phraseology:

> At first ... traditional phraseology simply contains built in rhythms. Later, the factor of tradition led to the preference of phrases with some rhythms over phrases with other rhythms. Still later, the preferred rhythms have their own dynamics and become regulators of any incoming phraseology.²⁴

The adonic, which became a verse-terminal boundary in the dactylic hexameter, may well have been such a 'built in rhythm', more so since it is an independent metrical unit with an extremely *rigid syllabicity. Right justification*, i.e. the tendency of the hexameter to display a progressive (as one moves from left to right *in the printed page*) rigidity by making the short syllables less prone to replacement by a long syllable, can be seen in the low ratio of substitution of the dactyl (– ⏑ ⏑) by a spondee (– –) in the fifth foot. Therefore, it can be argued that the terminal adonic, being a preferred rhythm, has evolved into a regulator of incoming phraseology, which in the case of πεφυζότες ἠΰτε νεβροί has been *conceptually detached* from the thematic environment of a simile and *dictionally translated* into the built-in rhythm of the terminal adonic.

In a nutshell, the examination of the outer and inner metric of verses XXI 6, XXI 528, XXI 532 and XXII 1 points to the participle πεφυζότες as the center around which the rest of the dictional elements were put into orbit. This participle had been 'extracted' from its 'natural' sequence (the simile πεφυζότες ἠΰτε νεβροί) and has created a series of allomorphs on the one hand, while preserving something of its ancient rust on the other, despite the adaptation to a new environment.²⁵

---

[23] See Kahane 2005:75.
[24] Nagy 1974:145; see also Nagy 1990a:37.
[25] It is certainly noteworthy that all the attestations of the form πεφυζότες are located in *Iliad* XXI and XXII and are only separated by a few verses. For the process of expansion and contraction of formulas, see Hainsworth 1968:74–89.

Genealogy of verses XXI 6, 528, 532 and XXII 1

The Formula πεφυζότες ἠΰτε νεβροί//-ούς (Stupefied Like Fawns)

The formula πεφυζότες ἠΰτε νεβροί is attested also as τεθηπότες ἠΰτε νεβροί//-ούς:

1. τίφθ' οὕτως ἔστητε τεθηπότες ἠΰτε νεβροί (IV 243)
2. τοὺς ἐξῆγε θύραζε τεθηπότας ἠΰτε νεβρούς (XXI 29)

The metrical form of the above verses is the following:

$$---\mid--\cup{}^{tr}\mid\cup-\cup\cup\mid-\cup\cup--\text{ (IV 243)}$$
$$---\cup\mid\cup-\cup{}^{tr}\mid\cup-\cup\cup\mid-\cup\cup--\text{ (XXI 29)}$$

These two verses are based on the same metrical, syntactic, structural (with respect to cola 3 and 4) and semantic pattern as far as their second hemistiches are concerned (since they are occupied by the formula τεθηπότες, -ας ἠΰτε νεβροί // -ούς).[27]

---

[26] Verse XXI 532 is an allomorph of XXII 1. The expression προτὶ ἄστυ is a traditional phrase (23 times in the *Iliad*, 7 times in the *Odyssey*) placed before the trochaic caesura (26 times). See Hoekstra 1964:118.

[27] The participle τεθηπότες is also attested in the nominative singular (τεθηπώς) in XXI 64 (ὣς ὥρμαινε μένων· ὁ δέ οἱ σχεδὸν ἦλθε τεθηπώς) and refers to Lycaon. The form τεθηπώς does not concern my research since it does not form part of the formulaic prototype that I have discussed above. The same applies to the form ταφών, which is connected to the root θαφ - of the verb τάφω, as is the case with τεθηπώς and τεθηπότες but it belongs to a different formulaic model.

We can therefore postulate an initial phase during which the built-in rhythm of the terminal adonic regulated the incoming phraseology of πεφυζότες ἠΰτε νεβροί and τεθηπότες, -ας ἠΰτε νεβροί // -ούς. The mental template these formulas stem from did not make its way into the system of Homeric diction in its entirety, but was broken down to its constituent parts. In the first phase, there was no formula contraction (as often happens in cases like this) that could have given a new coin, such as *πεφυζότες νεβροί, since the form πεφυζότες should always be followed by a vowel-initial word to avoid a cretic (– ᴗ –), which would of course be unacceptable for the hexameter. Nevertheless, in all the attestations of the form πεφυζότες, the terminal adonic (– ᴗ ᴗ – –) begins with an open syllable. At a later phase, the participle πεφυζότες was 'detached' from the ἠΰτε νεβροί and used independently.

It seems that the phrases πεφυζότες ἠΰτε νεβροί 'panic-stricken like fawns' and τεθηπότες, -ας ἠΰτε νεβροί // ούς 'stupefied like fawns' represent allomorphic manifestations of the same formula, as they have been developed upon the same semantic, metrical, and syntactic pattern. This observation is further corroborated by the fact that the kernel of this set expression is the simile (ἠΰτε νεβροί), which is localized at the most rigid and crystallized (and probably older) part of the hexameter, the terminal adonic (– ᴗ ᴗ – –).

After having established firm ground by having shown that we are in fact dealing with the same formula, it is now time to examine the function of these expressions within their immediate thematic environment.[28]

Migrating Formulas and Intertextual Imagery

In this second part, I will try to show how the mental pattern triggered by the formula πεφυζότες ἠΰτε νεβροί has 'migrated' from an intertextually reconstructed imagery to the dictional material of the epic tradition, at which point the diction is shaped into the given metrical and morphological constraints of the so-called Homeric *Kunstsprache*, an artificial language amounting to an amalgam of local dialects and various linguistic features that pertain to different historical periods.

It has been argued[29] that the simile in *Iliad* XXII 189–193 foreshadows the fatal pursuit of Hector by Achilles around the walls of Troy, the former being

---

[28] The preceding metrical and structural analysis is indispensable for the semantic investigation that will ensue. For it is not possible to trace the latent connotations of a formula unless one has acutely determined its pre-Iliadic (but epic in all probability) prehistory, its metrical structure, its place within the hexameter and finally its morphological variations.

[29] Richardson 1993:106.

compared to a young deer and the latter to a dog. Moulton[30] maintains that not only this particular simile but also the initial similes in *Iliad* XXII are all anticipatory, "since later in XXII the fawn image is expanded into one of the full-scale similes for the pursuit of Hector."[31]

As far as the participle πεφυζότες is concerned, Ameis-Hentze maintains that the poet preferred it instead of πεφευγότες "*von der die Flucht überdauernden Stimmung.*" Richardson[32] highlights the fact that this preference may be due to the influence of the word φύζα (panic-stricken flight),[33] constituting a more emphatic expression than φυγή (simple flight). This is also the interpretation offered by the scholia vetera (bT: καὶ τὴν μετὰ δέους κατάπληξιν οὕτω καλεῖ. ἔστιν οὖν δεδειλιακότες). It seems that the uncontrolled, panic-stricken flight of the deer facing great danger was the pretext for using the root *φυζ- explicitly for the *flight of the deer* (see *Iliad* IX 2: ... Φύζα, Φόβου κρυόεντος ἑταίρη).[34]

Notwithstanding the accuracy of the above observations, I will embark on a closer look at the thematic environment within which XXI 6, XXI 528, XXI 532 and XXII 1 are placed. In order to get a full picture of the semantic range covered by the participles πεφυζότες and τεθηπότες and examine their genetic interrelation, it is necessary to look at the narrative context:[35]

> Ἀργεῖοι ἰόμωροι, ἐλεγχέες, οὔ νυ σέβεσθε;
> τίφθ' οὕτως <u>ἔστητε</u> τεθηπότες ἠΰτε νεβροί,

---

[30] Moulton 1977:78–80, 76–87.
[31] Moulton 1977:79.
[32] Richardson 1993:54.
[33] According to Kirk 1985:357, the deer are "spiritless (ἀνάλκιδες, cf. ἀλκή 245) ... natural victims of carnivores in the poem's five remaining deer-similes ... they cover much ground in flight, stand still when tired, have no inclination to resist, but look puzzled." The poet used the expression φυζακινῆς ἐλάφοισιν (XIII 102) only for the Trojans (as he did with the form πεφυζότες) because he considered this unorganized, panic-stricken form of retreat as more appropriate to Asiatic than to Greek mentality. This is similar to the manner in which the two armies march into battle: the Trojans with shouting and uproar, whereas the Achaeans in silence. This deliberate distinction is made implicit by the particle αὐτάρ in XXII 3; the opposition alludes, through the different manner of movement of the two armies, to the different psychological state of the two sides. See also *Iliad* IV 422–438. The basic works on this topic are: Strassburger 1954 and Latacz 1977. For a more recent treatment of this theme, see Willcock 1993:141–147. For the first battle in the *Iliad* in which one can observe the distinction between the different ways the two armies march into battle, see Maronitis 1999:27–50.
[34] Moulton 1977:78–79 translates the participle πεφυζότες in the following way: "... who had run like fawns ..." In this way the thematic and emotional range of the form πεφυζότες is reduced to a simple expression of the Trojan retreat.
[35] The underlined phrases or words in the above passages determine the thematic environment of the formula πεφυζότες ἠΰτε νεβροί and of its allomorphs.

Chapter Nine

αἵ τ' ἐπεὶ οὖν ἔκαμον πολέος πεδίοιο θέουσαι,
<u>ἔστᾶσ'</u>, <u>οὐδ' ἄρα τίς σφι μετὰ φρεσὶ γίνεται ἀλκή</u>·
ὣς ὑμεῖς <u>ἔστητε</u> τεθηπότες, οὐδὲ μάχεσθε.
ἦ <u>μένετε</u> Τρῶας σχεδὸν ἐλθέμεν, ἔνθά τε νῆες
εἰρύατ' εὔπρυμνοι, <u>πολιῆς ἐπὶ θινὶ θαλάσσης</u>,
ὄφρα ἴδητ' αἴ κ' ὔμμιν ὑπέρσχῃ χεῖρα Κρονίων;

Argives, you arrow-fighters, have you no shame, you abuses?
Why are you simply *standing* there bewildered, like young deer
who after they are tired from running through a great meadow
stand there still, and there is no heart of courage within them?
Thus are you *standing still* bewildered and are not fighting.
Or are you *waiting* for the Trojans to come close, where the
    strong-sterned
ships have been hauled up along *the strand of the grey sea*,
so you may know if Kronos' son will hold his hand over you?

Iliad IV 242–249

ἀλλ' ὅτε δὴ <u>πόρον ἷξον ἐϋρρεῖος ποταμοῖο</u>
<u>Ξάνθου δινήεντος</u>, ὃν ἀθάνατος τέκετο Ζεύς,
ἔνθα διατμήξας τοὺς μὲν πεδίονδ' ἐδίωκεν
πρὸς πόλιν, ᾗ περ Ἀχαιοὶ <u>ἀτυζόμενοι φοβέοντο</u>
ἤματι τῷ προτέρῳ, ὅτ' ἐμαίνετο φαίδιμος Ἕκτωρ·
τῇ ῥ' οἵ γε <u>προχέοντο πεφυζότες</u>, ἠέρα δ' Ἥρη
πίτνα πρόσθε βαθεῖαν ἐρυκέμεν· ἡμίσεες δὲ
<u>ἐς ποταμὸν</u> εἰλέοντο <u>βαθύρροον ἀργυροδίνην</u>.
ἐν δ' ἔπεσον μεγάλῳ πατάγῳ, βράχε δ' αἰπὰ ῥέεθρα,
ὄχθαι δ' ἀμφὶ περὶ μεγάλ' ἴαχον· οἳ δ' ἀλαλητῷ
<u>ἔννεον ἔνθα καὶ ἔνθα ἑλισσόμενοι κατὰ δίνας</u>.
ὡς δ' ὅθ' <u>ὑπὸ ῥιπῆς πυρὸς</u> ἀκρίδες ἠερέθονται
<u>φευγέμεναι ποταμόνδε</u>, <u>τὸ δὲ φλέγει ἀκάματον πῦρ</u>
ὀρμενον ἐξαίφνης, ταὶ δὲ <u>πτώσσουσι καθ' ὕδωρ</u>,
ὣς ὑπ' Ἀχιλλῆος <u>Ξάνθου βαθυδινήεντος</u>
πλῆτο <u>ῥόος</u> κελάδων ἐπιμὶξ ἵππων τε καὶ ἀνδρῶν.

But when they came to the *crossing place of the fair-running river
of whirling Xanthos*, a stream whose father was Zeus the
    immortal,
there Achilleus split them and chased some back over the flat
    land

toward the city, where the Achaians themselves *had stampeded in terror*
on the day before, when glorious Hektor was still in his fury.
Along this ground they were streaming in flight; but Hera let fall
a deep mist before them to stay them. Meanwhile the other half
were crowded into the *silvery whirls of the deep-running river*
and tumbled into it in huge clamour, and the steep-running water
sounded, and the banks echoed hugely about them, as they outcrying
tried to swim this way and that, spun about in the eddies.
As before the *blast of a fire* the locusts escaping
into a river swarm in air, and the fire unwearied
blazes from a sudden start, and the locusts *huddle in water;*
so before Achilleus *the murmuring waters of Xanthos*
the deep-whirling were filled with confusion of men and of horses.

Iliad XXI 1–16

ὡς δ' ὑπὸ δελφῖνος μεγακήτεος ἰχθύες ἄλλοι
φεύγοντες πιμπλᾶσι μυχοὺς λιμένος εὐόρμου
δειδιότες· μάλα γάρ τε κατεσθίει ὅν κε λάβῃσιν·
ὣς Τρῶες ποταμοῖο κατὰ δεινοῖο ῥέεθρα
πτῶσσον ὑπὸ κρημνούς. ὃ δ' ἐπεὶ κάμε χεῖρας ἐναίρων,
ζωοὺς ἐκ ποταμοῖο δυώδεκα λέξατο κούρους,
ποινὴν Πατρόκλοιο Μενοιτιάδαο θανόντος·
τοὺς ἐξῆγε θύραζε τεθηπότας ἠΰτε νεβρούς,
δῆσε δ' ὀπίσσω χεῖρας ἐϋτμήτοισιν ἱμᾶσιν,
τοὺς αὐτοὶ φορέεσκον ἐπὶ στρεπτοῖσι χιτῶσιν,
δῶκε δ' ἑταίροισιν κατάγειν κοίλας ἐπὶ νῆας·

As before *a huge-gaping dolphin the other fishes*
escaping cram the corners of *a deepwater harbour*
in fear, for he avidly eats up any he can catch;
so the Trojans *along the course of the terrible river*
shrank under the bluffs. He, when his hands grew weary with killing,
chose out and took twelve young men alive *from the river*
to be vengeance for the death of Patroklos, the son of Menoitios.

Chapter Nine

These, bewildered with fear like fawns, he led out of the water
and bound their hands behind them with thongs well cut out of
    leather,
with the very belts they themselves wore on their ingirt tunics,
and gave them to his companions to lead away to the hollow
    ships.

Iliad XXI 22–32

ὡς δ' ὅτε καπνὸς ἰὼν εἰς οὐρανὸν εὐρὺν ἱκάνει
<u>ἄστεος αἰθομένοιο</u>, θεῶν δέ ἑ μῆνις ἀνῆκεν,
πᾶσι δ' ἔθηκε πόνον, πολλοῖσι δὲ κήδε' ἐφῆκεν,
ὣς Ἀχιλεὺς Τρώεσσι πόνον καὶ κήδε' ἔθηκεν.
ἑστήκει δ' ὁ γέρων Πρίαμος θείου ἐπὶ πύργου·
ἐς δ' ἐνόησ' Ἀχιλῆα πελώριον, αὐτὰρ ὑπ' αὐτοῦ
Τρῶες ἄφαρ <u>κλονέοντο</u> πεφυζότες, <u>οὐδέ τις ἀλκή</u>
<u>γίνεθ'</u>· ὃ δ' οἰμώξας ἀπὸ πύργου βαῖνε χαμᾶζε,
ὀτρύνων παρὰ τεῖχος ἀγακλειτοὺς πυλαωρούς·
"πεπταμένας ἐν χερσὶ πύλας ἔχετ', εἰς ὅ κε λαοὶ
ἔλθωσι προτὶ ἄστυ πεφυζότες· ἦ γὰρ Ἀχιλλεὺς
ἐγγὺς ὅδε <u>κλονέων</u>· νῦν οἴω λοίγι' ἔσεσθαι.
αὐτὰρ ἐπεί κ' ἐς τεῖχος ἀναπνεύσωσιν ἀλέντες,
αὖτις ἐπ' ἂψ θέμεναι σανίδας πυκινῶς ἀραρυίας·
<u>δείδια</u> γάρ, μὴ οὖλος ἀνὴρ ἐς τεῖχος ἅληται."
ὣς ἔφαθ'· οἳ δ' ἄνεσάν τε πύλας καὶ ἀπῶσαν ὀχῆας,
αἳ δὲ πετασθεῖσαι τεῦξαν φάος. αὐτὰρ Ἀπόλλων
ἀντίος ἐξέθορε, Τρώων ἵνα λοιγὸν ἀμύναι.
οἳ δ' ἰθὺς πόλιος καὶ τείχεος ὑψηλοῖο
<u>δίψῃ καρχαλέοι</u>, κεκονιμένοι ἐκ πεδίοιο
<u>φεῦγον</u>· ὃ δὲ σφεδανὸν ἔφεπ' ἔγχεϊ, λύσσα δέ οἱ κῆρ
αἰὲν ἔχε κρατερή, μενέαινε δὲ κῦδος ἀρέσθαι.

And as when smoke ascending goes up into the wide sky
from a burning city, with the anger of the gods let loose upon it
which inflicted labour upon them all, and sorrow on many,
so Achilleus inflicted labour and sorrow upon the Trojans.
The aged Priam had taken his place on the god-built bastion,
and looked out and saw gigantic Achilleus, where before him
the Trojans *fled* in the speed of their confusion, *no war strength
left them*. He groaned and descended to the ground from the
    bastion

and beside the wall set in motion the glorious guards of the
    gateway;
'Hold the gates wide open in your hands, so that our people
in their flight can get inside the city, for here is Achilleus
close by, stampeding them, and I think there will be disaster.
But once they are crowded inside the city and get wind again,
shut once more the door-leaves closely fitted together.
I am afraid this ruinous man may spring into our stronghold'.
He spoke, and they spread open the gates and shoved back the
    door bars
and the gates opening let in daylight. Meanwhile Apollo
sprang out to meet them, so that he could fend off destruction
from the Trojans, who, straight for the city and the lift of the
    rampart
dusty from the plain and throats *rugged with thirst, fled
away*, and Achilleus followed fiercely with the spear, strong
    madness
forever holding his heart and violent after his glory.
Iliad XXI 522–543

τόφρ' ἄλλοι Τρῶες <u>πεφοβημένοι</u> ἦλθον ὁμίλῳ
ἀσπάσιοι προτὶ ἄστυ· πόλις δ' ἔμπλητο ἀλέντων.
οὐδ' ἄρα τοί γ' ἔτλαν πόλιος καὶ τείχεος ἐκτός
<u>μεῖναι</u> ἔτ' ἀλλήλους καὶ γνώμεναι, ὅς τε <u>πεφεύγοι</u>
ὅς τ' ἔθαν' ἐν πολέμῳ, ἀλλ' <u>ἐσσυμένως ἐσέχυντο</u>
ἐς πόλιν, ὅν τινα τῶν γε πόδες καὶ γοῦναι σαώσαι.

ὡς οἳ μὲν κατὰ ἄστυ, πεφυζότες ἠΰτε νεβροί,
<u>ἱδρῶ ἀπεψύχοντο πίον τ' ἀκέοντό τε δίψαν</u>,
κεκλιμένοι καλῇσιν ἐπάλξεσιν· αὐτὰρ Ἀχαιοὶ
τείχεος ἆσσον ἴσαν, σάκε' ὤμοισι κλίναντες.

All this time the rest of the Trojans *fled* in a body
gladly into the town, and the city was filled with their
    swarming.
They dared no longer stay outside the wall and outside the city
to wait for each other and find out which one *had got away*
and who had died in the battle, so *hastily were they streaming*
into the city, each man as his knees and feet could rescue him.

> So along the city the Trojans, who had run like fawns, dried
> *the sweat off their bodies and drank and slaked their thirst,* leaning
> along the magnificent battlements. Meanwhile the Achaians
> sloping their shields across their shoulders came close to the
> rampart.
>
> *Iliad* XXI 606–XXII 4

By looking at the above passages we can pinpoint several common characteristics that they share:

a. expressions denoting an undisciplined, unruly, and disorderly flight due to sudden fear (ἀτυζόμενοι φοβέοντο, προχέοντο, φευγέμεναι, πτώσσουσι, φεύγοντες, δειδιότες, πτῶσσον, κλονέοντο, κλονέων, δείδια, φεῦγον, πεφοβημένοι, πεφεύγοι, ἐσσυμένως ἐσέχυντο),

b. exhaustion, distress of both the persecuted and the pursuer (expressed by the verb κάμνω and verbs denoting "standing in a place": ἔστητε - ἑστᾶσι - μένετε - μεῖναι) after a continuous pursuit,

c. complete feebleness of the persecuted (οὐδ' ἄρα τίς σφι ... γίνεται ἀλκή, οὐδέ τις ἀλκή // γίνεθ' ...),

d. reference to a water element either literally (πολιῆς ἐπὶ θινὶ θαλάσσης, πόρον ἷξον ἐϋρρεῖος ποταμοῖο, Ξάνθου δινήεντος, ἐς ποταμὸν ... βαθύρροον ἀργυροδίνην, ἔννεον ἔνθα καὶ ἔνθα ἑλισσόμενοι κατὰ δίνας, ποταμόνδε, καθ' ὕδωρ, Ξάνθου βαθυδινήεντος, ῥόος, ὑπὸ δελφῖνος μεγακήτεος ἰχθύες ἄλλοι, λιμένος εὐόρμου, ποταμοῖο κατὰ δεινοῖο ῥέεθρα, ἐκ ποταμοῖο), figuratively (δίψῃ καρχαλέοι, ἱδρῶ ἀπεψύχοντο πίον τ' ἀκέοντό τε δίψαν), or through its latent opposition to the danger emerging from the destructive force of fire (ὑπὸ ῥιπῆς πυρός, φλέγει ἀκάματον πῦρ, ἄστεος αἰθομένοιο).

Therefore, the emerging semantic framework (concerning the formula πεφυζότες ἠΰτε νεβροί) is that of uncontrolled fear seizing the pursued, who, at first, remain stunned due to panic and then attempt to escape. But what is the role of the water element?

Nagy[36] has convincingly shown that the words πῦρ and πόντος create a semantic framework that determines the *Trojan force* and the *danger the Achaeans are facing*, respectively. This specific poetic imagery has been frequently used by the poet and has almost developed into an Iliadic metonymy abundantly employed in Books IV-XV.[37]

---

[36] Nagy 1979:337–340.
[37] See Nagy 1979:335. The thematic motif of comparing the flight of pursued men to that of deer is already known from the Old Testament. See Rahlfs 1965, *Lamentationes Jeremiah*, 1.6 (καὶ ἐξῄρθη ἐκ θυγατρὸς Σειὼν πᾶσα ἡ εὐπρέπεια αὐτῆς· // ἐγένοντο οἱ ἄρχοντες αὐτῆς ὡς κριοὶ

Genealogy and Poetic Imagery of a Homeric Formula

From *Iliad* XVI onwards the picture on the battlefield changes. In contrast to previous Trojans victories, the Achaeans are now chasing the Trojans, due to Patroclus' and then Achilles' entry into battle. This shift in the course of the plot leads to an equivalent change in the roles of the two armies and, consequently, in the two poles of the imagery: now the fire symbolizes the force of Achilles, whereas the water element alludes to the salvation of the Trojans. Nevertheless, the difference between this and the previous imagery is not only seen as a reversal of the roles of victor and vanquished. The water element is only a mirage, a deceitful illusion supposedly leading the Trojans (who are now the pursued) to salvation, when most of them will be slaughtered by Achilles while attempting to get out of the river. The function of this imagery changes dramatically, since it now connotes that the balance between the initial victory of the Trojans and the subsequent prevalence of the Achaeans is misleading. The Achaeans will win the war and eventually sack Troy.

Death has often been linked to a sea journey, as the transition to the underworld requires a voyage by boat through the river *Acheron* and/or the lake *Acherousia*.[38] In Homeric eschatological mythmaking, the world of the living is separated from the world of the dead by a river constituting a border, literal and figurative alike, for a passage to Hades. Homeric eschatological beliefs[39] are consonant with the connection between the word πόντος and the concept of danger. It has been argued that the Greek word πόντος is related to the Sanskrit *pántāḥ* 'path, passage' and to the Latin *pons* 'bridge', and that the three forms connote *transition*, or, rather, *perilous transition*.[40]

The association of the formula πεφυζότες ἠΰτε νεβροί with the idea of imminent death is also dormant in the expression ἱδρῶ ἀπεψύχοντο (attested in *Iliad* XXII 2 just after πεφυζότες ἠΰτε νεβροί) and *mutatis mutandis* in the phrase ἀναπνεύσωσιν ἀλέντες (*Iliad* XXI 534). According to Sourvinou-Inwood, "[t]he word *psyche* is etymologically connected with *psycho*, breathe, as the cessation of breathing is the simplest and most obvious sign of death. The

---

οὐχ εὑρίσκοντες νομήν· // καὶ ἐπορεύοντο ἐν οὐκ ἰσχύι κατὰ πρόσωπον διώκοντες). See West 1997:248.

[38] See Barringer 1998:55. Cambitoglou, Aelian, and Chamay 1986:209 argue that the Nereids derive their eschatological dimension from their connection to water. This is exactly the reason explaining their link with funeral monuments like that at Xanthos, which dates from 390/380 BC. For more details on death and water and the image of Charon as a ferryman, see Lattimore 1976:13; Vermeule 1979:179; Sourvinou-Inwood 1981:15–39; 1996:61–62, 347–353; *LIMC* III.1:210–215.

[39] See Sourvinou-Inwood 1996:61.

[40] I owe this point made by Benveniste 1954:251–264 to Nagy 1979:339.

image of a dying person's last breath being released into the air provided the model for the visualization and representation of the departure from the body at the moment of death of the person's surviving component."[41]

Now I hope that the picture is much more clear. A brief sketch of the evolutionary process and semantic development of the above formula up to its present state can be outlined in the following way: it seems that the preverbal *Gestalt*[42] that existed in the formula πεφυζότες ἠΰτε νεβροί was that of panic-stricken, powerless deer, which were attacked by some carnivorous predator *when they were drinking water*, probably at some river bank.[43] This preverbal *Gestalt*, being innate in the mental template pertaining to this visual icon, was shaped into a formula placed in a dictional environment that recalled the initial, archetypal image from which the simile emanated. The participles πεφυζότες and τεθηπότες determine an emotional process that includes two chronologically distinct phases in the realization of the *Gestalt*: the confusion and perplexity in front of danger (τεθηπότες) and the panic- and terror-stricken flight (πεφυζότες). As the concept of πόντος symbolizes a *perilous transition*, so the water element alludes to *destruction*, to *imminent death*,[44] whence the simile of the deer for the panic-stricken Trojans. Needless to say, the thirst of the exhausted warriors recalls that of the deer who stop at the riverbanks to drink water.

The formula πεφυζότες ἠΰτε νεβροί is at the same time a simile, a part of which (even when found in isolation within the narrative) is surrounded by some common thematic elements and which consequently triggers in the singer's and the audience's mind the same connotations. This dictional and thematic material (as is the case with the short simile)[45] has acquired during centuries of long oral transmission by generations of bards a specific emotive tone, a special color that it preserved even when it entered Iliadic diction. This is a good example of how *radical complexity* and *overabundant systematicity* coexist within the web of Homeric diction and how *regular usage* has been

---

[41] See Sourvinou-Inwood 1996:57, and for a more detailed description of the journey to Hades, 56–66.
[42] For the concept of preverbal *Gestalt*, see Nagler 1967:269–311; 1974:8.
[43] For the role of the deer in ancient literature, see Keller 1913:277 and *RE* 16, VIII.2 s.v. Hirsch. For the deer in Homer, see Rahn 1953:277–297, 431–480. See also Rahn 1967:90–115, where the author shows how a deer's death in *Odyssey* x 157–160. is absorbed by the heroic tone of that specific scene. According to Dierauer 1977, in animal similes the emphasis often lies not in the *"Ähnlichkeit der Situation"* but in the *"Übereinstimmung der Gefühle"*. See also Schnapp-Gourbeillon 1981:31. The fullest investigation of this topic is that of Richter 1968:44–54.
[44] See *Odyssey* xiv 135, xxiv 291.
[45] See Bakker 1988:226.

followed by *pattern deviation* and *plurality*.⁴⁶ As a corollary to the combination of *complexity* and *systematicity*, we can see how the system has been able to create a delicate balance between *nucleus* and *periphery*⁴⁷ or *core* and *filler*.⁴⁸ A great deal of the semantic context of the aforementioned formula 'surfaces' in the Iliadic narrative even when the peripheral elements are not textually attested. Their semantic importance is so deeply built in the formula of which they are part that it is contextually 'present' even when πεφυζότες or τεθηπότες, -ας are not accompanied by the *periphery/filler* ἠΰτε νεβροί // -ούς. Therefore, the participle πεφυζότες points to the other pole of the semantic pair of the formula, the simile ἠΰτε νεβροί, even when isolated from it in the poem. In this way, the formula πεφυζότες ἠΰτε νεβροί reveals the multiple meanings of a poetic imagery consonant with Homeric eschatological beliefs, and all this through the dictional fossil of a formulaic expression.

In this light, *traditional referentiality* becomes a form of *intertextual cross-referencing*, since it alludes not to other identifiable texts but to a shared image-mapping⁴⁹ of a simile that stands for a *single* preverbal *Gestalt*. The conceptual pattern 'predator against prey' was further particularized into two distinct parts, the τεθηπότες part and the πεφυζότες part, referring to the dazzled or panic-stricken deer that are attacked by a carnivorous predator while drinking water. The intratextual diffusion and scattering of the constituent parts of a coherent *Gestalt* is balanced by their *intertextual* retrieval, even when not directly mentioned in a given performance. In such a complex oral medium as epic poetry, ellipsis, fragmentation, and deroutinization constitute manifestations of Homeric *entropy*,⁵⁰ which coexists with systematicity, canonization, and regularization. What is synchronically absent can therefore be diachronically present.

---

⁴⁶ See Kahane 2005:77–78.
⁴⁷ See Bakker 1995:116.
⁴⁸ See Visser 1987, 1988. See Russo 1997:253–260.
⁴⁹ See also chapter 12.
⁵⁰ On the term *entropy* and its implications, see Kahane 2005:70.

Part Four

INTERTEXTUALITY AND INTRATEXTUAL SEQUENCES

10

The Rhetorics of Supplication and the Epic Intertext
(*Iliad* I 493–516)

INTERTEXTUAL REFERENCES that do not belong to specific epic traditions can become thematically associated intratextual sequences in Homeric epic. One form of this arrangement consists of proximal sequences, where topics originating from different versions of a given mythical context are presented intratextually as part of a thematic chain. Cumulative arrangement with its built-in linearity leads to a compacting of material and a resulting dramatic intensification, since tattered pieces of myth are rewoven into a new, thick web of associations. In this chapter, I address, by way of a case study, Thetis' supplication to Zeus in *Iliad* I, a scene of special importance for the poem as a whole. In my analysis I will follow the deployment of the scene and examine how its structure and diction help us reconstruct the epic intertext from which it stems.

Although the *Iliad* moves on various levels and rotates between different poles,[1] one set of boundaries is Thetis' supplication to Zeus (forming the last part of the scene that begins with the meeting between Thetis and Achilles in *Iliad* I), and Priam's supplication to Achilles (in *Iliad* XXIV), which brings the epic to an end.[2] Thetis' supplication also functions as a nucleus that introduces themes running through the entire epic. Its importance lies in its hybrid nature, since it operates as a miniature model, or rather a pattern, presenting narrative threads that evolve and create larger units as the plot unravels. These themes

---

[1] I am not inclined to see a single thematic thread upon which the *Iliad* is composed and developed: anger, lament, and supplication are among the most important structural threads permeating the entire poem. Recent attempts to highlight one of these themes while underestimating others are bound to be one-sided once we acknowledge the multifariousness of the epic as well as the presence of multifaceted aspects, conjured up at times to create an exploding poetic and aesthetic polysemy.

[2] For a comparative analysis of supplication in the *Iliad* and the *Odyssey* with special emphasis on context, see Pedrick 1982:125–140.

Chapter Ten

include Achilles' short life-span, his liminality as a hero, the antithesis between honor and life, and the fulfillment of Zeus' will (Διὸς βουλή). Before I embark on a detailed stylistic analysis of *Iliad* I 493–516, I would like to summarize the findings in recent scholarship on Homer that are relevant to my research.

Supplication: From Theme to Speech-Act

"The plot of the *Iliad* traces a development between two successful supplications: Thetis' supplication to Zeus in Book I, in which she bids Zeus to honor her son (τίμησόν μοι υἱόν), and Priam's supplication to Achilles, by means of which Zeus conclusively honors Achilles and guarantees that he will have glory, or *kudos*."[3] Crotty, whose formulation I have just quoted, traces a poetics of supplication in the evolution of a deliberate contrast between the divine fate of Thetis and the mortal doom of her son Achilles. Zeus' will (Διὸς βουλή) is inaugurated with a prayer, which expresses the goddess' confidence "in her power to bring about her wishes (by offering an exchange of goods),"[4] but that is capped (in *Iliad* XXIV) by an old man's *supplication*, "which expresses the indifference of the world to the suppliant's wishes."[5]

The disparity between the immortality of the mother (Thetis) and the short life span of her son (Achilles) becomes a central theme around which the poem evolves and by which it differentiates itself from the previous tradition. In fact, a specific group of scholars, the so-called Neoanalysts, have strongly argued that the mother-son relationship (epitomized in the Thetis-Achilles pair) becomes one of the principal thematic areas where the *Iliad's* divergence from older epic poems, such as a pre-Homeric **Achilleis* (Kakridis) or **Memnonis* (Schadewaldt), can be observed. Thetis, for all her similarities to her Aethiopic counterpart Eos, will not grant immortality to Achilles as Eos did to Memnon in the post-Homeric *Aethiopis*,[6] but will offer him the chance to regain his honor, which, as she well knows, will definitely lead to his death. Consequently, "what Thetis asks Zeus to give Achilles is the opportunity to become the hero of the *Iliad*, to create the terms by which heroism will be redefined,"[7] as well as the terms by which the subject matter of the

---

[3] Crotty 1994:94.
[4] Crotty 1994:96.
[5] Crotty 1994:96.
[6] See Proclus' *Chrestomathy* 189–190 Severyns = 60–61 Kullmann: ἔπειτα Ἀχιλλεὺς Μέμνονα κτείνει· καὶ τούτῳ μὲν Ἠὼς παρὰ Διὸς αἰτησαμένη ἀθανασίαν δίδωσι ('Then Achilles slays Memnon, and Eos gives him immortality, having asked for it from Zeus').
[7] See Slatkin 1991:40. For a detailed analysis of the connection between the *Iliad* and the *Aethiopis*, see Kakridis 1949 and Schadewaldt 1965⁴. For the contents of the *Aethiopis*, see Proclus' summary

poem will be thematically verbalized, I might add. On the level of plot, Thetis' supplication unravels the first narrative thread of the poem, i.e. the fulfillment of Achilles' will, which is how the *Iliad* 'translates' his *wrath* (μῆνις) against Agamemnon. Thetis' supplication and its subsequent approval by Zeus become the driving forces of the plot until the moment its narrative *élan* is cut short, being subsumed and absorbed by another, even greater theme: Achilles' new *wrath* (μῆνις) against Hector. This new *wrath* will eventually come to an end through *a final supplication by Priam*, which will only be possible in its turn by a complete reversal of the order of meetings between Achilles-Thetis-Zeus in the beginning of *Iliad* I.[8]

Supplication forms one of the major subgenres used by the heroic performer.[9] Martin[10] has argued that, although speeches in the *Iliad* are highly stylized poetic versions of reality, they still retain their mimetic character, as they tend to reflect the poet's knowledge of how his contemporaries express their feelings and ideas. Archaic coloring and traditional elements are not absent from the speeches, but, as recent studies have shown,[11] it is there (in the speeches) that most of the innovations occur. In Martin's own words, "although we see Mycenaean memories in the narrative of Iliadic fighting, there is no comparable body of material for the poet to recall when reporting what Agamemnon, Odysseus, or Achilles says. Composition is less subject to tradition here. Speech is qualitatively different; unlike diegesis, it is the arena for pure mimesis."[12] This mimetic character observed in Homeric speeches

---

in Allen 1912:106; see also Severyns 1928:313–327. For all the relevant material concerning the Epic Cycle, see Allen 1912; Bernabé 1987; Davies 1988a; West 2003. For Proclus' summaries, I have used both the text of Severyns 1963 with minor changes and Kullmann's 1960 = 2002 paragraphization.

[8] The architectural symmetry of *Iliad* I and *Iliad* XXIV has been studied, most notably, by Whitman 1958. The order of meetings in *Iliad* I (Achilles-Thetis, Thetis-Zeus) is reversed in *Iliad* XXIV (Zeus-Thetis, Thetis-Achilles).

[9] Other such genres include prayer, lament, command, insult, and narration from memory. See Martin 1989:44 citing Basset 1938:70–71, who argues that these subgenres occupy 90% of the speeches in the *Iliad*. See also Bauman 1978:27, who maintains that speech-acts and speech-genres should not be distinguished in an oral culture.

[10] See Martin 1989:45.

[11] Griffin 1986:39–57 observed that there are some features in the diction of the Homeric poems which are more common in speeches (higher frequency of abstract nouns, more freedom with explanation of events in terms of what we call personifications, reservation of crucial moral terms from the narrative to the speeches, higher percentages of negative epithets with a-privative). Therefore, he argued that the narrative portions of the poem antedate the speeches, since the features mentioned above speak for their lateness. Similar views have been earlier maintained by Krarup 1948:1–17 and Fränkel 1962:68.

[12] Martin 1989:45.

Chapter Ten

may also be connected to the basic distinction Martin makes between *muthos* and *epos*: "[A] *muthos* focuses on what the speaker says and how he or she says it, but epos consistently applies to what the addressee hears."[13] Under this scope, the relation between Thetis and Zeus in *Iliad* I is reflected both in the kind of speech employed by the suppliant (Thetis) and in the form of speech-act she believes she is performing. For in *Iliad* I 419 she calls the speech that Achilles wants her to address to Zeus an *epos* although it is a kind of command, albeit in the form of a supplication. This leveling out of the observable distinction between the two terms (*muthos* and *epos*, respectively) can be explained by the fact that *muthos* refers to authoritative (marked) speech, and *epos* to non-(necessarily) authoritative speech. Thetis' designation of Achilles' speech in *Iliad* I 419 as an *epos* is therefore indeterminate and does not necessarily mean that she views Achilles' speech as an unimportant utterance. At the same time, her using of the term *epos* shows that she considers her speech to be non-authoritative and "focuses on message, as perceived by the addressee, rather than on performance as enacted by the speaker."[14] These scrupulous observations may help us understand and appreciate more fully the internal rhetoric of Thetis' speech as well as its importance for the weaving of the poetics of the *Iliad* as a whole.

Polysemy and Repetition

In his study of the poetic significance of formal repetition in Homer, Kahane[15] has pointed to the use of certain semantic markers, such as localization, meter, and verse-structure determining the range of meanings for a specific word, thus contributing to what is today considered to be an essential epic property, polysemy. To the basic denotation of a word, Kahane adds reference specification by the immediate verbal context and also a context-free thematic reference provided by pattern deixis. In this light, it becomes clear that semantic monopoly, to put it bluntly, is basically absent from the Homeric poems.

Since the 1960s there has been an increase in the publication of studies providing reassessment of the oral-formulaic theory.[16] Most of these studies

---

[13] Martin 1989:16.
[14] Martin 1989:12.
[15] Kahane 1994.
[16] Major contributions by Hainsworth 1964:155–164, 1968; Hoekstra 1964; Edwards 1966:115–179. Recent scholarship in: Visser 1987, 1988; Bakker 1988:151–195; Bakker and Fabricotti 1991:63–84. See also the surveys by Holoka 1973, 1979, 1990a, 1990b; by Edwards 1986, 1988; by Foley 1985, 1988.

The Rhetorics of Supplication

have modified our "Parryan" concept of a rigid formulaic system based on the assumption of orality:

> The phenomena investigated ... can, I suggest, be the product of an oral/traditional composition, but their existence does not preclude the possibility of literate composition. It is unlikely that they can be used as an argument either for or against orality and/or traditionality, except when making the very broadest points, and they neither contradict nor require us to modify our notions of Homeric formula or formulaic technique.[17]

Kahane's view reflects my own opinion with respect to the dilemma between oral versus literate composition. Let me add that localization of metrical shapes is not incompatible with oral modes of verse composition, but is not typical of works orally composed since statistical data concerning localization of *hapax legomena* for written hexameter poetry such as that of Apollonius and Callimachus closely parallel the ones referring to the *Iliad* and the *Odyssey*.[18] As far as structural formulas are concerned, one should bear in mind that "a literate poet imitating and/or innovating on the basis of an earlier Homeric, or oral, or traditional poem, or any two or all of these, would have certainly had time to choose positioning according to his own design. The literary poet could invent as many expressions as he chose ..."[19] Repetition can be of various sorts. It can include words, word groups, metrical and syntactical patterns, or even whole verses. The reproduction of these patterns is the result of the tradition working within the mind of the singer. Repetitive melodic, metrical, syntactical, and acoustical patterns form a grammar of poetry, "a grammar superimposed, as it were, on the grammar of the language concerned ... The speaker of this language, once he has mastered it, does not move more mechanically within it than we do in ordinary speech."[20] This is certainly true for the singer composing within the limits determined by the grammar of poetry. On the other hand, repetition refers to *pattern usage* and pertains more to reception than to composition. To make this point more clear: my view is that both an ancient audience and a modern reader "are not directly subject to the exigencies of oral composition,"[21] and so repetition

---

[17] Kahane 1994:5.
[18] See O' Neill 1942:105–178; Fantuzzi 1988.
[19] Kahane 1994:10.
[20] Lord 1960:35–36.
[21] Kahane 1994:16.

Chapter Ten

is significant for them since they do not operate at the level of the singer's compositional process, but on the level of the reception of his work.[22]

Sharing both a compositional and a reception-oriented aspect, polysemy and repetition allow traditional epic to build and also teach its listeners its own special poetic grammar. Under this scope, themes of cardinal importance to the plot are embedded in the audience's interpretive code and become 'members' of a larger 'family' of associations. They are constituent parts of a system that is intertextually derived on a compositional level, but intratextually functional on the level of its reception by the audience during the performance.

The scene that presents Thetis supplicating Zeus is divided into three discernible phases of unequal length: 1. An introductory portion (I 493–499); 2. Thetis' first appeal (I 503–510); 3. Thetis' second appeal, introduced by three "intermediate verses" (I 511–516).

Openings (I 493–499)

After the meeting between Achilles and Thetis at the seashore, Odysseus' delivery of Chryseis to her father followed by his propitiating sacrifice to Apollo, and a brief comment on Achilles' withdrawal from battle, the scene changes to describe the local and temporal circumstances under which the supplication will take place.

The *staging* of the supplication at Olympos is effectuated by the formulaic couplet of verses in I 493–494. They are emphatically related by their initial phrases, ἀλλ' ὅτε δή and καὶ τότε δή, and are strongly formulaic in their components:[23]

I 493: Adjective +Verbal Group (Verb + Subject)

I 494: Verbal Group (Verb + Subject) + Participial Phrase (expressing time like the adjective of the preceding verse).[24]

---

[22] See Nagler 1967, 1974 who has argued that literary values can be extracted from repetition. According to his theory, "phrases would be considered not a closed 'system classifiable as a subset of a larger system and susceptible of sub-classification within its own boundaries, but an *open-ended* 'family'," where each part of the group is an allomorph derived from a mental but real entity (the *Gestalt*), which expresses a preverbal template encompassing all the phrases of the same family at an abstract level.

[23] Kirk 1985:105.

[24] Verses 493 and 494 have the shape: ABC (A: initial phrases formed by a conjunction [ἀλλ'-καί], a temporal term [ὅτε-τότε], and the same particle [δή-δή]. In this way a sort of homoioarcton is created with an emphasis on verse 494 because of the excessive number of 't' sounds [ὅτε-τότε]. B: prepositional phrase [ἐκ τοῖο-πρὸς Ὄλυμπον]. C: verbal group]).

The Rhetorics of Supplication

The structural symmetry of these two verses gives an awe-inspiring tone to the passage. The syntactic predictability without abrupt change in the lining up of its components highlights the solemnity of the supplication scene.[25] The picture of all the gods returning to Olympos with Zeus at their head acquires the rhythm of a venerable, majestic pace, aurally perceptible through the repetition of a familiar sound at verse-initial position.

Recent studies on Homeric diction have drawn attention to the importance of the use of specific particles in the presentation of the story and, more significantly, in the participation of the audience in the unfolding of the plot. Bakker[26] notes the importance of drawing the listener into the scene and creating a shared basis for the narrator and the audience "as if they were actually jointly witnessing a given scene." Homeric diction uses particular particles, or clusters of particles, and temporal correlatives to achieve this goal, one of which is the 'pair' ὅτε-τότε. Their use is more common at significant breaks in the story (e.g. in the return of the gods from the Aethiopes in I 493–494), when the narrator most needs the participation of the listener. The singer attempts to create a shared basis, a common experience that unites narrator and audience as if they were present at the unfolding of a particular event or, to put it otherwise, as if they are both witnessing the same scene. Let us consider our present case (*Iliad* I 493–494):

ἀλλ' <u>ὅτε δὴ</u>
ῥ' ἐκ τοῖο δυωδεκάτη γένετ' ἠώς,
καὶ <u>τότε δὴ</u>
πρὸς Ὄλυμπον ἴσαν θεοὶ αἰὲν ἐόντες

But *when*
the twelfth dawn after this day appeared,
(and) then,

---

[25] The structure of these verses is due to the combined effect of meter and Greek word order on the *diachronic level*. On the *synchronic*, the formularity of these verses dictates the rhythm of the flow of speech. I follow Bakker 1997:184, who has argued that "meter emerges from discourse ... but at some point it becomes so rigid as to constitute a structure in itself, regulating the flow of speech." The structural formularity of these verses, which are uttered within a specific context (that of the preparation for the supplication scene) constitutes a speech ritual. Its function surpasses the grammatical and syntactical content of the construction 'conjunction + temporal particle + resumptive δή + prepositional phrase + adjective + verbal group' (see verses 493 and 494). Meter as well as word order are used as rhetorical devices, manipulating the segmentation and arrangement of the constituent parts of speech in order to reenact a specific ritual. In this way, *routinization* of ritual practice is reenacted through *routinization* of speech. See Bakker 1997:186–187.

[26] See Bakker 1997:79.

Chapter Ten

> the gods who live forever came back to Olympos all in a body[27]

By stressing the *here* and *now* of the events he is referring to, the external narrator[28] employs the correlatives ὅτε-τότε to make his account vivid.[29] The use of the apodotic καί in this sort of passage (see *Iliad* XVI 780; XVIII 350; XXII 209) coordinates what Chafe[30] has successfully called "regulatory intonation units," mapping out the flow of two "substantive intonation units," which create two balancing pairs.[31] In this way, the convergence between the time period of twelve days and the moment the gods return to Olympos is effectively brought to the present of the performance. It is as if the bard has said 'the gods are now (καὶ τότε δή) returning to Olympos, just at the point of completion of a twelve-day period (ὅτε δὴ ῥ' ἐκ τοῖο δυωδεκάτη γένετ' ἠώς)'. From this kind of utterance the audience is invited to 'notice' the twelve-day period and evaluate it *within the notion of time fostered by Iliadic song*. In accordance with what was said above on polysemy and repetition, Iliadic epic attempts to 'teach' its listeners its own poetic grammar and, in this case, its own *grammar of time*. In order to appreciate this kind of subtle system, we need to place it within the nexus of other relevant expressions of a twelve-day period. Such a time interval, typically expressed by ἠώς that is placed at verse-end,[32] bears a striking similarity to two other twelve-day periods in

---

[27] The translation is based on Lattimore 1951 but I have slightly altered it to emphasize the correlatives ὅτε-τότε.

[28] Or 'first narrator-focaliser', according to the terminology of de Jong 1987.

[29] For the epic's ability to create the illusion of a boundless, eternally dramatic present which is brought 'vividly' (ἐναργῶς) in front of the audience's eyes, see Bakker 2005:154–176.

[30] Chafe 1994:63–64.

[31] See Bakker 1997:79.

[32] Ἠώς occurs 27 times in the *Iliad*, 15 at the verse-end (as against 40 times and 35 times in the *Odyssey*, respectively). The pattern of twelve days occurs 6 times in the *Iliad* (I 493, XXI 46, XXI 81, XXIV 31, XXIV 413, XXIV 667). In *Iliad* XXI 46 and XXI 81 the pattern is used for Lycaon, who after being sold by Achilles to king Euneus in Lemnos and subsequently redeemed by the Imbrian Eetion who paid the ransom, was first sent to Arisbe, from where he fled and came to Troy where he enjoyed himself with his friends for eleven days (*Iliad* XXI 40–46). The twelfth day he returned to the battlefield where he was killed by Achilles. In *Iliad* XXIV 31 (= I 493) the pattern is employed for Apollo who asks the gods to act, since Hector's body is lying unburied for eleven days in Achilles' hut. Later in the same Book, the same pattern is used first by Hermes (XXIV 413), who informs Priam that the corpse of Hector has been preserved by the gods, and then by Priam (XXIV 667). The Trojan king tells Achilles that the Trojans intend to lament Hector for nine days, bury him the tenth day, build a grave-mound over him, and only on the twelfth day will they fight the Achaeans, if that must be (XXIV 664–667). In the *Odyssey*, the twelve days pattern is attested twice. In Book ii 374, Telemachus asks Eurycleia not to say to Penelope that he will go to Pylos and Sparta until eleven or twelve days have passed. In Book iv 588 Menelaus invites Telemachus to stay in Sparta for eleven or twelve days. In these two

Iliad XXIV.[33] Scholars have struggled to count the exact days described by the Iliadic plot, and have even developed theories about the way 'dawns' or 'days' should be numbered. They have thus failed to see that the symmetry between the beginning and end of the poem does not 'depend' on details of this sort. In cases like this, what really matters is the *synchronic description* of the 'twelve-day' period within archaic Greek poetry.[34] Such similarities are *diachronically* due to the fact that "the formula system developed around expressions such as δυωδεκάτη γένετ' Ἠώς | and | ἥδε δυωδεκάτη ... and so on."[35] On the other hand, "the analysis of system, or the *synchronic approach*, is *logically prior to a diachronic approach* because systems are more intelligible than changes."[36] In this light, the grammar of time employed by the Iliadic tradition indicates to the audience that the twelve-day period is a device that aims to open and close the poem. By being *synchronically observable* through its repetition, this time frame becomes functional on the level of the epic's performance, turning the relevant supplication scenes into 'oral indicators' of the song's beginning and end.

Taplin,[37] who has argued for a performance of the *Iliad* in three days to match the internal structure of the poem (according to his own reading) with the actual performance time, has noted the importance of the placement of specific characters or events at performance junctures. Thetis comes

---

instances in the *Odyssey*, as happened in the *Iliad*, the number twelve, when used to express a specific time span, modifies the word ἠώς (dawn).

[33] Achilles defiles Hector's body for eleven days (XXIV 31) and Priam asks for an eleven-day truce so that he can give his son's corpse a proper burial (XXIV 667). Taplin 1992:18n16 maintains that XXIV 31 "must refer to the stretch of time since the death of Hector, and so the tenth not the twelfth day of divine quarrelling (107–108). So Kirk I. 493–4 is wrong to refer 24.31 and 413 to two different lapses of narrative-time." See also Willcock 1984:312, who notes that the number twelve includes the three days spent on the Funeral Games and the nine days Achilles is keeping Hector's body in his hut unburied. Therefore, it is the tenth day since the beginning of the gods' division on the fate of Hector's corpse, and, consequently, there is no 'symmetry' between Books I and XXIV on this aspect.

[34] See Nagy 2003:40.

[35] Kirk 1985:105.

[36] Peradotto 1990:13. I owe this reference to Nagy 2003:40 (with respect to emphasis, I also follow Nagy).

[37] Taplin 1992:15–31 has argued that the *Iliad* may be divided into three parts of almost equal length. These parts are based on the observation of turning-points in the plot. Taplin's scheme runs as follows: Part I: I 1–IX 713 with significant structural subdivisions at I 492/3; IV 445/6; VII 482/8; Part II: XI 1 (Doloneia omitted) –XVIII 353 with subdivisions at XVI 123/4; Part III: XVIII 354–XXIV 804 with internal breaks at XXIII 56/7; XXIII 897/XXIV 1. Taplin proposes intervals between these parts according to the poet's sensitivity to audience response and further maintains (26) that the three-part structure of the *Iliad* matches a real 'Homeric' performance.

Chapter Ten

to the narrative foreground at crucial turning-points in the poem: at the beginning of part I (*Iliad* I 1 - IX 713) she visits Achilles and then supplicates Zeus (I 493–494); at the end of part II (XVIII 369) she ascends to Hephaestus' place in Olympos to carry a new request after having visited Achilles to ease his pain and grief at the loss of Patroclus; at the end of part III (beginning of *Iliad* XXIV) "her summons to Olympos leads into the concluding resolution of Achilleus' anger."[38] In this light, the return of the gods from the Aethiopes on the twelfth day places a time-boundary after which the fulfillment of the Διὸς βουλή 'will of Zeus' and the μῆνις 'wrath' of Achilles are practically set in motion. *Mutatis mutandis*, the use of an equivalent time frame towards the end of the epic reveals to the audience that the μῆνις 'wrath' of Achilles will end only when a second Διὸς βουλή 'will of Zeus' is implemented. The agent effectuating this implementation is none other than Thetis. Like a bard, she persuades the internal audience (Zeus in *Iliad* I and Achilles in *Iliad* XXIV) either to listen to the Iliadic song or to accept its closure. Under this scope, supplications, involving Thetis as the *suppliant* on the one hand, and Zeus or Achilles as *supplicandi* on the other, belong to a *synchronically conceived system* that opens and closes the *Iliad*.

The external audience is already aware (after Achilles' request that his mother supplicate Zeus) of the fact that the main players will be Thetis and Zeus. The characters' juxtaposition in verse I 495 brings about a half-verse cumulation leading from πάντες ἅμα to Ζεὺς δ' ἦρχε and subsequently creates an antithesis between Zeus and the rest of the gods.[39] The plethora of gods returning to Olympos stands in drastic contrast to their leader, who is designated by a short clause (Ζεὺς δ' ἦρχε). This distinction is, of course, based on hierarchy but it will become particularly relevant to both the ensuing supplication scene and to the entire system of supplications based on the special link between Zeus and Achilles.[40] Zeus, the only god mentioned by name, is *synchronically* presented as a separate and independent agent, whose oppo-

---

[38] Taplin 1992:21.

[39] See *Iliad* I 533, where Zeus' preeminent position among the Olympians is reflected by his being dictionally treated as a separate entity. There is no distinction between the rest of the gods, as they are acting as *a group, all at the same time* (θεοὶ δ' ἅμα πάντες). The juxtaposition of all the 'main players' (Thetis, Zeus, and the other gods) in a couple of verses (531–533) signifies the end of the supplication scene, which is capped almost in the same way as it began (with the necessary changes of course, since Thetis has to depart from Olympos). Verse 498 confirms the previous interpretation, as it is clearly stated that the son of Cronus was sitting apart from the other gods. There is a covert tendency in this passage to emphasize Zeus' separation from the rest of the gods, a point that is vital for the latent parallelism with Achilles.

[40] For the intertextual background of the Zeus–Achilles connection, see the rest of this chapter.

sition to the rest of the Olympians will become obvious as the plot unravels. In the previous scene, Achilles has just reminded Thetis of a story she used to tell him, according to which she had saved Zeus from a plan concocted by Hera, Poseidon, and Athena (*Iliad* I 396-406). The intertextual provenance of this enmity is intratextually reasserted by the various divine quarrels and rivalries observable in the Iliadic plot,[41] but it also needs to be mirrored on the micro-narrative of this supplication, considering that its hybrid nature makes it almost archetypal for the rest of the epic.

'Oral Dittography'

After the return of the gods to Olympos, the poet zooms his narrative lens on Thetis, whose ascending movement is described in detail. Her rise from the swell of the sea and subsequent ascent is presented as a gradual process comprising three distinct phases: rising from the sea (ἀνεδύσετο), ascending (ἀνέβη), and reaching the highest point of Olympos, where Zeus is seated alone, away from the other immortals (... ἄτερ ἥμενον ἄλλων // ἀκροτάτῃ κορυφῇ πολυδειράδος Οὐλύμποιο). The special care bestowed on the description of this movement is also observable in the three consecutive aural repetitions that facilitate the audience's perception of the meeting between the two gods. The associative syllabic repetition of *ane* in ἀνεδύσετο, ἀνέβη, which highlights Thetis, is followed by the assonance of *eur* (ηὗρεν-εὐρύοπα)[42] in verse I 498, which links the *suppliant* (Thetis) and the *supplicandus* (Zeus). The third syllabic repetition of *kro* (Κρονίδην - ἀκροτάτῃ κορυφῇ), giving emphasis to the word Κρονίδην,[43] results in the 'aural isolation' of Zeus. In this way, the listeners would have been able to follow acoustically the entire scene of Thetis' ascension, from the moment she rose from the sea until she 'found' Zeus in a state of 'pre-eminent isolation' away from the other immortals. The structural autonomy of these two couplets, as indicated by the repetition of the word 'Olympos' at verse-terminal position at the end of each distich, facili-

---

[41] See e.g. the 'The Deceit of Zeus' (Διὸς ἀπάτη) in *Iliad* XIV.
[42] Doubts may be raised against the ηὗρεν-εὐρύοπα vocalic repetition mainly because of the rough breathing of the former versus the smooth breathing of the latter. But it is not only modern sensibility that ignores the change of breathing. Such assonance is common in Ancient Greek. See e.g. Denniston 1952:124 citing numerous examples of this kind, like ἧμεν ἥμενοι (Euripides *Iphigenia in Tauris* 1339), ἕως σ' ἐῶσιν (Euripides *Orestes* 238), ἐκ δ' ἑλοῦσα (Euripides *Alcestis* 160). For the most detailed treatment of this phenomenon, see Norden 1915-1923³. See also Stanford 1967; Silk 1974:173, 224; *OCD* s.v. assonance.
[43] For the principal of *aural isolation*, see Silk 1974:187-191.

tates a significant change of rhythm. The first two verses devoted to Thetis (I 496-497) are marked by their intensive, accelerating rhythm, which is created by their four cola structure. Conversely, the other two (I 498-499) display a slower rhythm, due to their being comprised of three and two cola, respectively. This progressive decrease in the number of cola, a slowing down of the speed, *reflects* on a rhythmic register the initial acceleration of Thetis going up to mount Olympos and her deceleration, when she finds Zeus:

496: παιδὸς ἑοῦ // ἀλλ' ἥ γ' // ἀνεδύσετο // κῦμα θαλάσσης,[44]

497: ἠερίη δ' // ἀνέβη // μέγαν οὐρανὸν // Οὔλυμπόν τε.

498: ηὗρεν δ' // εὐρύοπα Κρονίδην // ἄτερ ἥμενον ἄλλων

499: ἀκροτάτῃ κορυφῇ // πολυδειράδος Οὐλύμποιο·

The analysis of the diction and style of the passage introducing the supplication scene has shown that the Iliadic tradition took great pains to highlight for its audience the movement of *both* Thetis and Zeus (accompanied by the other gods) toward mount Olympos. The placement of Thetis at the bottom of the sea, her usual abode, is expected, but Zeus' absence in the Aethiopes deserves further inquiry.

Divine journeys to the land of the Aethiopes are well known in Homeric epic.[45] They are mainly used to allow time for other *contemporaneous* actions to happen,[46] as in *Iliad* XXIII 205-207 and *Odyssey* i 22-27.[47] On the other hand, the situation described in *Iliad* I 493-499 results in the collapse of one of the basic assumptions of a supplication scene, according to which *the suppliant goes to the location of the supplicandus*. The mental template on which such a notion is based is reflected both in the regular terminology used for 'suppliant', 'supplication', and 'supplicate' in Greek language and in the diction employed by the Iliadic tradition. The typical words ἱκέτης 'suppliant', ἱκεσία 'supplication', and ἱκετεύω 'supplicate' are cognate to the verbs ἱκάνω / ἱκνέομαι 'to go towards, to approach'.[48] Although the verb employed in Thetis' meetings with

---

[44] The verb ἀνεδύσετο is hereby used with the accusative instead of the more usual genitive. See Kirk 1985:106 ad 496, who points to the fact that "the genitive 'out of the sea' is more to be expected than the accusative." See *Iliad* XIII 225 ἀνδύεται πόλεμον ('draw back from war'). See also Latacz et al. 2000:162 ad 496.

[45] See *Iliad* XXIII 205-207; *Odyssey* i 22-27.

[46] See Rengakos 2006:85-134.

[47] See Kirk 1985:97; West 1988:75.

[48] The use of ἱκνέομαι as 'supplicate' is attested already in Homeric epic. See e.g. *Iliad* XIV 260; *Iliad* XXII 123; *Odyssey* ix 266-267; xvi 424.

Achilles and Zeus in *Iliad* I is λίσσομαι, the 'approach' to the *supplicandus* by the *suppliant* is still inherent in the use of the verb εἶμι 'I will go', which is twice used for that purpose in the scene between Achilles and Thetis.[49]

The scene of Zeus' return from the Aethiopes seems rather 'vexing', since it will be subsequently followed by another movement, Thetis' ascension from the sea to Olympos. In fact, the Iliadic *staging* of this scene testifies to the existence of certain fissures in the narrative. One of them, perhaps the most important, concerns the antithesis between the description of Thetis' ascent and the lack of any details concerning the gods' journey of return. It seems as if Thetis' ascent to Olympos belongs to the kernel of this scene, given that she lives at the bottom of the sea, whereas the return of the immortals stems from another poetic environment, an epic tradition in which *the gods' journey to the Aethiopes would have been directly and internally linked to an ensuing supplication scene*.

Before embarking on a search for this tradition, I would like to stress the fact that the Iliadic epic explicitly states (I 424) that the gods go to the land of the Aethiopes κατὰ δαῖτα 'to feast'.[50] The feast is always offered by a host who invites his guests to his house or palace and offers them food, drink, and entertainment. Homeric epic highlights features pertaining to the feast offered to the immortals in the land of the Aethiopes, but carefully refrains from stating *who offered the feast*. Hesiodic epic (*Theogony* 984–985) tells us that the king of these pious people was Memnon, son of the goddess Ἠώς 'Eos/Dawn' and the mortal Tithonus. Given that the Homeric tradition explicitly refers to Eos and Tithonus (XI 1–2 = v 1–2) and that Memnon,[51] king of the Aethiopes and opponent of Achilles, belonged to an oral tradition prior to that of the *Iliad*, as can be argued from the content of the post-Homeric *Aethiopis* by Arctinus and relevant artistic representations, it is reasonable to focus on the figures of Eos and Thetis, Memnon's and Achilles' respective immortal mothers.

Greek epic constantly presents Eos, the Greek representative of the inherited Indo-European Dawn-goddess, *Ausos, in connection to various mortal heroes with whom she is united.[52] One of these heroes is the *Trojan* Tithonus,

---

[49] *Iliad* I 401 (ἐλθοῦσα); *Iliad* I 420 (εἶμ').
[50] In *Iliad* XXIII 205–207 and *Odyssey* i 22–27 the feast is part of a sacrificial ritual testifying to the piety of the Aethiopes.
[51] For *ellipsis* or implicit reference to Tithonus within the framework of a Homeric simile, see Danek 2006:66–67, who argues that Tithonus is missing from the list of Troy's elders because 'Homer' has *changed* the traditional simile based on the cicada-Tithonus imagery into a simile pertaining to the Iliadic, not to the Aethiopic content of this epic.
[52] For the relation between Indo-European *Ausos, Indic Uṣas, Aphrodite, and Thetis, see also chapter 5.

Chapter Ten

whom she abducts and attempts to make immortal. Since one of the most thorough versions of this myth comes from the *Homeric Hymn to Aphrodite* (5), it is advisable to examine it in detail, more so since the diction employed for Eos' supplication to Zeus may be relevant to Thetis' role in *Iliad* I:

> ὣς δ' αὖ Τιθωνὸν χρυσόθρονος ἥρπασεν Ἠώς
> ὑμετέρης γενεῆς, ἐπιείκελον ἀθανάτοισιν·
> <u>βῆ δ' ἴμεν</u> αἰτήσουσα κελαινεφέα Κρονίωνα
> <u>ἀθάνατόν τ' εἶναι καὶ ζώειν ἤματα πάντα</u>·
> τῇ δὲ Ζεὺς <u>ἐπένευσε</u> καὶ <u>ἐκρήηνεν ἐέλδωρ</u>·
> νηπίη, οὐδ' ἐνόησε μετὰ φρεσὶ πότνια Ἠώς
> ἥβην αἰτῆσαι ξῦσαί τ' ἄπο <u>γῆρας ὀλοιόν</u>.
> τὸν δ' ἤτοι εἵως μὲν ἔχεν πολυήρατος ἥβη,
> Ἠοῖ <u>τερπόμενος</u> χρυσοθρόνωι <u>ἠριγενείῃ</u>
> <u>ναῖε παρ' Ὠκεανοῖο ῥοῆς ἐπὶ πείρασι γαίης</u>·
> αὐτὰρ ἐπεὶ πρῶται πολιαὶ κατέχυντο ἔθειραι
> καλῆς ἐκ κεφαλῆς εὐηγενέος τε γενείου,
> τοῦ δ' ἤτοι εὐνῆς μὲν ἀπείχετο πότνια Ἠώς,
> αὐτὸν δ' αὖτ' ἀτίταλλεν ἐνὶ μεγάροισιν ἔχουσα
> <u>σίτῳ τ' ἀμβροσίῃ</u> τε καὶ εἵματα καλὰ διδοῦσα.
> ἀλλ' ὅτε δὴ πάμπαν <u>στυγερὸν κατὰ γῆρας</u> ἔπειγεν,
> οὐδέ τι κινῆσαι μελέων δύνατ' οὐδ' ἀναεῖραι,
> ἥδε δέ οἱ κατὰ θυμὸν ἀρίστη φαίνετο βουλή·
> ἐν θαλάμῳ κατέθηκε, θύρας δ' ἐπέθηκε φαεινάς.
> τοῦ δ' ἤτοι φωνὴ ῥέει ἄσπετος, οὐδέ τι κῖκυς
> ἔσθ' οἵη πάρος ἔσκεν ἐνὶ γναμπτοῖσι μέλεσσιν.

> So again Tithonus was seized by golden-throned Dawn from your family, a man
> like the immortals. *She went to ask* the dark-cloud son of Kronos for him *to be*
> *immortal and live for ever*, and Zeus *assented* and *fulfilled her wish* –foolish
> lady Dawn, she did not think *to ask* for youth for him, and the stripping away of
> *baneful old age*. So long as lovely youth possessed him, *he took his delight* in
> Dawn of the golden throne, *the early-born*, and *dwelt by the waters of Ocean at*

> *the ends of the earth*; but when the first scattering of grey hairs
> came forth
> from his handsome head and his noble chin, the lady Dawn
> stayed away from
> his bed, but kept him in her mansion and nurtured him *with food
> and ambrosia*,
> and gave him fine clothing. And when *repulsive old age* pressed
> fully upon him,
> and he could not move or lift any of his limbs, this is what she
> decided was the
> best course: she laid him away in a chamber, and shut its shining
> doors. His
> voice still runs on unceasing, but there is none of the strength
> that there used to
> be in his bent limbs.
>
> Homeric Hymn to Aphrodite [5] 218-238

Almost all of the thematic features in this epic narrative describing the myth of Dawn and Tithonus (Dawn's journey to Olympos and subsequent request to Zeus to offer immortality to Tithonus,[53] Zeus' assent, repulsive old age, Tithonus' delight while staying with Dawn, Dawn's appearance early in the morning, her sharing the same abode with Tithonus by the waters of the Ocean at the ends of the earth, her ability to nurture her consort with divine food) have left their traces in the Homeric epics and primarily in the Iliadic tradition, where they have been reshaped and tailored to the epic's needs. Before turning to the *Iliad*, I would like to draw attention to Eos' role in the 'Aethiopic' oral tradition, which basically corresponds to the second half of the (reconstructed) plot of the post-Homeric *Aethiopis* by Arctinus of Miletos. According to the summary offered by Proclus in his *Chrestomathy*, Eos had asked Zeus to grant to her son Memnon immortality after his death at the hands of Achilles:

---

[53] Kakridis 1944:159–176 has convincingly argued that Eos' request to Zeus to grant immortality to Tithonus was 'transferred' from her equivalent request for Memnon who could not ask Zeus on his own, since he had been killed by Achilles. In an older tradition, after being abducted by Eos Tithonus would have lived with her as an immortally youthful person. At that point there was no request whatsoever by Eos. Only at a later stage, when Tithonus was somehow connected to the cicada and the theme of his metamorphosis into an insect was developed, was there a need for an incomplete request from Zeus. Under the influence of Eos' request for Memnon, and given that she was Tithonus' wife and Memnon's mother, the tradition of the request for the son was passed on to the father.

ἔπειτα Ἀχιλλεὺς Μέμνονα κτείνει καὶ τούτῳ μὲν Ἠὼς παρὰ Διὸς αἰτησαμένη ἀθανασίαν δίδωσι.

Then Achilles slays Memnon, and Eos gives him immortality, having asked for it from Zeus.

189–190 Severyns = 60–61 Kullmann

In the *Iliad*, the similarities shared by Thetis and Eos are numerous but have been selectively reshaped. The following Iliadic passages display all the aforementioned features pertaining to Eos and Tithonus or Memnon, but applied now to the relation between Thetis and Peleus or Achilles:

(a) Journey to Olympos and subsequent request to Zeus (*Iliad* I 493–516) to offer Achilles not physical immortality but poetic immortality by making him the hero of the Iliadic tradition (notice the use of the formula κρήηνον ἐέλδωρ // ἐκρήηνεν ἐέλδωρ 'grant what I ask for'/ 'fulfilled her wish' in *Iliad* I 504 and in the *Homeric Hymn to Aphrodite* [5] 222).

(b) Zeus' assent: Zeus' assent is expressed both in *Iliad* I 524 and I 527 (κατανεύσομαι, κατανεύσω) and in the *Homeric Hymn to Aphrodite* [5] 222 (ἐπένευσε) by compound forms of the verb νεύω 'to nod in assent'.[54]

(c) Peleus' repulsive old age: XVIII 434–435.

(d) Tithonus' delight while staying in Dawn's abode (*Homeric Hymn to Aphrodite* [5] 226–227) becomes the gods' delight in visiting the Aethiopes (implicit in *Iliad* I 424: κατὰ δαῖτα 'to feast'), whom Memnon, the son of Dawn, rules (*Theogony* 984–985). Iris tells the Winds that she cannot feast with them in Thrace because she will go to the Aethiopes[55] by the streams of the Ocean, 'where they are making grand sacrifice to the immortals', and that she will there participate in the sacraments (*Iliad* XXIII 205–207). What is implicit in the *Iliad* becomes explicit in the *Odyssey*. In *Odyssey* i 25–26, it is overtly said that Poseidon had gone to the Aethiopes 'to accept a sacrifice of bulls and rams, and there he sat and enjoyed the pleasures of the feast' (ἀντιόων ταύρων τε καὶ ἀρνειῶν ἑκατόμβης. // ἔνθ' ὅ γε τέρπετο δαιτὶ παρήμενος· ...).

(e) The divine feast among the Aethiopes pertains to the 'fulsome banquet of the gods' (*Odyssey* viii 76), i.e. to their being 'expressly entertained

---

[54] Nodding assent (Naiden 2006:111) constitutes a variation from the norm, which is to raise the suppliant. Naiden observes that nodding is used by important *supplicandi*.

[55] Kakridis 1949:159–174 has argued that this episode may well be relevant to the same oral tradition (pertaining to the Memnon story), where the Winds would have been unwilling to blow on Achilles' pyre, since they were angry at him for having killed their brother Memnon. In that tradition, Zeus may have sent Hermes or Iris, after another request by Thetis (?), to the Winds, asking them to appease their anger and blow on Achilles' pyre, who deserved to be burnt.

as guests at a meal'.[56] Although Dawn's ability to nurture[57] is a stark feature of the *Homeric Hymn to Aphrodite* (5) 232, it seems more likely that the gods' feast among the Aethiopes is based on sacrificial practice (forming, at least later on, part of festivals like the *Theoxenia* and the *Theodaisia*).[58] In this light, it can be surmised that in another epic tradition the gods might have been entertained by Memnon *and* the Aethiopes, and that the Homeric tradition (especially the Iliadic one) has 'erased' Memnon's name, since he is incompatible with the *Iliad*'s plot. Needless to say, the Aethiopes could stay, as it happens in *Iliad* I 423-425, XXIII 205-207, and *Odyssey* i 22-27.

(f) Dawn's appearance early in the morning is transferred to Thetis. In *Iliad* I 497 and 557, she is described by the epithet ἠερίη 'early in the morning' or 'like a mist', which corresponds to Eos' epithet ἠριγένεια 'early-born'.[59] Interestingly enough, the other two attestations of this epithet are also associated with Dawn's abode and the Aethiopes. *Iliad* III 7 (ἠέριαι), referring to the cranes 'winging their way to the streaming Ocean, bringing to the Pygmaian men bloodshed and destruction', must be put next to fragment 150.17-18 (M.-W.) of the Hesiodic *Catalogue of Women*, which associates the Aethiopes to various mythical peoples, such as the Melanes, the Katoudaioi, and the Pygmies.[60] All these peoples are placed in the mythical imagination of the Greeks at the east end of the world, next to the streams of the Ocean. In *Odyssey* ix 52, the epithet ἠέριοι designates the attack of the Cicones 'early in the morning'.[61] Slatkin has rightly concluded that "[t]he use of ἠερίη and Thetis's early morning travels may evoke her ties to *Eos erigeneia* and the connection of their power with time, the defining factor of human life."[62]

(g) In the process of reshaping mythical material, the Iliadic tradition has incurred significant changes, one of which concerns Thetis' prophetic powers. In this respect, Eos and Thetis seem to be strongly opposed. In the *Homeric Hymn to Aphrodite* (5) 223-224, Eos is presented as unable to 'see' the future. She is called νηπίη 'foolish' (223), since she fails to see that immortality

---

[56] Burkert 1985:107.
[57] Dawn's ability to nurture seems to reflect the importance of light for vegetation. See also Herodotus III 18, where he describes the 'table of the sun' in the land of the Aethiopes, as a λειμών ('meadow') where every night the magistrates carefully store boiled flesh, and where anyone is allowed to go and eat *during the day*. Herodotus reports that the locals say that the earth itself brings forth the food.
[58] See Burkert 1985:107, 369n17-19, 390n82.
[59] See Schoeck 1961:41; Slatkin 1991:32-33n18.
[60] See West 1988:75.
[61] See Bechtel 1914:151; Chantraine 1968-1980 s.v.; Heubeck 1989:16.
[62] Slatkin 1991:33.

accompanied by old age would be destructive for a mortal. Conversely, in both the Aethiopic and in the Iliadic tradition Thetis is fully aware of Achilles' destiny, which she reveals to him.[63] Still, Thetis' prophetic powers undergo a significant 'internal' change. Whereas in the oral tradition on which the post-Homeric *Aethiopis* is based Thetis might have asked Achilles to abstain from battle (since she foresaw his death),[64] in the *Iliad* it is Achilles who asks her to set in motion a plan that will ultimately lead to his death. These considerations are readily applicable to some incongruities observed in Achilles' meeting with Thetis in *Iliad* I 351-427. It has been rightly argued that the first time Achilles speaks to his mother, he refrains from stating his request,[65] and, more significantly, the bard replaces the traditional praying formula ὣς ἔφατ' εὐχόμενος with the formula ὣς φάτο δάκρυ χέων (*Iliad* I 357). In Muellner's words, "the deletion of εὐχόμενος may be a covert statement that Achilles is less a man addressing a goddess than a god addressing a goddess, or which is similar, a man addressing his mother who happens to be a goddess."[66] What we see here at work is the different uses of Thetis' prophetic powers between the Aethiopic and Iliadic traditions. The 'ignorance' of Eos is contrasted to the 'wisdom' of Thetis, which in the *Iliad* undergoes a deeply moving dramatic shift, becoming the very means leading to Achilles' death.

(h) In the Homeric epics (*Iliad* I 423-425, XXIII 205-207; *Odyssey* i 22-27), the Aethiopes are located at the very same place where the goddess Dawn lives with Tithonus in the *Homeric Hymn to Aphrodite* (5), i.e. by the waters of the Ocean at the ends of the earth. Moreover, in *Iliad* XI 1-2 = *Odyssey* v 1-2 it is explicitly stated that Dawn rises from the bed she shares with Tithonus in order to bring light to both mortals and immortals. Interestingly enough, these verses (*Iliad* XI 1-2 = *Odyssey* v 1-2) are used 'alternatively' with *Iliad* XIX 1-2, where ... κροκόπεπλος ἀπ' Ὠκεανοῖο ῥοάων is employed as a 'variant' of ... ἐκ λεχέων παρ' ἀγαυοῦ Τιθωνοῖο.

(i) In the *Iliad*, Thetis visits Hephaestus and procures divine armor for Achilles, just as in the tradition reflected in the post-Homeric *Aethiopis*, Memnon has a Hephaestan-made armor (185-186 Severyns = 57 Kullmann):

---

[63] See Slatkin 1991:34-38.
[64] See Schoeck 1961:38-48, who argues that every time the *Iliad* is faced with the dilemma of Achilles' return to the battlefield, reference is made to a prophecy by Thetis. In the *Aethiopis* (186-187 Severyns = 58 Kullmann: καὶ Θέτις τῷ παιδὶ τὰ κατὰ τὸν Μέμνονα προλέγει ['And Thetis foretells to her son the events concerning Memnon']), since Thetis probably revealed to Achilles his own death after the killing of Memnon, she may well have advised him to abstain from the fighting. See Slatkin 1991:25n8.
[65] Muellner 1976:28.
[66] Muellner 1976:23.

Μέμνων δὲ ὁ Ἠοῦς υἱὸς ἔχων ἡφαιστότευκτον πανοπλίαν παραγίνεται τοῖς Τρωσὶ βοηθήσων 'Memnon, the son of Eos arrives, with Hephaestan-made armor, to defend the Trojans.'

Under the scope of the similarities presented above, I maintain that narrative fissures caused by the gods' journey to the Aethiopes and their hasty return to Olympos, where Thetis' supplication must take place, have to be set within the larger framework of the Thetis-Eos equation. In fact, we can posit a scene pertaining to the oral tradition that forms the background of the post-Homeric *Aethiopis*, in which Eos would have asked Zeus to offer immortality to her son Memnon after his death at the hands of Achilles *in return for the hospitality, sacrifices, and sumptuous feasts offered to the gods by Memnon when they visited the land of the Aethiopes by the streams of the Ocean.*[67] The Homeric tradition has concealed the feast offered by Memnon under the motif of the pious Aethiopes, who are depicted as offering sacrifices to the gods. The delight emphasized when the gods visit the Aethiopes in the Homeric poems mirrors the delight at the hospitality and feast offered by Memnon in a rival oral tradition.

Beneath the Iliadic tradition's attempt to 'erase' through stylistic sophistication the troublesome and rather idiosyncratic double movement of the *suppliant* (Thetis) and *supplicandus* (Zeus) in *Iliad* I 493–499 lies a deeper rupture of the mythical narrative. This rupture is due to the intertextual background of another oral tradition featuring Eos, and not Thetis, as Zeus' suppliant. This traditional background has acquired an *accretive* function in the *Iliad*, hence the duplication of movements toward Olympos and the *awkwardness* of the gods' feast in the land of the Aethiopes.

Such cases of *oral dittography*, where a single feature (Thetis' movement to Olympos) is doubled, giving the impression of a performative slip by the singer, reflect the reuse of a mythical template belonging to one oral tradition by another rival tradition. Contrary to palaeographical principles, this

---

[67] Slatkin 1991:64 rightly argues that "[t]he conventional form in which one god asks a favor of another does not include the reminder of a past favor or the promise of a future one on either part," and brings as evidence (64n10) *Iliad* XIV 190–192 and *Iliad* XXI 331–341. Under this scope, it is likely that Eos, unlike Thetis in *Iliad* I, would have recalled Memnon's (rather than her own) past services to the gods. See Slatkin 1991:64. Gould (1973:10–11) has argued that one of the consequences of supplication was *xenia*, a forming of a guest-host relation. Given that Eos' request for Memnon is a rather eccentric form of supplication, the *xenia* offered to the gods might have preceded the actual supplication. In fact, it may have been used as an argument for persuading Zeus to grant immortality to Memnon. Gods often appreciate piety and respect shown to them by mortals (cf. *Iliad* XXII 170-172). The literal *xenia* offered by Memnon and Eos in the Aethiopic oral tradition has been 'translated' into Thetis' request for a metaphorical *xenia* that should be granted to her though her re-integration into the community of the immortals (*Iliad* I 516).

narrative duplication is not to be remedied. Inscribed on the narrative of the Iliadic oral tradition, it has become indispensable and perfectly functional. The gods' absence in the land of the Aethiopes is necessary for the description of Odysseus' return of Chryseis to her father, Chryses, in *Iliad* I. This is, of course, the well-known *analytical-transitional* technique described by 'Zielinski's Law', according to which the epic poet describes action A up to a point, then transfers his audience to action B, returning to action A after B comes to a halt. Apart from the temporal exigencies of Iliadic narrative as studied by 'Zielinski's Law', the dictional underscoring of the power of Zeus, who is only mentioned by name and who is leading the gods to Olympos, functions as an introduction to his protagonist role in the ensuing meeting with Thetis. 'Oral dittography' is, then, not the equivalent of a textual protrusion, but a conscious by-product of a living oral tradition.

Preliminaries (503–510)

Once the spatio-temporal parameters (place = Οὔλυμπος—time = ἠερίη) have been given and the principal characters (suppliant = Θέτις and *supplicandus* = Ζεύς) have been introduced, the supplication is ready to begin.[68]

Intratextual Deroutinization, Part I

"Thetis crouched in front of Zeus, took his knees with her left hand and reached with her right hand to hold him under the chin. Then she spoke in entreaty to lord Zeus, son of Kronos." These verses describe the standard gestures[69] of supplication in a rather graphic way.[70] The progressive enjambment introduced by the run-over word σκαιῇ creates a chiasmus through its juxtaposition to δεξιτερῇ (*Iliad* I 500-501):

> λάβε γούνων // σκαιῇ
> δεξιτερῇ // ὑπ' ἀνθερεῶνος ἑλοῦσα

The harsh-sounding σκαιῇ-δεξιτερῇ cluster (reinforced by the enjambment) contrasts with the euphony of the ἀνθερεῶνος-λισσομένη sequence. This

---

[68] On the typology of supplication (approach, gestures, request and arguments, evaluation by the supplicandus), see Naiden 2006:29–104.

[69] On the standard gestures of supplication, see Naiden 2006:44–62. Thetis does not kiss Zeus' hand.

[70] These verses 'link' two distinct type-scenes, the 'arrival' and the 'supplication', by making the former part of the latter. See Arend 1933:28; Latacz et al. 2000:161.

contrast, which is reinforced by the hiatus, alludes to the antithesis between Thetis' emotional intensity and Zeus' majestic tranquility. Besides, the words pointing to Zeus (ἀνθερεῶνος and λισσομένη, the latter having Zeus as its notional object) are clearly euphonic, whereas those referring to Thetis (σκαιῇ-δεξιτερῇ), with their strident sequence of consonants making even their pronunciation strenuous, convey her emotional strain. These observations, stemming from the acoustics of the aforementioned expressions, reveal the special emphasis placed on the use of the σκαιῇ-δεξιτερῇ cluster. Surprisingly enough, this word combination does not pertain to either the Iliadic or to the Odyssean vocabulary of supplication. The following list of relevant verses shows that the use of both the left *and* right hands does not belong to the kinetic typology of supplication:

VIII 371: ἥ οἱ γούνατ' ἔκυσσε καὶ ἔλλαβε χειρὶ γενείου,

X 454–455: ἦ, καὶ ὃ μέν μιν ἔμελλε γενείου χειρὶ παχείῃ //

ἀψάμενος λίσσεσθαι, ...

XXI 68–69: ... ὃ δ' ὑπέδραμε καὶ λάβε γούνων // κύψας, ...

XXIV 478–479: χερσὶν Ἀχιλλῆος λάβε γούνατα καὶ κύσε χεῖρας //

δεινὰς ἀνδροφόνους, ...

On the contrary, the σκαιῇ-δεξιτερῇ cluster seems to be constantly employed within the context of an *aggressive attack against a rival or opponent*:[71]

Theogony 179: σκαιῇ, δεξιτερῇ δὲ πελώριον ἔλλαβεν ἅρπην

Iliad XXI 490: σκαιῇ, δεξιτερῇ δ' ἄρ' ἀπ' ὤμων αἴνυτο τόξα

The above verses, which have been composed in accordance to the 'law of the expanding members' (*Gesetz der wachsenden Glieder*), refer to Ouranus' castration by Cronus and to the conflict between Hera and Artemis, respectively. Cronus, following the precedent set by Ouranus' concealment of his own children in a place without light, swallows his children in his νηδύς 'womb', which becomes their metaphorical tomb. Before we go on, we should remember that soon after, Zeus will exploit, at full length, what he has learned both from the first and from the second phase of the succession myth. In

---

[71] The left hand is mentioned first as the one performing a secondary, ancillary role, whereas the right will actually carry out the main act of aggression. See West 1966:219 ad *Theogony* 179, who draws attention to "two Homeric exceptions to this rule: *Il.* 18.476 ff., *Od.* 19.480 ff."

Chapter Ten

order to avoid being overthrown by his predecessors, Zeus swallows his first wife Μῆτις ('Cunning Intelligence'). In this way, he places in his own womb the potential mother of his children, who would have been born from Metis' womb. This metonymical embedding of the previous phases of the succession myth constitutes Zeus' ultimate trick. By incorporating the strategies of his predecessors within his own plan and giving birth to a goddess (Athena) from his own head, Zeus is able to put an end to the succession myth, thus becoming the absolute and last ruler of the world.[72]

Through the scope of the continuum of narrative logic connecting the Hesiodic *Theogony* and *Iliad* I, it can be argued that the displacement of attack-oriented vocabulary to a supplication scene reflects a process of *deroutinization*, conjuring up features that stem from the mythical background of the Thetis-Zeus relationship. By alluding to the theogonic castration of Ouranus and to the past threat against Zeus' dominion by Athena, Hera, and Poseidon (see Achilles' speech to Thetis in *Iliad* I 396–406), the boundaries between supplication and cunning aggression are deliberately blurred. The audience is thus presented with a would-be threat to Zeus' rule, which will be the notional basis for the speech to follow. The listeners are invited to participate in an intertextual game, exploiting their knowledge not only of theogonic material but also of a marginal tradition (reflected later in Pindaric poetry),[73] according to which Zeus had helped Peleus marry Thetis to avert the prophecy that Thetis' future son by a god would have been able to overthrow him. Notwithstanding the limitations of its plot requirements, the Iliadic tradition lets its audience entertain the idea of a 'covert threat' to Zeus by Thetis. In this way, it makes clear to its listeners that this will be a rather oxymoronic supplication, not only because Thetis, being a goddess herself, is by definition an awkward suppliant, but also because of her special power and importance in a potential continuation of the succession myth.

The *Iliad*'s deliberate overriding of a familiar compartmentalization of dictional material and violation of type-scene based expectations culminates in an intratextual *deroutinization* of the supplication. Such deviation from traditional patterns functions like *an orange light* alarming the audience about the eccentricity or peculiarity of a given passage or scene. Disfluencies of this sort, though, are subsequently reinterpreted in the light of supra-segmental mythical variation, turning intratextual *fragmentation* into intertextual *integration*, a true hallmark of oral traditional poetry.

---

[72] Muellner 1996:92.
[73] See Pindar *Isthmian* 8.29–38.

Intratextual Deroutinization, Part II (503–510)

Crotty[74] has argued for a typology of supplication comprising a standard procedure:

> ... the person who is praying reminds the deity of past services performed[75] or of earlier displays by the god of benevolence to the one seeking his favor now. A future service may be promised, usually a sacrifice. The prayer concludes with the actual request, expressed concisely and directly.... The suppliant does not appeal to the god's pity but seeks to offer a kind of exchange: a favor now in light of past works pleasing to the gods or a promise of such a work in the future. The typical prayer, in other words, is similar to the kind of supplication used by warriors on the battlefield, in which the suppliant lays stress on his ability to repay his captor rather than on appeals to the other's shame or pity. The form of Greek prayer does not bespeak the suppliant's weakness; rather, *it casts the one praying in a position of strength*,[76] as one with the wherewithal to negotiate with the gods. It reflects a stance in which the suppliant has some claim to the god's benevolence because of past or future favors.

The aforementioned observations fit admirably within the intertextual background of the Thetis-Zeus relationship. Its intratextual *deroutinization* is hereby based on the use of certain features not pertaining to the typology of supplication but reflecting the very nature of warrior society, which is based on exchange rather than pity. In this way, Thetis' request mirrors the poetics of the *Iliad* as a whole and becomes the starting point from which the rest of the epic will evolve. The *hybridization* of this supplication can be better appreciated if it is compared to Chryses' supplication to Agamemnon and Menelaus in *Iliad* I 17–21. The optatives (δοῖεν, λύσαιτε) employed in Chryses' supplication have been changed into two (κρήηνον, τίμησον) and three (ὑπόσχεο, κατάνευσον, ἀπόειπε) imperatives during Thetis' first and second appeal.

Both the formula τόδε μοι κρήηνον ἐέλδωρ,[77] which recurs in supplication contexts and the duplication of imperative + dative construction in the ensuing

---

[74] See Crotty 1994:94–95.
[75] See Redfield 1975:136–137.
[76] The italics are mine.
[77] This formula is attested (with a slight variation) five times in the *Iliad*, always in the context of a prayer. In I 41 and I 455 from Chryses to Apollo, in I 504 from Thetis to Zeus, in VIII 242 from Agamemnon to Zeus, and in XVI 238 from Achilles to Zeus. It is a typical expression used by the

Chapter Ten

verse (τίμησόν μοι υἱόν) create an indirect reference to the Thetis-Zeus relationship by bridging the initial πάτερ with the word υἱόν. The semantic pair πάτερ-υἱόν has, as I have argued, wider implications; for it alludes to the intertextually attested background of a potential threat to Zeus by Achilles. In this way, the Iliadic tradition attributes to the supplication the connotations stemming from its intertextual substratum. The lack of a possessive pronoun or the adjective φίλος, which is regularly used in Homer as possessive, makes the dative μοι connote the person for whom the supplication is carried out as well as *the supplication's connection to the textual suppliant*. This amounts to an implicit indication that we are dealing with an *embedded supplication*, where the overt suppliant (Thetis) acts in the place and as a representative of the covert one (Achilles).

Conversely, the boundlessness of Thetis' grief over the shortness of Achilles' life, highlighted by the relative clause ὃς ὠκυμορώτατος ἄλλων // ἔπλετ᾽, counterbalances the 'concealed threat' born by the intertextual innuendo of the Thetis-Zeus relationship. At a critical juncture, where intertextual overtones are thrown into stark relief, the Iliadic tradition reminds its audience that Achilles is "the limiting case of human brevity"[78] and that in this epic the boundaries between divine immortality and human mortality are sharply and tragically drawn.[79]

Metrical factors and word order are then effectively orchestrated to highlight the motifs of τιμή 'honor' and γέρας 'prize', the former constituting the semantic nucleus of Thetis' supplication, the latter the terms by which the entreaty will be carried out. In particular, the two internal enjambments of verses 506 and 507, the alliteration of 'e', and the aural interplay between τίμησον 'honor' and ἠτίμησεν 'dishonored' on one hand, and the terminal assonance in the sound 'ras' (γέρας and ἀπούρας) assisted by the words' accentual pattern[80] on the other, accentuate τιμή 'honor' and γέρας 'prize', respec-

---

suppliant after the completion of his initial address to the deity, when he desires to express his appeal. It functions as an introduction to the verbalization of the petition, as if the suppliant is saying: "and now follows my request." See *Iliad* I 41. For ἐκρήηνεν ἐέλδωρ, see *Homeric Hymn to Aphrodite* (5) 222.

[78] Slatkin 1991:38.

[79] On the special diction devoted to Achilles' mortality, see Slatkin 1991:36–39.

[80] Of course, one could argue that the quantity of the final syllable ("ras") in γέρας and ἀπούρας is different (short in the first case and long by compensatory lengthening in the second: *ἀπούροντ-ς > ἀπούρας). This is certainly true, but since assonance does not necessarily depend on vowel quantity but on sound repetition, the difference between "ras" (γέρας) and "raas" (ἀπούρας) is aurally insignificant.

tively. The dictional and stylistic preoccupation with 'honor' and 'prize' is consonant with epic ideology and abides perfectly by the Iliadic heroic code.

Thetis asks Zeus, the divine ἄναξ, to grant Achilles that which Agamemnon, the human ἄναξ ἀνδρῶν, has deprived him of. The placement of ἄναξ ἀνδρῶν Ἀγαμέμνων and Ὀλύμπιε μητίετα Ζεῦ at the second part of the hexameter, after the trochaic caesura, reminds the audience that the restoration of Achilles' τιμή 'honor' will be effectuated only by discovering the divine-human disparity emblematized in the relationship between Achilles and Thetis.

Although Thetis uses the typical gestures of supplication, she still employs the *da quod dedi* strategy of reciprocity. Having restored Zeus' power in the past, she now begs him to restore her son's lost τιμή 'honor' by virtually menacing Agamemnon's kingship. The deliberate paradox of her supplication is based on the premise of reciprocity *only if seen from Achilles' point of view. On the contrary, from Agamemnon's point of view it is a threat to his superiority and preeminence among the Achaeans*. Thetis absorbs and verbalizes a request *in Achillean terms*, which makes her request even more eccentric, given that Agamemnon's power on the human level mirrors Zeus' preeminence in the divine realm. His initial silence (*Iliad* I 512: ἀλλ' ἀκέων δὴν ἧστο)[81] must be explained as a hesitation, which has both intertextual associations and intratextual affinities. In fact, the *Iliad* engages its listeners in an intertextually oriented misdirection[82] that is soon annulled. Intratextually, the hesitation between two courses of action is well interwoven with Thetis' impending second appeal. Besides, it is inextricably linked to complementary mythical material concerning an archetypal rivalry between Zeus and Achilles, who might have overthrown the father of gods and men if Thetis had been married to an immortal instead of Peleus.[83] From the point made above, it is clear that Thetis' supplication can be also read as a figurative delimitation of Agamemnon's power. This twofold *enjeu* becomes particularly intriguing if we recall that Agamemnon has previously spoken almost like Zeus "and declared his disgust for someone who has

---

[81] According to Montiglio 1993:184, Zeus' silence belongs to those kind of Iliadic silences situated in the midst of a "*réseau verbal*," which underlines and emphasizes their temporary nature. Montiglio notes that quite often silence in the *Iliad* denotes a suspension of speech and is perceived as a lack which will be surpassed by the intensity of another speech that will follow.

[82] On Homeric misdirection, see Duckworth 1933; Morrison 1992a, 1992b. On intertextual and intratextual misdirection, see Rengakos 2006:77–82 and 82–83, respectively.

[83] See Pindar *Isthmian* 8.29-38 and [Aeschylus] *Prometheus Bound* 167–176, 515–525, 755–765, 907–915, who constitute the earliest sources for this tradition. It has been argued (Reitzenstein 1900:73–105) that this version may go back to the same early source ('Hauptquelle'). See also Apollodorus' *Library* III 13.5. For all the relevant bibliography, see Slatkin 1991:70–77n19–26.

Chapter Ten

tried to speak as equal."[84] Thetis, and through her the Iliadic tradition, 'plays' with the notion of τιμή 'honor' in connection to κράτος 'power, authority'. Since Agamemnon, with his Zeus-like behavior, has dishonored Achilles, Zeus will figuratively dishonor Agamemnon by depriving him, and consequently the Achaeans, from κράτος (Agamemnon's source of authority and τιμή) and granting it to the Trojans.

It has been argued[85] that there is a link between the *Theogony*, where the central theme, according to a metonymic reading of its mythical narrative, is Zeus' μῆνις 'wrath' and the *Iliad*, which begins and is centered around the μῆνις 'wrath' of Achilles. Muellner[86] maintains that the *Theogony* functions as a *proem* to the *Iliad*, and so the very first word of the latter conceivably expresses the thematic nucleus of the former. The same author goes as far as to suggest that a variant of the myth about the marriage of Thetis and Peleus, symbolizing the starting point of Greek epic, alludes to an archetypal competition between Achilles and Zeus, which can be traced in a performance sequence between the two poems that summarizes the process of epic poetry's *raison d' être*, its ontogeny. The *Iliad* transforms divine into heroic μῆνις 'wrath', since the μῆνις 'wrath' of Apollo[87] causes, albeit indirectly, the μῆνις 'wrath' of Achilles. On the other hand, Zeus' Iliadic μῆνις 'wrath' is rather secondary, more so since it is used to support Achilles' wrath[88] at the end of *Iliad* I.

In this light, Thetis' appeal to Zeus acquires a figurative dimension. It reveals the existence of a latent reality, as Achilles' proximity to the divine results in a pathetic paradox.[89] The immortal mother (Thetis) appeals to the supreme deity (Zeus), begging him to grant her mortal son τιμή 'honor', the one thing that will lead to his death. While figuratively asking Zeus to 'kill' Achilles in terms of mortality, Thetis asks him to make Achilles the hero of the *Iliad*, to allow the poem to create its own subject matter.

---

[84] See Pucci 1997:194, 201. See also *Iliad* I 352-356.
[85] Muellner 1996:94-132.
[86] Muellner 1996:95-96.
[87] The *Iliad* achieves a remarkable displacement by replacing Achilles' (and for that matter, Patroclus') divine antagonist, Zeus, by Apollo.
[88] *Iliad* I presents a full circle of the μῆνις ('wrath') theme: the μῆνις ('wrath') of Apollo is appeased by Odysseus (when he takes Chryseis back to her father). Agamemnon's μῆνις ('wrath'), which is caused because he has no female slave is brought to an end by taking Briseis from Achilles, thus causing the latter's μῆνις ('wrath'). Thetis (as we pass to the divine world) persuades Zeus to validate Achilles' μῆνις ('wrath') even at the expense of provoking Hera's fear. In order to suppress the latter's protest, Zeus threatens Hera with his own μῆνις ('wrath'). Subsequently, this threat is averted by Hephaestus' cautionary narrative about Zeus' μῆνις ('wrath') against him.
[89] See Pucci 1997:194.

The Rhetorics of Supplication

The archetypal competition between Achilles and Zeus has a cosmic background. Pindar (*Isthmian* 8.29-38) relates a tradition according to which Thetis was destined to give birth to a child stronger than his father (εἵνεκεν πεπρωμένον ἦν φέρτερον, πατέρος // ἄνακτα γόνον τεκεῖν) if she had been united to Zeus (Ζηνὶ μισγομέναν) or to one of his brothers (Διὸς παρ' ἀδελφεοῖσιν) instead of a mortal. Vernant and Detienne have convincingly argued for the inherent link between the figure of Μῆτις ('Cunning Intelligence'), who is present in the *Theogony* but absent in the *Iliad*, and that of Thetis, being herself a figure of Μῆτις.[90] Furthermore, Briareos, who is summoned by Thetis, has saved Zeus from an internal Olympian threat (*Iliad* I 396-406) and has also, together with two other Hundred-Handers (*Theogony* 147-153), ensured Zeus' κράτος (*Theogony* 662) by defeating the Titans. Nagy[91] has rightly stressed the link between Thetis and Briareos: they both have cosmic powers and either live in the πόντος (Thetis) or have Πόντος (Briareos) or another sea-god like Nereus (Thetis) as their father. Whereas in the *Theogony* the threat to Zeus' supremacy comes from the Titans, it originates, in the tradition alluded to by *Iliad* I, from Athena, Poseidon, and Hera, who are all pro-Greek within the confines of the Iliadic plot. Interestingly enough, these three gods are all involved directly or indirectly in the 'Deception of Zeus' in *Iliad* XIV (Hera is the main agent, Athena helps her get 'ready' to seduce Zeus, and Poseidon frames the entire episode by his overt support to the Achaeans). What we see at work here is the process by which the Iliadic tradition has masked three potential cosmic rivals to Zeus' celestial supremacy into usurpers of his *will* within the world of heroes.

The multiple interconnections between Thetis, Briareos, Zeus, and Achilles show that the *Iliad* makes Zeus do for Achilles, on the human level, what he did not do for him on the divine. Achilles[92] will not become the best of gods, a deity more powerful than Zeus himself, because of the *unwillingness* on Zeus' part *in the non-Iliadic epic tradition*. Conversely, he will become the best of heroes (ἄριστος Ἀχαιῶν) through the *will* of Zeus *in the Iliadic tradition*. His potential father will restore his lost τιμή, thus doing, in the span of Achilles' lifetime, what Achilles could have done in the span of eternity. And yet Zeus' benefaction, albeit limited, will certainly lead to Achilles' death. By employing the phrase τίμησόν μοι υἱόν (*Iliad* I 505), the *Iliad* exploits the diverse intertextual background of the Zeus-Achilles and Zeus-Thetis relationships. In this

---

[90] See Vernant-Detienne 1978:127-164.
[91] See Nagy 1979:344-347.
[92] Nagy 1979:347.

235

way, the potential father (Zeus) will finally honor the son (Achilles) by leading him to his destined end.

In the theogonic tradition the figure of the *mother* (Gaia) or *wife* (Rhea) was responsible for initiating the overthrow of Ouranus and Cronus, respectively.[93] Contrarily, in the *Iliad* it is the figure of the *mother and potential wife* (Thetis) who will practically "ask" for the death of her son, rather than instigating the overthrow of her would-be husband (Zeus). Thetis' polytropic nature,[94] a cunning intelligence (μῆτις) endowed with knavery (πανουργία),[95] is implicit in her role in the supplication scene. Given that Thetis' deceptive force is mythically emblematized by her ultimate metamorphosis into a cuttle-fish (σηπία) in order to escape from the hands of Peleus, the paradox of her appeal to Zeus can be seen as a figurative metamorphosis from request into an intertextually-based threat and an intratextually asserted fame (κλέος) for her son.

Zeus, after thinking for a while in silence, will be faced with a second appeal. Thetis, the Iliadic counterpart of Hesiodic cunning intelligence (μῆτις), has one more cunning turn, one more undulating and twisting trick to put to use.

Intertextual Skewing and Intratextual Sequencing

The rhythmic hesitation inherent in verses 511–513 is reflected in the staccato effect of their condensed sense-units (ὣς φάτο ... ἀλλ' ἀκέων δὴν ἧστο ... γούνων / ... ἐμπεφυυῖα, ... αὖτις), preventing the swift flow of speech. This slow, interrupted tone stands in stark contrast to the vehemence of Thetis' appeal, which is about to start. The speed created by the accumulation of three imperatives (ὑπόσχεο, κατάνευσον, ἀπόειπε) and by the fluent integral enjambments[96] (allowing for only minimal interruption between the end of each verse and the beginning of the next) leads the attention of the audience directly to the next, final verse of Thetis' second appeal (516), in which the most important element of the speech is presented.

---

[93] For Ouranus, see *Theogony* 154–182 and for Cronus *Theogony* 453–480.

[94] The πανουργία ('cunningness') of Thetis has been interpreted by Slatkin 1986:22 as a result of her anger for not being allowed to marry a god. Thetis knows, as Loraux 1990:75 notes, that the price of the hegemony of Zeus is Achilles' death. 'Homer' has displaced wrath from the mother to the son as Thetis' maternal μῆνις ('wrath') has been absorbed by Achilles' anger. Loraux 1990:75 makes the point that between mother and son "*le deuil et la colère sont indivis*."

[95] See Vernant-Detienne 1978:159, who refer to the connection between Thetis and the cuttle-fish (σηπία). See also Herodotus (VII 191–192) and Aristotle, who calls the cuttle-fish πανουργότατον ('most cunning') among fish (*Historia Animalium* IX 37.59).

[96] See Kirk 1985:107.

The Rhetorics of Supplication

The critical term ἀτιμοτάτη (516) employed at the very end of Thetis' second appeal, symbolizing her recourse to the rhetoric of honor, will finally break Zeus' silence once and for all. By translating the intertextual background of an association between Zeus and Thetis into an intratextual sequence of appeals, the *Iliad* invites its listeners to appreciate the built-in teleology of Thetis' supplication. Since both reciprocity and honor have, within this framework, an 'intertextual past' and an 'intratextual future' (both Thetis and Achilles will be honored in the Iliadic tradition), it becomes clear that the *Iliad* is using Thetis as a poetic foil in order to keep from sidestepping the vexing paradox of her request, but to tailor it to its needs.

Reference or allusion to earlier stages of a rival oral tradition seems to be a constant feature of this supplication scene. This heavily loaded cross-referencing 'prehistory' can be described as a form of *intertextual skewing*.[97] Thetis' supplication to Zeus is retroactively affected by intertextual cross-references to other supplication scenes involving herself and Zeus or Eos (the *hypostasis* of the Indo-European Dawn goddess *Ausos) and Zeus. These epic versions are either explicitly (*Iliad* I 396–406) cited or implicitly[98] alluded to by the Iliadic tradition.

Extending Nagy's model of *diachronic skewing*, relevant to relay performance by rhapsodes,[99] to the supplication scene between Thetis and Zeus, we can observe a working analogy. The Iliadic tradition allows Thetis to create an intratextual sequence and continue her supplication by a second appeal exactly at the point where a rival tradition had left off. By employing the argument of loosing her honor (*Iliad* I 516: ὅσσον ἐγὼ μετὰ πᾶσιν ἀτιμοτάτη θεός εἰμι), Thetis carries on her supplication, which had ceased when she reminded Zeus of the help she had offered him in the past. Here on the level of cross-referencing, we can see what Nagy has observed on the level of rhapsodic performance. It is as if, to use an analogy, the Iliadic tradition has turned Thetis into an internal rhapsode, who takes the floor at the very point an earlier tradition has left off, only to make the epic of the *Iliad* begin.[100] The analogy is, I main-

---

[97] This term is based on Nagy's (1990a:394; 1996b:20n27; 2000:417–426; 2003:39–48) *diachronic skewing*, which designates situations "where the medium refers to itself in terms of earlier stages of its own existence."

[98] See the previous discussion. For Eos' supplication to Zeus in respect to Memnon in the *Aethiopis*, see 189–190 Severyns = 60–61 Kullmann. For an equivalent scene (with respect to Tithonus), see *Homeric Hymn to Aphrodite* (5) 218–238.

[99] Nagy 2003:43.

[100] See Nagy 2003:43, 44n19. See *Iliad* I 512 (ἀλλ' ἀκέων δὴν ἧστο) and *Iliad* IX 190–191: Πάτροκλος δέ οἱ οἶος ἐναντίος ἧστο σιωπῇ / δέγμενος Αἰακίδην, ὁπότε λήξειεν ἀείδων). See also *Iliad* I 513: ... καὶ εἴρετο δεύτερον αὖτις.

Chapter Ten

tain, especially apt; for it comes at exactly the point at which the plot is ready to commence, when Thetis asks Zeus to 'make the *Iliad* possible'. In this light, and pressing this analogy a bit more, Zeus becomes the narrative mirroring of the epic Muse, who is generically asked from the singer to endorse his request for a performance and subsequently 'allow the song to begin.' By mimicking bardic performance strategies, according to which the singer 'acknowledges' his inability to recall the deeds of the epic heroes without the help of the Muse or Muses (*Iliad* I 1; II 484–486; *Odyssey* i 1; i 10),[101] Thetis 'internalizes' her request and refers to her future loss of honor and recognition, should Zeus ignore her appeals. Under this scope, Thetis' supplication, starkly emphasized by its placement at the poem's beginning, becomes a stylized representation and conscious self-reflection of the aesthetics of epic performance.

---

[101] See Ford 1992:57–89.

11

Intertextuality and Intratextual Distality: Thetis' Lament in *Iliad* XVIII 52–64

Introduction

THE SCENE BETWEEN THETIS AND ACHILLES in *Iliad* XVIII 35–147 has attracted the interest of scholarly examination since the early analytical studies of Wilamowitz.[1] In line with the analytical approach to epic poetry that dominated 19th and early 20th century Homeric studies, Wilamowitz dissected the *Iliad* into smaller epic, poems arguing that the scene of the Nereids with Thetis lamenting Achilles had been the creation of the poet of Σ, who devised it in order to unite three independent epic poems antedating the *Iliad*, namely the *Patroclea, the *Shield of Achilles and the *Achilleis.

The rise of Neoanalysis resulted in the opening of new ground in the examination of this scene. Kakridis, Pestalozzi and Schadewaldt,[2] to name only the first major neoanalytical scholars, argued that Thetis' lament for Achilles in the *Iliad* was based on an older epic description of Achilles' funeral. The impact Neoanalysis had on the interpretation of this scene was overwhelming in the sense that it proved that the aforementioned scene had been a re-creation of older epic material and not the work of an incapable plagiarist, as the old analysis had maintained. Yet even between the so-called Neoanalysts there was no consensus with respect to the epic poem from which this scene derived. Kakridis, for example, spoke of an earlier *Achilleis, whereas Schadewaldt argued extensively in favor of a *Memnonis as the prototype upon which the *Iliad* had been composed.

From the brief presentation of the debate around the interpretation of this scene, it becomes clear that Thetis' lament for Achilles is an exceptional

---

[1] Wilamowitz–Moellendorf 1920².
[2] See Pestalozzi 1945; Kakridis 1949; Schadewaldt 1965⁴.

Chapter Eleven

event, especially (but not solely) because of its unsuitability to the Iliadic plot. Neoanalysis decisively turned the tide towards a Unitarian approach, according to which the peculiarities of this scene must be resolved through a *Quellenforschung*. In this chapter, I maintain that intertextual associations between Thetis' lament and an earlier poetic tradition (whether one believes in texts crystallized by writing in such an early period or not) can be better understood through intratextual sequences, which in this case are subgenre-oriented. Since the kernel of this scene is Thetis' lament itself, the idiosyncrasies and eccentricities of this γόος must be placed next to the typical structure and diction of the other Iliadic personal laments.[3]

Through a close examination of the composition of this speech, I will show how the Iliadic tradition has converted the intertextual background of Thetis' mourning for the dead Achilles into a highly original γόος, 'writing' its eccentricities against the typology of the other Iliadic personal laments. Distal intratextual sequences (since the γόοι are scattered throughout the entire poem) help understand the aberrance and liminality of Thetis' lament, matching the marginalization and liminality of its addressee, the epic's most atypical, but also greatest, hero.

Framing the Lament

The presentation and framing by the *diegesis* of Thetis' lamentation[4] will be our starting point. After the list of Nereids who accompany Thetis before she rises from the depths of the sea to speak to Achilles, we hear two verses (XVIII 50–51) preceding the actual utterance of the personal lament:[5]

τῶν δὲ καὶ ἀργύφεον πλῆτο <u>σπέος</u>· αἳ δ' ἅμα πᾶσαι	3
<u>στήθεα πεπλήγοντο</u>. Θέτις δ' ἐξῆρχε γόοιο·	0

The silvery *cave* was filled with these, *and together all of them beat their breasts*, and among them Thetis led out the threnody.

---

[3] In a previous study (Tsagalis 2004), I have argued that personal laments or γόοι constitute a subgenre that the *Iliad* has incorporated, tailored to its needs and plot requirements, and subsequently turned into an effective and indispensable constituent of its epic *Weltanschauung*.

[4] For a similar attempt concerning the antiphonal laments of Briseis and Achilles in *Iliad* XIX, see Pucci 1993:258–259.

[5] The numbers placed at the end of the verses refer to Higbie's 1990:29 classification of enjambment types: 1a stands for adding internal, 1b for adding external, 2a for clausal internal, 2b for clausal external, 3 for necessary, and 4 for violent enjambment. I have followed this classification instead of those of Parry 1929:200–220 and Kirk 1966:75–152 because I regard it as more precise and useful as a hermeneutic tool.

Verses XVIII 65-67 following Thetis' speech look similar to the ones preceding it:

ὣς ἄρα φωνήσασα λίπε <u>σπέος</u>· <u>αἳ δὲ σὺν αὐτῇ</u>   3
<u>δακρυόεσσαι</u> ἴσαν, περὶ δέ σφισι κῦμα θαλάσσης   3
ῥήγνυτο.

So she spoke, and left the cave, and the others together went with her in tears, and about them the wave of the water was broken.

There are striking similarities between these two pairs of verses: 1) they both designate the spatial surroundings (σπέος/cave) of Thetis and the Nereids, specifying the place where the personal lament will be uttered; 2) in both couplets the first verse ends with similar adonics (αἳ δ' ἄμα πᾶσαι / αἳ δὲ σὺν αὐτῇ) that have twice the necessary enjambment (type 3);[6] 3) the beginning of the second verse of each couplet is occupied by an expression describing the emotional stage of the group of mourners that accompany Thetis (στήθεα πεπλήγοντο / δακρυόεσσαι).

The word σπέος delineates the spatial frame of the personal lament. It does not simply determine the localization of Thetis and the Nereids but creates, through its repetition at the beginning and end of the personal lament, a framework encircling the speech. This ring functions *performatively*. It ascribes a specific quality to the γόος by denoting a displacement of the habitual *locus* of utterance, heretofore in front of the deceased's bier during the *prothesis*, to the divine environment of a sea-goddess. The specification of the spatial surroundings indicated by the dislocation of the typical personal lament environment entails important interpretive consequences, such as, on a primary level, the different nature of the mourner[7] in comparison to the mortals who are expected to perform the usual lament for the dead. Moreover, it attaches to the personal lament a distinct tone; the mourner utters her γόος

---

[6] The bibliography on enjambment is enormous but the most significant discussions are the following: Bassett 1926:116-148. Parry 1929:200-220 (= 1971:251-265); Lord 1948:113-124; Kirk 1966:75-152; Edwards 1966:115-179; Clayman 1977:85-92; Barnes 1979:1-10; Bakker 1990:1-21; Higbie 1990; Clark 1994:85-114; Friedrich 2000:1-19.

[7] Edwards 1991:150 notes that the epithet ἀργύφεον ('shining white') attributed to σπέος contrasts the halls of the immortals with the ugly suffering on the shore. Therefore, it also alludes, through the theme of divine versus human disparity, to the difference between this personal lament, which is expressed by a goddess and those expressed by mortals. Notice also that *Iliad* XVIII 30 (χερσὶ δὲ πᾶσαι), has almost the same terminal adonic as XVIII 50 (αἳ δ' ἄμα πᾶσαι), the former referring to the Nereids and the latter to the maids (δμῳαί).

Chapter Eleven

not only *in the physical absence* of the body of the deceased (as Thetis is in her cave at the depths of the sea), but also *in the virtual absence of a deceased* (since Achilles is alive). Thus, the reiteration of the word σπέος in the beginning and end of the speech has a multiple impact on its performance, far beyond its spatial localization.[8]

The first verse of each of the two couplets that frame the personal lament ends in a similar adonic (αἳ δ' ἅμα πᾶσαι / αἳ δὲ σὺν αὐτῇ). These phrases function as a refrain, exhibiting, through the repetition of equivalent semantic patterns placed at the same metrical slots and the two following necessary enjambments, a specific textual and poetic rhythm. The solemn approach of the chorus of mourners accompanying Thetis' lament with their gestures and tears is thus effectively expressed. Necessary enjambment, "revealing that the crucial element in a clause is the verb,"[9] results in a faster rhythm, not allowing even a minimal pause at verse-end. What follows is not an addition to a line of thought expressed in the enjambing verse, but the completion at the beginning of the second verse of the very kernel of the sentence. In necessary enjambment, which is the exact opposite of coterminacy,[10] semantic completion is effectuated by a run-over word or expression, making the mental leap to the next verse absolutely compulsory. The repetition of these necessary enjambments[11] closely conjoins the Nereids (to whom αἳ δ' (ἑ) refers in both cases) with the specific ritual gestures (στήθεα πεπλήγοντο / δακρυόεσσαι) described in the very beginning of the lines following the enjambed verses. In this way, the ritualistic aspects of the scene are tightly linked to their performers with an obvious impact on their intensity and rhythm.[12]

The beginning of the second verse of each couplet describes the emotional stage of the group of mourners. Verse XVIII 51 starts with a description of a corporeal gesture, (στήθεα πεπλήγοντο), the Nereids' beating of their own breasts. The same phrase is also attested in XVIII 31, referring this time to the female slaves (δμῳαί) of Achilles who beat their breasts while lamenting Patroclus. The expression "to beat one's breast" is only confined to females in the *Iliad*. Women beat their breasts as an external sign of excessive,

---

[8] One can recall the function of the scenery in Greek drama, which does not only localize the action but which also has wide interpretive consequences for the plot.

[9] Higbie 1990:49.

[10] Coterminacy is defined as the coincidence of semantic and structural completion within the boundaries of a single verse.

[11] Necessary enjambment is a higher-quality technique for reinforcing repetition patterns because it supersedes the hexameter verse boundary, indicating that analogies between the initial and closing frames go deep, at least deeper than the single verse. See Foley 1993:152.

[12] See Pucci 1993:258.

uncontrollable lamentation, whereas men express their grief with a series of immediate and violent gestures: they hit their face, raise their hands (Priam in XXII 33-34), roll in the dung (Priam in XXII 414), pull their hair (Agamemnon in X 15 and Priam in XXII 77-78), and put their hands on the breast of the deceased (Achilles in XVIII 317 = XXIII 18).[13] The phrases στήθεα πεπλήγοντο (XVIII 31 = XVIII 51), employed for the maidens and the Nereids, and χεῖρας ἐπ' ἀνδροφόνους θέμενος στήθεσσιν ἑταίρου (Iliad XVIII 317 = XXIII 18), used in Achilles' lament for Patroclus, extend both to the act being accomplished (beating versus putting) and to the receiver of this act (mourner versus deceased). The difference is important, more so since it refers to two distinct levels of lamentation. Whereas female mourners employ a self-destructive beating of their breast, Achilles places his own hands on the breast of his deceased friend. In this way, he covertly expresses both sharing the pain and taking an oath of avenging one death (that of his friend Patroclus) with another (that of Hector). This opposition between a female centripetal and a male centrifugal act seems to be the equivalent, on the level of corporeal gestures, to another antithesis on the level of sonority between the expressions ὀξὺ κωκύειν and βαρὺ στενάχειν, since in Homer the former is reserved only for women whereas the latter only for men.[14] Monsacré[15] has convincingly argued that women display a much more limited range of gestures compared to those of men. This may come as a surprise, but it is perfectly understandable if we keep in mind that, according to Monsacré, female grief:

> s' exprime toujours à l' intérieur d' un rituel au sens strict: la lamentation qui se passe dans des circonstances déterminées, suivant un code précis, qui ne semble leur laisser aucune marge de manoeuvre ... Face à l' expression féminine de la souffrance, figée dans un code

---

[13] Women also pull their hair (Andromache and Hecuba in XXIV 711). I have restricted my search only to the Iliad as I have done throughout this study due to the fact that my topic concerns only the older epic.

[14] On this opposition, see Arnould 1990:150-153. In Iliad XVIII 70-71 the expressions βαρὺ στενάχοντι and ὀξὺ κωκύσασα are found in two successive verses, the first referring to a male (Achilles) and the second to a female (Thetis) character. It seems that this scene is an allusion to Achilles' own death, which is directly connected to the theme of vengeance that may have arisen from another oral epic tradition. What has been stated above is true only for these two expressions as they stand: λιγύ, when used with κωκύειν, is restricted only to women but has a different treatment when used with the verb κλαίω (e.g. Iliad XIX 5: κλαίοντα λιγέως referring to Achilles). The same is the case with the compound στενάχειν of the verb ἐπιστενάχεσθαι, used for females only in the second part of the formula capping a γόος (... ἐπὶ δὲ στενάχοντο γυναῖκες). On κωκύειν, see also Krapp 1964:38 and Pucci 1993:258.

[15] Monsacré 1984:184.

Chapter Eleven

hyper-ritualisé, la douleur des hommes s' inscrit dans un registre plus large. À la douleur féminine, cantonnée à l' intérieur du seul rite, s' oppose la souffrance des hommes, libres d' utiliser pour s' exprimer tout le language gestuel de la société épique.

The idea of disfigurement expressed by the phrase στήθεα πεπλήγοντο is, therefore, inscribed on a larger register, comprising both female and male lament terminology. In *Iliad* XIX 282–286, the lament gestures performed by Briseis in front of the dead body of Patroclus are described in detail:

> And now, in the likeness of golden Aphrodite, Briseis / when she saw Patroklos lying torn with sharp bronze, folding / him in her arms *cried shrilly* (λίγ' ἐκώκυε) above him and *with her hands tore* (χερσὶ δ' ἄμυσσεν) / *at her breasts* (στήθεα) and *her soft throat* (ἀπαλὴν δειρήν) and *her beautiful forehead* (καλὰ πρόσωπα). / The woman like the immortals *mourning for him* (κλαίουσα) spoke to him.

With respect to this moving and powerful introduction to Briseis' ensuing γόος for Patroclus, Pucci[16] has argued that "Briseis utters her lament as she performs the rituals of mourning that comprehend the κωκύειν and the scratching of the breast, throat and face. She repeats ritualistic gestures that have their own ceremonial reason, intensity and rhythm."[17] The corporeal gestures of disfigurement positioned next to lament expressions such as λίγ' ἐκώκυε and κλαίουσα are further intensified, by virtue of being performed by slaves and not free women.[18] In this light, disfigurement implies self-effacement and symbolically mimics death through self-wounding. The female mourners' release of intense emotional force remains restricted within a hyper-ritualized code of expression. Women mourners tend to erase themselves as living human beings and figuratively assimilate into the condition of the dead. Their gestures are self-referential.[19] Given the rhythmic register on which the phrase στήθεα πεπλήγοντο is inscribed, one can detect a clear emphasis on the emotional preparation for a moving lament, in fact the most affecting in the *Iliad*.

The use of the verb δακρύω in XVIII 66 (δακρυόεσσαι) designates the appearance of tears in the eyes without any particular emphasis on their

---

[16] Pucci 1993:258.
[17] For a detailed analysis of Briseis' personal lament for Patroclus in *Iliad* XIX 287–300, see Pucci 1997:97–112; Dué 2002:5–7, 10–16, 67–78, 80–81; Tsagalis 2004:139–143.
[18] See Pucci 1997:97–112.
[19] See Reiner 1938:42; Neumann 1965:85–89; Anastassiou 1971:22.

flowing, as is the case with the substantive δάκρυ that is accompanied by various verbal forms and is more frequently used in the *Iliad*.[20] Given that the lament is framed by an 'introductory' expression of disfigurement (στήθεα πεπλήγοντο) and a 'capping' unmarked verb for grief, it becomes clear that the *diegesis* aims at creating an interplay between a corporeal gesture, symbolizing excessive grief, and a more restrained verbalization of mourning. The latter expression simply connotes an internalization of pain and suffering[21] that is consonant with the effect of the completion of the personal lament. The chorus of mourning Nereids, to whom both the expressions preceding (στήθεα πεπλήγοντο) and those capping (δακρυόεσσαι) the lament refer, have become less expressive, since the only role that will be assigned to them in the following verses is to return to the sea-depths and inform Thetis' father, the old man of the sea, of what had happened.[22] Therefore, the participle δακρυόεσσαι marks the completion of a concentric ring framing the personal lament and summarizing its emotional effect on the mourners (who are also, together with Achilles, the internal audience in this scene). The sonority of a violent corporeal gesture (στήθεα πεπλήγοντο) has been transformed after the utterance of the γόος to a silent (δακρυόεσσαι) internalization, a refined rationalization of mourning.

The pattern employed in the framing of Thetis' personal lament is built on components that indicate an internal emotional shift, a movement from excessive lamentation to restrained grief. Since this pattern is not observed in any other Iliadic lament, it seems reasonable that its intratextual differentiation from Iliadic practice may be relevant to the scene's heavy intertextual orientation. According to the Neoanalytical *credo*, Thetis' Iliadic lament for Achilles is based on her lament in the *Memnonis*, the pre-Homeric epic narrating the story of Memnon, whose plot corresponds to the second part of the post-Homeric *Aethiopis* by Arctinus of Miletos. Although we are in no position to know the form of Thetis' lament for Achilles in the Aethiopic tradi-

---

[20] Δακρύω is attested 5 times in the *Iliad* (I 349; X 377; XVI 7; XIX 229; XXII 491), whereas δάκρυ 27 times. See Monsacré 1984:171-172. The verb δακρύω may be indicating the appearance of tears in the eyes, i.e. the beginning of an emotional outburst, which will soon become δάκρυ χέειν 'to shed tears', i.e. to cry. See Watkins 1977:187-209, who argues that "denominative verbs are secondary and not subject to the same semantic restrictions as the noun itself." I owe this reference to Muellner 1996:9n11.

[21] Despite the fact that the verb δακρύω describes the appearance of tears on the face, I tend to interpret it as an internalization of pain, since their is no crying but only a simple mentioning of the tears, not even an emphasis on their shedding in the manner of expressions containing the word δάκρυ.

[22] See *Iliad* XVIII 140-144.

Chapter Eleven

tion, we can still speculate about the context of this γόος by combining (a) the information in Proclus' summary concerning the mourning for Achilles in the *Aethiopis* and (b) the Odyssean intertextual references to the lament for Achilles (*Odyssey* xxiv 58–62):

> καὶ Θέτις ἀφικομένη σὺν Μούσαις καὶ ταῖς ἀδελφαῖς θρηνεῖ τὸν παῖδα· καὶ μετὰ ταῦτα. ἐκ τῆς πυρᾶς ἡ Θέτις ἀναρπάσασα τὸν παῖδα εἰς τὴν Λευκὴν νῆσον διακομίζει.

> And Thetis, arriving with the Muses and her sisters, bewails her son. And after this, snatching him from the pyre, Thetis conveys her son to the island of Leuke.
> 198–200 Severyns = 65–66 Kullmann

> ἀμφὶ δέ σ' ἔστησαν κοῦραι ἁλίοιο γέροντος
> οἴκτρ' ὀλοφυρόμεναι, περὶ δ' ἄμβροτα εἵματα ἕσσαν.
> Μοῦσαι δ' ἐννέα πᾶσαι ἀμειβόμεναι ὀπὶ καλῇ
> θρήνεον. ἔνθα κεν οὔ τιν' ἀδάκρυτόν γ' ἐνόησας
> Ἀργείων· τοῖον γὰρ ὑπώρορε Μοῦσα λίγεια.

> The daughters of the Old Sea-god stood round you with bitter lamentations, and wrapped your body in an imperishable shroud. The Nine Muses chanted your dirge in sweet antiphony and you would not have seen a single Argive without tears in his eyes, such was the clear-voiced Muses' song.
> *Odyssey* xxiv 58–62

In light of the two aforementioned passages, it is clear that Thetis arrived (ἀφικομένη) at the Achaean camp accompanied by both the Muses and her sisters (Nereids). According to Proclus' summary, Achilles was lamented by both groups of mourners. Conversely, in the Odyssean version the Nereids 'stood round' (ἀμφὶ δέ σ' ἔστησαν) Achilles' body 'with bitter lamentations' (οἴκτρ' ὀλοφυρόμεναι) and 'wrapped' it 'in an imperishable shroud' (περὶ δ' ἄμβροτα εἵματα ἕσσαν), whereas the Nine Muses 'chanted the dirge in sweet antiphony' (Μοῦσαι δ' ἐννέα πᾶσαι ἀμειβόμεναι ὀπὶ καλῇ // θρήνεον).

Both versions seem to reflect the influence of an Aethiopic tradition[23] on the Iliadic and Odyssean traditions as well as on the post-Homeric *Aethiopis*

---

[23] The existence of a pre-Homeric *Memnonis* reflects the Neoanalytical approach, according to which the post-Homeric *Aethiopis* by Arctinus of Miletos is partly based on an older epic. From the point of view of oral poetics, one is able to argue for the existence of an 'Aethiopic' tradition feeding both the Iliadic tradition and the post-Homeric *Aethiopis*.

by Arctinus of Miletos. In this light, the *Iliad* appears to have framed Thetis' personal lament by its own plot requirements. The traditional staging of the lament employed by the Aethiopic tradition, i.e. the performance of the funeral lament next to the deathbed, is also observed by the subgenre of personal laments in the *Iliad* (as it is the case with the antiphonal laments for Patroclus by Briseis and Achilles in Book XIX, and for Hector by Andromache, Hecuba, and Helen in Book XXIV). The breaking of lament typology in *Iliad* XVIII is the result of the accommodation of intertextually relevant material to the exigencies of the Iliadic plot. In other words, the transfer of a scene belonging to the Aethiopic tradition into the *Iliad* has 'produced' a lament scene diverging from typical lament constraints. Of particular importance, this divergence becomes intratextually functional, standing apart from the typology of the rest of the Iliadic γόοι.

The presence of the Muses at the lament for Achilles in the Aethiopic tradition has been strongly debated. Both Stößel[24] and Danek[25] have argued that the Muses were not present at Achilles' lament in the plot of the pre-Homeric *Memnonis*. In order to explain their presence both in the extant Odyssean version and in the post-Homeric *Aethiopis* by Arctinus, Heubeck[26] suggests that the Muses *may* (the italics are mine) "have been introduced by the poet of the *Odyssey*." According to this interpretation, the Muses have been added because, within the context of *Odyssey* xxiv, the main point was the recognition of the highest κλέος that had been attributed to Achilles. In the Odyssean version, the Muses played the role of 'professional' ἀοιδοί, whereas the Nereids functioned like a chorus accompanying the lament, just as the Trojan women accompanied the lament for Hector by the professional θρήνων ἔξαρχοι in *Iliad* XXIV 719–722. Under this scope, the post-Homeric *Aethiopis* by Arctinus has been influenced by the *Odyssey*, hence Proclus' reference to both Muses and Nereids.

There are at least two serious problems with this interpretation, one external and the other internal. As far as the former is concerned, scholars have failed to notice that the absence of the Muses in the Iliadic version of Achilles' lament need not be due to the influence of an older, pre-Homeric *Memnonis-Stoff*, since it results from the very constraints governing the plot of the *Iliad*. The absence of a dead Achilles, i.e. of his body placed on a deathbed in the Achaean camp where the lament should take place, culminates in a re-localization of the lament by Thetis and the Nereids at the bottom of the

---

[24] 1975:51.
[25] 1998:472–473.
[26] 1992:366–367 (ad *Odyssey* xxiv 60).

Chapter Eleven

sea.²⁷ In other words, since it would have been absurd to have Thetis and her sisters lament Achilles while *standing in front of him in the Achaean camp*, then in order to tailor this unusual lament to its plot requirements, the *Iliad* needed to change its location and place it at the abode of Thetis and the Nereids, the bottom of the sea, where the problem of the absence of a dead body *disappears*. This necessary restriction leads directly to the elimination of the Muses from Achilles' Iliadic lament. The reason is very simple: the Muses cannot be placed at the bottom of the sea. The localization of the lament for Achilles at the bottom of the sea is clearly an Iliadic invention, since in the pre-Homeric *Memnonis (for those taking a Neoanalytical stance) the placement of the dead body of Achilles in the Achaean camp would have necessitated the performance of the lament by Thetis and the Nereids (and the Muses, according to my argumentation) on shore.

The second argument is, as I have mentioned above, internal. The presence of the Muses clearly symbolizes the honor and κλέος bestowed upon Achilles, especially within the context of the *Odyssey*'s final Book, where it is placed. Heubeck makes the attractive suggestion that the two groups of mourners (Muses and Nereids) in *Odyssey* xxiv correspond to the two groups of mourners (the professional ἀοιδοί and the chorus of Trojan women) in the first part of the lament for Hector in *Iliad* XXIV. What has escaped his notice is that in both of these cases we have a description of a formal θρῆνος, a lament sung by professionals and 'answered' by the bitter lamentations or inarticulate cries of a chorus of women. Whereas in *Iliad* XXIV this first part of the lament for Hector is followed by a second 'personal' phase in which three relatives (Andromache, Hecuba, and Helen) sing their personal laments or γόοι accompanied by a chorus of Trojan women (playing exactly the same role as in the formal θρῆνος), in the *Odyssey* there is *no mention whatsoever of a personal lament by Thetis*.²⁸ In fact, the *Odyssey* restricts itself to the presentation of only the

---

²⁷ Kullmann 1960:37 has argued that the scene in *Iliad* XVIII, in which Thetis, situated at the bottom of the sea, listens only to Achilles' and not to the maids' cries for Patroclus, is due to the poet of the *Iliad*, who cannot allow for the Nereids' lament to be lost under the lament of the maids. Given that both Patroclus and the maids are completely alien to Thetis, the poet of the *Iliad* effectively highlights the lament for Achilles. Once more, the intertextual background of this scene (in which Patroclus and the maids were absent) has been converted into an intratextual sequence 'surfacing' in the repetition of the phrase στήθεα πεπλήγοντο (XVIII 31, XVIII 51), which is attributed to both maids and Nereids. This grieving duplication is the result of the sequential, linear arrangement of two laments, one for Patroclus and the other for Achilles. The formulaic accretion of στήθεα πεπλήγοντο unveils the aberrant intertextual provenance of the two laments.

²⁸ See also Pindar *Pythian* 3.100–103, where Achilles placed on the pyre, is mourned by the Greek

formal θρῆνος, not the γόος for Achilles. Moreover, according to the Odyssean version, within the framework of the θρῆνος the Muses play the primary role, acting as professional singers, whereas the Nereids are downgraded to a secondary chorus. How is it possible that the Nereids, who were primary according to the Neoanalytical interpretation, have become secondary and vice versa for the Muses?

In this light, I maintain that either the pre-Homeric *Memnonis* or the Aethiopic tradition (for those who take an 'oral' stance and promote the importance of tradition instead of crystallized texts) would also be willing to confer special κλέος on Achilles. The lament for him needed to be special, and it is the presence of the Muses *together* with the Nereids that allows his θρῆνος to acquire cosmic significance. I suggest that, in the Aethiopic tradition, Achilles may have been lamented both through a formal θρῆνος and a γόος by Thetis, more or less in the manner of Hector in *Iliad* XXIV. The Muses, as professional singers, would have first sung the θρῆνος in the company of the Nereids, who would have been a chorus equivalent to that of the Trojan women at Hector's funeral. Then, a second phase would have followed in which Thetis would have uttered her personal lament for her son, accompanied by her sisters, the Nereids, who would again (as is the case with the Trojan women in *Iliad* XXIV) have answered to her γόος with their bitter lamentations. In fact, it is Hector's funeral in *Iliad* XXIV that has been shaped under the influence of Achilles' funeral in the Aethiopic tradition. The absence of Thetis' lament from *Odyssey* xxiv is explained as the result of this epic's attempt to highlight only the public, not the personal, aspect of Achilles' lament. Since Agamemnon's soul underscores Achilles' importance for the army, the personalized tone and intimacy of Thetis' γόος would have been quite inappropriate within this context. On the contrary, the *Odyssey* does not need to eliminate Thetis' preeminent role in the organization of funeral games for Achilles, since the games promote the public aspect of her son's life, i.e. his importance for the army.[29] In my view, it is perfectly plausible that the Aethiopic tradition would indeed have been an 'ideale Achilleis',[30] where both a formal θρῆνος by the Muses and the Nereids and a ritual γόος by Thetis would have been sung. With this in mind, the framing of Thetis' lament in *Iliad* XVIII is particular to its plot and bears the lasting imprint of the Iliadic tradition.

---

army, and *Isthmian* 8.56–60, where *only* the Muses are described as singing in his honor. I owe this reference to Burgess 2004:27.

[29] See in particular *Odyssey* xxiv 85–92, where special emphasis is laid on the admirable gifts set as prizes by the gods for the winners in the funeral games for Achilles.

[30] Danek 1998:473.

Chapter Eleven

Opening and Closure

After examining the oral-poetic frame that encompasses this personal lament, it is necessary to explore the diction of both the first two verses (52-53) by which Thetis addresses the Nereids and of the last two verses (63-64) capping the γόος proper:

> κλῦτε, κασίγνηται Νηρηΐδες, ὄφρ' εὖ πᾶσαι
> εἴδετ' ἀκούουσαι, <u>ὅσ' ἐμῷ ἔνι κήδεα θυμῷ</u>.

> Hear me, Nereids, my sisters; so you may all know
> well *all the sorrows that are in my heart*, when you hear of them
> from me.
>
> *Iliad* XVIII 52-53

> ἀλλ' εἶμ', ὄφρα ἴδωμι φίλον τέκος ἠδ' ἐπακούσω
> ὅττί <u>μιν ἵκετο πένθος</u> ἀπὸ πτολέμοιο μένοντα.

> Yet I shall go, to look on my dear son, and to listen
> to the *sorrow that has come to him* as he stays back from the
> fighting.
>
> *Iliad* XVIII 63-64

An internal ring is created by two distichs, an introductory couplet containing an address and exhortation to the Nereids to listen to her sorrows (κήδεα), and a closing couplet in which Thetis states her decision to go and listen to her son's mourning (πένθος). This ring consists of the following features:

1. The movement from her own sorrows (κήδεα) to her son's mourning (πένθος), reflecting the direction that the personal lament will follow.[31]

2. The emphatic repetition of εἴδετ' ἀκούουσαι + indirect clause (ὅσ' ἐμῷ ἔνι κήδεα θυμῷ) and ὄφρα ἴδωμι φίλον τέκος ἠδ' ἐπακούσω + indirect clause (ὅττί μιν ἵκετο πένθος ἀπὸ πτολέμοιο μένοντα), putting the emphasis on the perception of the sufferings of the mother and the mourning of the son. In the first case the Nereids are invited to learn the sufferings of Thetis, whereas in

---

[31] In *Iliad* XVIII 52-60 Thetis is the main subject of the four verbal forms: τέκον, θρέψασα, ἐπιπροέηκα, ὑποδέξομαι. In the last two verses before the final closing couplet, it is Achilles who comes to the foreground (ζώει, ἄχνυται). Although the initial invitation to the Nereids presents Thetis as the one in pain, her lament is centered around the fate of Achilles. This progressive withdrawal of Thetis and the ensuing focus on Achilles is in agreement with the scene of the dialogue that will immediately follow the personal lament. Mother and son will stand one in front of the other and describe in detail the fate of Achilles (Schadewaldt

the second Thetis herself will hear the mourning of her son. By equating the semantic rings of the opening and closing, the Iliadic tradition denotes that, in the process of the personal lament, Thetis takes the place that the Nereids occupied at the beginning, and Achilles the place that Thetis had when she began her speech. Synaesthetic knowledge—acquired by seeing (εἴδετ' / ἴδωμι) and hearing (κλῦτε, ἀκούουσαι / ἐπακούσω)—is deftly employed to mark the transition from the chorus of mourners (Nereids) to the individual lament singer (Thetis). In this way, mother and son are tightly linked in the world of lamentation and pain.

3. Both couplets constitute two separate blocks, independent from the rest of the speech. It would be tempting to hypothesize that they owe a considerable debt to a pre-Homeric *Memnonis and that the preverbal Gestalt[32] on which they are based reflects an attempt by the Iliadic tradition to diction-ally accomodate Thetis' personal lament, which did not really fit its narrative blueprint. Although such a hypothesis contains a fair amount of speculation, it is very likely that in the Aethiopic tradition Thetis would have come out of the sea together with the Nereids to lament Achilles. The first couplet, or at least the idea it expresses, may have complied with the plot line of the Aethiopic tradition, but the capping couplet is clearly an Iliadic invention. Moreover, both couplets commend themselves for the special care that the Iliadic tradition has bestowed upon them with respect to dictional selection. The use of φίλον τέκος in the accusative as object of ἴδωμι (Iliad XVIII 63), an Iliadic and Odyssean *hapax legomenon*, [33] the repetition of the same syntactical pattern (equivalent verbs + indirect clause), and the hortatory tone of the two blocks of verses speak for the meticulous verbalization of dictional material that is more rhetorical than funerary. This is the only occasion[34] where a personal lament begins and ends with two integral and almost autonomous couplets, clearly distinct from the rest of the speech. By displaying a linear rhythm "missing the layers of familiar echoes but exhibiting their forceful unrecognized meaning,"[35] these distichs covertly indicate the process of adjusting extratextual material to the *Iliad's* narrative plan.

1959[2]:252). Thetis summarizes in lament terminology what the ensuing dialogue will attempt to make more explicit.

[32] On the preverbal *Gestalt*, see Nagler 1967:269–311; 1974:8.

[33] This expression is always attested in the vocative (12 times in the *Iliad*; 4 times in the *Odyssey*).

[34] There are twelve personal laments in the *Iliad*: IV 155–182; VI 407–439; XVIII 52–64; XVIII 324–342; XIX 287–300; XIX 315–337; XXII 416–428; XXII 431–436; XXII 477–514; XXIV 725–745; XXIV 748–759; XXIV 762–775.

[35] Pucci 1993:261.

Chapter Eleven

Recasting a Formulaic Pattern

The personal lament proper begins with a really remarkable verse (*Iliad* XVIII 54):

> ᾤ μοι ἐγὼ δειλή, ᾤ μοι δυσαριστοτόκεια
>
> Ah me, my sorrow, the bitterness in this best of child-bearing

Verse XVIII 54 constitutes an introductory self-referential address, not referring to Achilles (the notional addressee of the speech) but to Thetis herself. It does not conform (despite the presence of ἐγώ,[36] μοι and δειλή, which recur in personal lament introductory addresses) to the pattern of the expanded address,[37] but deviates from it through the repetition of ᾤ μοι, ᾤ μοι (the only attestation of a double ᾤ μοι in both the *Iliad* and the *Odyssey*).[38] This is the only case in the entire *Iliad* where the exclamatory ᾤ is repeated in the same verse and the sole occasion the exclamatory ᾤ is attested in the Iliadic γόοι.[39] The verse is furthermore marked by the creation of the surprising epithet, δυσαριστοτόκεια, a truly enthralling coinage[40] and a *hapax legomenon* throughout all of Greek literature.[41] Ferrari has argued that in such an apostrophe as τέκνον, ἐγὼ δειλή (which begins Hecuba's personal lament in *Iliad* XXII 431), we can recognize a precise threnodic form (recurring in the "expanded" address that often begins a personal lament), "... *una giustapposizione immediata, una elementare frizione emotiva fra apostrofe nominale ... e pronome (o aggettivo) personale, fra 'tu' e 'io'*."[42] If we apply this observation to ᾤ

---

[36] Edwards 1991:151 implies that the use of ἐγώ in the beginning of a personal lament may be a sign of informality: "The first laments for Hektor begin in the same way: τέκνον, ἐγὼ δειλή, (Hecuba, 22.431), Ἕκτορ, ἐγὼ δύστηνος (Andromache, 22.477). The first hemistich is also used by Odysseus as the storm arises (*Od.* 5.299). The three final personal laments for Hektor begin, *perhaps more formally* (my italics), with a vocative without ἐγώ (24.725, 748, 762)."

[37] The expanded address is one of the typical features of the Iliadic personal laments. See Tsagalis 2004:32–36.

[38] For statistics on initial vocatives in Greek epic and drama, see Wendel 1929; Dickey 1996, although her study does not concern Homer, offers an interesting discussion of the various uses of vocatives in different contexts and authors.

[39] Vocative repetition preceded by ὦ within a single verse is attested one more time in the entire *Iliad* (VI 55: ὦ πέπον, ὦ Μενέλαε ...).

[40] See Pope 1985:1–8.

[41] Edwards 1991:151 notes on the use of this epithet: "The startling δυσαριστοτόκεια occurs only here, though Euripides has a reminiscence of it (*Rhesus* 909: μ' ἄπαιδα γέννας ἔθηκεν ἀριστοτόκοιο) and perhaps Stesichorus too S13.2–3 (*PMGF*) = S13.2–3 (*SLG*): ἐγὼν [μελέ]α καὶ ἄλασ-//τοτόκος κ]αὶ ἄλ[ασ]τᾳ παθοῖσα."

[42] Ferrari 1984:263.

μοι ἐγὼ δειλή, ᾤ μοι δυσαριστοτόκεια, we can see that this threnodic template is not at work, since the juxtaposition described above does not exist here. ᾤ μοι and ἐγὼ δειλή are not opposed to any "*apostrofe nominale*". Thetis does not address Achilles (therefore using the common proper-name vocative for speech introductions), but refers to herself (μοι, ἐγώ, δειλή). The "*apostrofe nominale*" is here replaced by δυσαριστοτόκεια set at the end of the verse. The anadiplosis of ᾤ μοι ... ᾤ μοι creates, through the repetition that it enhances, an intensification of the lament, verbalizing an emotionally strong throbbing by which Thetis addresses her own exceptional sufferings to bring herself to the foreground. The penthemimeral caesura coming after δειλή distributes the two ᾤ μοι to both the first and the second part of the verse, underlining the existence of a correspondence between the two parts: ᾤ μοι + ἐγώ + adjective (δειλή) / ᾤ μοι + adjective (δυσαριστοτόκεια). This emphatic correspondence is accompanied by a stronger beat in the second, more expanded part. This is the only time that ᾤ μοι ἐγώ(ν) begins the verse without being introduced by the formula ὀχθήσας δ' ἄρα εἶπε πρὸς ὃν μεγαλήτορα θυμόν.[43] Whereas in all other attestations of this word-group a secondary clause follows, here the internal verse break comes only after δειλή, without allowing ᾤ μοι ἐγώ to constitute a sentence. Thus, the two vocative clauses in asyndeton placed at the beginning of Thetis' speech and occupying an entire verse (XVIII 54) connote moments of high emotion.[44]

The epithet δυσαριστοτόκεια is clearly stronger than δειλή in closing the first part of the verse before the penthemimeral caesura. The latter is common in verse-initial addresses,[45] whereas the former constitutes a *hapax legomenon* in all of Greek literature. It is a triple compound (probably following the pattern of δυσ-άμ-μορος), but only with a single negative (δυσ-). Schadewaldt[46] and later Nagy[47] have observed that this epithet is then explained or rather developed throughout the process of the personal lament. Verses 55–56 explain -αριστοτόκεια, that is to say, the two last parts of this triple compound,

---

[43] See *Iliad* XI 403–404; XVII 90–91; XXI 552–553; XXII 98–99.
[44] See Higbie 1990:46–47; Beck 2005:161n24.
[45] The same epithet is attested 5 times in the *Iliad* (three times in personal laments: XVIII 54; XIX 287; XXII 431) always in addresses in character-text. The same expression is constantly used: ἆ δείλ' (XI 441, 452; XVI 837; XVII 201; XXIV 518) when a man is the addressee.
[46] See Schadewaldt 1965⁴:250.
[47] According to Nagy 1979:182 § 11n3: "The phrasing ἥ τ' ... ἔξοχον ἡρώων at 55–56 serves to elaborate on the compound epithet *dusaristotókeia* at 54, with the culminating theme conveyed by the epithet *éxokhos heróōn* 'the very best of heroes. (The element *dus-* 'bad, sad' of the compound *dus-aristo-tókeia* is meta-linguistic, in that it conveys the application of the epithet *-aristo-tokeia* 'mother of the very best' in the context of *o moi ... o moi*, the language of lamentation) ..."

since τέκον υἱὸν and ἀμύμονά τε κρατερόν τε, // ἔξοχον ἡρώων in verses 55-56 refer to -τόκεια and the -αριστο part of the compound, respectively. Finally, verses 59-60 explain the function of δυσ-. Thetis will not welcome her son to the house of Peleus in Phthia; Achilles will die in Troy.[48]

The first verse of the lament proper stands out as exceptional because of its deviation from the pattern of the *expanded address* that often begins a personal lament, and more significantly through the anadiplosis of ᾧ μοι and the use of δυσαριστοτόκεια. The Iliadic tradition captures the attention of any attentive listener by having Thetis accumulate, in the beginning of her lament, poetic innovations that produce an unfamiliar effect. Her emotional condition, that of deep pain, becomes the focus of attention as her lament is verbalized by way of the unknown and the unexpected.

By referring to the excellence of her son and to his prevalence among other warriors, Thetis virtually employs a variant form of the *comparison*, a typical feature of the Iliadic personal laments.[49] In this case, the comparison is one of ability on the battlefield, not of previous and present sufferings or losses of dear ones. This disguised *comparison* is verbalized by the *gradatio* (αὔξησις) ἀμύμονά τε κρατερόν τε, // ἔξοχον ἡρώων. The first two epithets simply characterize Achilles, whereas the third illustrates his excellence among heroes as the best warrior, a quality with which the *Iliad* has amply endowed him. In the word group ἔξοχον ἡρώων there is a latent superlative element picking up the second part of the compound δυσαριστοτόκεια, which also contains the superlative (αριστο-). The differentiation of Thetis' address is carried out not by avoiding the typical elements pertaining to the expanded address (such as the superlative), but by their different handling and placement, resulting in an important shift of emphasis. The first two epithets (ἀμύμονά τε κρατερόν τε) are paratactically linked without any particular impact on the picture the mother draws of her son. Contrariwise, the phrase ἔξοχον ἡρώων following in asyndeton shifts the stress. Achilles is not an ordinary warrior, but the best of the Achaeans, the one around whose wrath the whole *Iliad* has been composed.

---

[48] It seems that the *Iliad* ignores or rather deliberately disregards the fact that Thetis had left the house of Peleus and had been living with her father in the depths of the sea. See Willcock 1984 ad loc. But cf. Kakridis 1949:72 rejecting Bethe's proposal (1914:89; 1922:227) who had argued that verses 59-60 had been taken from the Ὁπλοποιία, which was, pace Bethe, an independent poem. Thetis could only have welcomed her son in the house of Peleus and not in the depths of the sea. Therefore, what she says should be read not as a sign of ignorance of her separation from Peleus after their marriage but as the prevalence of her maternal side, which brings her closer to mortals than gods, hence her helplessness.

[49] See Tsagalis 2004:36-39.

The effect produced is highly significant; for Thetis has prepared the ground for drawing an emotionally powerful picture, that of Achilles' life.

Verses 56 and 57 depict a vegetal imagery. Achilles is presented as ἔρνεϊ ἶσος 'like a young tree' and his nurturing (θρέψασα, a word referring to both plants and men) is likened to that of a shoot growing "in the pride of the orchard." Nagy has observed that Achilles in the *Iliad* and Demophon in the *Homeric Hymn to Demeter* (2) gain their immortality through "the permanence of the cultural institutions into which they are incorporated—cult for Demophon, epic for Achilles of our *Iliad*" and that, like the epithet ἄφθιτος // -ον, the effect amounts to "the *cultural* negation of a *natural* process, the growing and the wilting of plants, and also, by extension, the life and the death of mortals."[50] Moreover, in Homeric epic vegetal imagery is closely linked to lamentation. The phrase φυτὸν ὥς is only applied to Achilles in the *Iliad*[51] and the *Odyssey*, and the word ἔρνος is also used in a simile employed in the necrological vignette for the death of Euphorbus by Menelaus in *Iliad* XVII 53–60. Vegetal imagery, in a wider sense (containing also comparisons to trees), is typical of the Iliadic short obituaries.[52] In IV 482–487 Simoeisius is compared to a smooth poplar (αἴγειρος λείη), and in V 560 the two sons of Diocles are likened to high pine trees (ἐλάτῃσιν ἐοικότες ὑψηλῇσιν). The epithets θαλερός, deserved for Simoeisius in IV 474, and ἐριθηλές, used for the seedling to which Euphorbus is compared in XVII 53, also point to the same sort of imagery, since the verb θάλλω 'to thrive' describes literally the natural condition of bloom and figuratively human vigor.[53] In the context of lamentation vegetal imagery is employed for heroes who are likened to plants or trees. The reason for the consistency in the use of this kind of imagery is the *Iliad's preoccupation with the theme of premature death*. Nature and, in particular, vegetation offer a good opportunity for stressing a motif of great importance for Iliadic epic. The fate of the epic's greatest hero, Achilles, who is destined to die young (ὠκυμορώτατος), becomes the thematic pattern in relation to which the deaths of other heroes will be measured. By creating its own evaluation system, the Iliadic tradition opens up for its listeners its own horizon of expectations.[54] The contextualization of Thetis' personal lament indicates

---

[50] Nagy 1979:184.
[51] See *Iliad* XVIII 57 and XVIII 438.
[52] See Tsagalis 2004:179–192.
[53] Nagy 1979:183 § n2. refers to *Iliad* XXII 87 in which Hecuba uses the expression φίλον θάλος "in the context of conjuring up a future scene where Hektor will be laid out on the funeral couch and his mother will be mourning him."
[54] On this term, see Jauss 1982:28–32 (for ancient literature).

Chapter Eleven

that the nourishment of Achilles in the choicest spot of the orchard, i.e. in a *privileged place deserved only for the chosen ones*, is a covert reference to his aberrance from heroic norm, to the dramatic liminality that keeps him apart from the rest of his comrades. Thus, the vegetal imagery gives to the personal lament a wider scope, acquiring its full force only through a proleptic allusion to an extra-Iliadic event, Achilles' death.[55] Now let us turn to verses XVIII 57-60:

> τὸν μὲν ἐγὼ θρέψασα φυτὸν ὣς γουνῷ ἀλωῆς
> νηυσὶν ἔπι προέηκα κορωνίσιν Ἴλιον εἴσω
> Τρωσὶ μαχησόμενον· τὸν δ' οὐχ ὑποδέξομαι αὖτις
> οἴκαδε νοστήσαντα δόμον Πηλήϊον εἴσω.

> and I nurtured him, like a tree grown in the pride of the orchard.
> I sent him away with the curved ships into the land of Ilion
> to fight with the Trojans; but I shall never again receive him
> won home again to his country and into the house of Peleus.

Verses XVIII 57-60 contain a long period with two independent clauses in parataxis. Participles (θρέψασα, μαχησόμενοι, νοστήσαντα) play a dominant role. As Thetis explains the reason for her sufferings (κήδεα), the rhythm of her words slows down. She now draws carefully, with attentive small moves (flowing one after the other without any subordination that would divide them into primary and secondary), the circle of Achilles' life. τὸν μὲν ἐγὼ θρέψασα φυτὸν ὣς γουνῷ ἀλωῆς and τὸν δ' οὐχ ὑποδέξομαι αὖτις // οἴκαδε νοστήσαντα δόμον Πηλήϊον εἴσω form its temporal "diameter", since they refer to the beginning and end of her son's life. On the other hand, Ἴλιον εἴσω // Τρωσὶ μαχησόμενον determines its sharpened center, since it presents Thetis as responsible for the participation of Achilles in the war. The harmony of this description is the result of the juxtaposition of τὸν μὲν ... Ἴλιον εἴσω // Τρωσὶ μαχησόμενον with τὸν δ' ... // οἴκαδε νοστήσαντα δόμον Πηλήϊον εἴσω, expressing the alternation between past (first clause) and future (second). This juxtaposition strikes a balance between what has happened in the past and what foreshadows the future. It also equates dictionally what is semantically opposed, i.e. the happiness of the past with the grimness of the future. The emotional outcome of such an effect is

---

[55] In the sense that Achilles will not die in the *Iliad*, but in the *Aethiopis* (Proclus's *Chrestomathy* 191-192 Severyns = 62 Kullmann).

impressive, entailing a "rhythmic coterminacy"[56] that starts at verse 57 and reaches its culmination at verse 60.

Being deprived of any single lament term, these verses mark a slowing down of the rhythm, since the high pitch and emotional intensity of the expanded address appears to evaporate or at least to be diffused. What follows functions like a commentary, an explanation and development of Thetis' introductory outburst of pain.

Verses XVIII 57–60 are full of familiar expressions: γουνῷ ἀλωῆς (3 times in the *Iliad*); νηυσὶν ... κορωνίσιν (13 times in the *Iliad*, once with the variant νήεσσι); Ἴλιον εἴσω (6 times in the *Iliad*); Τρωσὶ μαχησόμενον (2 times in the *Iliad*); οἴκαδε νοστήσαντα (2 times *Iliad*); and δόμον Πηλήϊον εἴσω (2 times in the *Iliad*). These formulas create a *dictional intimacy*, as if Thetis were, through the use of familiar stereotypical vocabulary, to bring to the *expressive surface* of her speech the most basic external prolepsis of this epic, Achilles' future death at Troy. Achilles' short lifespan (being ὠκύμορος[57] and even ὠκυμορώτατος[58]) and his destined death at Troy are also allusively suggested by the rhyming of Ἴλιον εἴσω (58) with δόμον Πηλήϊον εἴσω (60). The acoustical representation of a semantic correspondence between Troy and Phthia reminds the audience of the opposition of the two poles between which Achilles' life has been spent. Through the aural link that the rhyming creates, an assimilation of the two places produces a dramatic summary of Achilles' life. Troy and Phthia are not simply two place names, but stand for *different states of Achilles' being*. In fact, they constitute an epic hero's poetic topography, stretching from heroic death and κλέος at Troy to unheroic νόστος to Phthia.[59] In his personal lament for Patroclus in *Iliad* XIX 315–337 (uttered antiphonally to Briseis' preceding lament) Achilles refers twice to both Troy and Phthia:

ὅς που νῦν <u>Φθίηφι</u> τέρεν κατὰ δάκρυον εἴβει
χήτει τοιοῦδ' υἷος· ὃ δ' <u>ἀλλοδαπῷ ἐνὶ δήμῳ</u>
εἵνεκα ῥιγεδανῆς Ἑλένης Τρωσὶν πολεμίζω.

who now, I think, *in Phthia* somewhere lets fall a soft tear

---

[56] I have borrowed the term coterminacy from verse-structure analysis. Coterminacy describes the conjunction of prosodical/metrical completion and semantic consummation. It is textually expressed by heavy or light punctuation 'reminding' the reader that in pre-pausal positions not followed by enjambment the tone should be neutralized for an instance, until the new verse begins in a distinctively different rhythm.

[57] See *Iliad* I 417; XVIII 95, 458.

[58] See *Iliad* I 505.

[59] See *Iliad* IX 410–416, where the antithesis between Achilles' two choices is epitomized in plain epic terms.

Chapter Eleven

> for bereavement of such a son, for me, who now *in a strange land*
> make war upon the Trojans for the sake of accursed Helen;
>
> *Iliad* XIX 323–325

> πρὶν μὲν γάρ μοι θυμὸς ἐνὶ στήθεσσιν ἐώλπει
> οἶον ἐμὲ φθείσεσθαι <u>ἀπ' Ἄργεος ἱπποβότοιο</u>
> <u>αὐτοῦ ἐνὶ Τροίῃ</u>, σὲ δέ τε Φθίηνδε νέεσθαι

> Before now the spirit inside my breast was hopeful
> that I alone should die *far away from horse-pasturing Argos
> here in Troy*; I hoped you would win back again to Phthia
>
> *Iliad* XIX 328–330

Achilles' highlighting of Phthia (*Iliad* XIX 323, 330) and Troy (*Iliad* XIX 330) makes evident that these two places are metonymically equivalent to his past, present, and future. Scyros, which is also mentioned in the above lament as the place where Neoptolemus grew up,[60] was the dwelling of Achilles according to a tradition that presented either his father Peleus[61] or his mother Thetis as unwilling to send him to Troy.[62] In the former, Lycomedes made Achilles dress like a girl and hide among the other women of his palace. In the end, he was discovered by Odysseus, who presented the women with baskets and weaving tools, but put weapons among them. While all the women were looking at the baskets and weaving tools, Achilles betrayed his identity by laying his hands on the weapons. He subsequently had to sail to Troy, leaving behind the daughter of Lycomedes, Deidameia, who was pregnant with his son, Neoptolemus. The *Iliad* seems to be unaware[63] of either variant version of the Scyros-episode, according to which Achilles hid on this island *before* the first gathering of the Achaean fleet at Aulis.[64] Conversely, the Iliadic tradition knows and alludes to an alternative version of the Scyros-episode featured in Proclus' summary

---

[60] See Proclus' summary of the *Ilias parva* in his *Chrestomathy* 217–218 Severyns = 76 Kullmann.

[61] According to the scholia on *Iliad* XIX 326 (Dindorf), it was Peleus who did not want to sent Achilles to Troy because he knew that he was destined to die there (Πηλεὺς δὲ προγινώσκων ὅτι μοιρίδιον ἦν ἐν Τροίᾳ θανεῖν Ἀχιλλέα, παραγενόμενος ἐς Σκῦρον πρὸς Λυκομήδην τὸν βασιλέα παρέθετο τὸν Ἀχιλλέα 'Since Peleus foresaw that Achilles was destined to die in Troy, he went to Scyros and entrusted Achilles to king Lycomedes').

[62] Hyginus *Fabulae* 96; scholia on *Iliad* I 417 (Dindorf). According to this version, it was Thetis who entrusted Achilles to Lycomedes, after she found out from Zeus that her son was destined to have either a short life in Troy or a long life if he were not to take part in the war.

[63] But is not, as I will show.

[64] Kullmann 1960:197.

of the *Cypria*. According to this version (130–131 Severyns = 27 Kullmann), "Achilles sets in at Scyros and marries the daughter of Lykomedes, Deidameia" (Ἀχιλλεὺς δὲ Σκύρῳ προσσχὼν γαμεῖ τὴν Λυκομήδους θυγατέρα Δηϊδάμειαν). These two traditions (Achilles hiding at Scyros versus Achilles arriving at Scyros after the Teuthranian expedition) are incompatible. Bernabé wrongly attributes to the *Cypria* (frs. 19 and 21 in *PEG* 1) the episode mentioned by the scholia on *Iliad* XIX 326. Davies, more cautiously, lists both of these fragments under 'fragmenta incerti loci intra cyclum epicum' (frs. 4 and 5 in *EGF*). The *Ilias parva* may have been a better guess (see *Iliad* XIX 326 and *Ilias parva* 4^A [= fr. 24 *incerti operis* in *PEG* 1], but also the problems arising from 4^B in *EGF*). In my view, the cyclic fragments reflect two rival traditions. In the first, Achilles, sent secretly to Scyros by either Thetis or Peleus to avoid going to Troy, has an affair with Deidameia, who will later on give birth to Neoptolemus. In the second tradition, Achilles arrives at Scyros because of a storm, sacks the island, and marries Deidameia, who gives birth to Neoptolemus.

The intertextual play the Iliadic tradition unravels is fascinating because of the different methods it employs in transforming the two aforementioned traditions. Kullmann, referring to the second tradition and taking a Neoanalytical stance, spoke of a *Kyprien-Stoff* and convincingly argued that the content of the *Cypria* is covered by thematic assumptions suiting the *Iliad*.[65] I would like to argue that the *Iliad* is aware of *both* of these traditions, attempting to modify Kullmann's formulation as far as the *Kyprien-Stoff* is concerned.

Thetis' analeptic statement in *Iliad* XVIII 58–59 (νηυσὶν ἔπι προέηκα κορωνίσιν Ἴλιον εἴσω // Τρωσὶ μαχησόμενον) and various other passages (IX 252–256; IX 438–440; XI 765–789)[66] show that the Iliadic tradition not only *erased* the unheroic character of Achilles' hiding in Scyros, it even exploited the intertextual background through a complete *reversal*. While Thetis and Peleus (standing for alternative variants of a multiform tradition) tried to secretly keep Achilles in Scyros, the Iliadic tradition starkly presents both Achilles' parents as *being willing* to send him to Troy. This pleonastic intensification of the *willingness* of Thetis and Peleus to send Achilles to Troy is the *Iliad's* polemical cry against a rival tradition. By adopting such a mythical viewpoint, the *Iliad* is able to deepen the *pathos* in Thetis' lament on the one hand, and make full use of the theme of Peleus on the other. Achilles' suffering for his aged father left back in Phthia, a motif of cardinal importance for the Iliadic plot

---

[65] Kullmann 1960:191, 196–198.
[66] See Kullmann 1960:258–260.

as shown by the Priam episode in *Iliad* XXIV, is significantly strengthened if Peleus had urged Achilles before his departure to Troy 'to be always best in battle and pre-eminent beyond all others' (*Iliad* XI 784: αἰὲν ἀριστεύειν καὶ ὑπείροχον ἔμμεναι ἄλλων). In this way, the Iliadic tradition was able to exploit the opposition between Phthia and Troy as emblems of heroic topography, the former standing for Achilles' would-be unheroic νόστος, the latter for his foreshadowed heroic death and winning of κλέος.

Kullmann was correct in assessing that the *Iliad* was aware of the thematic material reflected in the *Cypria*, arguing, with respect to *Iliad* XIX 326-337, that "*der Kyprieninhalt deckt sich mit den stofflichen Voraussetzungen der Ilias.*"[67] From the point of view of oral theory, instead of *Stoff*, we can speak of oral poetic traditions shaping each other during the Archaic period. The intertextual (inter-traditional) background of this scene has been thoroughly transformed by the Iliadic tradition, not through its *reversal* as in the previous case, but through its *duplication* and *re-orientation*. Schematically, the situation can be presented as follows:

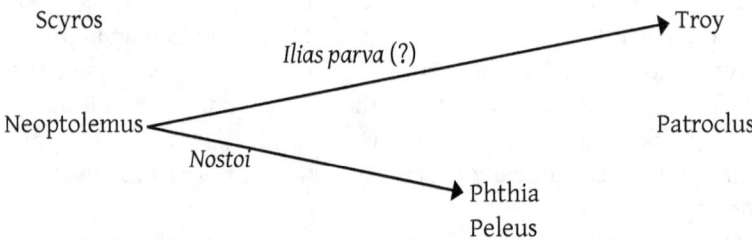

The arrows indicate that the only person who will indeed change location is Neoptolemus. In *Iliad* XIX 326-337, Achilles laments the dead Patroclus, who will not take Neoptolemus from Scyros and return to Phthia. He also refers to his father Peleus, whom he imagines as growing old in Phthia. Conversely, Neoptolemus will finally leave from Scyros but *not* return to Phthia. Instead, he will be brought by Odysseus to Troy, fight against the Trojans, and will only return to Phthia after the sack of Ilium. By combining Neoptolemus with Patroclus and Peleus, the Iliadic tradition is able to *duplicate* the Scyros element of the myth and integrate it into the poem's viewpoint. Scyros is no longer reminiscent of the hero's past, a place Achilles sacked after the Teuthranian expedition (according to the *Kyprien-Stoff* or *Cypria*-tradition), but a window to another hero's future. The *Iliad* is thus able to join past and future by exploiting intertextual associations 'bridged' through the theme of Patroclus' death and

---

[67] Kullmann 1960:198.

translated into an intratextual sequence of place names. Since the reference to Neoptolemus points both to the past and to the future, the two intertextual allusions acquire linearity in the course of Achilles' lament. In fact, Achilles' speech reaches a subliminal irony, since the audience knows that in the tragic universe of Iliadic heroism separated fathers and sons will never meet again. Achilles will neither return to Phthia (as a son) to meet Peleus nor to Scyros (as a father) to see Neoptolemus. Instead, Neoptolemus will come to Troy only *after* the death of Achilles and will finally return to Phthia *after* the death of Peleus.[68]

Under this scope, the polarity between Phthia and Troy highlighted by Thetis' personal lament is set against its intertextual background. *Reversal* on the one hand, and *duplication* and *re-orientation* of some of its ramifications on the other culminate in the re-contextualization and the subsequent effectiveness of this γόος due to its special dramatic impact.

In light of this digression, revealing the role and significance of the place-names for Achilles' fate, the rhyming at verse-end of the phrases Ἴλιον εἴσω and Πηλήϊον εἴσω declares their generic force, at the same time paralleling and contrasting them within the cycle of Achilles' life. The addition of internal enjambment effectuated by the hemiepes (Τρωσὶ μαχησόμενον: – ⏑⏑ – ⏑⏑ –) in verse 59 (Higbie's 1b type) curtails the continuity of the μέν-δέ clauses and makes possible the rhyming between Ἴλιον εἴσω (58) and δόμον Πηλήϊον εἴσω (60). As a result, a slower pace is produced with internal links added in parataxis that depict Achilles' life through the perspective of death. Then, Thetis (XVIII 61–62) returns to the present:

ὄφρα δέ μοι ζώει καὶ <u>ὁρᾷ φάος ἠελίοιο,</u>
<u>ἄχνυται, οὐδέ τί οἱ δύναμαι χραισμῆσαι</u> ἰοῦσα.

Yet while I see him live and *he looks on the sunlight, he has sorrows*, and though I go to him *I can do nothing to help him*.

The formula ὄφρα δέ μοι ζώει καὶ ὁρᾷ φάος ἠελίοιο is attested once more in the *Iliad* (XVIII 442), when Thetis visits Hephaestus for the making of Achilles' new shield.[69] The first verse of this couplet is a typical metaphor, often employed

---

[68] See Proclus' summary (*Ilias Parva* 217–218 Severyns = 76 Kullmann; *Nostoi* 299–300 Severyns = 111 Kullmann). Hector and Priam constitute the equivalent Trojan example, whose analogy to Achilles and Peleus is narratively exploited in *Iliad* XXIV.

[69] See *Iliad* XXIV 558, a verse that seems to have been a later interpolation since neither the scholia nor Eustathius mention it. See Richardson 1993:335 who notes: "... Herodian and Didymus discuss various explanations of ἔασας which assume that it stood on its own, and

Chapter Eleven

in a funerary or lament context. The phrase φάος ἠελίοιο might even be a smaller formula, more so since it is shaped as a pherecratean[70] and is always placed at verse-end.

Ἄχνυται standing in verse initial position after clausal internal enjambment (Higbie's type 2b) starkly inaugurates the use of lament terminology after the interlude of verses 57–60. Thus, eleven verses after the beginning of the γόος and only two before its end, we hear for the first time a term referring to the person whom Thetis is actually lamenting. This postponement, delaying the focus on Achilles, has kept the emotive tension of the personal lament suspended for its greatest part. Now, Thetis turns to her son and recapitulates the high key of her initial distress. The pitch is again raised as it was in verse 54, where the anadiplosis of ᾦ μοι and the epithet δυσαριστοτόκεια had expressed a true outburst of pain. Ἄχνυται conveys the hidden thematic seed planted by Thetis in the personal lament from its beginning. Thetis' singling out of Achilles is achieved through an emphatic, lugubrious cadence and the emotionally powerful, mournful tune of a mother's weeping.

Οὐδέ τί οἱ δύναμαι χραισμῆσαι ἰοῦσα contains the 'verb + infinitive formula' δύναμαι + χραισμῆσαι, which is attested, with some variation, 8 times in the *Iliad*. As Higbie has observed,[71] *Iliad* XI 120 and XVIII 62 = XVIII 443 are the only cases in which the aorist infinitive is used instead of the present, due to the flexibility of the formulaic system. Of interest for our analysis, only XI 120 and XVIII 62 = XVIII 443 do not have necessary enjambment. In all the other cases the infinitive is placed at the beginning of the next verse, producing necessary enjambment. Let us first review all of these cases before making some observations concerning XVIII 62:

> ὣς ἄρα τοῖς <u>οὔ τις δύνατο χραισμῆσαι</u> ὄλεθρον   1a
>
> so *there was no one* of the Trojans *who could save* these two
>
> *Iliad* XI 120

> ἄχνυται, <u>οὐδέ τί οἱ δύναμαι χραισμῆσαι</u> ἰοῦσα.
>
> sorrows, and though I go to him *I can do nothing to help him*
>
> *Iliad* XVIII 62 = XVIII 443

Sidonius read ἐπεί με πρῶτ' ἐλέησας in 557. Probably it is a late interpolation designed to complete the construction ἔασας, which stands on its own at 569, 684, and elsewhere."

[70] See Nagy 1974:49–102.
[71] Higbie 1990:160–161.

Intertextuality and Intratextual Distality

σύμπαντας· τότε δ' <u>οὔ τι δυνήσεαι ἀχνύμενός περ</u>   3
<u>χραισμεῖν</u>, εὖτ' ἂν πολλοὶ ὑφ' Ἕκτορος ἀνδροφόνοιο

all of them. Then *stricken at heart though you be, you will be able
to do nothing*, when in their numbers before man-slaughtering
    Hektor

Iliad I 241–242

θεινομένην· τότε δ' <u>οὔ τι δυνήσομαι, ἀχνύμενός περ</u>,   3
<u>χραισμεῖν</u>· ἀργαλέος γὰρ Ὀλύμπιος ἀντιφέρεσθαι

struck down, and then *sorry though I be I shall not be able
to do anything*. It is too hard to fight against the Olympian.

Iliad I 588–589

ἡ δ' εἴ πέρ τε τύχῃσι μάλα σχεδόν, <u>οὐ δύναταί σφιν</u>   3
<u>χραισμεῖν</u>, αὐτὴν γάρ μιν ὑπὸ τρόμος αἰνὸς ἱκάνει   0

and even if the doe be very near, *still she has no strength
to help*, for the ghastly shivers of fear are upon her also

Iliad XI 116–117

... <u>οἳ δ' οὐκ ἐδύναντο καὶ ἀχνύμενοί περ ἑταίρου</u>   3
<u>χραισμεῖν</u>, αὐτοὶ γὰρ μάλα δείδισαν Ἕκτορα δῖον.   0

... *who for all their sorrowing could do nothing
to help* their companion, being themselves afraid of great
    Hektor.

Iliad XV 651–652

καὶ γὰρ σοὶ ποταμός γε πάρα μέγας, <u>εἰ δύναταί τι</u>   3
<u>χραισμεῖν</u>· ἀλλ' οὐκ ἔστι Διὶ Κρονίωνι μάχεσθαι   1b

For here is a great river beside you, *if he were able
to help*; but it is not possible to fight Zeus, son of Kronos.

Iliad XXI 192–193

Of all the cases where δύναμαι + χραισμεῖν is used, there are three in which the expression ἀχνύμενός περ or its extended form ἀχνύμενοί περ ἑταίρου splits the formula by relocating it after δύναμαι and before the run-over word χραισμεῖν at verse-initial position. Higbie has argued that this formulaic expression "does not avoid enjambment by inverting its order, but does so by changing the form and shape of the infinitive, as in XI 120 and

Chapter Eleven

XVIII 62. In XI 116-17 and XXI 192-3, there is the regularizing tendency of the bucolic diaeresis as a convenient point to begin a phrase."[72]

In light of the aforementioned comparative stylistic analysis, it becomes obvious that verse XVIII 62 (= XVIII 443) is the only case in which the word group δύναμαι + χραισμεῖν, when joined by some form of the verb ἄχνυμαι, is not split and in which it remains unenjambed.[73] Consequently, XVIII 62 (= XVIII 443) marks a deviation from the formulaic pattern observed throughout the *Iliad*. The interpretive consequences of this change can be better appreciated if one observes that ἄχνυται precedes the formula δύναμαι + χραισμεῖν and is tied to verse XVIII 61 (= XVIII 442), which it brings to semantic completion. Achilles' and Thetis' grief and suffering are thus inextricably linked to Patroclus' life. What we see at work here is the effective *bridging* of Thetis and Patroclus, two figures not mythically connected.[74] In the Iliadic tradition, Achilles' grief and Thetis' helplessness are tightly linked to the theme of interdependence between Achilles and Patroclus. By creating an inseparable bond between Patroclus' life and Thetis, the Iliadic tradition has been able to devise a plan that presents two unrelated mythical figures through the dramatic scope of Achilles' involvement with both of them.

Thetis' Iliadic helplessness must be set against her intertextually asserted power. By violating its audience's expectations, the *Iliad* makes a profound statement concerning its stance not only towards a rival tradition, but also towards the heroic world as a whole. To this extent, the comparison between the *Iliad* and the *Aethiopis* is didactic. According to Proclus' *Chrestomathy* (185-190 Severyns = 57-61 Kullmann), 'Memnon the son of Eos arrives, with Hephaestan-made armor, to defend the Trojans. And Thetis foretells to her son events concerning Memnon. And when battle occurs Antilochus is slain by Memnon. Then Achilles slays Memnon, and Eos gives him immortality, having asked for it from Zeus' (Μέμνων δὲ ὁ Ἠοῦς υἱὸς ἔχων ἡφαιστότευκτον πανοπλίαν παραγίνεται τοῖς Τρωσὶ βοηθήσων· καὶ Θέτις τῷ παιδὶ τὰ κατὰ τὸν Μέμνονα προλέγει. καὶ συμβολῆς γενομένης Ἀντίλοχος ὑπὸ Μέμνονος ἀναιρεῖται, ἔπειτα Ἀχιλλεὺς Μέμνονα κτείνει· καὶ τούτῳ μὲν Ἠὼς παρὰ Διὸς αἰτησαμένη ἀθανασίαν δίδωσι). The *Iliad's* divergence and distancing from the *Aethiopis* is to be commended. Whereas in the latter epic Eos bestows immortality upon her son, Memnon, in the former Thetis is unable to avert her son's death. Achilles is not elevated, like Memnon in the *Aethiopis*, into divine

---

[72] Higbie 1990:161.

[73] In *Iliad* XI 120, necessary enjambment is also avoided but in that case the verb ἄχνυμαι is not used.

[74] See Kullmann 1960:37.

stature, on the contrary, he experiences death that not even his divine mother can forestall. The difference between the power of Eos in the *Aethiopis* (and, according to my stance, in the Aethiopic oral tradition) and the helplessness of Thetis in the Iliadic tradition epitomizes the dramatic perplexity and qualitative superiority of the latter.[75] The Iliadic stance on the world of heroes is much more thorough and critical in comparison to that of the Aethiopic tradition. Heroic immortalization is replaced by tragic death, which, despite its having been foreshadowed, remains disastrously inescapable.

Under this scope, XVIII 62 strongly represents an Iliadic viewpoint. It bestows upon Thetis' personal lament a tone of futility, stating the mother's acknowledgement of her inability to help her son. At the same time, through this gesture, the *Iliad* reconfirms its decision to foreshadow, continuously from its very beginning, the death of Achilles. The uniqueness of XVIII 62, summarizing not only the son's grief but also his mother's helplessness, is intratextually manifested through its divergence from a sequence of formulaic and semantic uses that recur in the *Iliad*. Once more, the eccentricities of Iliadic diction reveal intertextual ruptures, such as Thetis' helplessness and Achilles' grief, which are singled out here for their pathos and intensification.

It is impossible, of course, to prove the exact relationship between Thetis' personal lament in the *Iliad* and Thetis' lament for Achilles in the *Aethiopis*. Any such comparison would be, if anything, unsound since the actual text of the *Aethiopis* has been lost to us and a summary offered by Proclus is too short to support such a bold reconstruction.[76] It is better, albeit less ambitious, to restrict ourselves to the previous observation about verse XVIII 62 than to depart on an intriguing but groundless hypothesis that would be practically untenable at the raising of the first doubts. One of the most remarkable features of this personal lament is Thetis' ability to move on different emotional levels. The speed of an initial hortatory block of verses is followed in the first verse of the γόος proper by an outburst of lament. This is followed by a slow rhythm of the description of Achilles' life, emphasizing the antithesis between a happy past and a gloomy present. Having come full circle, the speech ends with a distich that recapitulates the speed of the introductory

---

[75] Memnon and Achilles are adversaries in the *Aethiopis*, but at the same time they share a parallel fate. In *Nemean* 6.50 Pindar uses the expression Μέμνονος οὐκ ἀπονοστήσαντος, which recalls οὐχ ὑποδέξομαι αὖτις / οἴκαδε νοστήσαντα in *Iliad* XVIII 59–60.

[76] Edwards 1991:150–151: "It seems unlikely that her [Thetis'] speech here could have owed more than occasional phrases to other versions, for her account of Akhilleus' life is framed in characteristic style by context-related couplets (52-3, 63-4; see also Lohmann 1970:54) and concludes with a reference to his present misery (61-2)."

couplet. This undulating movement, leaving and returning to the point from which it departed, might be a 'compositional innuendo' that implicitly points to the intertextual background of the entire scene.

The final juncture between ἰοῦσα / ἀλλ' εἶμι expresses Thetis' determination to go and visit her son despite her inability to assist him. In the majority of Iliadic personal laments, an ἀλλ' (ά) or νῦν is placed after the *comparison*,[77] referring to past sufferings and introducing the return to the present state of affairs. Here, this typical structural device, which recurrently makes possible the contrast between past and present, is reappropriated and recontextualized. Thetis implies that the real reason for her visit, amply stated in the introductory and closing couplets of her personal lament, is to share and alleviate Achilles' pain through her physical presence. In this way, the γόος itself covertly indicates *how* it has been adjusted to the Iliadic plot. The 'lament for the dead Achilles' (*Klage um den toten Achill*) featured in the Aethiopic tradition has been narratively 'disguised' as the 'lament for the disaster inflicted on a living man' (*Klage um das Unglück eines Lebenden*).[78]

Comparative Observations on the Diction of Thetis' Lament

The following comparative analysis of certain dictional features of Thetis' lament explores both the eccentricities and peculiarities of this γόος and the reasons lying behind them. I will first study certain elements pertaining to the Thetis' language in the *Iliad* and then resume the analysis of *Iliad* XVIII 52–64, concluding with an overall appraisal of the speech and its emotional force. I begin with a comparison between verses I 414, XVIII 54 and XXII 431, the first two of which are uttered by Thetis, the third by Hecuba in the initial verse of her personal lament for Hector in Book XXII.

> ὤ μοι τέκνον ἐμόν, τί νύ σ' ἔτρεφον αἰνὰ τεκοῦσα;
>
> ... Ah me, my child. Your birth was bitterness. Why did I raise you?
>
> *Iliad* I 414

> B. ὤ μοι ἐγὼ δειλή, ὤ μοι δυσαριστοτόκεια
>
> Ah me, my sorrow, the bitterness in this best of child-bearing
>
> *Iliad* XVIII 54

---

[77] See Tsagalis 2004:36–39.
[78] Kullmann 1960:37.

C. τέκνον, ἐγὼ δειλή· τί νυ βείομαι αἰνὰ παθοῦσα

Child, I am wretched. What shall my life be in my sorrows
Iliad XXII 431

These three verses share the following metrical, dictional and semantic similarities:

1. The word groups (A) ᾧ μοι τέκνον ἐμόν, (B) ᾧ μοι ἐγὼ δειλή, and (C) τέκνον, ἐγὼ δειλή, occupying up to position 5 in the dactylic hexameter, are in complementary distribution. The first is to the second as the second is to the third, and as the first is to the third, as illustrated in the following scheme:

(A)/(B): ᾧ μοι / ᾧ μοι
(B)/(C): ἐγὼ δειλή / ἐγὼ δειλή
(A)/(C): τέκνον ἐμόν / τέκνον

2. After the penthemimeral caesura, both (A) and (C) introduce a rhetorical question: τί νύ σ' ἔτρεφον // τί νυ βείομαι.

3. (A), (B), and (C) end with three *hapaxes* sharing similar semantic nuances: αἰνὰ τεκοῦσα / δυσαριστοτόκεια / αἰνὰ παθοῦσα.

Given that (B) and (C) belong to personal laments and (A) and (B) are expressed by Thetis, the question needing to be answered concerns the impact they have on the verbalization of Thetis' pain. In other words what do these verses show with respect to the manner Thetis expresses her grief?

The similarities and structural analogies between the laments reveal an underlying pattern upon which they are based, more so since they are all situated amidst a mournful context. Surprisingly enough, (B) seems to represent a sophisticated combination of all of these constituent elements. For the epithet δυσαριστοτόκεια also contains, albeit in a latent form, the idea expressed by τέκνον in cases (A) and (B), given that the last part (-τοκεια) of the triple compound epithet speaks of the relation between mother and son. In this respect, case (B) is a powerful combination of cases (A) and (C) with the addition of another characteristic pertaining to Achilles: the -αριστο part of the compound epithet designates the excellence of the lamented hero.[79]

Thetis' use of lament diction in referring to Achilles deviates from that employed by Hecuba with respect to Hector. Whereas ἔτρεφον αἰνὰ τεκοῦσα (I 414)[80] and -τοκεια (XVIII 54)[81] emphasize Thetis' motherhood, Hecuba uses

---

[79] See *Iliad* XVIII 10, where Achilles employs ἄριστος for Patroclus.
[80] Τεκοῦσα seems to be in ring form with τέκνον placed at the beginning of the verse. Here localization, euphony (τέκνον / αἰνὰ τεκοῦσα), and etymology tightly bind these phrases together.
[81] The following features point to the same interpretive direction: 1) the presence of τέκον in I 418 (ἔπλεο· τώ σε κακῇ αἴσῃ τέκον ἐν μεγάροισιν) and XVIII 55 (ἥ τ' ἐπεὶ ἂρ τέκον υἱὸν

Chapter Eleven

παθοῦσα, which is explained by βείομαι introducing the well-known polarity between life and death.[82] On the other hand, Thetis cannot stress a similar idea *because of her divine nature, which culminates in her disparity with her son, her experiencing of a different fate*.[83] Achilles' death cannot have an impact on Thetis' state of being because of her divine stature and immortality. Contrarily, the death of Hector entails wider implications by far surpassing the domain of his family. By standing for the inevitable fall of Troy, Hector's death gives Hecuba's agonizing question social and political dimensions.[84] This differentiation, being in agreement with one of the epic's main lines of thought, widens the *semantic horizon* of Thetis' diction. *For she not only describes the relation between mother and son, but also discloses the tragic distance separating them*.

A second comparative examination concerns verses XVIII 55–56, which describe Achilles as a special epic hero:

ἥ τ' ἐπεὶ ἄρ τέκον υἱὸν ἀμύμονά τε κρατερόν τε,
<u>ἔξοχον ἡρώων</u>, ...

since I gave birth to a son who was without fault and powerful,
conspicuous among heroes;

Thetis develops the idea of Achilles' excellence with respect either to his suffering or to his bravery (ἔξοχον ἡρώων). By paratactically accumulating epithets referring to her son's excellence on the battlefield, she deliberately reserves for him a special place that no other mortal can hold. Thetis employs a form of the three-colon crescendo containing three terms in an almost ascending climax of importance. The expression ἔξοχον ἡρώων placed at the end of this climactic structure deviates from the typical three-colon crescendo, which is normally restricted to a single verse. The typical form of this stylistic device is used in catalogues and basically concerns nouns, the last of which is accompanied by an epithet:

Ἄργός τε Σπάρτη τε καὶ εὐρυάγυια Μυκήνη

Iliad IV 52

ἀμύμονά τε κρατερόν τε), and 2) the absence of this verb from both of Hecuba's personal laments in *Iliad* XXII and XXIV.
[82] Verse XXII 431 is continued by: σεῖ' ἀποτεθνηῶτος. This is a different form of *death wish* (*Todeswunsch*), which is a typical device in Iliadic personal laments. See Tsagalis 2004:42–44.
[83] See Slatkin 1991:48–52.
[84] On Hecuba's personal laments for Hector, see Tsagalis 2004:154–161.

Intertextuality and Intratextual Distality

Ἴσανδρόν τε καὶ Ἱππόλοχον καὶ Λαοδάμειαν

Iliad VI 197

Δωρὶς καὶ Πανόπη καὶ ἀγακλειτὴ Γαλάτεια

Iliad XVIII 45

The three-colon crescendo can also be observed, though less frequently, in verses containing three epithets sequentially arranged:

<u>ἀφρήτωρ ἀθέμιστος ἀνέστιός</u> ἐστιν ἐκεῖνος

Out of all brotherhood, outlawed, homeless shall be that man

Iliad IX 63

Parataxis is a basic feature of the three-colon crescendo, more so since its members need to be tightly joined in order to be conceived as a single unit split in three parts.[85] In contrast to the above examples, the phrase ἔξοχον ἡρώων, designating Achilles as pre-eminent among other heroes, acquires a particular stress, being placed emphatically at verse-initial position. In this way, the linear arrangement of the crescendo's three members is interrupted, the run-over phrase ἔξοχον ἡρώων standing in to add internal enjambment to the previous verse. By achieving semantic completion at verse-end, the run-over expression ἔξοχον ἡρώων is effectively 'isolated' and emphasized. Once more, diction and stylistic manipulation of typical structures results in attributing a special tone to Thetis' lament.

Thetis' γόος in *Iliad* XVIII is also relevant to what Zeus tells her in *Iliad* XXIV 104–105. I have already shown that the Iliadic tradition transforms the motif of 'the lament for the dead Achilles' into that of 'the lament for a still suffering man' by having Thetis progressively 'move' from her own sufferings (κήδεα) to her son's cause for mourning (πένθος). The passages under discussion run as follows:

<u>κλῦτε</u>, κασίγνηται Νηρηΐδες, ὄφρ' εὖ πᾶσαι
εἴδετ' ἀκούουσαι, ὅσ' ἐμῷ ἔνι <u>κήδεα</u> θυμῷ.

---

[85] In tragedy, this device is used with great syntactical variety and often with a stress not on the length of its expanding members but on their sequential juxtaposition, as the ancient grammarians had observed. See Euripides *Heracles* 494: ἄρηξον, ἐλθὲ καὶ σκιὰ φάνηθί μοι, where the second member of the sequence is not longer than the first. In other cases the three-colon is continued to the next verse (Sophocles *Electra* 13, *Antigone* 901, Euripides *Heracles* 1226, 1390). This device was called by Behagel "*Gesetz der wachsenden Glieder*." I owe the reference to Allen 1973:118–119. This device had already been observed by the ancient grammarians. See Demetrius *On Style* 18, as well as Cicero *De oratore* III 186.

> *Hear* me, Nereids, my sisters; so you may all know
> well all the *sorrows* that are in my heart, when you hear of them from me.
>
> *Iliad* XVIII 52–53

> ἀλλ' εἶμ', ὄφρα ἴδωμι φίλον τέκος ἠδ' ἐπακούσω
> ὅττί μιν ἵκετο <u>πένθος</u> ἀπὸ πτολέμοιο μένοντα.
>
> Yet I shall go, to look on my dear son, and to listen
> to the *sorrow* that has come to him as he stays back from the fighting.
>
> *Iliad* XVIII 63–64

> ἤλυθες Οὔλυμπόνδε, θεὰ Θέτι, κηδομένη περ,
> <u>πένθος ἄλαστον</u> ἔχουσα μετὰ φρεσίν· οἶδα καὶ αὐτός.
>
> You have come to Olympos, divine Thetis, for all your sorrow,
> with an *unforgotten grief* in your heart. I myself know this.
>
> *Iliad* XXIV 104–105

In XXIV 104–105, Zeus's words confirm that Thetis has absorbed and internalized her son's πένθος. As Nagy[86] has shown, κλέος ἄφθιτον and πένθος ἄλαστον are linked with a specific correlation. The former describes, in the singer's own terms, the imperishable fame one can win through the accomplishment of noble deeds or can bequeath to an enemy if vanquished by him in battle. Conversely, the latter designates the unforgettable grief one experiences in defeat. Thus the wounding of Menelaus in *Iliad* IV 197 = 207 is described as κλέος for the Trojans but as πένθος for the Achaeans:

> ... τῷ μὲν κλέος, ἄμμι δὲ πένθος.
>
> ... glory to him, but to us a sorrow.

By employing, therefore, the language pertaining to the *Iliad*'s conception of the heroic code, Zeus situates Thetis' grief within the epic matrix of the world of heroes. In *Iliad* XVIII 52 Thetis starts her personal lament with a call to the Nereids to listen to her sufferings. The word she uses is κλῦτε, a term etymologically related to κλέος. By interweaving the semantics of the heroic term par excellence, κλέος, with the very fabric of her γόος, Thetis virtually asks the Nereids not simply to listen to her sufferings but to become the

---

[86] Nagy 1979:94.

internal audience of her lament song, her commemoration of Achilles' κλέος. The semantic congruity between κλῦτε and κλέος entails that Thetis' γόος will epitomize the very foundations upon which the Iliadic heroic world is based, i.e. that πένθος ἄλαστον 'unforgettable grief' becomes κλέος ἄφθιτον through its commemoration in poetry. Given that πένθος ἄλαστον 'unforgettable grief' is strongly associated with the ritual lament expressed by women for the dead, Zeus' words to Thetis in *Iliad* XXIV 104–105 reconfirm that her lament speech for Achilles in XVIII 52–64 has been decoded by the *Iliad* as a reactivation of Achilles' κλέος ἄφθιτον 'imperishable glory' through poetry.

The verbalization of Thetis' weeping reveals the special care in the choice of diction and in the internal organization of her speech. The heavily intertextual background of the entire theme of Achilles' death has been 'translated' by the Iliadic tradition into multiple idiosyncrasies, violating expectations and breaking constraints relevant to the subgenre of Iliadic laments. Situated within a scene savoring intertextual associations, which have worked their way into the fabric of the Iliadic plot, Thetis' γόος stands apart, exactly as Achilles stands apart from the rest of the Iliadic heroes.

12

Mapping the Hypertext: Similes in *Iliad* XXII

IN SPITE OF THE FACT THAT HOMERIC SIMILES have undergone exhaustive analysis, interest in them has been renewed in recent years, though the focus of research has shifted from studying their classification[1] to exploring their oral function[2] and the way they generate meaning.[3] Drawing both on the rich groundwork done on the field of simile categorization and on the solid foundations of narrative semiotics[4] and oral poetics, I will attempt to present the complex process by which Homeric poetry uses similes to create unexpected intratextual allusions. Martin has recently suggested that Homeric similes belong to a distinct rhythmic and narrative level.[5] Their special rhythmic characteristics need not be confused with metrical parameters. In fact, epic poetry has resorted to particularly refined ways of differentiating rhythm (as with the use of material with lyric undertones or with features pertaining only to the main narrative or to the speeches). Martin's interpretation rightly stresses the fact that, given the metrical exigencies and the restrictions of the dactylic hexameter, epic poetry virtually needed to 'invent' intricate methods for creating rhythmic variation. Operating on a special rhythmic and narrative register distinguished from that exclusively controlled by the omnipresent external narrator, the similes invite the audience to listen to an intradiegetic commentary on the central themes unraveled by the plot. Within this special universe, similes constitute a special phenomenon of epic language. Their formularity depends not on verbatim repetition of phrases filling certain metrical slots in the hexameter verse, but on their placement in given narrative junctures. The fact that similes never appear in speeches

---

[1] Fränkel 1921; Coffey 1957:113–132; Lee 1964; Bowra 1952:266–280; Scott 1974; Moulton 1977; Edwards 1987:102–110.
[2] Muellner 1990:59–101; Martin 1997:138–166; Bakker 2001a:1–23.
[3] Minchin 2001a:25–52 (= 2001b:132–160).
[4] For the semiotics of narration and its applicability to the Homeric epic, see Nimis 1987.
[5] 1997:138–166.

may be seen as a reflex of the formulaic nature of Homeric language on the level of dictional units larger than the formula. To gain as much as possible from the full range of the similes' referentiality, the audience needs to listen to them on a different key than the rest of the narrative. In this way, certain events, such as the fated conflict between Achilles and Hector in *Iliad* XXII, are presented on a register distinct from the plot, suggesting a level of sophistication devised with remarkable effectiveness by epic song.

Building on Goatly's theory on the function of metaphor,[6] Minchin[7] has recently suggested that the principle functions of the simile are as follows: (a) *explanation* and *modeling* of abstract or unfamiliar concepts; (b) *reconceptualization*, i.e. bringing forward covert meaning or obfuscatory associations in the narrative; (c) *filling lexical gaps* when "there is no word or form of words available to us to describe an action or an event—or, if there is, we cannot recall it at the moment we need it;"[8] (d) *expressing* emotional attitude; (e) *decoration and hyperbole*; (f) *cultivation of intimacy* between speaker and audience, when the examples selected by the speaker refer directly to the experience of his listeners; (g) *textual structuring*; (h) *enhancing memorability, foregrounding, and informativeness*; and finally (i) *prolonging* the audience's pleasure.

The cognitive basis of this classification has to its advantage, aside from its comprehensiveness, its emphasis on memory and conception. In this light, I maintain that the distinct performance register of the similes is also a mental pathway leading listeners to multiple conceptual strata. One result of the similes' different *experiential loads* is that they make available to the audience a *hypertextual* world of multiple image-mappings. In fact, the similes are equivalent to HTML, a 'Hyper Text Markup Language', employing effective formats, which (re)activate a sequence of images on a level distinct from the main narrative.[9] The cognitive background of the similes is of particular importance for understanding how they operate. Since the singer expects from his audience an evaluation of the similes' content, it is to be expected that this form of internal involvement by the listeners will entail the whole nexus of experiential multiformity and variety encoded in personalized visual images of familiar scenes of life. In this way, the condensed and highly fragmented picturing of the simile will conjure in the minds of the listeners a sequence of images defying both diachronic layering and language-oriented *storage* techniques, such as those employed in type scenes. The *hypertextual* world of

---

[6] Goatly 1997.
[7] Minchin 2001b:138–139.
[8] Minchin 2001b:138.
[9] For a *hypertextual* version of Homer, see Kahane 1997:333.

Chapter Twelve

similes is based on the power of image, not on words. The performance availability of similes and their *hypertextual* function was particularly helpful for the singing bard. After all, he did not need to repeat them accurately, as is the case with the constituent elements of type scenes. His audience would recognize their special performance register and become personally involved in their interpretation, their visualization. In the end, it was precisely the special rhythmic frequency of the similes to which both singer and audience would have to be attuned.

Similes as a 'Dramatic' Summary of the Main Narrative

Iliad XXII stands as the culmination of the entire epic, in which the dramatic conflict between Achilles and Hector finally takes place. This is in fact the epic's *telos*, the goal toward which the plot has been moving since its very beginning. It is no surprise then that the duel between the best of the Achaeans and the best of the Trojans that occupies the entirety of Book XXII includes no less than nine extended similes.[10]

> ὣς εἰπὼν προτὶ ἄστυ μέγα φρονέων ἐβεβήκει,
> σευάμενος <u>ὥς θ' ἵππος ἀεθλοφόρος σὺν ὄχεσφιν</u>,
> ὅς ῥά τε ῥεῖα θέῃσι τιταινόμενος πεδίοιο·
> <u>ὣς Ἀχιλεὺς λαιψηρὰ πόδας καὶ γούνατ' ἐνώμα</u>.

> He spoke, and stalked away against the city, with high thoughts
> in mind, and in tearing speed, *like a racehorse with his chariot*
> *who runs lightly as he pulls the chariot over the flat land.*
> *Such was the action of Achilleus in feet and quick knees.*
>
> *Iliad* XXII 21–24

> τὸν δ' ὁ γέρων Πρίαμος πρῶτος ἴδεν ὀφθαλμοῖσιν,
> <u>παμφαίνονθ' ὥς τ' ἀστέρ' ἐπεσσύμενον πεδίοιο</u>,
> ὅς ῥά τ' ὀπώρης εἶσιν, ἀρίζηλοι δέ οἱ αὐγαί
> φαίνονται πολλοῖσι μετ' ἀστράσι νυκτὸς ἀμολγῷ,
> ὅν τε κύν' Ὠρίωνος ἐπίκλησιν καλέουσιν·
> λαμπρότατος μὲν ὅ γ' ἐστί, κακὸν δέ τε σῆμα τέτυκται,
> καί τε φέρει πολλὸν πυρετὸν δειλοῖσι βροτοῖσιν·
> ὣς τοῦ χαλκὸς ἔλαμπε περὶ στήθεσσι θέοντος.

---

[10] Only the extended or long similes in *Iliad* XXII will be examined in this study. I will not deal with 'short' similes characterized as such by a single point of comparison (*tertium comparationis*).

The aged Priam was the first of all whose eyes saw him
as he swept across the flat land in full shining, like that star
which comes on in the autumn and whose conspicuous brightness
far outshines the stars that are numbered in the night's darkening,
the star they give the name of Orion's Dog, which is brightest
among the stars, and yet is wrought as a sign of evil
and brings on the great fever for unfortunate mortals.
Such was the flare of the bronze that girt his chest in his running.

Iliad XXII 25–32

ὡς δὲ <u>δράκων</u> ἐπὶ χειῇ ὀρέστερος ἄνδρα μένῃσιν
βεβρωκὼς κακὰ φάρμακ', ἔδυ δέ τέ μιν χόλος αἰνός,
σμερδαλέον δὲ <u>δέδορκεν</u> ἑλισσόμενος περὶ χειῇ,
ὣς Ἕκτωρ ἄσβεστον ἔχων μένος οὐχ ὑπεχώρει,
πύργῳ ἔπι προὔχοντι φαεινὴν ἀσπίδ' ἐρείσας.

But as a *snake* waits for a man by his hole, in the mountains,
glutted with evil poisons, and the fell venom has got inside him,
and coiled about the hole he *stares* malignant, so Hektor
would not give ground but kept unquenched the fury within him
and sloped his shining shield against the jut of the bastion.

Iliad XXII 93–97

<u>ἠΰτε κίρκος ὄρεσφιν</u>, ἐλαφρότατος πετεηνῶν,
ῥηϊδίως οἴμησε μετὰ τρήρωνα πέλειαν,
ἣ δέ θ' ὕπαιθα φοβεῖται, ὃ δ' ἐγγύθεν ὀξὺ λεληκὼς
ταρφέ' ἐπαΐσσει, ἐλέειν τέ ἑ θυμὸς ἀνώγει,
<u>ὣς ἄρ' ὅ γ' ἐμμεμαὼς ἰθὺς πέτετο</u>, τρέσε δ' Ἕκτωρ
τεῖχος ὕπο Τρώων, λαιψηρὰ δὲ γούνατ' ἐνώμα.

As when a hawk in the mountains who moves lightest of things flying
makes his effortless swoop for a trembling dove, but she slips away
from beneath and flies and he shrill screaming close after her

Chapter Twelve

plunges for her again and again, heart furious to take her;
so Achilleus went straight for him in fury, but Hektor
fled away under the Trojan wall and moved his knees rapidly.

Iliad XXII 139–144

<u>ὡς δ' ὅτ' ἀεθλοφόροι περὶ τέρματα μώνυχες ἵπποι</u>
<u>ῥίμφα μάλα τρωχῶσι</u>, τὸ δὲ μέγα κεῖται ἄεθλον,
ἢ τρίπος ἠὲ γυνή, ἀνδρὸς κατατεθνηῶτος,
<u>ὣς τὼ τρὶς Πριάμοιο πόλιν πέρι δινηθήτην</u>
<u>καρπαλίμοισι πόδεσσι·</u>

As when about the turn posts racing single-foot horses
run at full-speed, when a great prize is laid up for their winning,
a tripod or a woman, in games for a man's funeral,
so these two swept whirling about the city of Priam
in the speed of their feet.

Iliad XXII 162–166

<u>ὡς δ' ὅτε νεβρὸν ὄρεσφι κύων ἐλάφοιο δίηται</u>
<u>ὄρσας ἐξ εὐνῆς διά τ' ἄγκεα καὶ διὰ βήσσας</u>,
τὸν δ' εἴ πέρ τε λάθῃσι καταπτήξας ὑπὸ θάμνῳ,
ἀλλά τ' ἀνιχνεύων θέει ἔμπεδον, ὄφρα κεν εὕρῃ,
<u>ὣς Ἕκτωρ οὐ λῆθε ποδώκεα Πηλείωνα.</u>

As a dog in the mountains who has flushed from his covert
a deer's fawn follows him through the folding ways and the valleys,
and though the fawn crouched down under a bush and be hidden
he keeps running and noses him out until he comes on him;
so Hektor could not lose himself from swift-footed Peleion.

Iliad XXII 189–193

<u>ὡς δ' ἐν ὀνείρῳ οὐ δύναται φεύγοντα διώκειν -</u>
<u>οὔτ' ἄρ' ὃ τὸν δύναται ὑποφεύγειν, οὔθ' ὃ διώκειν -</u>
<u>ὣς ὃ τὸν οὐ δύνατο μάρψαι ποσίν, οὐδ' ὃς ἀλύξαι.</u>

As in a dream a man is not able to follow one who runs
from him, nor can the runner escape, nor the other pursue him,
so he could not run him down in his speed, nor the other get clear.

Iliad XXII 199–201

<u>οἴμησεν</u> δὲ ἀλεὶς ὥς τ' αἰετὸς <u>ὑψιπετήεις</u>,
ὅς τ' <u>εἶσιν πεδίονδε</u> διὰ νεφέων ἐρεβεννῶν
ἁρπάξων ἢ <u>ἄρν' ἀμαλὴν</u> ἢ <u>πτῶκα λαγωόν</u>·
ὣς Ἕκτωρ <u>οἴμησε</u> τινάσσων φάσγανον ὀξύ.

He made his swoop, like a high-flown eagle
who launches himself out of the murk of the clouds *on the flat land*
to catch away *a tender lamb* or *a shivering hare*; so
Hektor *made his swoop*, swinging his sharp sword.

Iliad XXII 308–311

<u>οἷος δ' ἀστὴρ εἶσι μετ' ἀστράσι νυκτὸς ἀμολγῷ</u>
Ἕσπερος, ὃς κάλλιστος ἐν οὐρανῷ ἵσταται ἀστήρ,
<u>ὣς αἰχμῆς ἀπέλαμπ' εὐήκεος</u>, ἣν ἄρ' Ἀχιλλεὺς
πάλλεν δεξιτερῇ, φρονέων κακὸν Ἕκτορι δίῳ,
εἰσορόων χρόα καλόν, ὅπῃ εἴξειε μάλιστα.

And as a star moves among stars in the night's darkening,
Hesper, who is the fairest star who stands in the sky, *such
was the shining from the pointed spear* Achilleus was shaking
in his right hand with evil intention toward brilliant Hektor.
He was eyeing Hektor's splendid body, to see where it might
best give way.

Iliad XXII 317–321

The size of the similes is so limited in comparison to their narrative 'mapping', namely the area of the main narrative they cover, that the term 'extended' or 'long' simile is rather misleading. The use of this terminology is relevant only in relation to the 'short' simile, even though it is not at all certain that the 'extended' simile has originated by simply adding material to some preexisting form of 'short' simile. Muellner[11] has argued that Homeric similes are, from the point of view of the narrative, compact forms of speech with special morphological characteristics that remain on a separate narrative (and perhaps rhythmic) register.[12] They present a sort of internal commentary on the plot, by which the external narrator makes a gesture towards his audience, sharing his viewpoint with them in the form of a narrative pause.

---

[11] Muellner 1990:59–101.
[12] The similes display a significant number of new forms, but this should in no way be interpreted as a sign of late-composition. The views of Shipp 1972²:7–144, 208–222 have been convincingly refuted by Chantraine 1955:73.

Chapter Twelve

The arrangement of the aforementioned similes is reflected in the structure of *Iliad* XXII and in the thematic classification of the material describing the dramatic conflict between Achilles and Hector. Schematically, the arrangement of similes can be better appreciated through their examination on both a *horizontal* and on a *vertical* axis. The *horizontal* (syntagmatic) axis runs as follows:

A. Introduction: Presentation of the two heroes:
 1. ἀεθλοφόρος ἵππος (Achilles)
 2. ἀστήρ (Achilles)
 3. δράκων ὀρέστερος (Hector)

B. Body: The chase
 1. κίρκος-πέλεια (Achilles—Hector)
 2. ἀεθλοφόροι ἵπποι (Achilles—Hector)
 3. κύων-νεβρὸς ἐλάφοιο (Achilles—Hector)
 4. ὄνειρος (Achilles—Hector)

C. Epilogue: Clash of the two duelists
 1. αἰετός—*ἄρς/ λαγωός (Achilles—Hector)
 2. ἀστήρ (Achilles)

This *horizontal* classification, following the deployment of similes in the main narrative, reflects an abbreviated form of the action in *Iliad* XXII. Before embarking on an examination of the similes' function, let us see how they may be organized on a *vertical* (paradigmatic) axis, where the similes are grouped according to the information they provide (see the table on the next page).

The vertical classification of similes shifts the point of interest from their linear arrangement to their thematic proximity, from the way they are placed to the way they overlap and connect.[13] If we attempt to 'read' these similes as a single thematic whole, we will find that the main theme of *Iliad* XXII, the death of Hector, is presented on four different levels: a) as a race; b) as a highlighting of the strength of Achilles; c) as a bestial, disastrous conflict; and d) as a necessity that is agonizingly prolonged.

---

[13] See Danek 2006:41–71, who has argued that 'Homer' aimed at a synchronization of two types of similes, the traditional or *Grundform*, with its objectified content and the innovative, 'Homeric' one with its subjective, plot-dependent overtones.

RACE	ACHILLES	CONFLICT	PERPETUATION OF THE PURSUIT
ἀεθλοφόρος ἵππος (Iliad XXII 21-24)	ἀστήρ (Iliad XXII 25-32)	δράκων - ἀνήρ (Iliad XXII 93-97)	ὄνειρος (Iliad XXII 199-201)
ἀεθλοφόροι ἵπποι (Iliad XXII 162-166)	ἀστήρ (Iliad XXII 317-321)	κίρκος - πέλεια (Iliad XXII 139-144)	
		κύων - νεβρὸς ἐλάφοιο (Iliad XXII 189-193)	
		αἰετός - *λαγωός (Iliad XXII 308-311)	

Intratextual Sequences and Hypertextual Imaging

The comparison of both Achilles (*Iliad* XXII 21-24) and of the two duelists (*Iliad* XXII 162-166) to *racing horses* forms an interpretive framework that encompasses all of *Iliad* XXII. This second dramatic 'Teichoscopia', with its carefully rendered staging, presents the best of the Achaeans and the best of the Trojans, who will soon fight for their lives before the entire Achaean and Trojan public. The battlefield becomes the scene where the fated conflict will unfold, while Hector's relatives on the walls of Troy and the Achaean army watching at a distance symbolize an internal audience following the unraveling of the plot. A careful analysis of the scope of these two similes shows how one small element relating one (Achilles) or two (Achilles and Hector) characters to horses has been skillfully elaborated with the addition of thematic material. This amplification technique results in a profound shifting of the focus of the aforementioned similes. The singer invites his listeners to get involved in the interpretive process and evaluate the simile for themselves.[14] In turn, realizing that the storyteller has situated them on a register distinct from that of the main narrative or *diegesis*, the listeners may use the simile as a *hypertextual gateway* that opens only to lead them into a universe of relevant

---

[14] See Minchin 2001b:143.

Chapter Twelve

but multiple personal image-mappings, which they will subsequently fuse into the condensed visualization offered by the singer, who tries to guide[15] or at least limit the scope of the interpretation. While the singer aims, using sequences of similes, to 'control their meaning', or, rather, to lead his audience into adducing for themselves the meaning that suits the epic's plotline, similes defy strict interpretation. While staring through this *hypertextual window*, the audience will have to discover for itself the covert message of the simile: why are Achilles and Hector compared to *racing* horses (ἀεθλοφόροι ἵπποι) and not to regular ones? Since listeners have different perceptions of racing horses and their image-mappings of such a scene will be colored by personal experience, it is fair to say that there are as many answers as there are listeners. First, the allusion to chariot horses accentuates the speed with which they move onto the battlefield.[16] Second, the similes of racing horses are presented to offset the tragic nature of the circumstances, that is, the fact that the conflict will directly impact on Hector's life. Third, these similes constitute a cross-reference to *Iliad* IX 123–124, in which Agamemnon promises that he will offer Achilles twelve racing horses as gifts in the event that the son of Thetis returns to battle. The gift-offering theme (seven tripods, ten talents of gold, twenty shining cauldrons), which is directed towards the restoration of Achilles' honor, comes to a rest only towards the end of the *Iliad*. Occurring after Patroclus' death, gift-offering simply looses the importance it might have had in the case of Achilles' earlier potential return to the battlefield. Agamemnon's promised gifts are finally given to Achilles only at the end of the poem, at a point when they are quite overdue, since Achilles' honor has been restored through the replacement of his μῆνις against Agamemnon by an even greater μῆνις against Hector. Achilles will acquire Agamemnon's racing horses too late, not as a persuasive means for his return to the war but as a reminder of the Fates' tragic ploy. In this light, it is all the more important that Achilles himself become a prize-winning horse in a race destined to finally lead to his doom. Expressed on a special narrative register, these two similes retrieve a *prima facie* trivial detail that has remained suspended and, thus, draw it out again. The study of similes in *Iliad* XXII centered on the racing horses shows that the battle between Achilles and Hector, which was ultimately fought for the prize of human life, is presented as a battle of special importance. As the heroes who participated in the struggle are not ordinary ones, but the best of

---

[15] See Nannini 2003:121.
[16] Interestingly enough, in *Iliad* XXII 162, the racing horses (ἀεθλοφόροι ἵπποι) are called single-hoofed (μώνυχες). Chariot horses are not hoofed in order to be able to run faster.

both the Greek and the Trojan side, so the horses to which they are compared are not regular, but racing, prize-winning horses.

The second category of similes (according to their placement on the *vertical* axis) includes two circumstances in which Achilles is compared to a star outshining the others in the night sky. In the first instance the star is considered to be the constellation of the Dog Star, in the second that of the Evening Star. In chapter eight, I have argued that the formula νυκτὸς ἀμολγῷ, which forms part of both of these similes, constitutes an implicit reference to the contrast between light and darkness. Since the aforementioned formula stands for a symbol of imminent danger with catastrophic consequences for those involved, the distinction between the constellations of the Dog Star and the Evening Star (*Iliad* XXII 25–32 and 317–321) is virtually blurred. What matters is not their astronomical accuracy but their thematic affiliation. Achilles is distinct, just as are the above-mentioned stars in the night sky. His brightness is a sign of disaster (*Iliad* XXII 31) or a foreshadowing of the fated blow of the spear that will strike the exposed portion of Hector's body, that not protected by his armor (*Iliad* XXII 319–321). Just as in the previous group of similes, the main theme is a combination of a covert reference to Achilles' preeminence in the battlefield and an allusion to Hector's impending death. By using the abbreviated form of the two similes, the singer aims at limiting the wide range of images drawn from the audience's common experience. At the same time, since both the Dog Star and the Evening Star would no doubt have conjured multiple visual memories of the night sky in the listeners' minds, the listeners would immediately evaluate the specific visualization offered by the storyteller. In contrast to the heroes of the past, for whom the audience had to rely on the singer's performance, the intimacy with the world described in the similes allowed listeners to freely exploit the plethora of personal image-mappings and to subsequently compare the singer's imagery to their own mental pictures. Some of the listeners would certainly have diverged from the bard's imagery, especially those whose mental *storage* of the 'night sky' was based on a very strong and clear mental pattern. In cases like these, however, the tradition might have welcomed 'visual interpolation', since the listener would have reappropriated the simile according to his personal imaging code and added or subtracted details tailoring the singer's 'guidelines' to his own experience.

The third group of similes is perhaps the most interesting, though the most problematic with respect to the ways in which it can be interpreted. It includes four similes (*Iliad* XXII 93–97, *Iliad* XXII 139–144; *Iliad* XXII 189–193; *Iliad* XXII 308–311), which all relate to scenes that come from the world of

Chapter Twelve

animals. The first simile is about a snake lying in wait in his lair. It digests poison and curls up inside its mountainous nest, sending vengeful glares toward its enemy as it watches him. Likewise, Hector, with unquenched anger inside him, does not retreat but waits for Achilles. The simile takes great pains at emphasizing (XXII 93: δράκων; XXII 95: δέδορκεν) the piercing glare of the snake. In order for the interpretive interplay to become fully comprehensible, this simile must be connected to a preceding one, placed before the supplication speeches of Priam and Hecuba and the internal monologue of Hector. At that point, the narrative had been interrupted by the presentation of the gleaming Achilles in a simile comparing him with the star shining brighter than the others in the night sky. The *Iliad* slightly postpones Hector's presentation (with the insertion of three speeches[17] at the beginning of *Iliad* XXII), by employing a simile that stresses the very same characteristic emphasized in the case of Achilles, i.e. his radiant gleam. This shine is surely connected with Hector's bitter wrath, an element that is justifiably surprising. If anyone were possessed by such fury, then it would surely be Achilles, who sought revenge for the death of Patroclus. The projection of the characteristics that suitably describe Achilles onto Hector represents a deliberate attempt to make the two appear similar as they approach their fated doom. The fact that in one of these similes the snake is placed in the mountains results in the tragic assimilation of the two heroes. Just as Achilles stands out like a bright star in the vast night sky, so Hector is like a snake secluded in the mountains but endowed with a piercing glare.

The second simile (*Iliad* XXII 139–144) describes a hawk in the mountains attacking a frightened dove that desperately tries to survive. The hawk's aggression, which forms the focal center of the simile, is manifested in the readiness by which the hawk's attack is effectuated (*Iliad* XXII 140: ῥηϊδίως), in the dove's fear (*Iliad* XXII 140: μετὰ τρήρωνα πέλειαν), in the frequency of the hawk's attacks (*Iliad* XXII 142: ταρφέ' ἐπαΐσσει), and last but not least in the predator's intense desire to capture the dove (*Iliad* XXII 142: ἐλέειν τέ ἑ θυμὸς ἀνώγει).

The third simile (*Iliad* XXII 189–193) refers to the pursuit of a deer's fawn by a dog. The simile implies the weakness of the fawn while overtly underscoring the dog's persistence in trailing the helpless animal. The simile's tenor reveals an interesting focalization-inversion, as the subject of the action is shifted from Achilles to Hector, in direct contrast to the simile's vehicle.[18] The

---

[17] Priam (38–76), Hecuba (82–89), Hector (99–130).
[18] For the relative (*Wie-Satz*) and the deictic (*So-Satz*), see Fränkel 1921, where the two parts of the extended Homeric simile are distinguished for the first time.

change of focal subject must be mainly interpreted in relation to the subsequent simile of the dream, in which neither the attacker is able to catch his prey nor the prey to escape. This endless chase, in the form of a narrative ring,[19] is supported by the continuous shifting of emphasis. In *Iliad* XXII 93-97, the focal center is Hector, then Achilles (*Iliad* XXII 139-144), then first Achilles and then Hector (*Iliad* XXII 189-193), and finally Hector (*Iliad* XXII 308-311). In this last simile, Hector is compared to an eagle swooping down through the clouds, striking a tender ewe or a fearful hare. Here too the emphasis lies on the predator's majestic movement (*Iliad* XXII 308: ὑψιπετήεις), the fear experienced by the animal under attack (*Iliad* XXII 310: ἄρν' ἀμαλὴν ἢ πτῶκα λαγωόν), and the duration of the attack (*Iliad* XXII 309: ὅς τ' εἶσιν πεδίονδε). The continuous shifting of focal center that characterizes the similes of this group shows that, in the *vertical* axis, the interchanging roles of the conflict's two protagonists may well indicate their dramatic assimilation on the narrative level.[20]

This third group, containing four animal similes, is the best represented within the simile sequence in *Iliad* XXII. This comes as no surprise, as animal similes constitute one of the largest categories of similes in the entire poem. The mental image the storyteller tries to bring up in his listeners' minds belongs to different phases of a single preverbal *Gestalt*.[21] Although the conceptual template is that of 'predator against prey', the snake simile pictures the initial phase of this mental pattern, the hawk and dog similes visualize the second phase, i.e. the pursue or chase, while the eagle simile zooms in on the final clash between predator and prey.[22] In this case, when the sequence of homologous similes is completed, the audience may reactivate in their memory this chain of image-mappings and interpret them *sequentially*. Under this scope, *visual interpolation* by the audience will 'correct' itself at the end, once multiple realizations of the mental pictures stimulated by the similes finally 'yield' to the sequential interpretation implicitly suggested by the storyteller.

The single dream simile belonging to the fourth simile group (*Iliad* XXII 199-201) is consonant with the aforementioned interpretation. By combining

---

[19] The simile of the dream (*Iliad* XXII 199-201) has the form: ABC (199) - ABC (200) - ACB (201), if A: οὐ δύναται, οὔτ' ... δύναται, οὐ ... δύνατο, B: φεύγοντα, ὑποφεύγειν, οὐδ' ... ἀλύξαι, C: διώκειν, οὔθ' ... διώκειν, μάρψαι ποσίν.
[20] On some reverse similes in the *Odyssey*, see Maronitis 1971:205-232 (especially 215-217) and Heubeck 1992:338-339 with further bibliography.
[21] See Nagler 1967:269-311; 1974:8.
[22] See chapter 9.

all the previously explored focal centers (the race, the imminent catastrophe, and the intentional shifting of roles), the dream simile encompasses the tragic character of the entire episode on a different narrative level: Achilles and Hector, without understanding that they are chasing and being chased by death, take on the roles of attacker and prey interchangeably, until they realize too late the final moment of defeat. The verbal repetitions that form the framework of the representational re-narration of the fated conflict in *Iliad* XXII 199–201 condense this last simile even further (A: οὐ δύναται, οὔτ' ... δύναται, οὐ ... δύνατο, B: φεύγοντα, ὑποφεύγειν, οὐδ' ... ἀλύξαι, C: διώκειν, οὔθ' ... διώκειν, μάρψαι ποσίν). The image of the dream creatively unravels the theme of the endless chase and, by blurring the roles and significance of the characters, converges the two heroes' fates, as they are both found in a dramatic deadlock. The emphasis given by the storyteller on verbal repetitions creates an almost single pathway for his listeners to follow in the visualization of the dream. The stress placed on never-ending pursuit would be particularly relevant to any listener's mental template of an agonizing dream. It is, perhaps, reasonable to argue that in this particular case the storyteller might have effectively directed his audience's visual imaging according to his own will.

I do not claim to have exploited the full semantic potential of the wide array of similes in *Iliad* XXII. By focusing my attention on their similarities, I have attempted to show that they represent a visual scope much wider than their limited size. In that respect, the extended simile is, narratively speaking, an abbreviated simile,[23] representing a 'summary' that designates "the textual compression of a given story-period into a relatively condensed statement of its main features."[24] I am not arguing for an acceleration of the narrative 'pace', as is the case with 'summaries' in pure narratological terms, but of a process of engaging the audience in filling in the necessary gaps in order to complete the comparison at hand. By keying the audience on a narrative register distinct from the external narrative, the similes allow the audience to participate in a dynamic interplay with their own experiential universe, which consists of multiple image-mappings, both converging on and diverging from the visualization suggested by any given simile. As a set of allusions to and comments on the story,[25] similes constitute an elaborate, memory-oriented cognitive

---

[23] Muellner 1990:66; Minchin 2001b:143–148.
[24] Markantonatos 2002:7–8.
[25] The term *story* designates all the elements of *myth* as they become distinguishable through a focalizer. See de Jong 1987:31–32, 35.

mechanism, allowing the audience to 'look' outside the narrative window and to enjoy the imagistic richness of their own ability to construct pictures.

In this way, *hypertextuality*, as a form of multilevel intertextuality, disrupts the conventional 'linearity' of song. What is perceived as a simile sequence throughout the performance is in fact a special rhythmic template that encourages the audience to make the leap to other sequences of image-mappings, regardless of intertextual or intratextual location. In this light, similes do not 'assimilate' the world of the main narrative to physical imagery. They rather allow the audience to conjure up the multiple visual worlds of mental images, engaging them in the most active evaluation of the performance and inviting them to *erase* and *(re)write* the oral palimpsest of epic song.

Bibliography

Translations

All translations of the *Iliad* are taken from Lattimore 1951, and of the *Odyssey* from Rieu 2003 (= 1946). For Aristotle I have consulted Halliwell 1995; for Herodotus, Waterfeld 1998; for the Homeric Hymns, West 2003; for Philostratus, Berenson, Maclean, and Aitken 2003 (= 2001); for Proclus, Burgess 2001; for Livy, Foster 1919; for Ovid's *Fasti*, Frazer 1989² (= 1931); for Propertius, Goold 1990; for Virgil, Fairclough 1918.

Concordances

I have also made ample use of both the *TLG* and the following concordances and formular analysis indices: Tebben 1977 (*Homeric Hymns*), 1994 (*Odyssey*), 1998 (*Iliad*); Pavese and Boschetti 2003 (*Iliad* and *Odyssey*).

Adam, A.-M. 1985. "Monstres et divinités tricéphales dans l' Italie primitive." *Mélanges de l' école française d' Athènes* 97:577–609.
Ahl, F. and Roisman, H. M. 1996. *The Odyssey Reformed*. Ithaca and London.
Alden, M. 1995. "Ναυσικά η Μαινάς." In Εὐχὴν Ὀδυσσεῖ: *Proceedings of the 7th International Symposium on the Odyssey*, ed. M. Païzi-Apostolopoulou, 335–351. Ithaki.
———. 2000. *Homer Beside Himself: Para-Narratives in the Iliad*. Oxford.
Alexiou, M. 2002. *The Ritual Lament in Greek Tradition*. 2nd ed. Revised by D. Yatromanolakis and P. Roilos. Lanham, MD.
Allen, G. 2000. *Intertextuality*. London.
Allen, T. W., ed. 1912. *Homeri Opera*. Vol. 5. Oxford.
———, ed. 1917–1919. *Homeri Opera*. Vols. 3–4. Oxford.
Allen, T. W. and Sikes, E. E., eds. 1904. *The Homeric Hymns*. Oxford.

Bibliography

Allen W. S. 1973. *Accent and Rhythm. Prosodic Features of Latin and Greek: A Study in Theory and Reconstruction.* Cambridge.

———. 1987. *Vox Graeca: The Pronunciation of Classical Greek.* 3rd ed. Cambridge.

Aloni, A. 1986. *Tradizioni arcaiche della Troade e composizione dell' Iliade.* Milan.

Alton E. H. et al., eds. 1978. *P. Ovidi Nasonis Fastorum Libri Sex.* Leipzig.

Ameis, K. F. and Hentze, C. 1889. *Anhang zu Homers Odyssee.* Leipzig.

Anastassiou, I. 1971. *Zum Wortfeld "Trauer" in der Sprache Homers.* Hamburg.

Anderson, W. S. 1964. "Hercules Exclusus, Propertius IV, 9." *American Journal of Philology* 85:1–12.

———. 1992. "The Limits of Genre." In *The Interpretation of Roman Poetry: Empiricism or Hermeneutics?*, ed. K. Galinsky, 96-103. Frankfurt am Main.

Arce, J. 1986. 'Cacus.' *LIMC* III 1:177–178.

Arend, W. 1933. *Die typische Scenen bei Homer.* Berlin.

Arnould, D. 1990. *Le rire et les larmes dans la littérature grecque d' Homère à Platon.* Paris.

Ashmole, B. 1967. "A New Interpretation of the Portland Vase." *Journal of Hellenic Studies* 87:1–17.

Athanassakis, A. N. 1976. *The Homeric Hymns.* Baltimore.

———. 1977. *The Orphic Hymns: Text, Translation and Notes.* Missoula, MT.

Austin, N. 1975. *Archery at the Dark of the Moon.* Berkeley.

———. 1994. *Helen of Troy and her Shameless Phantom.* Ithaca and London.

Autenrieth, G. 1984. *Homeric Dictionary.* London.

Bakker, E. J. 1988. *Linguistics and Formulas in Homer: Scalarity and the Description of the Particle per.* Amsterdam and Philadelphia.

———. 1990. "Homeric Discourse and Enjambment: A Cognitive Approach." *Transactions of the American Philological Association* 120:1–21.

———. 1995. "Noun-Epithet Formulas, Milman Parry, and the Grammar of Poetry." In *Homeric Questions: Proceedings of a Colloquium Organized by the Netherlands Institute at Athens*, ed. J. P. Crielaard, 97–125. Amsterdam.

———. 1997. *Poetry in Speech: Orality and Homeric Discourse.* London.

———. 1999. "Homeric ΟΥΤΟΣ and the Poetics of Deixis." *Classical Philology* 94:1–19.

———. 2001a. "Similes, Augment, and the Language of Intimacy." In *Speaking Volumes: Orality and Literacy in the Greek and Roman World*, ed. J. Watson, 1–23. Leiden.

———. 2001b. "The Greek Gilgamesh, or the Immortality of Return." In *Eranos: Proceedings of the 9th International Symposium on the Odyssey*, ed. M. Païzi-Apostolopoulou, 331–353. Ithaki.

———. 2001c. "Homer, Hypertext, and the World of Myth." In *Varieties and*

Consequences of Orality and Literacy/Formen und Folgen von Mündlichkeit und Schriftlichkeit: Franz Bäuml zum 75.Geburtstad, ed. U. Schaefer and H. Spielmann, 149–160. Tübingen.

———. 2005. *Pointing at the Past: From Formula to Performance in Homeric Poetics*. Cambridge, MA.

Bakker, E. J. and Fabricotti, F. 1991. "Peripheral and Nuclear Semantics in Homeric Diction: The Case of Dative Expressions for 'Spear'." *Mnemosyne* 44:63–84.

Barber, E. A., ed. 1960 (repr. 1978). *Sexti Properti Carmina*. 2nd ed. Oxford.

Barnes, H. R. 1979. "Enjambment and Oral Composition." *Transactions of the American Philological Association* 109:1–10.

Barringer, J. M. 1988. *Divine Escorts: Nereids in Archaic and Classical Art*. Ann Arbor.

Barthes, R. 1975. *S/Z* (trans. R. Miller). London.

Bassett, S. E. 1923. "The Second Necyia Again." *American Journal of Philology* 44:44–52.

———. 1926. "The So-called Emphatic Position of the Runover Word in the Homeric Hexameter." *Transactions of the American Philological Association* 57:116–148.

———. 1938. *The Poetry of Homer*. Berkeley and Los Angeles.

Baud-Bovy, S. 1973. "'Η ἐπικράτηση τοῦ δεκαπεντασύλλαβου στὸ ἑλληνικὸ δημοτικὸ τραγούδι." *Hellenika* 26:301–313.

Bauman, R. 1978. *Verbal Act as Performance*. Rowley, MA.

Bechtel, F. 1914. *Lexilogus zu Homer*. Halle.

Beck, D. 2005. *Homeric Conversation*. Washington, DC.

Benveniste, E. 1954. "Problèmes sémantiques de la reconstruction." *Word* 10:251–264.

Berenson Maclean, J. K. and Aitken, E. B. 2001. *Flavius Philostratus. Heroikos*. Atlanta.

Bernabé, A., ed. 1987. *Poetarum Epicorum Graecorum Testimonia et Fragmenta* (*PEG* 1). Leipzig.

———, ed. 2004. *Poetarum Epicorum Graecorum Testimonia et Fragmenta* (*PEG* 2). Munich.

Bethe, E., ed. 1900–1931 (repr. 1967). *Pollucis Onomasticon*. Vols. 1–2 (*Lexicographi Graeci 9.1–9.2*). Leipzig.

———. 1914. *Homer: Dichtung und Sage*. Vol. 1 (*Ilias*). Leipzig and Berlin.

———. 1922. *Homer: Dichtung und Sage*. Vol. 2. Leipzig.

Blazquez Martínez, J. M. 1983. "Gerión y otros mitos griegos en Occidente." *Gerión* 1:21–38.

Bibliography

Block, J. H. 1995. *The Early Amazons: Modern and Ancient Perspectives on a Persistent Myth*. Leiden.
Boedeker, D. 1974. *Aphrodite's Entry into Greek Epic*. Leiden.
Bömmer, F. 1957–1958. *P. Ovidius Naso. Die Fasten*. Vol. 1 (Einleitung, Übersetzung). Vol. 2 (Kommentar). Heidelberg.
Bowra, C. M. 1960. "Homeric Epithets for Troy." *Journal of Hellenic Studies* 80:17.
Boyer R. et al. 1989. *L' Homme Indo-Européen et le sacré*. Milan.
Bréal, M. 1863. *Hercule et Cacus: Étude de mythologie*. 2nd ed. Paris.
Brize, P. 1980. *Die Geryoneïs des Stesichoros und die frühe griechische Kunst*. Würzburg.
———. 1988. 'Geryoneus.' *LIMC* IV.1:186–190.
Brosse, J. 1993. *Mythologie des arbres*. Paris.
Burgess, J. 2001. *The Tradition of the Trojan War in Homer and the Epic Cycle*. Baltimore and London.
———. 2002. "Kyprias, the Kypria, and Multiformity." *Phoenix* 56:234–245.
———. 2004. "Untrustworthy Apollo and the Destiny of Achilles: *Iliad* 24.55–63." *Harvard Studies in Classical Philology* 102:21–40.
———. 2006. "Neoanalysis, Orality, and Intertextuality: An Examination of Homeric Motif-Transference." *Oral Tradition* 21:148–189.
Burkert, W. 1979. *Structure and History in Greek Mythology and Ritual*. Berkeley and Los Angeles.
———. 1983. *Homo Necans: The Anthropology of Ancient Greek Sacrificial Ritual and Myth* (trans. P. Bing). Berkeley.
———. 1985. *Greek Religion* (trans. J. Raffan). Cambridge.
Burnet, J., ed. 1900–1907 (repr. 1967). *Platonis Opera*. Vols. 1–5. Oxford.
Cairns, F. 1992. "Propertius 4.9: Hercules Exclusus and the Dimensions of Genre." In *The Interpretation of Roman Poetry: Empiricism or Hermeneutics?*, ed. K. Galinsky, 65–95. Frankfurt am Main.
Calame, C. 1977. *Les choeurs de jeunes filles en Grèce archaïque*. Rome.
Cambitoglou, A., Aelian, C., and Chamay, J. 1986. *Le peintre Darius et son milieu*. Geneva.
Campbell, D. A. 1993. *Greek Lyric: The New School of Poetry and Anonymous Songs and Hymns*. Vol. 5. Cambridge, MA.
Carpenter, T. H. 1986. *Dionysiac Imagery in Archaic Greek Art: Its Development in Black-Figure Vase Painting*. Oxford.
Càssola, F., ed. 1975. *Inni omerici*. Rome.
Cazzaniga, I., ed. 1962. *Metamorphoseon Synagoge*. Milan.
Chafe, W. 1994. *Discourse, Consciousness, and Time: The Flow and Displacement of Conscious Experience in Speech and Writing*. Chicago.

Chantraine, P. 1927. *Histoire du parfait grec.* Paris.
———. 1955. Review of G. P. Shipp, "Studies in the Language of Homer." *Transactions of the Cambridge Philological Society* 8 (1953). *Revue de philologie* 29:72–73.
———. 1968-1980. *Dictionnaire étymologique de la langue grecque.* Vols. 1–2. Paris.
———. 1986-1988. *Grammaire homérique.* Vols. 1–2. 6th ed. Paris.
Chatzis, A., ed. 1914 (repr. 1967). *Kaine Historia (Fragmenta). Der Philosoph and Grammatiker Ptolemaios Chennos.* Paderborn.
Cingano, E. 2005. "A Catalogue Within a Catalogue: Helen's Suitors and the Hesiodic Catalogue of Women (frs. 196-204)." In *The Hesiodic Catalogue of Women: Constructions and Reconstructions,* ed. R. Hunter, 118–152. Cambridge.
Clader, L. L. 1976. *Helen: The Evolution from Divine to Heroic in Greek Epic Diction.* Leiden.
Clark, D. 1987. *Studies in Odyssey 13-24,* (dissert. University of Cambridge). Cambridge.
Clark, M. 1994. "Enjambment and Binding in Homeric Hexameter." *Phoenix* 48:85–114.
———. 1997. *Out of Line: Homeric Composition Beyond the Hexameter.* Lanham, MD.
Clayman, D. L. and van Nortwick, 1977. "Enjambment in Greek Hexameter Poetry." *Transactions of the American Philological Association* 107:85–92.
Clayton, B. 2004. *A Penelopean Poetics: Reweaving the Feminine in Homer's Odyssey.* New York.
Coffey, M. 1957. "The Function of the Homeric Simile." *American Journal of Philology* 78:113–132.
Cole, S. G. 1993. "Voices from beyond the Grave: Dionysus and the Dead." In *The Masks of Dionysus,* ed. T. H. Carpenter and C. A. Faraone, 276–295. London.
Collins, L. 1988. *Studies in Characterization in the Iliad.* Frankfurt am Main.
Constantinidou, S. 1990. "Evidence for Marriage Ritual in *Iliad* 3." In Ἀφιέρωμα στὸν Ἰ. Καμπίτση. *Dodone* 19:47–59.
Cook, R. 1978. *The Tree of Life: Image for the Cosmos.* London.
Coulon, V. and van Daele, M., eds. 1928 (repr. 1967). *Aristophane.* Vol. 3. Paris.
Croon, J. H. 1952. *The Herdsman of the Dead.* Utrecht.
Crotty, K. 1994. *The Poetics of Supplication.* Ithaca and London.
Crudden, M. 2001. *The Homeric Hymns.* Oxford.
Cuny, A. 1936: "Gr. ΠΕΦΥΖΟΤΕΣ." *Revue des études grecques* 49:395–398.

Bibliography

Dalley, S. 1991. *Myths of Mesopotamia:. Creation, the Flood, Gilgamesh and Others*. Oxford and New York.

Danek, G. 1998. *Epos und Zitat: Studien zu den Quellen der Odyssee*. Vienna.

———. 2002. "Traditional Referentiality and Homeric Intertextuality." In *Omero tremila anni dopo*, ed. F. Montanari and P. Ascheri, 3–19. Rome.

———. 2006. "Die Gliechnisse der *Ilias* und der Dichter Homer." In *La poésie épique grecque: métamorphoses d'un genre littéraire*, ed. F. Montanari and A. Rengakos, 41–71. Entretiens sur l' antiquité classique 52. Geneva.

Danthine, H. 1937. *Le palmier-dattier et les arbres sacrés dans l' iconographie de l' Asie occidentale ancienne*. Paris.

Daraki, M. 1985. *Dionysos et la déesse terre*. Paris.

Davies, M., ed. 1988a. *Epicorum Graecorum Fragmenta (EGF)*. Göttingen.

———. 1988b. "Stesichorus' Geryoneis and its Folk-Tale Origins." *Classical Quarterly* 38:277–290.

———. 1989. *The Greek Epic Cycle*. London.

———, ed. 1991. *Poetarum Melicorum Graecorum Fragmenta*. Oxford.

———. 2002. "The Folk-Tale Origins of the *Iliad* and the *Odyssey*." *Wiener Studien* 115:5–43.

de Jong, I. J. F. 1987. *Narrators and Focalizers: The Presentation of the Story in the Iliad*. Amsterdam.

———. 2001. *A Narratological Commentary on the Odyssey*. Cambridge.

———. 2006. "The Homeric Narrator and His Own Kleos." *Mnemosyne* 59:188–207.

De Lannoy, L., ed. 1977. *Flavii Philostrati Heroicus*. Leipzig.

Del Corno, D. 1961. "I papiri dell' *Odissea* anteriori al 150 a. Cr." *Rendiconti dell'Istituto Lombardo, Classe di Lettere, Scienze morali e storiche* 94:3–54.

Denniston, J. D. 1952. *Greek Prose Style*. Oxford.

Derderian, K. 2001. *Leaving Words to Remember: Greek Mourning and the Advent of Literacy*. Leiden.

Detienne, M. 1973. *Les maîtres de vérité dans la Grèce archaïque*. 2nd ed. Paris.

Devambez, P. and Kauffmann-Samaras, A. 1981. 'Amazones.' *LIMC* I.1:586–653.

Dickie, E. 1996. *Greek Forms of Address: From Herodotus to Lucian*. Oxford.

Diels, H. and Kranz, W., eds. 1951–1952 (repr. 1966). *Die Fragmente der Vorsokratiker*. Vols. 1–2. Berlin.

Dierauer, U. 1977. "Tier und Mensch im Denken der Antike." *Studien zur Tierpsychologie, Anthropologie und Ethik*. Amsterdam.

Diggle, J. 1970. *Euripides: Phaethon*. Cambridge.

———, ed. 1981–1994. *Euripidis Fabulae*. Vols. 1–3. Oxford.

di Martino, M. G. I. 1997. 'Gerione.' *Enciclopedia Oraziana*, 383–384. Rome.

Dindorf, G. 1875–1877. *Scholia Graeca in Homeri Iliadem*. Vols. 1–4. Oxford.
Doherty, L. E. 1995. *Siren Songs: Gender, Audience, and Narrators in the Odyssey*. Ann Arbor.
Drachmann, A. B., ed. 1903–1927 (repr. 1966–1969, Amsterdam). *Scholia Vetera in Pindari Carmina*. Vols. 1–3. Leipzig.
Duckworth, G. E. 1933. *Foreshadowing and Suspense in the Epics of Homer, Apollonius and Vergil*. Princeton.
Dué, C. 2002. *Homeric Variations on a Lament by Briseis*. Lanham, MD.
Dumézil, G. 1943. *Servius et la Fortune: Essai sur la fonction sociale de louange et de blâme et sur les éléments indo-européens du cens romain*. Paris.
———. 1958. *L' idéologie tripartie des Indo-Européens*. Brussels.
———. 1968. *Mythe et épopée I: L' idéologie des trois fonctions dans les épopées des peuples indo-européens*. Paris.
Dümmler, F. 1890. "Hektor." In *Kyrene*, ed. F. Studnicza, 194–205. Leipzig.
Ebbott, M. 1999. "The Wrath of Helen: Self-Blame and Nemesis in the *Iliad*." In *Nine Essays on Homer*, ed. M. Carlisle and O. Levaniouk, 3–20. Lanham, MD.
Edwards, A. T. 1985. *Achilles in the Odyssey: Ideologies of Heroism in the Homeric Epic*. Meisenheim am Glan.
Edwards, M. W. 1966. "Some Features of Homeric Craftsmanship." *Transactions of the American Philological Association* 97:115–179.
———. 1969. "On Some 'Answering' Expressions in Homer." *Classical Philology* 64:81–87.
———. 1970. "Homeric Speech Introductions." *Harvard Studies in Classical Philology* 74:1–36.
———. 1980. "Structure of Homeric Catalogues." *Transactions of the American Philological Association* 110:81–105.
———. 1986. "Homer and Oral Tradition: The Formula, Part I." *Oral Tradition* 1:171–230.
———. 1987. *Homer: Poet of the Iliad*. Baltimore.
———. 1988. "Homer and Oral Tradition: The Formula, Part II." *Oral Tradition* 3:11–60.
———. 1991. *The Iliad: A Commentary*. Vol. 5. Cambridge.
Eliade, M. 1963. *Patterns in Comparative Religion* (trans. R. Sheed). New York.
Elmer, D. 2005. "Helen Epigrammatopoios." *Classical Antiquity* 24:1–39.
Else, G. F. 1957. *Aristotle's Poetics: The Argument*. Cambridge, MA.
Erbse, H., ed. 1969–1988. *Scholia Graeca in Homeri Illiadem*. Vols. 1–5. Berlin.
Evans, A. 1901. "Mycenaean Tree and Pillar Cult." *Journal of Hellenic Studies* 21:99–204.

Bibliography

Fairclough, H. R. 1918. Virgil. *Aeneid.* Vols. 1-2. New York.
Fantuzzi, M. 1988. *Ricerche su Apollonio Rodio: Diacronie della dizione epica.* Rome.
Faust, M. 1970. "Die künstlerische Verwendung von κύων 'Hund' in den homerischen Epen." *Glotta* 48:8-31.
Felson-Rubin, N. 1994. *Regarding Penelope: From Character to Poetics.* Princeton.
Ferrari, F. 1984. "Dizione epica e pianto rituale." *Rivista di filologia ed instruzione classica* 112:257-265.
Finkelberg, M. 1998. *The Birth of Literary Fiction in Ancient Greece.* Oxford.
———. 2002. "The Sources of Iliad 7." *Colby Quarterly* 38:151-161.
———. 2003. "Homer as a Foundation Text." *Homer, the Bible, and Beyond,* ed. M. Finkelberg and G. G. Stroumsa, 75-96. Leiden.
Finley, J. H. Jr. 1978. *Homer's Odyssey.* Cambridge, MA.
Finsler, G. 1924. *Homer.* 3rd ed. Leipzig.
Foley, J. M. 1985. *Oral-Formulaic Theory and Research. An Introduction and Annotated Bibliography.* New York.
———. 1988. *The Theory of Oral Composition: History and Methodology.* Bloomington.
———. 1991. *Immanent Art: From Structure to Meaning in Traditional Oral Epic.* Bloomington.
———. 1993. *Traditional Oral Epic: The Odyssey, Beowulf, and the Serbo-Croatian Return Song.* Berkeley and Los Angeles.
Fontenrose, J. 1959. *Python: A Study of a Delphic Myth and its Origins.* Berkeley and Los Angeles.
Forbes Irving, P. M. C. 1990. *Metamorphosis in Greek Myths.* Oxford.
Ford, A. 1992. *Homer: The Poetry of the Past.* Ithaca and London.
Forsdyke, J. 1956. *Greece before Homer.* New York.
Foster, B. O. 1919. *Livy.* Vol. 1. New York.
Foucault, M. 1979. "What is an Author?" In *Textual Strategies: Perspectives in Post-Structuralist Criticism,* ed. Josué V. Harari, 141-160. Ithaca.
Fowler, D. 2000. "On the Shoulders of Giants: Intertextuality and Classical Studies." In *Roman Constructions,* ed. D. Fowler, 115-137. Oxford.
Fowler, R. L., ed. 2000. *Early Greek Mythography (EGM).* Oxford.
Frame, D. 1978. *The Myth of Return in Early Greek Epic.* New Haven and London.
Fränkel, H. 1921. *Die homerischen Gleichnisse.* Göttingen.
———. 1926. "Der kallimachische und der homerische Hexameter." *Nachrichten von der Gesellschaft der Wissenschaft zu Göttingen.* 197-229.
———. 1962. *Dichtung und Philosophie des frühen Griechentums.* Munich.
Frazer, J. G. 1989. *Ovid: Fasti.* Vol. 5. 2nd ed (rev. trans. by G. P. Goold). Cambridge, MA.

Friedrich, P. 1978. *The Meaning of Aphrodite*. Chicago.
Friedrich, R. 2000. "Homeric Enjambment and Orality." *Hermes* 128:1-19.
Frontisi-Ducroux, F. 1986. *La cithare d' Achille: Essai sur la poétique de l' "Iliade."* Rome.
Gagliardi, P. 2006. "I lamenti di Andromaca nell' *Iliade*." *Gaia* 10:11-46.
Ghali-Kahil, L. B. 1965. *Les enlèvements et le retour d'Hélène dans les textes et les documents figurés*. Paris.
Goatly, A. 1997. *The Language of Metaphors*. London and New York.
Goldhill, S. 1991. *The Poet's Voice: Essays on Poetics and Greek Literature*. Cambridge.
Goodman, N. 1968. *Languages of Art: An Approach to a Theory of Symbols*. Indianapolis and New York.
Goold, G. P. 1990. *Propertius: Elegies*. Cambridge, MA.
Gould, J. 1973. "Hiketeia." *Journal of Hellenic Studies* 93:74-103.
Gow, A. S. F., ed. 1952 (repr. 1965). *Theocritus*. Cambridge.
Gow, A. S. F. and Scholfield, A. F., eds. 1953. *Nicander. The Poems and Poetical Fragments*. Cambridge.
Graver, M. 1995. "Dog-Helen and Homeric Insult." *Classical Antiquity* 14:41-61.
Griessmair, E. 1966. *Das Motiv der mors immatura in den griechischen metrischen Grabinschriften*. Innsbruck.
Griffin, J. 1977. "The Epic Cycle and the Uniqueness of Homer." *Journal of Hellenic Studies* 97:39-53.
———. 1986. "Homeric Words and Speakers." *Journal of Hellenic Studies* 106:36-57.
Grimal, P. 1986. *The Dictionary of Classical Mythology* (trans. by A. R. Maxwell-Hyslop). Oxford.
Grube, M. A. 1961. *Demetrius on Style*. Toronto.
Hainsworth, J. B. 1964. "Structure and Content in Epic Formulae: The Question of the Unique Expression." *Classical Quarterly* 14:155-164.
———. 1968. *The Flexibility of the Homeric Formula*. Oxford.
———. 1988. *A Commentary on Homer's Odyssey*. Vol. 1. Oxford.
———. 1993. *The Iliad: A Commentary*. Vol. 3. Cambridge.
Halliwell, S. 1995. *Aristotle. Poetics*. Cambridge, MA.
Hammond, M. 1987. *The Iliad: A New Prose Translation*. London.
Hansen, P. A., ed. 1983-1989. *Carmina Epigraphica Graeca*. Vols. 1-2. Berlin and New York.
Hansen, W. F. 1977. "Odysseus' Last Journey." *QUCC* 24:27-48.
———. 1990. "Odysseus and the Oar: A Folkloric Approach." In *Approaches to Greek Myth*, ed. L. Edmunds, 239-272. Baltimore.

Harrison, J. E. 1991. *Prolegomena to the Study of Greek Religion*. 3rd ed. Princeton.
Hartmann, A. 1915. *Untersuchungen zur Rekonstruktion der Telegonia des Eugamon von Kyrene I: Die mythographische Überlieferung*. Munich.
———. 1917. *Untersuchungen über die Sage vom Tod des Odysseus*. Munich.
Haynes, D. E. L. 1975. *The Portland Vase*. 2nd ed. London.
———. 1995. "The Portland Vase: A Reply." *Journal of Hellenic Studies* 115: 146–152.
Heath, M. 1989. *Unity in Greek Poetics*. Oxford.
Henrichs, A. 1987. "Myth Visualized: Dionysus and his Circle in Sixth-Century Attic Vase-Painting." In *Papers on the Amasis Painter and his World*, 92–111. Malibu.
———. 1993. "'He Has a God in Him': Human and Divine in the Modern Perception of Dionysus." In *Masks of Dionysus*, ed. T. H. Carpenter and C. A. Faraone, 13–43. Ithaca and London.
Hercher, R., ed. 1864 (repr. 1971). *De Natura Animalium*. Leipzig.
Hershkovitz, D. 1998. *The Madness of Epic: Reading Insanity from Homer to Statius*. Oxford.
Heubeck, A. and Hoekstra, A. 1989. *A Commentary on Homer's Odyssey*. Vol. 2. Oxford.
Heubeck, A., West, S., and Hainsworth, J. B. 1988. *A Commentary on Homer's Odyssey*. Vol. 1. Oxford.
Heyden, D. 1995. "Caves." In *The Encyclopedia of Religion*, ed. M. Eliade, 3:127–133. New York.
Higbie, C. 1990. *Measure and Music: Enjambment and Sentence Structure in the Iliad*. Oxford.
———. 1995. *Heroes' Names: Homeric Identities*. New York and London.
Hind, J. 1995. "The Portland Vase: New Clues towards Old Solutions." *Journal of Hellenic Studies* 115:153–155.
Hoekstra, A. 1964. *Homeric Modifications of Formulaic Prototypes: Studies in the Development of Greek Epic Diction*. Amsterdam.
Holmberg, I. 1995. "The Odyssey and Female Subjectivity." *Helios* 22:103–122.
Holoka, J. P. 1973. "Homeric Originality: A Survey." *Classical World* 66:257–293.
———. 1979. "Homeric Studies 1971–1977." *Classical World* 73:65–150.
———. 1990a. "Homer Studies 1978–1983: Part I." *Classical World* 83:393–361.
———. 1990b. "Homer Studies 1978–1983: Part II." *Classical World* 84:89–156.
Hölscher, U. 1967. "Die Atridensage in der Odyssee." *Festschrift Alewyn*, 1–16. Cologne.
———. 1990. *Die Odyssee: Epos zwischen Märchen und Roman*. Munich.

Holwerda, D., ed. 1991. *Scholia Vetera et Recentiora in Aves*, pars 2, fasc. 3. Groningen.
Holzinger, C. von. 1895. *Lykophron's Alexandra*. Leipzig.
Hooker, J. T. 1986. "Helen and the Duration of the Trojan War." *Parola del passato* 41:111-113.
Hornblower, S. and Spawforth, A. 1996. *The Oxford Classical Dictionary*. 3rd ed. Oxford.
Howald, E. 1937. *Der Mythos als Dichtung*. Zurich.
———. 1964. *Der Dichter der Ilias*. Erlenbach and Zurich.
Huxley, G. L. 1960. "Homerica II: Eugamon." *Greek, Roman and Byzantine Studies* 3:23-28.
Immisch, O. 1889. "Ad Cypria carmen." *Rheinisches Museum* 44:299-304.
Jacoby, F., ed. 1923-1958 (repr. 1954-1969). *Die Fragmente der griechischen Historiker*. Vols. 1-3. Leiden.
Jacoubet, H. 1924. "Note sémantique: ἀμολγός." *Revue des études grecques* 37:399-402.
Jakobson, R. 1952. "Studies in Comparative Slavic Metrics." *Oxford Slavonic Papers* 3:21-66.
———. 1985. *Selected Writings*. Vol. 7. Berlin.
Jakoby, C., ed. 1995. *Dionysii Halicarnasei Antiquitatum Romanarum quae supersunt*. Vol. 1. Leipzig.
James, E. O. 1966. *The Tree of Life: An Archaeological Study*. Leiden.
Jameson, M. 1993. "The Asexuality of Dionysus." In *The Masks of Dionysus*, ed. T. H. Carpenter and C. A. Faraone, 44-64. Ithaca and London.
Jamison, S. W. 1991. *The Ravenous Hyenas and the Wounded Sun: Myth and Ritual in Ancient India*. Ithaca and London.
Janko, R. 1992. *The Iliad: A Commentary*. Vol. 4. Cambridge.
Jauss, H. R. 1982. *Towards an Aesthetic of Reception*. Minneapolis.
Jeanmaire, H. 1951. *Dionysus: Histoire du culte de Bacchus*. Paris.
Jenkins, T. J. 1999. "Homêros ekainopoiêse: Theseus, Aithra and Variation in Homeric Myth-Making." In *Nine Essays on Homer*, ed. M. Carlisle and O. Levaniouk, 207-226. Lanham, MD.
Jouan, F. 1966. *Euripide et les legendes des Chants Cypriens: Des origines de la guerre de Troie à l' Iliade*. Paris.
———. 1980. "Le Cycle épique: État des questions." *Association Guillaume Budé, Actes du Xe Congrès*, 83-104. Paris.
Jourdain-Annequin, C. 1989. *Héraclès aux portes du soir: Mythe et Histoire*. Paris.
Kahane, A. 1994. *The Interpretation of Order: A Study in the Poetics of Homeric Repetition*. Oxford.

———. 1997. "Quantifying Epic." In *A New Companion to Homer*, ed. I. Morris and B. Powell, 326–342. Leiden.

———. 2005. *Diachronic Dialogues: Authority and Continuity in Homer and the Homeric Tradition*. Lanham, MD.

Kakridis, J. T. 1944. Ομηρικές έρευνες. Athens.

———. 1949. *Homeric Researches*. Lund.

———. 1960. Review of Günther Jachmann, "Der homerische Schiffskatalog und die *Ilias*." *Gnomon* 32:393–410.

———. 1971. *Homer Revisited*. Lund.

———. 1986. Ελληνική Μυθολογία. Vol. 2. Athens.

Kannicht, R. 1969. *Euripides Helena*. Vol. 2. Heidelberg.

———, ed. 2004. *Tragicorum Graecorum Fragmenta*. Vols. 5.1-5.2. Göttingen.

Kassel, R., ed. 1965. *Aristotelis de Arte Poetica*. Oxford.

Katz, M. 1991. *Penelope's Renown: Meaning and Indeterminacy in the Odyssey*. Princeton.

Keller, O. 1913. *Die antike Tierwelt*. Vol. 2. Leipzig.

Kepinski, C. 1982. *L' arbre stylisé en Asie occidentale au deuxième millénaire avant J.-C*. Paris.

Kerényi, C. 1976. *Dionysos: Archetypal Image of the Indestructible Life*. Trans. R. Mannheim. London.

Kern, O., ed.1963. *Orphicorum Fragmenta*. 2nd ed. Berlin.

Kirk, G. S. 1966. "Studies in Some Technical Aspects of Homeric Style: (I) The Structure of the Homeric Hexameter; (II) Verse-Structure and Sentence-Structure in Homer." *Yale Classical Studies* 20:75–152.

———. 1985. *The Iliad: A Commentary*. Vol. 1. Cambridge.

———. 1990. *The Iliad: A Commentary*. Vol. 2. Cambridge.

Klinger, F. 1964. *Studien zur griechischen und römischen Literatur*. Zurich and Stuttgart.

Kouremenos, Th., Parassoglou, G., and Tsantsanoglou, K., eds. 2006. *The Derveni Papyrus*. Florence.

Kourou, N. 2001. "The Sacred Tree in Greek Art: Mycenaean versus Near Eastern Traditions." In *La questione delle influenze vicino-orientali sulla religione Greca*, ed. S. Ribichini et al., 31–53. Rome.

Krapp, H. 1964. *Die akoustische phänomene in der Ilias* (dissert. University of Munich). Munich.

Krarup, P. 1948. "Verwendung von Abstrakta in der direkten Rede bei Homer." *Classica et mediaevalia* 10:1–17.

Kretschmer, P. 1921. "Literaturbericht für das Jahr 1917." *Glotta* 11:108.

———. 1924. "Ἀμολγός." *Glotta* 13:166–167.

Kroll, J. 1932. *Gott und Hölle*. Warburg.
Kullmann, W. 1955. "Die Probe des Achaierheeres in der *Ilias*." *Museum Helveticum* 12:253–273.
———. 1960. *Die Quellen der Ilias (Troischer Sagenkreis)*. Wiesbaden.
———. 1992. *Homerische Motive: Beiträge zur Entstehung, Eigenart und Wirkung von Ilias und Odyssee*. Ed. R. J. Müller. Stuttgart.
———. 1995. "The Two *Nekyiai* of the Odyssey and Their Oral Sources." In Ψυχὴν 'Οδυσσεῖ: *Proceedings of the 7th International Symposium on the Odyssey*, ed. M. Païzi-Apostolopoulou, 41–53. Ithaki.
———. 2002. "Procli Cyclicorum enarrationes paragraphis divisae." In *Realität, Imagination und Theorie*, ed. A. Rengakos, 156–161. Stuttgart.
Kumaniecki, K. F., ed. 1969. *M. Tulli Ciceronis de Oratore*. Leipzig.
Kyriakidis, S. 1978. Τὸ δημοτικὸ τραγούδι. Συναγωγὴ μελετῶν. Athens.
Laimou, A. A. 1999–2000. "Ο Τρωικός κύκλος στην προκλασική εικονογραφία της ανατολικής Ελλάδας." *Archaiognosia* 10:11–50.
Lange, K. 2002. *Euripides und Homer: Untersuchungen zur Homernachwirkung in Elektra, Iphigenie im Tauerland, Helena, Orestes und Kyklops*. Stuttgart.
Larson, J. 2001. *Greek Nymphs: Myth, Cult, Lore*. Oxford and New York.
Latacz, J. 1977. *Kampfparänese, Kampfdarstellung und Kampfwirklichkeit in der Ilias, bei Kallinos und Tyrtaeus*. Munich.
Latacz, J., et al. 2000. *HomersIlias: Gesamtkommentar*. Vol. 1. Munich and Leipzig.
———. 2003. *Homers Ilias: Gesamtkommentar*. Vol. 2. Munich and Leipzig.
Lateiner, D. 1995. *Sardonic Smile: Nonverbal Behavior in Homeric Epic*. Ann Arbor.
Lattimore, R. 1951. *The Iliad of Homer*. Chicago and London.
Lattimore, S. 1976. *The Marine Thiasos in Greek Sculpture*. Los Angeles.
Lazzeroni, R. 1971. "Su alcuni deverbali greci e sanscriti." *Studi e Saggi di Linguistica* 11:22–47.
Lecomte, C. 1998. "L' Εὐρωπία d' Eumélos de Corinthe." In *D' Europe à l' Europe 1: Le mythe d' Europe*, ed. R. Poignault and O. Wattel-de Croizan, 71–79. Tours.
Lee, D. J. N. 1964. *The Similes of the Iliad and the Odyssey Compared*. Melbourne.
Levaniouk, O. 1999. "Penelope and the Pênelops." In *Nine Essays on Homer*, ed. M. Carlisle and O. Levaniouk, 95–136. Lanham, MD.
Lloyd-Jones, H. and Wilson, N., eds. 1990. *Sophoclis Fabulae*. Oxford.
Lohmann, D. 1970. *Die Komposition der Reden in der Ilias*. Berlin.
Loraux, N. 1990. *Les mères en deuil*. Paris.
Lord, A. B. 1948. "Homer and Huso III: Enjambment in Greek and Southslavic Heroic Song." *Transactions of the American Philological Association* 79:113–124.

Bibliography

———. 1960. *The Singer of Tales*. Cambridge, MA.

———. 1991. *Epic Singers and Oral Tradition*. Ithaca.

Lowenstam, S. 1993. *The Scepter and the Spear: Studies on Forms of Repetition in the Homeric Poems*. Lanham, MD.

Ludwich, A., ed. 1889. *Homeri Odyssea*. Leipzig.

Lynn-George, M. 1988. *Epos: Word, Narrative and the Iliad*. Basingstoke, NH.

Lyons, J. 1977. *Semantics II*. London and New York.

Mackie, H. 1996. *Talking Trojan: Speech and Community in the Iliad*. London.

Macleod, C. W. 1982. *Homer. Iliad. Book 24*. Cambridge.

Maehler, H. post Snell, B., eds. 1971–1975 (repr. 1987–1989). *Pindari Carmina cum Fragmentis*. Leipzig.

Malkin, I. 1998. *The Returns of Odysseus: Colonization and Ethnicity*. Berkeley.

Manakidou, F. 2002. Στρατηγικές της Οδύσσειας. Συμβολή στο ομηρικό ζήτημα. Thessaloniki.

Mandilaras, G. B. 2003. *Isocrates. Opera Omnia*. Vols. 1–3. Leipzig.

Marg, W. 1956. "Das erste Lied des Demodokos." In *Navicula Chiloniensis, Festschrift F. Jacoby*, 16–29. Leiden.

Markantonatos, A. 2002. *Tragic Narrative: A Narratological Study of Sophocles' Oedipus at Colonus*. Berlin and New York.

Marks, J. 2002. "The Junction between the *Kypria* and the *Iliad*." *Phoenix* 56:1–24.

———. 2003. "Alternative Odysseus: The Case of Thoas and Odysseus." *Transactions of the American Philological Association* 133:209–226.

Maronitis, D. N. 1971. Ἀναζήτηση καὶ νόστος τοῦ Ὀδυσσέα. Ἡ διαλεκτικὴ τῆς Ὀδύσσειας. Athens.

———. 1990. " Ὁ ὁμιλητικὸς χῶρος καὶ τὰ σήματά του: ἀπὸ τὴν Ἰλιάδα στὴν Ὀδύσσεια." In *Proceedings of the 5th International Conference on the Odyssey*, ed. M. Païzi-Apostolopoulou, 105–123. Ithaki.

———. 1995. "Προβλήματα τῆς ὁμηρικῆς Ἑλένης." In *Εὐχὴν Ὀδυσσεῖ: Proceedings of the 7th International Conference on the Odyssey*, ed. M. Païzi-Apostolopoulou, 55–73. Ithaki.

———. 1999. Ὁμηρικὰ Μεγαθέματα: Πόλεμος, Ὁμιλία, Νόστος. Athens.

Marshall, P. K., ed. 1993. *Hygini Fabulae*. Stuttgart.

Martin, R. P. 1989. *The Language of Heroes: Speech and Performance in the Iliad*. Ithaca and London.

———. 1992. "Hesiod's Metanastic Poetics." *Ramus* 21:11–33.

———. 1997. "Similes and Performance." In *Written Voices, Spoken Signs: Tradition, Performance, and the Epic Text*, ed. E. J. Bakker and A. Kahane, 138–166. Cambridge, MA.

———. 2000. "Wrapping Homer Up: Cohesion, Discourse, and Deviation in the *Iliad*." In *Intratextuality: Greek and Roman Textual Relations*, ed. A. Sharrock and H. Morales, 43-65. Oxford.

———. 2001. "Just Like a Woman: Enigmas of the Lyric Voice." In *Making Silence Speak: Women's Voices in Greek Literature and Society*, ed. A. Lardinois and L. McClure, 55-74. Princeton.

Mascialino, L., ed. 1964. *Lycophronis Alexandra*. Leipzig.

Matthews, V. J., ed. 1996. *Antimachus of Colophon*. Leiden.

Mawet, F. 1979. *Recherches sur les oppositions fonctionelles dans le vocabulaire homérique de la douleur (autour de πῆμα - ἄλγος)*. Brussels.

Mayer, K. 1996. "Helen and the Διὸς βουλή." *American Journal of Philology* 117:1-15.

Mayer, M. 1883. *De Euripidis mythopoeia capita duo*. Berlin.

Meillet, A. 1923. *Les origines indo-européennes des mètres grecs*. Paris.

Merkelbach, R. 1969. *Untersuchungen zur Odyssee*. Munich.

Merkelbach, R. and West, M. L., eds. 1967. *Fragmenta Hesiodea*. Oxford.

Meuli, K. 1921. *Odyssee und Argonautika*. Berlin.

Mikalson, J. 2005. *Ancient Greek Religion*. Oxford.

Minchin, E. 2001a. "Similes in Homer: Image, Mind's Eye, and Memory." In *Orality and Literacy in the Greek and Roman World*, ed. J. Watson, 25-52. Amsterdam.

———. 2001b. *Homer and the Resources of Memory: Some Applications of Cognitive Theory to the Iliad and the Odysssey*. Oxford.

Monsacré, H. 1984. *Les larmes d' Achille: Le héros, la femme et la souffrance dans la poésie d' Homère*. Paris.

Montiglio, S. 1993. "La menace du silence pour l' héros de l' *Iliade*." *Métis* 8:161-186.

Morrison, J. V. 1992a. *Homeric Misdirection: False Predictions in the Iliad*. Ann Arbor.

———. 1992b. "Alternatives to the Epic Tradition: Homer's Challenges in the *Iliad*." *Transactions of the American Philological Association* 122:61-71.

Moulton, C. 1974. "The End of the Odyssey." *Greek, Roman, and Byzantine Studies* 15:153-169.

———. 1977. *Similes in the Homeric Poems*. Göttingen.

Muellner, L. C. 1976. *The Meaning of Homeric* εὔχομαι *through its Formulas*. Innsbruck.

———. 1990. "The Simile of the Cranes and Pygmies: A Study of Homeric Metaphor." *Harvard Studies in Classical Philology* 93:59-101.

———. 1996. *The Anger of Achilles: Mênis in Greek Epic*. Ithaca and London.

Müller, C., ed. 1855 (repr. 1965). *Geographi Graeci Minores*. Vol. 1. Paris.

Bibliography

Murnaghan, S. 1987. *Disguise and Recognition in the Odyssey*. Princeton.
Murray, G. 1934. *The Rise of the Greek Epic*. 4th ed. Oxford.
Mynors, R. A. B., ed. 1969 (repr. 1977). *P. Vergili Maronis Opera*. Oxford.
Nagler, M. 1967. "Towards a Generative View of the Homeric Formula." *Transactions of the American Philological Association* 98:269-311.
———. 1974. *Spontaneity and Tradition: A Study in the Oral Art of Homer*. Berkeley.
Nagy, G. 1974. *Comparative Studies in Greek and Indic Meter*. Cambridge, MA.
———. 1976. "Formula and Meter." In *Oral Literature and the Formula*, ed. A. B. Stolz and R. S. Shannon, 239-260. Ann Arbor.
———. 1979. *The Best of the Achaeans: Concepts of the Hero in Archaic Greek Poetry*. Baltimore.
———. 1982. "Hesiod." In *Ancient Authors*, ed. T. J. Luce, 43-73. New York.
———. 1990a. *Pindar's Homer: The Lyric Possession of an Epic Past*. Baltimore.
———. 1990b. *Greek Mythology and Poetics*. Ithaca and London.
———. 1996a. *Poetry as Performance: Homer and Beyond*. Cambridge.
———. 1996b. *Homeric Questions*. Austin.
———. 2000. "Distortion diachronique dans l'art homérique: Quelques précisions." In *Construction du temps dans le monde ancien*, ed. C. Darbo-Peschansky, 417-426. Paris.
———. 2003. *Homeric Responses*. Austin.
———. 2004. *Homer's Text and Language*. Urbana and Chicago.
Naiden, F. S. 2006. *Ancient Supplication*. Oxford.
Nannini, S. 2003. *Analogia e polarità in similitudine: Paragoni iliadici e odissiaci a confronto*. Amsterdam.
Nardo, D. 1996. 'Gerione.' In *Enciclopedia Virgiliana*, vol. 2. (2nd ed.), 698-699. Rome.
Neumann, G. 1965. *Gesten und Gebärden in der griechischen Kunst*. Berlin.
Nilsson, M. P. 1967. *Geschichte der griechischen Religion*. Vol. 1. Munich.
Nimis, S. 1987. *Narrative Semiotics in the Epic Tradition: The Simile*. Bloomington.
Norden, E. 1915-1923. *Die antike Kunstprosa vom VI Jahrhundert v. Christ bis in die Zeit der Renaissance*. Vols. 1-2. 3rd ed. Leipzig.
Nyberg, H. S. 1966. *Die Religionen der alten Iran* (trans. H. H. Schaeder). Osnabrück.
Ogilvie, R. M. 1965. *A Commentary on Livy, Books 1-5*. Oxford.
———, ed. 1974. *Titi Livii*. Vol. 1. Oxford.
O'Hara, J. J. 1996. *True Names: Vergil and the Alexandrian Tradition of Etymological Wordplay*. Ann Arbor.
Olson, S. D. 1997. "Odysseus' Winnowing-Shovel (Hom. *Od.* 11.119-37) and the Island of the Cattle of the Sun." *Illinois Classical Studies* 22:7-9.

O'Neill, E. 1942. "The Localization of Metrical Word-Types in the Greek Hexameter." *Yale Classical Studies* 8:105–178.
O'Nolan, K. 1969. "Homer and Irish Heroic Narrative." *Classical Quarterly* 19:1–19.
Orth, E. 1913. 'Hirsch.' In *RE* VIII.2:1936–1950.
Oswald, R. 1993. *Das Ende der Odyssee: Studien zur Strukturen epischen Gestaltens*, (dissert. Karls-Franzens University of Graz). Graz.
Otto, W. F. 1933. *Dionysus und Kultus*. Frankfurt am Main.
Page, D. L., ed. 1962 (repr. 1967). *Poetae Melici Graeci*. Oxford.
———. 1973. "Stesichorus: The Geryoneïs." *Journal of Hellenic Studies* 93:138–154.
———, ed. 1974. *Supplementum Lyricis Graecis*. Oxford.
Pallantza, E. 2005. *Der Troische Krieg in der nachhomerischen Literatur bis zum 5. Jahrhundert v. Chr.* Stuttgart.
Papadopoulou-Belmehdi, I. 1994. *Le chant de Pénélope: Poétique du tissage féminine dans l' Odyssée*. Paris.
Papageorgius, P. N. 1888. *Scholia in Sophoclis tragoedias vetera: e codice Laurentiano denuo collato*. Leipzig.
Parks, W. 1990. *Verbal Dueling in Heroic Narrative*. Princeton.
Parry, M. 1929. "The Distinctive Character of Enjambment in Homeric Verse." *Transactions of the American Philological Association* 57:200–220.
———. 1971. *The Making of the Homeric Verse: The Collected Papers of Milman Parry*, ed. A. Parry. Oxford.
Paschalis, M. 1981. "Ἡ εἰκόνα τῆς σπηλιᾶς στὶς Ὠδὲς τοῦ Ὁρατίου καὶ ἡ καταγωγή της." *Hellenika* 33:30–40.
———. 1997. *Vergil's Aeneid: Semantic Relations and Proper Names*. Oxford.
Pattichis, P. L. 1978. *Εὐριπίδου Ἑλένη*. Athens.
Pavese, C.O. and Boschetti, F. 2003. *A Complete Formular Analysis of the Homeric Poems, I–III*. Amsterdam.
Pedrick, V. 1982. "Supplication in the *Iliad* and the *Odyssey*." *Transactions of the American Philological Association* 112:125–140.
Peek, W. 1955. *Griechische Vers-Inschriften*. Vol. 1. Berlin.
Peradotto, J. 1990. *Man in the Middle Voice: Name and Narration in the Odyssey*. Princeton.
Pestalozzi, H. 1945. *Die Achilleis als Quelle der Ilias*. Zurich.
Petegorsky, D. 1982. *Context and Evocation: Studies in Early Greek and Sanskrit Poetry*, (dissert. University of California at Berkeley). Berkeley.
Petzl, G. 1969. *Antike Discussionen über die beiden Nekyiai*. Meisenheim am Glan.
Pfeiffer, R., ed. 1949 (repr. 1965). *Callimachus. Fragmenta*. Vol. 1. Oxford.
Phillips, E. D. 1953. "Odysseus in Italy." *Journal of Hellenic Studies* 73:53–67.

Pircher, J. 1979. *Das Lob der Frau im vorchristlichen Grabepigram der Griechen.* Innsbruck.
Pomeroy, S. 1975. "Andromache: un example méconnu de matriarcat." *Revue des études grecques* 88:16–19.
Pope, M. 1985. "A Nonce-word in the *Iliad.*" *Classical Quarterly* 35:1–8.
Powell, J. U., ed. 1925. (repr. 1970). *Collectanea Alexandrina.* Oxford.
Privitera, G. A. 1970. *Dionisio in Omero e nella poesia greca arcaica.* Rome.
Propp, V. J. 1975. *Morphologie des Märchens.* 2nd ed. Munich.
Pucci, P. 1979. "The Song of the Sirens." *Arethusa* 12:121–132.
———. 1987. *Odysseus Polutropos: Intertextual Readings in the Odyssey and in the Iliad.* Ithaca.
———. 1993. "Antiphonal Lament between Achilles and Briseis." *Colby Quarterly* 29: 258–259.
———. 1997. *The Song of the Sirens: Essays on Homer.* Lanham, MD.
———. 2003. "Prosopopée d'Hélène." *Le mythe d'Hélène,* ed. M. Bronze et al., 89–119. Brussels.
Purves, A. 2006. "Unmarked Space: Odysseus and the Inland Journey." *Arethusa* 39:1–20.
Rabel, R. J. 1989. "The Shield of Achilles and the Death of Hector." *Eranos* 87:81–90.
Radermacher, L., ed. 1901. *Demetrii Phalerei qui dicitur de Elocutione Libellus.* Leipzig.
Radt, S., ed. 1985. *Tragicorum Graecorum Fragmenta.* Vol. 3. Göttingen.
———, ed. 1999. *Tragicorum Graecorum Fragmenta.* Vol. 4. Göttingen.
Rahlfs, A., ed. 1965. *Septuaginta, id est Vetus Testamentum Graece iuxta LXX.* Stuttgart.
Rahn, H. 1953. "Tier und Mensch in der homerischen Auffassung der Wirklichkeit." *Mitteilungen zur Kulturkunde* 5.6:277–297; 5.7–8:431–480.
———. 1967. "Das Tier in der homerischen Dichtung." *Studium Generale* 20:90–115.
Ramersdorfer, H. 1981. *Singuläre Iterata der Ilias (A–K).* Königstein.
Redfield, J. M. 1975. *Nature and Culture in the Iliad.* Chicago and London.
Reiner, E. 1938. *Die rituelle Totenklage der Griechen.* Stuttgart and Berlin.
Reinhardt, K. 1961. *Die Ilias und ihr Dichter.* Göttingen.
Reitzenstein, R. 1900. "Die Hochzeit des Peleus und der Thetis." *Hermes* 35:73–105.
Rengakos, A. 2002. "Zur narrativen Funktion der Telemachie." In *La mythologie et l' Odyssée: Hommage à Gabriel Germain,* ed. A. Hurst and F. Létoublon, 8–98. Geneva.

———. 2004. "Die Argonautika und das 'kyklische Gedicht': Bemerkungen zur Erzähltechnik des griechischen Epos." In *Antike Literatur in neuer Deutung*, ed. A. Bierl et al., 277–304. Munich and Leipzig.

———. 2006. *Το χαμόγελο του Αχιλλέα: Θέματα αφήγησης και ποιητικής στα ομηρικά έπη*. Athens.

Reynolds, L. D. and Wilson, N. G. 1991. *Scribes and Scholars*. Oxford.

Richard, J. C., ed. 1983. *Origo Gentis Romanae*. Paris.

Richards, I. A. 1936. *The Philosophy of Rhetoric*. Oxford.

Richardson, N. 1993. *The Iliad: A Commentary*. Vol. 6. Cambridge.

Richter, W. 1968. *Die Landwirtschaft im Homerischen Zeitalter*. Vol. 2. Göttingen.

Rieu, E. V. 2003. *Homer: The Odyssey*. Rev. trans. by D. C. H. Rieu. London.

Rix, H. 1976. *Historische Grammatik der griechischen: Laut- und Formenlehre*. Darmstadt.

Robb, K. 1994. *Literacy and Paideia in Ancient Greece*. Oxford.

Robert, C. 1920. *Die griechische Heldensage*. 4th ed. Berlin.

Roos, A. G., ed. 1967. *Flavius Arrianus: Alexandri Anabasis*. Vols. 1–2. Leipzig.

Rose, V., ed. 1886 (repr. 1967). *Aristotelis qui ferebantur Librorum Fragmenta*. Leipzig.

Rosén, H. B., ed. 1987, 1997. *Herodoti Historiae*. Vols. 1–2. Stuttgart.

Rosen, R. 1990. "Poetry and Sailing in Hesiod's *Works and Days*." *Classical Antiquity* 9:99–113.

Russo, J. A. 1997. "The Formula." In *A New Companion to Homer*, ed. I. Morris and B. Powell, 238–260. Leiden.

Russo, J. A., Fernández-Galiano, M. and Heubeck, A. 1992. *A Commentary on Homer's Odyssey*. Vol. 3. Oxford.

Russo, J. A. and Simon, B. 1968. "Homeric Psychology and the Oral Epic Tradition." *Journal of the History of Ideas* 29:483–498.

Rüter, K. 1967. *Odysseeinterpretationen: Untersuchungen zum ersten Buch und zur Phaiakis*. Göttingen.

Rutherford, I. 2000. "Formulas, Voice, and Death in Ehoie-Poetry, the Hesiodic *Gynaikon Katalogos*, and the Odysseian *Nekyia*." In *Matrices of Genre: Authors, Canons, and Society*, ed. M. Depew and D. Obbink, 81–96. Cambridge, MA, and London.

Rutherford, R. B., ed. 1992. *Homer. Odyssey. Books 19–20*. Cambridge.

Rzach, A. 1922. 'Kyklos.' *RE* IX.2:2347–2435.

Sakellariou, M. 1958. *La migration grecque en Ionie*. Athens.

Schadewaldt, W. 1965. *Von Homers Welt und Werk. Aufsätze und Auslegungen zur homerischen Frage*. 4th ed. Stuttgart.

———. 1966 (repr. 1987). *Iliasstudien*. 4th ed. Berlin (repr. Darmstadt).

Schauenburg, K. 1957. "Zu Darstellungen aus der Sage des Admet und des Kadmos." *Gymnasium* 64:210–230, plates I–VIII.

Scheer, E., ed. 1908. *Lycophronis Alexandra*. Vol. 2. Berlin.

Schmidt, E. G. 1996. "Achilles und Helena—ein verhindertes antikes Traumpaar: Ps.-Hesiod, Frauenkatalog Frgm. 204, 87–92 M.-W." In *Worte, Bilder, Töne, Studien zur Antike und Antikerezeption: Bernhard Kytzler zu Ehren*, ed. R. Faber and B. Seidensticker, 23–38. Würzburg.

Schmitt, R. 1967. *Dichtung und Dichtersprache in indogermanischer Zeit*. Wiesbaden.

Schnapp-Gourbeillon, A. 1981. *Lions, héros, masques: Les représentations de l' animal chez Homère*. Paris.

Schoeck, G. 1961. *Ilias und Aethiopis: Kyklische Motive in homerischer Brechung*. Zurich.

Schroeder, L. Von. 1914. *Herakles und Indra: Eine Mythenvergleichende Untersuchung*. Vienna.

Schulze, W. 1892. *Quaestiones epicae*. Gütersloh.

Schweitzer, B. 1922. *Herakles*. Tübingen.

Schwyzer, E. 1934–1939: *Griechische Grammatik*. Vol. 1. Munich.

———. 1950. *Griechische Grammatik*. Vol. 2, ed. A. Debrunner. Munich.

Scodel, R. 2002. *Listening to Homer: Tradition, Narrative, and Audience*. Ann Arbor.

Scott, W. C. 1974. *The Oral Nature of the Homeric Simile*. Leiden.

Scully, S. 1990. *Homer and the Sacred City*. Ithaca and London.

Seaford, R. 1993. "Dionysus as Destroyer of the Household: Homer, Tragedy and the Polis." In *Masks of Dionysus*, ed. T. H. Carpenter and C. A. Faraone, 115–146. Ithaca and London.

Segal, C. 1971a. "Andromache's Anagnorisis: Formulaic Artistry in *Iliad* 22.437–476." *Harvard Studies in Classical Philology* 75:33–57.

———. 1971b. *The Theme of Mutilation of the Corpse*. Leiden.

———. 1994. *Singers, Heroes, and Gods in the Odyssey*. Ithaca and London.

———. 1997. *Dionysiac Poetics and Euripides' Bacchae*. Princeton.

Severyns, A. 1928. *Le cycle épique dans l' école d' Aristarque*. Liège.

———. 1938. *Le codex 239 de Photius*. Vols. 1–2 of *Recherches sur la Chrestomathie de Proclos*. Paris.

———. 1948. "Curiosités biographiques dans les poèmes d'Homère." *Bulletin de la classe des lettres de l' Académie royale de Belgique* 34:428–441.

———. 1953. *La Vita Homeri et les sommaires du Cycle. Étude paléographique et critique*. Vol. 3 of *Recherches sur la Chrestomathie de Proclos*. Paris.

———. 1962. "Ulysse en Élide." *Antiquité Classique* 31:15–24.

———, ed. 1963. *La Vita Homeri er le sommaires du Cycle. Texte et traduction*. Vol. 4 of *Recherches sur la Chrestomathie de Proclos*. Paris.

Shapiro, H. A. 1995. "Coming of Age in Phaiakia: The Meeting of Odysseus and Nausikaa." In *The Distaff Side: Representing the Female in Homer's Odyssey*, ed. B. Cohen, 155–164. New York and Oxford.

Sharrock, A. 2000. "Intratextuality: Texts, Parts, and (W)holes in Theory." In *Intratextuality: Greek and Roman Textual Relations*, ed. A. Sharrock and H. Morales, 1–39. Oxford.

Sharrock, A. and Morales, H. eds. 2000. *Intratextuality: Greek and Roman Textual Relations*. Oxford.

Shipp, G. P. 1972. *Studies in the Language of Homer*. 2nd ed. Cambridge.

Sicherl, M. 1956. Review of Albert Severyns, "*Recherches sur la Chrestomathie de Proclos III: La Vita Homeri et les sommaires du Cycle*." *Gnomon* 28:210–218.

Sicking, C. M. 1993. *Griechische Verslehre*. Munich.

Sideras, A. 1971. *Aeschylus Homericus: Untersuchungen zu den Homerismen der aischyleischen Sprache*. Göttingen.

Sifakis, G. M. 1988. *Γιὰ μιὰ ποιητικὴ τοῦ ἑλληνικοῦ δημοτικοῦ τραγουδιοῦ*. Herakleion.

Silk, M. S. 1974. *Interaction in Poetic Imagery*. Cambridge.

———. 1983. "LSJ and the Problem of Poetic Archaism: From Meanings to Iconyms." *Classical Quarterly* 33:303–330.

Simon, E. 1983. *Festivals of Attica*. Madison.

Singor, H. W. 1992. "The Achaean Wall and the Seven Gates of Thebes." *Hermes* 120:401–411.

Sistakou, E. 2001. "Παράδοση και νεοτερικότητα στον κατάλογο των Αργοναυτών (Απολλ. Ροδ. Αργ. 1.23–233)." *Hellenika* 51:231–264.

———. 2004. *Η άρνηση του έπους: όψεις του τρωικού μύθου στην ελληνιστική ποίηση*. Athens.

Slatkin, L. M. 1986. "The Wrath of Thetis." *Transactions of the American Philological Association* 116:1–24.

———. 1991. *The Power of Thetis: Allusion and Interpretation in the Iliad*. Berkeley and Oxford.

Small, J. P. 1982. *Cacus and Marsyas in Etrusco-Roman Legend*. Princeton.

Sodano, A. R. 1951. "Il mito di Pentesilea nel 1 libro dei μεθ' Ὅμηρον di Quinto Smirneo." *Annali Fac. Lett. Filos*. Napoli 1:55–79.

Solmsen, F., ed. 1970. *Hesiodi Opera*. Oxford.

Sourvinou-Inwood, C. 1981. "To Die and Enter the House of Hades: Homer, Before and After." In *Mirrors of Mortality: Studies in the Social History of Death*, ed. J. Whale, 15–39. London.

———. 1986. 'Charon.' *LIMC* III.1:210–225.

———. 1991. *'Reading' Greek Culture: Texts and Images, Rituals and Myths*. Oxford.

———. 1996. *'Reading' Greek Death: To the End of the Classical Period*. Oxford.

———. 2005. *Hylas, the Nymphs, Dionysos and Others: Myth, Ritual, Ethnicity*. Stockholm.

Spencer, D. 2001. "Propertius, Hercules and the Dynamics of Roman Mythic Space in *Elegy* 4.9." *Arethusa* 34:259–284.

Spiro, F., ed. 1903 (repr. 1967). *Pausaniae Graeciae Descriptio*. Vols. 1–3. Leipzig.

Stanford, W. B. 1963. *The Ulysses Theme*. 2nd ed. Oxford.

———. 1967. *The Sound of Greek: Studies in the Greek Theory and Practice of Euphony*. Berkeley.

Stockinger, H. 1959. *Die Vorzeichen im homerischen Epos: Ihre Typik und ihre Bedeutung*. St. Ottilien.

Stößel, H.-A. 1975. *Der letzte Gesang der Odyssee: Eine unitarische Gesamtinterpretation*. Erlangen and Nürnberg.

Strassburger, G. 1954. *Die kleinen Kämpfer in der Ilias*. Frankfurt.

Svoronos, J. 1888. "Ulysse chez les Arcadiens et la *Télégonie* d' Eugammon." *Gazette archéologique* 13:257–280.

Taplin, O. 1992. *Homeric Soundings: The Shaping of the Iliad*. Oxford.

Tebben, R. J. 1977. *Homer-Konkordanz: A Computer Concordance to the Homeric Hymns*. Hildesheim.

———. 1994. *Concordantia Homerica, Pars I, Odyssea, I-II*. Hildesheim.

———. 1998. *Concordantia Homerica, Pars II, Ilias, I-III*. Hildesheim.

Thilo, G. and Hagen, H., eds. 1881. *Servii Grammatici qui feruntur in Vergili Carmina Commentarii*. Vols. 1–3, ed 3. Leipzig.

Thompson, S. 1955. *A Motif-Index of Folk-Literature*. Vol. 1. Bloomington and London.

Thornton, A. 1984. *Homer's Iliad: Its Composition and the Motif of Supplication*. Göttingen.

Tomberg, K.-H. 1968. *Die Kaine Historia des Ptolemaios Chennos: Eine literarhistorische und quellenkritische Untersuchung*. Bonn.

Torres-Guerra, J. B. 1995. *La Tebaida Homerica come fuente de Ilíada y Odissea*. Madrid.

Touchefeu-Meynier, O. 1981. 'Andromache I.' *LIMC* I.1:767–774.

Trümpy, H. 1950. *Kriegerische Fachausdrücke im griechischen Epos*. Bâle.

Tsagalis, C. C. 2004. *Epic Grief: Personal Laments in Homer's Iliad*. Berlin and New York.

———. 2006. "Poet and Audience: From Homer to Hesiod." In *La poésie épique grecque: métamorphoses d' un genre littéraire*, ed. F. Montanari and A. Rengakos, 79–130. Entretiens sur l' antiquité classique 52. Geneva.

———. 2008 (forthcoming). "Μεταμορφώσεις του μύθου: Ο τρωικός κύκλος στους τρεις μεγάλους τραγικούς. In *Αρχαία Ελληνική Τραγωδία: Θεωρία και Πράξη*, ed. A. G. Markantonatos and C. C. Tsagalis, *Σήματα: Σύγχρονες προσεγγίσεις στην αρχαία ελληνική γραμματεία* 1. Athens.

Tsagarakis, O. 1982. "The Teichoskopia Cannot Belong to the Beginning of the Trojan War." *Quaderni Urbinati di Cultura Classica* 41:61–72.

———. 2000. *Studies in Odyssey 11*. Stuttgart.

Unger, E. 1926. "Lebensbaum." In *Reallexikon der Vorgeschichte*, ed. M. Eberts, VII:261–262.

van der Valk, M., ed. 1971–1988. *Eustathii Archiepiscopi Thessalonicensis Commentarii ad Homeri Iliadem pertinentes*. Vols. 1–4. Leiden.

van Groningen, B. A., ed. 1977. *Euphorion*. Amsterdam.

van Nooten, B. and Holland, G.B., eds. 1994. *Rig-Veda: A Metrically Restored Text*. Cambridge, MA.

van Raalte, M. 1986. *Rhythm and Metre: Towards a Systemic Description of Greek Stichic Verse*. Leiden.

van Thiel, H., ed. 1991. *Homeri Odyssea*. Hildesheim.

———, ed. 1996. *Homeri Ilias*. Hildesheim.

Veneri, A. 1986. 'Dionysos, the Literary Sources.' *LIMC* III.1:414–420.

Vérilhac, A. - M. 1978. ΠΑΙΔΕΣ ΑΩΡΟΙ. *Poésie funéraire*. Vols. 1–2. Athens.

Vermeule, E. 1979. *Aspects of Greek Death in Early Greek Art and Poetry*. London.

Vernant, J.-P. 1965. *Mythe et pensée chez les Grecs*. Paris.

———. 1996. *L' individu, la mort, l' amour*. Paris.

Vernant, J.-P. and Detienne, M. 1978. *Cunning Intelligence in Greek Culture and Society* (trans. J. Lloyd). Sussex, NJ.

Vernant, J.-P. and Vidal-Naquet, P. 1986. *Mythe et tragédie en Grèce ancienne*. Vols. 1–2. Paris.

Vian, F. 1959. *Recherches sur les Posthomerica de Quintus de Smyrne*. Paris.

———. 1963a. *Aux origines de Thèbes: Cadmos et les Spartes*. Paris.

———, ed. 1963b. *Quintus de Smyrne. La suite d'Homère*. Vol. 1. Paris.

———, ed. 1976–1996. *Apollonios de Rhodes Argonautiques* (trans. É. Delage). Paris.

Visser, E. 1987. *Homerische Versifikationstechnik: Versuch einer Rekonstruktion*. Frankfurt.

———. 1988. "Formulae or Single Words? Towards a New Theory on Homeric Verse-Making." *Würzburger Jahrbücher für die Altertumswissenschaft* n.s. 14:21–37.

———. 1998. 'Geryoneus.' In *Neue Pauly, Epo-Gro*, 4:981–982.

Bibliography

Vitelli, G. and Norsa, M. 1927. *Papiri Greci e Latini*. Vol. 8. Florence.
Vivante, P. 1982. *The Epithets in Homer: A Study in Poetic Values*. New Haven.
Vodoklys, E. J. 1992. *Blame-Expression in the Epic Tradition*. London.
Vogel, F. et al, eds. 1888–1906 (repr. 1964). *Diodori Bibliotheca Historica*. Vols. 1–4 Leipzig.
Voigt, E.-M., ed. 1971. *Sappho et Alcaeus. Fragmenta*. Amsterdam.
von Bothmer, D. 1957. *Amazons in Greek Art*. Oxford.
von der Mühll, P. 1946. *Odyssea*. Basil.
Voskos, A. I. 1974. Μελέαγρος - Ἀχιλλεὺς καὶ Φοῖνιξ. Συμβολὴ εἰς τὴν ἔρευναν τῆς ἑνότητος τῆς Ἰλιάδος. Nicosia.
Vox, O. 1975. "Epigrammi in Omero." *Belfagor* 30:67–70.
Vürtheim, J. 1907. *De Eugammonis Cyrenaei Telegonia, post De Aiacis origine, cultu, patria*. Leiden.
Waern, I. 1951. *GES OSTEA: The Kenning in Pre-Christian Greek Poetry*. Uppsala.
Wagner, R., ed. 1894a. *Apollodori Bibliotheca. Pediasimi Libellus de duoedecim Herculis Laboribus*. Leipzig.
———, ed. 1894b. *Mythographi Graeci*. Vol. 1. Leipzig.
Wahrmann, P. 1924. "Homer: ἐν νυκτὸς ἀμολγῷ." *Glotta* 13:98–101.
Waldner, K. 2000. *Geburt und Hochzeit des Kriegers: Geschlechterdifferenz und Initiation in Mythos und Ritual der griechischen Polis*. Berlin and New York.
Waterfeld, R., trans. 1988. *Herodotus. The Histories*. Oxford and New York.
Wathelet, P. 1988. *Dictionnaire des Troyens de l'Iliade*. Vols. 1–2. Liège.
Watkins, C. 1977. "À propos de ΜΗΝΙΣ." *Bulletin de la Société de Linguistique de Paris* 72:187–209.
———. 1987. "Two Anatolian Forms: Palaic aškumāuwa-, Cuneiform Luvian wa-a-ar-ša." In *Festschrift for Henry Hoenigswald on the Occasion of his 70th Birthday*, ed. G. Cardona and N. Zide, 399–404. Tübingen.
———. 1995. *How to Kill a Dragon. Aspects of Indo-European Poetics*. Oxford.
Weber, L. 1925. "Homerica." *Rheinisches Museum* 74:337–343.
Weicker, G. 1912. 'Geryoneus.' *RE* VII.1286–1296.
Welcker, F. G. 1882. *Der epische Cyclus oder die homerischen Dichter*. Vols. 1–2. 2nd ed. Bonn.
Wendel, C., ed. 1914. *Scholia in Theocritum Vetera*. Leipzig.
———, ed. 1935 (repr. 1974). *Scholia in Apollonium Rhodium vetera*. Berlin.
Wendel, T. 1929. *Gesprächsanrede im griechischen Epos und Drama der Blütezeit*. Stuttgart.
West, M. L., ed. 1966. *Hesiod. Theogony*. Oxford.
———, ed. 1978. *Hesiod. Works and Days*. Oxford.
———. 1985. *The Hesiodic Catalogue of Women*. Oxford.

———, ed. 1990. *Aeschyli Tragoediae*. Stuttgart.
———. 1997. *The East Face of Helicon: West Asiatic Elements in Greek Poetry and Myth*. Oxford.
———, ed. 1998–2000. *Homerus. Ilias*. Vols. 1-2. Stuttgart.
———. 2001. *Studies in the Text and Transmission of the Iliad*. Munich and Leipzig.
———. 2002. "'Eumelus': A Corinthian Epic Cycle?" *Journal of Hellenic Studies* 122:109–133.
———. 2003. *Homeric Hymns, Homeric Apocrypha, Lives of Homer*. Cambridge, MA.
West, S. 1967. *The Ptolemaic Papyri of Homer*. Cologne and Opladen.
———. 1988. *A Commentary on Homer's Odyssey*. Vol. 1. Oxford.
———. 1989. "Laertes Revisited." *Proceedings of the Cambridge Philological Society* 35:113–143.
Whitman, C. H. 1958. *Homer and the Heroic Tradition*. Cambridge, MA.
Wilamowitz-Moellendorff, U. von. 1895. *Euripides Herakles*. Vols. 1-2. 2nd ed. Berlin.
———. 1920. *Die Ilias und Homer*. 2nd ed. Berlin.
Wilamowitz-Moellendorff, U. von and Schubart, W. 1907. *Griechische Dichterfragmente*. Vol. 1. Berlin.
Willcock, M. M. 1964. "Mythological Paradeigma in the *Iliad*." *Classical Quarterly* 14:141–154.
———. 1977. "Ad Hoc Invention in the *Iliad*." *Harvard Studies in Classical Philology* 81:41–53.
———. 1984. *The Iliad of Homer*. London.
———. 1993. "Fighting in the *Iliad*." In *Σπονδές στον Όμηρο: Proceedings of the 6th International Conference on the Odyssey*, ed. M. Païzi-Apostolopoulou, 141–147. Ithaki.
———. 1996. "Neoanalysis." In *A New Companion to Homer*, ed. I. Morris and B. Powell, 174–189. Leiden.
Wilson, P. 1999. "The *aulos* in Athens." In *Performance Culture and Athenian Democracy*, ed. S. Goldhill and R. Osborne, 58–95. Cambridge.
Winkler, J. 1990. "Penelope's Cunning and Homer's." In *The Constraints of Desire*, ed. J. Winkler, 129–161. New York.
Wohl, V. J. 1993. "Standing by the Stathmos: The Creation of Sexual Ideology in the *Odyssey*." *Arethusa* 26:19–50.
Worman, N. 2001. "This Voice Which is Not One: Helen's Verbal Guises in Homeric Epic." In *Making Silence Speak: Women's Voices in Greek Literature and Society*, ed. A. Lardinois and L. McClure, 19–37. Princeton.
———. 2003. *The Cast of Character: Style in Greek Literature*. Austin.
Wyss, B., ed. 1936. *Antimachi Colophonii Reliquiae*. Vols. 1-2. Berlin.

Bibliography

Yarden, L. 1972. *The Tree of Light: A Study of the Menorah, The Seven-Branched Lampstead.* Uppsala.
Zagagi. N. 1985. "Helen of Troy: Encomium and Apology." *Wiener Studien* 19:63-88.
Zarker, J. W. 1965-1966. "King Eëtion and Thebe as Symbols in the *Iliad.*" *Classical Journal* 61:110-114.
Zumthor, P. 1972. *Essai de poétique médiévale.* Paris.

Index Locorum

Aelian
  De Natura Animalium I 56, 72
  Varia Historia III 42, 26; XII 36, 25
Aeschylus
  Cabiri, fr. 97 (*TrGF* 3), 20
  Heliades, fr. 69.7 (*TrGF* 3), 166, 170
  Memnon, frs. 127–130 (*TrGF* 3), 98
  Persians 624, 119
  Prometheus Bound 167–176, 515–525, 755–765, 907–915, 233
  Psychostasia TRI B VI, 1–5 (*TrGF* 3), 98; *Psychostasia*, frs. 279–280a (*TrGF* 3), 98
Agias 305 F 1 (*FGrHist*), 173, 174
Alcaeus fr. 283.7–8 (Voigt), 118; fr. 349 (Voigt), 20
Antimachus fr. 90 Wyss = fr. 63 Matthews, 191
Antoninus Liberalis *Metamorphoses* IV 13–14, 174; X 3, 26
Apollodorus
  Epitome I 23, 133; III 10, 50; V 1, 94; VII 34–37, 78; VII 38–40, 78; VII 40, 87
  Library I 6.1, 169; II 4.6, 176; II 5.10, 169, 174; II 106–112, 173; III [45] 5.6, 25; III 10.8, 103; III 107, 133; III 13.5, 233

Aristodemus of Thebes 383 F 7 (*FGrHist*), 16
Aristophanes *Lysistrata* 1182–1185, 56
Aristotle
  fr. 507 (Rose), 87; fr. 640.46 (Rose), 16
  Historia Animalium IX 37.59, 236
  Poetics 1451a8, 137
Callimachus *Aetia*, fr. 188 (Pfeiffer), 50
Cicero *De Oratore* III 186, 269
Demetrius *On Style* 18, 269
Derveni Papyrus col. XI 1–2, 169
Diodorus Siculus V 50, 12
Dionysius of Halicarnassos *Roman Antiquities* I 38, 177; I 38.2, 181; I 38–42, 173; I 39, 180; I 39.2, 181; I 39.3, 169; I 39.3–4, 181
Ephorus *Cumaeus* 70 F 129b (*FGrHist*), 174
Epic Cycle
  Aethiopis 178–181 Severyns = 54–55 Kullmann, 94; 184–190 Severyns = 57–61 Kullmann, 97; 185–186 Severyns = 57 Kullmann, 226; 185–190 Severyns = 57–61 Kullmann, 264; 186–187 Severyns = 58 Kullmann, 226; 189–190 Severyns = 60–61 Kullmann, 101

Epic Cycle, *Aethiopis*, cont.
210, 224, 237; 191–192 Severyns
= 62 Kullmann, 256; 198–200
Severyns = 65–66 Kullmann, 246;
199–200 Severyns = 66 Kullmann,
100, 104

Cypria 91–92 Severyns = 5
Kullmann, 53; 93–94 Severyns = 7
Kullmann, 53; 100–102 Severyns
= 11 Kullmann, 101; 106–109
Severyns = 14–16 Kullmann, 108;
130–131 Severyns = 27 Kullmann,
259; 152–153 Severyns = 38
Kullmann, 107; 152–156 Severyns
= 38–40 Kullmann, 107; 153–154
Severyns = 39 Kullmann, 107;
157–158 Severyns = 41 Kullmann,
93, 103; 158 Severyns = 41
Kullmann, 101; 159–160 Severyns
= 42 Kullmann, 96, 106, 107; 167–
168 Severyns = 49 Kullmann, 111;
Cypria PEG 1, fr. 1 = *EGF* fr. 1, 111;
PEG 1, fr. 19 = *EGF* fr. 4, 259; *PEG* 1,
fr. 21 = *EGF* fr. 5, 259; *PEG* 1, fr. 29
= *EGF* fr. 19, 48, 51

Ilias parva 217–218 Severyns = 76
Kullmann, 258, 261; *EGF* fr. 4^B,
259; *PEG* 1, fr. 19 = *EGF* fr. 19, 122;
PEG 1, fr. 24 = *EGF* fr. 4^A, 259

Nostoi 299–300 Severyns = 111
Kullmann, 261

Telegonia 306–330 Severyns =
114–130 Kullmann, 77; 327–330
Severyns = 128–130 Kullmann,
94, 95; 329 Severyns = 129
Kullmann, 95, 96; *PEG* 1, fr. 3 =
EGF fr. 2, 68; *PEG* 1, frs. 1–5 = *EGF*
frs. 1–2, 77

Eumelus *Europia PEG* 1, fr. 11 = *EGF* fr. 1, 1, 6, 18; *PEG* 1, fr. 13 = *EGF* fr. 3, 23

Euphorion fr. 2 (CA) = fr. 4 (van Groningen), 50

Euripides
  Alcestis 160, 219
  Alcmene fr. 104 (*TrGF* 5.1), 166, 170
  Andromache 29, 109; 1260–1262, 104
  Bacchae 337–339, 5; 556, 6; 821, 59;
    928–929, 59; 935–939, 59; 977, 5;
    1115–1116, 56
  Cyclops 4, 18; 68–69, 18
  Helen 98–99, 102–103
  Heracles 494, 269; 1226, 269; 1390, 269
  Iphigenia in Tauris 435–437, 104;
    1339, 219
  Orestes 238, 219
  Rhesus 909, 252
  Suppliants 993, 18

Gilgamesh VI iii–VII i, 175, 183

Hecataeus of Miletos 1 F 26 (*FGrHist*)
  = fr. 26 (*EGM*), 173, 174

Hellanicus of Lesbos 4 F 23 (*FGrHist*) =
  fr. 23 (*EGM*), 19; 4 F 111 (*FGrHist*)
  = fr. 111 (*EGM*), 173

Heraclitus B15 (D-K), 13

Herodotus I 84, 23; I 131, 181; II 121,
  80; III 18, 225; IV 8, 173; VI 61,
  122; VII 191–192, 236; IX 73, 133;
  IX 93, 171; IX 93.1–2, 169, 180; IX
  93–94, 161

Hesiod
  Catalogue of Women 150.17–18
    (M.-W.), 225; fr. 177 (M.-W.), 19,
    20; fr. 182 (M.-W.), 23; fr. 183 (M.-
    W.), 25; frs. 196–204 (M.-W.), 119,
    122, 134; fr. 204.78–85 (M.-W.),
    96; fr. 204.87–92 (M.-W.), 102; fr.
    204.89–92 (M.-W.), 96

Index Locorum

Shield 248–257, 119
Theogony 147–153, 235; 154–182, 236; 179, 229; 287–294, 173; 294, 169, 175; 453–480, 236; 662, 235; 969–974, 19; 975–978, 19; 979–983, 173; 982–983, 173; 984–985, 221, 224
Works and Days 126, 13
Homer
  Iliad I 1, 238; 1 – IX 713, 218; 4–5, 5; 17–21, 231; 24, 116; 41, 231;159, 126; 241–242, 263; 242, 7; 349, 245; 351–427, 226; 352–356, 234; 357, 226; 366, 21; 366–367, 21; 378, 116; 396–406, 97, 219, 230, 235, 237; 401, 221; 413, 217; 414, 266, 267; 415–416, 21; 417, 257; 418, 267; 419, 212; 420, 221; 423–425, 225, 226; 424, 221, 224; 455, 231; 492–493, 217; 493, 214, 215, 216; 493–494, 214, 215, 217, 218; 493–499, 214, 220, 227; 493–516, xxi, 100, 209, 210, 224; 494, 214, 215; 495, 218; 496, 220; 496–497, 220; 497, 220, 225; 498, 219, 220; 498–499, 220; 499, 220; 500–501, 228; 503–510, 214, 228, 231; 504, 224, 231; 505, 235, 257; 506, 232; 507, 232; 511–513, 236; 511–516, 214; 512, 233, 237; 513, 237; 516, 227, 236, 237; 524, 224; 527, 224; 531–533, 218; 533, 218; 557, 225; 588–589, 263
  Iliad II 339, 96; 484–486, 238; 488, 129; 514, 114; 532, 121; 571, 120, 121; 583, 121; 591, 120, 121; 607, 120, 121; 623–624, 80; 691, 21
  Iliad III 7, 225; 40, 116; 70, 107; 124, 122; 144, 133; 157, 116; 158, 116; 159–160, 116; 160, 116; 161–244, 106; 162, 115; 171, 128; 172, 114; 172–180, 113, 122; 173, 115, 116; 174, 118; 174–175, 117, 121; 175, 120, 121; 177, 124; 178–180, 117; 179, 125; 180, 114, 126; 186, 16; 189, 14, 16; 199, 128; 199–202, 128; 200–202, 117; 201–202, 128; 204–224, 128; 205, 132; 206, 131; 206–207, 131; 209, 132; 210, 132; 217, 132; 221–224, 130; 228, 128; 228–242, 130; 229, 131; 230–231, 132; 231, 132; 232–233, 131; 233, 132; 236–239, 132; 236–242, 133; 239, 120, 121; 240–242, 132; 242, 132; 244, 108, 133; 322, 9; 380–382, 100, 101; 400–401, 97; 401, 120, 121; 443, 120, 121
  Iliad IV 28, 140; 52, 268; 155–182, 251; 197, 270; 207, 270; 242–249, 198; 243, 193, 195; 245, 197; 378, 21; 402, 114; 406, 21; 422–438, 197; 422–440, 161, 162; 441, 7; 445–446, 217; 474, 255; 482–487, 255
  Iliad V 185, 4; 210, 120; 311–318, 100; 325–326, 121; 326, 120; 560, 255; 590–595, 17; 703–710, 17; 708–710, 17; 717, 4; 831, 4
  Iliad VI 55, 252; 101, 4; 130–140, 2, 11, 18, 26; 132, 1, 4, 5, 6, 7, 15; 132–133, 6, 15; 133, 11, 15; 133–134, 13; 134, 7; 135, 1, 8, 27; 136, 6, 8, 9, 12; 137, 8; 140, 5; 156, 120; 185, 9; 19, 9; 190, 15; 197, 269; 201, 15; 205, 14, 15; 250, 114; 344, 114; 345–347, 115; 357–358, 116, 126; 358, 126; 388, 11; 388–389, 11; 389, 1, 4, 5, 6, 7; 390, 11; 390–

Homer, *Iliad* VI, *cont.*
  391, 11; 390–493, 11; 392–394, 11;
  394, 12; 395–398, 11; 399, 6, 12;
  400, 8; 404, 12; 405, 12; 407–439,
  10, 251; 409–410, 13; 411, 9, 12,
  13; 414–428, 15; 416, 13, 21;
  418–419, 13; 420, 18; 422–423, 13;
  423, 15; 425, 14, 18; 425–428, 14;
  431–439, 14; 433, 22; 433–439, 23,
  24; 438–439, 22; 460–461, 117;
  467, 6; 467–468, 6, 8; 467–469, 8;
  483, 8; 498, 7

Iliad VII 89–90, 117; 131, 9; 217–218,
  9; 244, 17; 482–488, 217

Iliad VIII 41, 164; 42, 164; 43, 164;
  43–44, 164; 45–46, 165; 68, 165;
  69, 165; 69–74, 97; 73–74, 165;
  75–76, 165; 111, 4; 122–129, 164;
  122–132, 163; 127, 163; 131, 165;
  187–189, 14; 242, 231; 355, 4; 360,
  4; 371, 229; 413, 4; 494, 17

Iliad IX 2, 197; 63, 269; 123–124,
  280; 173, 116; 184–191, 34; 190–
  191, 237; 238, 4; 252–256, 259;
  283–289, 123; 285, 123; 351, 7;
  379, 140; 410–416, 257; 438–440,
  259; 478–482, 123; 481–482, 123

Iliad X 15, 243; 114, 114; 213, 41;
  231, 9; 338, 9; 377, 245; 433, 9;
  454–455, 229

Iliad XI 1, 217; 1–2, 221, 226;
  116–117, 263, 264; 120, 262, 263,
  264; 163, 22; 166–168, 22; 167, 22;
  172–178, 155, 156, 160; 186–194,
  160; 403–404, 253; 441, 253; 452,
  253; 537, 9; 548–557, 156, 160;
  649, 114; 671–761, 164; 672–673,
  84; 739, 84; 741, 84; 751–752, 100;
  762, 127; 765–789, 259

Iliad XII 80, 116; 291, 160; 299–308,
  157, 160; 308, 1

Iliad XIII 102, 197; 225, 220; 307, 9;
  431, 120; 485, 120; 748, 116

Iliad XIV 62–63, 9; 190–192, 227;
  210, 114; 226, 120; 260, 220; 323,
  26; 325, 1, 26

Iliad XV 5, 243; 128, 4; 299, 9; 323,
  161, 185; 323–326, 155; 323–327,
  160; 325, 161; 605, 4; 606, 4; 630–
  637, 166; 632–633, 166; 651–652,
  263; 674, 116

Iliad XVI 7, 245; 75, 4; 77, 7;
  123–124, 217; 245, 4; 698, 21;
  729, 9; 780, 216; 837, 253; 840, 7;
  855–857, 118; 857, 117

Iliad XVII 53, 255; 53–58, 255;
  90–91, 253; 201, 253; 207–208, 14;
  428, 7; 616, 7; 638, 7

Iliad XVIII 10, 267; 30, 241; 31, 242,
  243, 248; 35–147, 239; 45, 269;
  50, 241; 50–51, 240; 51, 242, 243,
  248; 52, 270; 52–53, 250, 265, 270;
  52–60, 250; 52–64, 239, 251, 266,
  271; 54, 252, 253, 266, 267; 55,
  267; 55–56, 268; 57, 255; 57–60,
  256, 257, 262; 58, 257, 261; 58–59,
  259; 59–60, 254, 265; 60, 257, 261;
  61, 264; 61–62, 261, 265; 62, 262,
  264, 265; 63, 251; 63–64, 250, 265,
  270; 70–71, 243; 95, 257; 140–144,
  245; 149, 7; 291, 120; 317, 7, 243;
  324–342, 251; 350, 216; 354–XXIV
  804, 217; 369, 218; 386, 114; 394,
  114; 425, 114; 434–435, 224; 438,
  255; 442, 261, 264; 443, 262, 264;
  458, 257; 476ff., 229; 510, 116;
  536–538, 119; 573–589, 158, 160;
  582, 160; 583, 160

Iliad XIX 1-2, 226; 229, 245; 282-286, 244; 287, 253; 287-300, 244; 313, 9; 315-337, 122, 251, 257; 323, 258; 323-325, 257; 324-325, 123; 325, xvii, 106, 109, 111, 133; 326, 259; 326-337, 260; 328-330, 258; 330, 258; 347, 120; 353, 120; 532, 195

Iliad XX 76, 9; 89-92, 107; 106-107, 108; 205-212, 101; 325, 100; 443-444, 100; 465, 120

Iliad XXI 1, 189, 190, 193, 194, 195, 197; 1-16, 199; 2, 203; 5, 4; 6, 189, 192, 193, 194, 195, 197; 22-32, 200; 30-31, 166; 33-34, 243; 37, 22; 40-46, 216; 46, 216; 64, 195; 75, 114; 77-78, 243; 82, 216; 93, 282; 95, 282; 98-99, 253; 192-193, 263; 331-341, 227; 411, 4; 460, 114; 479, 114; 482, 4; 488, 4; 490, 229; 522-543, 201; 528, 189, 192, 193, 194, 195, 197; 532, 189, 190, 192, 193, 194, 195, 197; 534, 203; 544, 21; 552-553, 253; 606-XXII 4, 202

Iliad XXII 21-24, 274, 279; 25-32, 275, 279, 281; 26-32, 155; 27-28, 166; 29, 193, 195; 29-31, 166; 30-31, 185; 37, 42; 46, 216; 70-71, 5; 87, 255; 93-97, 275, 279, 281, 283; 123, 220; 139-144, 276, 279, 281, 282, 283; 140, 282; 142, 282; 145, 22; 162, 280; 162-166, 276, 279; 170-172, 227; 189-193, 196, 276, 279, 281, 282, 283; 192-193, 264; 199-201, 276, 283, 284; 209, 216; 209-213, 97; 289, 17; 308, 283; 308-311, 277, 279, 281, 283; 309, 283; 310, 283; 317, 166; 317-19, 155, 167, 185; 317-321, 277, 279; 319-321, 281; 359-360, 167; 361-363, 118; 363, 117; 405-407, 127; 414, 243; 416-428, 251; 431, 253, 268; 431-436, 251; 451, 114; 460, 1, 4, 5, 7, 10, 11; 460-465, 10; 461, 10; 462, 9; 466, 167; 466-467, 10; 468-470, 10, 56, 127; 477, 252; 477-479, 8; 477-514, 251; 491, 245; 503, 6, 8

Iliad XXIII 18, 7; 56-57, 217; 89-90, 123; 205-207, 220, 221, 224-226; 897-XXIV 1, 217

Iliad XXIV 31, 216, 217; 57, 261; 77-84, 6; 104-105, 269, 270, 271; 113-114, 5; 114, 4, 5; 135, 4; 144, 117, 118; 413, 216; 426, 127; 478-479, 229; 479, 7; 509, 7; 518, 253; 558, 261; 569, 261; 603-604, 25; 604-667, 216; 667, 216, 217; 684, 261; 711, 243; 719-722, 247; 723-724, 8, 16; 724, 7; 725, 252; 725-745, 251; 748, 252; 748-759, 251; 762, 114, 252; 762-775, 251; 764, 115; 765, xix, 138, 139, 140, 141, 142, 147; 765-766, 139, 140, 142, 149; 767-772, 147; 775, 123

Odyssey i 1, 238; 3, 71; 8-9, 83; 10, 238; 12, 189; 22-27, 220; 25-26, 224; 32-43, 41; 231, 115; 261, 7; 298-300, 41; 299, 41

Odyssey ii 374, 216;

Odyssey iii 135-150, 95, 160-166, 95; 194-198, 41; 303-310, 41; 363-364, 121

Odyssey iv 3-9, 109; 240, 129; 240-264, 129; 266-289, 129; 278-279, 126, 129; 519-537, 41; 791-792, 168; 793, 168; 795-841, 185; 800-

Index Locorum

Homer, *Odyssey* iv, *cont.*
    801, 168; 805–806, 168; 806–807, 168; 809, 168; 812–813, 168; 824, 168, 185; 825, 186; 833–834, 186; 835, 168, 186; 839, 186; 839–841, 167; 841, 155

  Odyssey v 1–2, 221, 226; 121–124, 166; 125–128, 19; 299, 252; 396, 122

  Odyssey vi 23, 121; 32–33, 60; 76, 56; 105, 18; 117, 57; 127, 57; 133, 55; 138, 57; 160–167, 47; 163, xv, 57; 215, 57; 225–226, 59; 230–231, 59; 248, 56; 249–250, 56; 280–281, 59; 282–284, 59

  Odyssey vii 114–132, 61; 243, 115

  Odyssey viii 73–82, 54; 76, 224; 522, 122

  Odyssey ix 52, 225; 58, 184, 186; 154, 18; 266–267, 220; 350, 4

  Odyssey x 157–160, 204; 400–401, 32; 456, 32, 34; 456–465, 32; 457, 32; 458, 32; 460–462, 32; 464–466, 32; 488, 32; 488–495, 32; 489, 32; 504, 32; 504–540, 32; 505, 32; 506, 32

  Odyssey xi 19–20, 39; 100–137, 70, 82; 106–109, 81; 107, 83; 121–122, 71; 121–137, 71; 128, 83; 130–134, 85, 89; 134, 82; 200–201, 122; 260–265, 23; 321–325, 14; 325, 56, 60; 385–461, 41; 422, 39; 433–434, 39; 434, 39; 439, 39; 488–491, 85; 537, 4

  Odyssey xii 37–141, 82; 299, 185; 377–383, 175, 183; 382–383, 172; 450, 39; 453, 39

  Odyssey xiii 347–351, 86; 355–360, 86; 356, 18; 383–385, 41

  Odyssey xiv 135, 204; 403, 41

  Odyssey xv 197, 121; 268, 127; 390, 115; 402, 115; 422, 39

  Odyssey xvi 424, 220

  Odyssey xvii 240, 18

  Odyssey xviii 406, 4, 5

  Odyssey xix 107–307, 142; 136, 122; 137, 39; 171, 115; 192–193, 146; 204, 147; 204–209, 122; 204–223, 144; 222, 141, 142; 222–223, 139, 140, 141, 142, 143; 264, 122; 315, 127; 334, 41; 480 ff., 229

  Odyssey xxi 298, 4

  Odyssey xxii 209, 121

  Odyssey xxiii 105–110, 73; 248–249, 73; 249, 73; 263–287, 69; 267–268, 71; 281, 82; 296, 30; 297–xxiv 548, 36

  Odyssey xxiv 11–12, 164; 12, 168; 23, 31; 35, 31; 47, 18; 58–62, 246; 60, 247; 73–76, 3; 85–92, 249; 94, 41; 105, 31; 106–119, 34; 114–119, 34; 120, 31; 191, 31, 32, 34, 35; 191–192, 35; 191–202, 30, 33, 36; 192, 33, 34, 36; 192–193, 36; 192–202, xv, 30, 35, 40, 41; 194–198, 37; 195–199, 37; 196, 38; 199, 36, 37, 39; 199–202, 37; 200, 37, 39; 201, 41; 202, 37, 39, 41; 289, 127; 291, 204; 309, 141, 142; 309–310, 141, 142; 321–323, 142; 430–431, 84; 430–432, 88; 482–486, 88

Homeric Hymn to Aphrodite (5) 218–238, 100, 223, 237; 222, 224, 231; 223, 225; 224, 225; 226–227, 224; 232, 225; 257, 18

Homeric Hymn to Demeter (2) 386, 4

Homeric Hymn to Hermes (4) 6, 168; 7, 168; 8, 168; 12, 168; 14–15, 168; 17–18, 169; 23, 168

Homeric Hymn to Pan (19) 19, 18
Horace *Ars Poetica* 23, 138
Hyginus *Fabulae* 81, 103; 96, 258; 127, 95
Ibycus fr. 291 (*PMGF*), 104; S 151.5-7 (*PMGF*), 122
Idomeneus 547 F 1 (*FGrHist*), 19
Inscriptions 486 (*CEG*), 117
Ion of Chios 392 F1 (*FGrHist*), 17
Isocrates *Archidamus* (6) 19, 174
Livy I 7.4-8.1, 176
Lycophron *Alexandra* 143, 103; 146, 103; 577, 56; 578-580, 56; 581-583, 56; 795-804, 88; 1189-1213, 16
Lycus Rheginus 570 F 1b (*FGrHist*), 174
Nicander *Heteroeumena* fr. 38, 174
Origo gentis Romanae VI 1, 172
Orphic Hymns 34.12, 170
Ovid
 Fasti I 582, 180; I 543-586, 179; I 547, 179; I 553-556, 179; I 572, 180; I 574, 180
 Metamorphoses XIII 632-674, 50; 669, 50
Pausanias II 20.4, 12; II 22.1, 12; II 37.5, 12; III 19.11, 133; III 19.11-13, 103; III 24.10-11, 103; V 22.2-3, 99; VII 4.9, 17; VIII 44.4, 87; IX 18.5, 16; IX 39.9, 22; X 31.2, 52, 53
Pherecydes 3F 140 (*FGrHist*), 49, 51; 3F 18b (*FGrHist*), 173
Philostratus *Heroicus* 54.8-13, 103
Pindar
 Isthmians 6.32-33, 176; 7.3, 21; 8.29-38, 230, 233, 235; 8.56-60, 248

Nemeans 4.49-50, 104; 4.52, 174; 6.50, 265
Olympians 2.79-80, 104; 8.31-46, 23
Pythians 3.100, 248
Plato *Symposium* 179e, 104
Plutarch *Moralia* 294 CD (*Aetia Romana et Graeca* 14), 87
Pollux IV 861, 12
Propertius IV 9.12, 179; IV 9.41, 179
Proxenus *Epirota* 703 F 8 (*FGrHist*), 174
Ptolemaeus Chennus *Kaine Historia* IV 3, 103
Quintus Smyrnaeus *Posthomerica* I 671-674, 94
Rig-Veda 1.62.9, 171; 1.186.4, 171; 2.24.3, 172; 2.3.6, 171; 3.40.14, 171; 4.5.8, 182; 7.41.7, 171; 7.87.4, 172
Sappho fr. 16.7-11 (Voigt), 118
Scholia on Aristophanes' *Aves* 465c, 174; 465d, 174
Scholia on Homer's *Iliad* I 417 (Dindorf), 258; II 220 (Erbse), 94; III 126-127 (Erbse), 113; III 189 (Erbse), 14; III 242 (Erbse), 133; VI 130 (Erbse), 12; VI 433-439 (Erbse), 22, 23; XIV 319 (Erbse), 12; XIX 326 (Dindorf), 258; XXIV 765 (Erbse), 138; XXIV 765a (Erbse), 138
Scholia on Homer's *Odyssey* vi 164, 48, 51, 54
Scholia on Lycophron's *Alexandra* (Scheer) 212, 12; 570, 48, 50, 52; 580, 49, 50, 52, 56; 581, 49, 50, 51, 52, 53, 56; 815, 75, 88; 999, 94; 1194, 16
Scholia on Pindar's *Isthmians* 6.32, 176

Scholia on Pindar's *Nemeans* 4.84, 174
Scholia On Sophocles' *Philoctetes* 445, 94
Scholia on Theocritus' *Idylls* 4.20, 174
Scholia on Virgil's *Aeneid* VIII 190, 178; 203, 172
Scylax Caryandensis 26 (*GGM*), 174
Simonides fr. 558 (*PMG*), 104
Socrates of Argos 310 F 2 (*FGrHist*), 12
Sophocles
  Antigone 901, 269; 1128–1129, 18
  Electra 13, 269
  Fragments 28–33 (*TrGF* 4), 98; 453–461a (*TrGF* 4), 82
Stesichorus S13.2-3 (*PMGF*) = S13.2-3 (*SLG*), 252; frs. 181–186 S7–S87 (*PMGF*), 173; fr. 190 (*PMGF*), 96; fr. 192 (*PMGF*), 133; fr. 195 (*PMGF*), 1; fr. 201 (*PMGF*), 122
Telestes fr. 805(c) (*PMG*), 60
Theocritus *Idylls* 18.24, 120; 18.43–48, 105, 106; 25.7, 84; 25.29, 84; 25.43, 84; 25.54, 84; 25.108, 84; 25.129–144, 84; 25.160, 84; 25.193, 84; 26.1–9, 56
Vetus Testamentum, Lamentationes Jeremiah 1.6, 202
Virgil
  Aeneid VI 9–13, 179; VIII 200–275, 178; VIII 248, 176; VIII 254, 175; VIII 262–267, 178
  Georgics 1.477, 178

Index of Subjects

aberration, 46, 193
accretion, 193, 248
Achilleis, 67, 210, 239, 249
Achilles, ix, x, xvii, xviii, xxi, xxii,
 xxvii, 3, 4, 5, 7, 8, 10, 14, 15, 16,
 18, 19, 20, 21, 22, 34, 35, 38, 41,
 42, 54, 85, 93, 94, 95, 96, 97, 98,
 99, 100, 101, 102, 103, 104, 105,
 106, 107, 108, 109, 110, 111, 119,
 122, 123, 124, 125, 127, 129, 133,
 158, 160, 166, 167, 185, 186, 196,
 203, 209, 210, 211, 212, 214, 216,
 217, 218, 219, 221, 223, 224, 226,
 227, 230, 231, 232, 233, 234, 235,
 236, 237, 239, 240, 242, 243, 245,
 246, 247, 248, 249, 250, 251, 252,
 253, 254, 255, 256, 257, 258, 259,
 260, 261, 262, 264, 265, 266, 267,
 268, 269, 271, 273, 274, 278, 279,
 280, 281, 282, 283, 284
advance organizer, 160
allegory, 166
 solar, 164
Andromache, xiv, xv, xvii, 1, 2, 4, 5,
 6, 7, 8, 9, 10, 11, 12, 13, 14, 15, 16,
 18, 19, 20, 21, 22, 25, 27, 28, 56,
 110, 127, 167, 243, 247, 248, 252
apparatus fabulosus, 68

Babylonian, 175, 183, 184

catalogue, 1, 19, 26, 109, 126, 134, 268
 of Heroes, 134
 of Ships, 121, 133
 of the troops, 120
 of warriors, 120, 133, 134
cataphoric word-group, 194
Cattle of the Sun, xx, 70, 81, 83, 84,
 153, 154, 161, 164, 169, 175, 178,
 183, 184, 186
Circe, 32, 68, 72, 78, 79, 81, 82, 83, 84,
 85, 95, 175
core, 205
coterminacy, 192, 193, 242, 257
cross-reference, xii, xiii, xvi, xvii, 21,
 25, 44, 45, 63, 111, 237, 280
cross-referencing, xv, xxii, 44, 46, 47,
 205, 237

decasyllable, 190, 192
deep structure, xi, xx, 89, 156, 161, 188
deixis
 local, 185
 pattern, 120, 212
deroutinization, 205, 228, 230, 231
detachment
 conceptual, 194
diachrony, 191, 192
Dionysiac, xiv, 1, 2, 4, 5, 6, 7, 9, 10,
 11, 12, 13, 18, 28, 55, 56, 57, 58,
 59, 60

Index of Subjects

displacement, 128, 230, 234, 241

Eetion, xiv, 10, 14, 15, 18, 19, 20, 21, 216
ellipsis, xi, 205, 221
enjambment, 192, 193, 232, 236, 241, 257, 261, 262, 263, 264, 269
  adding
    external, 240
    internal, 240
  adding-unperiodic, 192, 193
  clausal
    external, 240
    internal, 240
  necessary, 240, 241, 242, 262
  necessary-periodic, 192, 193
  progressive, 228
  secondary, 193
  violent, 240
entropy, 193, 205
Epic Cycle, xii, 23, 50, 52, 67, 96, 135, 210
erasing, xiii
expanding members, 229, 269

filler, 205
formula, xix, xx, 7, 9, 18, 21, 31, 33, 34, 39, 71, 114, 115, 116, 122, 124, 127, 136, 137, 142, 153, 154, 155, 156, 160, 166, 167, 168, 170, 171, 178, 182, 184, 185, 186, 187, 188, 189, 190, 191, 192, 193, 195, 196, 197, 202, 203, 204, 205, 213, 224, 226, 231, 243, 253, 257, 261, 262, 263, 264, 273, 281
  accretion of. *See* accretion
  allomorph of, 7, 9
  and idiosyncracies, xxii
  and system, 35, 185, 213, 217, 262
  archetypal, 192
  composition of, 140
  contraction of, 194, 196
  deviation from, xxii, 116, 120
  direct referentiality of, 154, 188
  family of, 188
  introductory, 32
  localization of, 120
  migrating, 196
  misuse of, xviii, 113
  model of, 195
  naming, 125
  noun-epithet, 7, 136
  nuclear idea of, 7
  Odyssean, 124, 129
  paradigmatic, 113, 120, 121, 132
  pattern of, 34, 252, 264
  praying, 226
  prototype of, 193, 195
  range of, xx, 188
  repetition of, 137
  reshaping of, 115
  splitting of, 263
  staging, 35
  structural, 213
  structural unboundedness of, 189
  syntagmatic, 113, 129
  technique of, 213
  template of, 193
  truth-telling, 125
  xenia-, 125
fragmentation, xi, 137, 205, 230

genre-mixing, xviii, 113, 124
Gestalt, xx, 7, 31, 188, 189, 204, 205, 214, 251, 283

hapax legomena, 113, 213
Hector, xiv, xvii, 2, 4, 5, 6, 7, 8, 9, 10, 11, 12, 13, 14, 15, 16, 17, 18, 20, 22, 25, 27, 28, 54, 73, 97, 110, 114, 115, 117, 118, 120, 127, 138, 140, 147, 148, 149, 160, 163, 164, 165,

Index of Subjects

166, 167, 185, 196, 211, 216, 217, 243, 247, 248, 249, 261, 266, 267, 268, 273, 274, 278, 279, 281, 282, 284
Helen, ix, xvi, xvii, xviii, xix, 26, 64, 93, 94, 95, 96, 97, 99, 100, 101, 102, 103, 104, 105, 106, 107, 108, 109, 110, 111, 112, 113, 114, 115, 116, 117, 118, 119, 120, 121, 122, 123, 124, 125, 126, 127, 128, 129, 130, 131, 132, 133, 134, 138, 139, 140, 144, 147, 148, 149, 247, 248, 258
hypertextuality, xxiii, 273, 285

iconym, 154
image-mappings, xxiii, 273, 280, 281, 283, 284, 285
imagery, xx, xxii, 153, 154, 158, 160, 161, 163, 164, 165, 166, 167, 171, 172, 184, 185, 186, 189, 196, 202, 203, 205, 221, 255, 281, 285
imminent danger, xx, 166, 168, 186, 281
imminent death, xx, 203, 204
incompatibility, canonized, 193
indeterminacy, 38, 65, 66
integration, 227, 230
intertextuality, x, xii, xiv, xxv
　and diachronically diffused associations, xiv
　and intratextual sequences, xiv, xxi, 209, 239, 240, 279
　between recognizable song-traditions, xiv
　meta-traditional, xiv, 111, 113, 117, 126, 132, 133, 138, 148, 149
　oral, x
Iranian tradition, xx, 181, 182
isometric oscillation, 193
isometric parallelism, 193

labyrinthine, x, xiii, xx, 137
lament, xxii, 239, 240, 266
Lycurgus, 1, 2, 3, 4, 5, 6, 7, 8, 9, 11, 12, 15, 18, 21, 26, 57

maenad/maenadic, 2, 5, 10, 56, 59
meaning, proliferation of, xiii
Memnonis, 67, 97, 210, 239, 245, 246, 247, 249, 251
meta-cyclic, xii
meta-epic, xii
meta-traditionality, 91
mouvance, 65
multiform/multiformity, xi, 45, 191, 259

Nausicaa, xv, 44, 47, 54, 55, 56, 57, 59, 60, 61, 62
neoanalysis, 67, 135, 239
nucleus. *See* core

Odysseus, xv, xvi, xviii, xix, 5, 30, 31, 32, 33, 34, 35, 36, 38, 39, 40, 41, 42, 44, 46, 47, 48, 51, 52, 53, 54, 55, 56, 57, 59, 60, 61, 63, 64, 65, 66, 68, 69, 70, 71, 72, 73, 74, 76, 78, 79, 80, 81, 82, 83, 84, 85, 86, 87, 88, 89, 90, 107, 128, 129, 130, 140, 141, 142, 143, 145, 146, 147, 148, 149, 161, 164, 168, 172, 183, 184, 186, 211, 214, 228, 234, 252, 258, 260
Oinotropoi, xvi, 48, 49, 50, 51, 52, 53, 54, 55, 56, 57, 60, 61, 62
optional punctuation, 193
oral poetics, xi, 46, 68, 246, 272
orality, xi, 68, 213
oscillation principle, 124

palimpsest, ix, xi, 46, 285
Pan-Hellenic, xiii, xix, 111, 149

323

Index of Subjects

paradoxical taxonomy, 193
para-narrative, 133
pattern, xiv, xxii, 7, 25, 31, 32, 34, 51, 53, 115, 116, 120, 124, 138, 153, 175, 178, 182, 189, 190, 191, 192, 193, 195, 196, 205, 209, 212, 213, 216, 232, 245, 251, 252, 253, 254, 255, 264, 267, 281, 283
Penelope, ix, xv, xvi, 5, 30, 31, 33, 36, 37, 38, 39, 40, 42, 47, 63, 64, 65, 66, 68, 70, 71, 72, 73, 74, 75, 76, 78, 79, 81, 82, 83, 94, 95, 118, 127, 141, 142, 143, 145, 146, 147, 168, 185, 216
performance, xii, xiii, xix, xxi, 5, 35, 45, 63, 74, 86, 89, 113, 134, 136, 146, 154, 205, 212, 214, 216, 217, 234, 237, 242, 247, 248, 273, 281, 285
perilous transition, 203, 204
periphery, 205. *See also* filler
plurality, 205
poikilia, xii, xiv
polysemy, 209, 212, 214, 216

radical complexity, 204
reciprocity, 233, 237
reenactment, 12, 120, 134, 188
referentiality, 137, 273
 direct. *See* formula, direct referentiality of
 self-, 123
 traditional, 154, 187, 188, 205
regularity, 31, 113
 fluctuating, x, 112
right justification, 190, 191
rigid syllabicity, 194
routinization, 215

self-reflexivity, xvi, 42
signifieds, universe of, xiii
simile, xx, xxii, 146, 156, 157, 158, 159, 160, 161, 162, 166, 167, 185, 186, 189, 192, 193, 194, 196, 204, 205, 221, 255, 272, 273, 277, 279, 281, 282, 283, 284, 285
skewing
 diachronic, 237
 intertextual, 236, 237
song, x, xi, xii, xiii, xiv, xv, xvi, xvii, xix, xx, xxi, xxv, 2, 19, 28, 33, 35, 36, 38, 39, 40, 41, 42, 43, 44, 46, 63, 65, 67, 68, 71, 74, 99, 105, 110, 111, 112, 132, 133, 137, 144, 148, 149, 167, 192, 193, 216, 218, 238, 246, 271, 273, 285
speech-act, 212
supplication, xxi, 27, 98, 99, 100, 101, 209, 210, 211, 212, 214, 215, 217, 218, 220, 221, 222, 227, 228, 229, 230, 231, 232, 233, 236, 237, 282
symbiosis, x, 44, 46, 154
synchronic, 31, 124, 191, 192, 215, 217

Teichoscopia, xvii, 10, 106, 107, 108, 112, 113, 120, 121, 122, 125, 127, 128, 129, 132, 133, 134, 279
Teiresias, xvi, 69, 70, 71, 73, 74, 78, 79, 81, 82, 83, 84, 85, 86, 87, 88, 89
Telegonus, 68, 72, 78, 79, 81, 83, 84, 90, 94, 95
Telemachus, 5, 64, 65, 68, 72, 78, 81, 82, 94, 95, 127, 168, 216
text-fixation, 63
textualization, 63
theme, xviii, xxi, xxii, 5, 11, 39, 42, 45, 58, 64, 142, 167, 173, 184, 188, 197, 210, 223, 234, 241, 243, 253, 255, 259, 260, 264, 271, 278, 280, 281, 284
Thetis, ix, xxi, xxii, 3, 4, 6, 8, 12, 18, 20, 21, 93, 97, 98, 99, 100, 101, 104, 105, 108, 111, 122, 209, 210,

211, 212, 214, 217, 218, 219, 220,
221, 222, 224, 225, 226, 227, 228,
229, 230, 231, 232, 233, 234, 235,
236, 237, 239, 240, 241, 242, 243,
245, 246, 247, 248, 249, 250, 251,
252, 254, 255, 256, 257, 258, 259,
261, 262, 264, 265, 266, 267, 268,
269, 270, 271, 280
Tithonus, 100, 166, 221, 222, 223, 224, 226, 237
twenty-year
  epic, xix
  hero, xix, 135, 142
  time-span, xix, 148

variation, 12, 68, 128, 133, 224, 230, 231, 262, 272
Vedic, 170, 171, 172, 181, 182, 184, 186
visualization, xv, 204, 274, 280, 281, 284

web of myth, x, xii, xiii
wrath, xi, xviii, 20, 27, 109, 162, 211, 218, 234, 236, 254, 282
writing, ix, xii, xiii, xix, 67, 68, 87, 110, 191, 239, 240

Zielinski's Law, 228
Zitat, xvii

This book was composed by Ivy Livingston
and manufactured by Edwards Brothers, Lillington, NC

The typeface is Gentium, designed by Victor Gaultney
and distributed by SIL International

www.ingramcontent.com/pod-product-compliance
Lightning Source LLC
Chambersburg PA
CBHW071854290426
44110CB00013B/1144